What's New in *Virtual Reality Madness and More!*

- **Three new chapters.** Chapter 7, "Hardware for Virtual Worlds," covers some of the VR hardware you can add to your computer, while Chapters 14 and 15 are VR hardware and software buyer's guides.
- **Expanded coverage in all chapters.** Chapter 4, "Virtual Fun," covers a slew of new games, including Myst, Iron Helix, and DOOM. Chapter 10, "You Are the Star," now covers Adobe Premiere. Every chapter has coverage of new products.
- **New products on the CD-ROMs.** The *Virtual Reality Madness and More!* CD-ROMs contain a special edition of Virtus WalkThrough, and there are new demos of virtual-reality games and more!
- **Coverage of updated virtual-reality software.** Learn about the new Windows version of Vistapro, Distant Suns, Virtus WalkThrough, and Virtus VR.
- In addition, the book is packed with new images, a completely new color section, and more!

VIRTUAL REALITY MADNESS AND MORE!

Ron Wodaski and Donna Brown-Wodaski

SAMS PUBLISHING

This book is dedicated to our kids: Chanel, Chris, and Justen.

Copyright © 1994 by Sams Publishing

SECOND EDITION

International Standard Book Number: 0-672-30604-2

Library of Congress Catalog Card Number: 94-67508

97 96 95 94 4 3 2 1

Interpretation of the printing code: the rightmost double-digit number is the year of the book's printing; the rightmost single-digit, the number of the book's printing. For example, a printing code of 94-1 shows that the first printing of the book occurred in 1994.

Thanks to VictorMaxx Technologies, Inc. for providing the CyberMaxx head-mounted display pictured on the front cover. For more information on the VictorMaxx product line, please consult the product directory in Chapter 14, "VR Hardware."

Trademarks

Composed in 1Stone Serif and MCPdigital by Macmillan Computer Publishing

Printed in the United States of America

PUBLISHER
Richard K. Swadley

ACQUISITIONS MANAGER
Stacy Hiquet

MANAGING EDITOR
Cindy Morrow

ACQUISITIONS EDITOR
Gregory S. Croy

DEVELOPMENT EDITORS
Dean Miller
Angelique Brittingham

SOFTWARE DEVELOPMENT SPECIALIST
Wayne Blankenbeckler

PRODUCTION EDITOR
Fran Blauw

EDITORIAL COORDINATOR
Bill Whitmer

EDITORIAL ASSISTANTS
Carol Ackerman
Sharon Cox
Lynette Quinn

TECHNICAL REVIEWER
Brad Pillow

MARKETING MANAGER
Gregg Bushyeager

COVER DESIGNER
Tim Amrhein

BOOK DESIGNER
Alyssa Yesh

DIRECTOR OF PRODUCTION AND MANUFACTURING
Jeff Valler

IMPRINT MANAGER
Juli Cook

MANUFACTURING COORDINATOR
Paul Gilchrist

PRODUCTION ANALYSTS
Angela D. Bannan
Dennis Clay Hager
Mary Beth Wakefield

GRAPHICS IMAGE SPECIALISTS
Becky Beheler
Clint Lahnen
Jason Hand
Mike Reynolds
Dennis Sheehan
Susan VandeWalle

PRODUCTION
Mona Brown
Michael Brumitt
Elaine Crabtree
Kimberly K. Hannel
Stephanie J. McComb
Brian-Kent Proffitt
Kim Scott
Dennis T. Wesner
Holly Wittenberg

INDEXER
Charlotte Clapp

Overview

Contents

Part I Virtual Reality Is Here

Part II Virtual Fantasies

Acknowledgments

We have received outstanding cooperation from numerous companies whose software and hardware are reviewed in this book. It takes a lot of effort to ship dozens and dozens of products in both directions, and we'd like to take this opportunity to publicly thank everyone who helped out in this regard.

A special thanks goes to our three kids, Chris, Chanel, and Justen, who had to wait sometimes while Mommy and Daddy finished their chapters.

Thank you to Millie Brown, who helped with equipment acquisition and moral support.

We also want to tip our hats to all the folks in the various multimedia- and virtual-reality-related forums on CompuServe. If you aren't already a member of CompuServe, you're missing out on one of the world's best idea exchanges. We visit the various forums every day, both to answer questions and to learn. Multimedia in general and virtual reality in particular are fast-evolving fields. Electronic communication is the most effective way to keep up to date.

About the Authors

Ron Wodaski and **Donna Brown-Wodaski** reside on the shores of Puget Sound in Washington, where they use the back roads to the information highway to keep up with the latest advances in multimedia and virtual reality.

Ron started out as a journalist, but caught the computer bug when he bought one of the original Osborne computers as a word processor.

He designed and wrote custom software using BASIC and dBASE II for several years, eventually joining the dBASE team at Ashton-Tate until it was merged with Borland. Somewhere along the line, he graduated to C and then retired to Visual Basic and Toolbook. He has worn a number of different hats in the computer industry, including programming, test management, project management, and product design.

He currently writes books on a variety of computer subjects. Ron writes the *Ask Mr. Multimedia* column for *Multimedia World* magazine. Word has it that he is also *Dr. Multimedia* on America Online. He creates a monthly multimedia column for *Nautilus* (a CD-ROM magazine), and pens various fiction and science fiction stories. When no one is looking, he avoids computers entirely while kayaking or sailing the waters of Puget Sound.

Donna handles research and product-coordination duties, and co-authors books with Ron. She learned early on that the only good computer was one you could have fun with. She helped found Pearlsoft, one of the first companies to develop user-friendly database software. She then worked with Ashton Tate on dBASE IV 1.0, working closely with the core team to document and explain the new features.

Currently, Donna provides consulting and training services to a wide range of business clients.

Given her choice, she, too, would rather be out on the waters of Puget Sound.

Introduction

Virtual versus Artificial

If there is a phrase that is even more ambiguous than the word *multimedia*, it's *virtual reality*. These are two of the hottest buzzwords in the computer universe, and finding any two people who can agree on what they mean is a major accomplishment.

What is virtual reality (affectionately known as VR)? Here's my own home-grown definition:

> **Virtual reality is anything that isn't real, but does a good job of faking it.**

That's a pretty broad definition. Some folks would define virtual reality narrowly, in terms of goggles, gloves, and interactivity. I made my definition broad for a good reason. I also have some home-grown ideas about why anyone would want to mess around with virtual reality in the first place:

> **Virtual reality is for stretching and enhancing the imagination.**

Goggle/glove/interactive VR certainly does that, but so do a lot of other things that imitate reality. A few examples from actual virtual reality (AVR)[1] will demonstrate my point:

- Chemists can view complex molecules in real time and visualize new ways of creating materials.
- Students can roam through a computer representation of the solar system to learn about things like gravity and mass.
- Pilots can train without leaving the ground, or test expensive new aircraft designs without trashing the hardware in a crash.
- An artist can create worlds that are internally logical without worrying about troublesome things like the laws of physics.
- An architect and client can "see" a new building—even walk around in it—before the first spade of earth is turned.

It isn't important whether things are merely artificial or totally virtual. Debates about what is and is not virtual reality are quite beside the point. Is it fun? Is it useful? These are the kinds of questions that really matter when it comes to artificial/virtual reality.

---

[1] I know, this is begging the point, but consider how you would phrase it! This is a good place to note that I have made liberal use of footnotes throughout the text. I have stuffed three kinds of material into footnotes: technical stuff for those who like that kind of thing; obscure but interesting trivia; and fun, irreverent, and editorial comments.

For that matter, I don't see any substantial difference between the multimedia and virtual reality. They are just two different points along a continuum. If I haven't already angered the virtual-reality purists with my earlier definition, comparing it to multimedia ought to finish the job. Equating these two is not, however, madness. Adding sound, music, voice, video, animation, and other media to computers moves us closer to virtual reality on every desktop. Virtual reality provides a linking principal for the various media that make up *multi*media. You have to start somewhere, and multimedia is a good, solid step toward the virtual future. Ignore it at your peril!

What Virtual Reality Is

Whether you play with VR or use it as a tool, there is a common element involved: visualization. However, what you visualize may or may not actually correspond to reality. A materials engineer can use VR to visualize how materials interact with each other at the atomic level—even though no one can say for sure what an atom "looks like." Similarly, an artist can create virtual spaces that don't even obey the basic laws of physics. Does gravity always have to pull downward? Does mass really have to matter?[2]

If we set aside the term *virtual reality* for a moment, we can use these two terms:

- **Artificial reality**—Anything that looks, feels, or operates realistically, but isn't real.[3]
- **Virtual madness**—Stuff that breaks the rules of reality.

These are equally legitimate virtual pursuits. Both are a part of virtual reality. Some of us want to recreate reality, either just like it is (scientific VR) or as we would like it to be. Others want to push the envelope, to use VR to stretch—maybe even to the breaking point—the human intellect and imagination. VR gives us the ability to, at least temporarily, redefine what reality is.

Let's face it—a book is a simple form of virtual reality. Pictures are a simple form of virtual reality. Ever since someone first used language, pictures, and sounds to represent things in the real world, mankind has been involved with virtual reality. Computers are extending the range to the point where we can imagine a time when it might be impossible to distinguish between the real world and a virtual one.

My point is that such extreme examples of virtual reality are not the only things worthy of the name *virtual reality*. 3D modeling is both cool and virtual, just as 3D goggles are. So is a tele-robotic arm, landscape generation, 3D home design, and

---

[2]Pun intended.

[3]Naturally, the degree of realism will vary with the hardware available.

so on. I see virtual reality as a continuum, with cave paintings at one end and total-immersion, full-body alternate reality at the other end. This book is about the stuff in the middle—it's new enough to be interesting and fun, it's (mostly) inexpensive so you can afford it, and it's virtual enough to excite and tantalize your imagination.

The Cost of Virtual Reality

It would be great if a reality built out of electrons and photons did not cost anything, but that just isn't the case. You can get started in virtual reality easily and inexpensively, but if you plan to seek out a high degree of realism and real-time imaging, you had better have a decent budget. Here are the facts of life in the virtual universe:

- It takes lots and lots of pixels to create high-resolution images. If you want fancy graphics, the two most important components in your system become the video subsystem and the CPU. Get the best you can afford in both areas.
- If you want stereo and 3D imaging, multiply the preceding by two.
- If you plan to use video, every part of your system will need to be an above-average performer. This includes your hard disk (larger and faster are better), the video system (accelerator cards are a must; look for ones that support Video for Windows in hardware), and the CPU (486/66 or better; a Pentium is a good choice).
- Rendering is a time-intensive process. I had no trouble creating animation with 3D Studio that required 5 or 6 hours to render. Plan on using your computer to render at night or on the weekend.

You don't need to have the most expensive computer components to work with virtual reality. Patience will often substitute for cash. The only time it will not work that way is when you need real-time performance, such as with digital video. For example, some of the cutting-edge software on the CD may require more hardware than you have installed. It's not the software that's at fault; it's the bit-hungry, byte-mangling requirements of multimedia and virtual reality that are the problem. If you are serious about virtual reality, you'll have to either invest time and patience or upgrade your hardware. If you just want to explore, the hardware you have now may be fine. I recommend at least a fast 386 with 4M of memory if you want to create 3D images. The larger your hard disk, the better. I would recommend at least a 340M or 500M disk if you're shopping for one, but it doesn't cost much more to move up to a gigabyte or more these days. Don't short change yourself with false economy if virtual reality appeals to you. I use a Pentium 66 (shortly to be upgraded to 90 MHz) with 16M of RAM, a hot Diamond Stealth 64 video card with 4M of memory, 24-bit color, 2.7 gigabytes of hard disk, and a FAST Movie Machine with Motion JPEG for video capture. Some days, I wish I had more—but that's life on the cutting edge, and virtual reality is right there on the cutting edge.

Magic, Realism, and the Imagination

This book is intended to work like a cookbook. If you want to cook a meal, the first thing most of us do is drag out a good cookbook and see what we can create with the food at hand. A good cookbook provides:

- A list of ingredients.
- The procedure for mixing the ingredients.
- Instructions for the actual cooking—oven temperature, how long to boil, and so on.
- Basic descriptions of fundamental procedures—poaching fish, sautéing onions, and so on.

We can convert these into their computer equivalents:

- A list of the hardware and software you'll need.
- The procedures for getting things to work together.
- How to use all this cool stuff—menu choices, file formats, procedures for creating models and worlds, and so on.
- Basic descriptions of fundamental procedures—rendering in three dimensions, interactive solutions, and so on.

As I write this, the image that comes to mind is of the three witches in *Macbeth.* "Bubble, bubble, toil and trouble..." That's the recipe for virtual reality. Mix and match reality and imagination in the strongest concentrations you can stand and see what comes out—goblins and ghosts, major distortions of space-time, or a fly-through of your new kitchen. The only limit to what you can do with virtual reality is right between your ears. Hold on tight, get ready for adventure: it's time for the amazing, 16.7-million color journey into the computer/mind spaces of *Virtual Reality Madness and More!*

Ron Wodaski

August 1994

I

VIRTUAL REALITY IS HERE

1

VIRTUAL REALITY HAS ARRIVED

The first edition of this book began with a simple assertion:

Virtual Reality has arrived.[1]

What was true a year ago is even more true today. In fact, virtual reality has more than arrived: it's moving in and settling down. Consider the evidence:

- Head-mounted devices[2] have come down from $6,000 to less than $1,000.[3]
- Several competing software products are now available for creating your very own virtual universes. Several even work in Windows, formerly the wasteland of virtual reality.
- Fancy VR trackballs and six-degrees-of-freedom[4] gizmos are now in the price range of mere mortals (translation: less than $1,000).
- A 3D-creation package for Windows (Caligari trueSpace—more about that later) is now available.

For decades, virtual reality has been nothing more than speculation and promises. Today, you can buy virtual-reality hardware and software right in your favorite computer store. Science fiction buffs have been waiting with barely suppressed glee for just this moment.

But this is just the beginning. We haven't arrived at the culmination of virtual reality; this is the moment of its birth. There is plenty of room to grow. You still can't get taste from your computer, nor can you surround yourself with the smell of the ocean shore in the morning. It's still all about sight and sound, with just a touch of tactile sensation thrown in for a tease.[5]

---

[1]I have chosen to make liberal use of footnotes throughout the text—sometimes for fun, and sometimes to expand a thought or follow a useful tangent. You have been warned!

[2]In the movies, when you see folks with half or more of their heads covered in a spacey-looking helmet, that's an HMD.

[3]Although you still can spend $6,000 and more if you really feel you have to.

[4]The six degrees of freedom (don't you just love that phrase out of context?) are up/down, left/right, forward/backward, pitch, roll, and yaw. Still confused? There is more on this kind of stuff later. Stay tuned.

[5]Example: data gloves. Still in the development stage, these devices enable you to use your hands as an input device without benefit (or encumbrance) of a mouse or keyboard. Much like a padded glove, these babies still sport wires all over the place and outrageous price tags. With any luck, by the time we're ready to write the next edition of the book, real data gloves will be available. For now, there's not much beyond the Mattel Power Glove.

I have to confess that it is enormous fun to write about virtual reality. VR, as it often is called, is by far the coolest thing to happen on computers since electrons first danced to the whims of programmers. In the first edition, I wrote: "I can't tell you how many times I went storming through the house to find my wife or one of the kids to show them some stunning apparition on my computer screen." This time around, my wife Donna is writing portions of the book—I guess she got the VR bug. I can't tell you how many times she came running through the house to tell me about some exciting discovery that you'll be reading about in this book. We can only hope you'll have as much pleasure discovering the possibilities as we did.

This book is arranged like a cookbook. You'll find cool recipes that you can mix up in your own home. We have tried to stick mostly with software and hardware that anyone can afford, but sometimes we found stuff so utterly cool and amazing that we included it even if it was expensive. Examples include such software as 3D Studio and SuperScape, and such hardware as head-mounted devices and fancy VR input devices like the Spaceball.

In this chapter, you start with a form of VR that is easy to visualize and work with: Vistapro. As you move through the book, you learn more and more about the concepts and techniques of virtual reality. Along the way, I've tried my best to include lots of fun stuff.[6]

Beginning at the Beginning

Virtual reality is an extremely broad term. It has come to refer to almost anything that has anything at all to do with three dimensions on computers. The original use of the word, back when VR was all in the imagination, referred mostly to complete immersion systems. This meant complex headsets to project a 3D visual space, and a bodysuit full of electronics to send and receive signals about your own body position. Using such a system, you would feel just like you were in a virtual world. More important, you could interact with that imaginary universe.

Such hardware is, in fact, available today. It requires a lot of supporting hardware, however, and represents the farthest edge of VR—in terms of cost and capability. It is not necessary, however, to start with such complex hardware and software at all. To my way of thinking, virtual reality starts in the imagination. Mankind was

[6]This reflects my theory of learning: we learn better and faster when we are having fun. Remember advanced math and how boring it probably was? What if you had been using what you were learning to build a remote-controlled airplane, or to design a more efficient racing-boat hull? It seems so obvious, you gotta wonder sometimes about the educational system.

born with the ability to visualize in three dimensions—that's where VR begins. The computer can only build on or enhance our own built-in VR abilities. For our purposes, virtual reality will encompass the full range of 3D and virtual software and hardware. Some of it will be interactive, and some will be static. But everything will meet the critical requirement for inclusion in this book: it has to be fun.

One of the most fascinating aspects of virtual reality is the creation of virtual landscapes. In this chapter, you learn how to build natural and fantastic landscapes using a product called Vistapro. Vistapro is a wonderful program that I enjoyed a great deal. It isn't often that I find a program that is this enjoyable and fun to use. I have included an earlier version of Vistapro on the CD-ROMs. It does not have all the features described in this chapter; you need to upgrade to the latest version to enjoy all the features. It is a complete version, however, and you can save the files and images that you create with it to your hard disk.

Planets 'R' Us: Vistapro 3.0

RECIPE

1 Copy program
2M or more available extended (XMS)[7] memory
1M hard disk space
1t patience

Instructions: Load the landscape of your choice and arrange ingredients in a pleasing setting. Render slowly on a fast machine until done. Serve with animation or morphing, or season with 3D Studio or Vream for exciting variations. Good rendering is like homemade bread: It has to sit a while before it's ready. Don't be in a hurry.

[7]It's easy to get confused between EMS and XMS memory. *XMS,* or *extended memory,* is faster because your computer can work with bigger chunks of it. *EMS,* or *expanded memory,* is slower because it requires a lot of juggling of memory space. If software gives you a choice, choose XMS.

Vistapro now ships on a CD-ROM, and most of the stuff that was optional last year is now included. The Vistapro CD-ROM edition includes the following goodies, most of which are covered in this chapter:

- Vistapro itself
- MakePath Flight Director for animation
- Vistamorph for landscape special effects
- Landscapes, including Ayers Rock, Mars,[8] and National Parks—a total of more than 3,000 landscapes for your rendering pleasure
- Image and animation samples
- MIDI and audio-music tracks
- A 3D bungee-jump animation

Figure 1.1 shows a typical landscape created with Vistapro.[9] It is based on a natural landscape in southwestern Oregon: Crater Lake. The vertical scale has been enhanced to emphasize details; and the sky, lighting, and angle of view were chosen to reflect the purpose for the image: a desktop for Windows. There's lots of clear space in the sky for icons.

Figure 1.1. A landscape created with Vistapro 3.0.

---

[8]There is more than 200M of Mars data.

[9]The CD-ROM includes numerous generated landscapes as well. These landscapes come in all sizes, so you can have fun no matter what computer you have. Images range from basic 8-bit images to 1024×768, 24-bit, photo-realistic images. There are even some 3D images for use with red/blue 3D glasses.

This image appears exactly as it was created in Vistapro. As you learn how to work with Vistapro, you can control precisely how the image appears: realistic or dreamy, sharply defined or obscured by fog. And after creating a landscape, you can enhance realism further by altering the image using paint programs, such as Photoshop from Adobe. Figure 1.2 shows a fanciful Mars landscape at local dawn, including artificial lens flare for a nice touch of ultra-realism.

Figure 1.2
A Vistapro image enhanced in Adobe Photoshop for Windows.

It's easy to create a landscape in Vistapro. The program includes mapping data for a number of real locations, from Big Sur in California to the Alps in Europe. You also can create fractal landscapes—scenes based on the science of fractal[(10)] imagery. To create a landscape, you just set a number of parameters and press the Render button (see fig. 1.3 to view a rendering in progress). To make life even easier, Vistapro comes with presets you can use to quickly set up for rendering.

I have included a demo version of Vistapro on the CD-ROMs that accompany this book. You can use the demo version to explore the capabilities of the program. Unlike most demo programs, it is full-featured; you can even save your work to disk. This demo, however, is the prior version of Vistapro for the PC, version 1.0. (The first PC version is 1.0, and the second version is 3.0. There was no version 2.0, so you aren't getting some horribly out-of-date version of Vistapro—just the

---

[10]*Fractal* comes from the word *fraction*. It refers to the use of fractional dimensions to create interesting, lifelike images. You draw on paper in two dimensions, and experience life in three dimensions, for example. A fractal image might have a dimension of 2.65, instead of a simple, straightforward 2 or 3.

last version. Is that clear?) You also can get Vistapro add-on products that enable you to create morphs[11] and animations. With these add-ons, you can create landscapes that grow and change before your eyes, or you can animate a fly-through of a landscape.

Figure 1.3. A Vistapro landscape partially generated.

The opening screen of Vistapro is shown in figure 1.4.[12] The landscape is on the left, and various controls are on the right. In this section, we look at how you can use the controls to create fractal landscapes, to modify existing landscapes, and to render landscapes in a variety of interesting ways.

Perhaps the nicest thing about Vistapro is that you can use it to do wonderful things without having to worry a whole lot about the complexities of 3D. Drawing software is awkward to use in 3D because it requires you to think in three dimensions. With Vistapro, you can rely on basic map-reading skills.

---

[11]The term *morph* is a shortened version of the word *metamorphosis*. A morph involves a visual transformation of one image into another. The movie *Terminator 2* used numerous morphs of a police officer turning into the liquid-metal terminator. Many commercials also feature morphs these days, such as a car morphing into a tiger.

[12] Vistapro originally was written for the Amiga, so the interface isn't PC standard. However, Vistapro is easy to use and shouldn't present any usage problems once you learn a few quirks. Quick tip: A *gadget* is really a text box, and you have to press Enter to complete your entry.

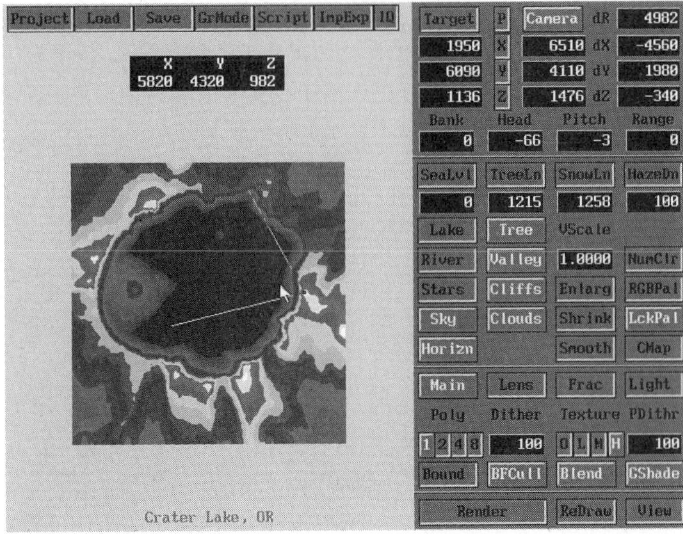

Figure 1.4 The Vistapro screen.

Setting Up for Rendering

Vistapro normally involves three steps. You can spend more or less time at each step to perfect your landscape:

- Create or select a map
- Set scene parameters
- Render

You can create a map in various ways, and you always can load one of the many maps supplied with the program. Vistapro uses Digital Elevation Modeling (DEM) to describe the 3D coordinates of a landscape. The sample files included with the program rely on USGS[13] mapping data and are extremely accurate.

Instant Virtual Reality

In the following sections, you learn how to fine-tune the various settings available in Vistapro to produce exactly the kind of landscape you want. You don't have to twiddle the dials, however, to get results. To follow along with this example, you can use the demo version supplied on disc or the regular version of Vistapro 3.0. To begin, load one of the supplied DEM files by clicking the Load menu and dragging to the Load DEM option. (Refer to fig. 1.4 to locate the menu bar at the top left of the Vistapro screen.) Pick any file on the list, such as CRATERLA.DEM, and click it. Click the Load button at the upper left to load the file.

---

[13]That's the United States Geologic Survey.

There's a tiny little button at the right of the menu, labeled IQ. Click this button to display a list of predefined settings:

Low—This setting renders very quickly, but the results are crude. This is useful when you want to check the general appearance of the landscape quickly.

Medium—This setting is useful for slower computers or to get a (relatively) quick look at your landscape.

High—This setting yields useful results—images that look realistic and can be used in desktop publishing or other situations that require detailed images.

Ultra—This sets Vistapro for extremely high-quality rendering. It takes longer to render images, but the results often are stunning.

User—You also can define your own settings.

The button you pick depends on what you would like to see, and also on the speed of your computer.[14] If you are using a 386/25 or slower machine, I would recommend the Medium setting for your first rendering. For faster computers, High or even Ultra is fine.

Clicking one of the IQ buttons sets numerous parameters; you may notice some of the settings on the right side of the screen changing. Don't worry about those settings yet. The only button you are interested in is at the bottom left of the controls: Render. Click it, and watch as the landscape is created bit by bit on-screen. The speed of rendering varies dramatically with the speed of your computer and with the level of quality you set. Rendering can take from a few seconds to a minute.

The border of the screen flashes when the rendering is complete. To save the rendering, press Esc, and then click the Save menu. Select the image type you want to save. For this exercise, I would suggest using Save PCX. This option saves your landscape rendering as an 8-bit PCX image.

Basic Settings

One setting makes a dramatic difference in the appearance of your rendered images: the screen resolution. By default, Vistapro assumes that you have the most

---

[14]Rendering is a CPU-intensive activity. Until recently, personal computers were simply too slow to be used for rendering. If you feel badly about the time it takes to render, consider this: Until the 486 CPU came along, most rendering was done on supercomputers like the Cray.

basic VGA display hardware installed.(15) If you have a Super VGA card, however, don't despair: if it includes support for VESA,(16) you can use Super VGA resolutions for rendering.

Display cards support the VESA standard in two ways:

- Right in the hardware
- Using a TSR(17) program

If your card supports VESA in the hardware, you don't need to do anything to use Vistapro at Super VGA resolutions.(18) Vistapro checks your video card to see whether it supports VESA automatically.

If your card uses a TSR to support VESA, you need to load that program before you run Vistapro to get Super VGA support. Consult the documentation that came with your video card for information.

If you have VESA support (and most recent video display cards do support VESA), you gain access to the Super VGA resolutions. Vistapro supports a number of Super VGA resolutions, ranging from 640×400 to 1280×1024. Most video cards that support 1280×1024, however, don't support it under VESA, so the highest resolution you are likely to be able to use is 1024×768. This is more than adequate for most needs. To set the resolution, use the GrMode menu button. This menu also enables you to turn on support for 24-bit color. If you choose to use 24-bit color, keep in mind that the file sizes for high-resolution images can get very large—1024×768×24 bits is 2,359,296 bytes (2,304K).

Not all video-card drivers support VESA as well as they should. If you encounter problems—such as a black or gray screen, vertical bars, or scrambled images—you should contact the video-card manufacturer for an updated VESA driver.

---

15 The default resolution is 320×200 and 256 colors (sometimes called MCGA). This is a standard VGA resolution.

16 There is a long story behind VESA. Every display adapter has its own way of doing SuperVGA; for a long time, there was no standard way of implementing Super VGA. This was a big problem for software companies, who had to write different software for each Super VGA display card or pass up support for Super VGA. VESA changed that by creating a standard interface for Super VGA resolutions (800×600, 1024×768, and so on).

17 Terminate and Stay Resident.

18 The demo version of Vistapro supplied on the CDs may not support some or all Super VGA resolutions.

If you are working with the demo version of Vistapro from the CD-ROMs, disk file size doesn't matter—you can't save to disk anyway. However, if you only have the minimum amount of memory required by Vistapro installed (2M) you may be limited to the lower screen resolutions.

Camera and Target

In the "Instant Virtual Reality" section earlier in this chapter, the view you saw used the default camera and target locations. In this section, you learn how to set up your own camera and target positions.

Figure 1.5 shows the controls for camera and target. Notice the three columns at the top, and a row of settings at the bottom. The first column, at the left, defines the Target location in 3D coordinates. The middle column defines the Camera location, and the far right column shows the delta[19] between the Target and Camera coordinates. You can use the small buttons between the Target and Camera settings to lock one or more of the settings. You use the bottom row of settings to change the orientation (heading) of the camera. All distances are measured in meters and all headings are measured in degrees.

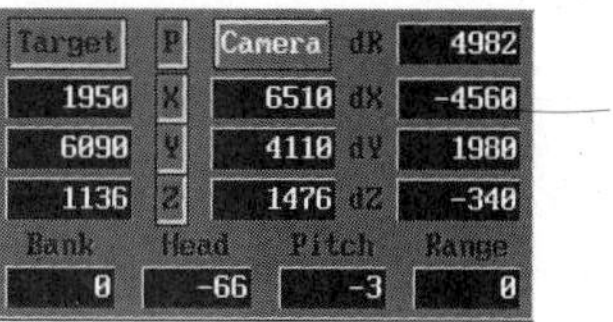

Figure 1.5. Camera and Target controls.

When you work in two dimensions, only two coordinates are needed to specify a location: height and width. Working in three dimensions requires three coordinates to specify a location: height, width, and depth. The first two dimensions, height and width, are referred to using the letters **x** and **y**.[20] The third dimension, depth, uses the letter **z**. These letters are a standard shorthand way of referring to the three dimensions; you'll see these letters over and over in this book and elsewhere.

You can see the letters **x**, **y**, and **z** in the columns under the Camera and Target controls. Notice the column of buttons between the Camera and Target columns; you use these buttons to lock the current position of the camera and target along any one dimension. If you want to prevent any changes to height, for example, simply click the **z** button before moving the camera or target.

---

[19]Delta is a Greek letter used by scientists and mathematicians to indicate change or difference.

[20]These are called *Cartesian coordinates*, as you may have learned in high school algebra or math class.

Moving the camera or target is very easy. Click the appropriate button at the top of the column, either Camera or Target. Then click anywhere on the map; the camera or target then moves to the new location. Both are marked by a tiny square, and the camera angle is displayed by two lines radiating from the camera. Objects within the angle are included in the rendering.[21]

The third column shows the delta, or difference, between the target and the camera. The top number, **dR**, is the actual range distance (a straight line, in meters) from the camera to the target. The three figures below **dR—dX**, **dY**, and **dZ**—represent the distance in the **x**, **y**, and **z** directions. For example, if the camera is at 1,000 meters and the target is at 500 meters, then **dZ** is equal to -500 meters.

Four settings are located at the bottom of the Camera/Target area. These settings control the orientation of the camera, including such things as tilt and rotation. Vistapro uses the technical terms[22] for each kind of orientation. To understand the terms, imagine that you are five years old again and playing airplane with your friends. Your arms are out to the side and serve as your wings. Most of these measurements describe a rotation of one kind or another, so most measurements are expressed as degrees:[23]

> **Bank**—If you lower your left wing (arm),[24] that is a bank to the left (counterclockwise) and it is expressed as a negative number. If you lower your right wing, that is a bank to the right and is expressed as a positive number. A bank of -10 means that the left wing is lowered 10 degrees.
>
> **Head**—Heading describes the direction you are facing. North is 0; south is 180 degrees. Rotation to the right (clockwise) is a positive number; rotation to the left is a negative number. If you refer back to figure 1.4, where the heading is -66, you see that this means the camera is facing roughly west northwest.
>
> **Pitch**—If you lean forward or backward, you can change your pitch. If you pitch forward (nose down), that's a negative number. If you pitch backward (nose up), that's a positive number. A positive pitch of 90 degrees puts your nose right on the ceiling.

---

[21]Because the camera view is 3D and the map view is 2D, you will find that objects outside the angle may show up in the rendered landscape. If you set the camera overlooking the valley, for example, objects in the valley show up for some distance outside the indicated angle.

[22]These terms are taken from aviation and often are used to describe the movements of an aircraft.

[23]There are 360 degrees in a complete circle. Thus, a quarter rotation is 90 degrees, and a half rotation is 180 degrees.

[24]Of course, the right wing (arm) goes up at the same time.

Range—This is not a measurement in degrees; it uses meters. It is a setting you can use to eliminate portions of the view from the rendering. If you enter 1,000 meters, for example, objects more than 1,000 meters away are not rendered. Similarly, if you enter -500, objects closer than 500 meters are not rendered.

By default, the camera is placed 30 meters above the height of the landscape at the location you choose. This placement prevents nearby objects from obscuring the view. You can change the camera height by entering a new number in the Camera Z control.[25] You don't need to make any changes to Bank, Head, Pitch, or Range to get useful renderings. Vistapro sets these when you locate the target or camera.

For a dramatic point of view, change the camera height to 500 or 1,000 meters above the height of the map location.

Trees and Clouds, Lakes and Rivers

The middle portion of the control panel contains a number of parameters that have a major impact on the appearance of your rendered landscape (see fig. 1.6). You can add a number of natural features, including such things as lakes and rivers, clouds, stars, cliffs, and so on.

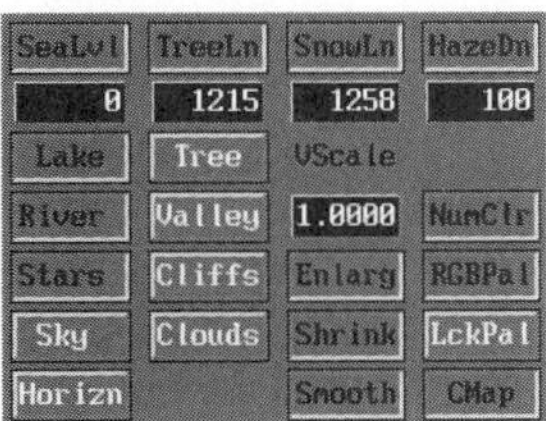

Figure 1.6. The Vistapro middle control panel.

The middle control panel also includes settings for various boundaries, such as the distance at which haze becomes apparent and the tree line. Using these settings, you can create a very natural-looking landscape.

Four kinds of settings are located on the middle control panel:

- Boundaries
- Natural features

[25]You can change the settings in any of the controls manually at any time before rendering.

- Scale and textures
- Colors

You learn about each of these settings in the following subsections.

Boundaries

The Boundaries settings enable you to establish the location of basic natural boundaries in the landscape. You can use these settings to make subtle adjustments to the landscape. You can add haze to increase the sense of distance in the landscape, for example.

There are four Boundaries settings you can control:

SeaLvl—Use this setting to change sea level. If you enter 500, for example, all portions of the landscape at or below 500 meters are changed to 0 meters. All portions of the landscape above 500 meters are lowered by 500 meters. The result is that everything at or below sea level is flattened. To set sea level based on the map, click the SeaLvl button and then click the map to indicate an elevation.

TreeLn—Vistapro can render trees in the landscape. This number defines the height in meters above which trees will not grow. This reflects the way trees actually grow in natural settings. As with many of its features, Vistapro uses artificial intelligence to decide where, exactly, to put trees. Steep slopes have a lower treeline and flat surfaces have a higher tree line. Again, this reflects the way trees behave in nature. To set a tree level based on the map, click the TreeLn button, and then click the map to indicate an elevation.

SnowLn—This is the lowest level at which Vistapro draws snow on the landscape. As with the tree line, Vistapro bends the rules to generate a realistic-looking snow line. To set a snow level based on the map, click the SnowLn button, and then click the map to indicate an elevation.

HazeDn—This is the haze distance; a value of 0 eliminates haze, values up to about 1,000 give progressively more haze, and values over 1,000 generate a thick fog.[(26)] To have Vistapro calculate a typical haze value, click the HazeDn button.

---

[26]In most cases, such foggy scenes aren't very useful—almost all of the detail from the landscape is lost. One type of landscape that sometimes benefits from severe haze is a seacoast, where some fog and a jutting headline can look terrific.

Natural Features

Version 3.0 of Vistapro gives you control over a number of natural features in the landscape. Such features can make a dramatic difference in the appearance of the rendered image. Table 1.1 lists the various settings you can control.

Table 1.1. Natural Features in Vistapro 3.0.

Feature	*Description*
Lake	Click this button, and then click a point in the map. All points at that elevation then define a continuous shoreline surrounding a lake. Be careful with this setting; if there is a break in the proposed shoreline, the lake may spill over into places you didn't intend.
River	Click this button, and then click a point on the map. Vistapro then calculates a river course for you. If the river isn't wide enough for your needs, click at an adjoining point to widen the river.
Stars	Use this option in place of Sky for a nighttime effect. You can choose large or small stars. Unless you intend to output to video tape, small stars are your best bet. ***Important:*** If you don't change the landscape colors, they still render in daytime colors!
Sky	Causes Vistapro to render a sky. If you have a bitmap you want to use as a sky, turn Sky off and use the Load/Background menu selection to load your bitmap.
Horizon	Causes Vistapro to render a horizon line. If you don't want a distant horizon, or if you have your own background, click to turn off this setting. In most cases, you will want Horizon on.(27)

continues

[27]If you set a very high camera elevation, having Horizon on usually improves the appearance of the image. A high camera elevation may show the edges of the map, and a carefully chosen horizon color can make this less noticeable.

Table 1.1. continued

Feature	*Description*
Tree	Turning on this setting causes Vistapro to add trees to the landscape. You don't see the trees until you render. The dialog box that you use to define the type and density of trees is described later in this section.
Valley	Determines the extent to which a valley changes the tree line or snow line. Clicking this setting opens a dialog box with two values. **Valley Width** determines how much valley effect is used. The default value is 100. **Valley Scale** determines the extent of valley effect at each valley point. Larger numbers expand the range of the valley effect, and smaller numbers restrict the range. The default is 8.
Cliffs	This defines which portions of the landscape are steep enough to be considered cliffs. Special colors are used to render cliffs. In some cases, a more natural look results if Cliffs is turned off. You need to experiment to see the effect on a given landscape.
Clouds	Turning on this setting causes Vistapro to add clouds to the sky. You don't see the clouds until you render. The dialog box that you use to define the type and density of clouds is described later in this section.

All these controls have noticeable effects on the rendered image, but several have a big impact on the final rendered image. We'll look at those controls in detail now.

LAKE

The Lake setting is powerful and dangerous, but it can add a touch of realism to a scene. You can change the colors for water to create different moods.[28] The most important thing to learn is the relationship between the point you click and the

[28]See the "Colors" section, later in the chapter.

shape of the lake. Fortunately, Vistapro enables you to preview the appearance of the lake before you finalize it.[29]

RIVER

It takes a little experimentation to develop a knack for getting rivers to look right. A single click to create a river is seldom enough to get a useful river effect; it's more like a creek effect. To create natural-looking rivers, look for the characteristic land forms on the map. Figure 1.7 shows a close-up of a portion of a map, and the best areas for starting a river are marked. Figure 1.8 shows the results of a single click to create a river; figure 1.10 shows a river created from multiple clicks. Note that there are several tributaries to the river, and that the river is wider.

Figure 1.9 shows the results of rendering the river in figure 1.8. Note that the river is almost invisible. Figure 1.11 shows a rendering of the river in figure 1.10. In this case, the river fits the scale of the landscape much better.

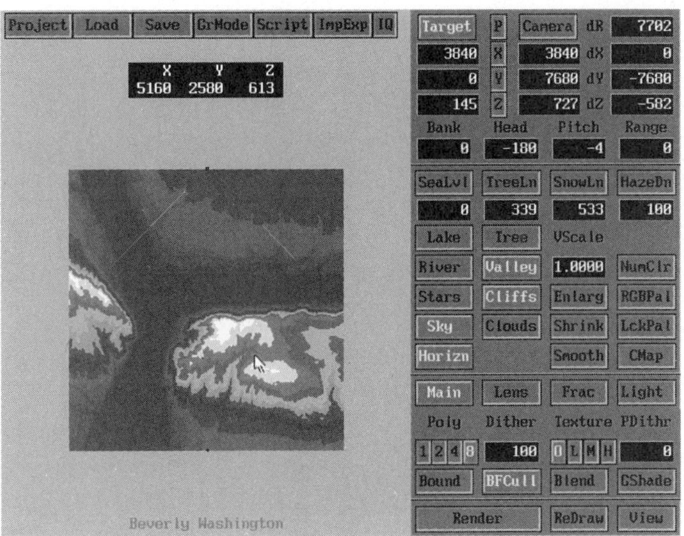

Figure 1.7. A detail of a map, showing good locations for originating a river.

---

[29] Unfortunately, the dialog box that asks you `Accept Lake?` often covers the preview area. You need a quick eye to determine whether the lake will work for you, because you may see only the preview for a fraction of a second. If in doubt, I highly recommend saving your work before creating a lake!

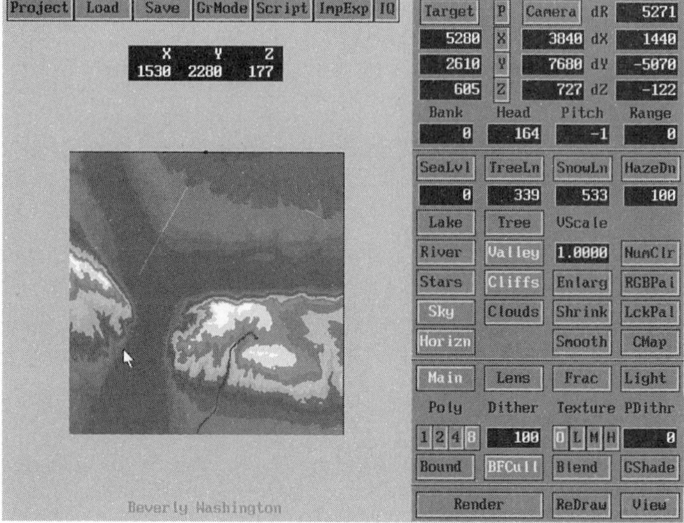

Figure 1.8.
A river created with a single click of the mouse.

Figure 1.9.
A rendering of the river created in figure 1.8.

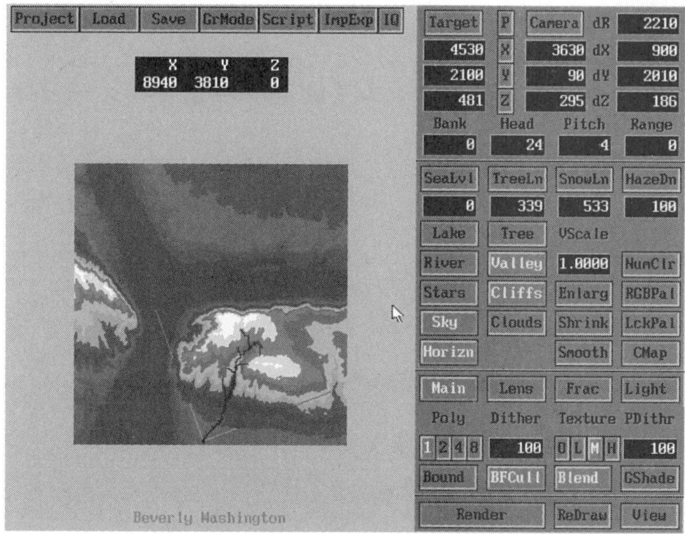

Figure 1.10. A river created with multiple mouse clicks.

STARS

It's easy to add stars to your images: Just click the Stars button to enable that feature. This action only changes the appearance of the sky, however, which now includes a dark background and lots of stars. The landscape colors don't change. The resulting image won't look bad, but if you want a realistic nighttime scene, you need to edit the landscape colors. Refer to the the "Colors" section later in this chapter for more information.

Figure 1.11. A rendering of the river created in figure 1.10.

Like other additions to the landscape, such as trees and clouds, the starry sky renders consistently. If you create an animation, you can count on the stars behaving like real stars. That is, they appear to move as the animation point of view changes.

TREES

The newest version of Vistapro, version 3.0, improves greatly on the original in this area. Vistapro 3.0 is capable of rendering realistic-looking trees. You pay a price for such realism, however: Rendering time increases dramatically if you set the quality of tree images very high. Unless you are rendering a final image, you probably want to render trees at modest settings.

Clicking the Trees button when it is off displays the dialog box shown in figure 1.12.

The first thing to notice is that there are four kinds of trees: Pine, Oak, Cactus, and Palm (see fig. 1.13 for an example of pine trees). Most types of terrain in Vistapro are similar to this figure. Each terrain type has a range of colors used to render the terrain. The default colors for trees are four shades of green, naturally. Because Vistapro offers several colors, you can generate more varied and interesting textures for the many kinds of terrain.

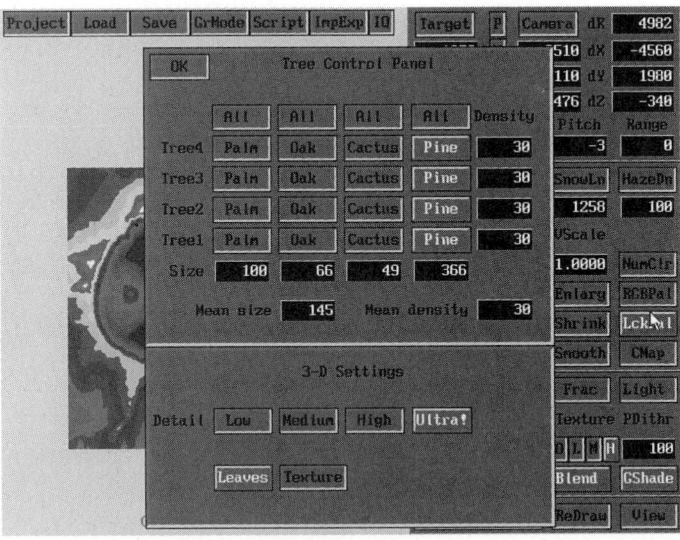

Figure 1.12. The dialog box for defining the characteristics of trees.

The Trees dialog box is a lot like a program within a program. It controls the rendering of trees, which are complete, discrete, fractal objects. The top half of the dialog box enables you to define the types of trees that appear at specific elevations, as well as the size and density of trees at each elevation.

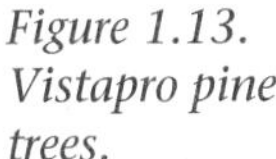

Figure 1.13. Vistapro pine trees.

If you want to have more pine trees at high elevations and more oak trees at low elevations, for example, you can set Tree4 as Pine, Tree3 as both Pine and Oak, Tree2 as Pine and Oak, and Tree1 as Oak.

The density of trees you use varies with the landscape. If you want a sparse look, try settings of 10-30. If you want a loose forest, try a setting of 50. Higher settings give you a full forest, and you cannot see individual trees. Size also varies, depending on the landscape. You may need to experiment with different sizes until you get the look you want. A flat landscape probably looks best with smaller trees, and a deep valley with steep cliffs may look better with taller trees. When in doubt, simply accept the default settings.

You can control the overall size and density of all tree types using the Mean Size and Mean Density settings.

The Tree Control Panel also contains settings for 3D rendering of trees. You can choose different levels of detail: Low, Medium, High, and Ultra. As a general rule, match the tree detail to the image size. If you are rendering at 320×200, Low detail is fine. Any additional detail simply gets lost. Even at 1024×768, only trees closest to the camera benefit from the extra detail.

The two buttons at the very bottom of the Tree dialog box, Leaves and Texture, further refine the appearance of trees. The Leaves button does just what you would expect: It adds leaves to the trees. The Texture button adds fractal textures to leaves and branches of trees. If you don't use 3D settings for trees, they are created as stick figures, as shown in figure 1.14. Figure 1.15 shows a rendered image with leaves, and figure 1.16 shows the same image with texture instead of leaves. All these images were rendered at 1024×768 with an IQ setting of Ultra.

CLOUDS

Your landscape needs a good set of natural-looking clouds to be complete. It just wouldn't do to have a gorgeous, natural landscape sitting under a completely artificial sky, now would it? A click of the Clouds button displays the dialog box shown in figure 1.17. This box contains just a few buttons and controls, but it doesn't take much to create a pleasing sky.

Figure 1.14. Two-dimensional trees: oak (a) and palm (b).

a

b

Figure 1.15. Oak (a) and palm (b) trees with leaves.

a

b

Figure 1.16. Palm trees with texture. Note that these are not substantially different from trees without texture at this resolution (640×480).

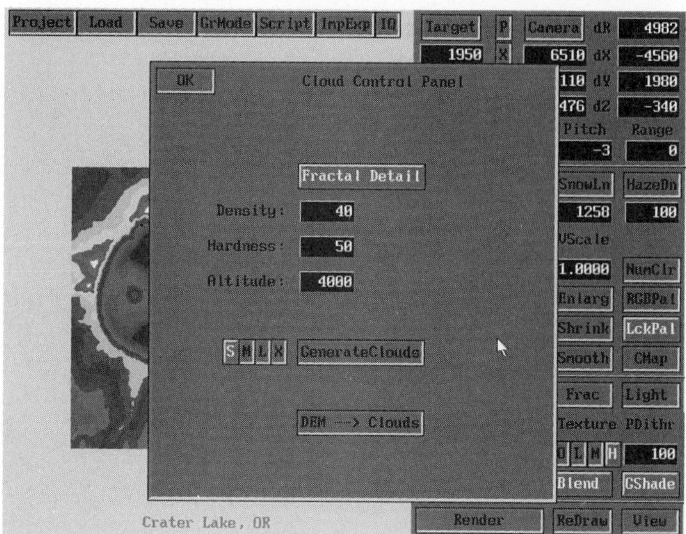

Figure 1.17. The Clouds dialog box.

Table 1.2 lists the various cloud controls.

Table 1.2. Vistapro Cloud Controls.

Control	*Description*
Fractal Detail	Adds fractal details to clouds for a more realistic effect.
Density	Determines the total cloud coverage. Higher numbers result in more clouds.
Hardness	Sets fluffiness. Lower settings result in fluffy, fleecy clouds.
Altitude	Determines the height of clouds. Clouds always are created higher than the camera's height.
S/M/L/X	Click one of these buttons to determine the size of the clouds, ranging from small to extra large.
GenerateClouds	After you have the settings the way you want them, click this button to generate the clouds.
DEM —> Clouds	Creates clouds based on the DEM data of the current landscape. You can use this setting to create clouds and then save them with the Save/Clouds menu item.

You can use the DEM —> Clouds button for a very interesting effect: skywriting. Create a PCX file in your favorite Image Editor that contains text, and then load it into Vistapro using the PCX —> DEM selection on the ImpExp[30] menu. Then use the DEM —> Clouds button to create clouds shaped like the text.

Figure 1.18 shows simple, medium clouds without any fractal detail, and figure 1.19 shows clouds with fractal detail added. The differences are subtle, but then so are clouds.

Scale and Textures

Just to the right of the controls for natural features is the third column of buttons in the middle control panel: scale and texture settings. The three scale settings and one texture setting are shown in table 1.3.

---

[30]Import/Export.

Figure 1.18. Clouds without fractal detail.

Figure 1.19. Clouds with fractal detail (most noticeable just to the right of top center).

Table 1.3. Vistapro Scale and Texture.

Control	*Type*	*Description*
VScale	Scale	Determines the vertical scale factor
Enlarg	Scale	Enlarges a portion of the map to full map size
Shrink	Scale	Shrinks multipart maps to the next smaller size
Smooth	Texture	Smoothes rough edges in the map

VERTICAL SCALE

Every point on the map is multiplied by the number you enter into the VScale box. This number increases or decreases the height of all points on the map. If you enter a value of 2.0000, for example, every point becomes twice as high. If you enter a value of 0.5000, every point is half as high. Because the lowest level on the map is always 0, numbers greater than 1 have the effect of increasing the vertical relief of the map.[31] Numbers between 0 and 1 reduce vertical relief.

You also can enter negative numbers. These numbers turn the map "inside out." That is, mountains become valleys and valleys become mountains. This can produce some very interesting effects.

ENLARGE

This control enables you to enlarge a portion of a map to full map size. This setting can be useful when you generate a map using fractals[32]—if you see an interesting portion of the map, you can enlarge it and work with just that portion of the map.

After enlargement, the map is smoother than it was because the partial map does not have the same level of detail as the full map. You can use the Fractalize button in the lower control panel to artificially add realistic detail.

SHRINK

Shrink is not the exact opposite of Enlarge. A little background is necessary. Vistapro can work with several sizes of maps. The smallest size, 258×258 data points, is appropriately called Small. The standard-size map is called Large, and it is 514×514 data points. You can load one standard Vistapro DEM file or up to four small DEM files. The largest size; Huge, is 1026×1026 data points and can contain up to 16 small files; four standard files; or one giant, extra-big, huge file.

---

[31]This is a fancy way of saying that the mountains get higher in relation to the valleys.

[32]See the "Fractal Magic" section.

The Shrink command shrinks the current map by one step in this hierarchy. Thus, a huge file shrinks to large, and a large shrinks to a small. A small file can't be shrunk any farther.

This business of combining DEM files to view larger areas is new in version 3.0 of Vistapro. Vistapro loads all files in a larger view if you set the image size to Automatic.(33)

SMOOTH

You seldom need to use smoothing with a DEM file that represents real data, but smoothing can be very useful when you are creating maps by other means. Smoothing removes the "rough spots" in the data. Look at figure 1.20, for example, which shows a map generated using fractals. The texture is extremely rough. Now look at figure 1.21 after smoothing has been applied; the texture is noticeably smoother.(34)

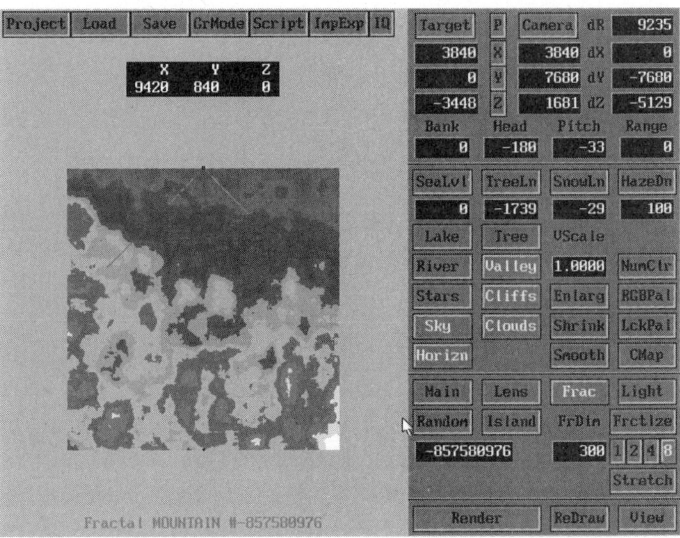

Figure 1.20.
A map with very rough texture.

Use smoothing when the map details are too complex to make out clearly.

33This is set on the Project menu: Set DEM Size.

34You can use smoothing several times to tame a particularly rough landscape. Smoothing tends to affect high points more than low points, however, so overuse can reduce the overall height of the terrain. You might need to apply a larger vertical scale after repeated smoothing.

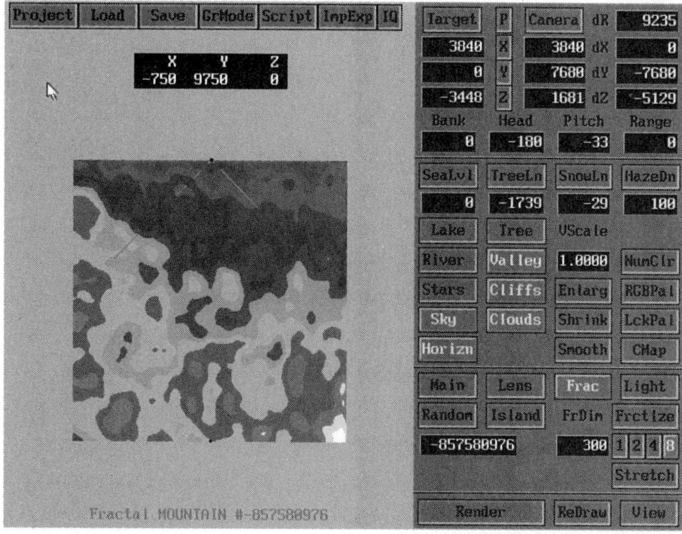

Figure 1.21. The same map after smoothing has been applied.

Colors

This brings us to the last column of controls in the middle control panel. There are four buttons, as explained in table 1.4.

Table 1.4. Vistapro Color Controls.

Control	*Description*
NumClr	Rendering normally uses all 256 colors in the 8-bit palette. If you plan to edit the image in a paint program, this setting enables you to use fewer colors for a rendering. You then can use the remaining palette slots for additional colors in a paint program. If your paint program supports 24-bit color, this setting is not necessary.
RGBPal	Normally, Vistapro selects the colors for a palette prior to rendering the image. This button enables you to force Vistapro to select a palette based on colors that actually appear in the rendered image. You must enable 24-bit support on the GrMode menu first, however.

continues

Table 1.4. continued

Control	*Description*
LckPal	This setting locks the color palette. Normally, Vistapro calculates a separate palette for each image. This button forces Vistapro to use the current palette for rendering.
CMap	Clicking this button activates the Color Map dialog box, which is described in this section.

Under most conditions, you don't need to do anything at all with this group of buttons. You can blissfully go on generating image after image without ever visiting this section of the screen. However, for special purposes, these are handy settings to have around.

After you have played around with Vistapro for a while, it can be fun to play around with the colors in a scene. You may want to render a nighttime scene, for example, or perhaps a Mars landscape appeals to you. The CMap button gives you the power to completely control the colors used by the system to render images. You can even save color settings to disk for later use. Figure 1.22 shows the ColorMap control panel.

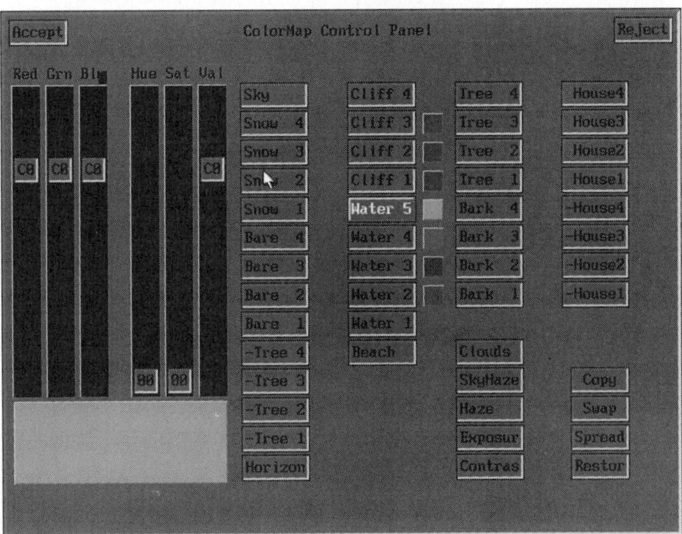

Figure 1.22.
The ColorMap control panel.

The ColorMap control panel has a zillion buttons, and it's both easy and complex to use. The easy part is setting individual colors. To set a color, click the button (such as Sky) and then adjust the Red/Green/Blue or the Hue/Saturation/Value sliders until you have the color you want. The hard part is creating a set of colors that gives you scenes that look the way you want them to look.

I've tried many techniques for developing a coherent set of colors, and only one method works consistently well: working within groups of colors, and then with groups of colors. Generally, I make one pass through all the color buttons, starting with Sky and working through the buttons, one color at a time. When I get to the first color in a group, I spend some time creating a color that is just right. The higher-numbered colors, such as Snow4, are located at higher elevations and are usually the brighter colors.[35] If I set a bright color in the 4 position, I then can set the exact same color in the 3 position, and then use the Value slider to darken it a little. This method enables me to maintain tight control over color values inside a group. If you want to vary hue or saturation instead of value, of course, you simply can change that slider instead.

Using this technique, you wind up with four colors that change predictably. The color may not be exactly what you want, or it may not work well with other color groups, but you now have a controlled situation that makes it easier to edit the entire color group, if that is necessary.

After I set up all the colors in all the color groups, I render a sample image to see the effect of the colors. If it is not the effect I want, I go back to the ColorMap and adjust the colors in whichever groups are causing a problem. If the snow is too dark, for example, I lighten each of the colors in the Snow group by the same amount.

This process requires a light touch and some patience, but you can create some amazing-looking scenes if you are willing to take the trouble to create your own color map.

Bottom Control Panels

The bottom control panel can take on four different appearances, depending on which of the four buttons at the top of the panel you click. These panel variations are listed in table 1.5, and are described in detail in this section.

---

[35]If you have some special color scheme in mind, of course, you may want the reverse.

Table 1.5. Vistapro Bottom Control Panel.

Variation	*Description*
Main	Enables you to set rendering parameters and establish basic geometry for rendering. You also need to have this panel active to start rendering.
Lens	Enables you to adjust angle of view for camera and create red/blue 3D images.[36]
Frac	Gives you access to fractal features, which include such goodies as adding fractal detail to a map or creating a complete fractal landscape.
Light	Enables you to adjust lighting angle and set shadow style.

The controls in the bottom control panel are settings that you use frequently. The most important panel to understand is the Main panel, because its controls have a major impact on the appearance of your rendered image.

MAIN

Getting the right settings on the Main control panel can make or break your rendering (see fig. 1.23). Knowing what to expect for various settings is the key to both natural and fantasy landscapes. You learn about the panel button by button in this section.

POLY

A properly rendered landscape doesn't show it, but it is made up of perfectly ordinary polygons.[37] These four minibuttons determine the size of the polygons used for rendering. Smaller polygons lead to more detailed renderings. Thus, a setting of 1 uses the smallest polygons and a setting of 8 uses the largest polygons. Figure 1.24 shows a landscape rendered with a polygon setting of 8, and figure 1.25 shows the same landscape rendered with a setting of 1. For these examples, to emphasize the effect of changing the polygon setting, no special smoothing or texturing capabilities were used.

[36]You need red/blue 3D glasses to get the stereo effect.

[37]If you didn't learn about polygons in geometry class, read on. A *polygon* is a flat shape bounded by three or more lines that meet at vertices (a *vertex* is a fancy name for a corner). The simplest polygon is a triangle, and most 3D programs build more complex objects out of triangular polygons. A rectangle or an octagon is also an example of a polygon. Polygons with sides of equal length are called *regular polygons*.

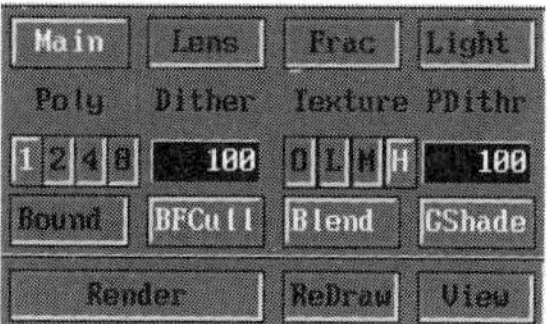

Figure 1.23. The Main version of the bottom control panel.

Large polygons are useful in the early stages of designing a landscape. You can check lighting angle, for example, without taking a lot of time for a detailed rendering. If all you want to know is whether a given cliff face is in light or shadow, a quick rendering is all you need.

After you have the gross features of the landscape worked out, however, you need to use progressively smaller polygon settings to see what your landscape looks like.

DITHER

Vistapro determines what color to use for a given polygon based on its altitude.[38] By itself, this creates a banding effect that doesn't look natural. You can use this setting to determine the amount of dithering between adjacent bands of color.[39]

A value of 100 provides a modest amount of dithering—just enough to blend adjoining areas slightly. Higher values smooth the transitions more; values of more than 1,000 make it impossible to distinguish one area from another. A value of 0 turns off dithering completely.

TEXTURE

Texture is a very powerful feature that has a lot to do with how natural your landscapes look. Without texture, color alone is used to suggest landscape features. Unless you want an unnatural look for your landscape, texture is a good idea. However, texture adds quite a bit of time to the rendering process.

Vistapro offers four minibuttons for setting texture levels. *O* stands for *Off*, and the remaining buttons set texture levels of Low, Medium, and High. When you set the texture level to Low or more, you are asked to choose between Shadow and Altitude texturing.

Shading texture is less CPU-intensive than altitude texture. If you click Shading, Vistapro breaks each polygon into smaller polygons and uses a slightly different

---

[38]Strictly speaking, this is not true. Vistapro considers other things besides altitude when deciding what color to use. A polygon on the side of a mountain might be below the snow line, for example, but Vistapro may decide to render it as snow or as a cliff instead of the color based on height. Vistapro takes a large number of values into consideration during rendering. Many of these values are intended to create the most natural-looking landscapes.

[39]*Dithering* is a simple mixing of pixels from one area with the pixels in an adjoining area.

color for each polygon.[40] Altitude shading uses fractal technology to break the larger polygon into smaller polygons, each of which is shaded and colored individually. This shading creates extremely realistic features. If realism is your goal, make sure that you set Altitude shading to On.

Figure 1.24. A landscape rendered with a polygon setting of 8.

Figure 1.25. A landscape rendered with a polygon setting of 1.

---

[40]If you choose to use shading texture, try clicking the GShade button as well. This turns on Gourand shading, a technique that is very effective for fantasy style landscapes. It normally is not useful to use Gourand shading with Altitude because Gourand obliterates the details generated by altitude shading.

PDITHR

PDithr stands for *pixel dithering*. Pixel dithering is different from regular dithering. Regular dithering affects the boundaries between landscape colors. Pixel dithering applies to every pixel in the image. Generally, a little pixel dithering—100 to 250 units—is a good thing. This is particularly useful in the sky. Vistapro uses only a few colors for the sky, and pixel dithering improves the situation.

BOUND

Clicking this button enables you to *mark* (set a boundary for) an area. During rendering, only the portion of the map within the boundary area is rendered.

BFCULL

BFCull stands for *back-face culling*. When this button is enabled, polygons facing away from the point of view are not calculated. It's hard to think of a situation in which you wouldn't keep this feature turned on. The only example that comes to mind involves putting the camera inside a mountain, where you would want to see the complete underside of the mountain.

BLEND

Blend is yet another control that is easy to confuse with dithering. If the Blend button is enabled, Vistapro averages the colors of a polygon with those of the polygons surrounding it. This action improves the appearance of distant portions of the rendering, and you have to decide for yourself whether the reduced intensity of color in the foreground is worth the result.

GSHADE

This button controls Gourand shading. This form of shading is used by a variety of 3D software products including 3D Studio. GShade is very effective at eliminating boundaries between polygons. However, this setting also has a tendency to make the landscape look less realistic because it decreases the apparent level of detail in the image. GShade is very useful for creating fantasy landscapes with a romantic feel to them. Figure 1.26, for example, shows a landscape generated with a realistic effect, and figure 1.27 shows the same landscape using Gourand shading.

Figure 1.26.
A landscape rendered without Gourand shading.

Figure 1.27.
A landscape rendered with Gourand shading.

Lens

Vistapro uses the image of a camera to describe the point of view used for the rendering. The analogy isn't carried very far,[41] but it is useful and does make it easier to get a feel for what the rendering looks like. After all, who hasn't had at least some experience with a camera these days?

Figure 1.28 shows the appearance of the bottom control panel when the Lens button is enabled. A number of buttons are located on this panel, but most of them are for special purposes. In fact, for most uses, you don't need to mess with the Lens settings at all.

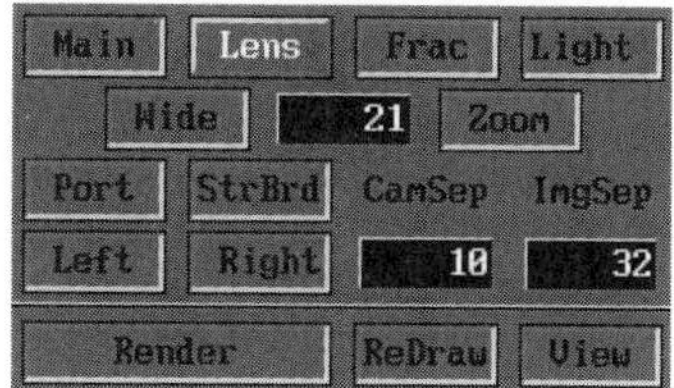

Figure 1.28. The Lens version of the bottom control panel.

The primary control you have over the lens is focal length. In nontechnical terms, your choices range from wide angle to telephoto. However, the numbers don't correspond to the focal length values for the most common lens in use today for 35mm cameras. Lower numbers represent wider fields of view and higher numbers represent narrower fields of view. If you click the Wide button, you get a 90-degree field of view. This view is useful for most situations. In real life, a wide-angle lens is the lens of choice for landscape photography, and that's generally true for Vistapro as well.

The manual for Vistapro points out that you can set very, very high values for the focal length, but you need to move the camera very far away from the scene. You can enter a value of 30,000, for example, but the camera must be 1 million meters away from the scene to get any kind of useful image.

---

[41]For example, 3D Studio uses extensive camera terminology and technique. You can roll or dolly the camera, and you can set a very wide range of lens characteristics.

The remaining controls enable you to create 3D images using red/blue images (you need red/blue glasses to view the images) and panoramic images. The procedure for creating red/blue 3D images is straightforward and is explained well in the Vistapro manual. However, even though the actual procedure is simple, it takes some intense experimentation to determine the correct values for effective 3D images. Expect to spend some time getting the hang of it. The key variables are camera separation and image separation. To get started, follow the manual's instructions exactly, and then vary the settings for your own viewing requirements.

If you do render 3D images, avoid large foreground objects when you are getting started. Large objects can make it difficult to get a good 3D effect. I also suggest making sure that there is no glare on the screen; bright reflections will almost certainly spoil the 3D effect.

Figure 1.29 shows what a red/blue 3D image looks like. This image is in black and white, but there are a number of images on the CD-ROMs that you can view with special glasses.

Figure 1.29.
A red/blue 3D image (see text for explanation of double image).

To create a panoramic series of images, you need to render three times: once in the usual way, then once with the Port[42] button enabled, and once with the StrBrd (Starboard) button enabled. To make sure that the images meet properly at the edges, use a setting of 16 for the focal length (just click the Wide button). Figure 1.30 shows a single image created from three views (Port, Normal, and Starboard).

Figure 1.30. A panoramic image created from three separate renderings.

Fractal Magic

The Fractal bottom control panel enables you to modify an existing landscape with fractal details or to generate random landscapes. Figure 1.31 shows the controls available in this control panel.

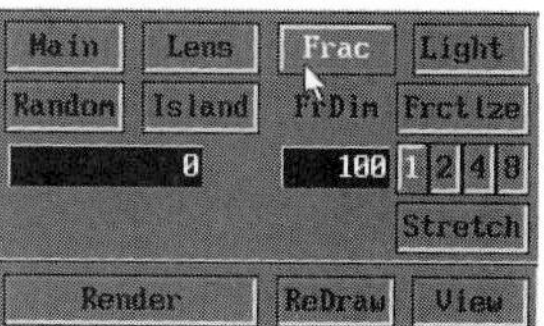

Figure 1.31. The Fractal version of the bottom control panel.

[42]Do you, like most of us, get confused when it comes to *port* and *starboard*? As a public service, I am offering some assistance in getting these two terms into your brain. Ignoring the fact that *left* and *right* would be just as easy to put on the buttons in Vistapro, there are some easy mnemonic devices you can use to tell your port from your starboard. Device 1: the word *left* has four letters, and so does *port*. Ergo: *port* is *left*. Device 2: *Left* comes before *right* in the dictionary, and *port* comes before *starboard*, so *port* is *left* and *starboard* is *right*. Device 3: As Phil, my development editor noted, "the ship left port" is also a convenient way to remember that *port* is *left*. The interesting thing about both of these words is that they are based on words that describe both sides of a ship. *Port* comes from the word *porthole*, meaning a small circular hole in the side of a ship; portholes can be on any side of a ship. Starboard comes from "steer bord." A *bord* is the side of a ship (any side), and *steering* is just what you think it is. How these came to refer to specific directions is anyone's guess; the terms have been in use in English for more than 400 years! I guess it's too late to make a change.

The Random button enables you to generate random fractal landscapes. Directly below the Random button is a text window where a random number appears if you click the Random button.[43] Vistapro generates the fractal landscape as a new map. The other controls in the Fractal control panel affect the nature of the new landscape.

A number such as 1,232,832 generates a completely different landscape than its opposite, -1,232,832. You also can enter numbers directly into the text window and press Enter to generate a landscape.

The Island button generates the landscape as an island; that is, the edge of the map is at 0 elevation. As with all landscapes, you have to fill the sea with water yourself; use the SeaLvl button or the Lake button—either will work well.

The FrDim setting controls the height and roughness of the generated terrain. The default value is 100. Higher values result in higher, rougher landscapes and lower values result in smoother, lower terrain.

The Frctlze button adds fractal detail to existing landscapes. It uses the setting of FrDim to determine what to do. High values of FrDim result in a roughening of the landscape and low values smooth out the landscape. This button also relies on the setting of the Fractal Divisor buttons immediately below it. The Fractal Divisor buttons determine the scale of the fractalization. A setting of 1 adds fractal noise in very tiny changes, whereas a setting of 8 probably changes the overall look of the landscape. This button works exactly in reverse when you generate a landscape; a small fractal divisor generates large landscape features and a high setting results in many small mountains.

The Stretch button changes a landscape by stretching it vertically. Peaks get higher, and valleys get deeper. If you set a low value in the Fractal Divisor buttons, only small features get stretched—a good effect for nightmare landscapes. At high values of the Fractal Divisor, only larger features are stretched. You can stretch repeatedly with different Fractal Divisor settings to get different effects. Figure 1.32 shows a landscape before stretching, and figure 1.33 shows the same landscape after stretching. Yes, that's Mount St. Helens in both figures.

---

[43]You can enter your own number here as well. In fact, if you find a random landscape that you like, you can note the number and re-create it anytime you want.

Figure 1.32. A landscape before stretching.

Figure 1.33. A landscape after stretching with a fractal divisor of 4 (twice) and with a fractal divisor of 1 (once).

Lighting

The Lighting control panel also affects the appearance of the landscape map. A set of concentric circles is overlaid on the map, as shown in figure 1.34. Each circle represents a different lighting angle. At the 0 circle, the light is right on the horizon. At the circle marked 45, the light is exactly halfway between zenith[44] and the horizon. The number represents the number of degrees the light is above the horizon; zenith is 90 degrees. To set the light location,[45] click the Custom button on the Light control panel, and then move the mouse around on the map until the light is coming from the direction you want, at the angle you want.

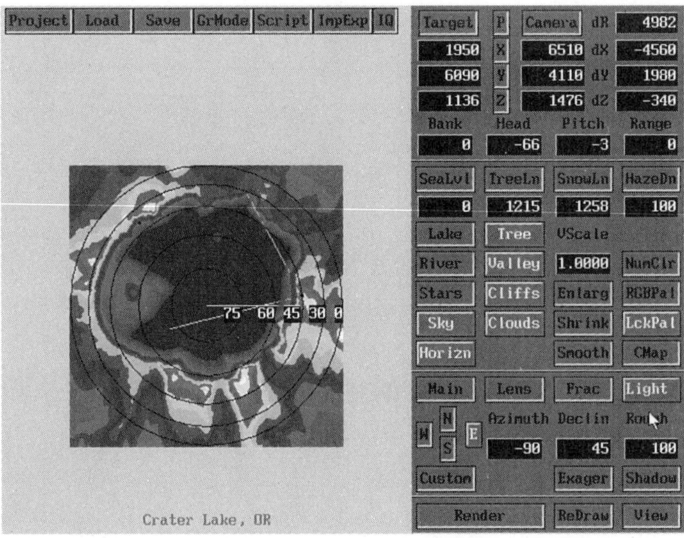

Figure 1.34. The Lighting version of the bottom control panel.

The angle of lighting and the direction in relation to the camera can make a huge difference in the appearance of the landscape. Generally, you want to light from the side at intermediate angles. A bad lighting location can ruin your rendering, however, while a creative lighting angle can create a mood or effect that enhances the appearance of the rendering. For examples of the effects of different lighting setups, refer to figures 1.35 through 1.40. All figures show the same landscape, with shadows turned on and exaggeration turned off. Roughness is set to 100 in all figures.

---

[44]*YATT: Yet Another Technical Term. Zenith* is the point in the sky directly overhead.

[45]It may help to think of the light as the sun on a cloudless day, because that's the effect you get from setting the lighting angle and position.

Figure 1.35. A landscape with the light right behind the camera; note how flat-looking the scene is.

Figure 1.36. The same landscape as figure 1.35, but lit from the right side at a 45-degree angle.

Figure 1.37. The same landscape as figure 1.35, but lit from the left side at a 45-degree angle.

Figure 1.38. The same landscape as figure 1.35, but lit from overhead (high noon).

Figure 1.39. The same landscape as figure 1.35, lit from behind and slightly to one side.

Figure 1.40. The same landscape as figure 1.35, lit from a low angle to simulate sunrise.

You can set basic lighting positions using controls in the Lighting control panels. The N/S/E/W buttons put the light at North, South, East, or West, respectively. The Declination is the lighting angle, expressed as degrees away from the horizon (which is 0). The Azimuth control refers to the rotational angle of the light, with South being 0 and North 180 degrees. The Rough setting controls the apparent roughness of the landscape, and is used with shading texture.[46] Useful values range from 0 to 300; higher values should be used only when you need an unnatural look. Figures 1.41 and 1.42 illustrate the effect of different roughness settings.

Figure 1.41. A landscape rendered with shadows on and a roughness setting of 0.

The Exager button exaggerates the effects of lighting. Instead of a gradual transition from light to shadow, the transition is more abrupt. This effect enhances the apparent detail in the image, but you should experiment with each landscape to see whether it works. In particular, using exaggeration with low lighting angles can put large, flat areas into near-total darkness.

The Shadow button does just what you would expect: It adds shadows to the landscape. This is a must for natural-looking landscapes. Only terrain casts shadows; trees and clouds do not. Rendering takes longer with shadows on.

[46]In case you forgot, you set shading texture in the Main bottom control panel when you select the amount of texture to apply—the O/L/M/H buttons control texture, with O being Off (no texture), and the other buttons setting Low, Medium, and High texture values, respectively. After you click L, M, or H, you are asked to set altitude or shading texture.

Figure 1.42. A landscape rendered with shadows on and a roughness setting of 300.

Figure 1.43 shows a landscape rendered with shadows off, and figure 1.44 shows a landscape rendered with shadows on.

Figure 1.43. A landscape rendered without shadows.

Figure 1.44. A landscape rendered with shadowing turned on.

Using PCX Files as Maps

This is one of the coolest features of Vistapro. You can import PCX files for a variety of applications and in a variety of ways. You can import a PCX graphic that has nothing at all to do with a landscape, for example, such as the face in figure 1.45.

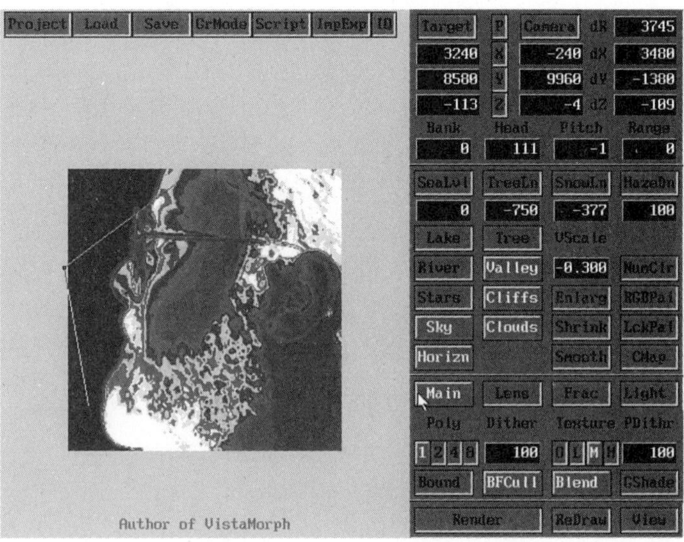

Figure 1.45. The face of the programmer of Vistapro imported as a landscape.

Although the map looks like a face, the rendered landscape doesn't resemble a face at all; figure 1.46 shows a cliff corresponding to the nose in the map. Before rendering the image, I created a sea in front of the nose and added fog to obscure the medium and distant portions of the landscape. Note that the scale setting in figure 1.45 is set to -0.300. As a result, the original peaks were turned into valleys and the original valleys were turned into mountains.[47] Figure 1.47 shows how the landscape looks with a scale setting of +03.00; it is a photo negative of figure 1.45.

Figure 1.46. A rendered landscape from the PCX file imported in figure 1.45.

As a matter of fact, I preferred working with this version of the file. Figure 1.48 shows why. I call it "The Valley of the Ear in Morning Light." As you can see if you look at the original on the CD-ROMs,[48] this image is lit by a low light angle. I also massaged this image slightly in Adobe Photoshop for Windows. I selected just the portions of the "snow" that are facing the sun, and tinted them ever-so-slightly pink to make it look more like an authentic sunrise. Vistapro does not support such detailing, but it's not hard at all to add such effects in a photo-realistic paint program; all you need is a "magic wand" tool that selects areas of similar color.

---

[47] Which hints at a more general consideration: Just importing a PCX file is seldom all you have to do to get a good landscape. You may have to make major adjustments in order to get good results. Be prepared to play and massage until you have something workable. Instant art this is not!

[48] To find images on the CD-ROMs, look for them by the figure number in the index.

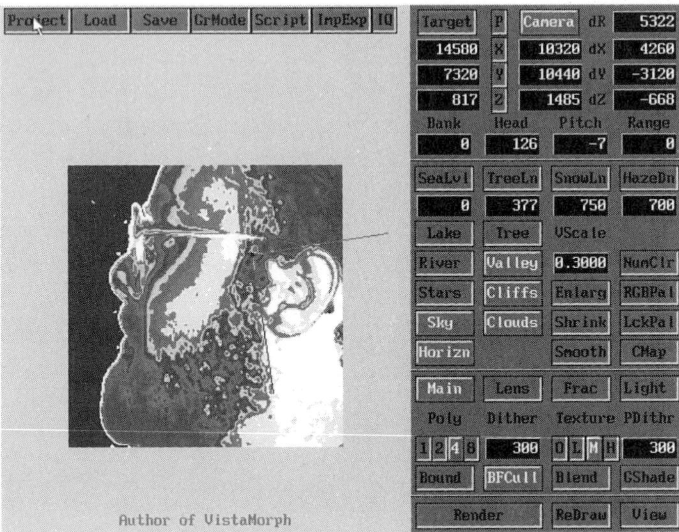

Figure 1.47. A reversed scale setting for the map in figure 1.45.

Make sure that the PCX file is large enough to fill the map area (which is usually 514×514). If the file is smaller, you may get skewing or other undesired distortion.

Figure 1.48. The Valley of the Ear in Morning Light.

It's not as easy as it might look to get a map that looks like the PCX file you import, however. I took a frame from a video I prepared for a different book I wrote (see fig. 1.49), converted it to a PCX file, and imported it. The resulting map (shown in fig. 1.50 from a very high camera angle) bore only the slightest resemblance to the image, but as you can see in figure 1.51, it nonetheless provided some interesting renderings. Figures 1.52 and 1.53 show details from a landscape generated from a slightly different version of the same image. Before converting the image from a BMP to a PCX file, I loaded it into BitEdit[(49)] and reordered the palette according to brightness. Vistapro maps the incoming image according to the order in which colors exist in the palette. If the colors are in random order, you see a random result, as shown in figure 1.50. If you order the palette entries in some way, you get more consistent results.

If you don't think you have an interesting landscape for rendering, try different camera angles and target locations. Almost every landscape has features in it somewhere that give you a pleasing rendering.

Figure 1.49. An image of the author for importing into Vistapro.

[49]This is a bitmap editor that comes with the Video for Windows retail package.

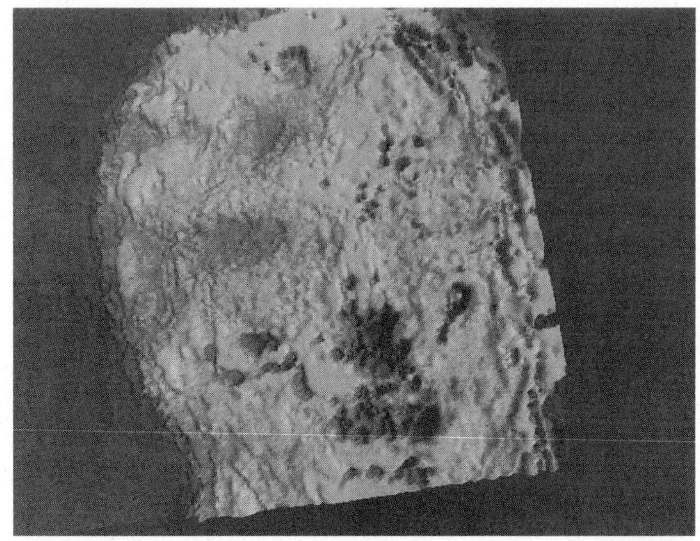

Figure 1.50.
A rendering of the image from figure 1.49; note that it bears little relation to the original image.

Figure 1.51.
A rendering at a low camera angle at a point just below the "nose."

Figure 1.52. A rendering of a broad valley from a different PCX image of the author.

Figure 1.53. The same valley as in figure 1.52, but from a much lower camera angle.

Figures 1.52 and 1.53 illustrate how important it is to experiment with different camera angles and targets. The mood of your image can vary dramatically with different placements.

Animation

Vistapro does a great job rendering single images, but the program really comes into its own when you generate a series of images and combine them into an animation. You could do this manually, of course, by adjusting the camera angle to a slightly different position for each image. However, you would need at least 15 frames for each second of animation.

If you use fewer than 15 frames per second, the image flickers too obviously. Even more frames per second would be better (cartoons and movies use 24, and video uses 30), but many computers don't support such high frame rates—see my book, *PC Video Madness*, for a complete discourse on this subject—and that can get mighty tedious to do manually. The answer is a Vistapro add-on program called Flight Director. Flight Director, also available from Virtual Reality Labs, uses Vistapro's script capabilities to generate a series of images that correspond to a flight path through a landscape.

Figure 1.54 shows a Flight Director screen. It looks something like the Vistapro screen, but only superficially. The concept behind Flight Director is simple. You click a series of points on the landscape map, and this becomes a flight path that a Vistapro camera follows. You can see the flight path superimposed on the map in the left half of the screen in figure 1.54.

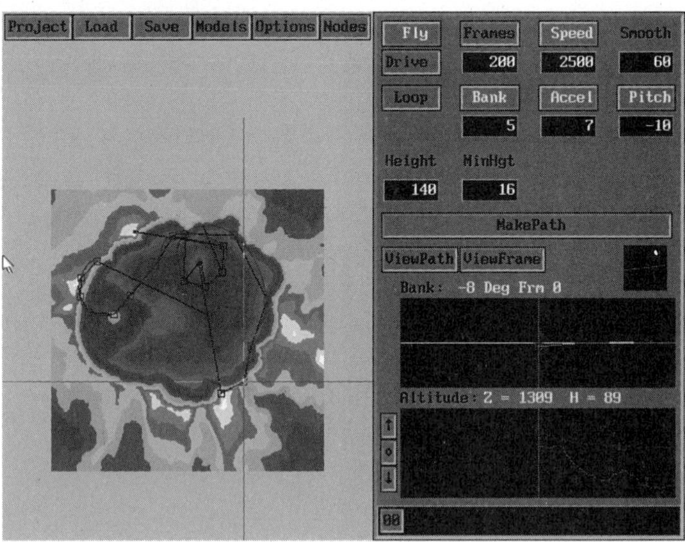

Figure 1.54. The Flight Director screen.

The crosshairs over the map mark the current cursor position. Each of the small squares along the flight path is called a *node,* and each node can have its own target. Flight Director interpolates camera and target positions between nodes, creating a smooth flight path. After you place all the nodes and add any targets,(50) click the MakePath button to generate a path. To see the result in Wireframe(51) mode, click the ViewPath button, which flies you through the animation in the space normally occupied by the map (see fig. 1.55).

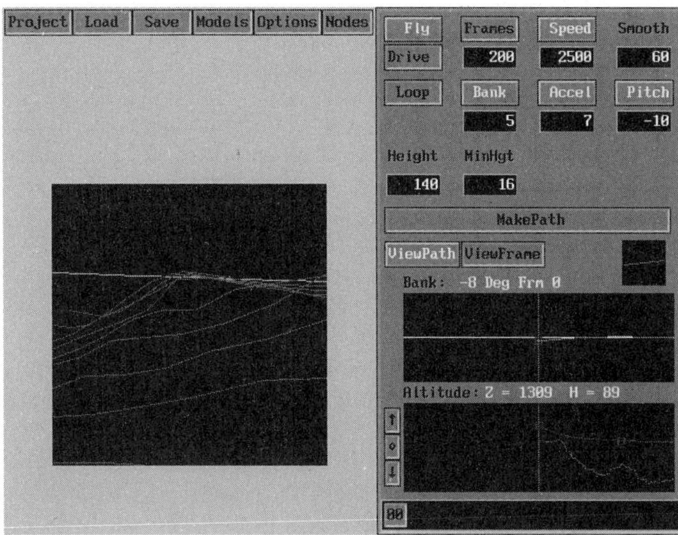

Figure 1.55. Wireframe animation of the flight path.

Flight Director enables you to choose the type of imaginary vehicle making the journey from the Models menu (see fig. 1.56). Not all the vehicles fly; in addition to a glider, jet, cruise missile, and helicopter, you will find a dune buggy and a motorcycle.(52)

---

50 If you don't add any targets, Flight Director assumes that you simply want the camera to point forward.

51 *Wireframe* refers to the act of rendering 3D objects using outlines instead of solid shapes. It's a lot easier and faster to render wireframes than solids.

52 Use caution when working with the land-based vehicles; the path is close to the ground, and actually may go underground if the landscape is very rough. This does not look very good, so watch out for it in the wireframe preview. You can tell you're underground if the landscape is suddenly overhead instead of below.

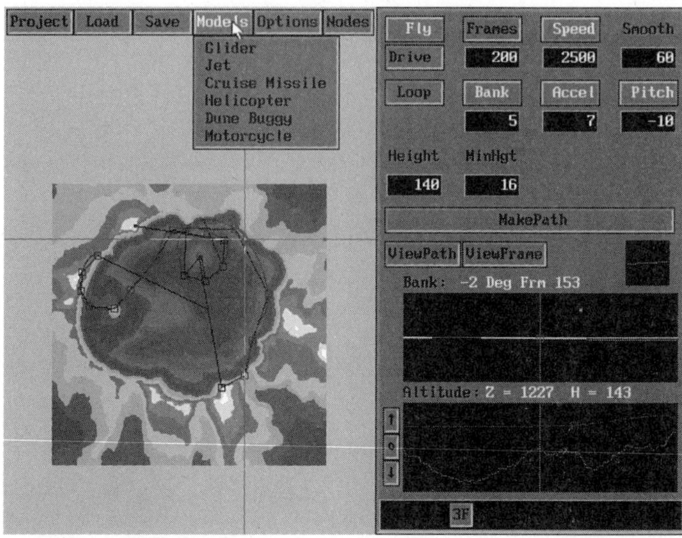

Figure 1.56. Choosing the kind of vehicle.

Let's take a moment to look at the controls in Flight Director. You may never use them; when you pick a vehicle, Flight Director sets default parameters that match the vehicle's characteristics. You may want to fine-tune those characteristics, however, or you may want to try something completely different.

Refer to figure 1.56, where you can see a number of buttons and text windows at the top right of the screen. You can choose to set Fly or Drive buttons, which correspond to the two types of vehicles on the Models menu. You also can determine whether the pace of the fly-through[53] is adjusted for the number of frames, or whether it proceeds at a constant speed and generates as many frames as are needed. If you want the number of frames to control the animation, click the Frames button and enter the number of frames. If you want speed to be the deciding factor, click the Speed button and enter an appropriate speed. I find that 2,500 is a good starting point for speed, but you can change that number for different effects.

You also can set numeric values for Bank, Accel, and Pitch, which control the limits of these activities for the vehicle. Banking refers to action in turns. Aircraft bank one way, while land-based vehicles bank in the opposite sense. A motorcycle, for example, banks into a turn, while a glider banks the opposite way. Acceleration controls the degree to which a vehicle changes speed as it rises and falls. A high Accel value means that the vehicle changes speed more dramatically.

---

[53]Granted, you can fly or drive, but for simplicity's sake I'll use the term *fly-through* in this section to refer to both.

You also can control Pitch changes. Higher values enable the vehicle to pitch forward or backward to a greater degree as it ascends and descends.

The Height text window tells Flight Director how high above the ground elevation to place nodes. For flying vehicles, a good range is from 100 to 200 meters. For ground vehicles, set a low value like 15 to 30 meters. Keep in mind that these numbers are for nodes only. Flight Director makes an effort to ensure that the path doesn't go through the ground, but this is not a guarantee. Raise these numbers for rough terrain to avoid running into the ground. The MinHgt text window tells Flight Director the minimum height above ground to maintain; this is also an effective way to keep from running into the ground. Settings of 5 to 15 meters (15 to 45 feet) will work, but use higher numbers for rough terrain.

The Smooth button also affects the relationship between the vehicle and the ground. High values of smoothing round off the rough edges of the path, but in rough terrain this can run you into the ground. If in doubt, check the path in Preview mode (click the View Path button).

The Loop button causes the last node to loop back to the first node, creating an animation that can be looped.

If you don't want to purchase Flight Director, but would still like to create animations, see "Scripting in Vistapro," later in this chapter, for some ideas that may help you create simple animations.(54)

The procedure for creating a flight path is simple:

- Click to place nodes indicating the path you want to follow.
- Select a model or set the various control settings manually.
- Click the MakePath button to create the path.
- Check the path with the ViewPath button.

If you find that you want to change a node, you can delete it and add a new one using the Node menu, or you can use the Bank and Altitude windows to move the node with the mouse (see fig. 1.56). After moving a node, you must use the

---

[54] Scripting won't be useful in the demo version of Vistapro that is on the CD-ROMs, because you need to save animation frames to the disk before you can link them into an animation. You need the full working version of Vistapro to create animation with Flight Director or scripts.

MakePath button again to re-create the path. Use the Save menu to generate a script that you can load into Vistapro.[55]

Figure 1.57 shows four frames from an animation from one of the files on the CDs. If you look closely, you'll see that each frame is slightly different. The sequence is taken from one of the Crater Lake fly-throughs.

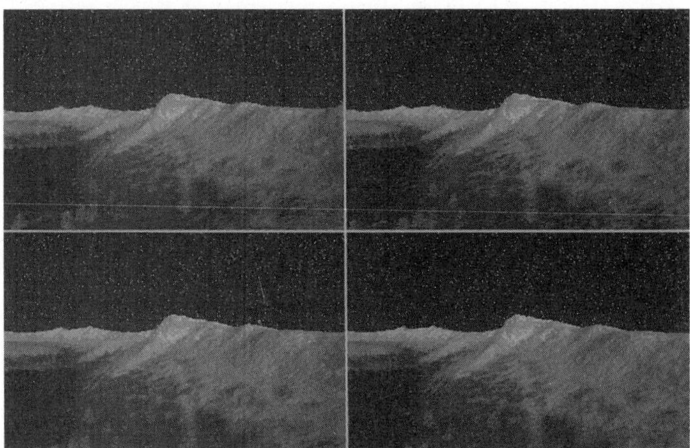

Figure 1.57. Four frames from an animation (a fly-through over Crater Lake, OR).

TIP

Lock the palette before creating animations.[56] This action ensures that a single palette is used for all the files. Locking the palette is necessary for using the animation player that comes with Vistapro, and makes life easier with most other programs. You may get better results, however, with some programs that can create a single palette from multiple palettes. Examples include Animator Pro and good old VidEdit.

---

[55]To load the script, just use the Script menu in Vistapro. Select one of the Run items (which one you use depends on the kind of file you want to generate—Targa, BMP, or PCX), and then click the name of the Script file you created in Flight Director. You need to supply a base name, such as PIC, to which Vistapro appends numbers for each file—PIC00001.PCX, PIC00002.PCX, and so on. Vistapro now happily creates all the images necessary for the animation. You can load the resulting files into a program such as Animator Pro or VidEdit to create an FLI, FLC, or AVI file. Before you start, make sure that the image size and all settings are correct. The most common mistake with a script is to have the wrong landscape loaded!

[56]Use the LckPal button in Vistapro to lock the palette. If you are using Vmorph (see the next section) to create the animation, set Lock Palette on the Setup menu.

See Chapter 6, "I Can Fly!", for an exciting use of a landscape animation in 3D Studio.

Morphing

Now you'll learn something that literally will make the earth move: morphing landscapes. It won't exactly happen under your feet, but you can create animations of a wide variety of landscape changes. In this section, you learn how to create an animation that grows a rugged, mountainous landscape out of flat terrain using Vmorph, another add-on program for Vistapro.

Figure 1.58 shows the starting landscape. However, this is not the place to get started; you start with the last frame, for reasons that will be clear shortly. Figure 1.59 shows the last frame.

Figure 1.58. The starting landscape for a morph.

I created this landscape using the Fractal control panel; I simply clicked the Random button and took what showed up. Because the morph is intended to show a landscape rising up, the key is to use the vertical-scaling capabilities. It's very simple: for the ending image, I used a vertical scale of 2.0 and saved the file as END.DEM. For the starting image, I used a vertical scale of 0.2 and saved it as START.DEM.

Figure 1.59. The ending landscape for a morph.

Don't save the file as an extended DEM file. Vmorph can't handle the extended file format.[57] If you want to include such things as clouds in the morph, you need to use scripts. See "Scripting in Vistapro," later in this chapter, for an example.

Figure 1.60 shows the opening screen of Vmorph. Vista Morph is not included on the CDs. It is an add-on program that you can purchase from Virtual Reality Laboratories, the folks who sell Vistapro. It's much easier to work with than it looks. There's a menu at the top, frame numbers from left to right,[58] and buttons with actions you can take on the left. You only need to use one of the buttons to create a morph: LOADDEM. You load START.DEM to start the morph and END.DEM to complete it.

---

[57]Extended DEM files contain information beyond simple landscape data—cloud settings, tree settings, and so on.

[58]The frame numbers are confusing; they read from left to right and bottom to top. That is, the number 10 shows up with 0 on the top and 1 on the bottom.

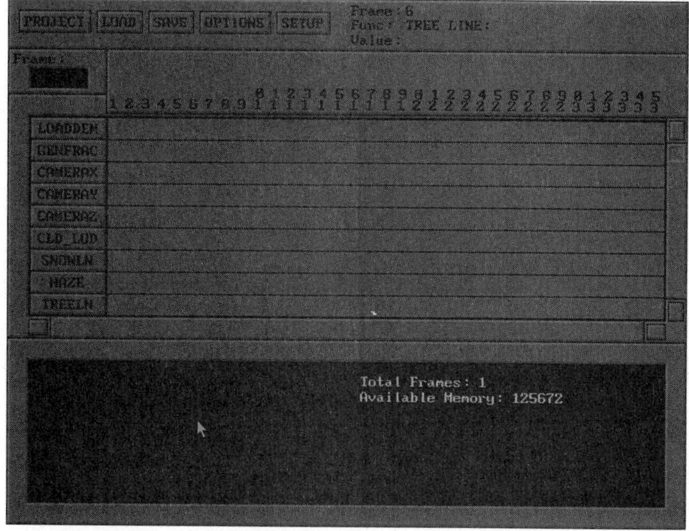

Figure 1.60. The opening screen of Vmorph.

Step 1: Click on the line marked LOADDEM in the space for frame 1 (see fig. 1.61). A dialog box appears. Enter the name of the file to load (START.DEM) and click OK.

Step 2: Click again on the line marked LOADDEM, but this time in the space for frame 60 (see fig. 1.62).[(59)] A dialog box opens. Enter the name of the file to load (END.DEM) and click OK.

Step 3: Click the right mouse button to toggle the menu, and then click the Morph button. The dialog box shown in figure 1.63 appears. Don't enter text into the text windows directly. Click on the LOADDEM line in frame 1, and then in frame 60. The values are entered into the Morph dialog box automatically. You need to change only one value: set a value of .75 for Ease.[(60)]

Step 4: Set global values for the morph on the Setup menu: Lock Palette On and Graphics Mode 320×200. Set the palette to frame 1.

Step 5: Time to generate the script. Click the Save menu and enter a name for the script file in the text window (see fig. 1.64). After the script is saved, exit Vmorph.

Step 6: Load Vistapro. Click the script menu selection Run PCX, which displays the dialog box shown in figure 1.65. Click the file name of the script file you created in step 5.

---

[59]Use the slider button at the bottom right to move to frame 60.

[60]Ease controls the pace of the morph. If the Ease value is less than 1, the morph starts fast and then slows down. If the Ease value is greater than 1, the morph starts slow and then speeds up.

Step 7: After the script loads, you see a dialog box asking for the base picture name. This is a three-character prefix that is used for each of the image files generated. The first file name in the example would be PIC00000.PCX, the next PIC00001.PCX, and so on. After you click OK, the script runs. The script repeatedly uses Vistapro to create frames; the process can take a long time. I once created a very long fly-through of the Big Sur area. It had more than 1,600 frames and took two and a half days to generate. This isn't as bad as it seems; I added trees, which can triple the rendering time.

Step 8: Enjoy! You can use the PCX2FLC utility to create an animation, or you can load the bitmaps into VidEdit (Video for Windows) as a DIB sequence[61] and add sound appropriate to such earth-shattering goings on. The PCX2FLC utility is easy to use—it has a command-line interface. To create an animation, use the command line

```
pcx2flc pic -b -s
```

where `pic` is the base picture file name, `-b` tells the program to use compression to reduce file size, and `-s` tells the program to optimize for playback speed. These settings ensure playback on the widest variety of hardware. The output file in this example would have the file name PIC.FLC.

See "Scripting in Vistapro" for an example of a script created by Vmorph.

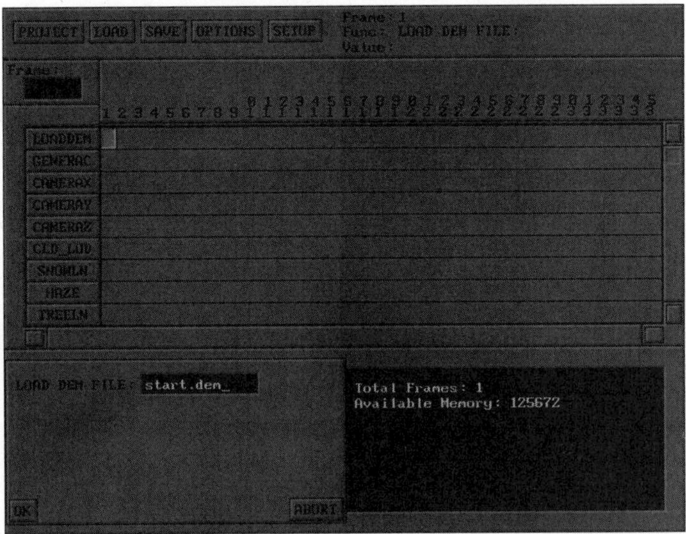

Figure 1.61. Loading a DEM file in frame 1.

[61]You can use a utility like Image Pals in Windows to convert all the files in one shot, or you can use the Run BMP24 menu choice instead of Run PCX to generate bitmap files directly. However, 24-bit files are much larger, so you need much more disk space—192,000 bytes per frame, to be exact, for a 320×200 animation.

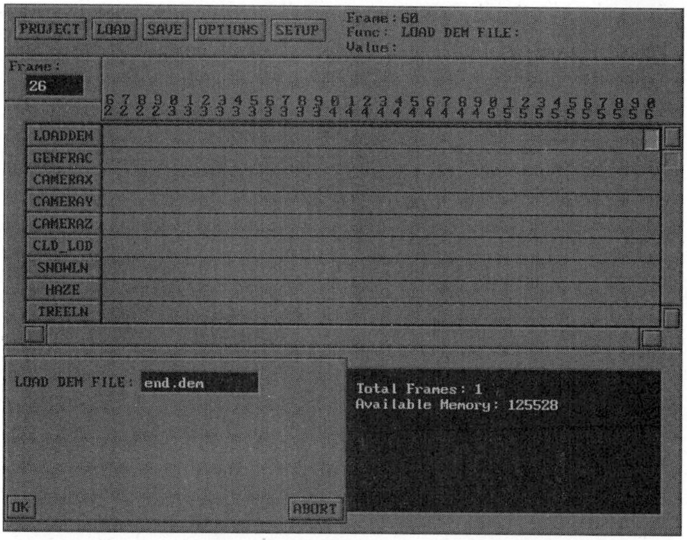

Figure 1.62. Loading a DEM file in frame 26.

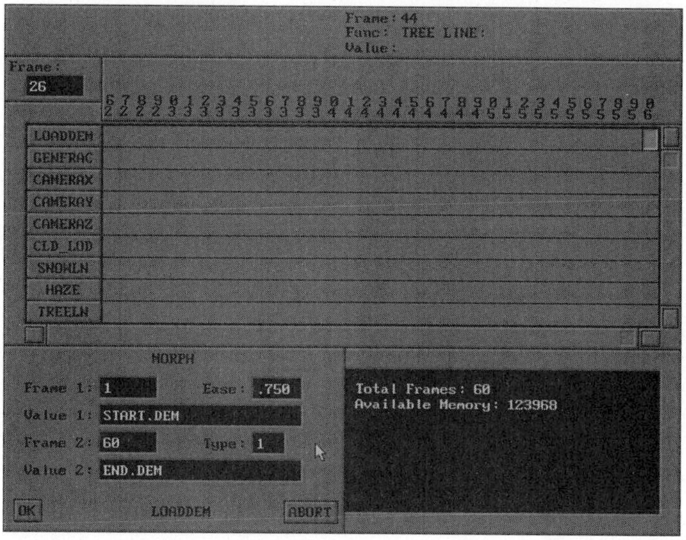

Figure 1.63. Setting the morph values.

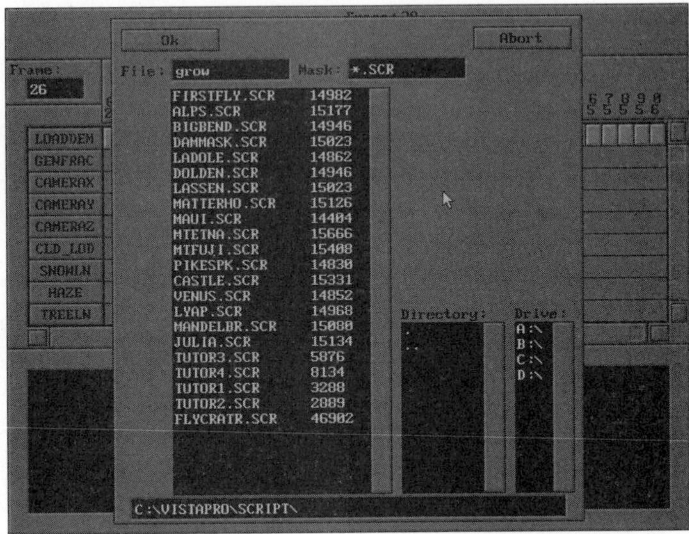

Figure 1.64.
Generating the script file.

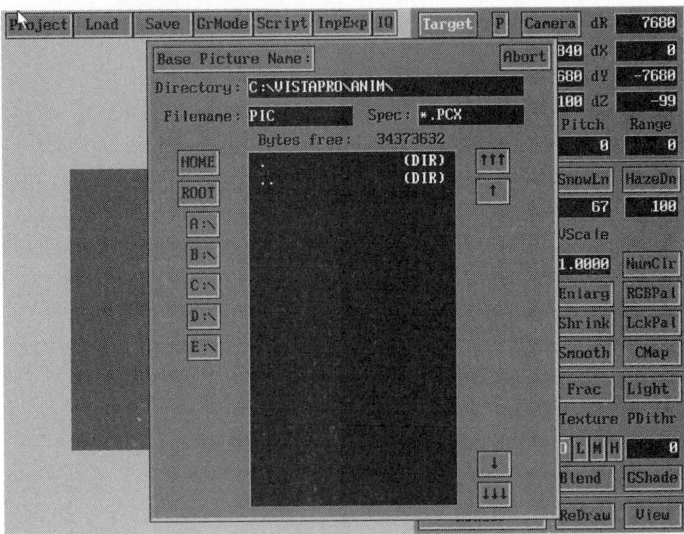

Figure 1.65.
Selecting a script.

Figure 1.66. Four sample frames from a morph animation (frames 1, 20, 40, and 60).

Vistapro Gallery

All the images in this section were created with Vistapro. Some of the images were further modified in a paint program. Typical reasons for using a paint program include adding a sun, adding special effects such as lens flare, adding objects or people to the landscape, and using the landscape as a background.

Figure 1.67. A view of El Capitan, a famous rock-climbing destination.

Figure 1.68. The same view as in figure 1.67, but using Gourand shading. Note how this softer shading gives the image a very different feel.

Figure 1.69. A fractally generated landscape in late afternoon light.

Figure 1.70. This landscape is similar to that in figure 1.69, but no cliffs and a body of water give it a much more serene look. Note that there is no sky haze, giving the landscape a hyper-real look.

Figure 1.71. Even the simplest landscape looks good in a Vistapro rendering.

Figure 1.72. A slightly fractalized version of the Mandelbrot set.[62] A Mandelbrot DEM file is one of the sample files that comes with Vistapro. As supplied, the landscape has sheer cliffs and isn't too exciting. I applied smoothing and a little fractal texture to create a more realistic appearance.

Figure 1.73. Two renderings of a valley using the same data. The rendering on the left was done using normal height, and the rendering on the right used a height setting of 2.000.

[62]The *Mandelbrot set* is a famous set of points in fractal history. See Chapter 7, "Hardware for Virtual Worlds," for information about fractals.

Figure 1.74. A fanciful landscape created from one of the DEM files supplied with Vistapro 3.0.

Scripting in Vistapro

One of the most powerful aspects of Vistapro is its support for scripting. Just about every feature of Vistapro can be controlled in a script. The easiest way to create a script is to use Vmorph to generate a script. If necessary, you can edit the generated script in a text editor to make final changes. You usually can accomplish everything you need to right in Vmorph, however.

Figure 1.75. This landscape was created from a PCX image that was imported with the PCX—>DEM menu selection. The extreme vertical drop is typical of an abrupt change in the PCX from a light shade to a dark shade.

Figure 1.76. This landscape also is based on an imported PCX that was converted to a DEM file. The image has a haunting quality that I really like; it's one of my favorite Vistapro landscapes.

In the "Morphing" section earlier in this chapter, I outlined an eight-step procedure for creating a morph in Vmorph. In this section, you learn how to tweak the script to produce the most realistic-looking animations.

Remember that column of buttons at the left of the Vmorph screen? Refer back to figure 1.61. To set up the necessary parameters, all we need to do is click in frame 1 in the rows corresponding to several important buttons. The most important settings are shown in table 1.6.

Table 1.6. Morph Settings.

Setting	*Description*
Altitude Texture	One of the most important settings for photo-realism is altitude texture. We are rendering at 320×200, so there's no need for ultimate quality. I used a setting of `ALTITUDETEXTUREMEDIUM`.
Blending	Blending is most effective on distant portions of the landscape. With a setting of `BLENDON`, distant objects are not too sharply defined.

Setting	*Description*
Dithering	With only 256 colors in a palette, dithering is critical for realism. This is one of two dither settings, and it controls dithering between color bands. I used the same value that Vistapro uses as a default: DITHER 100.00.
Shadows	Just for fun, I used Vmorph to create a varying sun angle during the animation. Setting SHADOWSON emphasizes the movement of the sun.
Lighting Angle (Azimuth)	Moving the sun during the animation gives the impression of time-lapse photography. A setting of SUNAZIMUTH 90.00 starts the sun in the east. It moves approximately 3 degrees (1/60×180) in each frame. The exact change from frame to frame is affected by the Ease setting of .75.
Pixel Dither	This is one of two dither settings. This setting controls the amount of dithering in all pixels, whereas the Dither setting refers only to the color bands. I used a setting of PIXELDITHERRANDOM 100.00. This provides a modest amount of dithering; too much dithering ruins the realistic effect.
Polygon Size	All the settings listed here are important, but none is more important than Polygon Size. For realism, always use a setting of POLYGONSIZE1 when rendering. This creates the smallest possible polygons.

continues

Table 1.6. continued

Setting	*Description*
Backface Culling	Rendering speed increases if you set BACKFACECULLINGON. This means that unseen portions of the landscape are not rendered.
Palette Locking	Setting LOCKPALETTE ensures that all frames use the same palette as frame 1. This is necessary if you are using PCX3FLC to create the animation.

You can set each of these values by clicking in frame 1 in the corresponding row in Vmorph. An appropriate dialog box appears, enabling you to enter or click on the required value or setting. The only exception to this is the lighting angle. This works just like the morphing you did on the LOADDEM line. Click frame 1 in the row marked SunAzimuth and enter a value of 90 (that's East). In the same row, click frame 60 and enter a value of -90 (West). Then click the Morph menu button at the top of the screen to display the Morph dialog box. Click frame 1, then frame 60, and then click OK in the dialog box to create the intermediate settings in frames 2 through 59.[63]

If you set these values correctly, you see the following script lines for frame 1, following the default settings:

```
ALTITUDETEXTUREMEDIUM
BLENDON
DITHER 100.00
SHADOWSON
SUNAZIMUTH 90.00
PIXELDITHERRANDOM 100.00
POLYGONSIZE1
BACKFACECULLINGON
RENDER
LOCKPALETTE
; Frame: 1 END
```

[63]You can use this technique to morph any numeric values in a script, between any two frames.

The wide variety of available commands gives you a high degree of control over scripting. With a little effort, you can create some amazing animation. You also can use Vmorph to add such things as cloud map loading for each frame to increase realism. To load a cloud map, all you need is a command like this for each frame:

```
CLOUDLOAD CLOUD\MORPH1
```

The file name is MORPH1. You do not need to specify the CLD extension.

Creating animations is fun, but it's also fun just to play them. I have included many animations created with Vmorph (as well as an animation player) on the CD-ROMs for your enjoyment.

Listing 1.1. A Vistapro Script Generated by Vmorph.

```
Vista Script File
CamX,  CamY,  CamZ, Bank, Hdng, Ptch,
; Frame: 1 BEGIN
DEFAULTDIRDEM DEM\
DEFAULTDIRCMAP CMAP\
DEFAULTDIRCLOUD CLOUD\
DEFAULTDIRSCRIPT SCRIPT\
DEFAULTDIRFOREGROUND TGA24\
DEFAULTDIRBACKGROUND TGA24\
DEFAULTDIRIQ IQ\
LANDSCAPESIZEAUTO
GRMODEVGA320X200
GRMODEVESA640X480
LOADDEM DEM\START.DEM
ALTITUDETEXTUREMEDIUM
BLENDON
DITHER 100.00
SHADOWSON
SUNAZIMUTH 90.00
PIXELDITHERRANDOM 100.00
POLYGONSIZE1
BACKFACECULLINGON
RENDER
LockPalette
; Frame: 1 END
; Frame: 2 BEGIN
SPAWN META DEM\START.DEM DEM\END.DEM DEM\METALTMP.DEM 1 59 1 0.75 1
LOADDEM DEM\METALTMP.DEM
SUNAZIMUTH 83.90
LOCKPALETTE
RENDER
; Frame: 2 END
; Frame: 3 BEGIN
SPAWN META DEM\START.DEM DEM\END.DEM DEM\METALTMP.DEM 2 59 1 0.75 1
LOADDEM DEM\METALTMP.DEM
```

continues

Listing 1.1. Continued

```
SUNAZIMUTH 80.85
RENDER
; Frame: 3 END
;
; Frames 4 through 57 are pretty much the same.  For each
; frame, the parameters for the SPAWN command are
; incremented, and the sun azimuth angle is changed to give
; the impression that the sun is moving across the sky
; ;during the morph.
;
; Frame: 58 BEGIN
SPAWN META DEM\START.DEM DEM\END.DEM DEM\METALTMP.DEM 57 59 1 0.75 1
LOADDEM DEM\METALTMP.DEM
SUNAZIMUTH -86.95
RENDER
; Frame: 58 END
; Frame: 59 BEGIN
SPAWN META DEM\START.DEM DEM\END.DEM DEM\METALTMP.DEM 58 59 1 0.75 1
LOADDEM DEM\METALTMP.DEM
SUNAZIMUTH -90.00
RENDER
; Frame: 59 END
; Frame: 60 BEGIN
LOADDEM DEM\END.DEM
SUNAZIMUTH -90.00
RENDER
; Frame: 60 END
```

Vistapro for Windows

I found Vistapro completely addictive—it was just about impossible to stop playing with it. I suppose that it makes one feel like a kind of superman, able to forge complete landscapes out of mere electrons. There was only one thing stopping me from becoming a complete addict: Vistapro ran under DOS, and I spend most of my time in Windows.

I am no longer safe. Virtual Reality Laboratories sent me a soon-to-be-released Windows version of Vistapro. Now I have this program at my fingertips and I don't know how I'm going to get my work done.

The Windows interface is almost exactly like the DOS interface, as you can see in figure 1.77. A few of the buttons have moved to new homes, but by and large, anyone familiar with the DOS version can find their way around in the Windows version.

Even though the version I looked at was a prerelease version, I found it very stable. I was able to generate images easily. Figure 1.78 shows an aerial shot of Maui that I created with the Windows version of Vistapro.

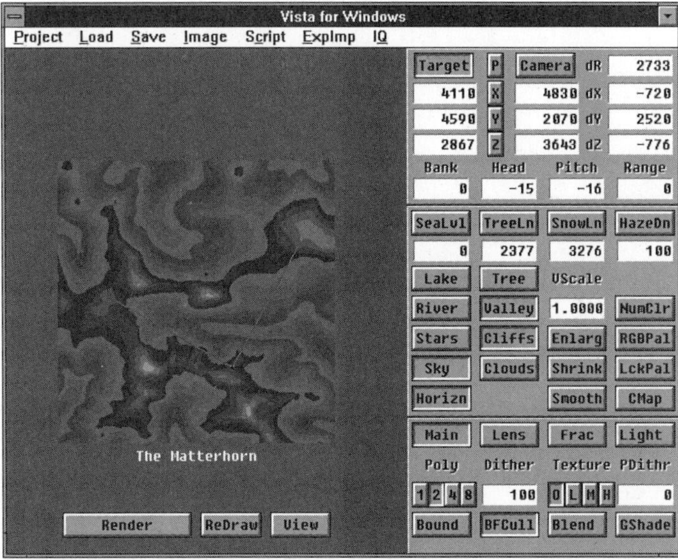

Figure 1.77. The Windows interface of Vistapro.

Figure 1.78. An aerial view of Maui created with the Windows version of Vistapro.

As you can see, all the detailed features of the DOS version are available in Windows. The trees are nicely detailed, shadowing is very effective, and the water even has waves. I was extremely pleased with performance on my 486/66. In general, I prefer the Windows version over the DOS version. Perhaps this is just because of my preference for working in Windows, but the capability to render in the background is an especially useful feature that the DOS version does not offer.[64]

Figure 1.79 shows another image that I generated with the Windows version. This is a random fractal landscape with a lake of black lava. It is an almost hyper-real landscape, very rich in detail and extremely effective at fooling the eye.

Figure 1.79. An imaginary landscape that looks almost photographic.

Figure 1.80 shows another side of the capabilities of Vistapro for Windows. This is a nighttime, moonlit landscape from the vantage point of a valley near the Matterhorn. It has an eerie, almost supernatural quality. It would make a great movie set!

[64]Watch out, however—rendering uses up a lot of your computer power, and some tasks aren't much fun while rendering is going on. Solitaire is fine; word processing may get tedious.

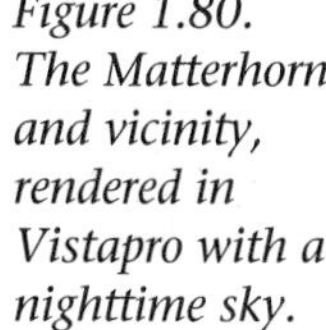

Figure 1.80. The Matterhorn and vicinity, rendered in Vistapro with a nighttime sky.

Speaking of the Matterhorn, I learned a little tip that I'd like to pass on to you. In general, when I render, I use the highest possible quality settings. Compare figure 1.81 to 1.82, however. Note that figure 1.81 is much more realistic than figure 1.82. The primary difference between these two figures is the polygon setting. Figure 1.81 uses a very high (and therefore coarse and, one would assume, less realistic) setting of 8. However, when coupled with altitude shading, this gives the rock face of the mountain an extremely realistic look. There is one flaw, that nearly horizontal line at the base of the Matterhorn, but this seems a small price for a touch of reality.

Figure 1.82, on the other hand, shows more detail, but the rock face is much less realistic. The small polygon size—a setting of 1 was used—results in a kind of pebbly surface, quite unlike the actual surface of your average mountain.

Overall, I can't overstate how pleased I was with the Windows version of Vistapro. I do try to restrain myself when recommending software, but Vistapro has to be an exception. It's been wonderful fun to play with. The Windows version just makes it that much more tempting.

Figure 1.81.
A more realistic view of the Matterhorn, rendered in Vistapro. See text for details and compare to figure 1.82.

Figure 1.82.
A less realistic view of the Matterhorn, rendered in Vistapro. See text for details and compare to figure 1.81.

Related Products

Several related products are available from Virtual Reality Laboratories that are worth a mention here. These products use some of the same techniques used in Vistapro, but address different issues and tasks. Two of the more interesting are the Mars Explorer and Distant Suns.

Mars Explorer

I recently read a pair of science fiction novels set on the planet Mars. They are *Red Mars* and *Green Mars,* by Kim Stanley Robinson. Both novels include settings at various places on Mars, and use the scientific names for these places—Olympus Mons, and so on. As I read along, I got more and more confused. I kept thinking that I would enjoy this so much more if I had a handy reference to the surface features of Mars.

Mars Explorer to the rescue! This program enables you to explore a large portion of our planetary neighbor in detail. The program is supplied on CD-ROM, and has a simple and very handy interface (see fig. 1.83).

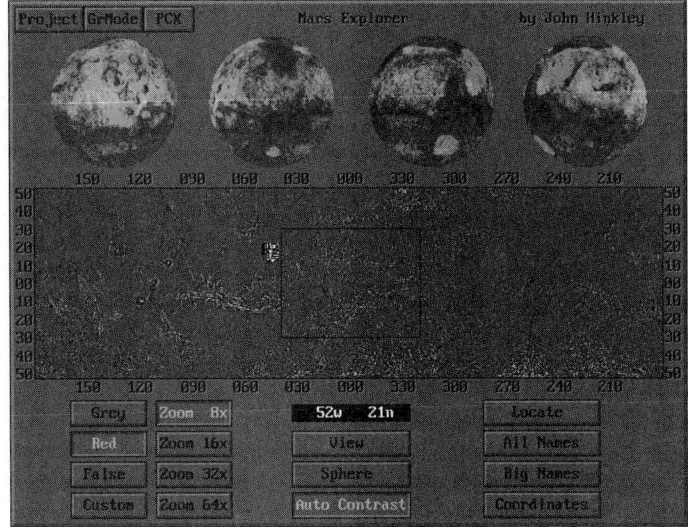

Figure 1.83. The Mars Explorer user interface.

The four global views of Mars at the top are purely ornamental; the meat and potatoes of this program is the map at the center of the screen. The black box encloses an area of Mars that you can view in greater detail. The exact nature of those details is determined by the buttons at the bottom of the screen. See table 1.7 for a description of what each button does.

Table 1.7. Mars Explorer Buttons.

Button	*Function*
Grey	Displays the Mars map in grey.(65) Useful if you are using a monochrome monitor on your portable computer during a Mars landing.
Red	Mars' nickname, the Red Planet, is based on its natural color. Red displays Mars as it was meant to be seen.
False	You also can view Mars in false colors, but I couldn't find a good reason to use this selection.
Custom	If you care to take the time, you can define your own 256 false-color scheme for viewing Mars.
Zoom buttons	Enables you to see various levels of detail. See figures 1.84 through 1.86 for examples of zoom capabilities. At larger zoom factors, the little black box gets smaller, because you are viewing a smaller area of the planet.
View	Views the area within the little black box.
Sphere	Displays a revolving sphere animation of Mars. Awesome, but once you've seen it... figure 1.87 shows a single frame from the animation.
Auto Contrast	These images were collected by a spacecraft orbiting high above the Martian surface, and image contrast is quite poor. The software attempts to correct for this problem if this button is clicked. You also can make manual adjustments to contrast to suit your own tastes.

[65]*Grey* or *gray*? The spelling *grey* is your clue that this program was developed originally in Great Britain, where they have grey skies. I live near Seattle, where we have gray skies.

Button	*Function*
Locate	Displays a list of Martian features to view.
All Names	Shows all names in the Martian place-name database when you view an image of the surface. See figure 1.88 for an example.
Big Names	Shows just the really important place names when you view an image.
Coordinates	Searches using Martian surface coordinates.

A gallery of Mars Explorer features follows.

Figure 1.84. A view of the area around Olympus Mons at a view factor of 8x. At this setting, you can make out only the major features of the planet. It's hard to get a sense of scale, but Olympus Mons is 600 kilometers across and 25 kilometers high! For comparison, the original Mt. Olympus is a little less than 10,000 feet high.

Figure 1.85. A view of the area around Olympus Mons at a view factor of 32x. The mountain now fills more than half the height of the image, and many more details are visible.

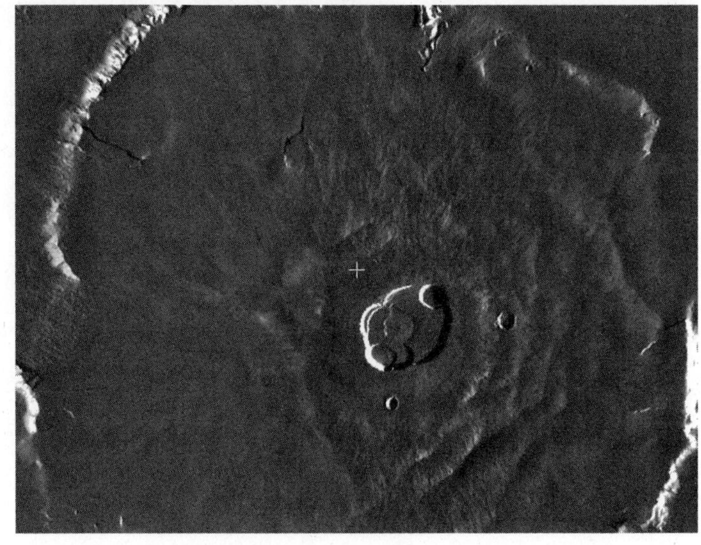

Figure 1.86. A view of the area around Olympus Mons at a view factor of 64x. The mountain is now bigger than can be shown, and the finer details of its surface are clearly visible.

Figure 1.87. A single frame from the animation of a revolving Mars.

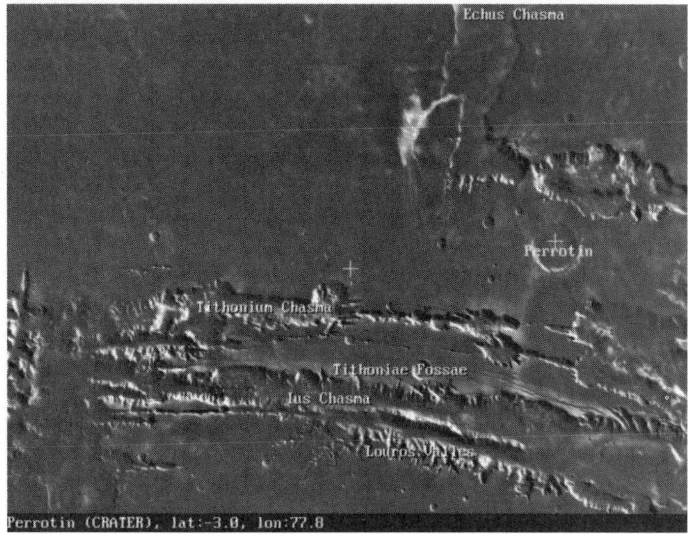

Figure 1.88. A view of the Tithonium Chasma showing place names; Perrotin crater is selected at middle right. Note that the latitude and longitude of the crater are displayed at the bottom of the screen. This example includes only the major place names. With all place names set, dozens of names would be shown.

Just for fun, I loaded several of the Mars DEM files that come on the Vistapro CD-ROM into Vistapro for Windows (see fig. 1.89). I used a total of 12 files, creating a region 4 wide by 3 high in order to encompass all of Olympus Mons.[(66)]

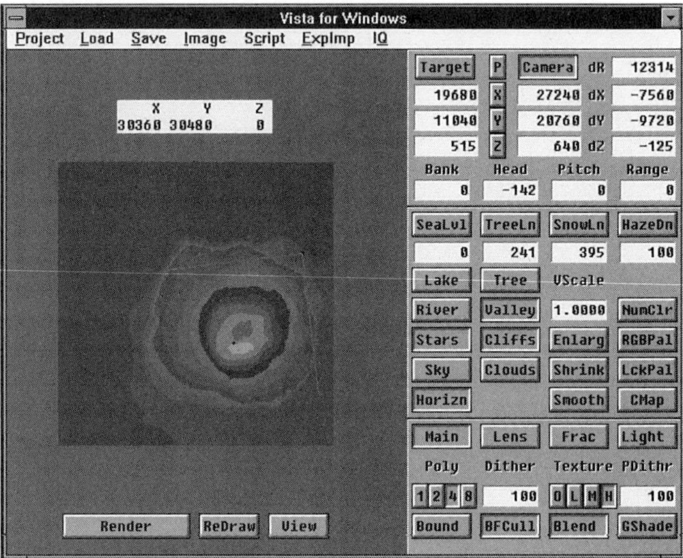

Figure 1.89. Vistapro for Windows with the DEM files for the Olympus Mons region loaded.

I rendered the scene with the vertical scale exaggerated by a factor of 7—Olympus Mons is so large that it looks almost flat from any normal vantage point. Figure 1.90 shows the resulting rendering. This image also is reproduced in the color section of the book, and can be found tucked away in the IMAGES directory on the CD-ROMs.

The Vistapro CD-ROM comes with a very large number of Mars DEM files, covering a large portion of the planet. You easily can render any scene you want by loading the appropriate region's DEM files.[(67)]

---

[66] The files are arranged by latitude and longitude, so they were easy to find using the opening screen of Mars Explorer as a guide.

[67] As if Vistapro weren't already addictive enough, now I've got another planet to fool around with! No wonder I never seem to get to Comdex.

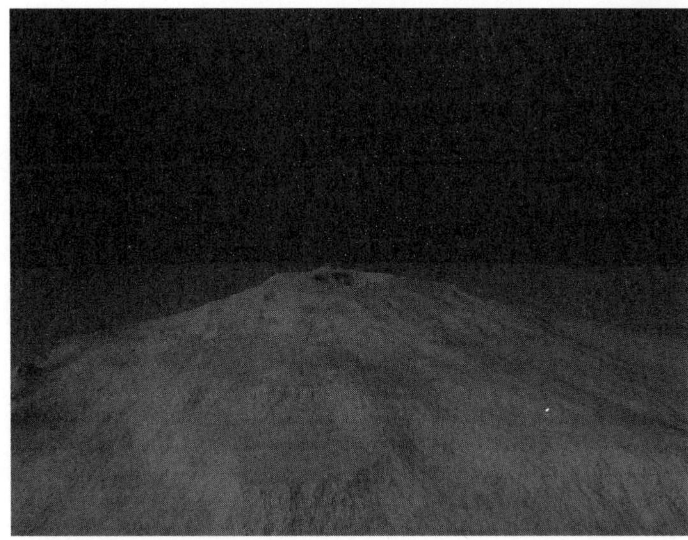

Figure 1.90. A rendering of the landscape around the Olympus Mons on Mars, courtesy of Vistapro for Windows.

Distant Suns

While Vistapro and Mars Explorer use much of the same technology, Distant Suns (also from Virtual Reality Laboratories) is a completely different kind of program. Distant Suns enables you to tour the universe, but the emphasis is on accurate facts, not realism. I have been an astronomy buff since I was knee high to a 14-inch monitor, so I couldn't resist the temptation.(68)

I may be stretching the term *virtual reality* to make it cover Distant Suns, but it's well worth the stretch. Figure 1.91 shows one of the many views of the universe that Distant Suns offers. In the figure, you are somewhere out in the solar system,(69) watching comet Halley make its orbit around the sun. The comet is located just above the word `Mercury`. If you look closely, you even can make out the tail. The toolbar under the Distant Suns menu is set to animate Halley's orbit at the rate of two days per frame, which is just right to give it a nice graceful transition near the sun.

68Given my confession of addiction to Vistapro and this reference to temptation, you might be getting the idea that my interests in computers are out of control. You are correct.

69From the looks of things, it appears that your viewing position is somewhere beyond Mars and within the orbit of Jupiter.

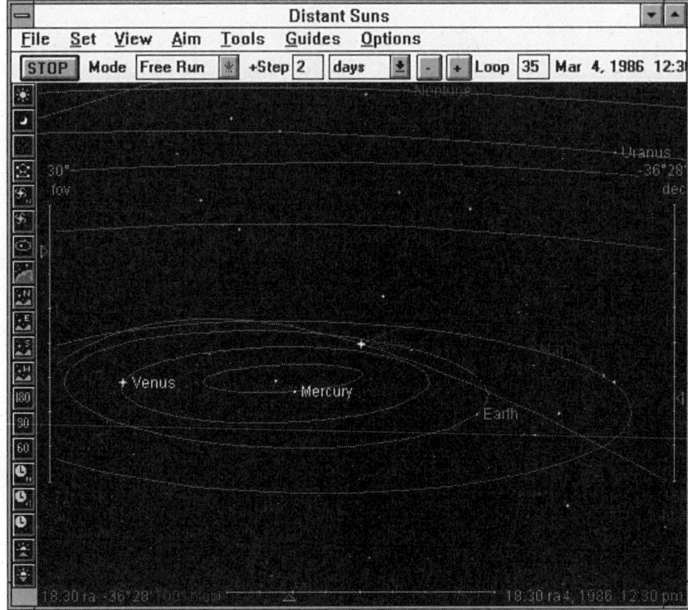

Figure 1.91. Distant Suns animating the orbit of comet Halley as of March 4, 1986.

You also can use Distant Suns to view the universe in more traditional, technical astronomical terms, as shown in figure 1.92. You can easily center the view on an astronomical object of interest, using the Search & Aim dialog box shown in figure 1.93. The view is centered on the now-famous star Betelgeuse.[70]

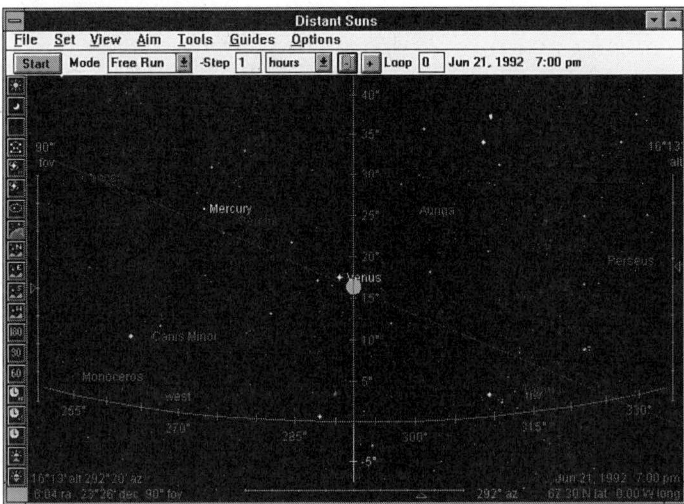

Figure 1.92. A view of the starry skies centered on the sun.

[70]Famous of course, because of the movie starring Michael Keaton some years ago. Fame has its price, of course; how many of us can spell the name correctly?

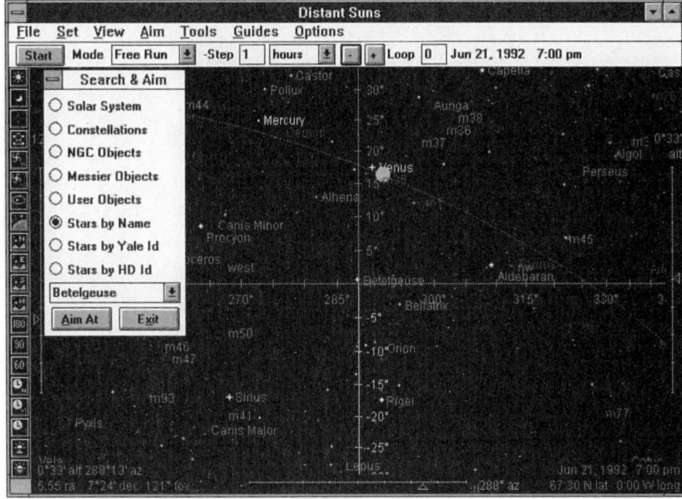

Figure 1.93.
The Search & Aim dialog box lets you center the view on just about any heavenly object.

Distant Suns is full of neat features. There is a detailed lunar map, for example, as shown in figure 1.94. Another clever aid to celestial navigation is shown in figure 1.95—the Rise/Set guide. This guide adjusts to the date you select, and shows graphically the rising and setting times of the principal heavenly bodies.

Figure 1.94.
Distant Suns includes a lunar map.

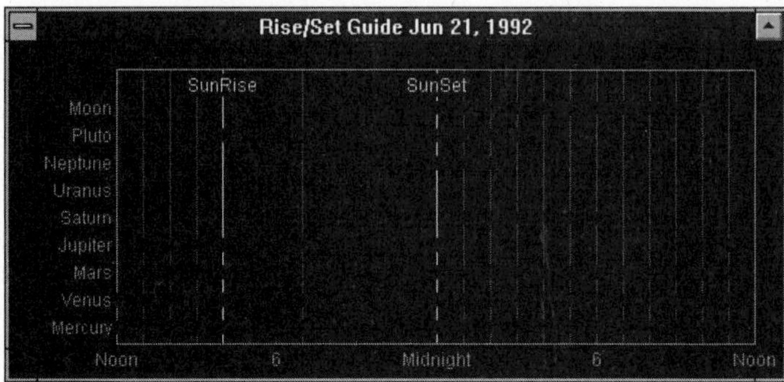

Figure 1.95. The Rise/Set guide enables you to see what heavenly bodies are available for viewing in the night sky.

It was a lot of fun to work with Distant Suns. The capability to create animation of sky movements was especially interesting, and the detailed and comprehensive nature of the information will amuse and inform anyone with an interest in astronomy. The documentation is straightforward and very useful, and it contains a wide variety of useful facts. You can even learn how to select an appropriate telescope if you tire of virtual skies and want to spend some time gazing at the real thing.

Also included is a huge library of astronomical images. There is a large library of images from the lunar orbiter flybys, as well as a number of images from planetary exploration. Figure 1.96 shows just one of the hundreds of images from the CD, a close view of the asteroid Gaspra.

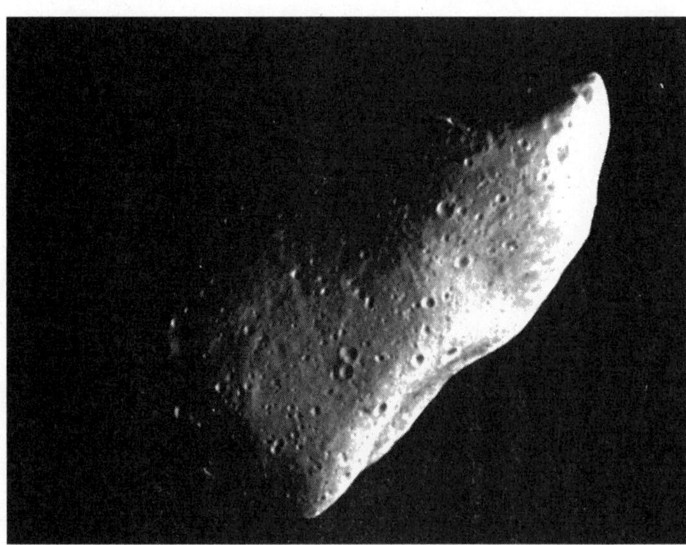

Figure 1.96. A photograph of the asteroid Gaspra from the collection of images on the Distant Suns CD.

I have hardly covered even the high points of Distant Suns. The program's capabilities go on and on. It was clearly a labor of love by its creator, which makes it doubly enjoyable for the user.

Hitch Your Wagon to a Star

I hope that I have been able to convey the excitement and pleasure I experienced using Vistapro. Software comes and goes, but there are certain packages that offer more than usual, and I certainly put Vistapro and Distant Suns into that category. There's something about creating photo-realistic renderings that I found exciting, and Vistapro is easy to use and powerful. Distant Suns has enough meat to satisfy the hungriest astronomical purist. These programs don't offer every single feature you might want, but then again, neither of them costs a fortune, either. Vistapro, in particular, is one program no virtual-reality enthusiast should be without.

There is a demo version of Vistapro on the CD-ROMs; give it a whirl and see if you don't agree.(71)

---

71 You might think I get a commission, I'm selling this program so hard. Unfortunately, I don't get a penny.

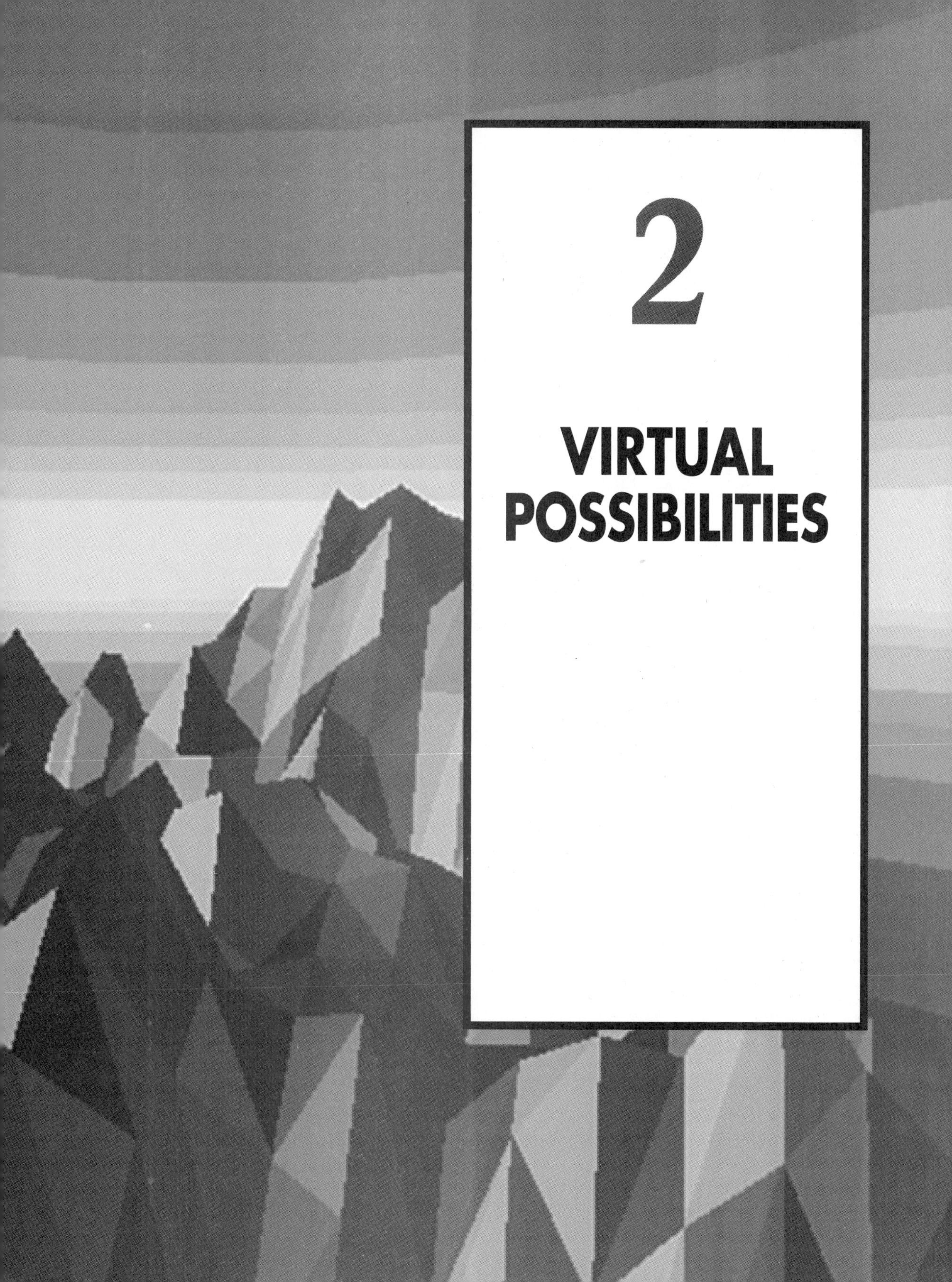

2

VIRTUAL POSSIBILITIES

In Chapter 1, "Virtual Reality Has Arrived," you learned how to get a running start in virtual reality using Vistapro. In this chapter, virtual reality moves indoors with three easy-to-use but powerful products: Virtus WalkThrough, Virtus VR, and Virtual Reality Studio. Like Vistapro, these programs offer an inexpensive way to explore virtual spaces.[1]

These programs don't offer all the fancy control and details of the high-end packages, such as Superscape, but they are a blast to use as you'll see in this chapter. Before the blast, however, a little background on VR. There's a lot of discussion about just what, exactly, qualifies as VR. Prepare yourself for a radical definition of the concept.

Artificial Reality

Virtual reality is a buzzword these days, and a hot one at that. It's so hot, in fact, that the meaning changes almost daily as companies try to associate their products with the words. I'd like to step back from the craziness and intensity of buzzwords and talk in a more generic sense about the underlying concepts of virtual reality. I use the term *artificial reality* as a starting point.

Not only does using this term avoid the confusion surrounding *virtual reality*, but in many ways *artificial reality* is more accurate. I don't expect everyone to suddenly switch to using new terminology, but it might take some of the heat, confusion, and too-high expectations out of the air. To that end, a definition of the term artificial reality is necessary.[2]

> **artificial reality**— *n.*; anything at all that stimulates the mind or senses to create a simulacrum of reality *in the imagination.*

I have deliberately created a definition that stresses results, not the technique used to achieve those results. The emphasized phrase—*in the imagination*—stresses the

---

[1]Virtus WalkThrough is particularly appealing—you already own it. I have included it on one of the CD-ROM discs that comes with this book. This is a real deal—the genuine article, and already paid for. What's the catch? A simple one—you can have a lot of fun with Virtus WalkThrough, but you also can upgrade to the Professional version. See the back of the book for details.

An early version of VR Studio, Version 1.0, is included on the CD-ROM that comes with this book. You can find information about that version in Appendix A, and the complete manual is supplied on the CD-ROM. Including Version 2.0 of Virtual Reality Studio would have made the price of the book quite high. Version 1.0 enables you to play and explore inexpensively. This chapter covers the latest version, 2.0. This version is available at many software outlets and by mail order.

[2]Truth be told, I hate definitions, because as soon as you create one, someone comes along and points out the deficiency of the definition. Defining terms such as *artificial reality* is doubly dangerous because the terms are so vague.

kind of results that matter. Virtual reality need not be virtually real to be interesting, useful, or fun.[3]

For some time, virtual reality had a very definite meaning: full bodysuits, helmets, and other paraphernalia associated with full-body total immersion into an electronic reality.[4] Pieces of that total picture have begun to arrive, and the term *virtual reality* has shifted to describe those first arrivals. The term has then been stretched further to mean just about anything three dimensional. This is an extremely broad range of meaning, and it is useful to break artificial realities into categories. The following sections cover these categories, beginning with the most modest forms of artificial reality and ending with the ultimate forms of virtual reality. The range reflects the current state of the art and projections of what might be possible in the future.

Text

Text may strike you as an unusual form of artificial reality, but it is useful to look at how text serves in that role. For centuries, books have been the cutting edge of artificial reality. Think about it: you read words on a page, and your mind fills in the pictures and emotions—even physical reactions can result. Text is important because all our expectations[5] are based on what we've experienced with books.[6]

Text forms a baseline on which we can measure the success of various kinds of artificial reality. Although there are many ways that images, sounds, and other sensory communication can expand the capabilities of text, there are qualities of the reading experience that will be challenging to reproduce. If you are not convinced, think about books that have been converted to movies. Most of the time, even if the movie is regarded as being as good as the book was, the movie has to leave out a lot of the story—the overhead of telling a story in pictures is a lot higher than for text.

---

[3]The day when virtual reality becomes virtually indistinguishable from reality is a long way down the pike. We can't let that little fact spoil the party!

[4]In some ways, I like that term—*electronic reality*—best of all. But buzzwords have never thrived on accuracy, have they?

[5]Except those based on television.

[6]Kids, of course, who are growing up today don't necessarily base their expectations on books. Many do, however—my son Justen loves books, but he's also a nut about his Sega and Nintendo systems, as well as PC games like Stunt Island. Books provide a depth of stimulation that most games and PC programs can't match. The nonvisual, low-tech nature of text actually gives it an advantage over all other forms of artificial reality. It's a lot easier to simulate, and stimulate, if the technical overhead is reduced. This seems obvious, but it's a critical obstacle that must be overcome in the development of virtual reality.

2D Still Images

Photographs have been with us for a little more than a century, and their capabilities are described in the phrase "a picture is worth a thousand words." This is true in two senses: a picture—specifically, a photograph—is both accurate and detailed. Nonetheless, comparing pictures and words is, to drag in another old bromide, like comparing apples to oranges. Text is good at certain things, and pictures are good at others. You can't, for example, look behind what is in a 2D picture, nor can you take pictures of many things—the state of a man's mind, the inside of a volcano, or a molecule.

Most of the time, pictures and text are used together. This reflects their complementary aspects. Each is good at different things, and best when used together. Neither one is truly superior to the other.

3D Still Images

This is a technology that is both common and in its infancy. Primitive 3D still images have been with us for decades, but it has been holograms that have made quality 3D images possible. However, from a commercial standpoint, holography is mostly a failure—there are no widespread commercial uses of holograms as images. Holograms are used for such things as credit cards and packaging precisely because they are complicated to reproduce.

Technically speaking, however, 3D images represent an interesting twist in the move toward more sophisticated artificial reality. The simulacrum of the third dimension is vivid, even if the image quality is often second rate or worse.

Animation

Neither 2D nor 3D images have a quality that reality thrives on: movement. Animation—the trick of using flickering images to fool the eye—adds the dimension of time to artificial reality in ways that still images never can. A series of still images on a page, for example, or even a series of slides, provides only an intellectual sense of movement and change. Animation, even when very abstractly done, conveys a sense of immediacy that is very powerful.

Video

I was tempted to include video with the discussion of animation, but the two technologies are different enough to merit separate consideration. Video, after all, captures an image of reality and preserves it, and that is an entirely different kind of artificial reality than animation. Animation is truly and totally artificial—most of the time. Some of the most fascinating animation sequences are actually based on video.

The process starts with a standard video of some real action—a fish swimming or a couple dancing. An artist then uses this as an underlay for an animation, substituting a series of drawings for the video frames. The effect looks like a virtuoso animation, when in reality, it is just a series of tracings.

Sound

Multimedia computers, upgrade kits, and sound cards are in the process of revolutionizing how we think of computers. The ability to listen to sounds appropriate to a context can make the computer interaction much more pleasant, and often more interesting, effective, and informative. You can use sound for everything from using a cat's meow instead of a beep for errors, to controlling your computer with voice commands.

Unfortunately, the majority of the sound cards installed on computers today isn't of very high quality, and most uses of sound do not use high-fidelity recording techniques. High-quality stereo sound is as important for computer use as it is in a home stereo system. Until there is general use of noise-free, accurate sound equipment on computers, we'll be missing something. In terms of numbers, we must move from the 8-bit, mono, 22 kHz sounds of today to true CD-quality sound (16-bit stereo with 44 kHz sampling).

3D Motion

We are just beginning to witness serious efforts to portray the third dimension in ordinary media. Films such as *Jaws III* featured 3D, for viewers using special glasses, but the investment in equipment to create such films made them unusual. Technology has just begun to swing to the point where you can create 3D motion pictures on your own.

In most cases, some form of glasses is required to decode the 3D information in each image of an animation or video sequence. Unlike conventional 3D glasses, video 3D glasses are high tech. They use shutters that direct subsequent frames of the video to each eye in turn. Chapter 13, "The Virtual Future," covers this kind of technology in greater detail.

This kind of technology is right at the edge of what is available to the average computer enthusiast today. Developments in this area will make up the bulk of serious progress in virtual/artificial reality over the next several years.

3D Input Devices

One of the most frustrating aspects of current 3D technology is the lack of a convenient way to manipulate 3D objects. Whether you are using a simple 2D video monitor or sophisticated, 3D head-mounted displays, if you do not have the capability to manipulate objects with a 3D input device,[7] the possibilities are limited.

As you will see repeatedly in the examples in this book, programmers and game designers have developed many clever techniques for manipulating 3D objects using 3D tools. Almost without exception, this is a tedious, frustrating, and inexact way to work. Current experiments with head-mounted tracking devices, 3D mice, and interactive gloves have not yet resulted in a low-cost, easy-to-use solution to the problem.

Head-Mounted Displays

Often called HMDs, these range from goggles to full-sized, head-encircling units. You can buy a head-mounted display today for less than $10,000, but most of the software that uses such expensive hardware is highly specialized. You can find software that enables you to visualize complex organic molecules in 3D, for example, but there is nothing available yet that addresses more pedestrian activities. The high cost of HMDs is the current root of that problem.

Very few inexpensive head-mounted displays exist, and they tend to make serious compromises. Human vision is marvelously wide-angle, for example. Creating a screen that is small and light enough to be placed in front of your eyes, and still curved enough and wide enough to give you a natural field of vision is beyond the range of affordable technology. Some simple units are available for less than $1,000, but they were just being announced as this book went to press.

Another serious problem involves data rates. Filling larger displays with data takes serious computing power—more than is available currently, particularly if the HMD is at all light and portable.

Wide-Angle Displays

Thus, the next step after HMDs is HMDs with a field of vision approximately the same as we humans take for granted. Personally, I would expect this to be a major step, and one that has the potential to revolutionize artificial reality. Until the field

---

[7]The world is waiting for a 3D manipulation device that will make 3D interaction as easy as 2D mouse-based or pen-based interaction.

of vision is wide enough to engage the two kinds of vision we possess, the experience will be marred by whatever shows up in our peripheral vision—whether it be simply blackness or "real reality."

Display technology also must advance to a point where the large numbers of pixels needed for true wide-angle displays can be displayed cheaply and, just as important, instantly.[8]

Tactile Feedback

What would life be like if your mouse went bump when you reached the edge of the computer screen? That's *tactile feedback*—a physical sensation coming back from the computer to tell you what's going on. Vibrating mice are with us today, but there is a real lack of software that supports such technology.[9]

A mouse represents just the barest beginnings of tactile feedback technology. Gloves that give you a sensation of picking up objects are a much more advanced form of tactile feedback.

Head and Body Tracking

If only the computer could, like a friend in a conversation, keep track of our head or body position, we could communicate so much more easily with the computer. Voice recognition is nice, but what if you could signal the equivalent of an OK button by just nodding your head? Pointing with a finger is one of the most natural gestures, but it is completely mysterious to a computer.

Current ideas about how to implement tracking are somewhat intrusive. Video games, for example, are making use of large (3 to 4 feet in diameter) circular sensors placed on the floor. Experimental head-tracking devices often require you to wear something on your head, although there are experiments with video cameras built into monitors.[10] The computer analyzes the video image to try to determine where your head is facing.

---

[8]The very nature of digital imaging is both a blessing and a curse. The blessing comes in the form of very exact image representation. The curse takes the form of high data rates to reproduce precise colors and large, complex—and therefore interesting—images.

[9]What we really need is a mouse that will resist movement if you try to do something inappropriate. Wouldn't it be great if the mouse offered resistance when you tried to move the mouse cursor out of a modal dialog box, for example? (A modal dialog box is an item that you must deal with before you return to the program that spawned it.)

[10]How would you feel if the computer were constantly watching you with a video camera?

Nonvisual Sensory Output

Now we are moving into the realm of future possibilities. Senses such as smell and touch are a lot harder to integrate into a computer connection. The sense of smell, for example, is extremely complex—and very personal. One person's great smell is another person's stink.

Given that we are only just beginning to be able to reproduce a limited number of scents chemically, and that the most desirable scents are tremendously subtle and natural, the sense of smell may not be computerized for quite some time. Touch is equally complex. Touch receptors are located all over the body, with different kinds of receptors in different areas. It seems highly likely that initial attempts to integrate touch will focus on areas of the body with large numbers of touch receptors, such as the hands.

"Extrasensory" Input and Output

The possibility of involving non-sensory data in the loop also exists. This can be done as a simulation or by mapping—for example, converting infrared data into sounds (mapping bright objects in the infrared to high pitches, and dim objects to low pitches), or mapping it to the visible spectrum (bright as blue, dim as red, for example). Ultimately, this possibly could be done more directly by mapping sensor data right into the brain.[11]

Total Immersion

The ultimate goal of artificial reality would be to create an experience that would be indistinguishable from the real McCoy. This seems like total hype at this stage of the game, and the proper forum for such ideas may well have to remain on the Holodeck of the Enterprise for the time being.

Artificial Is a Matter of Degree

If there is anything to be learned from my attempt at classifying the forms that virtual reality might take, it is that there are many degrees of artificial. Some degrees are more realistic than others, and some do a better job of creating the experience of reality than others. The "reality" is that there are multiple dimensions involved, and there is no single line from the simple to the complex. Artificial

---

[11]This is far out, highly speculative stuff. It is, however, interesting to think about the possibility of extending human senses via computers.

reality is made up of a large number of intersecting needs and technologies, and all of it is bounded by what we actually can afford to do, as individuals and as a society.

Creating Virtual Spaces with Virtus WalkThrough

One big difference between the first edition of this book and the present edition is the power of the available VR software. However, there is a second difference that's just as important: the software is getting easier to use. Two products from Virtus exemplify the best of both worlds: Virtus WalkThrough and Virtus VR. Both products take full advantage of the Windows interface, and that makes them easy to use. Both products also offer significant power for creating virtual worlds.

Virtus WalkThrough offers more pure power, while Virtus VR is designed for the beginner. I am extremely pleased that Virtus has allowed us to include a complete version of Virtus Walkthough on the CD-ROM discs that come with this book. It serves as a great introduction to an even more powerful product: Virtus WalkThrough Pro. The Pro version was not available at the time this edition was being written, but the early indications are that it will be a real powerhouse.

If you haven't already installed the version of Virtus WalkThrough on the CDs, this is a good time to do so. It will enable you to follow along as I describe how to use the product.

WalkThrough Tools

Take a look at the WalkThrough interface. There are three parts:

- The Plan View, where you add and modify objects.
- The WalkThrough windows, where you move through the virtual environment.
- A floating toolbar, which changes appearance depending on what you are doing.

Figure 2.1 shows the main window, with the Plan View on the left and the WalkThrough window on the right. Note that the Plan View includes rulers at the left and top so that you can tell where you are in your world. When you start WalkThrough, the Plan View shows a top view of your world, but you easily can switch to a right, left, bottom, back, or front view.

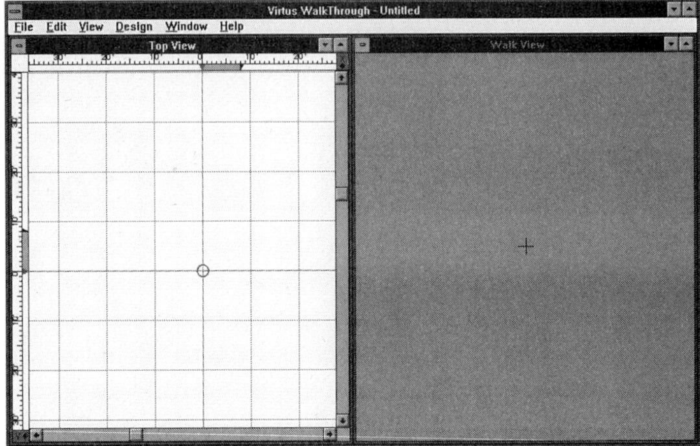

Figure 2.1.
The basic Virtus WalkThrough window.

The floating toolbar, shown in figure 2.2, is filled with useful tools. Table 2.1 lists the capabilities of the initial set of tools. Note that some tools actually serve several different purposes. In addition, there are some tools that are not displayed until you access certain features of the program.[12] Overall, you'll find that there are a lot of tools with a lot of power.

Figure 2.2.
The Virtus WalkThrough toolbar.

[12]This means, in effect, that the toolbar is context sensitive. It will display only the tools you can use at any given point in time.

Table 2.1. The Virtus WalkThrough Tools.

Icon	*Description*
	Create 8-sided object
	Create 6-sided object
	Create square object
	Create triangular object
	Create multisided object
	Create irregular object
	Create rectangular object
	Make object opaque
	Make object translucent (use when you want a surface to look like glass)
	Make object transparent (use when you want a surface to be invisible)
	Inflate normal[13]
	Inflate double-pointed
	Inflate double-rounded
	Inflate pointed normal
	Inflate rounded normal

continues

[13]*Inflation* refers to the way an object is built up. If you are creating a box, for example, you would draw a rectangle in the Plan View. If inflation is normal, you'll get a box. If inflation is set to pointed, you'll get a pyramid.

Table 2.1. continued

Icon	*Description*
	Inflate pointed reverse
	Inflate rounded reverse
	Move object
	Rotate object
	Zoom in
	Zoom out
	Zoom to fit box
	Enable x-y motion (useful for control when using the tumble editor)
	Enable x-z motion
	Enable y-z motion
	Place on front (used only in Surface Editor)
	Place through (used only in Surface Editor)
	Place on back (used only in Surface Editor)
	Open Surface Editor
	Open Tumble Editor
	Open Lighting Editor
	Color bar: change color

Icon	*Description*
	Start recording moves (use to record movements in the WalkThrough window)
	Stop recording
	Play the recorded moves
	Color picker
	Tape measure
	Select object
	Lock object (prevents changes)
	Hide object (if the scene gets too crowded, temporarily hide objects)
+/–	Add/remove handle (use to revise shape of existing objects)
	Connect surfaces
	Slice (cut off a part of an object)
	Scale
	Skew

WalkThrough Basics

Table 2.1 lists a lot of tools; they may seem intimidating at first, but as you work with them you'll see that they are all useful. In this section, you learn how to use many of these tools.

To start, click on the Rectangle tool to activate it. When a tool is active, any action you take in the Plan View utilizes that tool. Click and drag out a rectangle in the Plan View (see fig. 2.3).

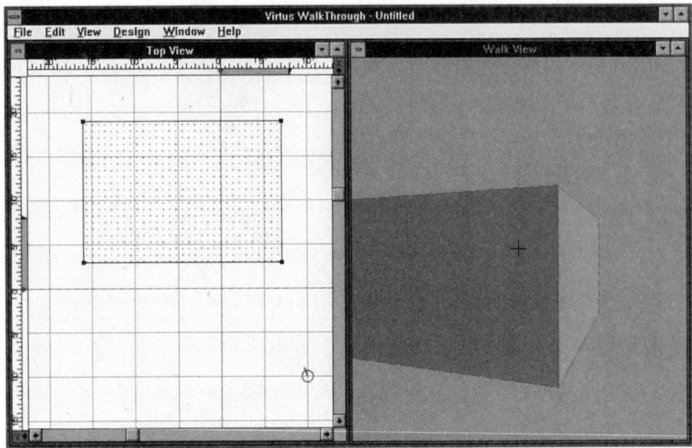

Figure 2.3.
Creating a box.

Although you only dragged out a rectangle, the result was a 3D box, as you can see in the WalkThrough window. If you don't see the box in perspective as it is shown in figure 2.3, you can use the WalkThrough window and your mouse to maneuver around until you get a good view of the box.

Figure 2.4 shows the effect of various mouse clicks on your position in the WalkThrough window. Where you click in relation to the central cross hairs controls how you move. Click below to move back, and above to move forward. Clicking to the left turns left, and clicking to the right turns right.

You can move in more complex ways as well, as shown in figure 2.5, using the Shift or Control key with mouse clicks.(14)

When the WalkThrough window is active, the toolbar changes to the version shown in figure 2.6. Instead of tool icons, it contains a zoom slider and a cube for tumbling your point of view. When the Tumble Editor is active, you can click and drag this cube to change the orientation of an object. Figure 2.7 shows the cube rotated so that the left side (that's the side with the "L" on it) is facing toward you.

---

[14]You also can use the Plan View to change your viewpoint. See that little circle below the rectangle in figure 2.3? You can drag it around, and it represents the viewer's position. To change the direction of view, hold down the Control key and drag out from the center of the circle. Experiment to see how this effect works.

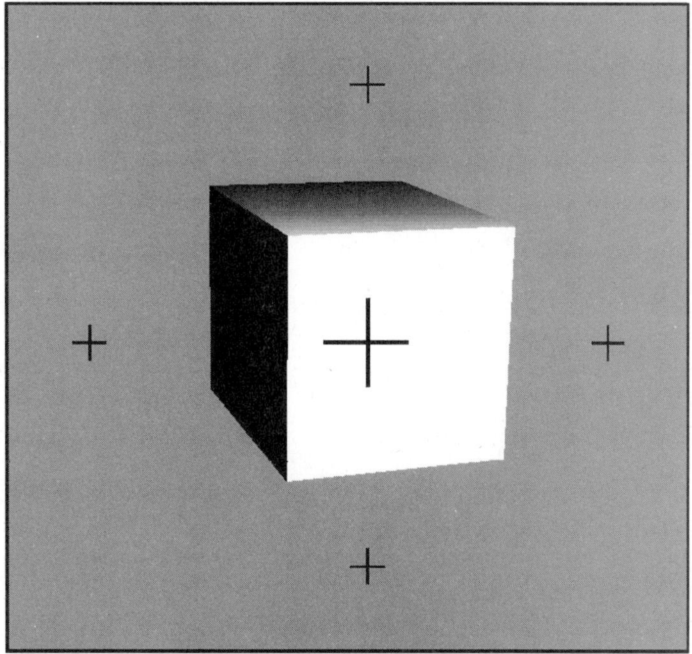

Figure 2.4. Moving around in Virtus WalkThrough.

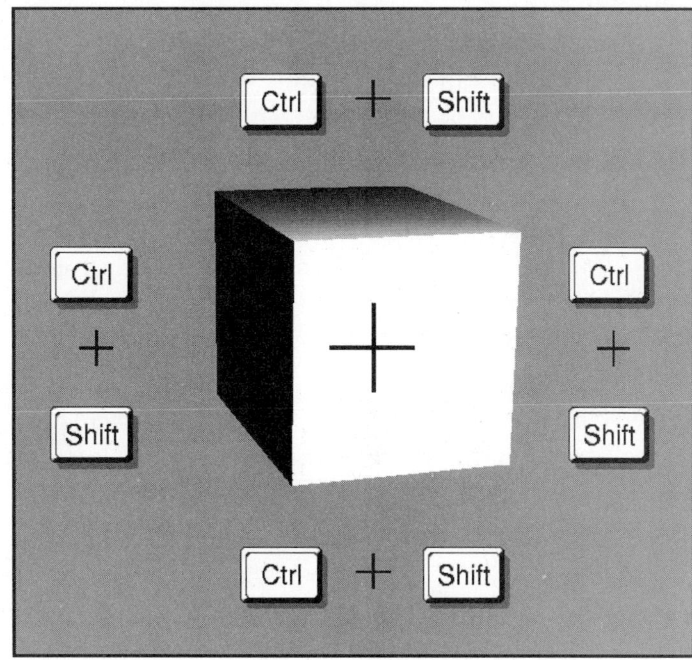

Figure 2.5. Additional movements using the mouse and Control/Shift keys.

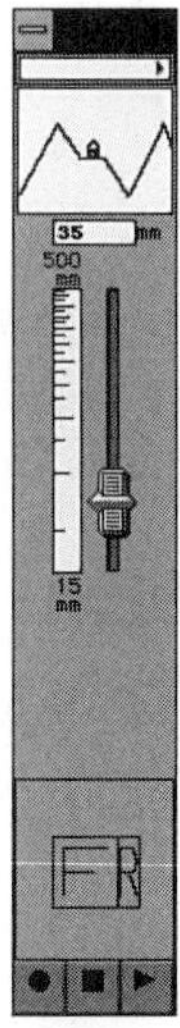

Figure 2.6. The toolbar for the WalkThrough window.

Figure 2.7. The Tumble Cube in action.

By clicking on other Object Create tools, you can create all kinds of objects. To create an eight-sided column, for example, click on the eight-sided tool, and then click and drag in the Plan View (see fig. 2.8).

What you see now are two rather boring gray objects. Let's add some color. Click on the Color Picker bar and drag down to open the Color dialog box (see fig. 2.9). The top of the box shows colors used recently (just one right now!), and the bottom part of the box shows a wider range of colors. For full 24-bit color picking, click on the upper left of the palette. You can use the Windows Color common dialog box to choose any color you want.

Many of the tools on the toolbar have a small black triangle at the lower right. This triangle indicates that there are some alternate tools available. To see the flyout bar displaying the alternate tools, click and drag on the tool. Figure 2.10 shows two alternate inflation tools: Pointed Inflation at the left, and Rounded Inflation at the right.

It takes a while to remember where all the alternate tools are located—not to mention all the different things they can do for you. After you commit the tools to memory, however, you'll find them extremely flexible.

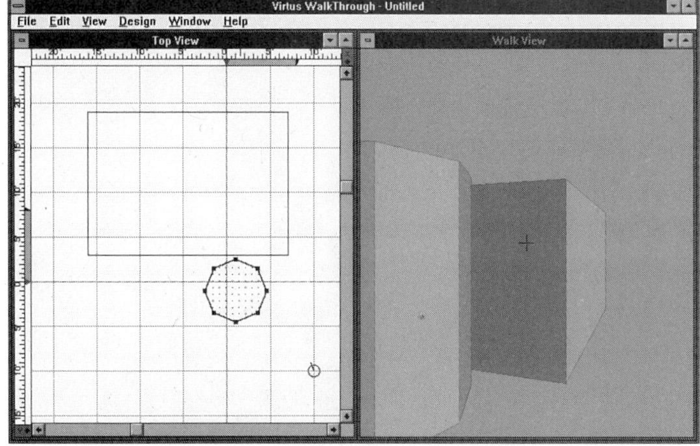

Figure 2.8. Adding a second object.

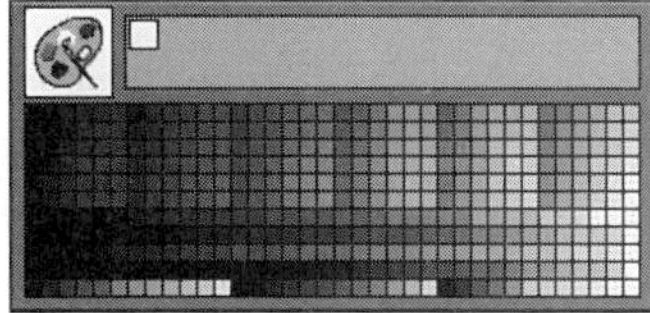

Figure 2.9. Choosing a color for an object.

Figure 2.10. Alternate tools make the toolbar very flexible.

Speaking of rounded inflation, click on the box in the Plan View to select it. You know it's selected when it has black boxes (called *handles*) at the corners. Then click on the Rounded Inflation tool while the flyout bar is extended to activate it. Because you activated the tool when an object was selected, it changes the inflation of the object. Figure 2.11 shows the result: a rounded rectangle.

If you had wanted to round the bottom surface, you would have used the Reverse Rounded Inflation tool, just to the right of the Normal Inflation tool.

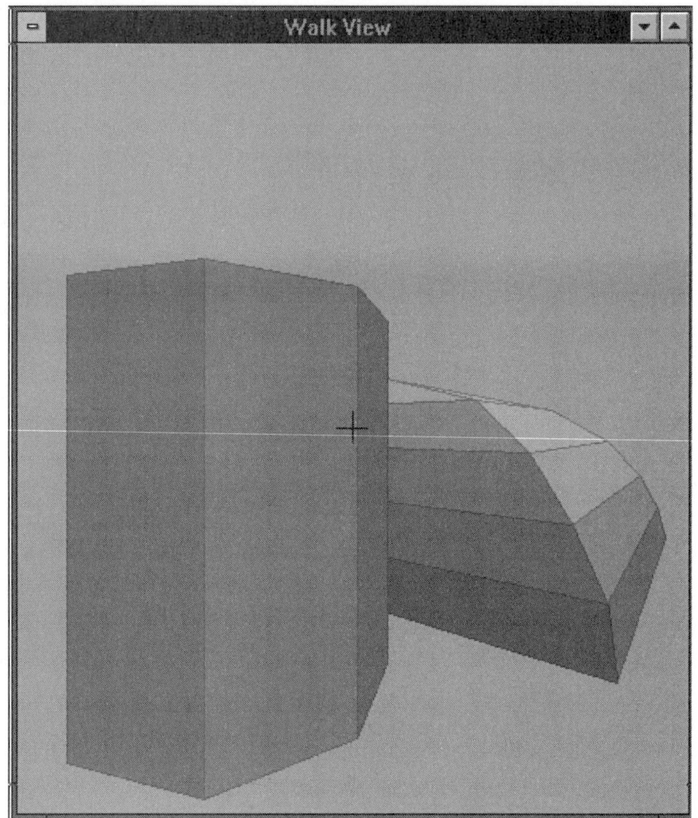

Figure 2.11. Rounding the rectangle.

To see an example of pointed inflation, select the column and then activate the Normal Pointed tool to change the inflation of the column. The result is shown in figure 2.12.

Figure 2.12. Changing the column to use pointed inflation.

If you view these objects from the top in the Plan View (see fig. 2.13), you can see that the objects appear quite a bit different from those with normal inflation. Later in this section, you learn how to add additional handles to these objects to make them more realistic.

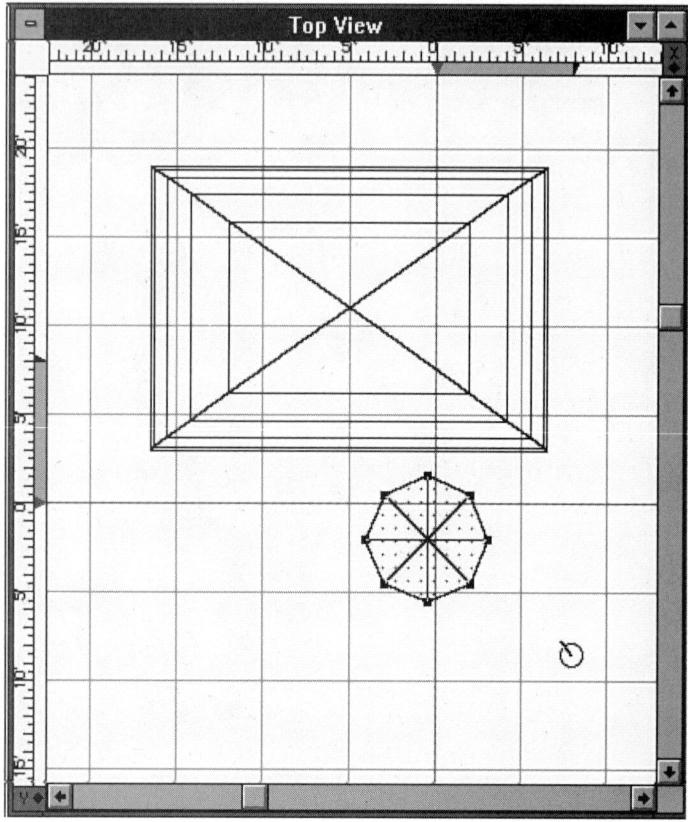

Figure 2.13. The top view of objects with altered inflation.

Wouldn't it be amusing if we made the pointed column look like glass? It's easy to do. Just select the column, and then click on the Transparent tool. Presto! As you can see in figure 2.14, you've got glass.

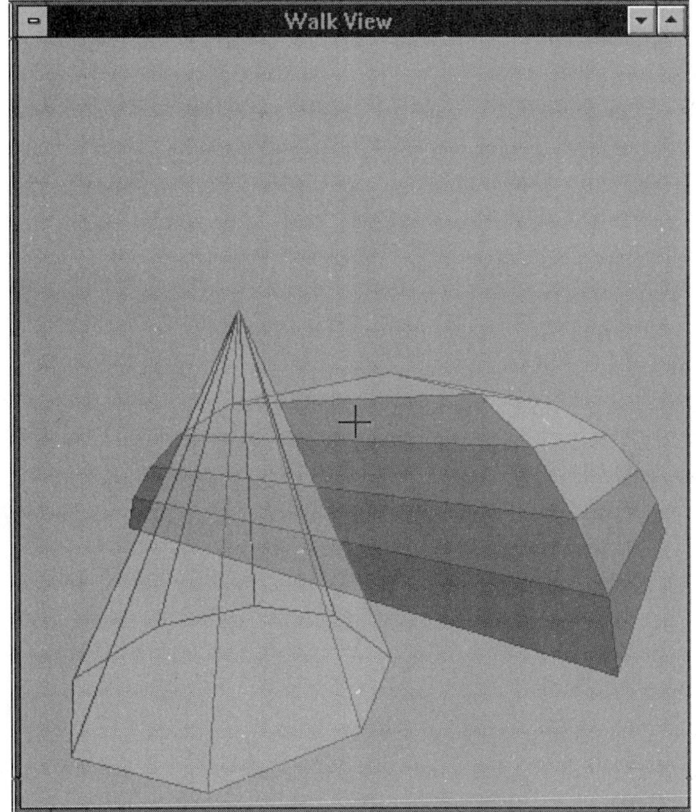

Figure 2.14. Making an object translucent is easy: just click on the Transparent tool.

So far, we've been creating and altering objects by using the Top View in the Plan View. You can change to other views using hot keys, or by using the View menu (see fig. 2.15). I found myself changing views often as I worked on various aspects of a project.

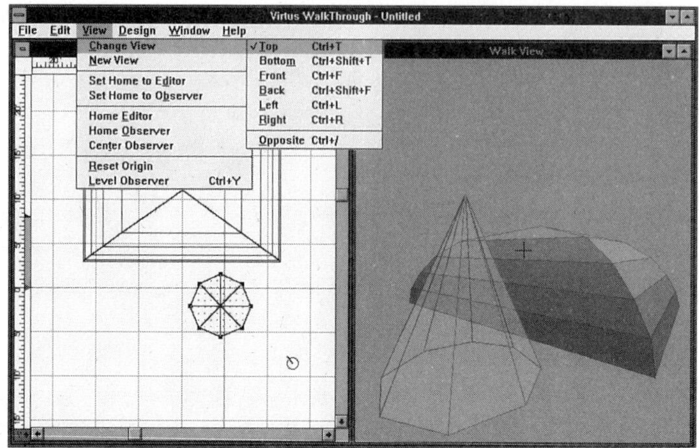

Figure 2.15. Changing your point of view in the Plan View.

Many features in the toolbar also are accessible by hot keys and the menus. As you can see in figure 2.16, for example, the Edit menu contains many, many selections, including options for changing object transparency, undoing skew/scale/rotate, using inflation, and so on.

After you have created an object, there are many different ways to refine its shape. You can change the scale of an object simply by dragging a corner, or you can grab an edge and move an entire side of an object in or out, up or down. Figure 2.17 shows the rounded rectangle with the left edge moved in toward the object center.

The change is even clearer from a side view, as shown in figure 2.18.

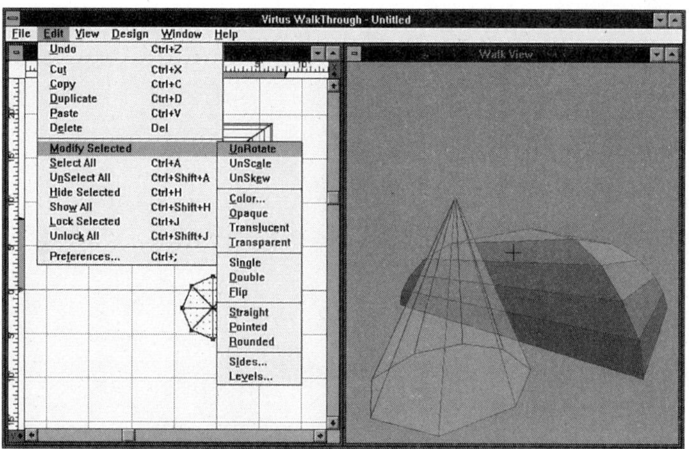

Figure 2.16. Editing object characteristics using the menu.

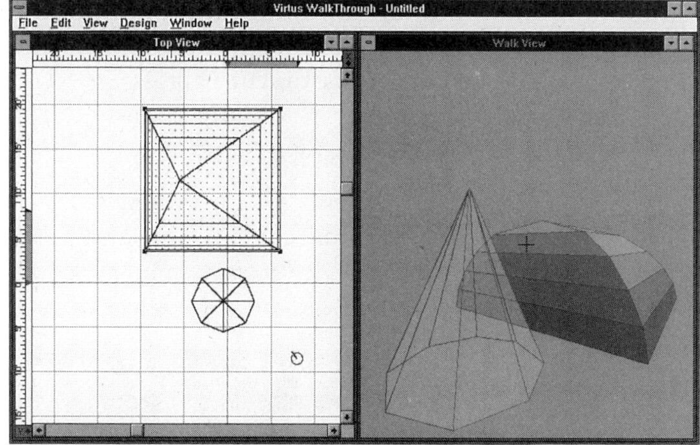

Figure 2.17.
Changing the shape of an object by dragging an edge.

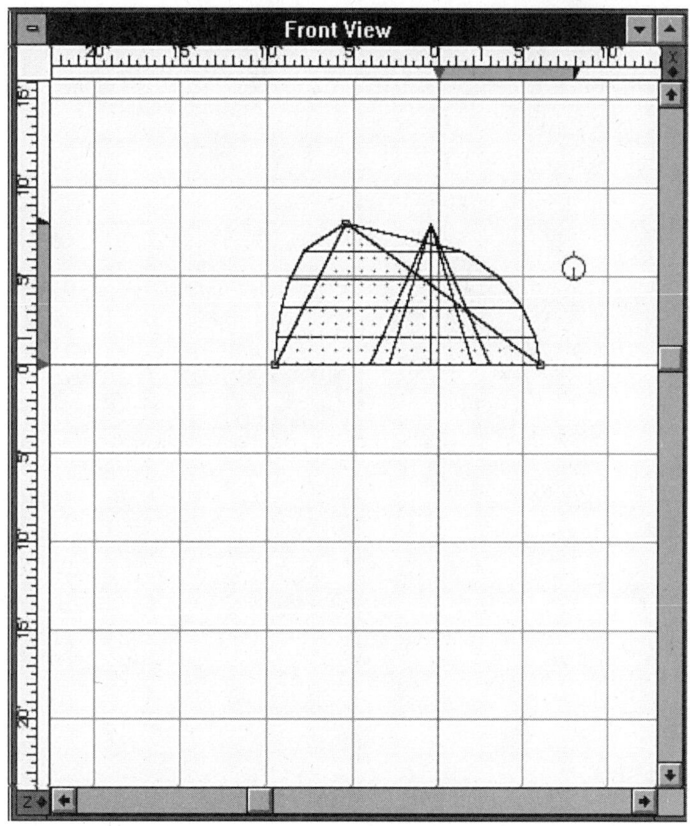

Figure 2.18.
A side view of the modified rounded rectangle.

Although the rounded rectangle is rounded, it isn't very smoothly rounded. It's easy to refine the outline using the Add/Remove handle tool.(15) Click the tool to activate it, and then place the cursor cross hairs on an edge, click, and drag out the new handle.(16) I did this repeatedly to the outline of the rounded rectangle, and you can see the result in figure 2.19.

Adding handles to an object is an extremely useful way to modify the shape of basic objects to make more complex objects. Figure 2.20 shows a simple rectangle that had two handles added to make a more complex shape.

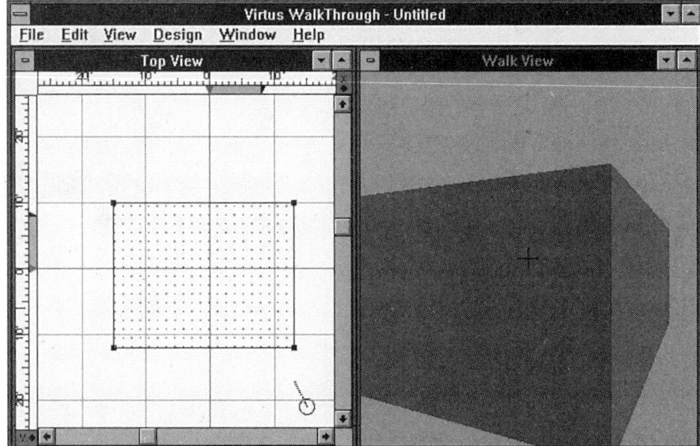

Figure 2.19. Adding new handles to an object.

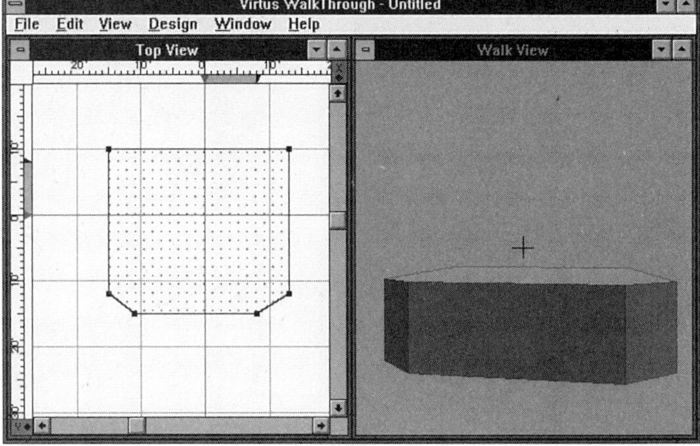

Figure 2.20. Building complex shapes from simple shapes by adding handles.

15That's the tool with the plus/minus sign on it.

16To remove a handle, click on it while the Add/Remove handle tool is active, and drag it away.

So far, we've been focusing on creating and modifying objects. You also can select one surface of an object and modify it. This gives you a very fine level of control over the shape and characteristics of your objects. It's also easy to do. Click on an object to select it, and then click on the Shape Editor tool. Then click on the edge of the surface you want to edit.[17] In the Top View shown in figure 2.20, for example, click on the line between the two handles that were added to the basic rectangle. This action opens the Shape Editor with just the surface in question displayed (see fig. 2.21).

One easy trick: Make the surface into a glass-like material. Make sure that the surface is selected in the Surface Editor (make sure that it has those little black handles at the corners), and click on the Transparent tool. You might want to try the same thing with the two surfaces to the right and left; the result should look something like figure 2.22.

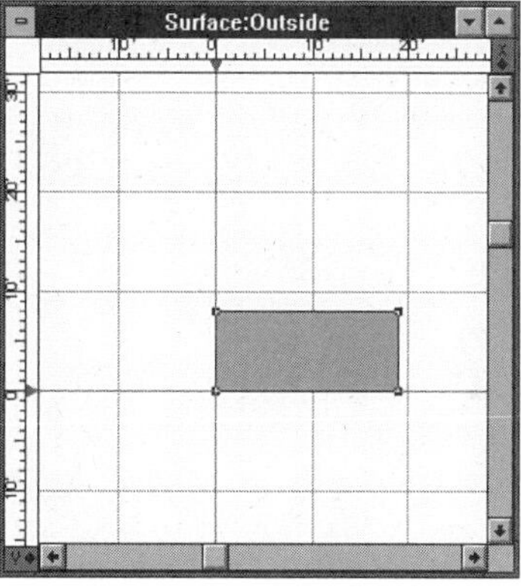

Figure 2.21. Using the Shape Editor.

You use the Tumble Editor to change the orientation of an object. Figure 2.23 shows the Tumble Editor in action. When the Tumble Editor is active, you change the orientation of an object by dragging the mouse across the cube that appears at the bottom of the toolbar.

Another good use for the Tumble Editor involves the Slice tool. You can orient the object in a convenient position, and then draw a line through it with the Slice tool. Every part of the object on one side of the line is removed. It's something like passing a hot knife through butter. The result of some carving with the Slice tool is shown in figure 2.24.

---

[17]There is a bit of a trick to this. In some cases, you'll click on an edge, but you won't get the surface you intended in the Shape Editor. Usually, simply changing to a different view in the Plan View gives you the surface you want.

Figure 2.22. Making surfaces translucent.

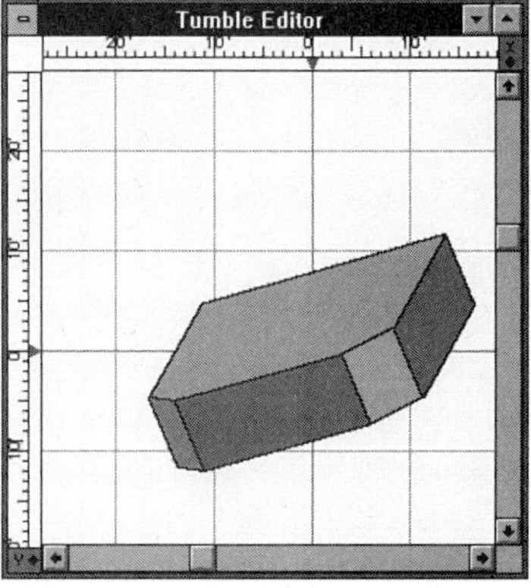

Figure 2.23. Using the Tumble Editor.

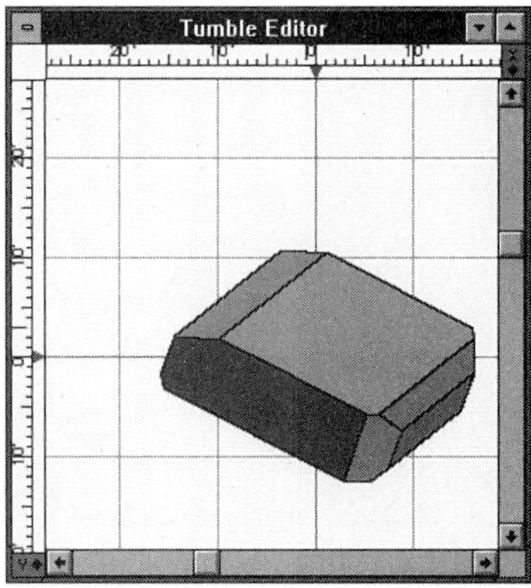

Figure 2.24. The effects of using the Slice tool.

WalkThrough Libraries

Virtus WalkThrough offers a lot of power for creating objects, but you don't have to create everything from scratch. Several libraries of objects can save you a lot of time and trouble. Even more important, as your skill with WalkThrough grows, you can create your own objects and store them in your own libraries. This is an extremely powerful technique for building more and more sophisticated virtual worlds.

When you install Virtus WalkThrough, you also install a number of useful libraries. You get two additional libraries if you send in your product registration (for the full retail version, that is). Libraries give you enormous power, because whatever you can create, you can store in a library.

Figure 2.25 shows a typical Library view—the list of library contents on the left, and a standard WalkThrough window on the right. You can view the object from any angle, and switch easily from one object to another.

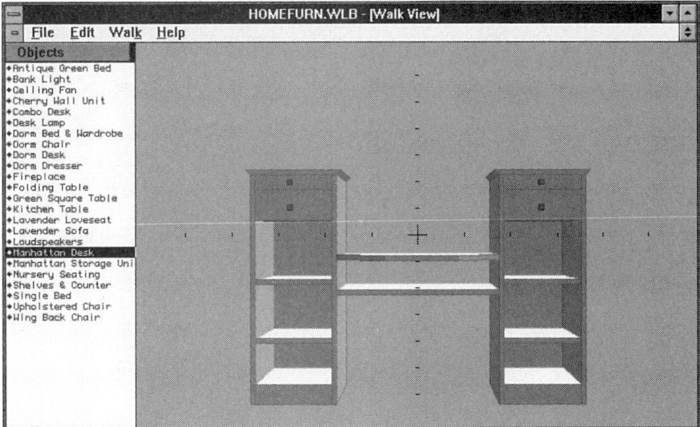

Figure 2.25. A typical WalkThrough library object.

Adding a library object to a virtual world is simple: copy it to the Clipboard, and then paste it into your world. That's all there is to it.

There are a large number of preferences for maneuvering through a library; the navigation preferences are shown in figure 2.26.[18] You can choose a wide-angle or telephoto lens, or even change the type of lens to match the view.

[18] You also can use these same preferences in WalkThrough itself.

Figure 2.26. Setting WalkThrough preferences.

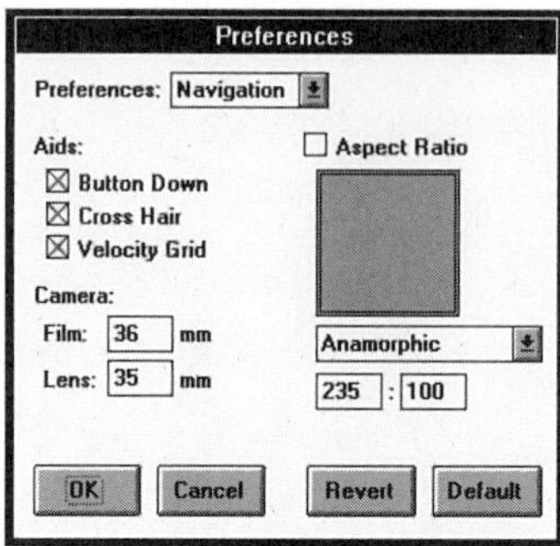

One of the more fascinating libraries contains human figures, every one of which is named Brutus. Some of the figures are very amusing; four are shown in figure 2.27.

Figure 2.27. Brutus, hero of the Virtus libraries, in four different incarnations.

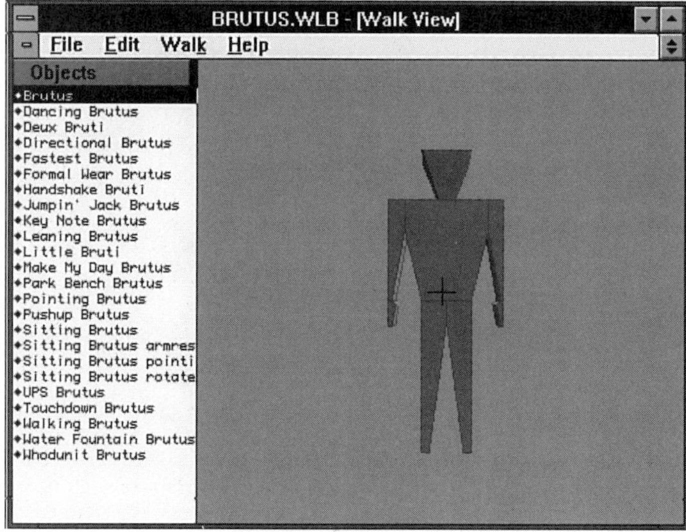

a

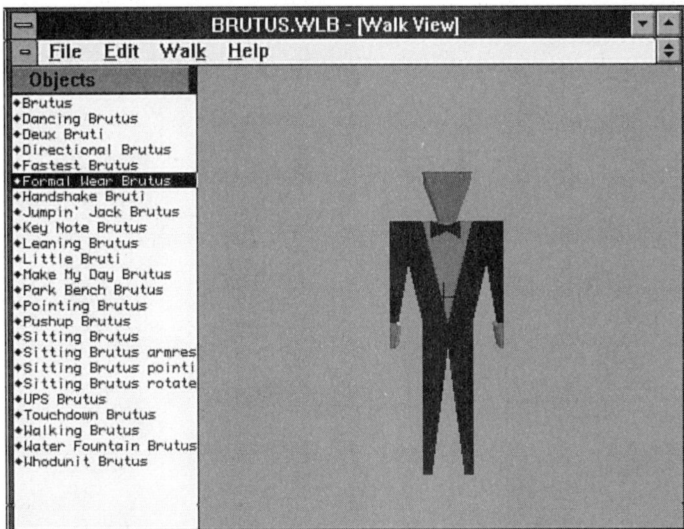
BRUTUS.WLB - [Walk View]
File Edit Walk Help
Objects
Brutus
Dancing Brutus
Deux Bruti
Directional Brutus
Fastest Brutus
Formal Wear Brutus
Handshake Bruti
Jumpin' Jack Brutus
Key Note Brutus
Leaning Brutus
Little Bruti
Make My Day Brutus
Park Bench Brutus
Pointing Brutus
Pushup Brutus
Sitting Brutus
Sitting Brutus armres
Sitting Brutus pointi
Sitting Brutus rotate
UPS Brutus
Touchdown Brutus
Walking Brutus
Water Fountain Brutus
Whodunit Brutus

b

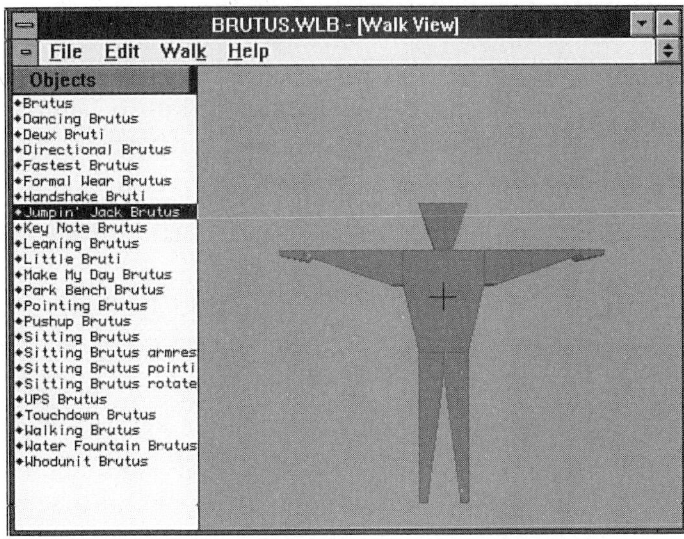
BRUTUS.WLB - [Walk View]
File Edit Walk Help
Objects
Brutus
Dancing Brutus
Deux Bruti
Directional Brutus
Fastest Brutus
Formal Wear Brutus
Handshake Bruti
Jumpin' Jack Brutus
Key Note Brutus
Leaning Brutus
Little Bruti
Make My Day Brutus
Park Bench Brutus
Pointing Brutus
Pushup Brutus
Sitting Brutus
Sitting Brutus armres
Sitting Brutus pointi
Sitting Brutus rotate
UPS Brutus
Touchdown Brutus
Walking Brutus
Water Fountain Brutus
Whodunit Brutus

c

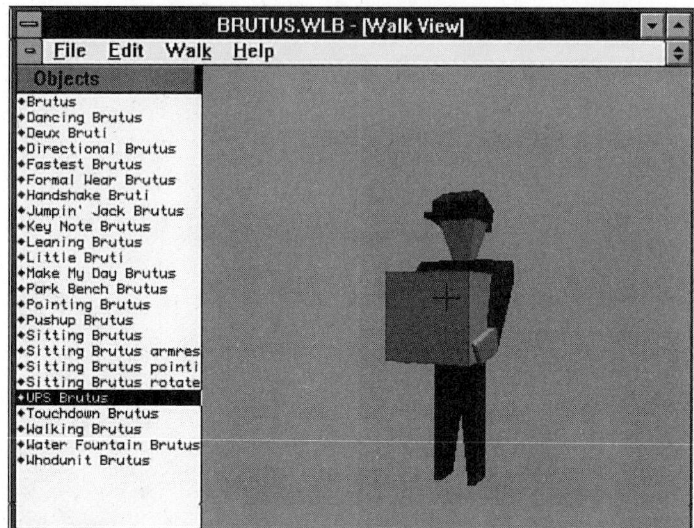

d

Building a WalkThrough House

Let's take everything you've learned about Virtus WalkThrough and apply it to a virtual world. I always seem to gravitate to building virtual houses—let's try a house with a bow window. The window will demonstrate the finer points of creating details in Virtus WalkThrough.

We'll start with some of the techniques you learned earlier. Start with a rectangle, just like the one we created earlier (see fig. 2.3). This will be the basic shape of our house. Now create a smaller rectangle at the "front" of the house, using the Rectangle tool in the Plan View.

If you did not already create the second rectangle touching the house, drag the window so that it lines up with the front edge of the house now.

This smaller rectangle will become the bow window. The first step toward that goal is to add two new handles to the front of the window, which is done almost exactly as we did back in figures 2.19 and 2.20, but on a smaller scale.

The window needs more curvature, so, one at a time, move the front corners back. Simply click on a handle and drag it to move it.

We're getting close—just one more thing to do. Make sure that the Plan View is the active window, and then press Ctrl+F to switch to the front view. Click on the window you are building to select it, and then click on the top edge and move it down a small amount (see fig. 2.29 for guidance). Then do the same with the lower edge. The result should look like figure 2.28.

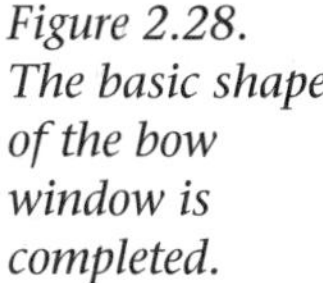

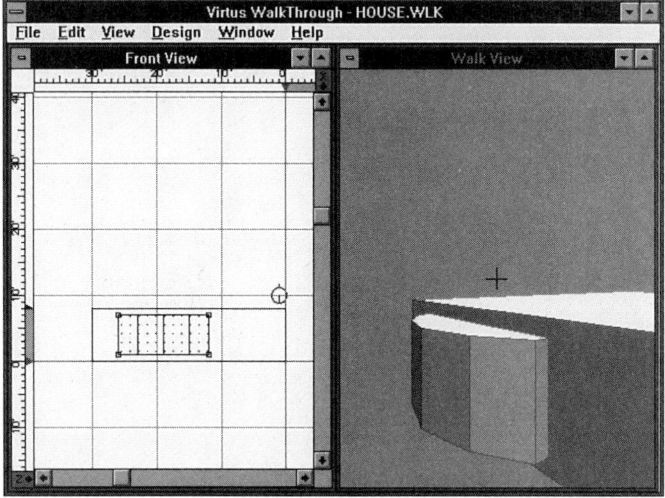

Figure 2.28. The basic shape of the bow window is completed.

We now have the shape of a bow window, but it's not transparent. We'll need to add some window panes. This part can get a little tricky, so pay close attention. We are going to select each panel of the bow window, and operate on it in the Surface Editor. Selecting the panel you want may require some experimentation, because it's not always obvious which line to click on to select a panel.(19)

To start, click to select the window, and then click on the Surface Editor icon. Now click on any of the vertical lines that border the panels; this opens the Surface Editor with a single panel, ready for editing.(20) Click on the Rectangle tool, and draw a window pane, as shown inside the panel (see fig. 2.29). Click on the Transparent tool, and that should make the window look like glass.

Repeat these steps for each of the panels. Experiment with using different vertical and horizontal lines to activate the Surface Editor—it's not always obvious which line to click to select a panel. You'll wind up with four panes in four panels, as shown in figure 2.30. You'll also want to make the back of the window transparent; simply select that surface, click on the Surface Editor icon to activate the Surface Editor, and then activate the Transparent icon.(21)

---

[19]This is mostly annoying, rather than a big bother. If you select the wrong panel, you know it immediately in the Surface Editor. Just close the Surface Editor, and try a different line. If clicking on the two vertical sides of a panel doesn't do the trick, for example, try clicking on the top or bottom line of the panel. Eventually, you'll get the surface you need.

[20]Make sure that the Place Through icon is active; otherwise, the objects you are creating will be above or below the surface, instead of on it.

[21]Otherwise, the back of the window object will prevent you from seeing into the house.

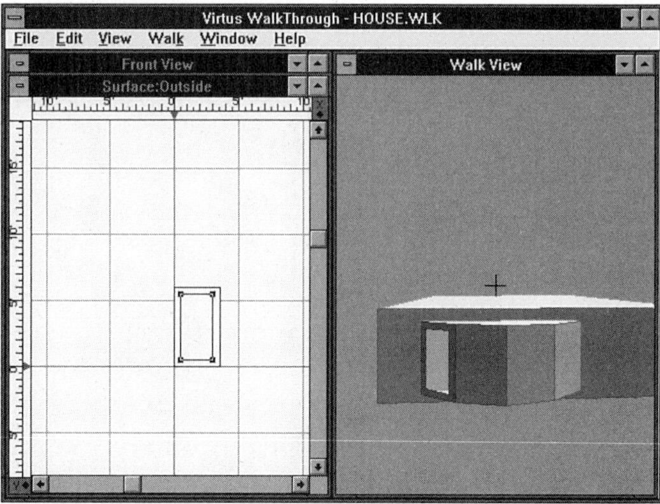

Figure 2.29. Adding a pane to one of the panels.

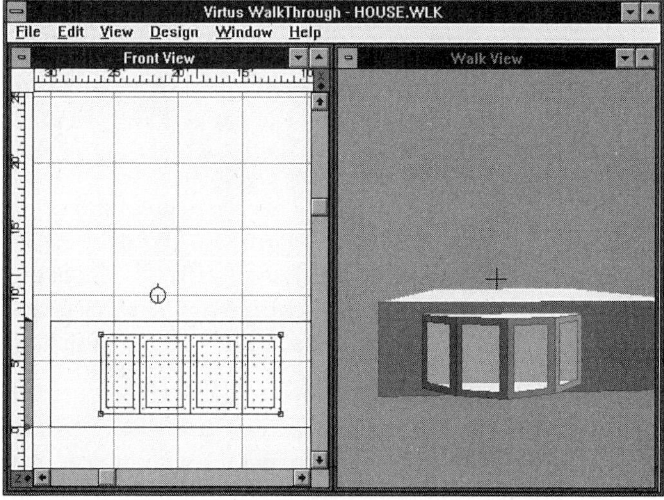

Figure 2.30. The completed bow window.

A window is nice, but a door to get into the house would be even nicer. We'll use the Surface Editor again, but this time, select the front of the house after you activate the Surface Editor icon. Align the Plan View so that you can see and work on the right side of the front surface. Again using the Rectangle tool, drag out a rectangle for a large entryway (see fig. 2.31).

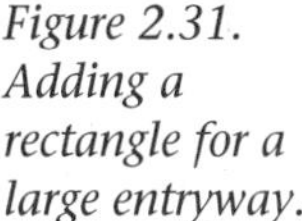

Figure 2.31. Adding a rectangle for a large entryway.

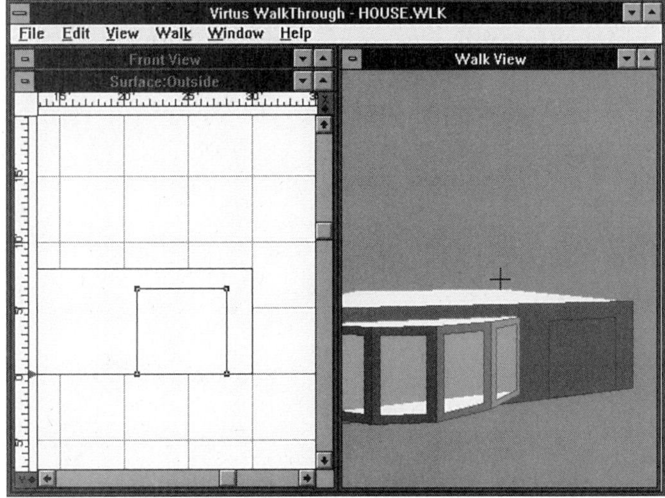

While you have the front wall selected, you'll need to make an opening in it for the window—otherwise, you'll look through the window box and see just the front wall of the house! Simply drag out a rectangle the same size as the bow window, using the rulers to guide placement.[22]

Let's add some additional detail for the entryway. You'll be adding four elements, in the following order (peek ahead to fig. 2.32 to see where the objects go):

1. Add a side light to the entryway, and make it translucent.

2. Add the door.

3. & 4. Add two windows to the door, and make them translucent.

You can select each of these objects in turn and give them a color. I chose dark brown for the entryway frame, a lighter brown for the door, and a slight blue tint for the glass. You can give the front of the house a color, but I wanted my house all one color, so I didn't add any color until after I closed the Surface Editor.

Figure 2.33 shows the results of adding the additional detail (including adding color). It's now very clear what the overall object is—the window and door are detailed sufficiently to read clearly.[23] What we need now, of course, is a roof.

---

[22]Hint: Look at the house in the Plan View from the front, and note the exact boundaries of the window object.

[23]If you are feeling ambitious, try creating a little doorknob for the door. Hint: Create a box, and then modify the inflation to rounded on both ends.

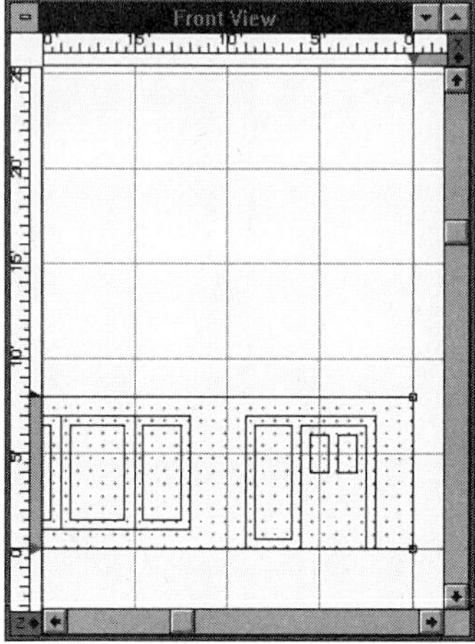

Figure 2.32.
Adding details to the entryway.

When you are building a complex model, Virtus WalkThrough enables you to create separate layers for each group of objects. So far, we've been working with the default layer, but we easily can add a new layer for the roof (and for anything we might place there, like a chimney). The New Layer menu option opens the dialog box shown in figure 2.34; all you have to do is name the layer. Layers make it easier to manage a large environment with lots and lots of objects.

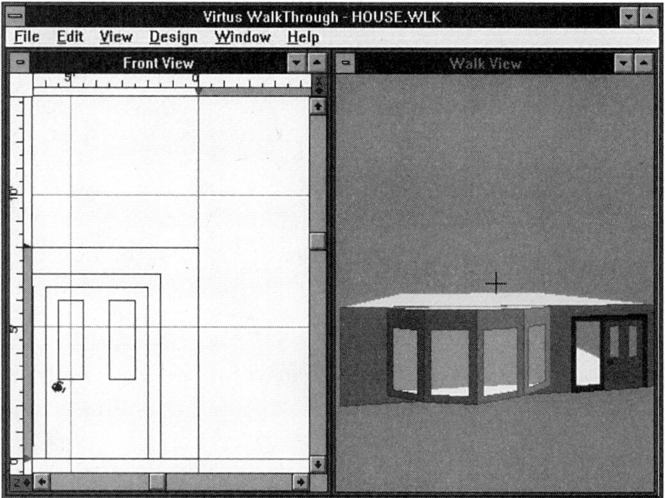

Figure 2.33.
A view of the front of the house.

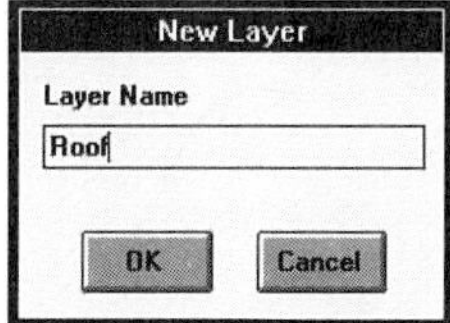

Figure 2.34. Adding a new layer.

When creating the roof, it's important that we locate it above the house. Look at figure 2.35, which shows the roof already added, from a front view. See that little gray bar along the left-hand ruler? That bar has small black handles that you can use to define the inflation height of new objects. Before creating the roof, I simply set that bar to eight feet. To create the roof, switch to Top view and drag out a rectangle, being sure to slightly overlap the house—that's what a roof does in real life.

The roof is just a blocky box so far, however, as you can determine by moving around in the WalkThrough window. Let's use the Slice tool to lop off pieces of that box, leaving a nice, normal roof. Select the roof, and then select the Tumble Editor icon. This displays the Tumble Editor, and you can change the orientation of the roof object by dragging the mouse over the little cube in the toolbar. Arrange the roof object so that you are viewing it from the front; you can double-click on a face of the roof to level it in the Tumble Editor. The result of your effort should look like figure 2.36.

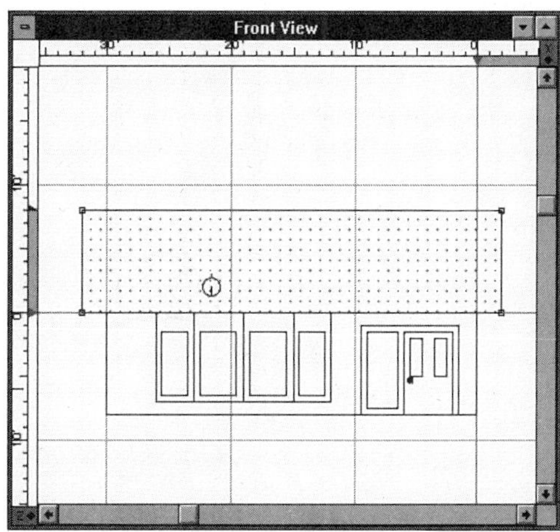

Figure 2.35. Adding a roof of the correct height.

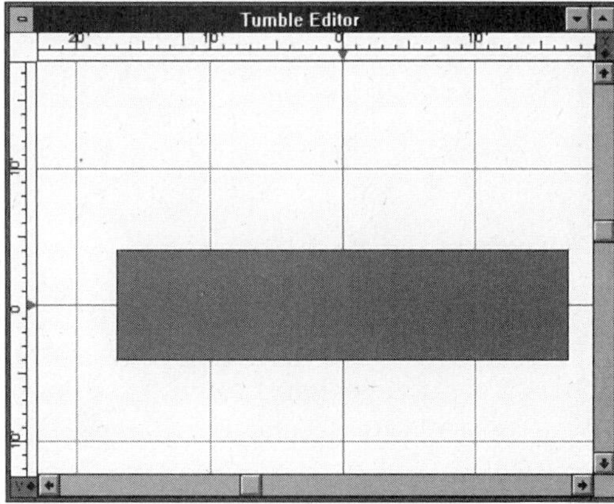

Figure 2.36. Using the Tumble Editor.

Now select the Slice tool, and position the cross hairs at the mid-point of the top of the roof. Click and drag to the lower right-hand corner of the roof, and release the mouse button. The result should be a removal of a section of the roof, as shown in figure 2.37.

To create a matching slope on the other side of the roof, place the cross hair at the lower left corner. Then click and drag to the top center, and release the mouse button. This removes a corresponding section of the roof object, leaving a much more normal-looking roof profile (see fig. 2.38).(24)

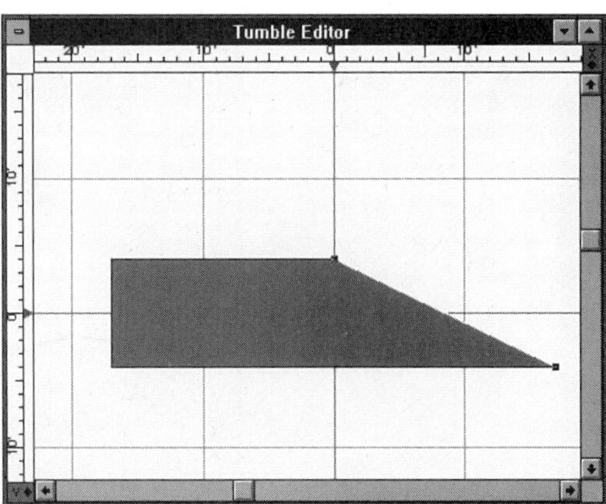

Figure 2.37. Removing a portion of an object with the Slice tool.

---

24 If, instead, you click and drag from the top center to the lower left, you'll remove the roof, and leave the part that was supposed to be removed. If you make this mistake (or any others!), press Ctrl+Z to undo the error.

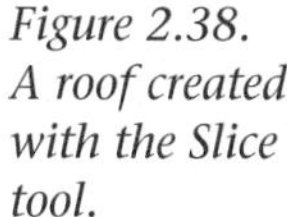

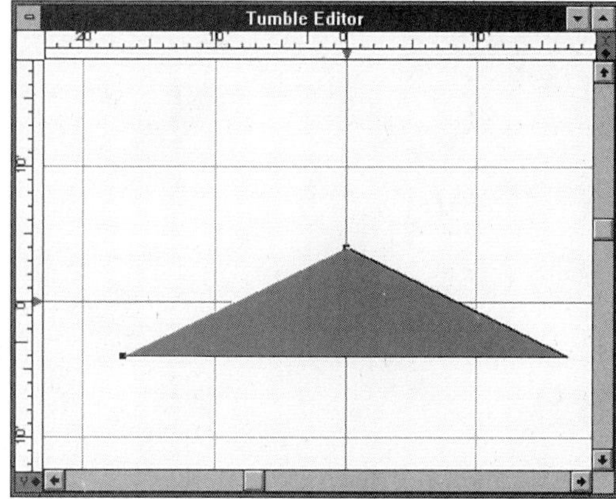

Figure 2.38. A roof created with the Slice tool.

If you would like to create a hip roof, tumble to a side view, double-click on the roof to orient it to face you, and then use the Slice tool to remove additional portions of the roof object (see fig. 2.39).

Figure 2.40 shows the completed house and roof in the WalkThrough window. Note that you can see through the windows, as though they were glass.

You can add a ground object by dragging out, for example, an eight-sided object with only one foot of inflation—use the gray bar at the side of the Plan View to limit the size of the inflation.

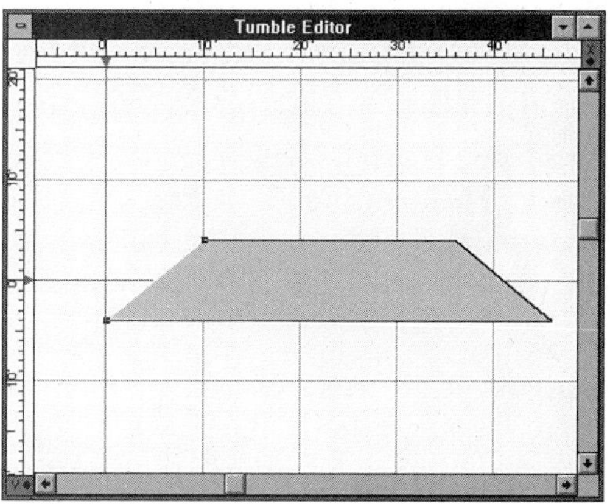

Figure 2.39. The roof modified to the hip roof style.

Figure 2.40. The house now has a roof.

Other nice touches include adding furniture using the various libraries. To open a library, use any of the Library icons in the Virtus WalkThrough program group. When you find an object you want to add to the house, use the Edit/Copy option in the Library window and the Edit/Paste option in the Plan View window.[25]

Creating Virtual Spaces with Virtus VR

Virtus WalkThrough is both powerful and fun, but for an easy start with VR, it's hard to beat another Virtus product: Virtus VR. Best of all, Virtus VR runs under Windows, so there's nothing at all to getting it up and running. Install, and play!

Figure 2.41 shows what Virtus VR looks like when you start it. The left portion of the window, called the Gallery, contains objects you can place into a virtual environment. The top window is where you do your work of creating and modifying objects and the environment. It's called the Plan View. The bottom window is the Walk window, where you easily can walk through a virtual environment using the mouse.

For beginners, there is a collection of buildings, environments, and objects that enables you to get started right away. In figure 2.41, the objects were pretty ordinary—cylinders and boxes and other boring (but necessary!) 3D shapes. Virtus VR also comes with some pretty detailed objects for various kinds of environments—the home, kitchens, offices, and even farms. As an example, let's decorate the Oval

[25] I have included the house on the CD-ROM for your viewing pleasure, and there are a number of interesting models included with the Virtus software when you install it onto your hard disk.

Office of the White House.(26) Figure 2.42 shows the Plan View of the White House, and figure 2.43 shows an outside view.

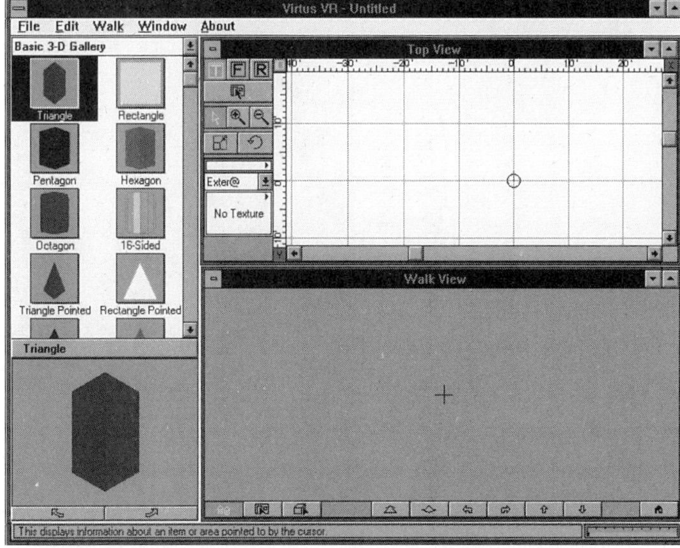

Figure 2.41. Virtus VR looks like this before you start building a world.

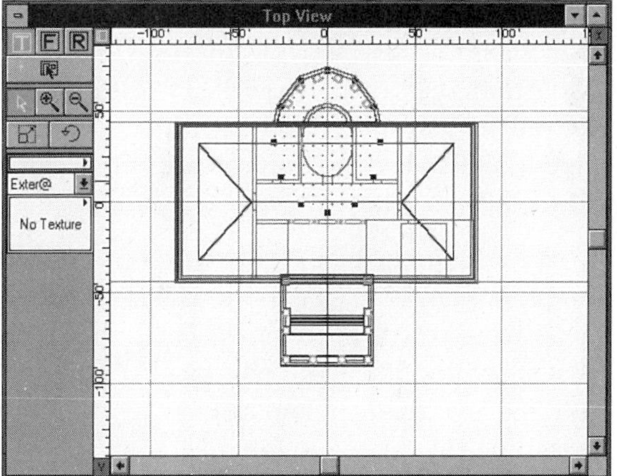

Figure 2.42. A plan of the White House.

---

[26] You guessed it: The plans for the White House are conveniently included with Virtus VR.

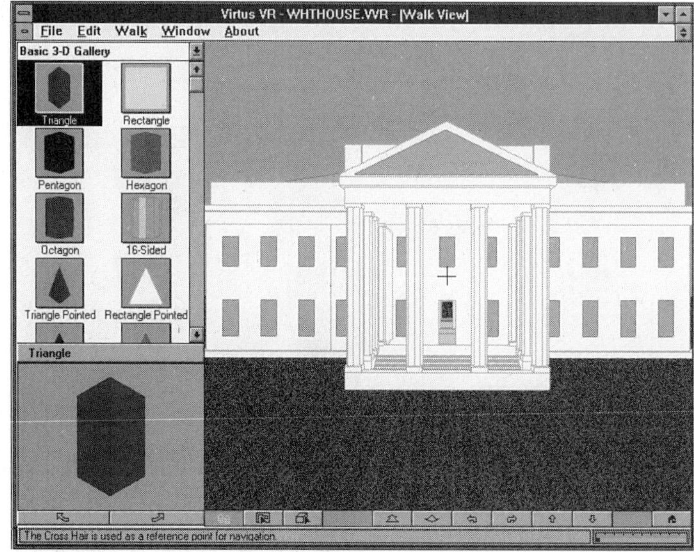

Figure 2.43.
An outside view of the White House.

You can use the Walk window to get to the Oval Office. By clicking above the cross hairs at the center of the window, you can move forward. To move backward, click below the cross hairs. Clicking to the right or left makes a turn. You can combine these moves by clicking on a diagonal.

By combining these moves, you easily can find your way in any virtual world. To move from the view in figure 2.43 to the inside of the Oval Office, you would move forward and down to enter the front door, and then go straight back to the office. Figure 2.44 shows the unfurnished interior of the Oval Office, as included with Virtus VR.

Notice in figure 2.44 that I have selected the Office 3D gallery instead of those boring simple shapes. Now you'll find chairs and desks at the left of the Virtus VR window. To place one of these objects in the virtual Oval Office, just click and drag the object into the Plan View, placing it where you want. You can resize the object, move it, rotate it, and change the color or surface texture of the object.

For fun, look at the little window at the bottom of the gallery—you can use the left and right arrows to rotate an object and see it from all sides. Figure 2.45 shows an office chair as it is being rotated.

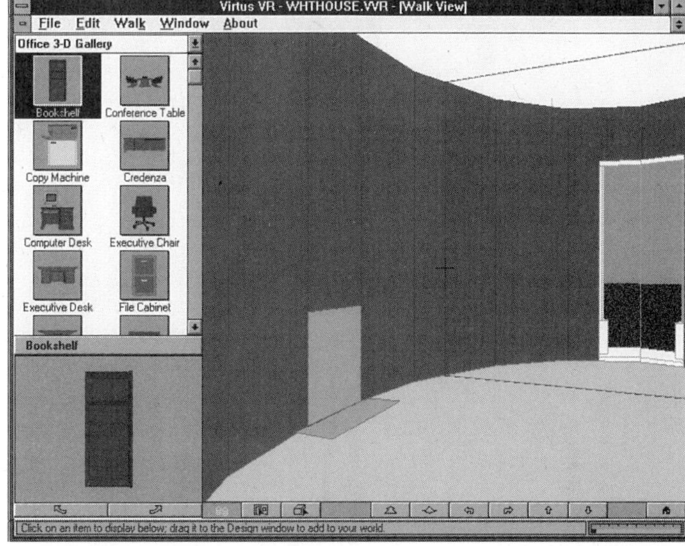

Figure 2.44. Inside the Oval Office.

Figure 2.45. Various views of an office chair.

Figure 2.46 shows the Plan View and the WalkThrough window, with a chair and desk now installed in the Oval Office. Both items can be seen in both windows.

You also can create your own buildings and rooms from scratch, or create an outdoor scene. Figure 2.47 shows a fun living room, with fireplace and furniture, that I created in about 15 minutes with Virtus VR.

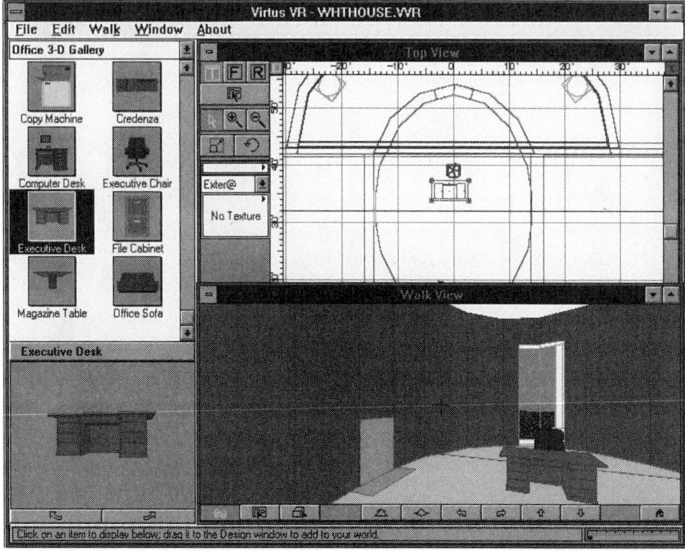

Figure 2.46.
A partially furnished oval office.

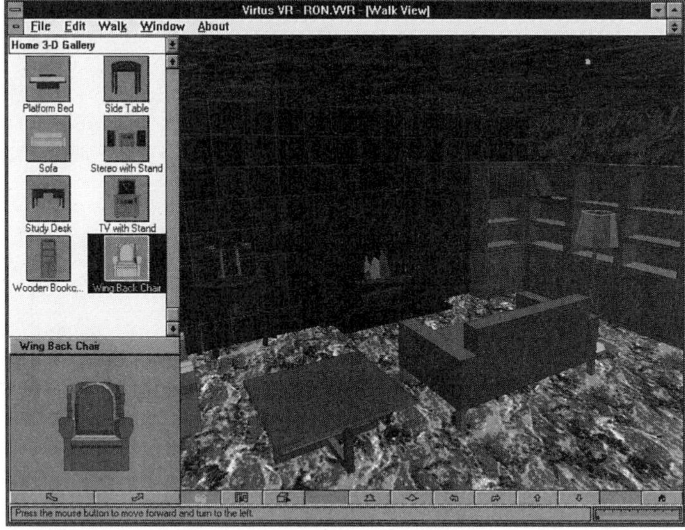

Figure 2.47.
A living room created from scratch with Virtus VR.

Let's look at how the living room was created. I began with a simple box, as shown in figure 2.48.

To do anything interesting with this box, we'll need to use some of the tools in the toolbox. The toolbox is located at the left of the Plan View.

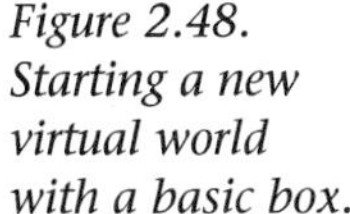

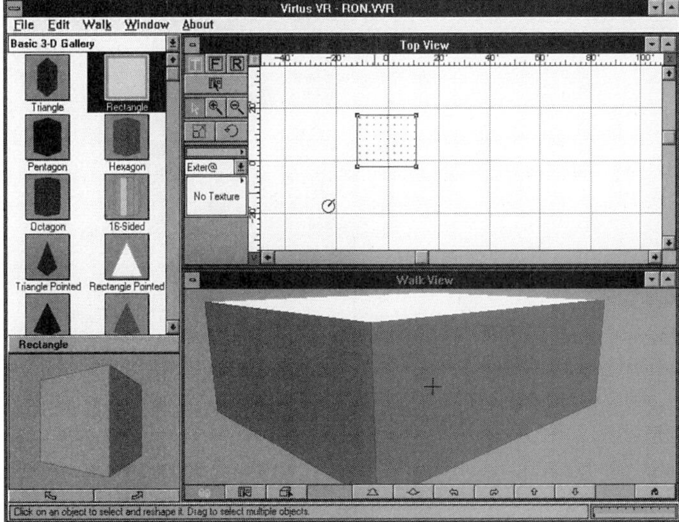

Figure 2.48. Starting a new virtual world with a basic box.

The easiest thing to do is to change the object's color. Click and drag downward on the Color panel to display the Color Selection palette (see fig. 2.49). The last 30 colors you used are displayed at the top, with a larger number of colors below. If you want to be very precise about the color you use, click on the Little Palette icon, and you get a standard Windows Color Picker dialog box. Figure 2.50 shows the object with color applied.

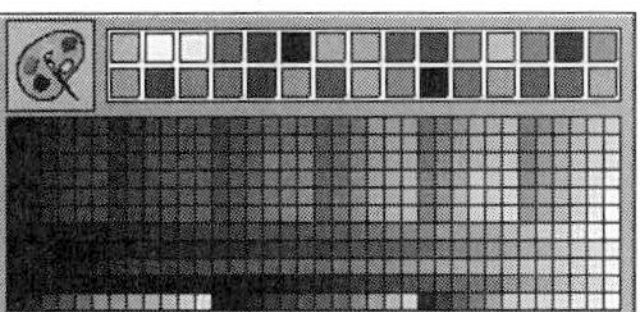

Figure 2.49. Selecting a color for an object.

Colors are nice, but there are more interesting ways to add details to an object in Virtus VR. Click and drag downward on the Texture panel to display a list of available textures you can apply to an object.[27] Figure 2.51 shows a few of the textures supplied with Virtus VR, and figure 2.52 shows an object that has a texture.

27There are several Texture libraries supplied with Virtus VR. The small panel above the Texture panel enables you to select from the available collection of textures.

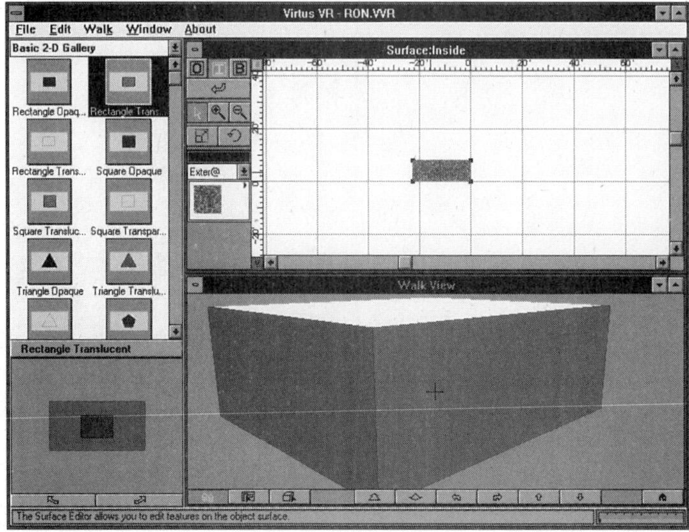

Figure 2.50. Applying a color to the object.

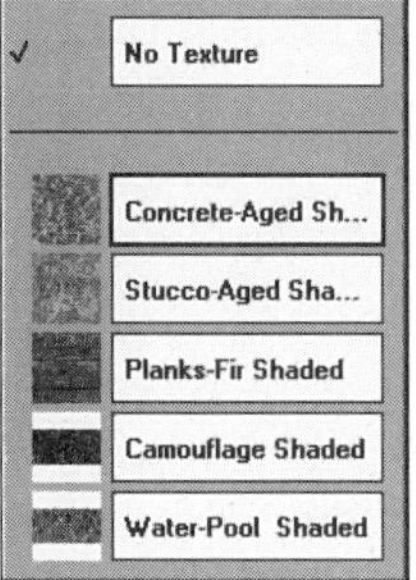

Figure 2.51. Some of the textures supplied with Virtus VR.

Now we have a box with a texture, but that's still hardly an amazing feat. Let's add a window and a door—then we'll have something! To switch to a new gallery, click on the small panel at the top of the gallery, and select one of the Window galleries. To place a window on what is now becoming a building, simply click and drag the window of your choice into the Plan View.[28] Figure 2.53 shows a window on the building, and figure 2.54 shows a door added. I switched to the Door gallery, of course, before clicking and dragging the door into place.

[28]Of course, you should rotate the Plan View to make sure that the surface you are looking at is the one that gets the window!

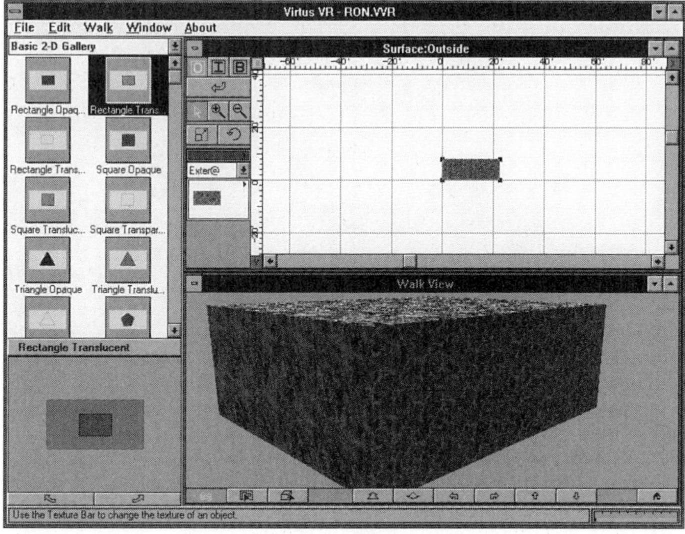

Figure 2.52. An object with a texture applied to it.

Figure 2.53. A window turns the box into a building.

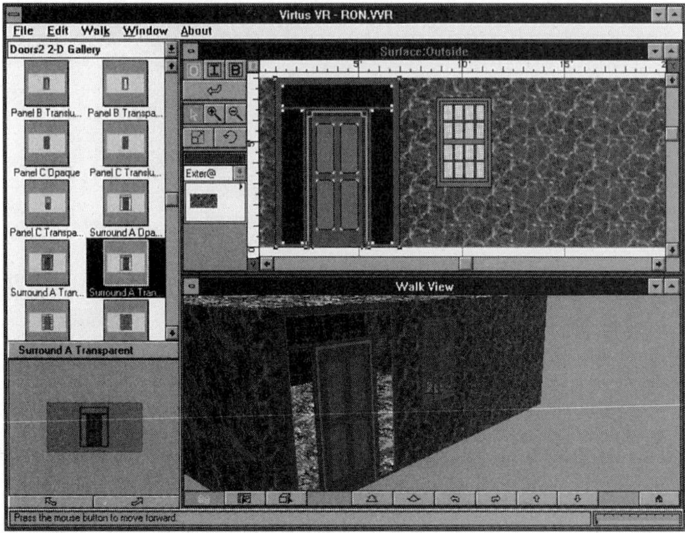

Figure 2.54. *Adding a door makes it a bit more real.*

You now can use the mouse to move through the door and into the interior of the building. Switching to the Home 3D gallery gives us some very useful objects to add to our burgeoning virtual world, such as the fireplace shown in figure 2.55.

Next, I added a couch, a small table, and a lamp. The room looked a little spare, so I dressed it up with a row of bookcases on the right-hand wall (see fig. 2.56).

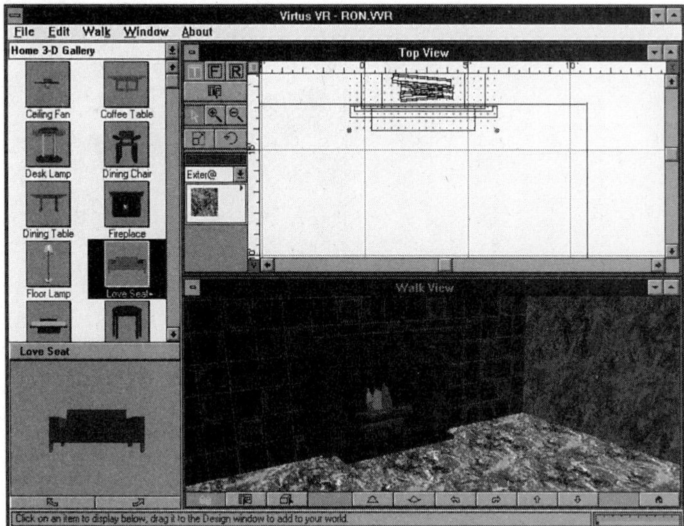

Figure 2.55. *Adding a fireplace to the interior.*

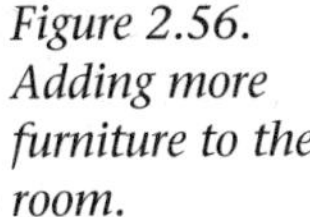

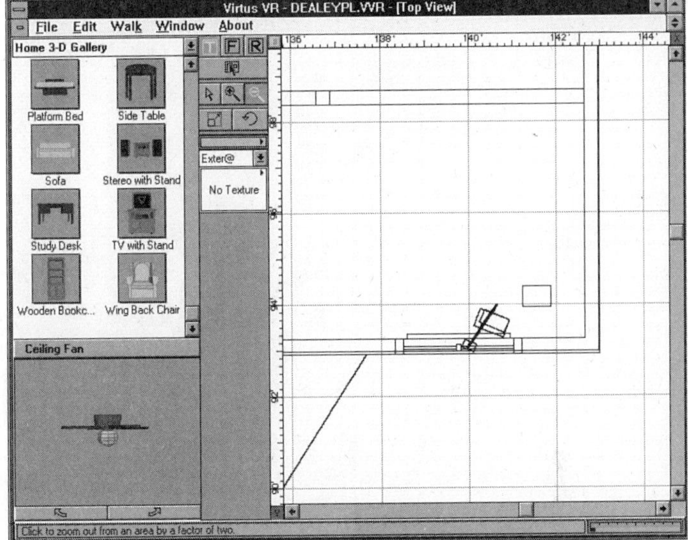

Figure 2.56.
Adding more furniture to the room.

I had thought that the bookcases would add a nice realistic touch, but they wound up looking so bare that I just had to make some books to put on the shelves. This was very easy to do—I simply created a box, shrunk it down to the size of a book, and gave it a brown color (see fig. 2.57 for the Plan View of the book in the bookcase). One book, of course, makes hardly any difference. I used the Object Duplicate command to create a whole row of books; figure 2.58 shows the result.

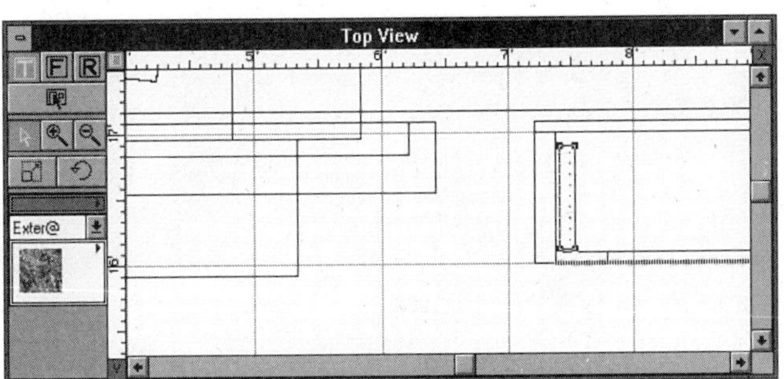

Figure 2.57.
One book created in Virtus VR.

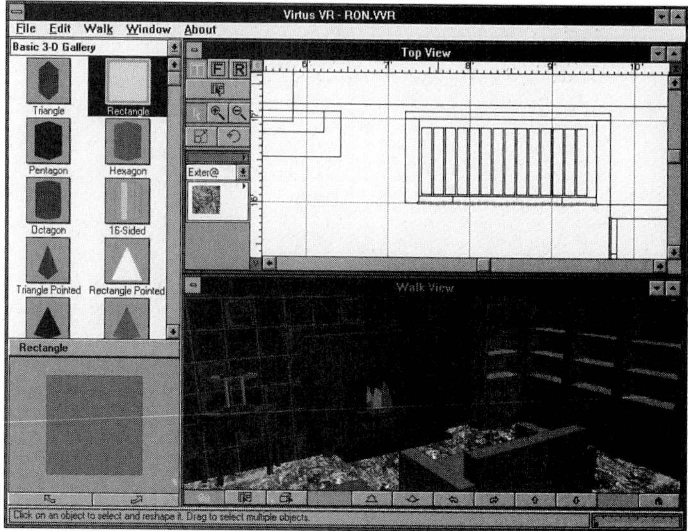

Figure 2.58. Adding some books to a bookcase.

To make the scene a bit more realistic, I took a moment to "knock" the books out of their perfect alignment (see fig. 2.59). I then added one more book in one of the other bookcases, and tilted it to suggest realism (see fig. 2.60). I could have gone on to add more books, but the scene looks like someone is in the process of moving in, and that was realistic enough for me.

I did add a few more touches, such as a wing chair and a floor lamp, to create the final scene, as shown in figure 2.61.

Of course, you could take the scene further. You could add one of the characters from the People gallery to our virtual world. In figure 2.62, I added a woman seated on the couch, and moved the point of view to a position on the couch looking at her.

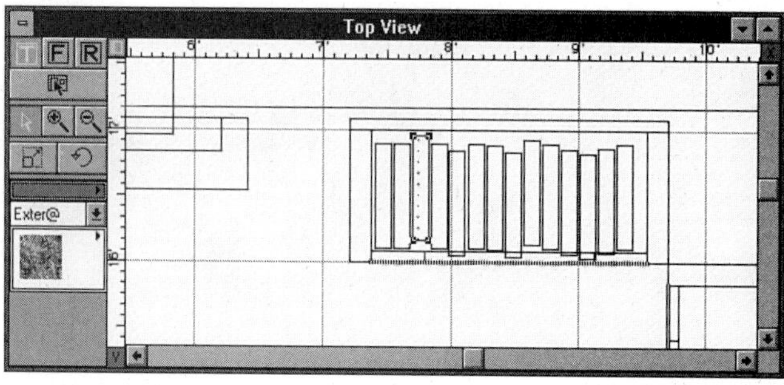

Figure 2.59. Loosening up the arrangement of books.

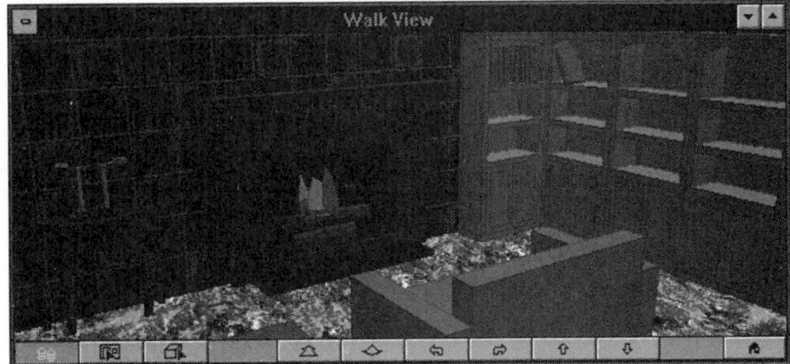

Figure 2.60. The scene with more books in the bookcases.

Figure 2.61. The completed virtual world.

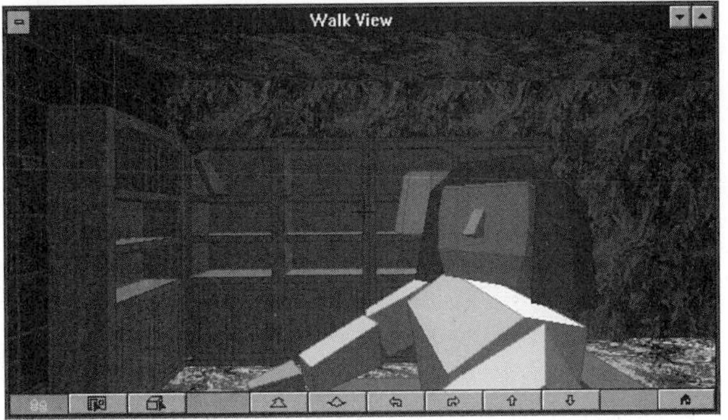

Figure 2.62. People in the virtual world.

If you want, you can record your movements in a virtual world for later play back. You also can export recorded movements to an FLC file. This animation format is supported by many products, such as Autodesk's Animator Pro.

I enjoyed Virtus VR a great deal. It's simple, but it's very easy to use, and provides enough entertainment and flexibility to make it a really good deal. If you have any interest in exploring the possibilities of virtual reality, this is a great place to start.

Creating Virtual Spaces with VR Studio 2.0

One of the things I did not emphasize in my progressive section of artificial reality technologies was image resolution. There is a simple rule that explains the importance, and the problems, of high resolutions: For a given CPU, the higher the image resolution, the longer it takes to display a single image. It may be acceptable to take a second or two to display a high-resolution image when you are using a paint program, but when you want 15 or more frames displayed per second, that's no good at all.

Virtual Reality Studio 2.0 enables you to move your viewpoint around a virtual space. This means that the display changes constantly to reflect the new position of your viewpoint. To make the movement fluid, it operates at low (standard) VGA and MCGA resolutions. You have a choice of 640×480 and 16 colors, or 320×240 and 256 colors. Neither of these is what anyone would describe as realistic, so we must ask the question: Without realism, is this virtual reality at all?

That's really a trick question, because we are operating under the definition given earlier for artificial reality. By these standards, Virtual Reality Studio qualifies. There is an even more important standard that also applies: is it fun?[29] VR Studio is fun.

It takes a bit of learning to get comfortable with VR Studio, however. The interface suffers from the usual difficulties of manipulating 3D objects with 2D tools. The approach used by VR Studio uses indirect object manipulation. Instead of selecting and dragging objects, you select an object and move it using Control buttons. To move a cube, for example, you select it, and then use the object mover controls to move it up, down, to lengthen it, or to rotate it. You also can use similar controls to change your point of view. Truth be told, this system works better for

---

[29]This standard comes into play (sorry for the pun) again in Chapter 4, "Virtual Fun," where you learn that even inexpensive games can be a fun dose of virtual/artificial reality.

changing your point of view than it does for moving and changing objects. Nonetheless, it does work.

VR Studio is one of the software packages that has its own personality. This is evident in the unique user interface, and in the manual. The following passage, for example, is taken verbatim from the manual:

> *The commands for making absolute moves are detailed in the reference manual, which, as you may be realizing, will have to be digested in full with gravy and two vegetables before you get the maximum out of this rather horrifyingly complex program that you thought "might be a bit of fun."*

Learning a complex, idiosyncratic program is a bit less of a strain when the manual describes the situation clearly.[30]

I also must warn you that VR Studio has some bugs. These bugs are more frustrating than serious, but you should keep an eye out for anomalies. Save your work often. The calculations for visual representation of a 3D space in two dimensions are complex, and VR Studio sometimes gets things wrong. An object that should be on one side of a wall, for example, might wind up on the other side, but only at certain angles. This is unfortunate, but when you consider the cost of VR Studio relative to other 3D packages, a little tolerance of such things is reasonable. In other words, despite such problems, I think that VR Studio is a useful and interesting program. However, the door of opportunity for an inexpensive and fun VR package is still open.

The opening screen of VR Studio is shown in figure 2.63. There is a menu at the top, a view in the middle, and a whole lot of controls at the bottom. There is also a small information window imbedded in the Control Panel.

It would be fun to start creating an object, but it is a lot more sensible to look closely at that Control Panel first. You live and die by the Control Panel—if you learn to use it right off the bat, if you treat it as an end in itself, you suffer a lot less frustration. It's very much like learning to play the piano—if you can't relate the notes on the page to the keys on the piano, you are in trouble.

Two chunks of controls are worth knowing about. The chunk to the right of the little display panel controls the movement of your viewpoint. The chunk arranged in a line at the bottom consists of buttons that access some of the most commonly used features of the menus. Let's look at the controls for moving around in the scene first.

---

[30]Just adding silly comments, of course, isn't enough to make me feel better. The documentation for Imagine also is spotted with silly comments, but, unlike the VR Studio docs, Imagine's aren't possessed of a painfully accurate self-knowledge.

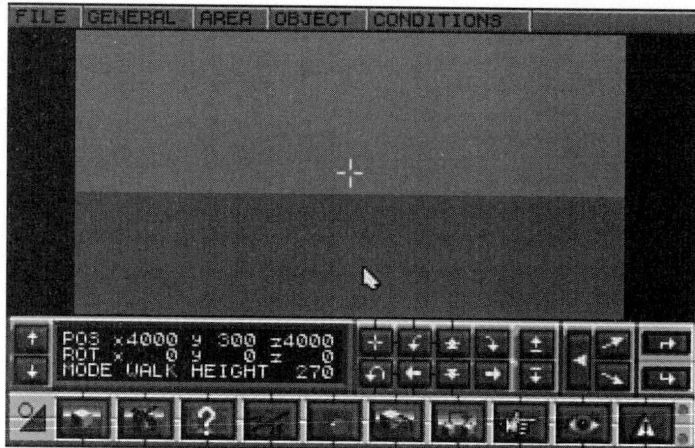

Figure 2.63. The opening screen of Virtual Reality Studio 2.0.

Moving your viewpoint is tricky. I used the piano analogy earlier, but that doesn't quite capture the experience of learning how to move around in VR Studio. The best analogy for that part of the process is learning to ride a bicycle. There will be times when you mean to turn left, but you'll turn right by mistake.[31] After you learn the nuances of the controls, however, you'll find it easy to set a useful viewpoint. The key is to learn to use controls in groups. If you want to get a better look at a part of your universe, for example, you may need to rotate left, look "up," back up, look "down," and then zoom in. This all becomes second nature after a few hours.

Here's a list of the controls that explains what each one does:

Cross hairs—A small cross hair marks the center of the viewport. Clicking this button toggles the cross hairs on and off. Most of the time, you can leave them off.

Reverse—Turns you 180 degrees from your current heading. In other words, it reverses your direction. This control is useful for navigating in architectural spaces. After you enter a door, for example, you can turn right around with no fuss or bother.

Rotate Left—Rotates your view to the left, which has the effect of rotating the universe to the right. It takes some practice to get this correct. Most people tend to associate the rotational direction with the universe

---

[31]Just after I learned how to ride a bicycle, and was oh so proud of myself, someone behind me yelled, "Your back wheel is turning backwards!" Rube that I was at the tender age of seven, I turned around to look and crashed ingloriously.

rather than one's own point of view. Don't be surprised if you find yourself reaching for the wrong rotate button for the first few sessions with VR Studio.

Forward—Moves you forward. This is a relative forward, not absolute. This has subtle, but important, effects on your navigation. If you are looking down on a scene, moving forward moves you down—forward is whatever direction you happen to be facing. If you are looking from above, and want to move "forward" instead of down, you need to look ahead before moving forward, and then look down again. The keys that look up and down are near the bottom right of the screen (with diagonal arrows in them).

Rotate Right—Rotates your view to the right, which has the effect of rotating the universe to the left. (See the explanation for Rotate Left.)

Up—Moves you straight up. No matter what direction you are facing, this button moves you vertically. See the forward button for an important difference between these two buttons. You almost always need to look down if you make large vertical movements.

Left—Moves you to the left. Leftward movement is always relative to your current position. Because the rotate keys rotate your point of view, not the universe, you almost always need to use the rotate controls with the left and right controls to walk "around" an object.

Back—Moves you backward. This is a relative backward, not absolute. This has subtle, but important, effects on your navigation. If you are looking down on a scene, moving backward moves you up—backward is the opposite of whatever direction you happen to be facing. If you are looking from above, and want to move "backward" instead of up, you need to look ahead before moving backward, and then look down again. The keys that look up and down are near the bottom right of the screen (with diagonal arrows in them).

Right—Moves you to the right. Rightward movement is always relative to your current position. Because the rotate keys rotate your point of view, not the universe, you almost always need to use the rotate controls with the left and right controls to walk "around" an object.

Down—Moves you straight down. No matter what direction you are facing, this button moves you vertically. See the Back button description for an important difference between these two buttons. You almost always need to look down if you make large vertical movements.

Level—This button faces you forward without changing other aspects of your viewpoint. If you are looking down from a great height and click this button, for example, you will be looking straight ahead at a great height.[32]

Rotate Up—This button rotates your point of view upward.

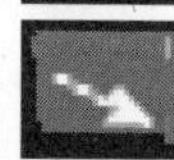

Rotate Down—This button rotates your point of view downward.

Roll Right—Rotates your point of view clockwise.

Roll Left—Rotates your point of view counterclockwise.

I strongly suggest practicing with these controls to move around in a simple universe. Let's create a cube. Click on the little Cube icon control at the bottom left of the screen (see fig. 2.63 for the location of this control). The dialog box in figure 2.64 appears.

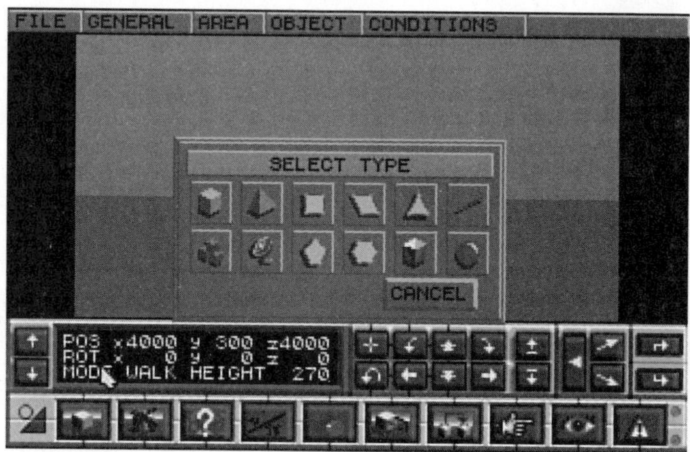

Figure 2.64. Creating an object in VR Studio 2.0.

[32]And you most likely will see nothing at that point, unless you have some very tall objects in your universe.

The dialog box displays icons for the 12 kinds of objects you can create in VR Studio. Select the icon of the cube in the upper left corner. This deposits a cube in the virtual universe (see fig. 2.65).[33]

Now you have a reference point that enables you to see the effects of using the various controls. If you try to move up or down, you discover that your movement is very limited. That's because VR Studio's default vehicle is walking. Use the General/Mode/Vehicle menu option to change your vehicle to Fly2 (see fig. 2.66). This allows for more natural movement—particularly the capability to move up and down. When you are creating a virtual universe, it is critical to move up and get an overview of your handiwork. The best use of the Walk mode is for cruising through a virtual universe that already has been built.

To test your maneuvering skills, try the movements shown in table 2.2 using the point-of-view controls. If you like to solve puzzles on your own, you may want to try to find a method to make the movements listed on the left before peeking at the methods I used, listed in the right-hand column.

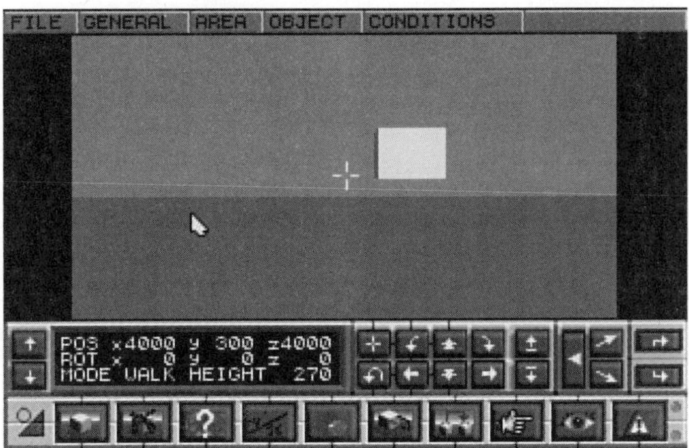

Figure 2.65. A virtual cube in a virtual space.

33Although VR Studio only has a limited number of basic shapes, you can change their sizes and relative proportions, and you can combine objects into groups to form more complex shapes. In general, however, the limited number of basic shapes means that you won't be able to create very realistic images.

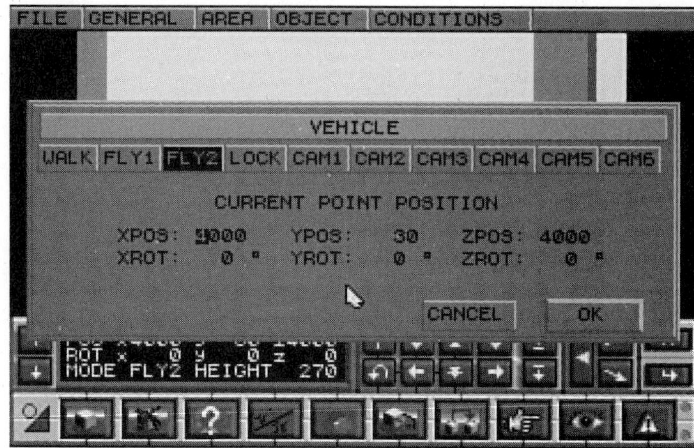

Figure 2.66. Changing your vehicle type.

Table 2.2. Point-of-View Controls.

Movement	*Method*
Move down to the ground	Press the down control until you can't move down any more.
Look at the cube from above	Move forward, left, up, down, or right until the cube is right in front of you. Then press the Up and Rotate Down controls in tandem[34] until you are above the cube looking down.
Look at the cube from the right side	Use the Right and Rotate Left controls in tandem to gradually shift your point of view around to the right side of the cube. This is a tricky set of moves, but you will often find the need to use it.
Look at the cube from below	Move forward, left, up, down, or right until the cube is right in front of you. Then press the Down and Rotate Up controls in tandem until you are below the cube looking up.

[34] *In tandem* means click one, then the other, and repeat until you are where you need to be.

Movement	*Method*
Move to one of the cube's faces and then shift to a view looking out from that face	Move forward, left, up, down or right until the cube is right in front of you. Then press the Reverse control to change your point of view 180 degrees.

Before you learn how to modify the cube's shape, take a look at that bottom row of controls. From left to right, these controls do the following:

Create object	Displays a dialog box that enables you to choose what kind of object you want to create.
Delete object	Lists current objects and enables you to select one for deletion.
Set/modify conditions	This is covered in detail in Chapter 9, "The Model is the Thing." By setting conditions, you can control what happens to an object during an interactive session.
Object attributes	Displays a dialog box that enables you to set a variety of object attributes. Two of the most important attributes involve sensors and transporters, topics covered later in this section.
Object color	Displays the controls for changing object colors. You can change the color of each face of an object.
Modify object	Displays the controls for modifying the shape and orientation of an object.
Copy object	Creates a copy of the selected object.
Select object	Changes the currently selected object.
View full screen	Displays the current workspace without the controls.
Reset point of view	Resets your point of view to ground level. It also resets your vehicle mode to Walk.[35]

The first thing to do is to make that simple little cube more interesting. Let's build a house with Virtual Reality Studio—it will show off the program's features and

[35]This is frustrating, especially if you ever click this button by mistake.

capabilities. Start by clicking the Modify Object icon at the bottom of the screen. This displays the most common VR Studio dialog box: Select Object (see fig. 2.67).

Before you carry out a command, you always must specify what object the command applies to. Even though you have created only one object, a cube, you will note that there are two objects listed, and our cube is number 2. Object number 1 is something called a *cuboid*. This is a default object that exists in every new virtual space—it is the ground.(36)

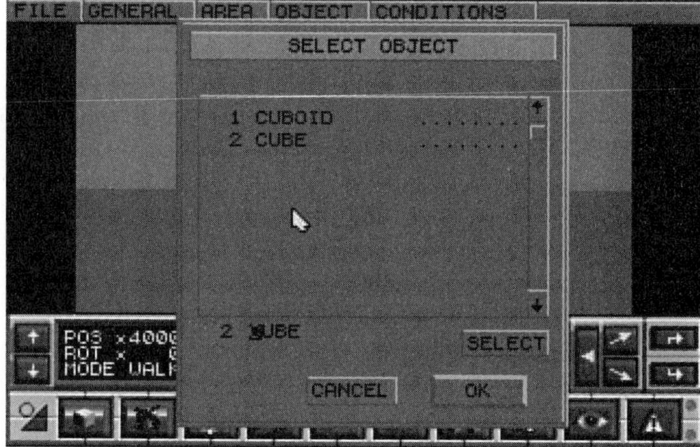

Figure 2.67. Selecting an object.

To select the cube, you can click object number 2, or you can click the Select button and then click on the cube in the scene. After you have many objects, it is much easier to select objects in the scene.(37) You can use the Object Attributes button to access a dialog box that enables you to name your objects, but in the heat of creation, it's often easy to overlook this step.

After you select the object you plan to modify, the Object Editor appears and takes over the lower half of the screen (see fig. 2.68). This awesome array of buttons and

---

36What is the difference between a cube and a cuboid? After a thorough review of the too-brief documentation that comes with VR Studio, I could find no reference to explain *cuboid*. Unfortunately, there isn't an index where I could look it up. I give VR Studio a B- for the documentation. The documentation that exists is written clearly. However, the lack of an index and the omission of a comprehensive reference section will frustrate you sometimes.

37One exception to this is the group. When you group objects, the group exists, but cannot be selected by clicking on the scene. You must choose the group by name from the Select Object dialog box. If you click on a group in the scene, you merely select the object of the group that you happened to click on.

controls looks imposing, but after a little practice, I found it easy to use. The top portion of the Object Editor should look familiar—it is nothing more than the controls for moving your viewpoint. The bottom half consists of five clusters of similar controls. Each set of controls modifies related attributes of the currently selected object.[38]

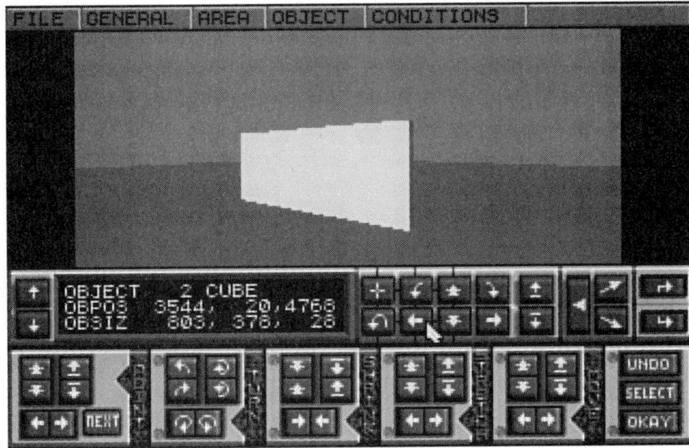

Figure 2.68. The Object Editor screen.

The labels for each of the control clusters are not easy to distinguish in black and white. From left to right, they are

Point	Moves individual points
Turn	Rotates objects
Shrink	Reduces the size of objects
Stretch	Increases the size of objects
Move	Moves objects

Each of these control clusters contains six buttons that behave identically, with the exception of the Rotation controls, which I will describe separately. A typical cluster (Move) is shown in figure 2.69.

The two buttons at the left move the object away from you or toward you. The two buttons at the right move the object up and down. The two buttons at the bottom move the object left and right. The other controls have similar functions. Consider the Stretch controls, for example. The top left button stretches out the

---

[38]Once you are in Object Edit mode, the rules for selecting objects change. You can select objects simply by clicking on them. Groups, however, still must be selected "the old fashioned way"—use the Select button at the lower right of the Object Editor.

object edge farthest away from you, and the button immediately under it stretches the face closest to you. The two buttons at the right stretch the object vertically, and the remaining two buttons stretch it horizontally. These buttons enable you to stretch in two directions along each of the three axes—up/down, left/right, and in/out. The Shrink control cluster is the exact opposite—it pulls in where the Stretch controls push out. The Point controls move individual points on an object, and the Rotate controls rotate to varying degrees, as specified on the icon for each button.

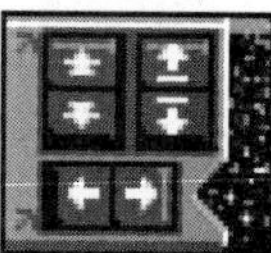

Figure 2.69. The Object Editor's Move control cluster.

The Point control cluster adds a Next button, which advances you to the next movable point on the object.[39]

To create a house, the cube must be transformed into an exterior wall. This is done easily using the Stretch and Shrink control clusters. Use the Left and Right Stretch buttons to pull the cube out horizontally, and then use the Stretch Up button to increase its height. Use one of the Shrink Toward/Away buttons to slim down the thickness of the wall. You can use the Viewpoint controls to move around and see what you are doing from a different perspective. Because several adjoining faces of the cube have identical colors, you may not be able to see clearly without changing your point of view. The wall should look like the example in figure 2.70.

If you will be adding any of the clip art objects that come with VR Studio (such as couches, tables, and chairs), you can load one of them now to check the size of your wall. To load an object, refer to the clip art handbook that comes with VR Studio to find the file name, and then use the File/Load Object menu option to load the object (see fig. 2.70). Figure 2.71 shows a desk and chair loaded and placed into the scene.

After you have your first wall, you simply can duplicate it over and over, stretching and shrinking the copies to make the remaining walls. Clicking the Copy Object icon at the bottom of the screen displays the dialog box shown in figure 2.72.

When you copy an object, you can specify the relative position of the new object.

[39]Not all objects have movable points, and not all points on an object are movable. The Next button takes you to legally movable points only.

You also can specify the object position in coordinates. In figure 2.72, the selected relative position for the new wall is Right. Figure 2.73 shows the result. The new wall is placed immediately to the right of the old wall.

This looks like one big wall, but it is not. Click the Modify Object button at the bottom of the screen, and select the new wall. Move it to the right, using the Move control cluster in the Object Editor (see fig. 2.74).

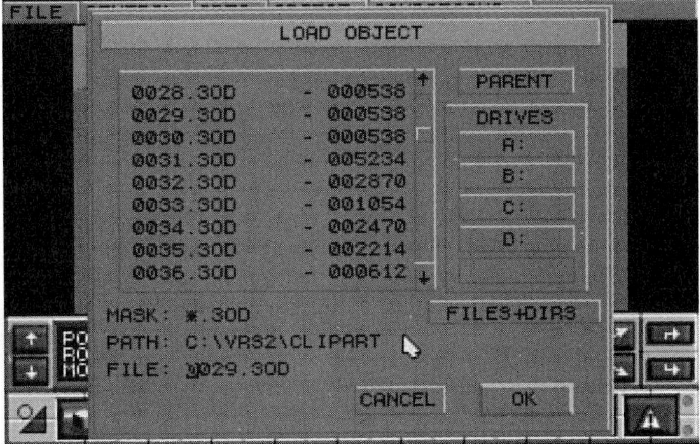

Figure 2.70. Loading an object from available clip art.

Figure 2.71. A desk and chair loaded into the scene.

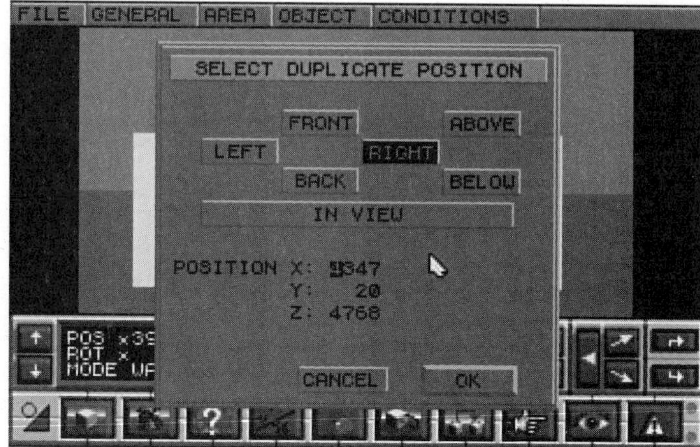

Figure 2.72. Copying an object.

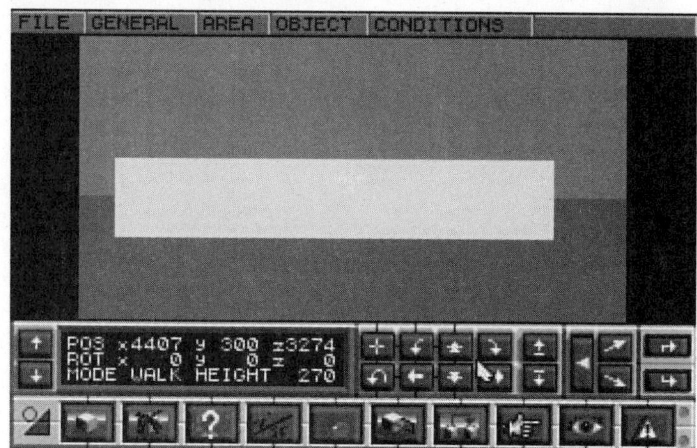

Figure 2.73. Adding a second wall to the right of the first wall.

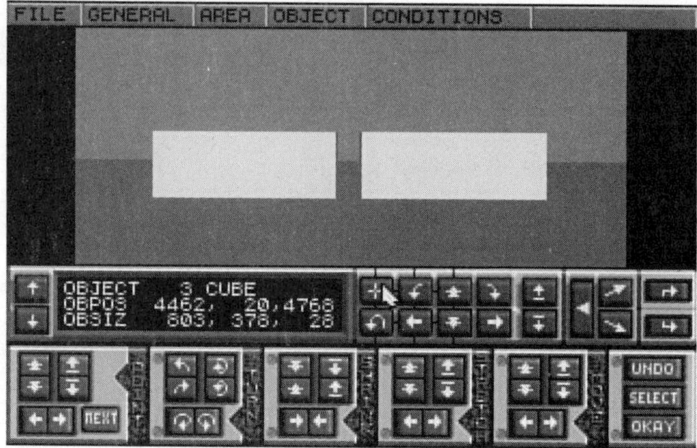

Figure 2.74. There are now two walls.

You now can use the Rotate control cluster to rotate the new wall 90 degrees (see fig. 2.75) and then move it next to the first wall and align the corners (see fig. 2.76).

You can add objects to the scene at any time. Figure 2.77 shows a couch being added.

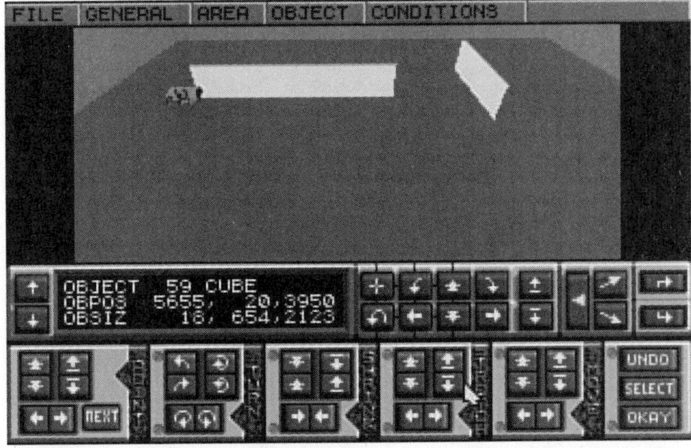

Figure 2.75. Rotating an object.

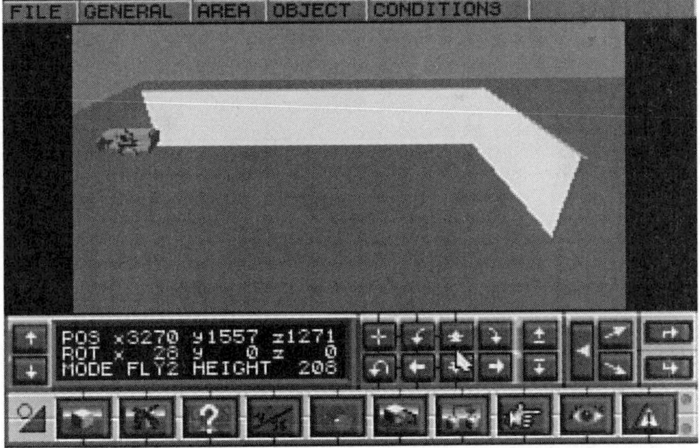

Figure 2.76. Aligning the two walls.

Figure 2.78 shows the scene after a chair and a third wall have been added. The third wall was added by copying the second wall, and specifying Left for the placement. VR Studio finds the nearest position to the left of the wall where it can place the new wall, which is (conveniently!) at the edge of the first wall, just like in figure 2.76.

Figure 2.77.
Adding a couch.

Figure 2.78.
Adding a third wall.

The house will be a little small, however, if you do not stretch out the new wall. Figure 2.79 shows the third wall stretched out (done, of course, with the Object Editor), and yet another wall added. This new wall is an interior wall, but it was added like the previous walls and then stretched and shrunk to fit. You can see the beginnings of the floor plan.

Figure 2.80 shows a few more walls added in the same fashion. To make the house interesting, I deviated from a simple square.

There is no grid in VR Studio, so it can be challenging to correctly line up walls at the corners. Here is where whatever practice you have at moving around comes in very handy. If you take a moment to position the point of view near the corner (see fig. 2.81), it becomes very easy to line up walls and other objects precisely.

Figure 2.82 shows how to add a bedroom, complete with bed and closet, to the house. The bed was added using the same steps used to add the desk, and the walls were made from copies of existing walls.

Figure 2.83 shows the addition of walls for a bathroom (on the left) and a kitchen. I also added a rather overdone dining room table[40] opposite the soon-to-be-finished kitchen. This is yet another stock object from the clip art that accompanies VR Studio.

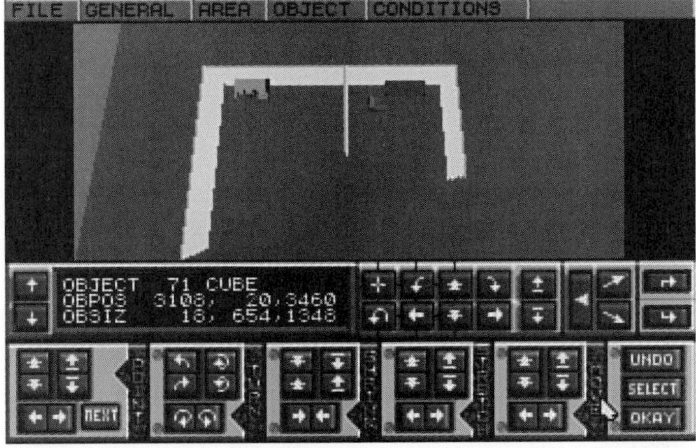

Figure 2.79. You can stretch and shrink new walls after you add them.

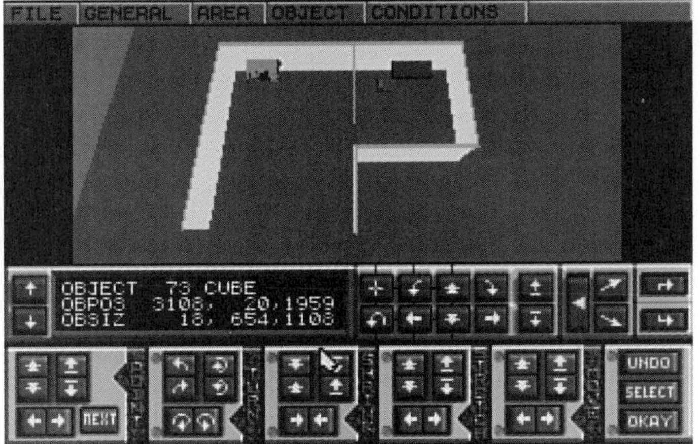

Figure 2.80. Additional walls give further definition to the room.

---

[40]As my editor noted, the table would make an excellent TV tray for Henry VIII.

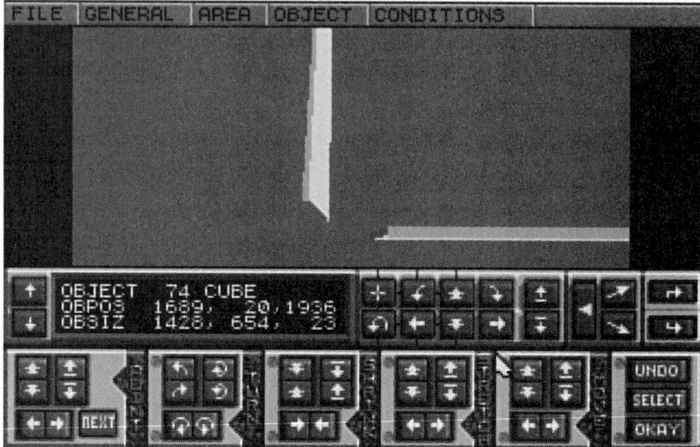

Figure 2.81. Lining up walls at the corners.

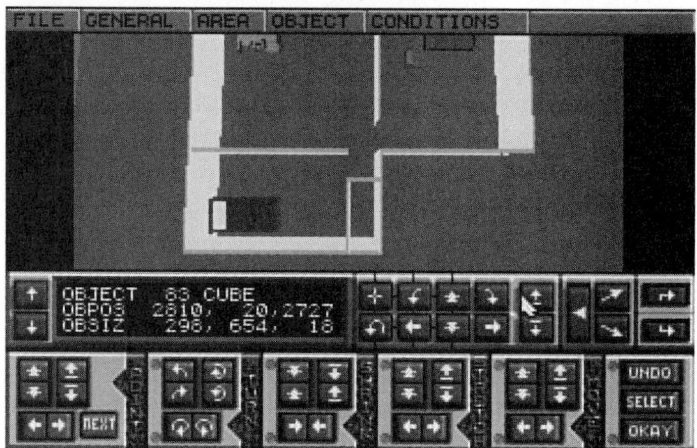

Figure 2.82. Creating a bedroom.

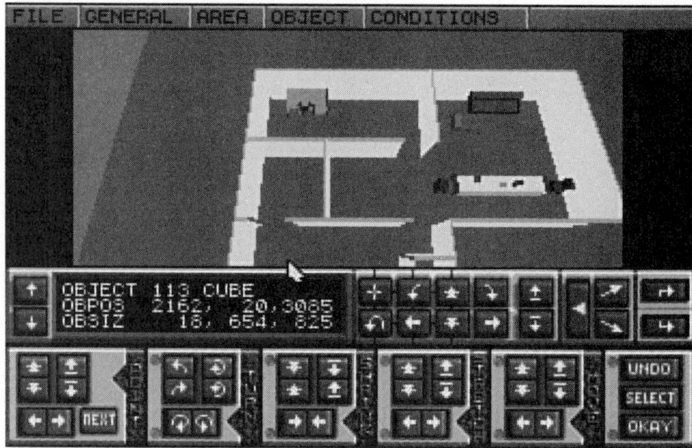

Figure 2.83. Adding a bathroom and kitchen to the house.

The kitchen really ought to have cabinets. To create them, you can return to the basics. Create a cube, as shown in figure 2.84. Figure 2.84 also shows the Color Editor. The available colors are shown at the bottom center of the screen. The six faces of the current object are shown at the left, and you can put a different color on each face. To choose a color, click with the left mouse button. To set a color, right-click on the corresponding face at the lower left.[41]

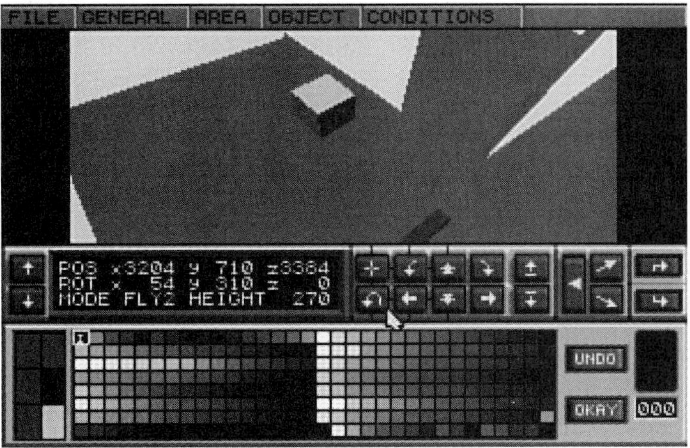

Figure 2.84. Using a cube as the basis for kitchen cabinets.

To create cabinets, use the Object Editor to stretch the cube into a counter. You then can copy and Shrink/Stretch to put a U-shaped set of counters in the kitchen. If you want, you can add a refrigerator or stove from the clip art collection.

To add a roof to the house, create a pyramid[42], and then stretch it to extend just a bit past the edges of the floor plan. The final result looks something like figure 2.85.

After you add a roof, you can locate the point of view inside the house to continue adding furniture, appliances, or whatever you want to the decor. Sometimes, just to be perverse, VR Studio places the new object or group above the roof. VR Studio uses rules to make sure that it doesn't place one object where another one already exists, and the results therefore are sometimes unpredictable. If this happens, just lift your point of view above the roof to find the object. Then slide the roof aside and drop the object through the opening (see fig. 2.86).

---

41 This arrangement of coloring the faces by clicking on one of the squares at the lower left is bothersome. It is almost impossible to keep the faces straight. (Sorry, another pun just slipped out.) Fortunately, you can right-click on an object face to set its color.

42 You can create a pyramid just like you create a cube—click on the pyramid shape instead of the cube shape in the dialog box for creating objects.

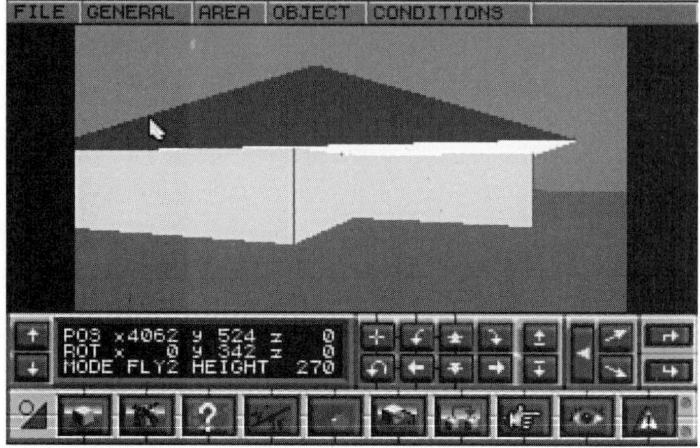

Figure 2.85.
An outside view of the completed house.

This exterior view is quite plain. The house needs some windows and doors. You can add these using the Create Object button at the bottom of the screen. Instead of using a solid object, simply add a few rectangles. These can be sized and colored to suit your tastes. Figure 2.87 shows an outside view with a door and a window added at the front entrance of the house.

So far, this door is just a flat rectangle placed against the house. However, VR Studio enables you to create entrances and transporters that move you to an entrance. To create an entrance, move to the position that represents the entry point. In this case, that's the inside of the wall where the door was placed—just inside the living/dining room. Click the Area/Create Entrance menu option to make this spot an entrance. To see the attributes of the entrance, click the Area/Edit Entrance menu option. This displays the dialog box shown in figure 2.88.

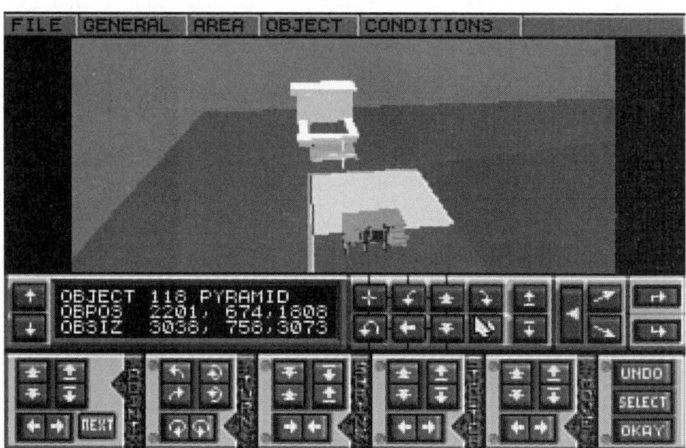

Figure 2.86.
Adding an object after the roof is on.

Figure 2.87. An outside view with a door and window added.

Notice that both the position and rotation coordinates of the entrance position are editable. This means that to create an entrance, you must set not only the position, but the orientation as well. In this example, the entrance is intended to mimic the act of walking through a door, so the orientation points into the room.

Figure 2.88. Editing the attributes of an entrance.

Now that you have an entrance, you can create a transport that takes you to it.[43] Select the exterior door, and modify its attributes using the Object/Edit Attributes menu option or the Object Attributes button at the bottom of the screen. Either method displays the dialog box shown in figure 2.89.

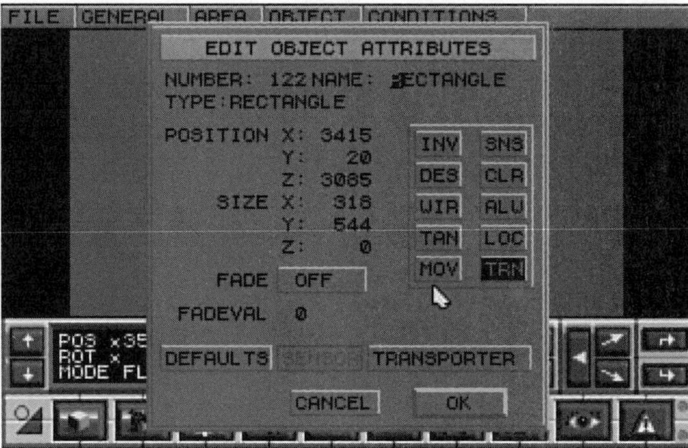

Figure 2.89. The Object Attributes dialog box.

Many attributes are available for editing, but only one is of interest for creating a transporter: the TRN button. Click it to activate the Transporter button. Clicking the Transporter button enables you to select the area and entrance that the object will transport to (see fig. 2.90).

Now when you collide with the door (that is, when you "walk" into it) you are transported to the living/dining room, at the location you set as the entrance. To create a way back out, you must create another door on the inside of the wall,[44] create an entrance near the outside door, and then make the inside door a transporter.

---

[43]The term *entrance* is a little misleading. An entrance need not be located in an entry point. You can move to a point far away from the house, for example, and make that an entrance. Such jumps lend themselves well to game situations.

You also can create multiple areas in a project. You can create one kind of space in one area, and a completely different kind of space in a different area. A transporter in one area can take you to an entrance in a different area.

[44]Don't copy the outside door to make the inside door. VR Studio will not be able to properly keep track of the entrances, and you won't be able to transport properly no matter how much you edit the various attributes and objects.

This concludes the tour of the basic features of Virtual Reality Studio 2.0. For information about the advanced features of VR Studio, see Chapter 9, "The Model is the Thing." Even if you never do anything beyond creating interesting custom universes, however, you'll get a lot of enjoyment out of VR Studio.[45]

Figure 2.90. Selecting the entrance for a transporter.

---

[45] However, a warning to the wise. VR Studio has some bugs that can be frustrating. Most of these bugs don't show up until you try to create a large number of objects. I strongly suggest that you save your work frequently, and that you check the state of all objects before saving over an older version of the scene. This precaution will enable you to restore from an older version if something goes wrong. You also should contact Virtual Reality Laboratories to see whether you have the latest version of the package. The latest version I received was 2.07. They are making an effort to clean up the bugs.

3

VIRTUAL POWER

3D Modeling

Most of the pictorial art throughout history was created without any accurate attention to the third dimension. At best, the third dimension was stretched in virtually[1] unrecognizable ways. There are good reasons for this. The most important reason is simple to state:

Drawing in three dimensions is not natural.

Before you start calling me an idiot for making such an inane pronouncement, think about this for a minute. What is natural about 3D is viewing in three dimensions. Living in three dimensions does not automatically qualify anyone for drawing in three dimensions. There is some effort involved. If you don't believe me, pull out pencil and paper and draw a circle. Heck—don't even worry too much about getting the sides perfect; if you were working on a computer, the computer could align things for you.

Done with the circle? Good. Now draw a sphere.

Not as simple, right? Good. Now we're on the same wavelength.

I am making this point as a warning. If you have never drawn in three dimensions with a pencil, don't expect the computer to suddenly make it easy. It's not the mechanics of drawing in 3D that are difficult; it's thinking in 3D that's hard. Once you break through the barrier, however, and start thinking in 3D, it gets easier and easier. If you haven't already had a 3D-drawing "Aha!" experience, you will at some point. It may seem like work until you reach that stage, however. So don't give up if it seems frustrating—you'll miss the best part of 3D if you do. Which leads me to the following statement:

With a little effort, you can make drawing in three dimensions a perfectly natural activity.

In other words,[2] 3D drawing is an acquired taste.

Working in Three Dimensions

There are two ways to work in three dimensions: intuitive and mechanical. The intuitive method is exciting, once you acquire the skills, but good old mechanical drawing has its advantages, too. For starters, it offers a frame of reference that I can describe. It's like the notes in a musical score—it's a way of describing

[1] Unintentional play on words, but I'll take credit for it anyway.

[2] And in keeping with the recipe idea, of course.

something, but it is not that something. Just as it takes practice to turn notes into music, it takes practice to turn mechanical drafting into interesting virtual spaces.

When working in two dimensions, we traditionally use Cartesian[3] coordinates to define points in the 2D plane. Figure 3.1 shows a typical Cartesian coordinate system. There is a vertical axis, called the *y axis*, and a horizontal axis, the *x axis*. The point where these two axes meet is called the *origin*. The origin is at distance zero on both axes, and we can describe this point as (0,0).

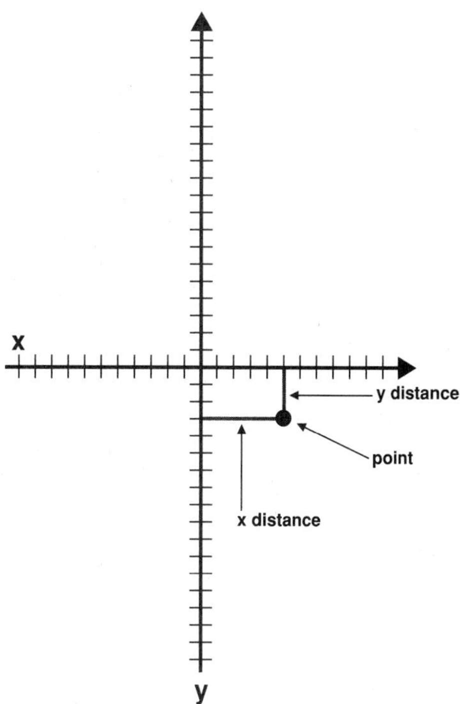

Figure 3.1. The Cartesian (x,y) coordinate system.

To define a point, we need merely mention its distance from the origin along both axes. A point 5 units to the right of the origin along the x axis and 3 units below the origin on the y axis, for example, has the coordinates (5,-3). By convention, the x coordinate is given first. There are an infinite number of such points in the 2D plane.

[3]Named after the great mathematician René Descartes, who slept until noon. They never tell us those things about famous people, and we don't find out until it's too late to develop such delicious eccentricities in ourselves.

To describe points in 3D space, we merely add a third dimension. The third axis is called the *z axis*.[4] A three-dimensional coordinate system is shown in figure 3.2.

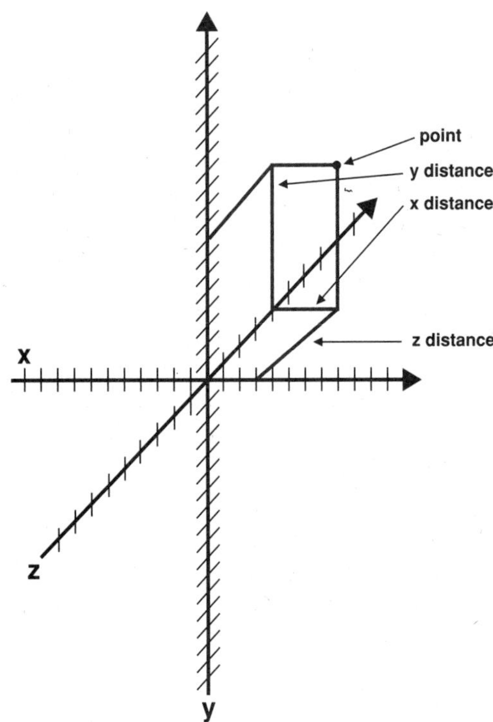

Figure 3.2. A three-dimensional coordinate system.

To specify a point in a three-dimensional system, we need to supply three numbers. Each number represents the distance from the origin along each respective axis—x, then y, then z. If we take the same point as in the preceding example, and lift it 83 units up from the origin, its coordinates are (5, -3, 83).

Now, we have not merely an infinite number of points in a plane, but an infinite number of planes in space—and each plane has an infinite number of points in it. The level of complexity has just gone from infinity to infinity squared.[5]

I suppose all those infinities would be more manageable if we didn't have to find a way to represent them on two-dimensional surfaces. Paper is two-dimensional;

---

[4] I'll bet you saw that coming.

[5] Of course, I'll leave the question of how one squares infinity to the mathematicians.

the computer screen is two-dimensional. Thus, the allure of fancy virtual-space-creating goggles: they offer the promise of being able to draw and work in three dimensions using clever tricks to fool the eye (see Chapter 8, "Seeing is Believing").

The problem is, such goggles cost thousands of dollars, have limited capabilities,[6] and the range of software written for them is, well, almost zero.[7] For a while yet, we'll have to make do with representing three dimensions in two dimensions. The rest of this chapter is dedicated to the proposition that as long as we're calling it virtual reality, degrees of virtuality are a reality—for the time being. After all, a perfectly rendered, highly detailed 3D scene on your computer monitor beats the heck out of nothing at all.

trueSpace from Caligari

RECIPE

Recipe for Instant 3D

1 copy trueSpace
1 glance at documentation

Instructions: Make a few basic shapes, and then stretch 'em around a bit so they look like real stuff. Paint liberally, then render. Great for hors d'oeuvres, parties, screen savers, and so on.

---

[6]Don't move your head too quickly, for example—the computer will choke trying to update the scene to keep up and will shatter any illusion of reality.

[7]Not that there aren't software programs, of course, but so far there aren't any spreadsheets or word processors—that is, the kinds of software you and I use every day. Drawing programs are limited to special-purpose applications, such as rendering the chemical structure of complex molecules.

One of the great truisms of working in 3D is that it's horribly difficult to create 3D objects while working with a 2D interface like a computer screen. Elsewhere in this book, we talked about the costs and benefits of various kinds of 3D and six-degrees-of-freedom input devices, as well as about various 3D viewing devices. The primary hazard with anything truly 3D is cost. In addition, you are limited to software that supports the 3D devices of your choosing.

Until 3D input and output becomes more economical, what we really and truly need is a 3D-modeling environment that works well in a 2D computer world. I'm a big fan of the interface in 3D Studio, but I'm also the first to admit that it takes serious study and practice to use it effectively—and even after a year of close study, you will find that there are things that are just plain hard to do with it. 3D Studio's first requirement is power, and sometimes that requires some sacrifice in the interface. This is fine if you absolutely must have it all, but sometimes it would be nice to just have a comfortable, easy-to-use interface for 3D modeling.

Well, there is one, and it's called trueSpace. With most 3D modelers, I find myself going through a frustration phase, where nothing makes any sense, and I keep waiting for everything to click into place.[8] With trueSpace, I was up and modeling in minutes, and I could hardly wait to learn about the next cool feature. I have arranged for a trial version of trueSpace on the CD-ROMs, and I recommend it highly. It's not cheap, but it's not thousands of dollars, either. It's what I would call affordable, and it's plenty good enough for real work, even if 3D Studio still is the professional's choice.

trueSpace Explained

Because I'm really impressed with trueSpace, I'm going to provide an extra-detailed tutorial. Even so, I simply can't go into all the cool and interesting 3D stuff you can do with this product. If you like what you see, start exploring with the trial version on the CDs.

The trueSpace interface, shown in figure 3.3, may seem overwhelming at first, but it's very well organized and slowly will begin to arrange itself into accessible categories after several hours of use. trueSpace runs in Windows, but the default interface plays around a bit with the realities of life in Windows. I wound up preferring the upside-down interface, although it put me off at first. I found it more natural to have the vast array of toolbars at the bottom of the working window, but if you don't like that arrangement, you can change it in the Preferences settings.

---

[8]Actually, it's usually more like a squishing sound, as my hopes get dashed by reality.

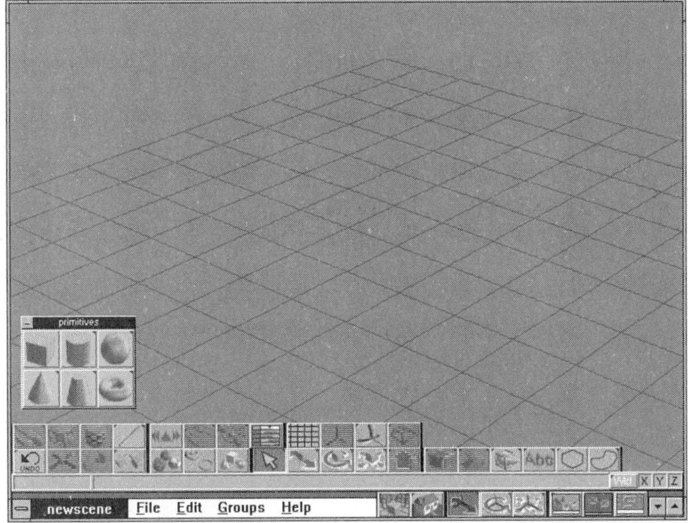

Figure 3.3.
The trueSpace opening screen.

Let's take a detailed look at the interface, because it's at the heart of using trueSpace effectively. The Caption bar, located at the bottom left of the screen, contains some of the usual Windows stuff: the Control Menu, the window caption, and a menu (File, Edit, Groups, and Help). To the right of the menu is a row of icons. These icons control the 3D viewpoint in the main window. They don't affect objects—just your view of the objects.

Above the icons, you will find a status bar. Pointing at any icon or tool displays a text message letting you know what that tool does. This makes it easier to learn how to use trueSpace—of all the kinds of software that benefit from a status bar, 3D modeling is at the top of the list.

Above the status bar are two rows of icons/tools. These seem intimidating at first, but you'll find that the tools are arranged logically into groups. It takes a while to get a good feel for which groups contain which tools, but once it falls into place, trueSpace really starts to feel like a 3D-modeling sports car.

When you first start, some of the tools are gray, because they can't be used until you have created an object. If you haven't created an object, you can't exactly rotate one, for example.

There's also an example of a Control Panel in figure 3.3, located above the tool groups and to the left. The Control Panel contains several basic geometric shapes[9]—a cube, a sphere, a torus,[10] and others. To create an object, just click on a shape and presto!—you've got one.[11]

The trueSpace Toolbox

Before we try to create any models, let's take a look at the basic complement of trueSpace tools. I hope you are impressed with the number of tools, because I have a nice surprise for you—many of those tools expand into two additional possibilities. By clicking and holding on a tool, you often can display a row of variant tools, from which you can pick one tool to work with. When you click on the tool for picking only part of an object, for example, you can choose among picking a vertex, a face, an edge, and so on.

By right-clicking on a tool, you often can open a dialog box for establishing settings for the tool. Right-clicking on the Rotation tool, for example, enables you to determine which axes you can rotate around (x, y, and/or z).[12]

I can't cover all the possibilities here in the book, but you can explore using the trial version on the CDs.

What I can do here is to provide a breakdown of the basic tools in the basic tool groups. Let's take a took at the tools available in trueSpace first, and then look at how they are used for modeling, surface mapping, and rendering.[13]

Editing Tools

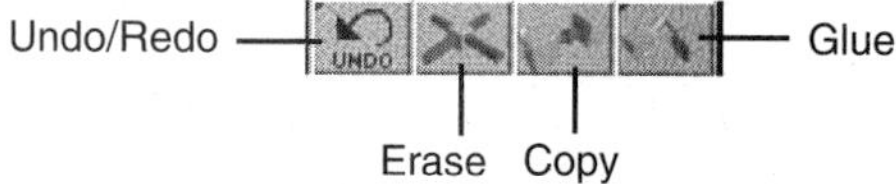

Figure 3.4. The Editing tool group.

[9]Referred to in 3D-speak as *primitives*.

[10]*Torus* is the technical term for a doughnut shape.

[11]One of the things I like about trueSpace is that it doesn't make you think in strict terms. With most 3D modelers, you can't just create a shape—you have to decide how big it should be and where it should be right off the mark. That's nice and scientific, but some of us would rather just get a default shape, and then push and shove it into place and shape afterward.

[12]Each axis can be selected independently, so you can rotate using one, two, or all three axes—yet another example of flexible, high-powered modeling in trueSpace.

[13]Keep in mind that many of these tools have variants. A tool with a little triangle in the upper right corner has variants. A tool with a little triangle in the upper left corner has a Control Panel for settings.

Undo/Redo—Does just what you would expect: undoes your last action or redoes an action that you just undid.

Erase—Deletes the current object.

Copy—Makes a second copy of the currently selected object.[14]

Glue—Enables you to attach objects hierarchically. An object can be a child or a sibling of another object, and you can unglue if necessary. If you create a torso, for example, an arm normally would be attached as a child object.

Library Tools

Figure 3.5. The Library tool group.

Material Library—Opens the current material library in a dialog box, enabling you to select a material to apply to an object or a face.

Path Library—Opens a dialog box with a list of predefined spline paths.

Primitives Panel—Enables you to create instantly simple geometric shapes such as cubes and spheres.

Navigation Tools

Four groups of navigation tools exist: Object, View, Point, and Deform. All these groups make use of the Coordinates Property Panel (see fig. 3.6).

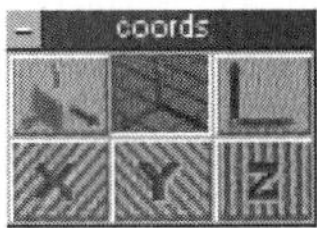

Figure 3.6. The Coordinates Property Panel.

This panel enables you to select the active axis or axes for allowable movement. The left mouse button controls movement on the x and/or y axis, while the right

[14]To select an object, click on it with the arrow cursor.

mouse button controls movement on the z axis.[15] The top row of buttons in the panel are used to constrain motion to three, two, or one plane.

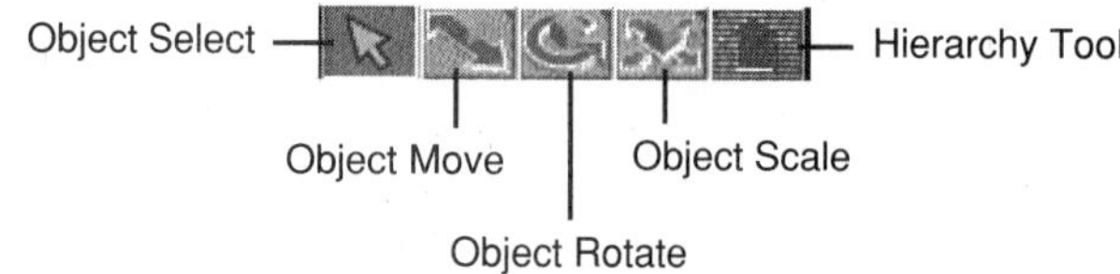

Figure 3.7. The Object Navigation tool group.

Object Select—Selects an object. When this tool is active, click on it.

Object Move—Moves the current object by clicking and dragging.

Object Rotate—Rotates the current object along one or more axes by clicking and dragging.

Object Scale—Increases or decreases the size of the current object by clicking and dragging in one or more dimensions.

Hierarchy Tool—Moves up or down in an object hierarchy.

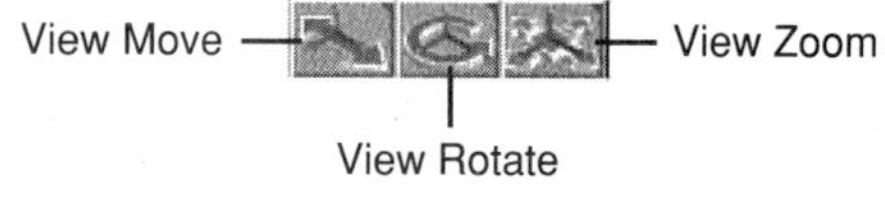

Figure 3.8. The View Navigation tool group.

View Move—Moves the viewpoint.

View Rotate—Rotates the view.

View Zoom—Zooms in or out.

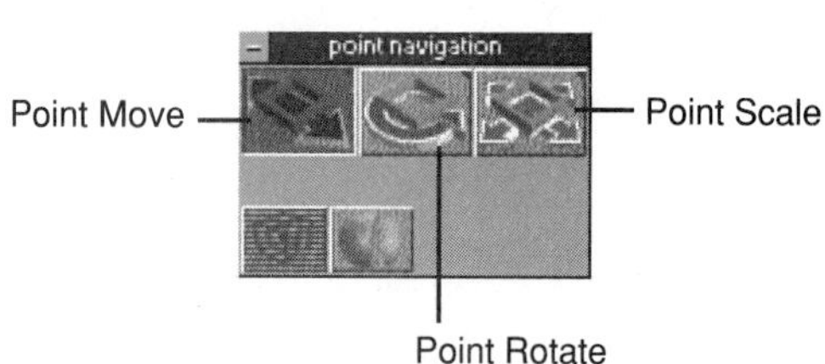

Figure 3.9. The Point Navigation tool group.

---

[15]In other words, to move on the x axis, deactivate the y axis in the Coordinate Control Panel, and then drag the left mouse button in the view to make the change. To move on both the x and y axes, activate both axes and then drag with the left mouse button pressed. To move up and down on the z axis, click with the right button and drag. It sounds complicated, but after you do it a few times, you'll see how easy and convenient it is.

Point Move—Moves the currently selected point(s).(16)

Point Rotate—Rotates the currently selected point(s).

Point Scale—Scales (enlarges or shrinks) the currently selected point(s).

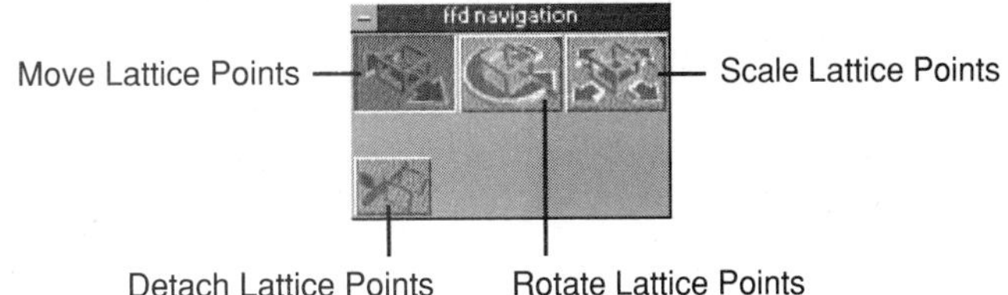

Figure 3.10. The Deform Navigation tool group.

Move Lattice Points—Moves selected points on a deformation lattice.

Rotate Lattice Points—Rotates selected points on a deformation lattice.

Scale Lattice Points—Scales selected points on a deformation lattice.

Detach Lattice Points—Detaches the lattice from one object so that you can use it to deform a second object.

Modeling Tools

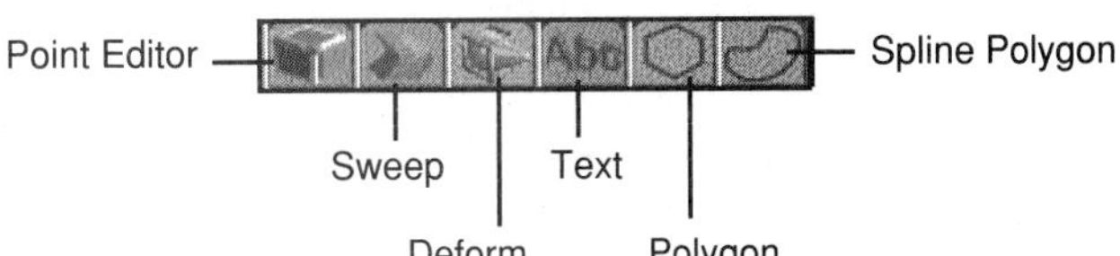

Figure 3.11. The Modeling tool group.

Point Editor—Edits portions of an object. Variants are Edit Points, Edit Edges, Edit Faces, and Edit Context.(17)

Sweep—Sweeps an object or face through space to create a more complex object.(18) Variants are Sweep, Tip, Lathe, Sweep Macro, and Bevel.

Deform—A very powerful tool! Creates a lattice that can be deformed in a free-form mode for complex modeling operations. This one tool is enough to make trueSpace a first-class 3D modeling product.

---

[16] Use the Point Edit tool in the modeling group, of course, for selecting points. You'll see a little "P" below the arrow cursor when you are in Point mode. Always select an object before you select Point mode—you can select only points on the current object.

[17] Edit Context enables you to edit a combination of points, edges, and/or faces.

[18] You see an example of a Sweep late in the tutorial.

Text—Creates 3D text objects from TrueType fonts. Variants are Text Vertical and Text Horizontal.

Polygon—Creates polygons in a single plane.[19]

Spline Polygon—Creates rounded shapes in a plane.

Rendering Tools

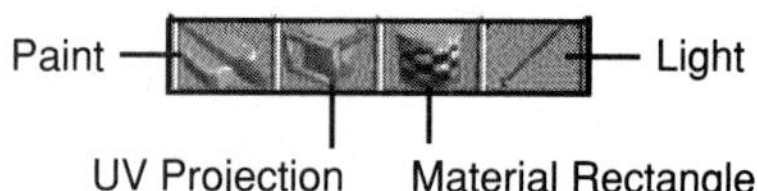

Figure 3.12. The Rendering tool group.

Paint—Creates new materials and applies the materials to objects or portions of objects. Variants are Paint Face, Inspect Face, Repaint Face, and Paint Object.

UV Projection—Applies textures to objects. There are three kinds of texture mapping: Planar, Cylindrical, and Spherical.[20] The Control Panel associated with this tool (as always, right-click to see it) clearly displays the results of each mapping choice using examples.

Material Rectangle—Creates material rectangles that can be positioned on an object's surface interactively.

Light—Adds lights and cameras to the workspace. Variants are Infinite Light, Local Light, Spotlight, and Camera.

Animation Tools

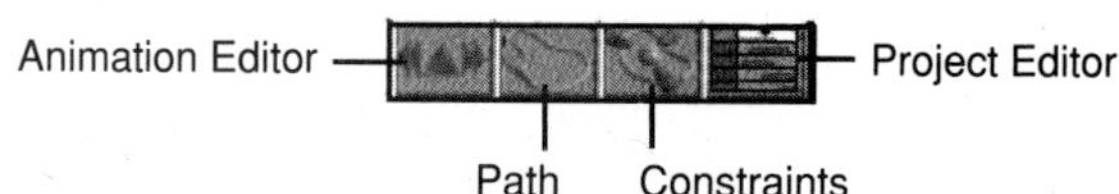

Figure 3.13. The Animation tool group.

Animation Editor—Opens the Animation Control Panel. You can add animation frames, set key frames, and play an animation. See the tutorial that follows for details.

Path—Draws or edits paths for objects that are animated.

---

[19]Shapes you create in a single plane are very useful for further editing with the Sweep.

[20]Planar mapping is flat mapping. Cylindrical mapping applies a texture, the way a label is applied to a can of refried beans. Spherical mapping applies the map to the surface of a sphere.

Constraints—Forces an object to behave in certain ways. There are two variants: one that forces an object to always face some other object, and one that forces an object to always face in the direction it is moving.

Project Editor—A timeline-based window that enables you to adjust the timing and relationships involved in an animation.

Utility Tools

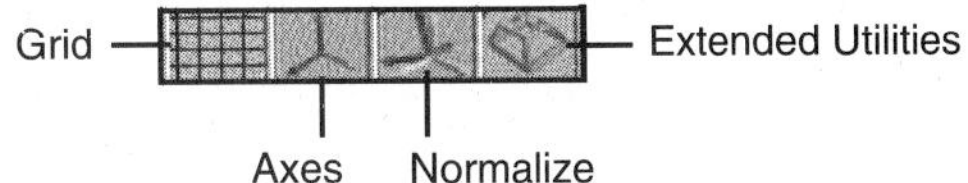

Figure 3.14. The Utility tool group.

Grid—Turns snap-to-grid on and off.

Axes—Displays and/or modifies the axes for an object.

Normalize—Returns an object to its original state. Variants are Normalize Location, Normalize Rotation, and Normalize Scale.

Extended Utilities—A collection of several variants not included elsewhere. Includes the capability to subdivide the faces of an object, mirroring, and others.

Window (View) Tools

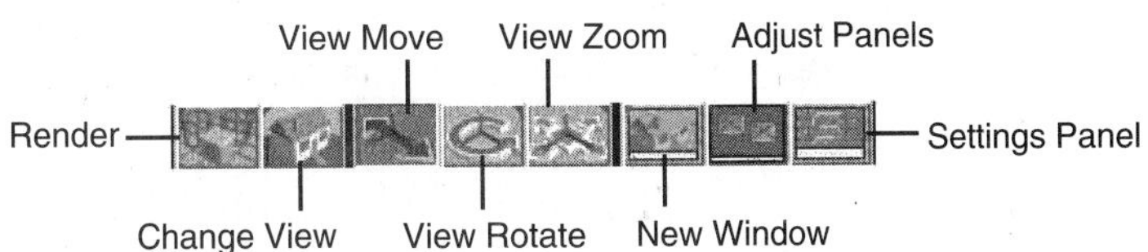

Figure 3.15. The Window (View) tool group.

Render—Renders an image of the window's contents. Variations include Render Object, Render Scene, Redraw Wireframe, and Render Scene to Disk. Rendering shows you the materials used on the surface of objects.

Change View—Changes to a different view, such as top, front, perspective, and so on.

View Move—Moves your viewpoint. Use the left button and drag in the workspace to move in the x and y planes; use the right button to move up and down. Click on this tool with the right button to open a Control Panel that enables you to constrain movement to just one or two planes.

View Rotate—Rotates the view; left and right mouse buttons work as in View Move.

View Zoom—Zooms the view; left and right mouse buttons work as in View Move.

New Window—Opens a new window with its own View controls.

Adjust Panels—Controls state and position of any and all open Control Panels. Variants include Dock All Panels and Close All Panels.

Settings Panel—Opens a Control Panel that enables you to adjust various global settings.

Getting Started with trueSpace

If the amount of detail in the preceding section seems overwhelming, I need to make two things perfectly clear:

- This is typical of life with 3D software and should not be held against trueSpace.[21]
- There's a lot more to trueSpace than what you've seen so far.

If this seems overwhelming, think for a moment about what's going on when you use a product like trueSpace. Not only does the software have to deal with all the variables of point of view and object rotation and all the rest, but it has to provide you with the easiest possible ways to interact with these. This is a major job, and until recently, it has required far more computing power and sophistication of software to get the job done. So don't be daunted; be impressed and hang in there. If there is one product that offers a (relatively!) easy path into 3D modeling, it's trueSpace.

Enough talk; let's do something![22] Begin the way any universe must begin: with a little light. Actually, let's create an Infinite Light; it's more in keeping with one's god-like role. Click on the Light tool in the Render group to create the light. Figure 3.16 shows the result: a single light has appeared in the universe.

But there is no one to see this light—let's create a camera to record the scene. This is as easy as creating a light—just click with the left mouse button on the Light tool, and a row of variant tools appears. Click on the tool that looks like a camera, and a camera appears in the universe (see fig. 3.17). It's not an impressive-looking camera, but its only job is to provide a point of view—it won't show up if you render the scene.[23]

---

[21]If you did not already know this, then you probably skipped ahead to this chapter.

[22]The following tutorial is based on the tutorial you'll find in the documentation for trueSpace. I have spiced it up with my own comments and observations, of course.

[23]Try it if you aren't the trusting kind.

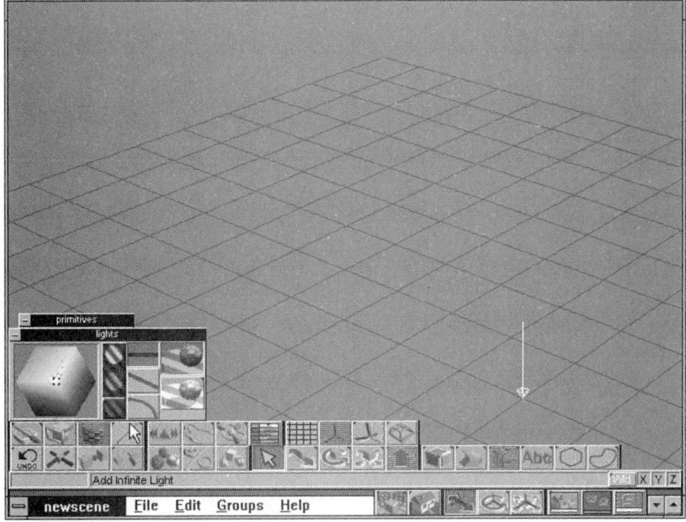

Figure 3.16. A universe with just one light in it.

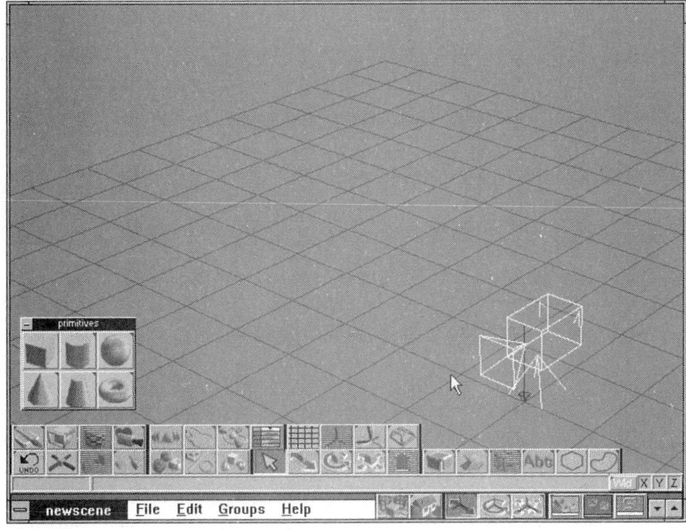

Figure 3.17. A camera in the universe.

A camera[24] can be moved just like any other object. If you look closely at figure 3.17, you'll note that the camera is just pointing off in any old direction, and we need it to point toward the scene we are about to create. To move the camera, click on the Object Selection tool, and then click on the camera. The camera turns white to show that it is selected. To rotate the camera, click on the Object Rotate tool,

---

[24]And lights, for that matter.

and then drag the mouse to perform the rotation. ***Hint:*** You usually want to rotate the camera in only one plane at a time, and that's usually the horizontal plane. To do this, you must rotate the camera about its vertical axis (the y axis). To constrain movement to just the y axis, right-click on the Object Rotate tool to open the Coordinates Control Panel (see fig. 3.18). By default, all three axes are active (x, y, and z), so all three buttons are pressed.[25]

Figure 3.18. The Coordinates Control Panel can be used to constrain rotation about an axis.

To deactivate the x axis, click the x button—it turns lighter (see fig. 3.19). Now, when you click with the left button and drag, the object rotates only around the y axis. You do not need to turn off the z axis; to rotate about the z axis, you must click and drag with the right mouse button.

Figure 3.19. The Coordinates Control Panel.

Click on the Object Rotate tool once more to activate it.[26] Now click and drag with the left mouse button anywhere in the scene to rotate the camera. Experiment with dragging left and right, up and down, and observe the effect it has on object rotation. The camera should wind up pointing straight ahead into the scene, as shown in figure 3.20.

It often is convenient to create a small window in which to work. Click on the New Window tool in the Window group to open a new window. Position the window at the upper left of the main window, as shown in figure 3.21.

You can control the point of view in the new window independently of the main window. Use the View tools to change the zoom, scale, and position in the new window. An easier and, in our case, more useful approach is to make the new

---

[25]A button looks darker when it is pressed. Sort of like people, I guess.

[26]And, at the same time, dismiss the Coordinates Control Panel.

window show us what the camera sees. Click on the new window's Change View tool with the left mouse button (and hold it), and then click on the Camera icon (see fig. 3.22 for the result).

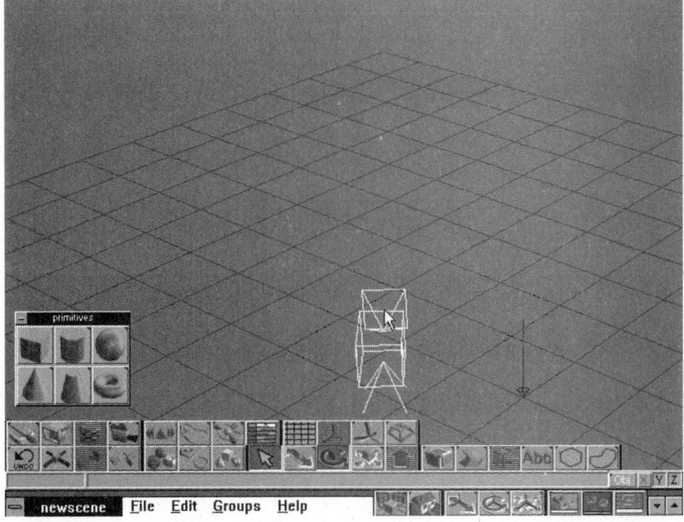

Figure 3.20. Rotating the camera to face into the scene.

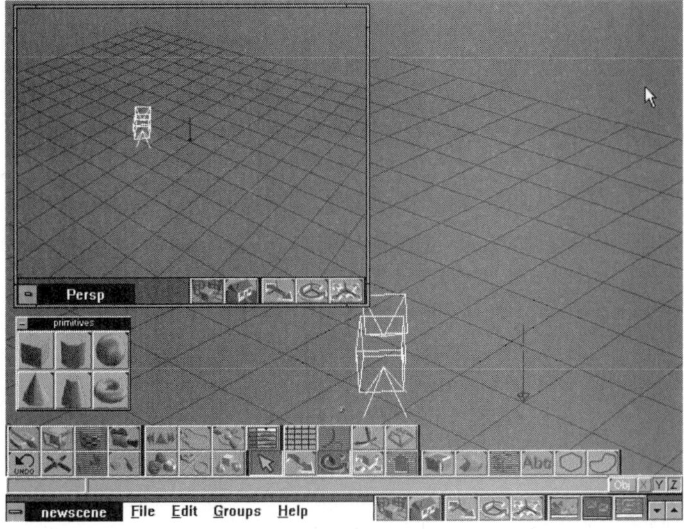

Figure 3.21. Adding a new window.

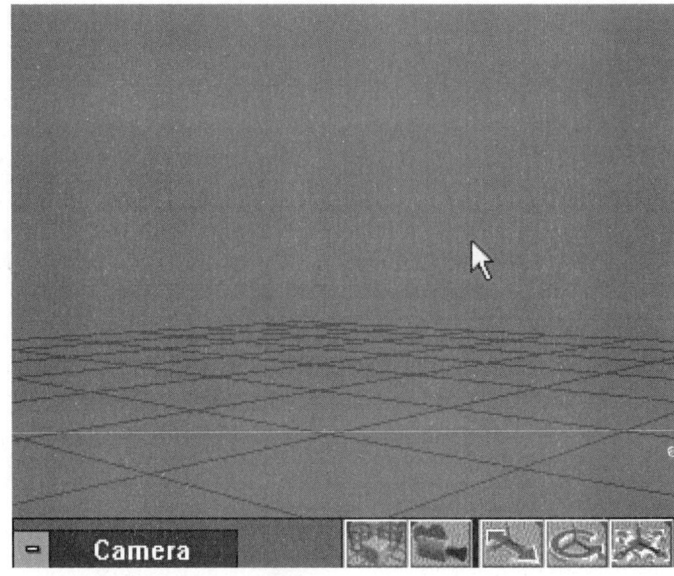

Figure 3.22. The new window now shows the viewpoint of the camera.

Now on to the meat of this exercise: let's create something interesting! Click on the Vertical Text tool in the Model group. This places a large cursor in the drawing space. Type in a word, such as **Multimedia!** The word shows up in the workspace (see fig. 3.23).

All we've done so far is create a flat bit of text—let's make it 3D. Click on the Sweep tool to extend the text into the third dimension (see fig. 3.24).(27)

We are going to use the view in the working window at the upper left for rendering this scene later on. Right now, as you can see in figure 3.24, we can't see very much of the text. To move the text, click on the Object Move tool and then click with the left mouse button and drag until the text shows clearly in the working window (see fig. 3.25). You may need to click and drag more than once to get the text where it needs to be. If you have trouble keeping track of your position, think in terms of moving the text in front of the camera. To move the text up and down, you can use the right mouse button instead of the left. Note in figure 3.25 that, in the main window, the text is positioned directly in front of the camera.(28)

27By doing this, we automatically are using the default settings for a Sweep. Right-click on the Sweep tool to change the default settings.

28If you feel up to it, you also can move the camera around to point at the text, but this is much trickier!

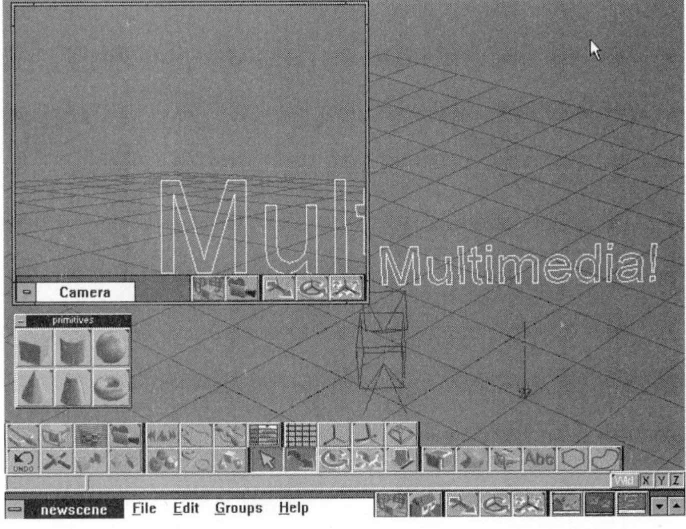

Figure 3.23. Adding text to a scene.

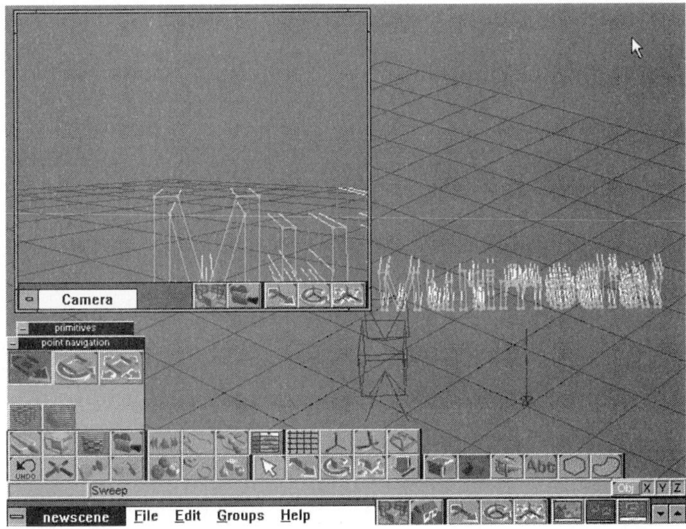

Figure 3.24. Now the text is 3D.

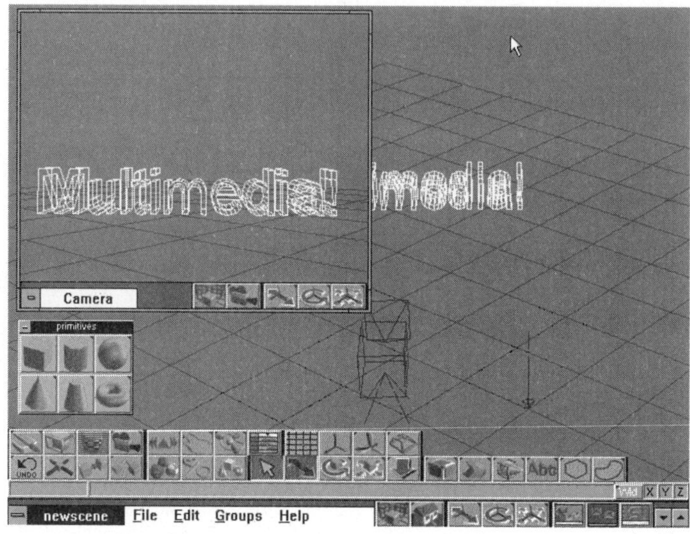

Figure 3.25. Moving the text so that it appears centered in the working window.

Creating an Animation

We now have an object, but it's nothing fancy so far. To make it more interesting, let's create an animation using the Animation Editor. It's surprisingly easy to do. Begin by clicking the Animation tool in the Animation group. This displays the Animation Editor, as shown in figure 3.26.

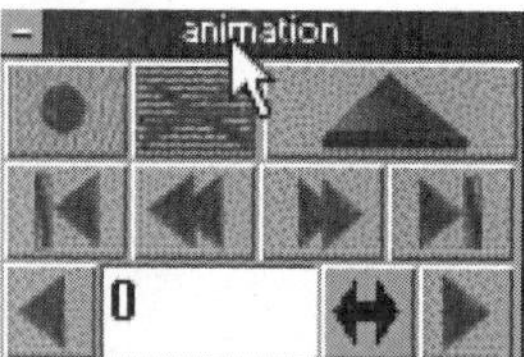

Figure 3.26. The Animation Editor.

The first job is to set up the beginning of the animation. Let's move the text back away from the camera—click on the Object Move tool, and then click and drag to move it away from the camera, but try to keep the text centered. Your result should be something like what is shown in figure 3.27.

The next job is to create additional frames. Click in the Current Frame box of the Animation Editor, type the number **30**, and press Enter (see fig. 3.28). This adds the frames and jumps you to frame 30. Frame 30 looks a lot like frame 0, but that's because we haven't added any changes. Using the Object Move tool, drag the text until it fills the screen from side to side (see fig. 3.29).

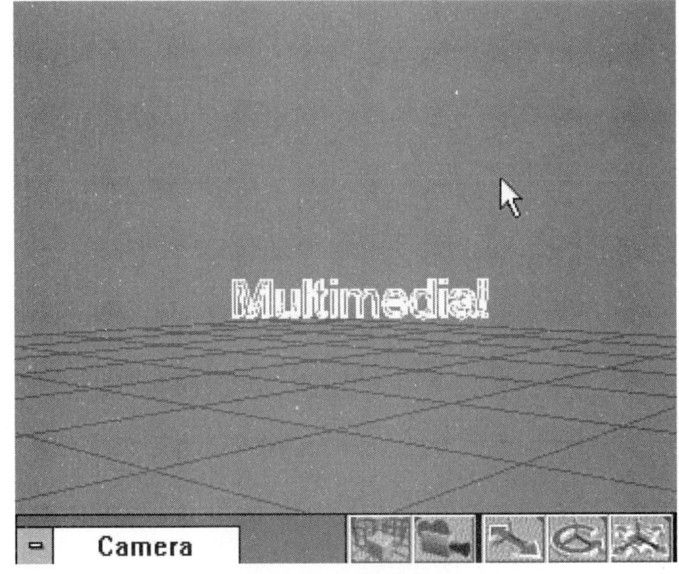

Figure 3.27. Moving the text away from the camera to create the beginning of the animation.

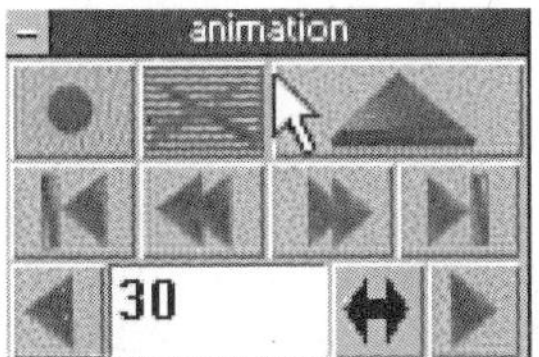

Figure 3.28. Adding new frames.

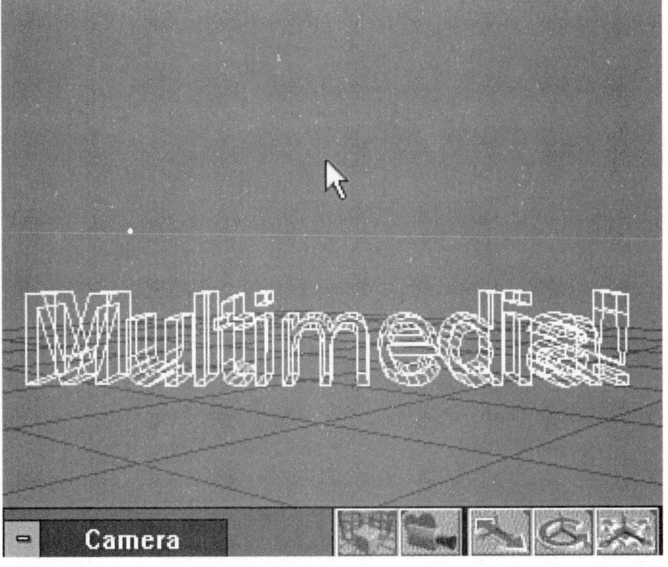

Figure 3.29. Moving the object to a new position in frame 30.

To record the changes in this frame and make it a key frame, click on any tool (such as Object Rotate, because we'll be using it next), and then click on the Record button in the Animation Editor. This locks the changes to the current frame.

What's a Key Frame?

When cartoons and animation first were created, the artists had to draw every frame of the animation by hand. Before they did this, however, they would render certain frames in the animation. They might draw every tenth frame, for example, and then fill in the frames between. This was an early example of key frames. It didn't save much time overall, but it did help the animators to get a handle on the huge task before them.

When you are creating an animation on a computer, you have a huge advantage. You can specify just the key frames, and have the computer fill in the other frames for you. A *key frame* usually marks a point where an object's animation starts or stops, changes direction, or otherwise becomes different. In the tutorial, you created a position for the text object at frame 0 and again at frame 30. The computer calculates all the intervening positions for you.

This makes your job as master animator easy. Think how tedious it would be to have to position the object in every frame—and how much harder still to make it move smoothly!

To view the animation, simply click the large Play button at the upper right of the Animation Editor. All you see is a wireframe animation, but it shows the movements quite clearly.

As amusing as this animation is,[29] we can do better. Go back to frame 0 (just click the Go To Start button), and (if you haven't already) click on the Object Rotate tool. Rotate the text so that it faces away from you, as shown in figure 3.30.

Now, the text object has two (count 'em!) motions at the same time—it is moving toward the camera, and it is rotating as well. To see the result in action, click the Play button.

But there's more! Set the frame number to 45, using the same technique you used to set it to 30. Click the Record button, then the Object Move button, and then Record again. This locks the position in frame 45 and makes it the same as the position in frame 30. This holds the object's position for 15 frames.

[29]Yes, my tongue is firmly in cheek.

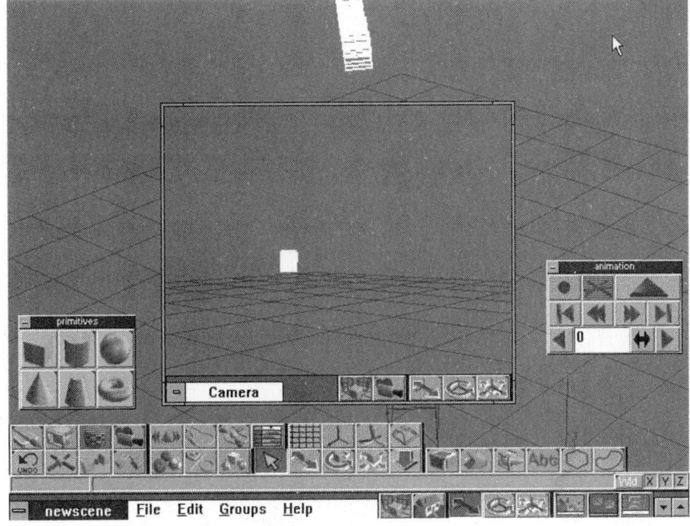

Figure 3.30. Rotating the object at frame 0.

Play the animation to see the result—it's not quite what you may have expected! Instead of holding still, the text more or less oozes back and forth. By default, the animation tries to smooth out transitions, but in this case, that works against our intentions. It's easy to fix—we simply tell the computer not to smooth things. Right-click on the Path tool in the Animation group to open the Spline Control Panel (see fig. 3.31). Click on the Sharp Corner icon; it tells the software we don't want smoothing. Click the Previous Key button in the Animation Editor to move to frame 30 (the previous key frame), and click the Sharp Corner icon again. Now both ends of the sequence have smoothing turned off. Play the animation to see the result.

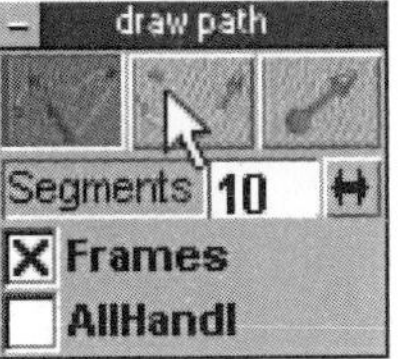

Figure 3.31. Changing properties of the object's path.

Let's add more action to the animation. Use the Current Frame box in the Animation Editor to go to frame 75 (just type **75** and press Enter). We'll add two motions. First, rotate the text object backward about 45 degrees (see fig. 3.32).[30] Second, move the object up (right-click and drag) near the top of the working

---

[30]Hint: Use the Object Rotate tool, of course.

window (see fig. 3.33). Third, drag the object toward the camera until it moves out of the frame. Because you raised the object, it passes over the camera and out of view (see fig. 3.34).

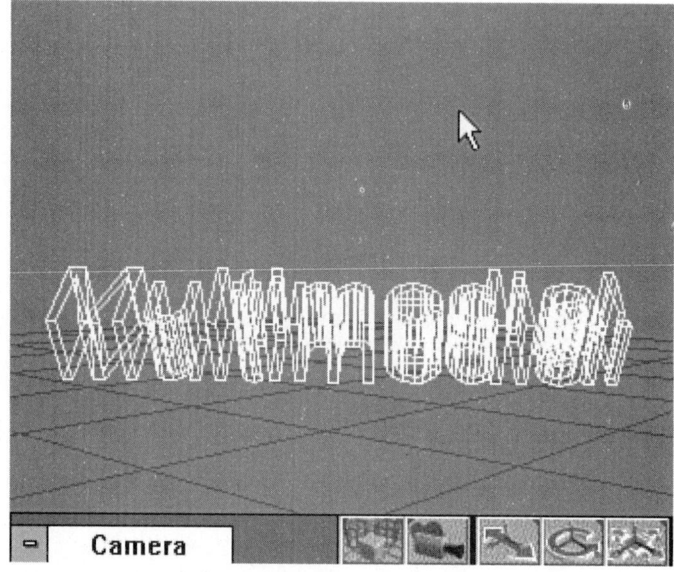

Figure 3.32. Rotating the object backward using the Object Rotate tool.

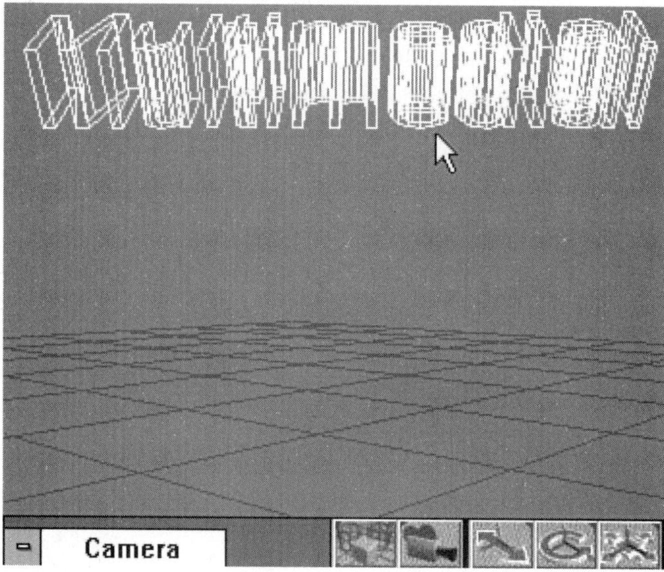

Figure 3.33. Raising the object by right-clicking and dragging.

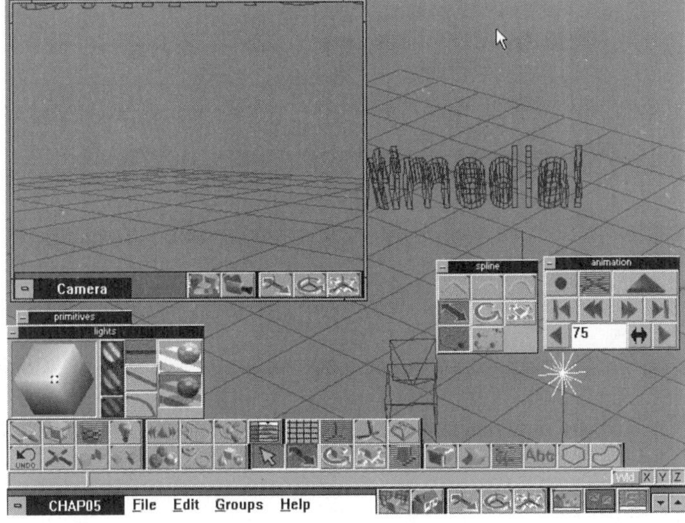

Figure 3.34. Moving the object until it disappears from the camera's view.

The result of these two combined movements (which occurs between frames 45 and 75) is a rotation and flying out of the scene—a nice dramatic finish to the animation. You can play the animation using the Play button on the Animation Editor, but that only displays the animation in Wireframe mode. To create a fully rendered version, click and hold on the Render button, and choose the Render to File tool (it's at the top of the variants). This opens the dialog box shown in figure 3.35.[31] To save the animation to an AVI file, make sure that you select AVI File *.AVI in the List Files of Type box.

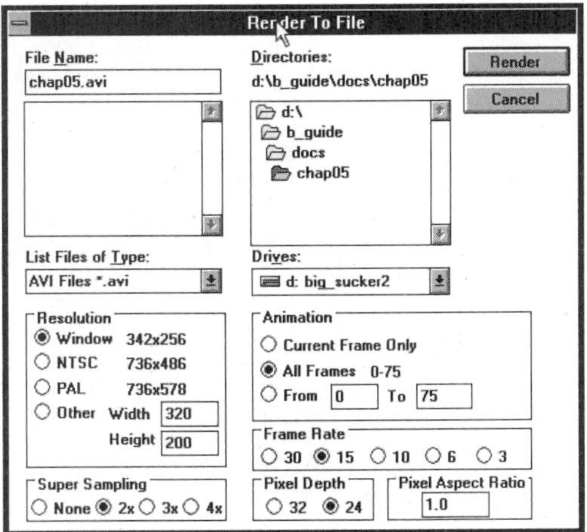

Figure 3.35. This dialog box enables you to render your animation to an AVI file.

[31]Note: The trial version on the CDs may not enable you to render to a file.

After you click the Render button, you can specify a video-compression method. This saves some file space. RLE encoding gives you a relatively clean image, but Cinepak or Indeo usually provides significantly higher compression rates. The dialog box shown in figure 3.36 is used to specify the compression method and the amount of compression used.

Figure 3.37 shows a single rendering—the surface material isn't too fancy, but we cover more of that in the next section of this tutorial.[32]

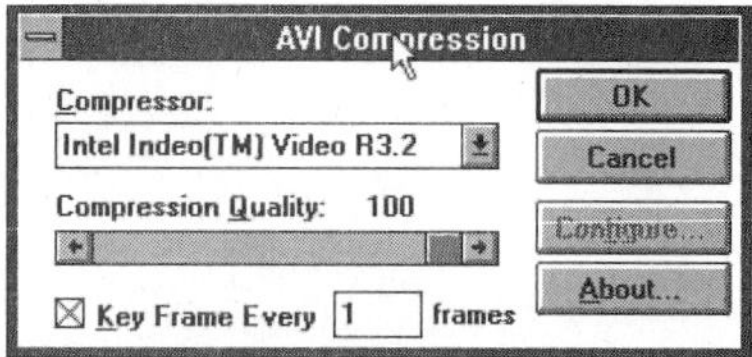

Figure 3.36. Choosing a compression method.

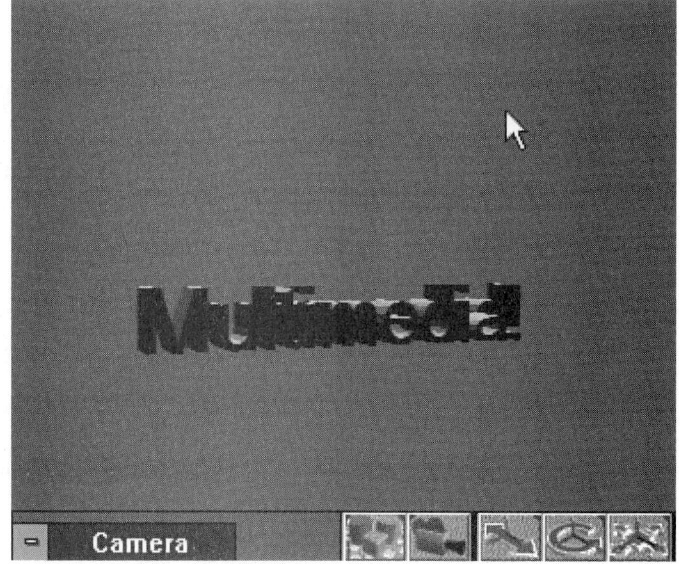

Figure 3.37. A rendered frame from the animation.

Modeling in 3D

Enough fooling around with simple stuff—let's build ourselves a super-futuristic jet fighter. Here's the fun part: we'll start with a simple cube and build a jet fighter without anything except all the cool tools in trueSpace.

---

[32]If you want to get a look at the completed animation, it's on the CDs.

Creating the cube is easy. If the Control Panel with the various primitive shapes is not already visible, click on the Primitives tool in the Libraries group to display it (you can see it at the left of figure 3.38). Simply click on the cube to create a cube, as shown in figure 3.38.

We're going to use the Sweep tool to stretch out some high-tech wings for our fighter, but first we have to slope in the sides and shrink it down a bit. Start with the Point Navigation Control Panel (see fig. 3.39). You can open the panel by clicking on the Point Editor tool. A small "p" is attached to the cursor to remind you that you are in Point Edit mode. There are several ways to edit points; make sure that you choose the Face Edit mode—click and hold, and then select the Face Edit variant.[33]

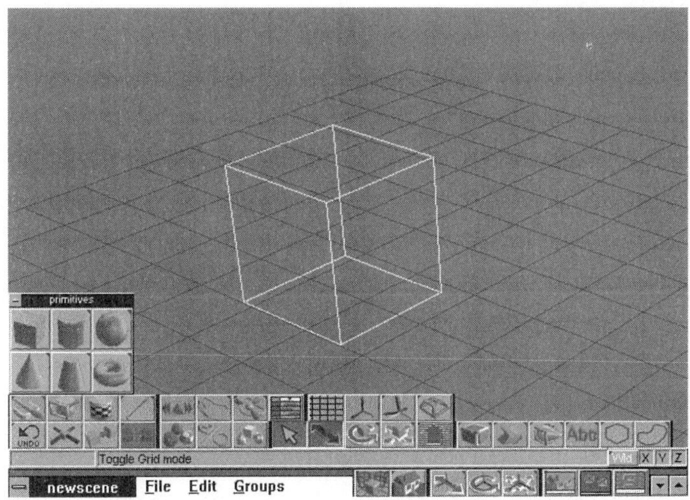

Figure 3.38. Creating a simple cube.

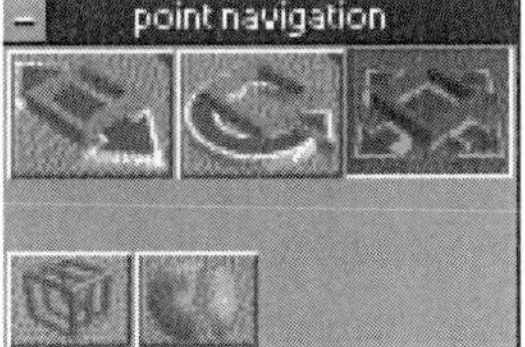

Figure 3.39. The Point Navigation Control Panel. From left to right: Move, Rotate, and Scale.

[33]It's the one with a face highlighted.

To select a face, just click on it. If you need to select a hidden face, that means you'll need to use the Window Navigation tools to change your point of view until you can click on the face you want. For this example, click on the top face of the cube. Then click on the Scale icon in the Point Navigation Control Panel. Click and drag to reduce the size of the top face (see fig. 3.40).

You also can move the points—click on the Move icon in the Point Navigation Control Panel, and then right-click and drag to move the top face downward.(34) Use a combination of scaling and moving until you have deformed the cube to the shape shown in figure 3.41.

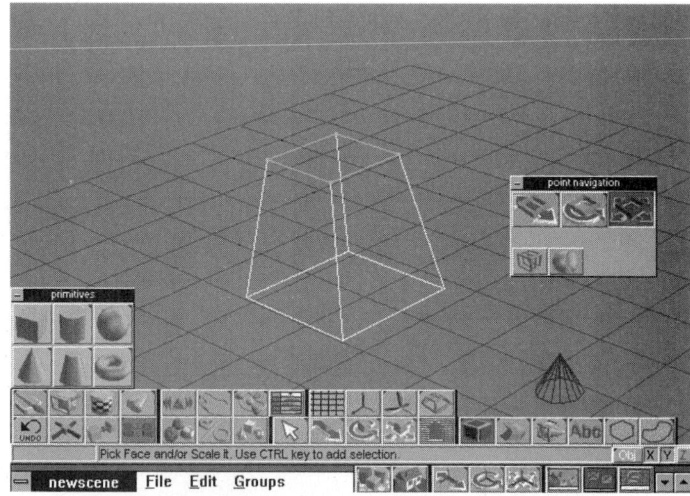

Figure 3.40. Scaling a single face on an object.

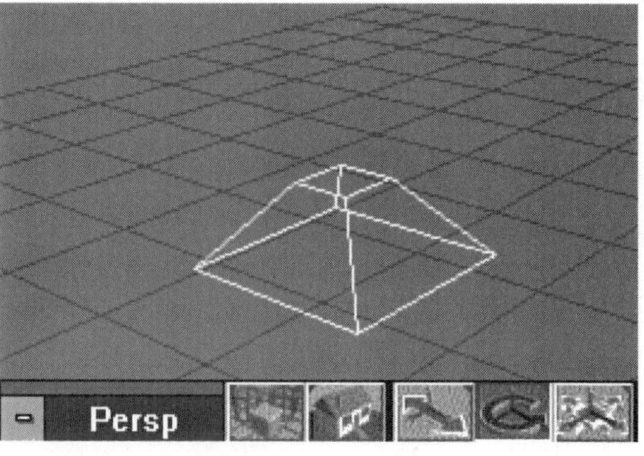

Figure 3.41. It doesn't look much like a cube now!

[34]Remember: Right-clicking lets you move on the z axis.

The next step is a bit tricky—you need to select faces on opposite sides of the former cube. The first side is easy to select; if you haven't messed around too much, you still have the Point Selection tool handy. Click on the right-hand face, and then use the Window Navigation tools to rotate and move your point of view until you expose the opposite face. Hold down Ctrl for a multiple selection, and then click on the face you want—both faces now are selected.

You used the Sweep tool earlier to expand text into the third dimension. This time, right-click the Sweep tool to open its Control Panel (see fig. 3.42). Set the z axis to 1, instead of the default .5 (one half unit). Click the object one time with the Sweep tool active to sweep out the two selected faces. Each face expands in its own direction, as shown in figure 3.43.

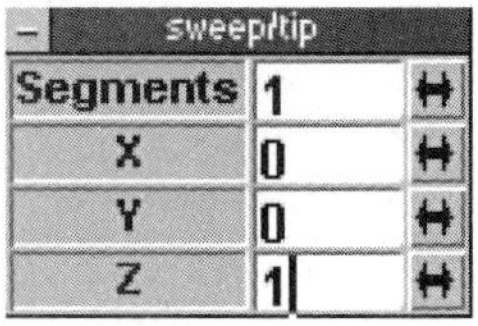

Figure 3.42. Changing the settings for the Sweep tool.

sweep/tip	
Segments	1
X	0
Y	0
Z	1

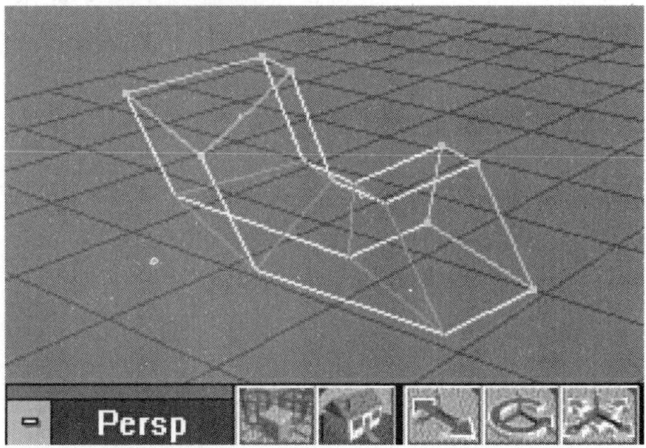

Figure 3.43. The object after one click of the Sweep tool with the modified settings.

Click three more times on the Sweep tool to make a nearly complete circle around the object (see fig. 3.44). Depending on the exact angles in your object, you may need to click two or perhaps four times instead of three—just make sure you don't overlap the edges. Use the Undo tool if you go too far.

Figure 3.45 shows a rendering of the object in three dimensions.

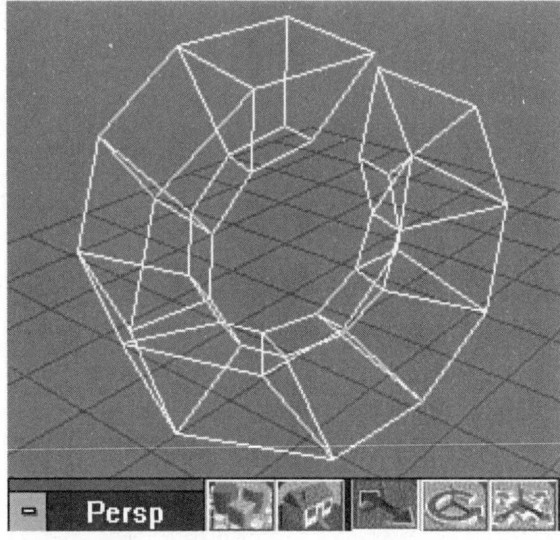

*Figure 3.44.
The object after three additional sweeps.*

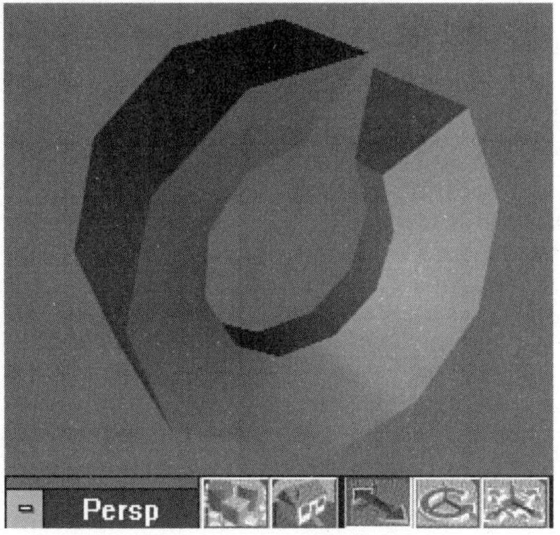

*Figure 3.45.
A rendering of the object so far.*

Now select the end faces, which are facing each other across the open part of the circle. As before, select the face that you can see, and then rotate either the object or your point of view until you can see the opposite face to click on it. If you aren't careful, you might select the wrong face as I did (see fig. 3.46). Remember to hold down the Ctrl key to select additional faces.

Now use the Scale tool to shrink these two faces almost to a point, as shown in figure 3.47. These will be the wing tips of the jet.

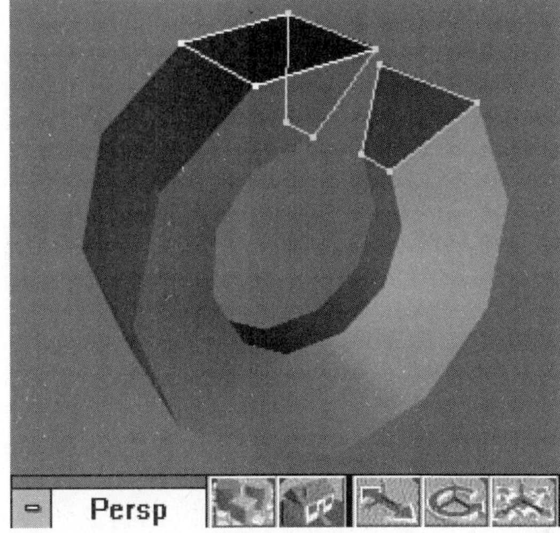

Figure 3.46. Selecting several faces.

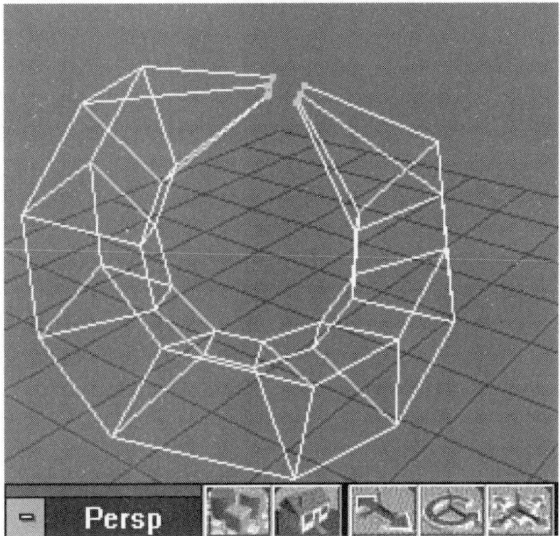

Figure 3.47. Scaling the two end faces.

For our next trick, we will subdivide one face into many smaller faces and then deform it to make the nose of the fighter. The face to select is the one from the original object that is shown at the bottom front of figure 3.47. Peek ahead to figure 3.48, which shows the face subdivided into smaller faces. When you have the right face selected (the hazards of working with 3D models in 2D should be very evident right now!), click the Utility pop-up menu and select the far right icon, Quad Divide. Click the icon three times to generate the result shown in figure 3.48.

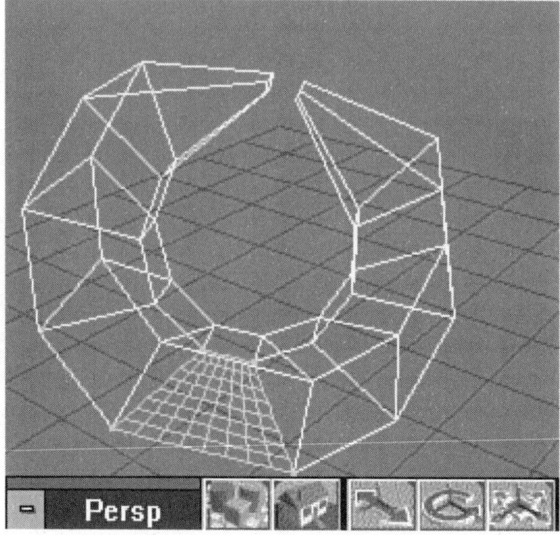

Figure 3.48. The result of using Quad Divide on a face.

Now for some real fun—let's do some deforming. Click on the Deform tool in the Model group. This adds a green box to the model. Any deformations you make to the green box are applied to the model. The first step is to subdivide the box vertically, creating a bilaterally symmetrical lattice. Click outside the lattice and drag upward just until a single, vertical line appears in the lattice. If more than one line shows up, you need to back up your drag. Figure 3.49 shows the lattice with its vertical division.

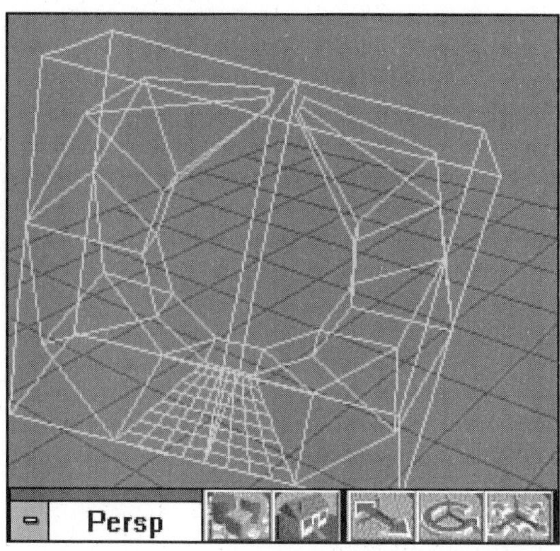

Figure 3.49. The deformation lattice has been devided into two equal halves.

Click on the bottom of the lattice at the vertical division, and then click to select it. If you do this correctly, you see the lines connected to that vertex turn white to indicate that they are selected. In the Deformation Control Panel, click on the Move tool at the left (see fig. 3.50).

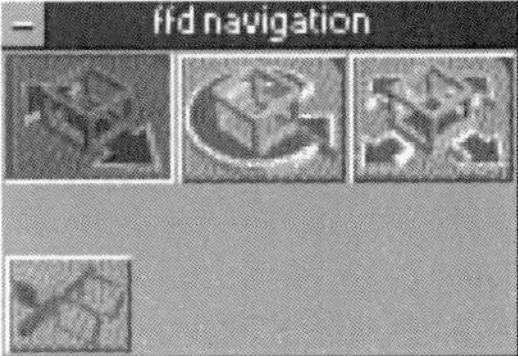

Figure 3.50. The Deformation Control Panel (FFD Navigation).

Now click and drag down and to the left to drag out the front of the jet fighter. Drag several times until you have the nose pulled out. Figure 3.51 shows a rendering of the fighter. It has the right shape, but the surface isn't much like a fighter, is it?

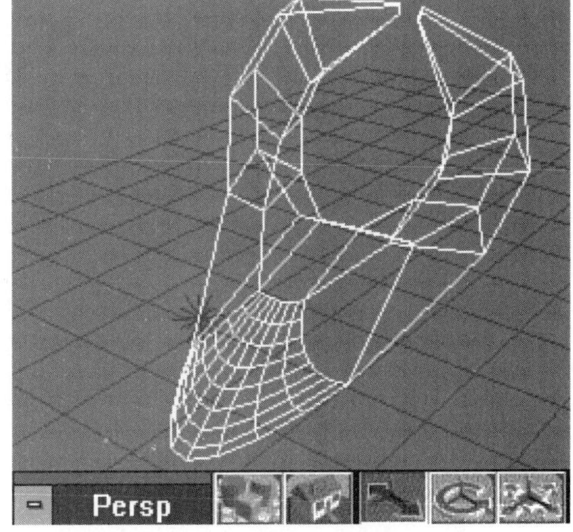

Figure 3.51. The deformed object is really starting to look like a space-age fighter.

Click on the Material Library tool in the Materials group. As shown in figure 3.52, this displays a series of spheres—one with each material in the current library.(35) Pick a material that you like (I chose the blue, shiny material) by clicking on it.

---

[35]This means, of course, that you can load different libraries. Experiment by clicking at the bottom of the Material Library dialog box to see what you can do.

You also will see other dialog boxes open, such as the Shader Attributes Control Panel (see fig. 3.53) and the Material Control Panel (see fig. 3.54).

Figure 3.52. You can select a material from the Material Control Panel.

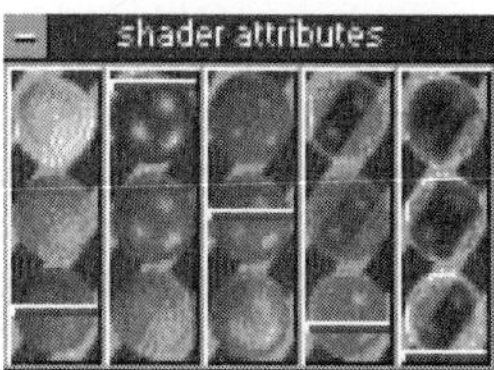

Figure 3.53. The Shader Attributes Control Panel.

Figure 3.54. The Material Control Panel, showing a detailed rendering of a sphere using the currently selected material.

After you select a material, you can click on the Paint tool and proceed to paint the object one face at a time (see fig. 3.55), or paint the entire object using a single material (see fig. 3.56). You use different variants of the Paint tool to determine which method of painting you will use.

This completes the tutorial. If you want to experiment, you can create an animation for the fighter, or you can experiment with applying several materials to various parts of the surface, one face at a time (subdivide faces if necessary to achieve the level of detail you want). You can create a glass-like material (use the Shader if necessary), for example, and then paint that material onto some of the subdivided faces at the nose of the fighter to simulate windows for the pilot.

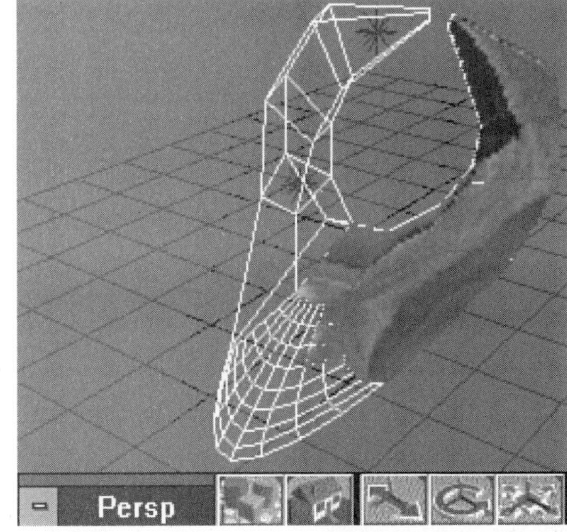

Figure 3.55. Painting an object one face at a time enables you to use multiple materials for a single object.

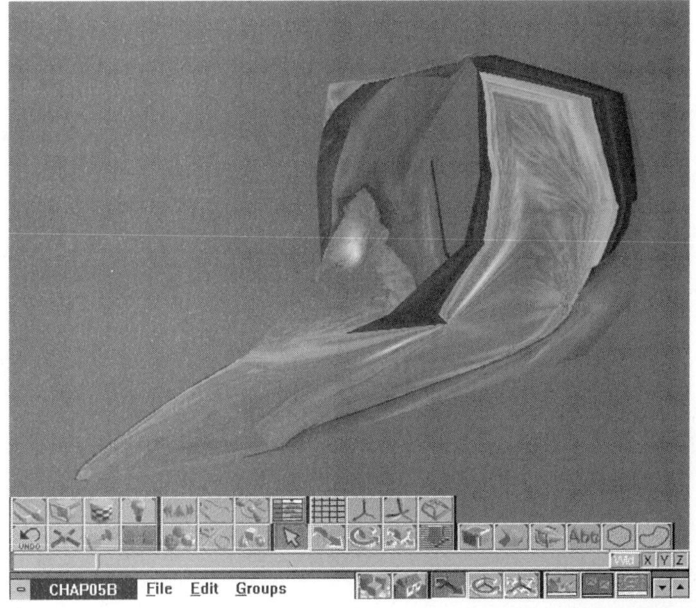

Figure 3.56. If the entire object will use the material, add the material in one step.

Video and 3D Modeling Software

One of the most fascinating ways to work with 3D modeling packages is to add video images. Many 3D packages support some form of animation, and video enables you to mix virtual and real in sometimes powerful ways. In this chapter, you explore ways to use 3D modeling to enhance videos. In Chapter 10, "You Are the Star," you learn how to put video images into a virtual space. You can put an image of yourself in a dream reality, or you can put a product video inside a virtual-space presentation for a sales meeting.

Working with video adds a whole new dimension to 3D modeling.[36] And the reverse is true as well: Adding 3D modeling to video creates some visually stunning possibilities. In this section, you learn how to use several 3D-modeling packages to create digital special effects for video files.

Issues with Video

Using video is not a trivial step. The results can be stunning, but if you are not already working with video, you may be surprised by the effort and technology required. It's not daunting by any means; with a minimum investment of time and money, you definitely can add videos or use 3D software to enhance your videos. Read through this section carefully to see whether you will be able to assemble the components you need. A minimum setup requires the following:

- A video source. Right now, it's expensive to buy video clips, so you'll probably want a video camera. You can spend anywhere from $400 to $2,000 for a new camera (more if you want professional Windows software). The retail price of this piece of the puzzle is the least of your worries—street prices are around $100, and it may even wind up as an integral part of Windows.
- A tripod. This is a minor item that can make a huge difference in quality. A tripod ensures steady images, which is very important when working with small image sizes. Make sure that you get a true video tripod with a fluid head.[37]

---

[36] Did he really say that? Ouch!

[37] A fluid head smoothes out motion when you pan the camera. Don't get a tripod for a still camera; it probably won't have a fluid head.

- A video capture card. A card that compresses video in real time is ideal; expect to spend around $500 for such a board. The Intel Smart Video Recorder is a good choice, but more boards are coming out all the time.
- A fast computer. I recommend at least a 486/33, 500M of hard disk space, fast seek time (12-millisecond average seek or better), and a very, very fast Windows accelerator video display card.
- Video for Windows software. The retail price of this piece of the puzzle is the least of your worries—street prices are around $100, and it may even wind up as an intregal part of Windows.
- 3D-modeling software. Good choices include the two packages I describe in detail later in this chapter—3D Studio 2.0 from Autodesk and Imagine 2.0 from Impulse. Imagine is much more affordable ($495 retail) than 3D Studio ($2,995).[38]

Some optional goodies to make life a little easier:

- A video monitor for displaying the incoming video signal.
- Remote controls for all your equipment so you're not jumping up and down all the time to adjust things.
- A video output card to send animation to videotape.
- A second deck for dubbing and editing of video material outside the computer. (If you do this, consider Video Director from Gold Disk; it could make your life substantially easier.)
- A high-end video-capture system. Standard video-capture cards, like the Intel Smart Video Recorder, are limited to image sizes of 320×240 and 15 frames per second (fps). Full-motion, full-frame video is 640×480 and 30 fps. For many applications, the smaller image size is fine—it enables you to display text as well as the video image on your computer screen. If you want to output edited video to tape, however, you'll need high-end equipment. Expect to pay from $5,000 to $50,000 for a full setup.

Obtaining Source Material

If you haven't worked with video before, you may be surprised to find out what's involved. It's not as simple as pointing a camera and pressing the Record button.

---

[38]Don't let the price difference fool you—Imagine is extremely powerful. Autodesk markets 3D Studio to folks who already are using things like AutoCAD, which is a limited market—thus the high price. If all you want to do is work in 3D modeling, then Imagine may be all you need. A warning, however: Imagine is extremely idiosyncratic. If you don't have an artistic orientation, you might find it frustrating. It also is challenging to learn to use well.

After you get the steps down, however, it's pretty easy to do. There are many nuances to learn, of course, but I've had so much fun integrating video into my applications that it's never been a bother.

Let's assume that you are working with the Intel Smart Video Recorder,[39] and that you have a videotape with a sequence you'd like to capture. It might be a shot of a new product showing how it is used, or it might be the president of a company making pithy comments during a keynote address at a symposium on flywheel manufacturing. The complete process works like this:

0. Before you do anything else, defragment the hard disk you will use for capture. This is a must! A fragmented disk can seriously cut into your ability to capture video. The time spent hunting for the next available sector results in lost data. After you defragment, run VidCap (the Video for Windows Capture program) and use File/Set Capture File to create a large capture file. Allow from 10M to 25M per minute of video, depending on the card you are using and the image size you plan to capture. Refer to the manual that comes with your capture card for guidance, or experiment.
1. Queue the videotape to a point several seconds before the beginning of the sequence you want to capture. Most decks take a few moments to get started. Pause the tape.
2. Run the VidCap application that comes with Video for Windows, (or any other application that supports video capture). Click on the Capture Video icon or choose Capture/Video from the menu.
3. Set the Capture options you want to use. For general use, I suggest Video Options set to 15 fps, 160×120, and the Indeo Video codec.[40] For audio, start with 8 bits, 22kHz, and mono. After you get this much working, you can experiment with other settings. Click OK when everything is set the way you want it.
4. Another dialog box appears; clicking OK starts recording. Don't do that yet! Every second of video capture chews up lots of disk space. Start video

---

[39]I keep mentioning this card because it is far and away the most convenient to use. Just in case you think I'm biased or that Intel is paying for the endorsement, I'll mention some other cards that also do a good job. The Video Spigot, from Creative Labs, has excellent image quality, and comes with some clever options that give you more choices when it comes to playback. The Pro Movie Spectrum, from Media Vision, also does a good job, but I thought the image quality wasn't quite as good as in the Spigot. If you need overlay, consider the Bravado 16 from Truevision. It comes with an add-on, real-time, compression module; has room for a VGA-to-video daughter card, and has excellent image quality. The only hassle is that it won't enable you to have more than 15M of memory in your system.

[40]*Codec* is a made-up word that has two possible origins. Some say it refers to encoding and decoding, and some say it refers to compression and decompression. Either way, it refers to a computer algorithm that handles both capture and playback. Take your pick.

playback, and after about a second (or when your deck is up to speed and playing with a clean image), click the OK button to start capture. When you have the entire sequence (plus a little extra, just in case), press Esc on your keyboard and then the Stop button on the video deck.

5. You now have the video sequence on your hard disk, but you are not done. Run VidEdit (it also comes with Video for Windows), and open the Capture file. Use Video/Compression options to set parameters for the file. If you want the file to be able to play satisfactorily on 386 machines, set the following compression options:

   - CD-ROM 150K/second
   - No change
   - Key frame set to 1

   Now use File/Save As to save the file with a new name. You now can use the Capture file to capture another sequence. This technique has the advantage of enabling you to use the same unfragmented Capture file over and over. In addition, it gives you the most compact file sizes and data rates for the best playback on slower machines.

If you want more detailed information about using video, you can find it in my book, *PC Video Madness*, also from Sams Publishing. It contains a wealth of information about working with video on the PC.

Image Quality

Because you will almost certainly be working with video-image sizes in the range of 160×120 to 320×240, you'll need to pay special attention to image quality at several steps in the overall process. When you are shooting video, try to fill the frame with the subject. This makes the subject stand out, even at smaller image sizes. A steady camera is also very important—use a tripod whenever possible. You can find a decent video tripod for as little as $50.

During or after capture, when you compress the video[(41)] you need to make some decisions that affect image quality. Uncompressed video isn't practical; full-motion, full-frame video occupies 1.5 gigabytes per minute![(42)] The more you compress, the lower the image quality. You need to find a balance point between quality, image size, frame rate, and the speed of the playback machine.

---

[41]Compression is a complex area. There are no general guidelines for how to compress. Tradeoffs are involved. Higher compression results in smaller files and enables you to play back on slower machines. Image quality is reduced, however. You have to experiment to find out what you prefer.

[42]That's why video is supported mostly in small sizes like 160×120 or 240×180.

Life with Palettes

I have a saying regarding video playback: "24 bits or bust." A little history is necessary to explain why this is so.

When Windows was born, only 4 bits of data were available for specifying colors. That yields a grand total of 16 possible colors. You cannot do photographic-quality images with 16 colors. You can fake it using dithering, but the results are not very pleasing.

The next step forward was to 8-bit color; that gives us 256 colors to work with. Actually, it's a little better than that; the design used to implement 256-color support lets you pick which 256 colors you want to use at any one time from a universe of more than 16 million colors. The selection of colors in use at any one time is called a *palette*. If you want to display an image that uses colors different from those in the current palette, you need merely switch to a different palette. Presto! You can display images that use a wide variety of colors.

The reality isn't quite so presto. If you have an image displayed on-screen when you change the palette, the colors in that image get changed—there's only one palette, and if you change it, everything changes. This is the Achilles heel of using palettes. Every time you change the palette, any images already on-screen get their colors scrambled. This can be so severe that you can completely lose any suggestion of what the first image actually shows.

Thus, my slogan: 24 bits or bust. 24-bit color gives you instant, simultaneous access to all 16+ million colors. And at today's prices—less than $130 for 24-bit video at 640×480—24-bit color is very affordable. Not only that, but 24-bit color looks dramatically better than any palette ever will. If you don't want the overhead of pushing all 24 bits around for every pixel on your screen, 16-bit color does a good job. It avoids the palette problems, provides enough color for general use, and has one-third less calories than true color.

And here's the clincher: The best codecs automatically store video data as 24-bit color. If you don't have 24-bit in your system, it fakes it—it dithers the image to use the current set of 256 colors to display the image. This is OK, but you miss seeing how good the video image really is. If you are going to work with video, use the best possible video display card you can afford. The results are worth it. If you must keep costs down, or if you want to work at high resolutions like 1024×768 or 1280×1024, 16-bit color is also very good and is an excellent compromise.

At the very high end, 32 bits of color are used. This includes 24-bit color, plus an 8-bit alpha channel. The alpha channel is used to define transparent and translucent areas of the image. Some hardware, such as color scanners, uses 32, 48, or even 64 bits of color information, but these are not often encountered in the everyday computer world. All of this says nothing about display technology; would you believe there is already research being done on using lasers to project images directly onto the retina of your eye? Now *there's* a technology that has SAFE stamped all over it!

3D Studio

Have you ever been in a situation where you knew what you had to do, didn't like doing it, and had to do it anyway? That's the position that I'm in when it comes to writing about 3D Studio from Autodesk. First, the good news: I love what I can do with this program. Next, the bad news: the software costs almost $3,000 and uses a hardware dongle[(43)] as well. These are major inconveniences in this day and age of $99 software. Why, in the very next section I'll be describing the wonders of a product that retails for one-sixth of that. The question becomes why bother with an expensive product like 3D Studio?[(44)]

Because there are times when nothing else will do. As you see in this section, 3D Studio can do some really fantastic effects.

---

[43]The word *dongle* has an interesting origin, or so I've read in the ads from a company that sells them to software vendors. The ad said that the inventor of the little hardware clump (which you attach to your parallel port so the software knows you are the true and legal owner of the software) was named Don Gull. I'm just a teensy-weensy bit skeptical on that one.

[44]Especially when Autodesk sent it to me at no cost, and I should be grateful and keep my mouth shut.

RECIPE

1 video file (AVI)
1t Video for Windows
1t Animator Pro
4 cups 3D Studio
4M-8M of memory
1 math coprocessor/486 CPU
1 VESA-compatible video display card

Instructions: Convert the AVI file to an FLC file, and then attach it as a texture map to an object in 3D Studio. Animate the object to create a digital special effect—wipes, explosions, flips, flying videos—you name it. Convert back to AVI and serve.[45] Makes an excellent appetizer in multimedia titles, or serve between courses to clear the palette.

Getting Started

Before you can use a video file in 3D Studio, you need to convert it to a file format that 3D Studio can read: FLC or FLI. These are animation file formats. The conversion process is easy, but you need extra software to pull it off. The easiest method uses Animator Pro, but there is a slower method that you can use if you don't have Animator Pro. I'll explain both methods in this section.

Start with the file open in VidEdit. From the File menu, choose Extract. The dialog box shown in figure 3.57 appears.

The List Files of Type box is the key to the process. Select DIB Sequence. Then enter a file name in the form

***xxxxnnnn*.bmp**

where *xxxx* is a unique name, and *nnnn* is the first number in a sequence, such as 0001 or 0000. The name you enter becomes the first file name in a numbered sequence of files. In the example in figure 3.57, the file names are FACE0000.BMP,

---

[45]Actually, this concoction might be best described as a kind of club sandwich: 3D Studio in the middle, Animator Pro on both sides of that, and VidEdit on the outside. A little mayo, and you've got lunch at your desk.

FACE0001.BMP, and so on. There will be one file for each frame in the video. It's a good idea to verify that you have enough disk space for the bitmaps. You can use this formula to estimate how much space you'll need:

<width> * <height> * <bit_depth/8> * <number_frames>

If you have a video sequence that is 160×120, using 24-bit color and 103 frames, for example, you need

160 * 120 * (24/3) * 103

or

15,820,800 bytes—that's 15.5 megabytes

Remember to use the BMP extension; some programs don't know to look for the default DIB extension that VidEdit uses. You can use more or less than four characters for each portion of the name; just make sure that there are enough characters in the numeric portion. If you have 103 frames in your video, for example, you must have at least three characters for the numeric portion of the name. All the following are valid sequence names:

FACE01.BMP

X000001.BMP

V1.BMP

ICEFALL1.BMP

When you have a satisfactory name entered for the initial file in the sequence, click the OK button. You see a message box telling you the progress of the operation.

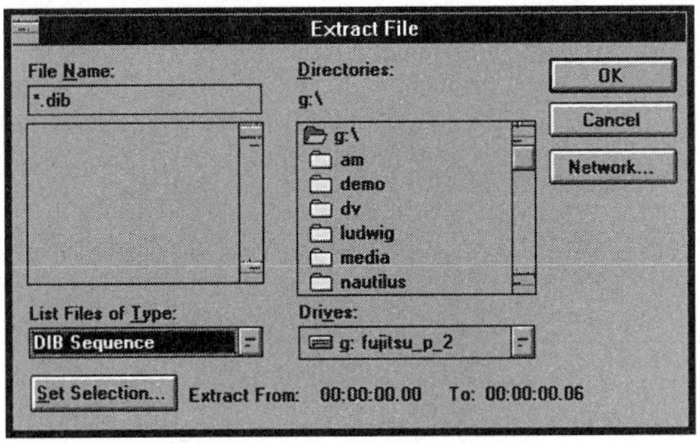

Figure 3.57. The Extract File dialog box in VidEdit.

After you have the DIB Sequence, you have two choices about how to get it into 3D Studio:

- Load the bitmaps into Animator Pro to create an animation (FLC) file.
- Convert the bitmaps to a file format that 3D Studio can read.

Let's look at how to use Animator Pro to handle this task first. Open Animator Pro and click the POCO menu. Click Numpic, as shown in figure 3.58.

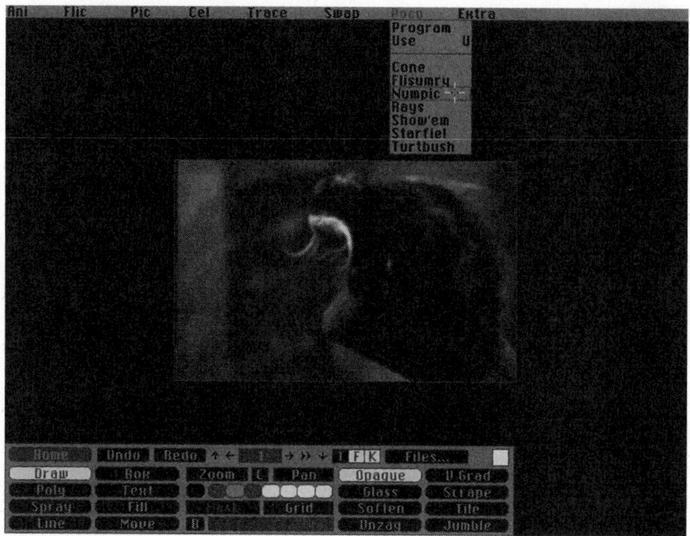

Figure 3.58. The POCO menu in Animator Pro.

This opens a dialog box that enables you to work with numbered file sequences (see fig. 3.59). To load the images you created in VidEdit, choose option 2: Load Pics as Flic. If the current animation is not the same size as the incoming images, you are asked whether you want to resize the FLC file to match the incoming image size; answer Yes.

Wait patiently while each file is read; this is especially necessary if you saved the bitmaps as 24-bit images, because Animator Pro analyzes each image and performs color reduction to 8-bit color.[46]

---

[46]VidEdit also gives you the option to perform color reduction. Use the Video/Video Format menu option to make the change. If you are wondering which program does the job better, all I can say is that VidEdit does it a lot faster, although you do have the extra step of creating a palette after you reduce the number of colors (otherwise you wind up with a grayscale image). There is an advantage to using Animator Pro, however. Animator Pro creates a separate palette for each frame. 3D Studio is capable of handling the creation of a unified palette during rendering. Because you can use lights in 3D Studio, the colors needed for the final images are likely to be different from the colors used earlier in the process.

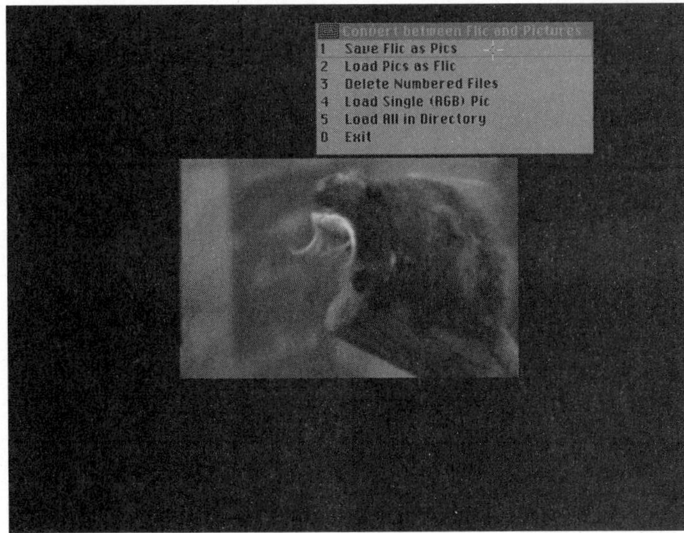

Figure 3.59. The Animator Pro dialog box for importing/ exporting numbered files.

Once you have an FLC file, it's time to run 3D Studio.

If you don't have Animator Pro and want to use AVI files in 3D Studio, follow this procedure:

1. Create a DIB sequence, as described previously, using VidEdit.
2. Use an image program to convert each of the bitmap files to a file type that 3D Studio can work with. I suggest Targa files (*.TGA). You can do this one image at a time with a paint program,(47) or you can use a utility like Graphic Workshop (shareware) or Image Pals (commercial software). Either of these products enables you to perform mass-conversion operations. The process still takes time, but you don't have to sit there and initiate each conversion.
3. In 3D Studio, instead of specifying an FLC file for the texture map, you would specify a file containing a list of the image files, in the order you want to use them.

Creating Objects in 3D Studio

The opening screen of 3D Studio is shown in figure 3.60. There are four viewports, a menu at the upper right, and several icons at the lower left.

---

[47] Talk about tedious! I had three AVI files, each with 562 frames, that I used in a single 3D animation. Converting one at a time would have taken me—let's see, at 35 seconds per image, and 3 × 562 images, that's—16.4 hours! Whew!

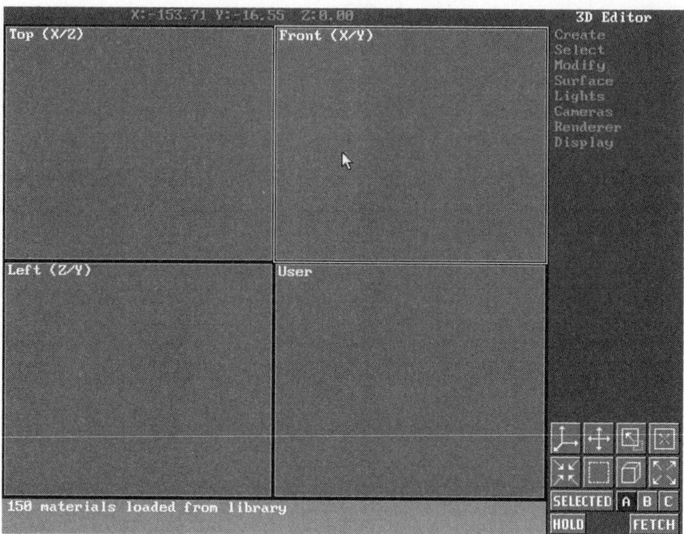

Figure 3.60. The opening screen of 3D Studio.

The standard types of viewport follow:

Top—This shows your 3D creation from above.

Front—A front view of the scene.

Left—A view from the left side.

User—A 3D view, sometimes referred to as an *orthographic projection.*

There are additional viewport types available, but you can display only up to four at one time.

Unlike the menus you may be familiar with in most graphic programs, 3D Studio's menu is vertical. Clicking on a top-level menu item, such as Create, displays the next level of commands (look ahead to fig. 3.63 to see an example).

The icon group at the lower right of the screen gives you access to a number of common actions (see fig. 3.61).

In this example, you learn how to use 3D Studio to create one style of video transition. You can apply the same basic techniques to a wide variety of special effects, however. I'll offer some suggestions at the end of this section. In the example, we'll shrink one video to reveal another video behind it.

You need precise sizes for your objects, so turn on Snap using the View menu (see fig. 3.62). I also turn on Grid Points to show the locations that I'm snapping to. The most common video file size is 160×120 pixels, so we'll create an object with exactly those dimensions. To create an object, choose Create from the menu at the upper right, and then click Box (see fig. 3.63).

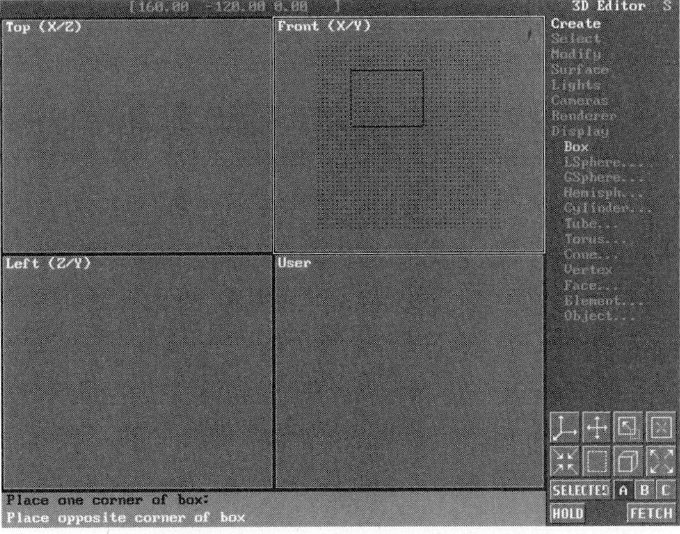

Figure 3.61. The 3D Studio icon group.

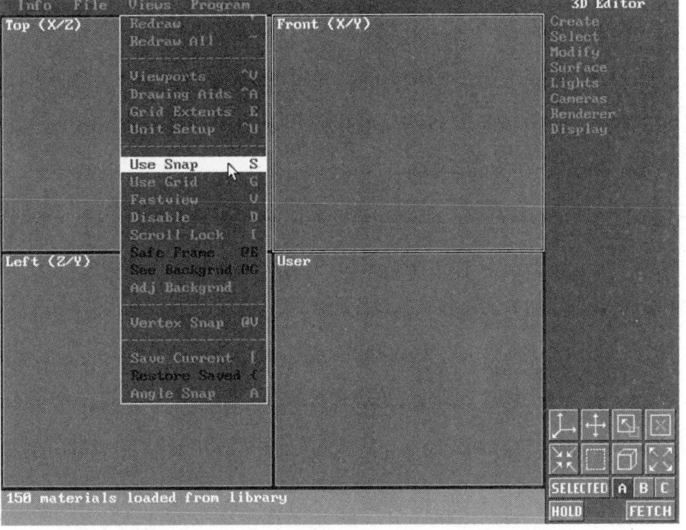

Figure 3.62. Turning on Snap in 3D Studio.

Click anywhere in the upper left of the Front viewport, and drag the mouse until you have a rectangle that is exactly 160 units[48] wide and 120 units high. You can verify the exact size at the top of the screen (see fig. 3.63). Note that 3D Studio prompts you for the required action at the bottom of the screen in a status bar.

48 3D Studio doesn't use any specific real-world measurement system; a unit can be anything you want it to be—feet, inches, meters, miles, etc.

After you define the rectangular shape, you are asked to set the depth of the box. Unless you want to attach the video to a box with depth, set the depth to be minimal by clicking twice in the same place—once to anchor the depth setting and once to define its length as zero. The completed, ultra-thin box is shown in figure 3.64.

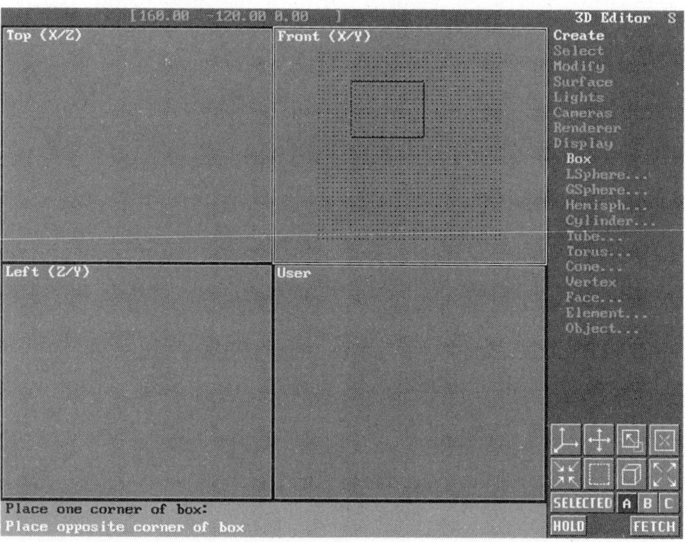

Figure 3.63.
Creating a box.

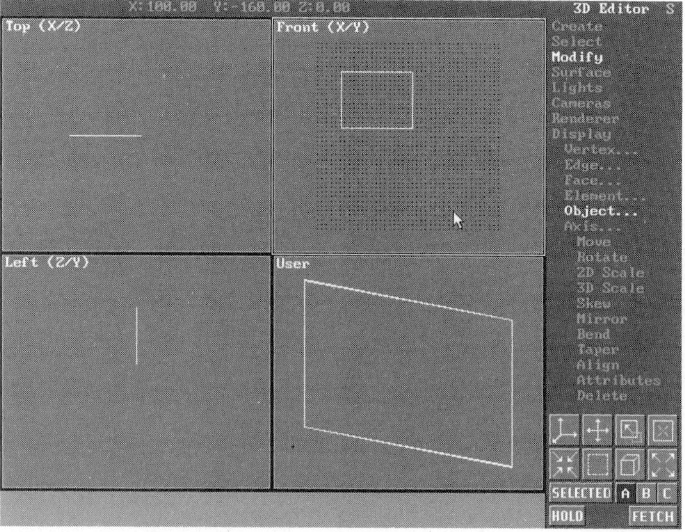

Figure 3.64.
A 160×120 box defined in 3D Studio.

Now click on the Modify menu and choose Object/Move. To create the second object,[(49)] hold down the Shift key when you click on the object we just created. This clones the object, giving us a second ultra-flat box just the right size, as shown in figure 3.65. After creating the clone using Move, you need to reposition the new object to cover the first object.

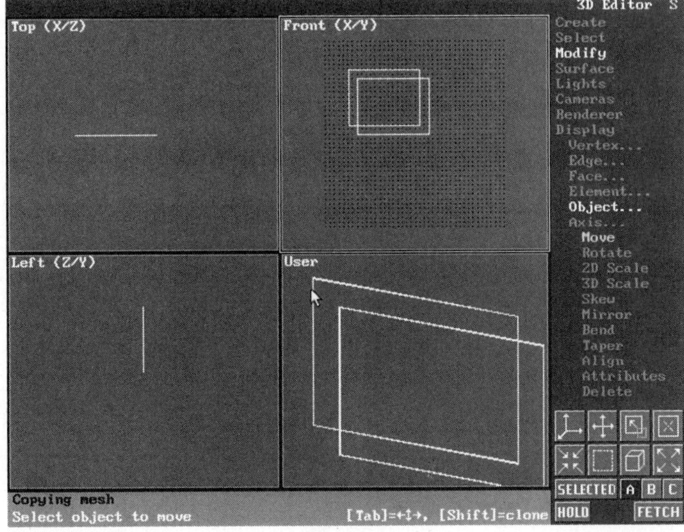

Figure 3.65.
A cloned object.

Mapping

You add a video sequence to an object as a texture map. To apply a map, you need to define mapping coordinates so that 3D Studio knows where to position the bitmaps and at what scale. In this case, the object is the same proportion as the video, 160×120, so the easiest way to do this is to fit the map to the object. Use the Surface/Mapping/Aspect/Region Fit[(50)] menu option to display the mapping coordinates. Figure 3.66 shows (in the upper right viewport) mapping coordinates that are both offset from and larger than the object. The crosshairs are located at the upper left corner of the object to define the upper left extent of the map, and you just need to click and drag to the lower right corner of the object to properly fit the mapping coordinates.[(51)]

---

[49]For the second video sequence, of course.

[50]This business of putting slashes between menu commands is the standard way of referring to 3D Studio menu options, and is used throughout this section.

[51]If you try to render an object that has a map but no mapping coordinates, you get an error message. It can't be done!

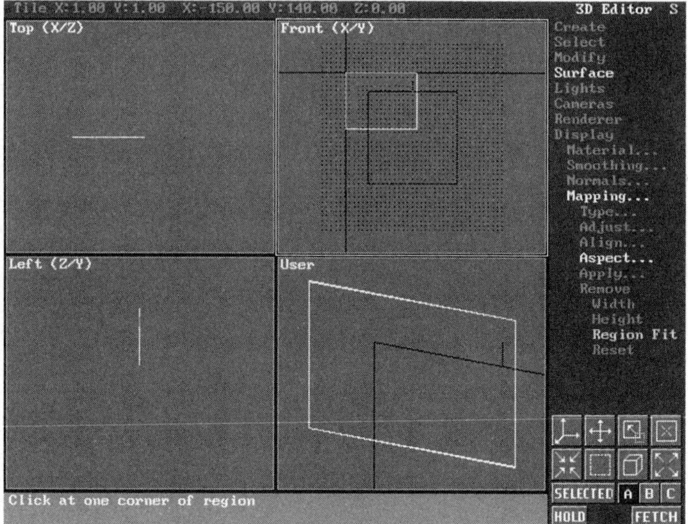

Figure 3.66. Default mapping coordinates.

Figure 3.67 shows mapping coordinates properly applied. The image has been zoomed to show just the object being worked on. Note that there is a small vertical line at the top of the rectangle; this little handle defines "up" for the map. Fortunately, it's already pointing in the right direction. If it weren't, we would use the Surface/Mapping/Adjust/Rotate option to change it.

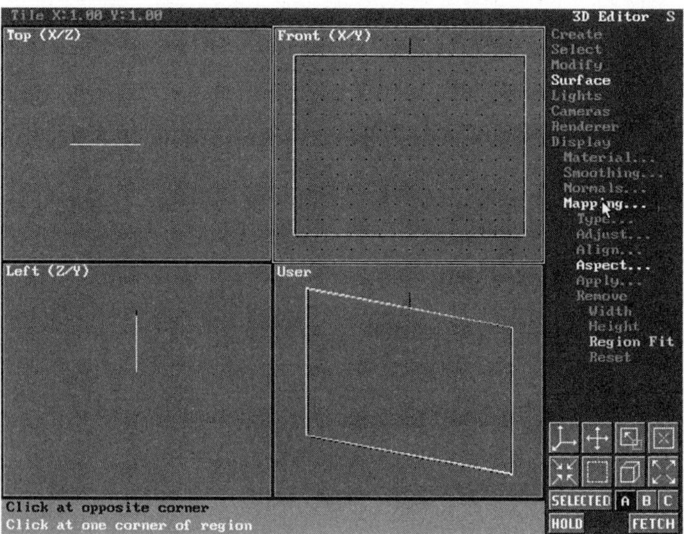

Figure 3.67. Mapping coordinates fitted to an object. Note "handle" at the top, indicating "up."

The next step is to apply the coordinates to both objects, using Surface/Mapping/Apply/Object. In order to apply the mapping coordinates, we need to select an object. With one object on top of the other, as in this case, however, you can't do that by clicking—the click always selects the object on top. To select an object by name, simply press the H key instead of clicking. This displays a list of objects from which to choose (see fig. 3.68). When you choose the object from the list, the action specified by the current menu option is applied to that object. You can apply the same mapping coordinates to both objects.

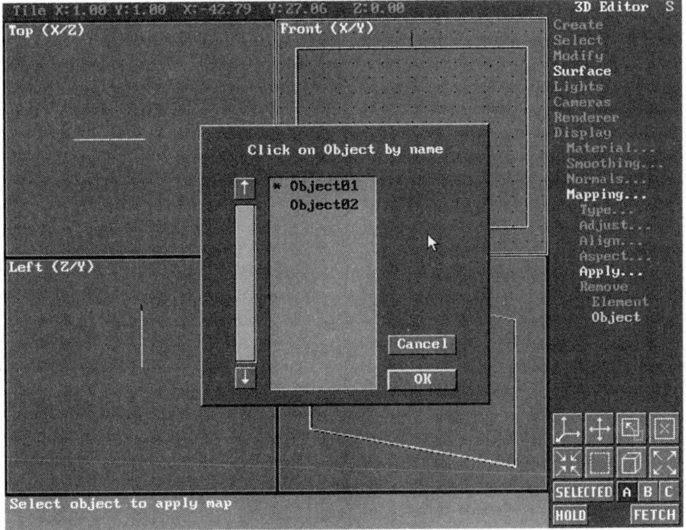

Figure 3.68. Selecting objects by name.

Materials

You can use the Materials Editor to create new surface materials in 3D Studio. To start the Materials Editor, press the F5 key. The Materials Editor screen is shown in figure 3.69.[52] The blank squares at the top of the screen are slots for new materials. The controls at the middle of the screen are used to set the color and characteristics of the material. The four groups of buttons at the bottom of the screen are the ones we are interested in—they control mapping. Before we start, however, move the mouse to the top of the screen to activate the menu and click Option/Cube. The default setting renders to a sphere; because you'll be rendering to a flat surface, the cube gives a more representative example.

---

[52]Due to the limitations of the screen-capture software, I had to use a reduced screen resolution to show 256 colors in the Materials Editor. The images in this section were taken at 320×240×256 colors; if you have a SuperVGA adapter, you almost certainly will want to use 640×480×256 colors.

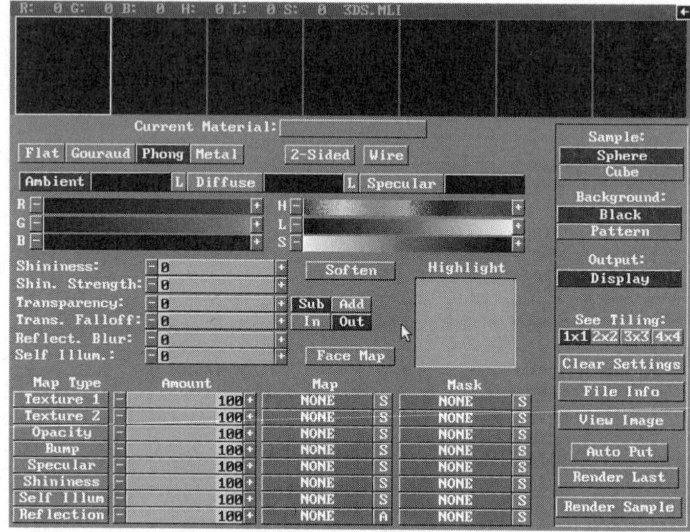

Figure 3.69. The Materials Editor screen in 3D Studio.

It's very easy to create a texture map. Click on the Texture Map file name button (see fig. 3.70). This opens a dialog box that enables you to select the file you want to use. Click the file name, and then click OK. The file name is displayed on the Texture Map file name button. To see what the texture map will look like, click the Render button (see fig. 3.70). A small-scale rendering is displayed in the current material slot at the top of the screen.

Figure 3.70. An example rendering of a texture map.

That's all there is to it. We won't be using any of the other features in the Materials Editor for this example. If we want to, we can set characteristics such as shininess, rendering quality, transparency, and more. We also can create bump maps (to determine surface texture based on an image file) or reflection maps (to determine what will reflect off of the surface).

To save the material, press the P key to put the material into the material library. A dialog box asks you for the material name; enter any name that fits in the space provided. Spaces are OK. Because we have two objects, each with a different AVI file, in this case, you also would create a second material using a second FLC file. After you put both materials into the library, press the F3 key to return to the 3D Editor.

Next, you'll want to apply the new material to the objects. Use the Surface/Material/Choose option to select one of the new materials, as shown in figure 3.71. In this case, the material is called Monkey Antics. Click OK when you have the right material selected.

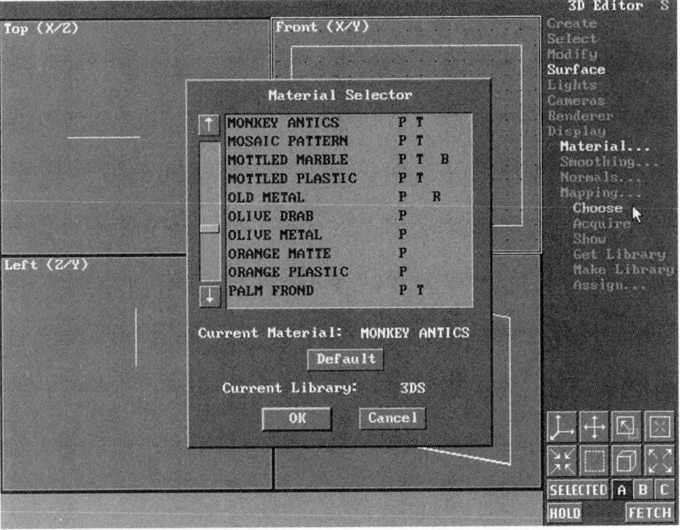

Figure 3.71. Selecting a new material with the Material Selector.

To apply the material to an object, use Surface/Mapping/Assign/Object. Then choose the second new material and apply it to the other object.

At this point, both rectangles are in the same plane, and you need to move one of them in front of the other. You can use Select/Object/Single to make one of the rectangles the current object, and then move the selected object. Press the H key to open the Click on Object by Name dialog box, and select whichever object you want to move to the front; then click OK.

Now use Modify/Object/Move, which changes the cursor to a small box with arrows, as shown in figure 3.72. Click in the Top viewport to activate it,[53] and then press Tab until the little arrows are pointing up and down. To move the currently selected object, click the Selected button at the bottom right, and then use the mouse to move the selected object just ever so slightly downward. Because we are working in the Top viewport, this has the effect of moving the object toward the front. Figure 3.72 shows how little of an offset is necessary.

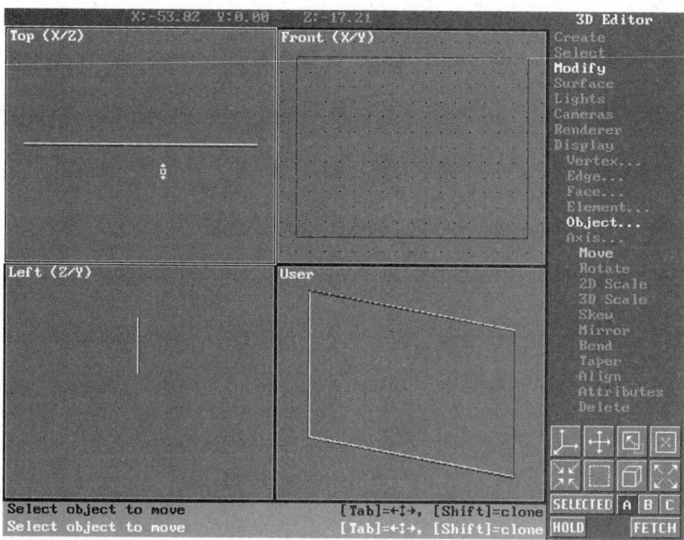

Figure 3.72.
Moving an object.

This is a good time to check your work. Use the Renderer/Render menu option, and click in the User viewport to select it as the view to render. You should see the Render Still Image dialog box (see fig. 3.73); if you don't, click the User viewport a second time.[54] Make sure that the Disk button is not highlighted, and then click the Render button to render to the screen. During rendering, you see a Rendering in Progress dialog box (see fig. 3.74).

---

[53] Only if it is not already activated.

[54] If the User viewport wasn't the active viewport, it won't render on the first click. The first click in a viewport always has the effect of activating it, rather than carrying out a menu action. This is a safety feature; it prevents you from taking actions you don't want to take and enables you to move to a different viewport and continue the current operation there.

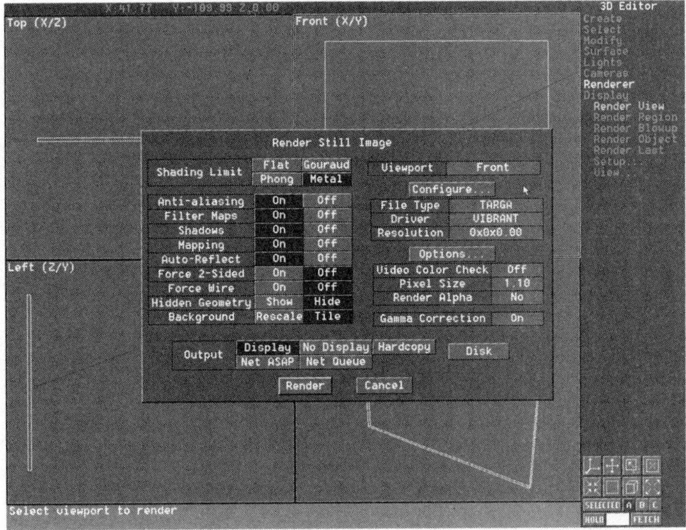

Figure 3.73. Rendering a still image.

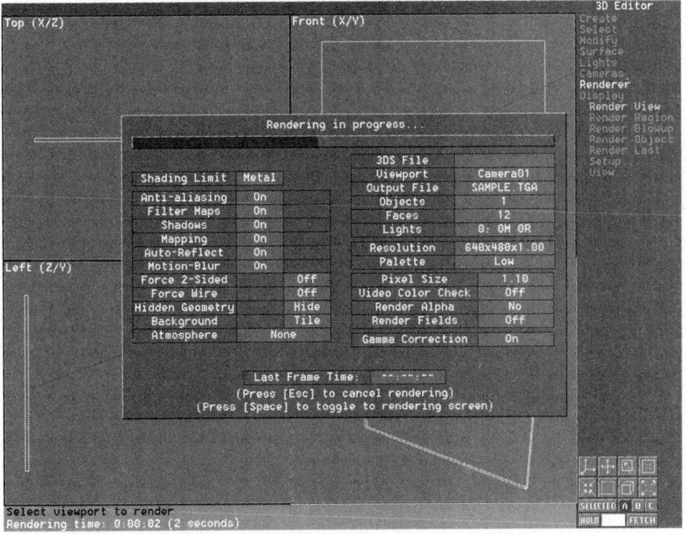

Figure 3.74. The Rendering in Progress message box.

After a few moments, you see a rather dim image, as shown in figure 3.75. You probably won't be able to recognize the image at all. The reason for this is simple: this is virtual reality—there is almost no light to illuminate the scene unless we add the light.

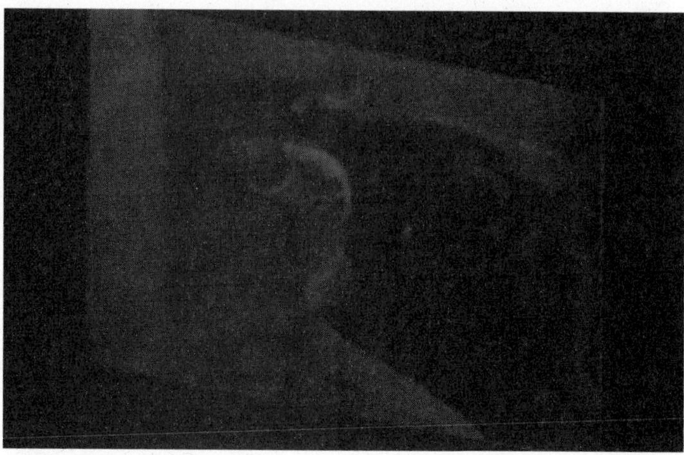

*Figure 3.75.
A rendered scene, but with inadequate lighting.*

By default, the ambient light in a scene is set to a value of 77. There are 256 possible values, from 0 to 255; a value of 77 represents 77/256 or 30 percent of full lighting—not much at all. The default value is displayed if you choose Lights/Ambient from the menu, as shown in figure 3.76. I suggest a setting in the range of 200 to 255 for adequate lighting. If you want colored lighting for special effects, use the RGB or HSL settings to create the color you want.

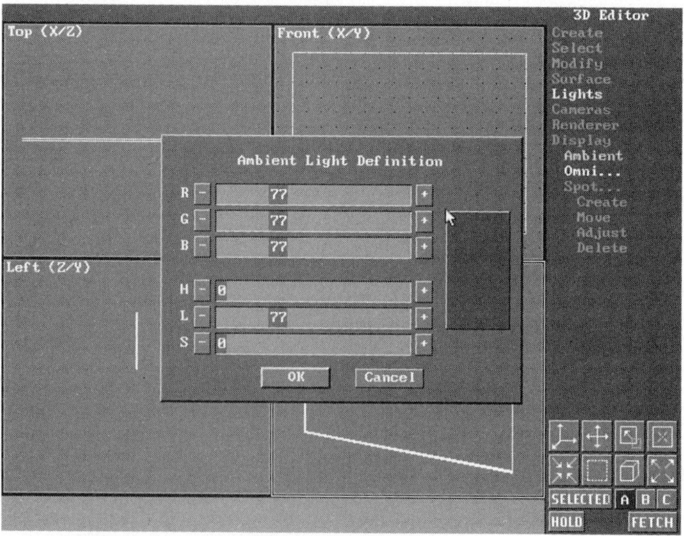

*Figure 3.76.
Adjusting ambient lighting.*

If you choose Renderer/Render again and render the scene to the screen, you see more natural results (see fig. 3.77).

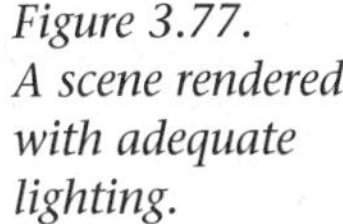

Figure 3.77.
A scene rendered with adequate lighting.

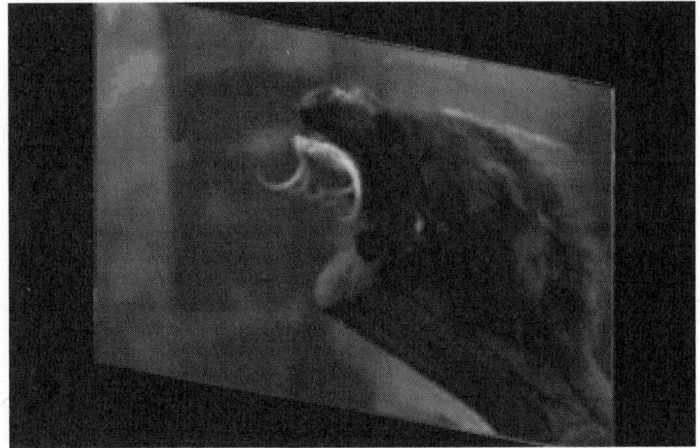

3D Studio also enables you to create two special types of lights. These are Omni lights, which are point sources of light; and Spotlights, which cast shadows and have adjustable light cones. You can create quite intricate lighting arrangements by using several kinds of lights in different positions.

Animating

Here's a summary of what we've done so far:

- Converted the AVI file to an FLC file or a series of TGA files
- Created two objects the same size as the video images
- Applied mapping coordinates to the objects
- Created two materials using texture maps—one for each video file
- Assigned the new materials to the objects
- Adjusted lighting values

Everything is now in place; it's time to animate. Animation takes place in the Keyframer, which you can access by pressing the F4 key. The opening screen of the Keyframer is shown in figure 3.78. It's similar to the 3D Editor screen, but there are some important differences. The four viewports are the same, but the menu is different. There are two new buttons above the icons: Track Info and Key Info. These buttons enable you to modify key points along the animation track to fine-tune the animation or to delete key animation events.

The buttons below the icons are standard VCR-style controls for moving from frame to frame or for playing the animation sequence.

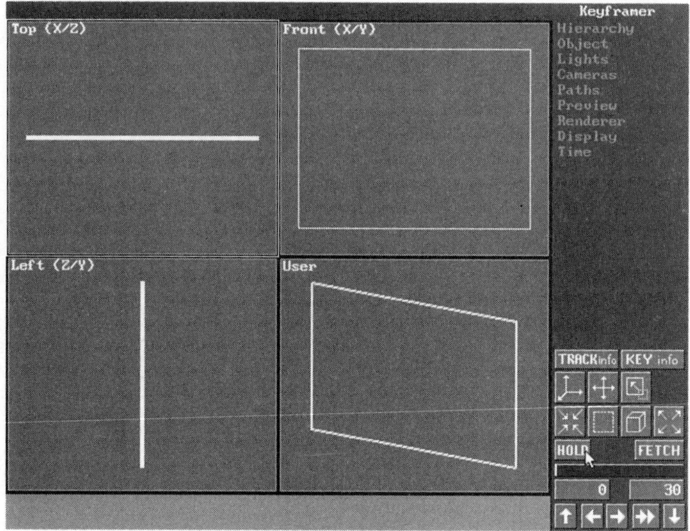

Figure 3.78. The Keyframer screen.

You can view an animation in several ways. You can use a standard viewport, such as Front view, which gives you a plane view (flat, no perspective). You also can render from the User viewport, which gives you an orthogonal view (3D, no perspective). Or, you can create a camera, which gives you full 3D and perspective. For our purposes, the flat, no-perspective view is ideal—there will be no distortion of the rectangle during the special effect. The Front viewport is best, of course, but there is empty space around the objects. We want to fill the frame with the image.

Figure 3.79 shows the Zoom icon in action. The upper left corner of the object has been clicked, and you then can drag the mouse to mark the lower right boundary of the viewport.

Figure 3.80 shows the result of this zoom. The left and right borders of the object now are coincident with the viewport. Don't worry about the fact that the tops and bottom of the objects aren't lined up with the viewport. You can set the aspect ratio of the rendering so that only the actual object appears in the scene. Of course, if you wanted black space around the image, you would adjust the zoom factor accordingly.

Using the Keyframer, you do not have to create every frame of the animation. In fact, in this case, we can create a single key frame, and the Keyframer generates all the intervening frames. Use the controls at the bottom right to move to the last frame. By default, the Keyframer creates 30 frames. At 30 frames per second, that's two seconds of video—about right for an effect.

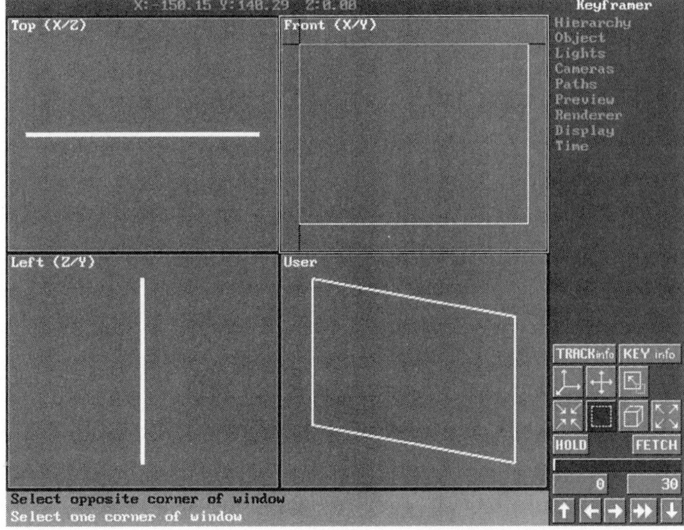

Figure 3.79. Adjusting the zoom factor of a viewport.

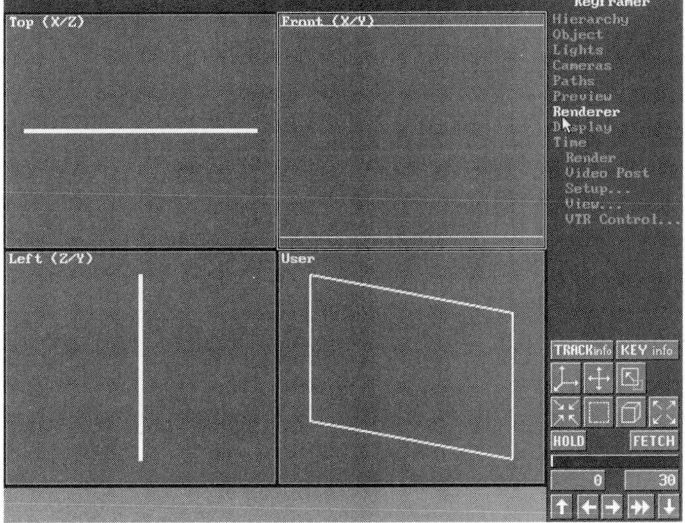

Figure 3.80. The zoom has been adjusted to match the object and the viewport.

This is a good point to talk about how to select the proper parts of your video sequence for the effect. Let's suppose that you have one video sequence that is 33 seconds, and a second sequence that is 14 seconds. For this example, you would export the last two seconds of the first video, and the first two seconds of the second video. After you complete generation of the effect, you splice the pieces together like this:

31 sec. of first video + 2-second effect + last 12 sec. of second video

This yields a total of 45 seconds of video. We lost two seconds because two seconds of each video now are playing simultaneously.

Back to the Keyframer: We now are at frame 30, the last frame in the sequence. The desired effect is to have the front video shrink away to nothing at the center of the other frame. Choose Object/Scale, and then click on the front object (use the H as described earlier if you want to select it by name). Drag the mouse sideways to change the scale of the object. Depending on your screen resolution, you may need to zoom in and scale the object a second time to make it small enough to "disappear" during the rendering. Any size below 1 unit will be smaller than a single pixel in the final rendering. Figure 3.81 shows the scaling operation in progress, and figure 3.82 shows the completed scaling.

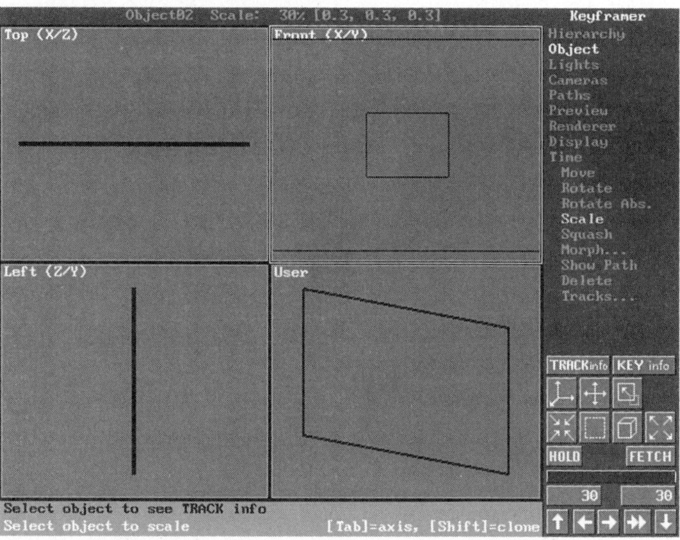

Figure 3.81. The scaling operation in progress.

To show that the Keyframer really does create all the intervening frames, look at figure 3.83. It shows frame 15 of the animation—yes, the front object is exactly halfway along in the shrinking process.

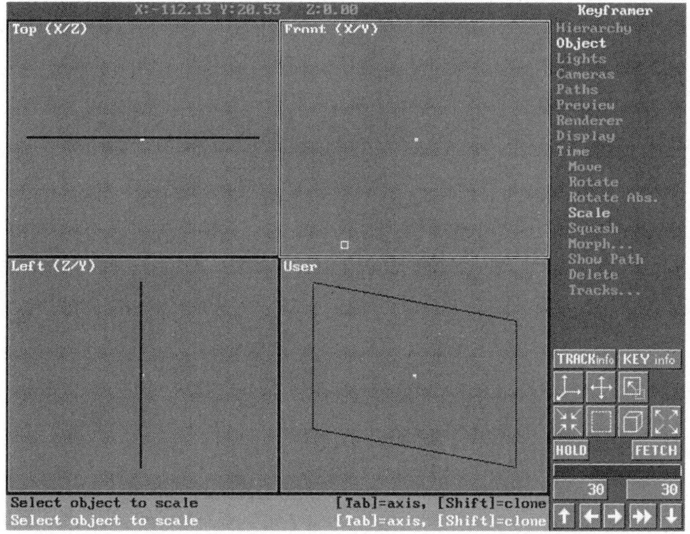

Figure 3.82. The scaling operation completed.

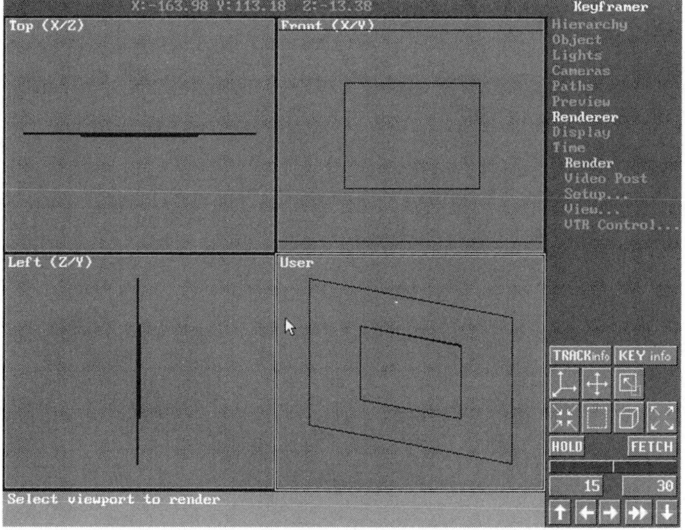

Figure 3.83. Frame 15 of the animation.

Rendering the Animation

After you create the animation sequence as a wireframe model, as outlined earlier, you are ready to render the animation as an FLC file. Before you render, you need to configure the system. Choose Renderer/Setup/Configure, which displays the dialog box shown in figure 3.84.

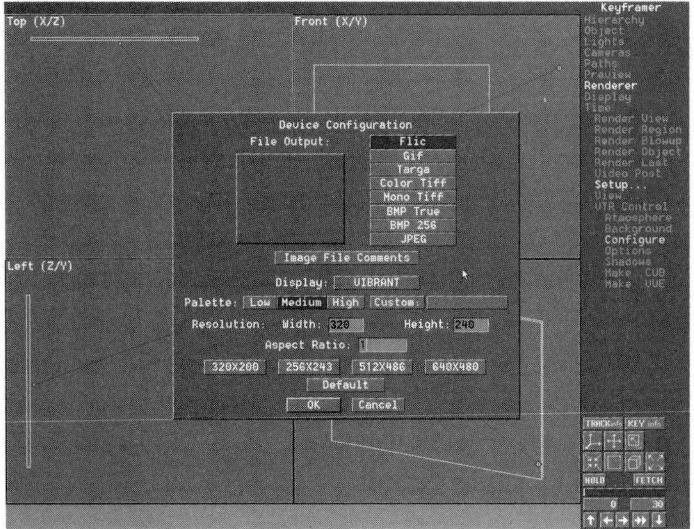

Figure 3.84. Configuring for rendering.

I suggest turning off compressed output—make sure that the Compressed button is not highlighted. This keeps image quality at the highest possible level. You have the option of outputting as an FLC file or a series of images. If you plan to use Animator Pro to output BMP files, go ahead and save your work as an FLC file. If you want to use a utility to convert numbered files to bitmaps, select the file format you want—GIF, TGA, or TIF.

There are three palette choices listed, but only two of them are worth considering: Medium and High. Refer to table 3.1 for information about the palette choices. For most cases, the Medium setting is fine.

You also need to set an appropriate image size. You can set three parameters: Width, Height, and Aspect Ratio. Width and Height are obvious: Use numbers that are in the same proportion as the objects. In this example, I have used 320×240, exactly twice the size of the originals. The primary consideration when deciding on image size is the machine you plan to use for playback. The smaller the image size, the better it plays on slow machines. Set the aspect ratio to 1. This is the ratio of pixel width and height.

After you have the configuration set, it's time to render. Choose Renderer/Render from the menu, and click in the viewport you want to render (Front). This displays the dialog box shown in figure 3.85.

Table 3.1. Rendering Palette Choices.

Choice	*Description*
Low	The Renderer creates an optimal 256-color palette for the first frame and then uses that palette for all subsequent frames. Unless the first frame is highly representative of the remaining frames, this is not a good option.
Medium	The Renderer creates an optimal 256-color palette for each frame in the animation and then combines the palettes into one optimal palette.
High	Each frame is rendered with 24-bit color. After rendering is complete, a single, 256-color palette is calculated. This option takes the most time, but gives the best results. It also uses a lot of disk space—72M in the case of a 562-frame animation I created.

For this example, accept the default settings for rendering. You can test the animation by picking a representative frame and rendering a single frame. Click the Single button, make sure the Disk button is not highlighted, and then click the Render button. You are asked whether you want to render to the screen only; click OK. When rendering is complete, you see an image like the one in figure 3.86. This is frame 15—the front image has shrunk halfway.

If the image meets your approval, it's time to render the complete animation. Choose Renderer/Render to redisplay the Render dialog box. This time, click the Disk button to highlight it and click the All button. After you click the Render button, you are asked to supply a file name. If you chose to render as a series of numbered frames, enter a name like **FILE*.GIF** or **FILE*.TGA**, depending on the file format you want. Otherwise, enter a file name of up to eight characters. Depending on the complexity of the animation, the image size, and the palette setting, the time to render each frame can vary from a few seconds to a few minutes.

If you rendered the animation as an FLC file, there are two ways to import it into VidEdit. You can run Animator Pro and use the POCO/Numpic menu option to save the file as a series of BMP files. You then can load the files as a DIB Sequence in VidEdit using the File/Insert menu option (see fig. 3.87). Or you can simply use the File/Open command and load the FLC file into VidEdit. In many cases, using File/Open works just fine. In some cases, you may find that the conversion did not work properly.[55] In such a case, you have to go back to Animator Pro and create bitmaps to insert.

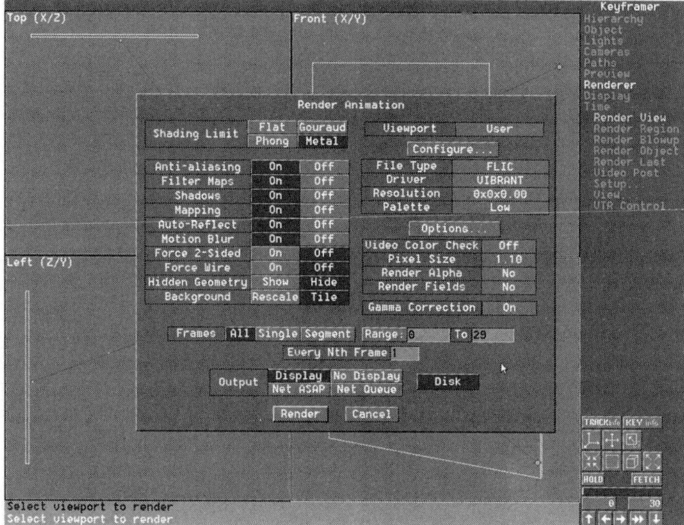

Figure 3.85. Setting up for rendering.

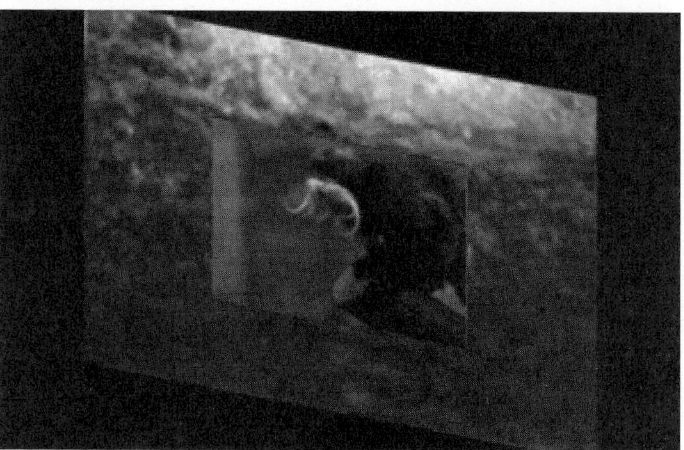

Figure 3.86. A rendered frame from the animation.

55Symptoms of incorrect importing include bits of prior frames floating around in the current frame, misalignment of images (horizontal or vertical offsets within the image frame), size distortion, and so on.

If you rendered the animation as a series of image files, use a utility like Image Pals or Graphic Workshop to convert the files to DIBs with a BMP extension. You then can use File/Insert to import the images (see fig. 3.87).

Figure 3.88 shows the entire 30-frame animation as a series of bitmaps loaded in the Image Pals utility program. The first frame is at the upper left, and the animation progresses from left to right, top to bottom.

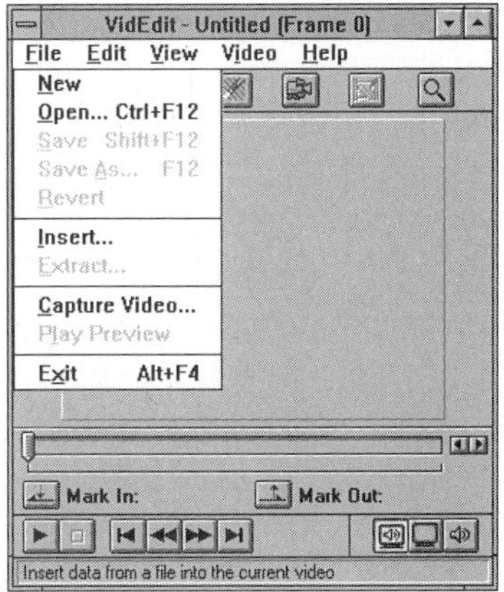

Figure 3.87. The File/Insert menu in VidEdit.

Finishing Up with VidEdit

After you have a series of bitmaps, you are ready to finish up the process using VidEdit. Figure 3.87 shows the File/Insert menu option, and figure 3.89 shows the dialog box that this menu option opens. To load a DIB sequence, first select DIB Sequence in the list box at the bottom left of the dialog box. Note that the default extension is *.DIB. Change it to *.BMP and press Enter. This displays all BMP files in the current directory (left of center in figure 3.89). Click the first file name in the sequence you want (FADE0001.BMP in this example) and click the OK button. This displays the dialog box shown in figure 3.90. Click DIB Sequence in the list, and then click OK.

VidEdit reads in the file. A message box appears, showing progress of the operation if there is a large number of DIBs to load. Figure 3.91 shows the sequence loaded into VidEdit. After you have the sequence in VidEdit, you can fine-tune frame rate, add audio, and so on—all the things that VidEdit is designed for.

If we assume that we started with one video sequence of 33 seconds and a second one of 14 seconds, you need to perform the following steps in VidEdit to complete the process:

- Open another instance of VidEdit and use Edit/Copy to copy the first 31 seconds of the first video to the Clipboard.
- Go to the original instance of VidEdit, move to the beginning of the special effect, and use Edit/Paste.
- Go to the second instance of VidEdit and open the second video file. Use Edit/Copy to place the last 12 seconds of the video into the Clipboard.
- Go to the original instance of VidEdit, move to the end of the file, and use Edit/Paste.
- If you will be saving the video using a 24-bit codec, skip to the next paragraph. If you will be using an 8-bit codec, choose Video/Create Palette and click the Paste Palette button when it appears. Then save the file as described in the next step.
- To save the file, use appropriate settings. If you want to ensure that the video will be viewable on the widest range of computers, use the parameters shown in figure 3.92. When using Indeo in particular, a key frame setting of 1 ensures that you will avoid any ghosting or weird delta frame[56] effects on slower machines.

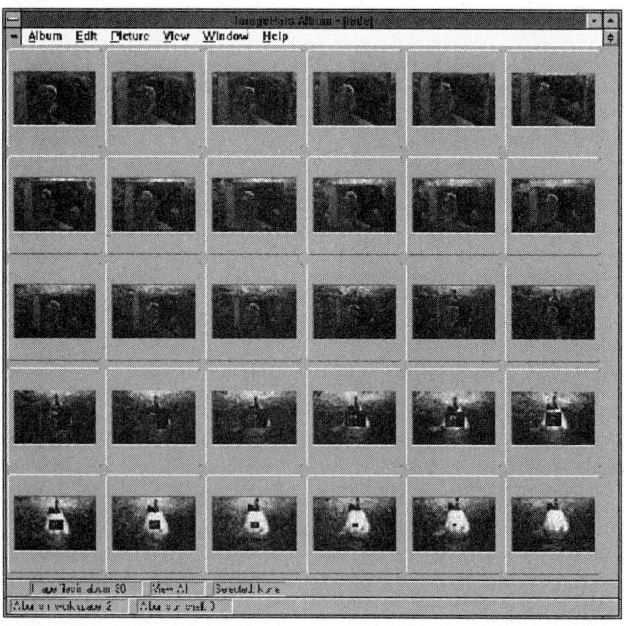

Figure 3.88. *A 30-frame animation as a series of bitmap images in Image Pals.*

[56]A *delta frame* is a frame between key frames. The Greek letter Delta has been used for many years by mathematicians and scientists to indicate change; a delta frame only contains information about changes, not an entire frame of data.

Insert File
File Name:
fade0001.bmp
expl0072.bmp
expl0073.bmp
expl0074.bmp
expl0075.bmp
expl0076.bmp
fade0001.bmp
fade0002.bmp
fade0003.bmp
Directories:
d:\avi4book\dibs
d:\
avi4book
dibs
OK
Cancel
List Files of Type:
DIB Sequence
Drives:
d: big_sucjer2

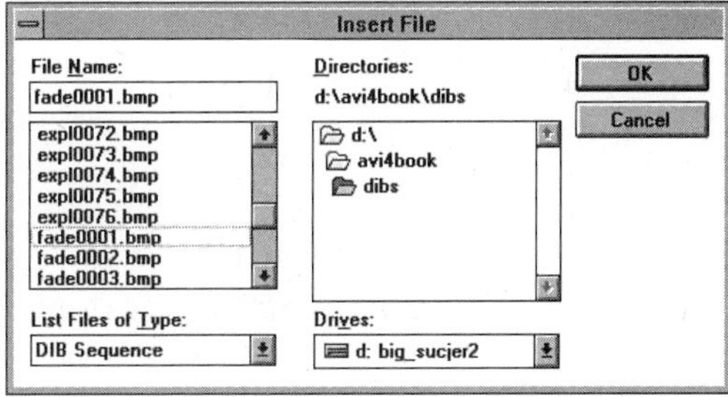

Figure 3.89. Selecting the first file in a DIB sequence.

Insert File
Select the file format:
Autodesk Animation
DIB Sequence
Microsoft AVI
OK
Cancel

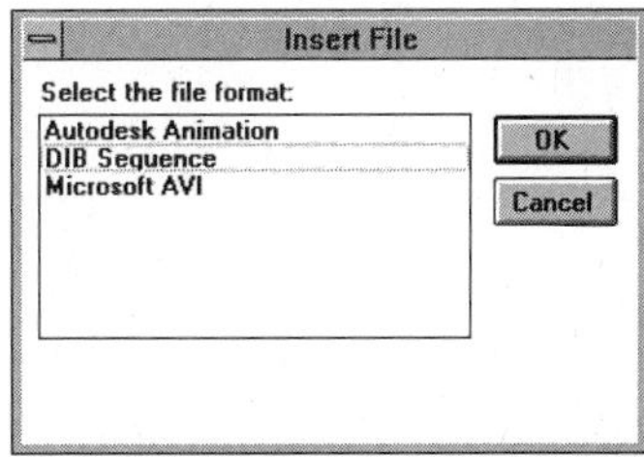

Figure 3.90. Inserting a DIB sequence.

VidEdit - Untitled (Frame 12)
File Edit View Video Help
Mark In:
Mark Out:
12 / 31
INS
K
Audio/Video

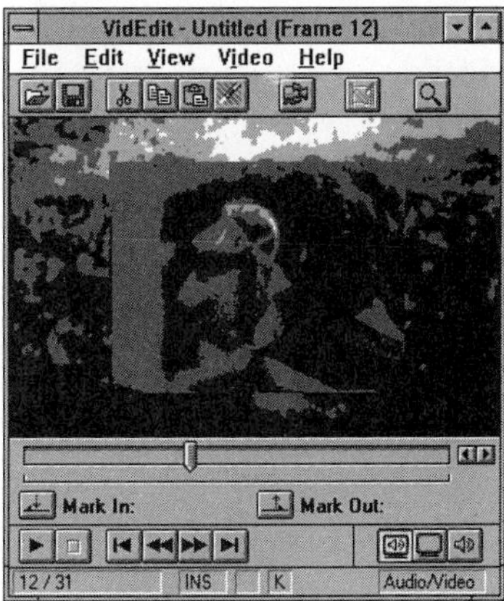

Figure 3.91. A video special effect loaded into VidEdit.

Save Video File
File Name:
fade.avi
3d2.avi
badland1.avi
c_horse1.avi
c_horse2.avi
clnthorn.avi
d2eye_f.avi
deer.avi
dkwngslw.avi
dog_cat.avi
Directories:
d:\avi4book
d:\
avi4book
dibs
hold
misc
wave
OK
Cancel
Drives:
d: big_sucjer2
Save Copy
Compression Options...
Stream audio
150K data rate
Intel Indeo(TM) Video

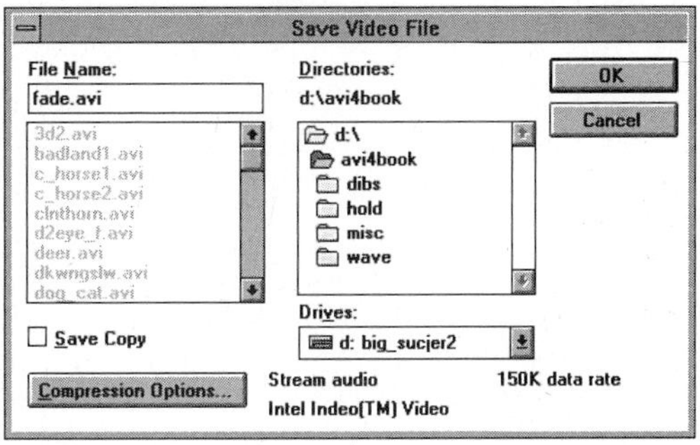

Figure 3.92. Setting Compression options in VidEdit.

Imagine 2.0

Imagine is a 3D-modeling package that originated on the Amiga. I can sum up Imagine in one sentence: It is a really cool product that can be frustrating to learn how to use. A love/hate relationship is almost inevitable with Imagine. There are times, while using the program, when I ask myself, "Why am I using this program?" Sooner or later, the answer comes knocking: I'll find a way to create a truly organic object that would be nearly impossible to create using a different program.

But that doesn't quite describe what it's like to get started with Imagine. After all, you can't use a program until you learn how to use it! Without qualification, I would say that Imagine was the hardest program to learn that I have encountered. You would think that it would have to be pretty darn useful to still get reviewed in this book, and you would be correct. To give you a clear idea of how Imagine works, I will take you through its operations one tiny step at a time. For that reason, this particular section is much more detailed than many other sections.(57)

RECIPE

4 cups Imagine
4-8M of memory
1M expanded memory
1 math coprocessor/486 CPU
1 VESA-compatible video display card
1 truckload patience

Instructions: Allow adequate time for preparation; ingredients may not blend properly at first. Using Imagine is a lot like making whipped cream: Stop too soon, and you'll have nothing but the time you spend; get it just right, and you'll have a delight. This is a real chance to let out your inner artiste.

---

[57] I almost feel obligated to do this—the manual that comes with Imagine has a long list of faults. #1: The manual was written for the Amiga, where Imagine was born, and there is absolutely no attempt to translate for the PC user. #2: There is no index. #3: (and I'm just getting started) It's nearly impossible to find the information you need in the narrative because it wanders around quite a bit. #4: The manual is written as though the author knows what you want to do and why,

The opening screen of Imagine is appropriately perplexing. It's just a logo, with no menu in evidence (see fig. 3.93). To access the menu, you need to click at the top of the screen. To get started, click on the Project menu, and then click New.(58) If you never even got to the opening screen, chances are you don't have any expanded memory. It's easy to add. Look at the line for emm386 in your CONFIG.SYS file. If it says `noems`, change it to `1024` instead. This gives you 1M of expanded memory. You can allocate more if you have 8M or more of system memory.

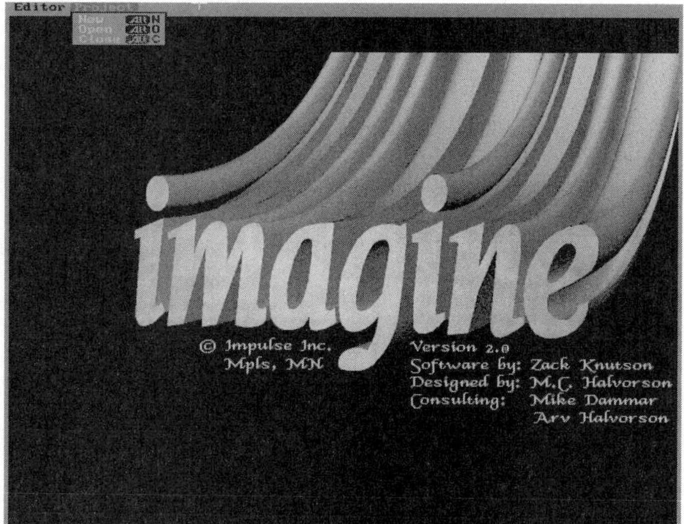

Figure 3.93. The Imagine opening screen.

After you name the project, you see the screen shown in figure 3.94. Click the New button to create a rendering subproject, which displays the dialog box shown in figure 3.95. There are many buttons and text windows, but you only need to understand a few of them to get started. Most important: Rendering method and Picture size. Set Scanline for the rendering method; this gives you most of the

---

57 (cont'd) and I think that's patronizing and out of place in a good software manual. #5: The entire manual is written as a single tutorial. There's no reference section at all. One good point: The information is all there if you can be patient enough to extract it. Author Phillip Shaddock, a good friend of mine, was writing the manual for version 3.0 of Imagine at the same time that I was writing the second edition of this book. Phil's efforts should dramatically improve the manual for Imagine.

58 Many menu selections also have corresponding key sequences to activate them. I've never used an Amiga, so I can't judge the portions of the interface that were carried over from the Amiga. However, some of them make no sense at all on the PC. To activate Alt key sequences, for example, you must use the right Alt key. The left Alt key—the one most of us use—won't do it.

features you want in solid modeling, but without ray-tracing features.[59] This is good for seeing what your image looks like without spending a lot of time getting there. When you finish the design, you can render with the Trace setting, which gives you full ray-tracing capabilities. Set an image size that meets your needs—320×200 or 640×480 is a good starting place.

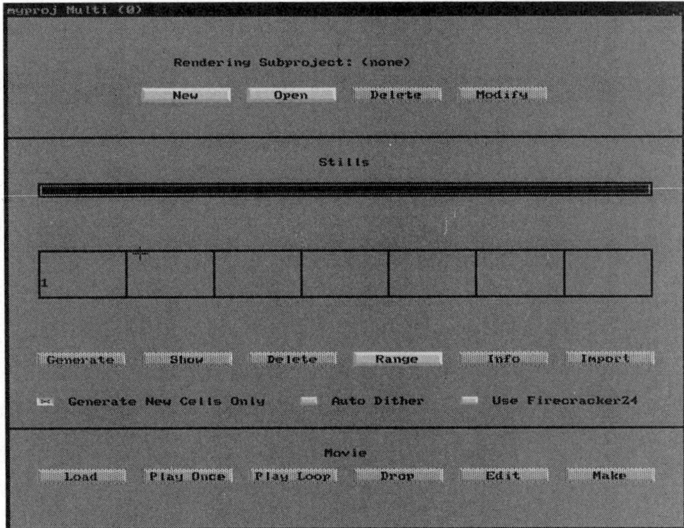

Figure 3.94. The Project Editor screen.

Imagine comes from the Amiga, so the text windows take a little getting used to. You can't just enter text; you must press Enter to "lock in" the text you've entered. If you don't press Enter, the text change does not take place. Exiting an Imagine dialog box is a two-step process: press Enter to exit the text window, and click an OK button to exit the dialog box.

Completing this step takes you back to the Project Editor. Click at the top of the screen to activate the Editor menu, shown in figure 3.96.

Imagine uses a number of what it calls *Editors*. Each Editor is its own distinct program, although some Editors resemble each other. Table 3.2 contains a brief description of each Editor and its capabilities.

---

[59] *Ray tracing* involves creating an image by tracing the path of light rays in the scene. This is a very exact way of handling complex phenomena like reflections, but it takes longer to render this way.

Figure 3.95. Creating a rendering subproject.

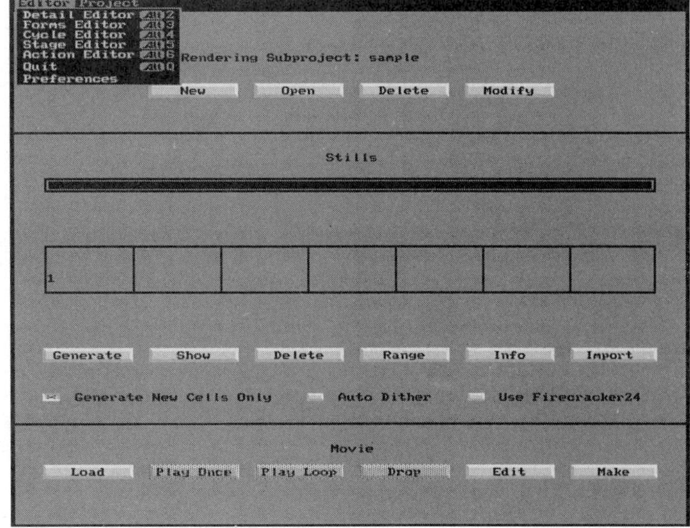

Figure 3.96. The Imagine Editors.

Table 3.2. Imagine Editors.

Editor	*Description*
Project	Where you manage your entire 3D project.
Detail	Does just what its name implies: Enables you to finish the details on objects that you created elsewhere. You can apply

continues

Table 3.14. continued

Editor	*Description*
	surface textures, for example, to objects you created in the Forms Editor.
Forms	Where you can create forms or objects interactively by moving the points on the surface of the object. You can create amazingly organic objects with this Editor. Typically, you'll create a basic form for an object here and then finish it in the Detail Editor.
Cycle	Enables you to set up repetitive motions for an animation.
Stage	Enables you to load various objects and put them into motion. It uses tweening[(60)] to create intermediate frames.
Action	You can apply the finishing touches to your animation here, including many special effects like explosions and rotations.

For this example, you'll start with the Forms Editor. In many ways, it's one of the most impressive aspects of Imagine. Short of the day when you can have a headset and gloves that enable you to modify a 3D object directly, Imagine gives you some interesting tools to work with in the Forms Editor. That's the good news. The bad news is that it's going to take time and practice, practice, practice to get good at it.

Figure 3.97 shows the opening screen of the Forms Editor.[(61)] There are four windows on the screen. Clockwise from the upper left, they are

Top—The object viewed from above.

Perspective—An adjustable perspective view of the object.

Right—The object viewed from the right side.

Front—The object viewed from the front.

---

[60]*Tweening* is a common concept in animation programs. It's similar to morphing: You create a start position and an end position, and the software creates all the intermediate positions.

[61]To get to the Forms Editor from any other Editor, use the Click menu at the top of the screen. It's right there on the Editor Menu.

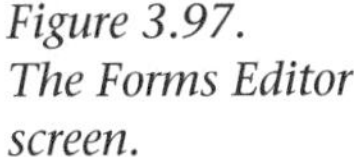

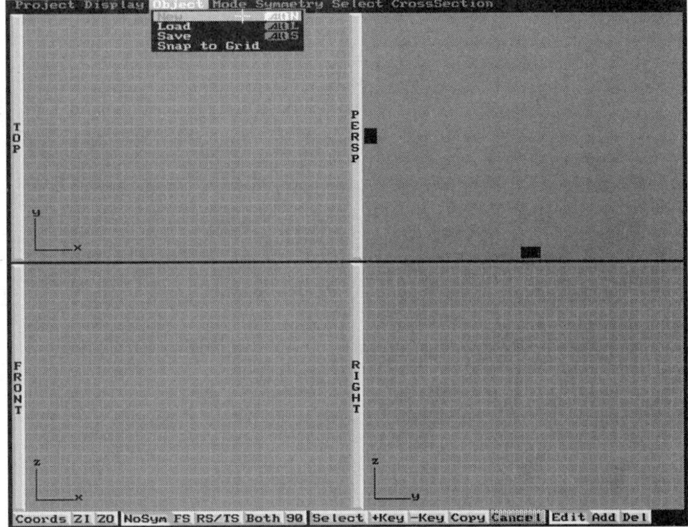

Figure 3.97. The Forms Editor screen.

This is a fairly standard variation on the presentation of 3D objects but, as you see shortly, it's not exactly what it seems to be. To create an object use the Click menu at the top of the screen and choose Object/New. This displays the dialog box shown in figure 3.98.

There are a lot of things going on in this dialog box that require an explanation. What are *slices*? What's a *former view*?(62) Let's interrupt the tutorial for a bit here to talk about how Imagine creates objects.

An object is made up of points and slices. Points are just what you expect—a point is a point is a point.(63) Slices also are just what the name implies. They are important because they enable you to establish some degree of control over your 3D objects. Think of a cucumber. It's basically a cylinder with its ends closed over. But it's a rounded shape; where do you put the points? The answer: at the slices. Take that cucumber and slice it up at intervals of, say, one inch. Then put it back together and you've got a typical Forms Editor object.

Keep that image in mind and refer again to figure 3.98. You are being asked to supply the number of points and the number of slices. If you enter 8 for the number of slices, it's like cutting the cucumber into 8 equally spaced slices. If you enter 16 for the number of points, you get 16 points—on each slice. That's a total of 128 points for the object.

---

[62]It's not the last view, I'll tell you that much!

[63]With apologies to Gertrude Stein.

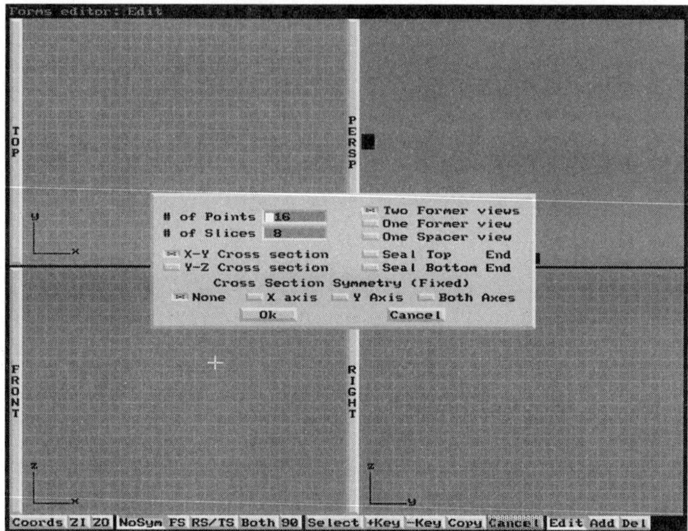

Figure 3.98. Creating a new object in the Forms Editor.

As for the other items in the New Object dialog box, a former view is nothing more than a view window in the Forms Editor. For certain kinds of objects, you can work with fewer windows when you need to modify only one or two dimensions of the object. For now, click the One Former View button. X-y and y-z cross sections refer to the orientation of the object in the Forms Editor view windows; for now, accept the default. As for sealing the top and bottom ends, all that does is close off the object instead of making it a hollow tube.

The buttons near the bottom of the dialog box regarding symmetry can be safely ignored for now; click None. These buttons enable you to create objects that are symmetrical in one or two directions. Your face is bilaterally symmetrical, for example—there is a single axis down the middle of your face with the same features on either side of that line.

Click OK to close the dialog box, and you see something like figure 3.99.

It's time for another digression into the ways and means of Imagine. There are some minor points about the display that make a big difference in how you work with Imagine compared to, say, 3D Studio.(64) The first thing to notice, if you can make it out in the figures, is that each of the view windows(65) has a small "axis indicator" in the lower left corner. There are two axes in each view—one pointing up

---

64Think of it this way: Imagine is a right-brain kind of program. Any sense it makes probably will appeal to the creative side of your brain. 3D Studio is more of a left-brain, intellectual type of program. Here's another way to look at it: Learning to use Imagine is like learning to play a musical instrument. Learning to use 3D Studio is like learning calculus.

65Except for the Perspective window, which uses sliders to adjust the point of view.

and one pointing to the right. Each axis is labeled with a letter: x, y, or z. It takes a while to get used to thinking in terms of axes, but this might help: The x axis goes from left to right, the y axis goes from front to back, and the z axis goes up and down.

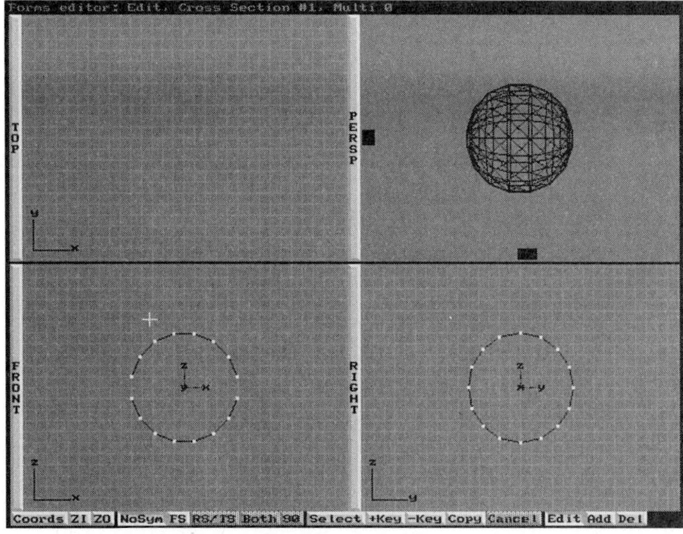

Figure 3.99. A newly created object in the Imagine Forms Editor.

Look closely at the Front view in figure 3.99. This is not just an ordinary front view of the object. Notice that the last two points on the right and left of the circle are not connected like the other points are. Let's go back to that cucumber idea. Think of figure 3.99 as a front view of a very, very fat cucumber. Those unconnected points are the two tips of the cucumber, and each pair of points defines a slice of the cucumber. Here's the punch line: If you move one of these points, you aren't really moving a point. You are adjusting a slice. We'll move some points and slices around shortly; for now, let's get back to describing the interface.

The Perspective view in figure 3.100 uses wireframe modeling. This makes it hard to visualize the object when there are many points, and in 3D modeling, there are almost always too many points. Imagine also lets you display the Perspective view as a solid, or even shaded.(66) Use the Display/Shaded menu option to change the Perspective display (see fig. 3.101 for the result).

66The shaded view actually only shows up under certain circumstances. You can enlarge any one view window to full screen by clicking on the vertical bar to the left of the view window. In full-screen mode, the Perspective window shows shading. If you must, peek ahead to figure 3.101.

Clicking on the left margin of any view window enlarges it to full screen, as shown in figure 3.101. Because we selected shading, a light source has been added to show the object more clearly as a 3D object. You can switch to the other view windows using the buttons at the right of the screen labeled Front, Right, and Top.

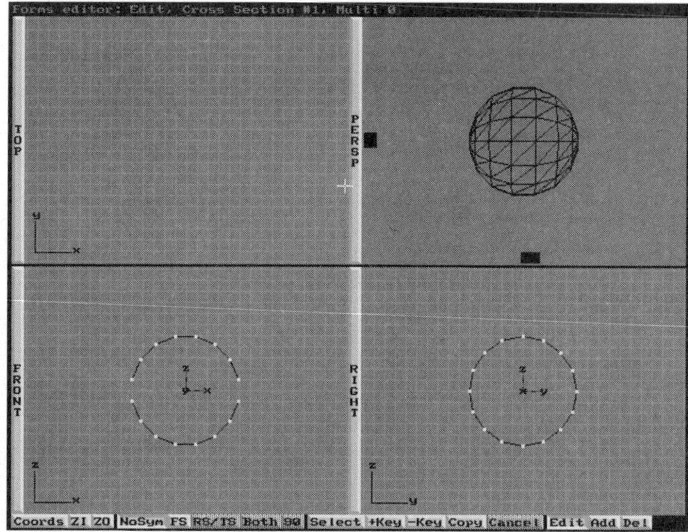

Figure 3.100. Using solid modeling to display the Perspective view.

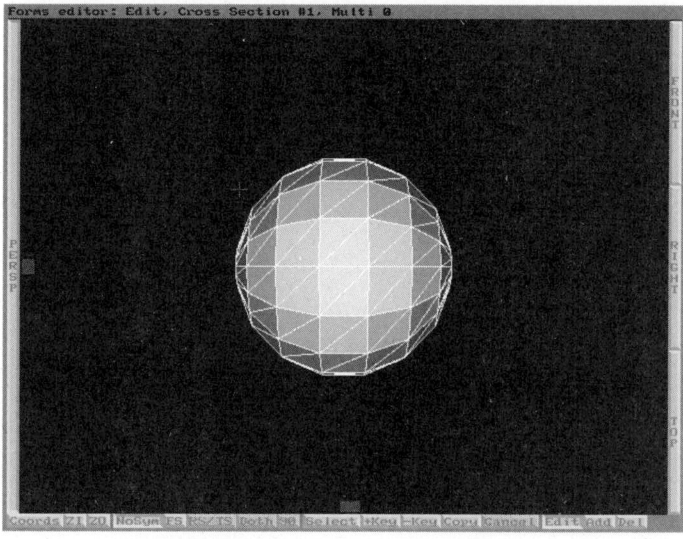

Figure 3.101. A shaded view of the object.

Let's get daring and move a point. Click on a point near the middle top of the Front view and move it close to the center of the object.[67] When you are done moving the point, look at the Perspective view (upper right of figure 3.102). Notice that you didn't move just one point; you adjusted an entire slice of the object. Figure 3.103 shows a 3D shaded view of the object.

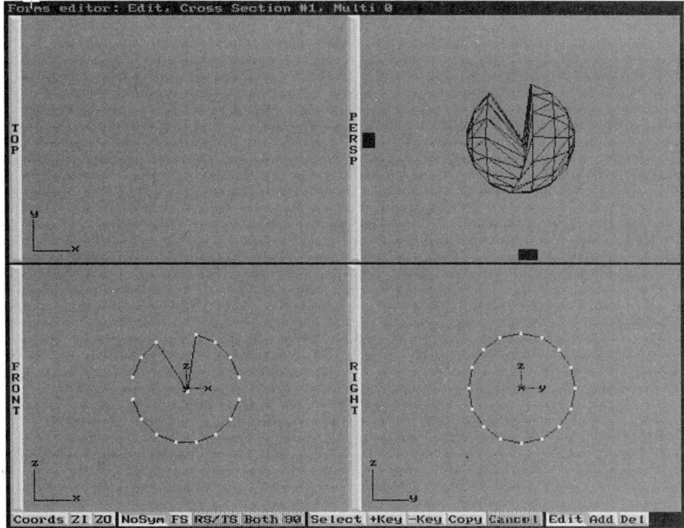

Figure 3.102. Moving a point on a slice in the Front view.

Because we created this object without any symmetry, we are free to move any point on any slice. If we create an object with bilateral symmetry, moving one point on a slice moves the corresponding point on the other side of the slice like a mirror image. Look at figure 3.104, for example. It shows an object that is bilaterally symmetrical.[68]

Time for another lesson in the ways and means of Imagine. Notice that the Right view window hasn't changed one bit, even though we have made dramatic changes to the shape of the object. Remember that the Front view isn't really a true front view. The Right view isn't really a true right view, either. You aren't seeing a front view of the entire object. You're seeing a front view of a single slice. Because all the

[67]While you are moving the object, you'll see a little axis indicator telling you that the z axis is up and the x axis is to the right. This duplicates what already is being displayed in the lower left of the Front view window, so I don't exactly understand why it happens.

[68]Most of the time, when you create a new object, it shows up as a sphere. You then can deform it to whatever shape you want. You can use a type of Snap to Grid feature to easily make perfectly square or rectangular objects.

slices are still circular (even if they are different sizes), the Right view is still circular, too. To change the slice that is shown in the Right view, use the Select button at the bottom center of the screen. You can display only key slices in the Right view. To make a slice a key slice, click the +Key button (to the right of the Select button). You can use the -Key button to make a slice a nonkey slice again. The idea behind key slices is simple. If a slice is not a key slice, it adapts itself to changes made to key slices. In other words, nonkey slices assume positions between key slices.

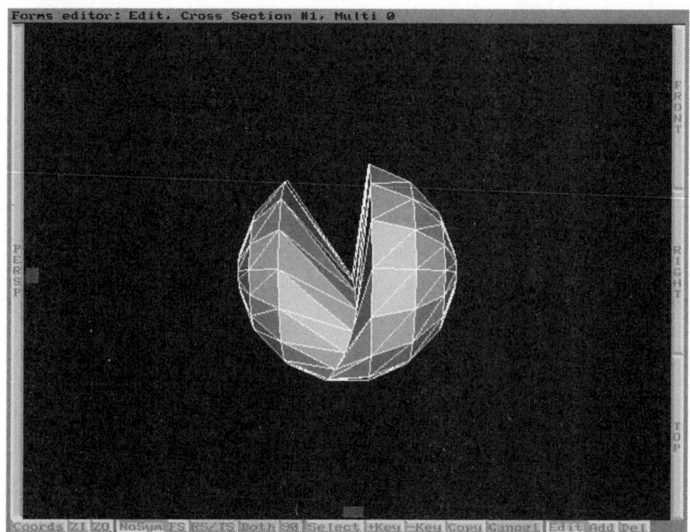

Figure 3.103. The result of moving a point on a slice.

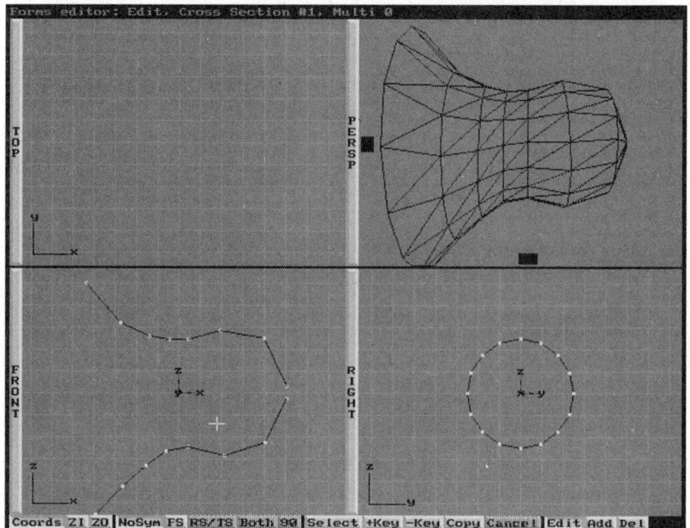

Figure 3.104. An object with two-fold symmetry.

Figure 3.105 shows a shaded 3D view of the new object.

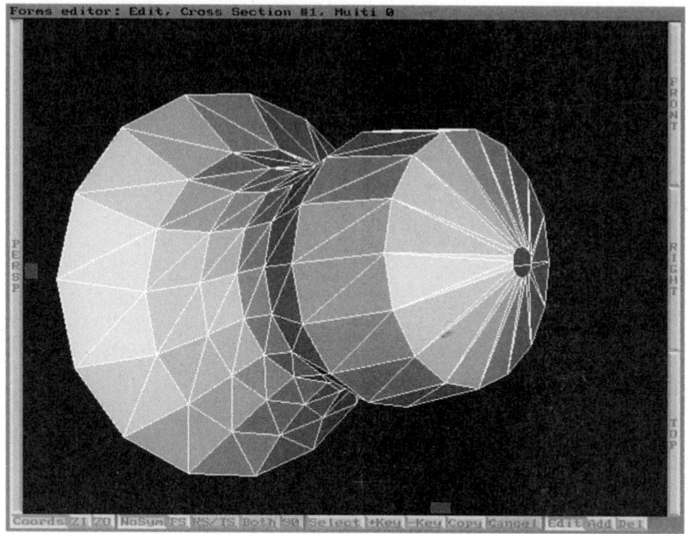

Figure 3.105. A shaded view of the new object.

You can work with more than one point at a time in Imagine. The Select menu enables you to pick the method you'll use for selecting active points: Click, Drag Box, or Lasso. Click is the method we've used so far; to modify a point, you just click on it. The Drag Box method is familiar to anyone who has used a Windows drawing program (see fig. 3.106). To drag a box around some points, choose Select/Drag Box from the Click menu at the top of the screen, and then click and drag a box around the points you want to select.

The points you selected, and the lines between them, now are highlighted and you can work with just those points. The Object/Snap to Grid menu option, for example, would operate on the selected points, moving them to the nearest grid points.[69]

You can create some pretty fancy shapes with the Forms Editor. Look at figure 3.107, which shows a car form from the samples that come with Imagine. A shaded view of the form is shown in figure 3.108. It doesn't look exactly like a car; you can add things like wheel wells and fenders in the Detail Editor.

---

[69]This is dangerous! If more than one point gets moved to the same grid point, you'll have no indication of the situation. This can get very confusing if you are not aware of the possibility.

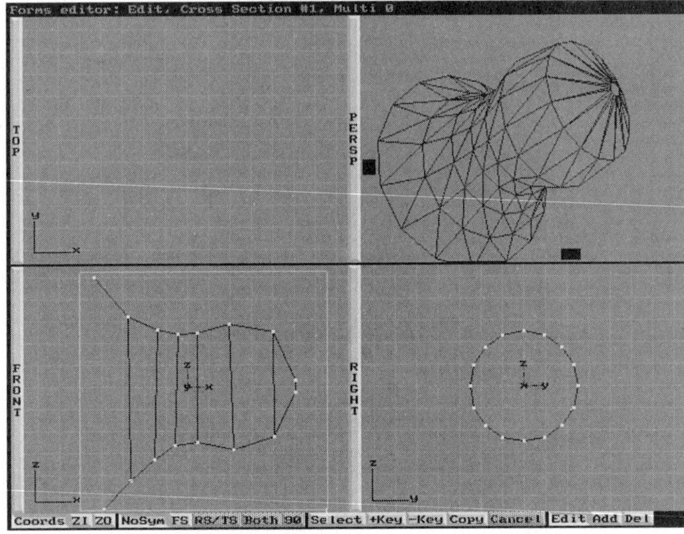

Figure 3.106. Selecting points with a drag box.

Fun with the Forms Editor

Let's try a little experiment to see if I can make it clear how an object responds to your manipulations in the Forms Editor. To start, create an object with eight slices and eight points. Before you click OK to create the Object, choose One former view. In the Front view, rearrange the points to make a rough outline of the letter A (see fig. 3.109).

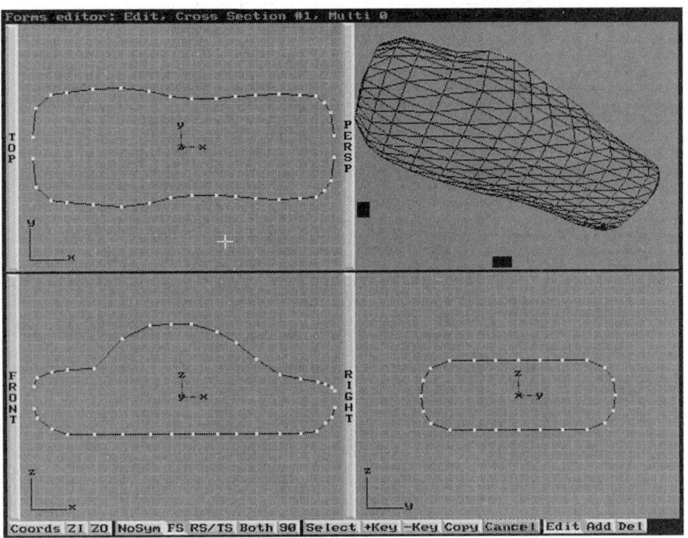

Figure 3.107. A more complex shape created with the Forms Editor.

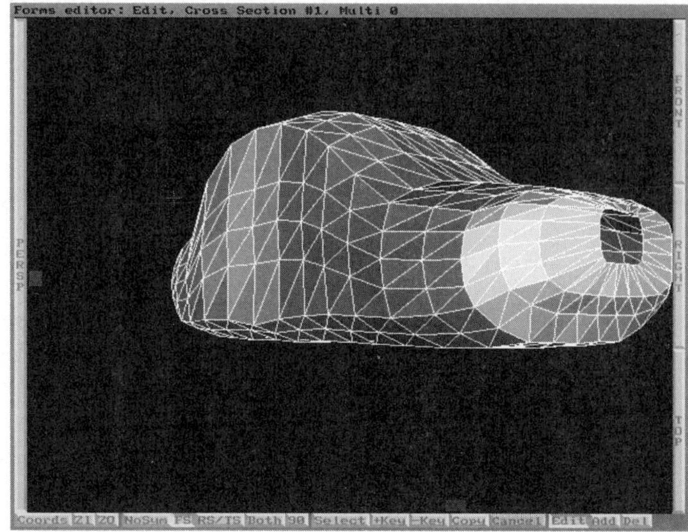

Figure 3.108. A shaded view of the object in figure 3.107; it's a car! Sort of.

Make one of the slices near the center of the letter form a key slice, and then use the Select button to select it. This slice is now the one showing in the Right view. Click Select/Lock to turn on Snap to Grid. Now move the points in the Right view to form a square. Look at the Perspective view, and note the contortions the form makes to switch from a circular slice, to a square slice, and then back again.

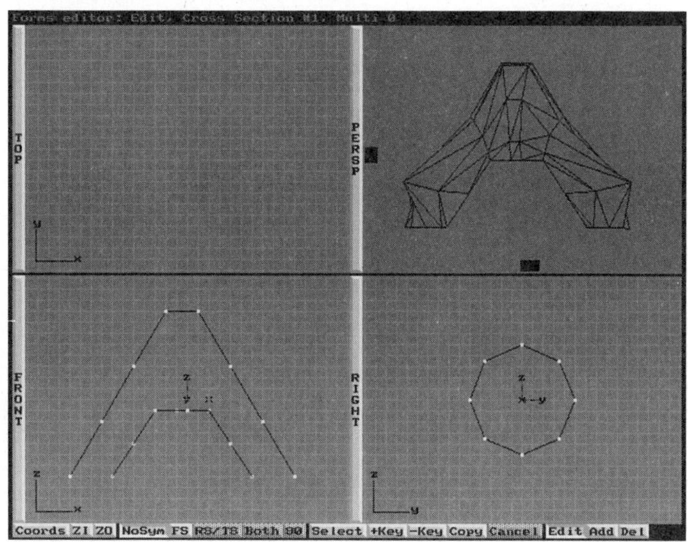

Figure 3.109. Fun with the Forms Editor.

Now rearrange the points in the Right view to form a diamond shape, as shown in figure 3.110. In addition, change the angle of view in the Perspective view to show the object more clearly. Note that the middle slice does, indeed, now have a diamond shape.[70]

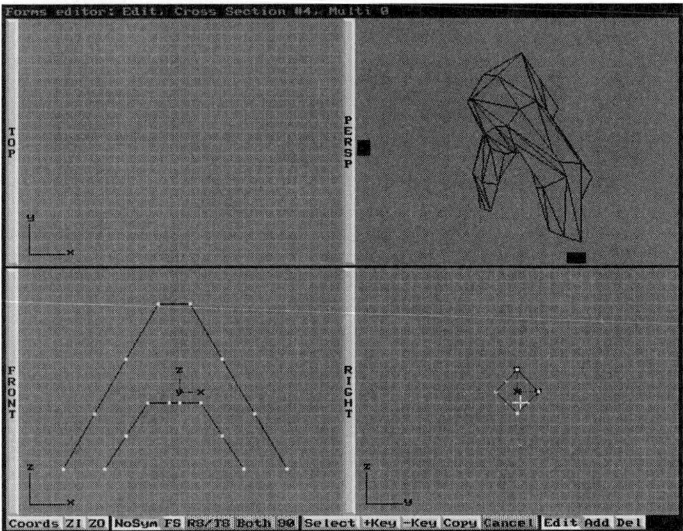

Figure 3.110. Yet another variation of the middle slice.

Now let's get weird. Move the top point of the diamond in the Right view way to the right, as shown in figure 3.111. Look at the Perspective view—there is the point way out to the right. Notice how the lines from other slices automatically adjust themselves to create intermediate positions.

Let's try a more useful set of transformations in the Forms Editor. Create a new object, again with eight slices and eight points. Choose No Symmetry, and Two former views. In the Front view, rearrange points until you have something like what I've done in figure 3.112. That's right: we're making a fish. Figure 3.113 shows a shaded view of the fish form.

The form is a little fat for an angel fish. In the Top view, move the points to narrow each slice (see fig. 3.114). Align the points that define the tail until they actually touch each other. Note how this changes the appearance of the slice in the Right view. This is not thin enough, however; you also need to move the points in the Right view to about the same distance apart as you did in the Top view.

---

70 With a little more effort, we could have a great robot shape here!

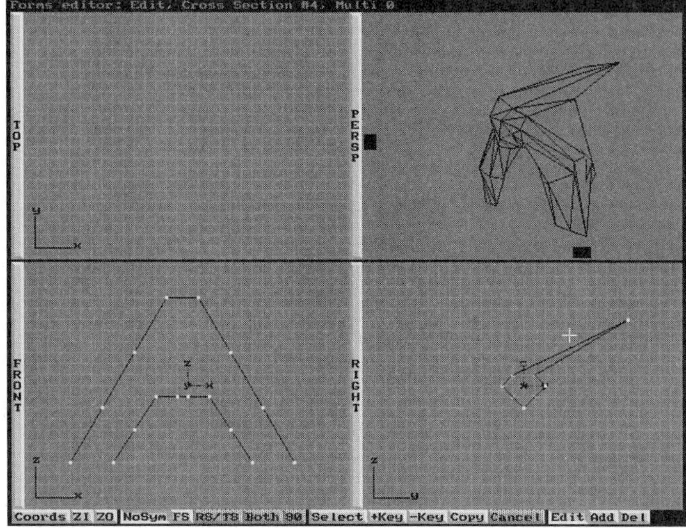

Figure 3.111. Far out to the right in the Forms Editor.

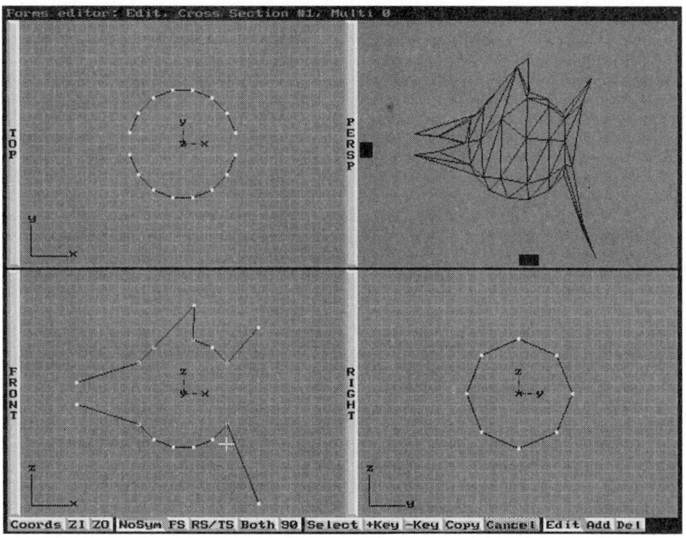

Figure 3.112. Creating a fish in the Forms Editor.

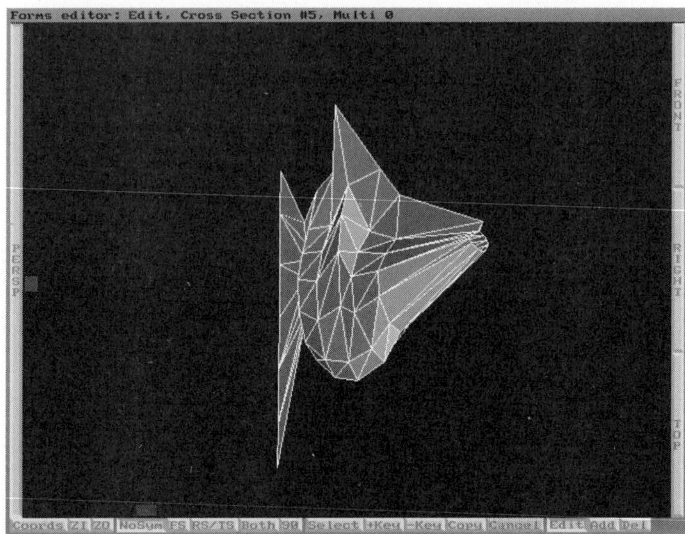

Figure 3.113. A fish form.

So far, we have just a fish floating in space. There is no reference point, but we can create one easily by adding something called a *ground*. The result in shown in figure 3.115.

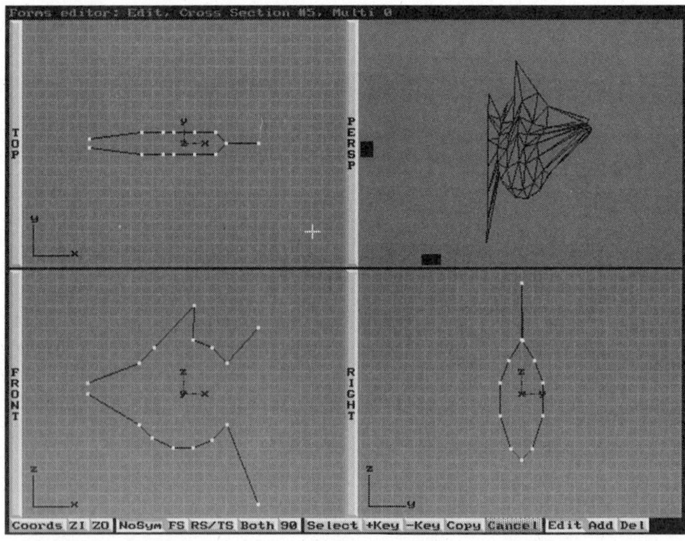

Figure 3.114. Narrowing the fish form for a realistic appearance.

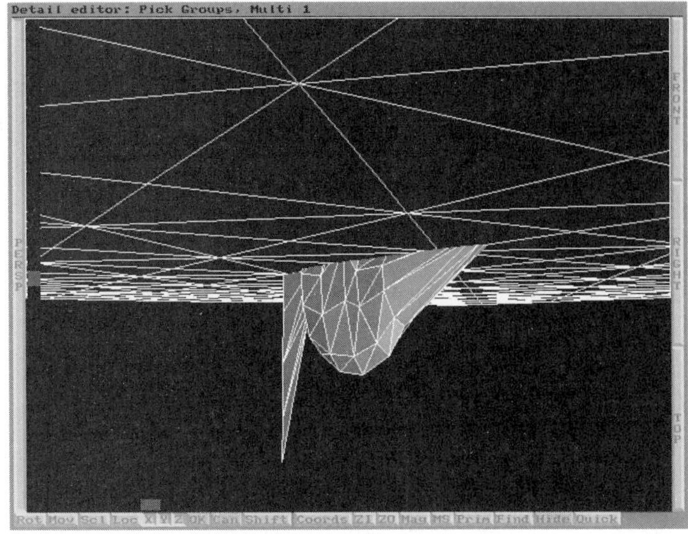

Figure 3.115. Oops—fish and ground share a common center.

Because objects are all created at the origin of the workspace, the ground cuts the fish in half. We need to move either the fish or the ground, and it's easy to do. Click the Move button at the bottom left, and then use the mouse to click and drag the ground below the fish (see fig. 3.116). The result of the move is shown in figure 3.117.

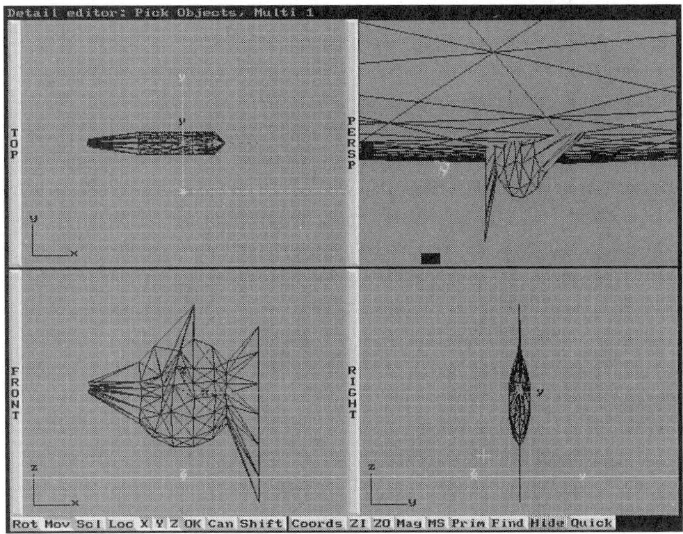

Figure 3.116. Dragging the ground to a new position after clicking the Move button.

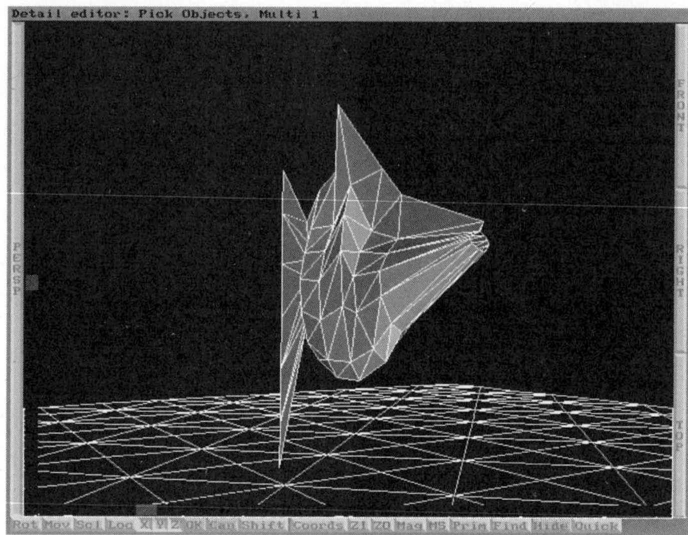

Figure 3.117. The result after moving the ground below the fish.

Now you can do a quick render by clicking the Quick button at the lower right of the screen. The result is shown in figure 3.118. Hmm... it sort of looks like a fish, but we're definitely not done yet! It's time for the Detail Editor.

Figure 3.118. A fish rendering.

The Detail Editor looks like the Forms Editor, but the menus are quite different. Once again, there are strange but important new concepts to learn. The most important concepts are Select and Pick. Selecting appears to mean nothing more than making an object appear orange, but you can't Pick an object unless it's

Selected. There's a menu option called Pick Selected, and that's what it does.[71] There are also several other methods for picking an object, such as Pick Last. Whatever method you use, Pick the fish. This enables you to access the Object/Attributes menu option, and this is where the fun really starts. This displays the Attributes Requester (Amiga talk for the Attributes dialog box), as shown in figure 3.119. You can set a large number of attributes—color, reflectivity, hardness, shininess, textures, and more. Providing a complete description of attributes is beyond the scope of this book, however. For this example, I gave the fish a bright blue color and made it mildly reflective and shiny. This gives a quick approximation of the surface attributes of a typical tropical fish.

Even so, there's more to do. At the very least, we should add an eye to our fish. We can create a simple sphere, and then Move it and Scale it so that it looks just right (see fig. 3.120). I set attributes of color black, shininess 100%, and white spectral reflection for the eye. Again, these are just quick approximations of the natural characteristics of an eye. The result isn't too bad (see fig. 3.121).

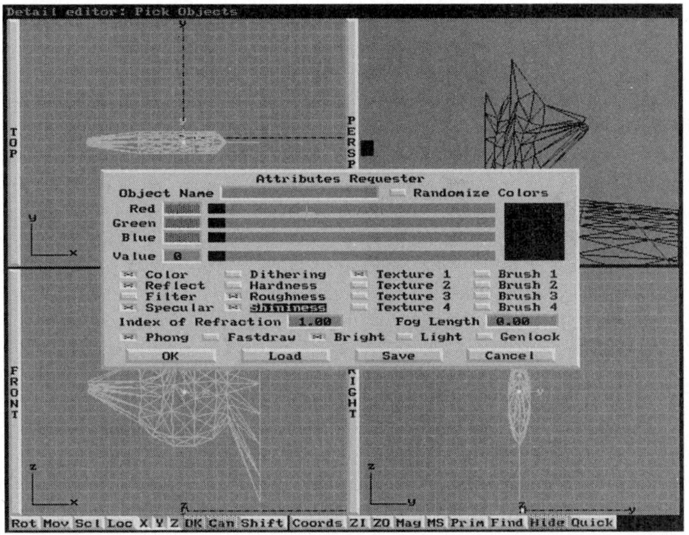

Figure 3.119. The Attributes Requester in the Detail Editor.

[71]Editorial comment: This complexity about selecting and picking makes the Detail Editor more painful than it needs to be but, like the other quirks of Imagine, you get used to it if you stay with it long enough. It adds significant difficulty to the learning process.

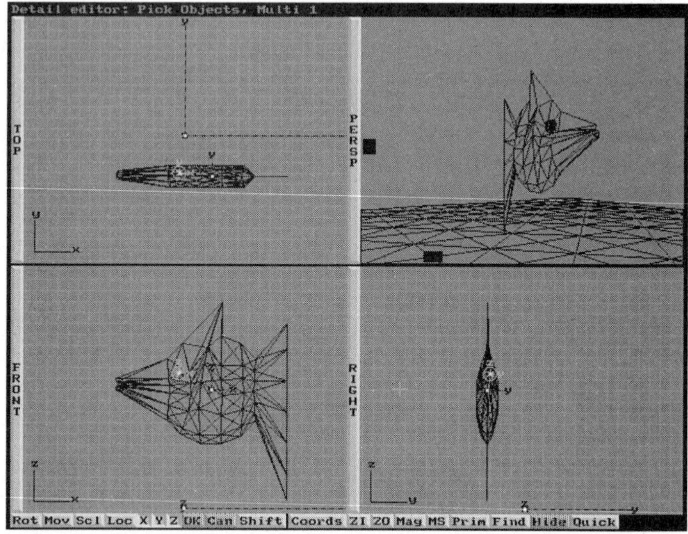

Figure 3.120. Adding an eye to the fish object.

Figure 3.121. A rendering of the fish, eye, and ground.

Summary

This section only hints at what you can do with Imagine. Despite its idiosyncratic interface and poor documentation, Imagine has some interesting and powerful capabilities. If you have time and patience, you can do much more than what I've shown here, including sophisticated animation.

Architectural Space

Computers are digital. That means that some things are easier than others. When it comes to virtual reality, straight lines are easier than curves. For that reason, some of the most advanced VR applications involve architecture. Not that buildings don't have curves, but the vast majority of the lines, edges, and faces are straight. This makes for a certain degree of simplicity.

Not so simple is the sheer number of those lines, edges, and faces. In fact, this is a good place to illustrate the volume of data involved in creating a virtual space. Consider the lowly Cape Cod style of home, for example. What would it take to simulate the process of opening the front door, crossing the living room, walking up the stairs, and then examining the details of an upstairs window frame?

Indoors

The answer is, it would take a lot. I want to impress on you just how much it does take, however, because this is the central issue of virtual reality. Until there are ways of handling the massive amounts of data involved, all the headsets in the world won't help a bit.

Let us go then, you and I, up to that front door. What do we see as we stand before it? There's the door itself, of course. This one is made of wood. "What kind of wood," we must ask. And is the wood painted, stained, oiled, varnished, or covered in some other way? Is there a window in the door? How many panes of glass are in the window? Is the glass simple, clear, flat glass; or is it stained glass, or perhaps cut or etched glass? How fancy is the frame around the window? What about the hardware on the door—brass, pewter, chrome, or something else? Is there weather stripping at the base of the door? What about the threshold at the base of the door frame? And what about the door frame—what kind of wood is used there, and is it a fancy molding with difficult-to-reproduce, complex curves? And then there are the latch and the notch for it in the door frame. And don't forget to consider where the light is coming from. Is it a sunny day? Are there any clouds? Is there a porch light—or, for that matter, a porch? Light surfaces reflect light; what effect does that have on the scene?

Assuming that we've been able to generate an image that can handle all of that, now we have to put it in motion—and that means starting all over again. Even a little motion changes things. As we open the door, the lighting angle changes constantly. But that's just part of the problem. As the door opens, it reveals a bit of the living room inside—with its rugs, walls, paintings, trim, couches, chairs, baseboard, electrical outlets, and more.

Now that I have you convinced of the difficulty of the task, it's time to look at a software package that does (sort of) just the things I've described. If you think this was merely a clever ploy to prevent you from being overly disappointed with the limited capabilities of low-end architectural-rendering software, you're right.[72] In order to render 3D scenes, or to enable you to move through the scenes, low-end software had to make some serious compromises.

Let's look at a software package called 3D Plan from Autodesk. It's a very easy program to use, and it provides some intriguing VR capabilities in an inexpensive package. Figures 3.122 and 3.123 show two views created with 3D Plan. Figure 3.122 shows a view across a backyard pool, and figure 3.3 shows a view through sliding glass doors into the interior of a cabin.

The opening screen of 3D Plan is shown in figure 3.124. The bulk of the screen is the area where the 3D view will be shown. Information about the current view is displayed at the bottom, and the menu is located at the right of the screen. There are five menu options, and they are listed in table 3.3.

Figure 3.122. A backyard virtual reality.

Table 3.3. 3D Plan Menu Options.

Option	*Function*
File	Loads and saves files
View	Establishes your point of view and the basic type of rendering
Display	Contains parameters for fine-tuning the rendering

[72]It's easy to expect too much from VR software if you don't consider the true nature of the task at hand.

Option	Function
Action	Enables you to move your point of view
Color	Changes the colors of objects in the rendering

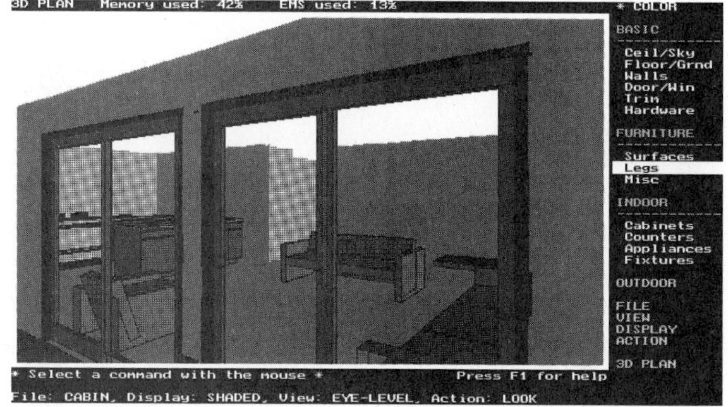

Figure 3.123. A view into the interior of a cabin.

RECIPE

1 DWG file
4 cups 3D Studio
2M of expanded memory
1 EGA or better display card

Instructions: This is an easy-to-prepare, light dessert. Images aren't very detailed—no Super VGA support—but the results are quick. Plan ahead: you can't do anything unless you have prepared some DWG files in advance. Use Generic 3D, AutoCAD, or any of the Home Design modules available from Autodesk.

3D Plan works with any EGA or better color display card, but I highly recommend using a VGA display. 3D Plan does not use any Super VGA capabilities you may have. This is unfortunate, because VGA resolution—and its 16 colors—doesn't provide a very realistic image.

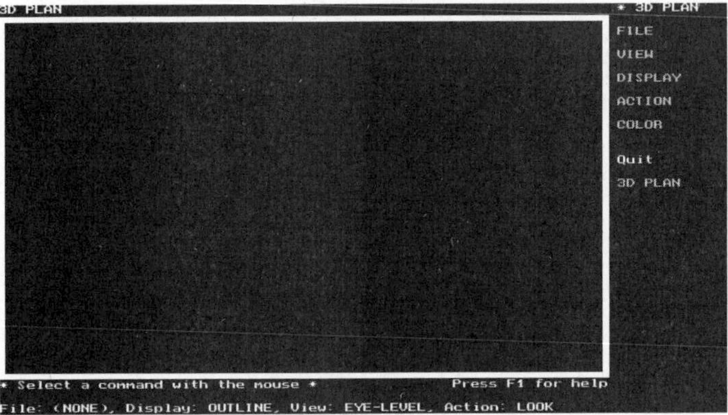

Figure 3.124. The 3D Plan opening screen.

To create a rendering, click on the File menu at the upper right of the screen. This displays a menu with several items; click on Load 2D. You can load only a 2D drawing that uses the DWG file format. You can use products like Generic CADD (also from Autodesk) to create plan drawings, or you can use the much simpler Home Series of drawing products (yes, also from Autodesk). The Home Series software comes in packages labeled Kitchen, Bathroom, and so on. You can create a plan in one of the Home Series packages and then view it in 3D with 3D Plan.

3D Plan comes with several sample DWG files. Figure 3.125 shows the plan file HOME.DWG during the loading process. 3D plan applies a little artificial intelligence during the loading process. It follows a few simple rules to determine what is, and is not, a wall in the plan drawing. When it has things pretty well figured out, 3D Plan displays only the walls. Most of the walls are in bold, indicating that they are selected. You can click on a wall to deselect it, and it does not appear in the 3D rendering. This can be useful. If you want to look at a kitchen in 3D, for example, it might be easier if you eliminate a wall or two. If you deselect a wall accidentally, just click on it again to reselect it.

Press Enter when you have the walls the way you want them.[73] 3D Plan then completes the loading process. You see the complete Plan View, including any 3D

[73]If the drawing has no walls—for example, a landscape drawing showing just trees and shrubs—3D Plan does not pause during loading to ask about walls.

objects that were placed in the view with the drawing program used to create the plan. Figure 3.126, for example, shows a complete Plan View from the HOME.DWG file.[74]

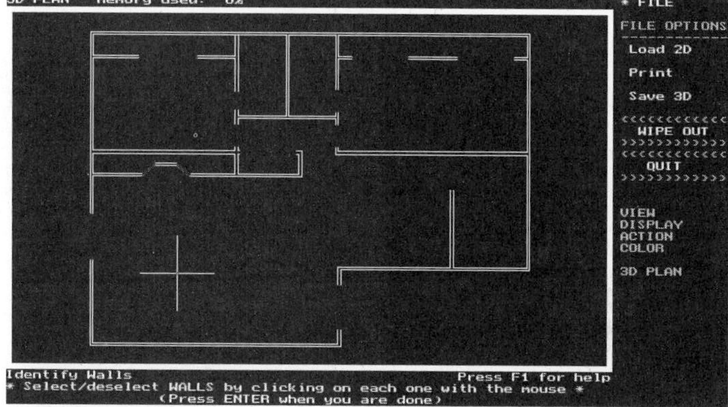

Figure 3.125. Selecting walls during loading.

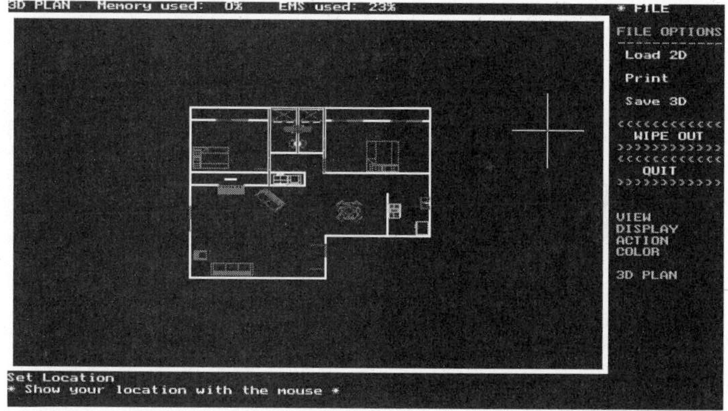

Figure 3.126. A Plan View in 3D Plan.

Your next task is to establish your position and point of view. Click anywhere on the Plan View to set your position; a crosshair with one long leg appears (see fig. 3.127). Slide the mouse back and forth to face the long leg in the direction you want to view. In this example, the viewpoint is just inside the front door in the living room, looking off toward the dining area.

---

[74]This is a good spot to put in a few words about what a *Plan View* is. If you have ever taken a class in mechanical drafting (I had one in high school), you are familiar with floor plans. That's all a Plan View is—a view from above showing the location of objects in the plan. Objects include walls, furniture, electrical lines, and anything else that might exist in an architectural drawing.

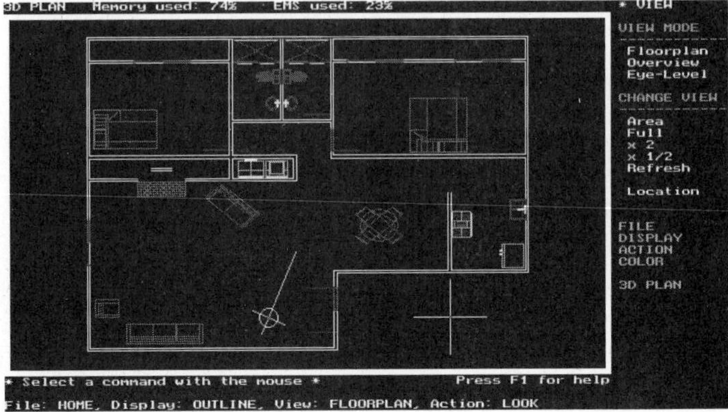

Figure 3.127. Setting the point of view.

Click on View to go to the View menu, where you see three possible View modes:

Floorplan—Shows the Plan View. This is a 2D-viewing mode.

Overview—A 3D view of the entire plan. This view ignores the viewpoint you just set.

Eye-level—A view at eye level from the viewpoint you just set.

You also can use this menu to change views. You can zoom in or out, for example, or use the Area selection to pick a specific area to view. To select an area, just click and drag out a box with the mouse.

Click on Eye Level, and you see something like the view shown in figure 3.128. The first thing you will no doubt notice is that it is a Wireframe view. If you have even a moderately fast computer, you can switch to a more pleasing rendering mode.

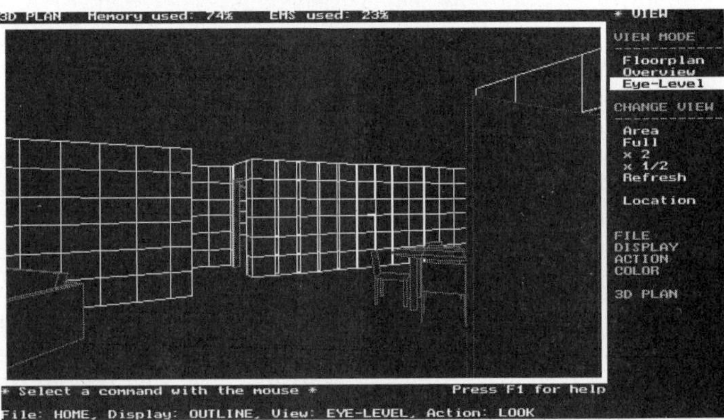

Figure 3.128. An eye-level view in 3D Plan.

Click on Display, which switches you to the Display menu. You see three display modes listed on the menu:

Outline—This is Wireframe mode.

Solid—Colors all objects in the scene using the current color scheme.

Shaded—Shades the solid view using simple rules about lighting. There is also a subchoice, Edge. If edges are on, you see a black line at the edge of each object.

Figure 3.129 shows a view using the Solid display mode. This is an improvement, but it's hard to tell where one wall ends and the next begins. Let's try Shaded mode (see fig. 3.130). This is as good as it gets. 3D Plan isn't a photo-realistic rendering program. It does, however, provide an inexpensive way to visualize what a new kitchen layout will look like, or to get an idea of what your new house will feel like. You could even use it to try out a new furniture layout. These are minor but worthy applications for virtual reality.

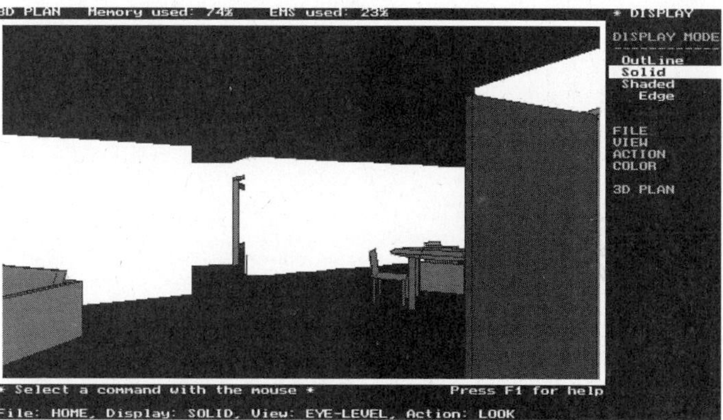

Figure 3.129. The Solid display mode.

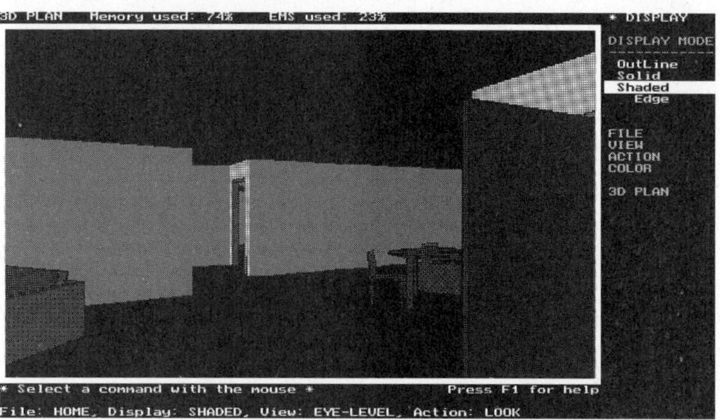

Figure 3.130. The Shaded display mode.

The rendering quality may not be detailed, but 3D Plan does have some additional VR features. You can move through the virtual space using the arrow keys, for example. There is a short delay while the program recalculates the view. The left- and right-arrow keys turn left and right, and the up- and down-arrow keys move the point of view forward and backward. Figure 3.131 shows a view of HOME.DWG from the dining area into the living room, for example. Figure 3.132 shows the view a few steps toward the living room.(75) This is much more intuitive than resetting the viewpoint using those crosshairs. In fact, it is this simple feature of being able to move through the 3D space that makes 3D Plan useful.

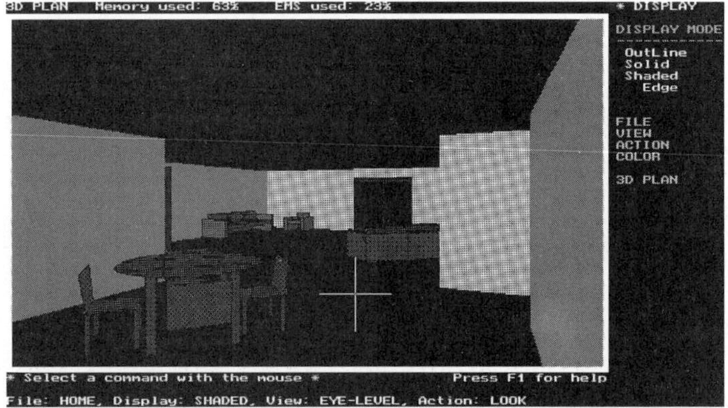

Figure 3.131. Another view in 3D Plan.

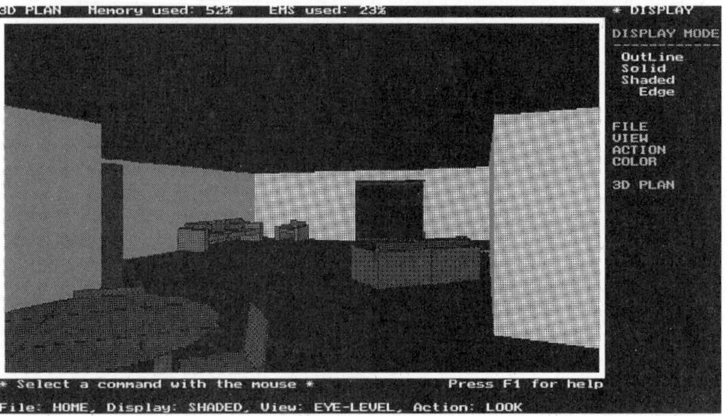

Figure 3.132. A step forward in the virtual space. Compare to figure 3.131.

---

75 This movement is precise. Each key press moves you the same number of feet or rotates you the same number of degrees. You can use the Ctrl key to magnify the motion. Pressing the left-arrow key, for example, rotates you one degree to the left, and holding down the Ctrl key and pressing the left-arrow key rotates the view 15 degrees.

If you aren't happy with the appearance of the image, you have limited control over the colors used. 3D Plan is limited to VGA's 16 colors, and there are more than twice that number of object categories, so colors have to be shared. You can set the color of a variety of object types. You can assign different colors to furniture, carpet, walls, ceiling, doors, door frames, and so on. Figure 3.133 shows the same view as in figure 3.132, but with different colors.

In addition to the eye-level view, you can look at your project using the Overview mode, as shown in figure 3.134.

3D Plan is one of the plainer programs that makes use of virtual reality, but it does a great job within its limited sphere.

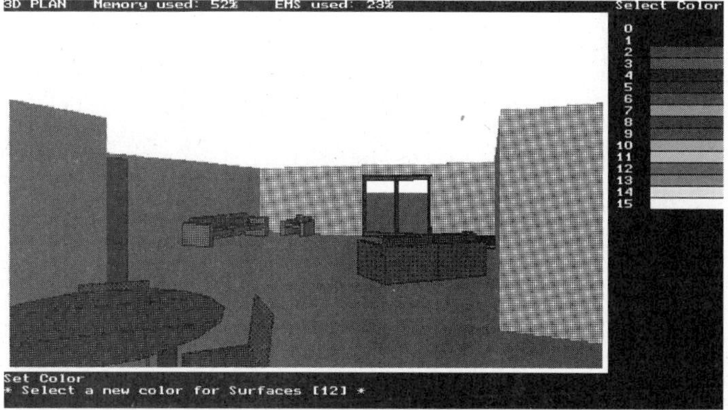

Figure 3.133. Setting different colors in 3D Plan.

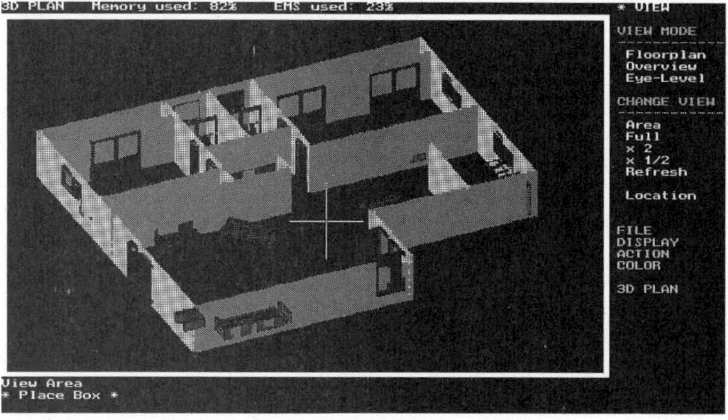

Figure 3.134. Using the Overview mode.

Outdoors

If rendering indoor spaces is challenging, outdoors is even more so. The variables that are so overwhelming indoors only become more numerous. In addition, nature enters the picture—grass, clouds, trees, and other detailed, complex objects.(76) Granted, there are techniques for dealing with such objects, but this greatly increases the load on the computer.

One way around this is obvious: Don't bother to render all the details. Of course, it helps if you do a great job with what you do render—the missing details are less noticeable. Figure 3.135 shows a rendering of a cathedral created in 3D Studio.(77)

Figure 3.135. A rendering of a cathedral in 3D Studio.

There's no lawn, no trees, and the windows look glued on, but this rendering is still impressive.(78) If the rendering itself isn't sufficient to impress you, there's a flying animation of a trip around and over the cathedral on the CD-ROMs.

---

76 The science of fractals is what enables computers to render such objects in anything even approaching a reasonable amount of time. It would be impossible to render every blade of grass in a lawn or every leaf on a tree.

77 The source file is one of many, many samples provided with 3D Studio. 3D Studio comes with a CD that has hundreds of files of all kinds that you can use to create renderings, or to use within your own renderings.

78 It's even more impressive in color, of course.

Sometimes, the problem isn't too many details; sometimes, in order to achieve a realistic rendering, you need to remove details. Objects fade with distance—in the real world, a distant mountain shows almost no details.[79] Fog is similar (see fig. 3.136).

Figure 3.136. Virtual fog.

Unfortunately, a lack of detail is sometimes simply unavoidable. It takes time to add the little details that add the extra touch of realism, and time isn't always available.[80] Figure 3.137 shows a portion of the same virtual space used for figure 3.136. This portion of the file doesn't have a lot of detail. That doesn't matter in the view of figure 3.136 because the street level is so far away, and obscured by fog as well. If you look at figure 3.136 carefully, you'll see that there are several cars down there on the street—just enough to suggest the idea of cars in the street. You don't realize how empty the streets are until you get down there and look.

Speaking of details, I decided to render a view of this cityscape at night, using low light levels. The first rendering looked wrong, and it didn't take long to figure out why: There were no lights at street level. The cars didn't have headlights or taillights. There were no streetlights. The traffic signals (you can see a few in fig. 3.137) didn't signal. It would take a lot of effort to add all those lights. To see just how much work it would take, I added headlights to each of the cars.

---

79 You can create a hyper-real landscape by leaving out the haze, of course.

80 At least right now it takes time. Perhaps someday, after we've all taken the time to create all the wonderful details of everyday life electronically, all we'll have to do is pull virtual stuff out of a virtual library—light bulbs, sidewalks, front doors, pottery, sofas, and ice cream cones.

Figure 3.137. A cityscape without a lot of details.

A lot more work was involved than I expected.[81] I couldn't just go to the car menu and click on headlights; I had to use what was available to create headlights. I'll describe what it takes to create a single headlight. Step one is to create a light located just above a car's bumper. This involves clicking in one view to place the light, and then clicking a second time to place the light's target.[82] I then had to zoom in and out a bit to make sure that the light was, in fact, next to that car's bumper. Why, you ask? When working in Front, Top, or Side view, an object may look like it's where it is supposed to be, but it may actually be a million miles away—there's no way to tell what's going on in the third dimension without switching to another view. This is the bane of existence in the virtual fast lane.

Once the list exists, you must adjust it. A light has a couple of nested cones: the central cone (the hotspot), where the light is brightest, and the outside cone, where the light is weaker (called *falloff*). I set the width of the hotspot at 15 degrees, and the falloff at 45 degrees. I then made sure that the light was aimed slightly downward, just like a real headlight. Unfortunately, when I rendered the scene, I couldn't see any evidence whatsoever that I had just spent some time creating headlights. I had to make two changes to make the lights visible.

The first problem was with the street. A very dull, black material had been created to simulate the street, and it wasn't reflecting any of the light. A real street, of course, is black, but it reflects some light. I had to go into the Materials Editor and muck around with the characteristics of the street. I added a little shininess and modified the way that the material responded to light. I went back and forth a few times until I had it right.

---

[81]I did this in 3D Studio; I don't know why I expected that it wouldn't take time.

[82]In 3D Studio, lights have targets.

Figure 3.138. The city at night, courtesy of 3D Studio.

The second problem involved the nature of lights in 3D Studio. You can see the effects of a light, but you won't see the light itself. So I had to add little globes just behind each light and set properties in the Materials Editor so that the globes glowed enough to look like headlights.

The result of all this effort is shown in figure 3.138. It's like one of those Waldo books: can you find the headlights? After all the work, you can't even see them at this point in the animation (frame 92 of 150). That's more of life in the virtual fast lane.

In the last few frames of the animation, when the point of view is much closer to street level, the headlights are quite noticeable (see fig. 3.139).

Of course, while working with the model in Wireframe mode, I had little idea of what the headlights would look like. Figure 3.140 shows a screen from 3D Studio during the creation process. The view at the upper left shows a car from above, with two lights and two targets (the vertical lines connect lights and targets). The view at the bottom left is a close-up from the side of the small spheres that show up as the bright lights in figure 3.139, and the view at the bottom right shows an overview of a portion of the city with cars in it.

The point of this is that there is an enormous amount of effort and care that goes into a photo-realistic virtual space. It gave me a real appreciation for the details of everyday life. Virtual Rome cannot be built in a day.

Figure 3.139. Virtual head-lights in frame 143 of 150.

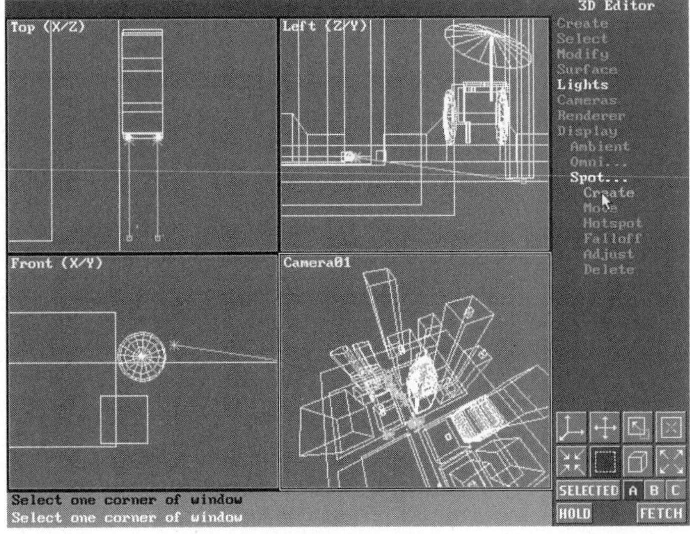

Figure 3.140. Creating headlights in 3D Studio.

4

VIRTUAL FUN

Even the most hard-core computer user probably wishes computers were more fun. Not that software vendors haven't tried—the next time you visit your local software store, compare the shelf space used for software and for games. In most cases, you'll see at least as much space devoted to games as to business software—sometimes more.

While you're in the store, ask the manager a simple question: which games are selling the best? The answer: 3D games sell better than any other category. The same is true of shareware games—titles like DOOM and Wolfenstein 3D are the hottest thing going. As a public service,[1] you'll find a number of 3D shareware games on the CD-ROMs that come with this book. Check the table of contents on the disc for instructions.

3D and the Inner Child

A little kid lurks inside every computer user. That much is clear from the huge number of games on dealer shelves. What is it about 3D games, and even the use of 3D in business software, that makes it so appealing? Was it the new features that made Windows 3.0 such a smashing success, or was it really those 3D buttons?

Without a moment's hesitation, I'll assert that Windows succeeded because it used 3D in small but important ways. The 3D look gave Windows legitimacy in a way that no other feature could. Think about it: before the 3D look, Windows was an interesting also-ran, sitting on as many bookshelves as hard disks. Put a little 3D in, and wham!—a revolution occurs.

Microsoft offers a lot of reasons for the success of Windows 3.*x*, such as

- The huge product roll-out, with live video conferences in cities all over the United States;
- The all-new GPF to replace the all-too-common UAE; and
- The addition of sound and other multimedia support.

These are not the reasons why Windows became a success. No one who actually buys Windows ever goes to such conferences; they're for guys in suits with big offices. GPF, UAE—gimme a break here; a crash is a crash, even if it only brings down the system half as often. As for multimedia, how many computers were already set up for multimedia when Windows was introduced?

---

[1]As if putting games on the CD is anything but a cold-blooded appeal to the child in every reader. Hi. I'm the author's alter-ego, Clarence. The author has certain obligations to his editor and society, but I don't. I'll be watching over Ron's shoulder throughout this chapter, and you can count on me to give you the real story.

I'm exaggerating here, of course,[2] but I'm doing it to make a point. Maybe 3D didn't put Windows on tens of millions of computers overnight, but it makes a Big Difference:[3] Buttons are really *buttons* now, not just little pictures with lines around them.

More precisely: virtual buttons. Remember those Fisher-Price crib toys that provide a row of buttons? Each button does something cute when the baby pushes it—a cow makes a "moo" sound, a door opens to reveal a picture of a turkey,[4] or a bell rings. That's what a toolbar is: the adult version of that old crib toy.

Many[5] psychologists define play as "anything that provides a large reward for a small effort." Do you see the connection? A simple little click on a toolbar button gives you big dialog boxes. No need to hunt through menus to find the commonly used tools (that's work); just click on a picture (that's play).

What does all this have to do with virtual reality? The answer is coming right up.

Virtual Reality as a Game

When a new computer product enters the market, it tends to sputter and flop around a bit before it becomes well known and successful.[6] During this time, whole legions of news reporters, computer columnists, and magazine editors spend infinite hours of their time theorizing about

- Why the new product came into being;
- Whether it represents an Entire New Category of software;
- Who will use the new software;
- What implications for the industry are inherent in the new software; and
- Whether anyone will actually spend money on it.[7]

---

[2]Like heck! He's silly enough to believe every word of what he's saying.

[3]With apologies to Douglass Adams for stealing the device of capitalizing Big Ideas.

[4]Hey—this is sounding more and more like software as we go along!

[5]Some.

[6]Unfortunately, some flounder, sputter, and do painful things to your computer even after they become successful!

[7]Do you know why we face a glut of monstrously huge software products these days? It's harder to pirate a piece of software that requires 10 pounds of documentation. If you ever spent some time at the photocopier making pirate documentation, those days are now officially over.

If you look through the computer press, you find exactly these kinds of discussions going on about virtual reality. Everyone is acting as though VR is some kind of New Thing. It's not new at all. In fact, at every stage of computing, as soon as the CPU power grows enough to support the next level of VR, it gets added. The most notable additions of VR to the common computing repertoire are listed in table 4.1.

Table 4.1. Virtual Reality That We Already Use.

Item	*VR Justification*
The mouse[8]	A device which, although not as sophisticated as a Power Glove, still allows you to move around in a virtual space.
GUI (Graphical User Interface)	Virtual desktop—that's what they called it at first, remember?[9]
3D buttons	Buttons have evolved from a mere box-shaped outline to a complete simulation with an animated click—how virtual does it have to be?
The toolbar[10]	Crib toy for adults

Soon, we'll have useful speech recognition and other advances, too. Speaking of speech, there's an interesting demo program on the CD-ROMs—InCube. As with all stuff on the CD-ROMs, just check the table of contents on the disc to find what you need.[11]

Cool Games

Since shortly after computers first arrived into our lives, one category of software has been driving the development of new technology more than any other: games. It is in games that the latest advances in multimedia and VR show up first. Games are where the risks are taken, the advances made. In our endless search for

[8]Can anyone explain why the price of a mouse varies from $19.95 to more than $100 for exactly the same functionality??? I mean, let's get real here.

[9]And you thought virtual reality was new...

[10]Didn't anybody patent this thing? They're everywhere—even places where they don't work. Somebody could've made a mint on this idea.

[11]Isn't organization wonderful? If he really cared, he'd tell you where it was.

knowledge and cool stuff to pass on to you, dear reader, we have left no CD unturned in our effort to find the coolest of the cool—the games that make your hair stand on end.

We looked at many games, and some were good and some were (horror of horrors!) boring. There are three major categories:

- Action games like DOOM, Blake Stone, Raptor, and Bio Menace. You are involved in a life-or-death struggle with an enemy and must shoot your way out of danger.
- CD adventure games like Myst, Iron Helix, Return to Zork, and Stunt Island. These are less adrenaline-raising games that sometimes offer subtle clues to unlocking puzzles.
- "Educational" games like SimCity 2000 and Math and Word Rescue. You build, test yourself, answer questions, or otherwise engage your mind in fun and playful ways.

Many games run only in DOS,[12] and they will test your ingenuity before you even play them. The DOS games require a ***lot*** of memory in order to run. Blake Stone, for example, requires 615,000 bytes of free conventional memory. You can't even think of playing such a game without DOS 6.2. If you haven't already done so, you should set up separate game-only CONFIG.SYS and AUTOEXEC.BAT files that set up your system for absolute minimum memory requirements. Before playing games, reboot with the minimum memory configuration. If you are unsure about how to set up for lots and lots of memory, I have some good news: Each of the games we reviewed had a help or README file that gave tips on how to optimize your system memory. MS-DOS 6.*x* manuals can help you out, too.[13]

A few adventure games run under Windows, and many of these, too, have unique system requirements that are listed with the game. When it comes to games, ignore the README files at your peril.

---

[12]Windows adds some overhead that can slow down games. As we were writing this chapter, Microsoft announced a new Windows interface for games that promises to greatly speed up graphics performance. Look for new Windows game titles by late 1994.

[13]The MS-DOS 6 manuals have a detailed section in the User's Guide on how to make more memory available. It has step-by-step instructions on how to optimize memory by using MemMaker. MemMaker looks over your existing memory configuration and suggests an optimum memory configuration for your machine. It increases efficiency by moving device drivers and memory-resident programs into available UMBs (upper memory blocks), and fine-tunes memory by changing the order of commands in your startup files. If you don't like the new memory configuration, you can always undo it. Once you find a satisfactory memory configuration, you can set up separate CONFIG.SYS and AUTOEXEC.BAT files for each configuration. See your DOS manual for details. I experimented with MemMaker and came up with a bare-bones configuration that I use for all VR DOS games. A word of warning, however: MemMaker is playing with fire and may occasionally backfire. When this happens, you should have a backup copy of your original configuration files to fall back on.

Don't assume anything when you start out to play a new game. These puppies are pushing the outer envelope of what can be done on a PC, and each game probably has some special requirements you'll need to know about. Read the README file carefully, and look for items relating to specific hardware or software you use regularly.

Installation procedures for several of the DOS games will ask you to specify an interrupt (IRQ), I/O, MIDIPORT, DMA channel, and so on. If you have not already installed your sound card, keep track of this information as you go. If you installed your sound card some time ago (like I did) and didn't record the settings, run the configuration or setup program.

I have a Sound Blaster sound card, and the configuration program (SBCONFIG.EXE) is located in the SB16 directory. See the end of this chapter for information about setting up a Sound Blaster 16; other sound cards will have similar procedures.

Memory management for DOS games is critical. Some third-party memory managers may not work properly with some games. Read the game documentation carefully if you are using a memory manager other than the one that ships with DOS.

Action Games

DOOM v1.2

DOOM is a shoot-'em-up action game that really gets the adrenaline going.(14) I (Donna) had never played an action game like DOOM, and none of the video arcade games prepared me for this experience. Probably the closest experience I can

---

[14]I have always preferred the tamer sort of adventure games, such as Myst or Return to Zork, that challenge a player to find clues and unlock hidden mysteries. But I have to admit, I got a real rush the first time I played DOOM. I could hear beasts growling in the background, and cautiously crept forward, peering around corners. I totally panicked when I saw a monster coming at me,

think of was sitting in the theater watching the *Terminator* movies. *This* is what it's like to actually lose yourself in an alternate reality. No helmet, no tactors,[15] not even total immersion, but each time I play the game I am totally caught up in this nightmare reality.[16]

I experienced an interesting physical reaction after playing some VR games. I am particularly susceptible to motion sickness, which may explain why I was affected and the rest of my family wasn't. After playing Raptor for about an hour, I felt very dizzy. The computer monitor was moving up and down as if I were sitting in a boat that was rocking up and down.

Something similar occurred after I had been playing DOOM for several hours. I had had a particularly busy morning, and decided to take off an afternoon and play DOOM—to really get a feel for the game and see how far I could get. There were no phone calls or interruptions, and I lost track of time. For that period of time, I was a marine fighting for my life.

When I came back to my "normal" reality, I realized I was staring at my computer screen, completely tense. My back was stiff and my palms were sweaty. I got up and walked out to the mailbox to relax. For a brief period of time, I was disoriented. My eyes had trouble adjusting to the sun, and I was slightly dizzy. I had no idea I had been so intensely involved in the game, but I can see how moving from one reality to another can affect you physically. I've read the reported side effects from extended use of HMDs and can see how this is possible. Although the effects quickly passed, I thought I'd pass this along. The moral of the story: Stay cool. Remember! It's just a game. Isn't it?

14(cont'd)and reacted at a very primal level. I experienced the same emotions I would in any life-threatening situation—and received an adrenaline rush that lasted throughout the game. So this is what all the fuss is about—you get a natural high! And the game is addictive. I watched Ron and my son sit at the computer for several hours trying to shoot their way out of a maze—and die several times before finally succeeding. Playing DOOM is a great way to get out your frustrations after a particularly trying day. "Take that, Sucker!" has a whole new meaning when you're standing with a machine gun in your hands facing a huge monster belching flames and smoke at you!

15*Tactors* are devices that provide tactile feedback.

16That's why we measure virtual reality success in human terms, not in artificial terms such as interactivity. Like a good book, good VR is involving. If it makes you sweat, it's good VR.

Setting Up Memory

DOOM uses DOS-protected mode, which means that it takes advantage of extended memory.[17] To configure DOOM for best use of memory, set up a minimum memory configuration and do the following:

- DOOM requires that you have 4M of RAM installed to run. Also: Make sure you have 3M of free RAM available.
- Do not use any memory managers such as EMM386 or QEMM, and so on. If you must, use the NOEMS option.
- Do not use any disk-caching programs like SMARTDRV.
- Load all the drivers and TSRs high that you can using DEVICEHIGH (CONFIG.SYS) or LOADHIGH (AUTOEXEC.BAT), as appropriate.[18]
- Use the MEM command with the /c switch to examine the layout of your machine's memory. This tells you how much memory each driver or TSR is using, and the size of contiguous memory blocks available for loading high. For best results, type

  mem /c | more

  to avoid information scrolling off the screen.[19]
- Load your mouse driver because you'll want the option of using your mouse and keyboard simultaneously with DOOM. You also can use a joystick as an alternative, but the keyboard/mouse combination worked very well for us.

Okay—Let's Play

Before you begin the game, read the README file by typing **readme** in the DOOM directory. It contains the DOOM Manual and Getting Started instructions, provides registration information, and lists brief descriptions of new features in version 1.2

---

[17]Some games use expanded memory; always check their documentation. We (like many folks running Windows) use the NOEMS parameter on EMM386.EXE in our CONFIG.SYS file. That meant changing the CONFIG.SYS file before using some games.

[18]I would strongly recommend not loading DOS games onto DoubleSpace compressed drives. When you use DoubleSpace, you lose about 50K of conventional memory—and that's a big chunk that your games may require. You can free up additional conventional memory by not loading your DoubleSpace driver into memory. If you have a minimum memory configuration in your startup files and have DoubleSpace drives you don't need, reboot your system setup with minimum memory configuration. When the message `Starting MS-DOS...` appears, press Ctrl-F8. This tells DOS not to load the DoubleSpace drives. Press Y to step through the commands in CONFIG.SYS and AUTOEXEC.BAT.

[19]Suggestion: Put this line in a batch file so you can run it easily and often.

and bugs fixed from version 1.1. The README file also provides background information on the game to give you some perspective on your adventure. It also provides the details of your mission, should you decide to accept it. You'll learn about the weapons provided, armor and health bonuses, and all the other features of the game. The end of the README file contains instructions for multiplayer and network play.[(20)]

Figures 4.1 and 4.2. Beginning screens for DOOM to select the game and episode.

When you are ready to begin the game, you are presented with a series of menu options. You can select a new game, load or save an existing game, or quit. The Options item lets you exit the game; turn messages (displayed at the top of the screen) on or off; and change the level of graphic detail, screen size, mouse sensitivity, or sound volume. The Read This! item contains an About screen and a brief list of navigation keys. You can access this menu at any time during the game by pressing Esc. I soon developed a habit of saving my game at the beginning of a level. I used the Quicksave feature whenever I completed a sticky task and didn't want to start over again.[(21)]

---

[20]Yes, you can involve your friends in the frenzy of DOOM. You can play by modem, or over a network. You can join with your friends to kill the bad guys, or you can try to kill each other. DOOM is very flexible that way. One Sams editor reports that it's fun to play DOOM by modem while using speaker phones for a conference call!

[21]And there are plenty of sticky tasks. There are times when you will be overwhelmed by the challenges, and it's nice to have a quick way of returning from the dead to have at it again.

If you choose the option for a New Game, you are given an opportunity to choose between three games.[22] Once you choose a game, you must determine your skill level. The highest level (naturally!) is Nightmare.

If you do not select any of the options, the game begins a self-running demo.[23] The demo takes you through a quick tour of the game and is useful for finding secrets, hidden passageways, and other hints and tips. When I get stuck on a level, I go through the demo again and try to pick up some tricks. But there's nothing like the first time you play the game and get to navigate through the corridors and up the stairs by yourself. Turning a corner, not knowing what to expect, is what DOOM is all about.[24]

Figure 4.3.
In the lobby with only a pistol for protection.

You begin DOOM in the lobby with a pistol in front of you. The only weapons you have at your disposal at first are a pistol and your fists. The optimum fun for me is using a mouse for navigating and firing your weapon, and the keyboard for switching weapons or pressing the space bar to open doors.

It takes a while to get the hang of navigation. I found myself bumping into walls or falling off stairs, with an echoing grunt from the character I'm playing. Or shooting at every strange sound. In the background are the growls and gun shots from your opponents.[25]

---

[22] If you are playing the shareware version (that is, you haven't registered), you have only one game to play—the first in the series. To play the other two games, you must register and they will be sent to you.

[23] You will be amazed the first time you watch the demo—particularly when you find yourself with a chainsaw in your hand. Ugh! My son's reaction? "Oh, wow! Who's the bad guy? Are we the bad guy? Can I play?" Hint: You'll see some interesting possibilities during the demo. It moves at a very fast pace, but pay attention—you can get some great ideas for later, when you are playing the game.

[24] I often find myself shouting out things like "Take that!" or "Yikes!" as the game unfolds—DOOM is very involving.

[25] You will even hear grunts from the other side of a wall—that's your clue that there's something there. After you've killed all the bad guys, if you still hear growls and grunts, there's more to do. Your job becomes finding the hidden doorway that will lead you to the next battle.

It doesn't take long to learn how to position yourself to go around corners or to climb a stairway. Unlike some VR products (VREAM, for example) you cannot go through objects. They provide resistance. Walls, for example, act just like walls.[26]

Figures 4.4 through 4.7. Navigating stairs to gather bonus armory points and armor.

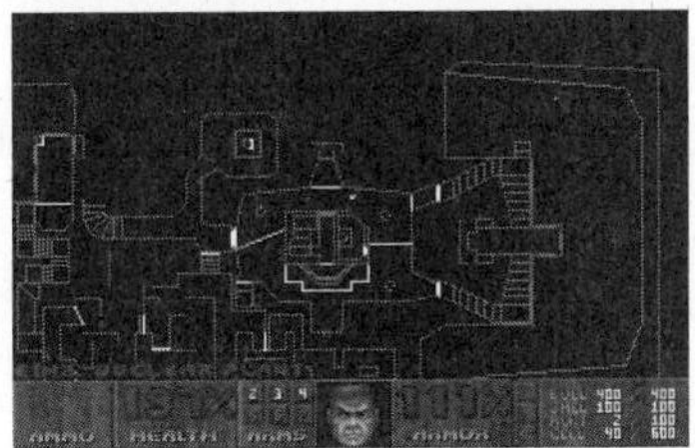

[26]Some walls are actually secret doors, but I won't spoil the fun by revealing too much.

One of my first accomplishments was to successfully climb the stairs off the lobby, and recover a vest and armor bonus. As you can see, the graphics are realistic but not high resolution. Color is used effectively to help clue you in. The vest is a bright green, while the armor bonus has a dull green fluorescent glow. The object of the game is to gather bonus points, weapons, ammunition, and secrets before moving to the next level. And, of course, to blast your adversaries to smithereens!

When you kill an enemy, his carcass lies there. Figure 4.6 shows the remains of an enemy on the left side of the screen under the window. Not only must you look at the carnage, but you can pick up his ammunition if you move over his body. Gruesome, huh?

You soon learn how to use your weapons to greatest advantage. Although the machine gun is extremely effective at picking off a large number of opponents, you quickly run out of ammunition. If you find a backpack, you can carry extra ammo. But the most effective way to fight your enemy is by alternating between a variety of weapons. Skill is important: You can nail even the baddest of bad guys with your shotgun if you fire without missing a beat.

You learn how to advance, retreat, and take cover behind corners or panels. Rather than bumping into walls, you learn how to use them to protect you from oncoming shots and blasts of fire. For some real fun, try charging your enemies and engaging them hand-to-gun.

Figures 4.8 through 4.17. A view of 360-degree rotation in the tower.

SCREEN SHOT

SCREEN SHOT

SCREEN SHOT

SCREEN SHOT

One of my most important discoveries was learning how to use the mouse to move around and turn.[27] Your movements are bidirectional, and you cannot jump or crouch. But you have the ability to control the speed and direction of your character. In the screen shots shown in Figures 4.8 through 4.17, you get a 360-degree view of the turret. The room looks outside onto some mountains and an outdoor area, and you can see from the screens how realistic the graphics are.

Figure 4.18.
Flip the switch.

During your travels, you will encounter rooms with a switch on the wall. If you press the space bar (or double-click the mouse button) you activate a switch that will open a door or reveal a hidden passageway. You have to go searching to find the door or passageway, as it isn't always obvious. And some of the hidden accesses have a time limit. If you don't move fast enough, you lose out.

---

[27]DOOM also supports the Logitech Cyberman, an inexpensive six-degrees-of-freedom input device. The hand controller buzzes and shakes when you are shot.

Notice the status bar at the bottom of the screen in Figure 4.18. It provides useful information on the amount of ammunition you have available, the percentage of health left (0% means you die!), the weapons at your disposal, and the percentage of armor you have for protection against oncoming fire. The "mug" in the middle is more than a self-portrait. It alerts you to the direction in which an enemy can be found, and as you lose health, the face shows the effects. There is also a color indicator if you find color-coded keys to high security areas, and the information on the far right tells you how many bullets you have for each of your weapons.

Sometimes you have to swim through pools of poison to flip a switch. If you take too long, the poison kills you. If you aren't careful and fall into a deep well of poison, you may not be able to get out.

Figure 4.19.
A pool of poison.

Figure 4.20.
A radiation suit.

Occasionally you will be lucky enough to find protective gear like these radiation suits. They are only effective for a brief period of time, so you must act fast before the effects wear off. They are good protection if you must swim through poison to reach secret rooms.

In some screens, you can see a medical kit in the far left background. Take note of these, even if your health is good and you aren't in need when you find one. If you have a particularly rugged shoot-out, you may want to backtrack to a secure area and pick up some health bonuses, medikits, and stimpaks. They can mean the difference between life and death.

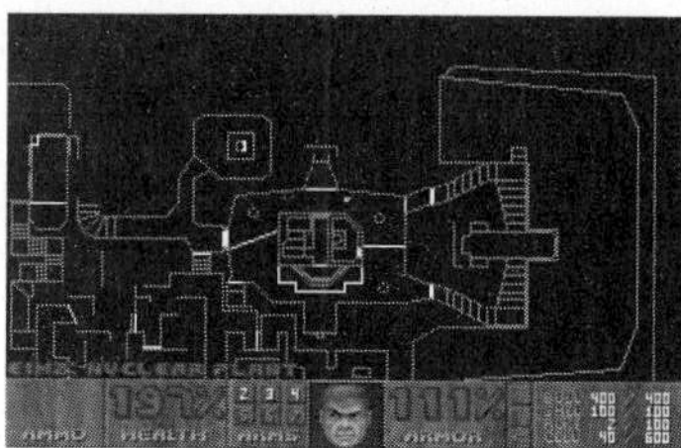

Figure 4.21. An automap diagram of the Nuclear Plant.

There are many mazes and corridors you must search through. It's easy to get lost and end up going in circles. The Tab key lets you easily toggle to a map that displays a schematic diagram of the building you are in. You can't see your opponents, but you can find entrances and corridors and get a different perspective on things.

Each level has an Exit door. When you have killed as many opponents as you can find, gathered as many items as you can use or carry, and can't find anymore secrets, it is time to exit. If you are not ready to exit, simply go back out the way you came, take note of where the exit was for future reference, and go look around some more.

Figure 4.22. Tally your points at the end of a level.

When you press the lever to exit, you are presented with a screen that tallies up the percentage of kills, items recovered, and secrets found. The goal, naturally, is to have 100% before exiting. You carry the items found with you to the next level. So, if you found a shotgun, chain gun, or chainsaw, you have the option of using them in the next level. Otherwise, you must rapidly search out new weaponry.

Figure 4.23. Your new target is the Nuclear Plant.

When you have completed one level and are ready to move on to the next, you are given a topographical map that shows the next building you must secure. You can press the Tab key to see an automap with a schematic diagram of the building.

Be on your guard when you begin a new level. The beasts get bigger and meaner as the game progresses. Some of them are nearly invisible—just an outline of a figure that comes out of the middle of nowhere.

You can save up to six games and start wherever you left off. The Pause button on your keyboard temporarily pauses the game if you are interrupted.

DOOM is the kind of game that will keep your interest for hours on end. It's a real blast![28]

---

[28]If you will pardon the pun.

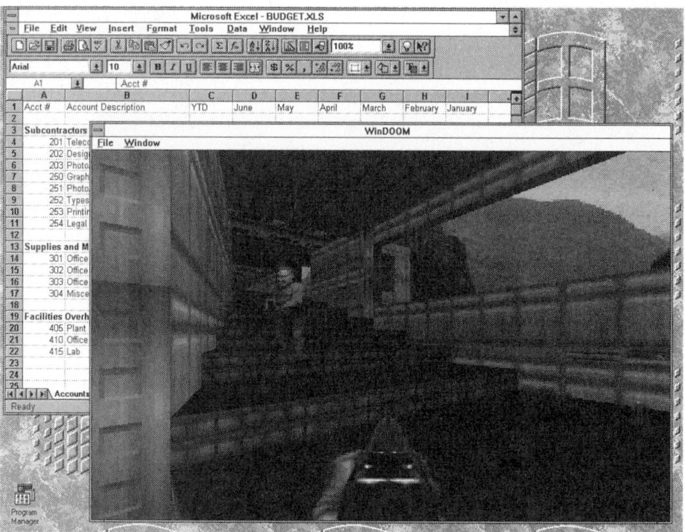

Figure 4.24.
Screen shot of WinDOOM.

Windows Version of DOOM

id Software is currently working on a Windows version of DOOM that will be available around Christmas 1994. It will have improved graphics and screen resolution. So mark your calendar.

Raptor

Raptor is a DOS-based game that puts you in the cockpit of a plane with turbine engines. You earn money on each mission, with which you can purchase additional weapons.[29]

During setup and installation, you select the game control type: mouse, keyboard, or joystick; music card; and sound device. If you have a sound card, the music and sound effects greatly enhance the game. The music in the opening sequence is really deep and full, and creates a feeling of anticipation.

If you select the option for a New Mission from the main menu, you are given the opportunity to select your call sign. You can select your pilot ID picture by clicking on ID with the mouse button. I chose a red-headed female and gave her the call sign Babe. Is this fantasy time, or what?

---

[29] Unless, of course, you fail and go down in flames.

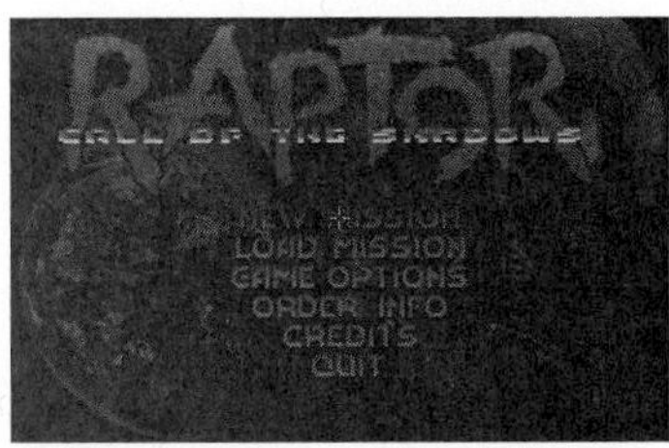

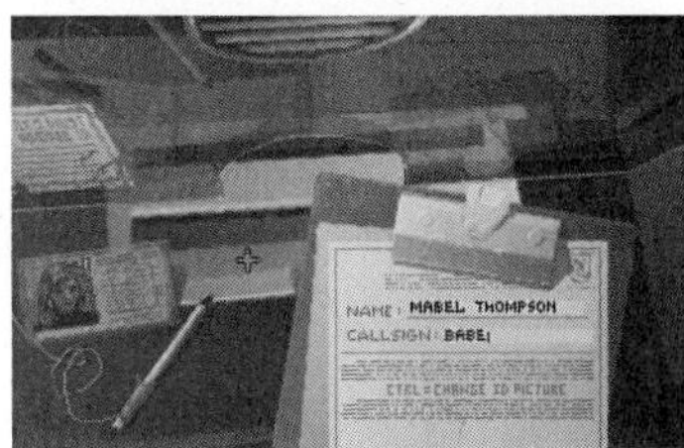

Figures 4.25 and 4.26. Raptor's main menu and call sign.

Figures 4.27 and 4.28. Choose the level of difficulty and your weapons.

Once you have selected your call sign, you have to select the level of difficulty. Training mode lets you familiarize yourself with the game and its controls, but you can't earn any money. Rookie is the easy level, with Veteran for medium difficulty and Elite for the brave (or foolhardy).

Once you pick the difficulty level, you enter the Hangar, where you have the opportunity to save the game (press F2 inside the hangar), enter the Supply Room to purchase supplies with money awarded in previous missions, fly a new mission, or leave the Hangar and return to the main menu.

Figure 4.29.
The Hangar.

The Supply Room offers an opportunity to select as many weapons as you can afford. I recommend starting out with lots of shields. It took me a while to figure out I had tons of ammo and could shoot it out the entire game. But I took a lot of hits and went down in flames the first couple of times. The plane is maneuverable, and a smart pilot will dodge incoming fire.

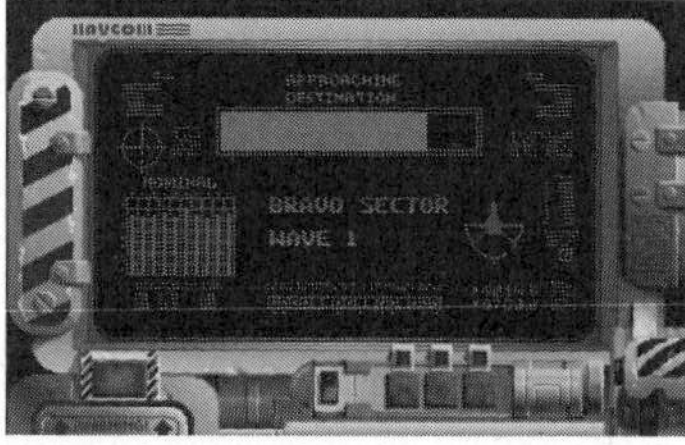

Figure 4.30.
The Flight Computer for Raptor.

After you select your weapons, you select a mission. The flight computer is displayed on your screen as your approach your destination. Be ready, 'cause you are about to take on several types of aircraft, ending with the mother of all aircraft!

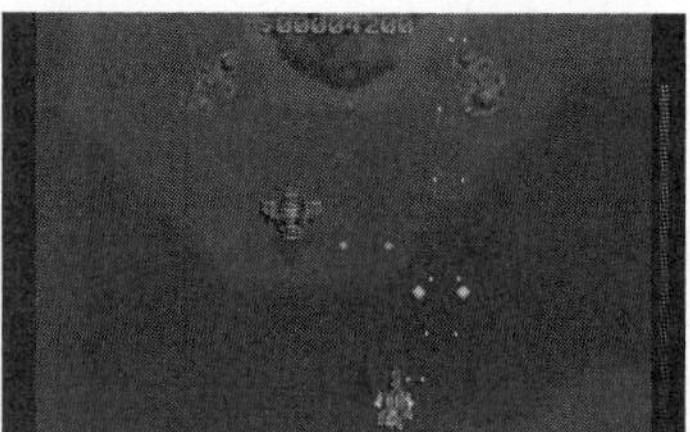

Figures 4.31 and 4.32.
Some aircraft give off a golden glow that awards you extra money. And you can increase your weaponry by destroying some land-based operations.

Ever watch the movie *Top Gun*? That's what Raptor reminded me of. On a much smaller scale, of course, but this is the first flight simulator I've used and it was fun to feel like I was flying an aircraft.

Navigation is pretty simple. Moving the mouse sideways causes a lateral move of the plane, and moving forward and backward repositions the plane accordingly.

The graphics may not be at the level of games like Myst or Zork, but they were good enough to make the game really enjoyable. Some of the planes produce a golden glow when destroyed and give you a bonus if you pick them up. Missiles also destroy buildings on the land, and occasionally they can add to your firepower.

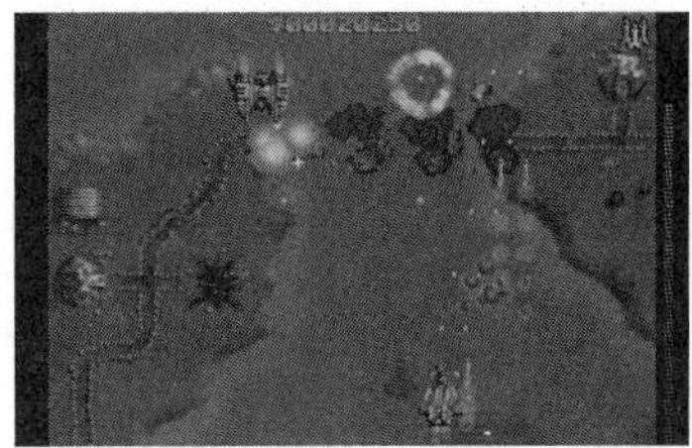

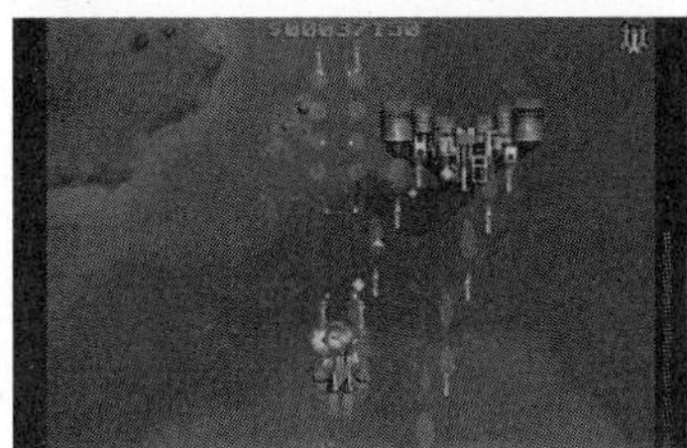

Figures 4.33 and 4.34. An enemy plan going up in flames and the mothership.

The graphics are pretty detailed, and enemy planes go up in flames. And just when you thought you had it made, you hear a deep rumble, see a large shadow coming in your direction, and encounter the mothership.

If you successfully complete your mission, you have money with which to buy additional weapons.

The game has limited navigation; for example, you can't turn your ship around. But you have quite a bit of maneuverability, and can move forward on the screen to take an aggressive posture, or fall back if you run into too many oncoming planes at once.

Raptor requires quick reflexes and an itchy trigger finger. You can outmaneuver the enemy if you play the game a couple of times. But it is a low-stress way to release a little frustration and have some fun. Raptor comes with an 11-page pamphlet but is intuitive enough to play by just sitting down and poking around.

Blake Stone

Blake Stone comes with a colorful manual that includes a comic book. My expectations were high for this game: it is the follow-up to Wolfenstein 3D: a classic of 3D gaming.

The colorful flyer gives the game a PC-13 rating, stating it is not recommended for younger viewers due to realistic depictions of violence. What a hoot!

Figure 4.35. The banner displayed when you start up Blake Stone.

I was impressed with the PC-13 screen that displays when you start up Blake Stone but still wasn't sure whether the game's creators were putting me on.

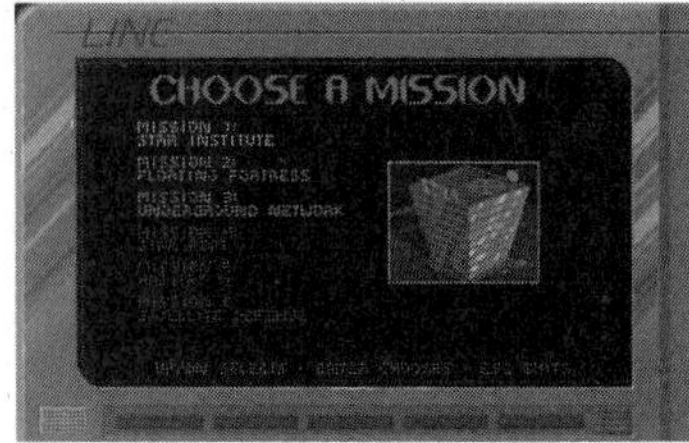

Figures 4.36 and 4.37. Startup screens for Blake Stone (choosing a mission and difficulty level).

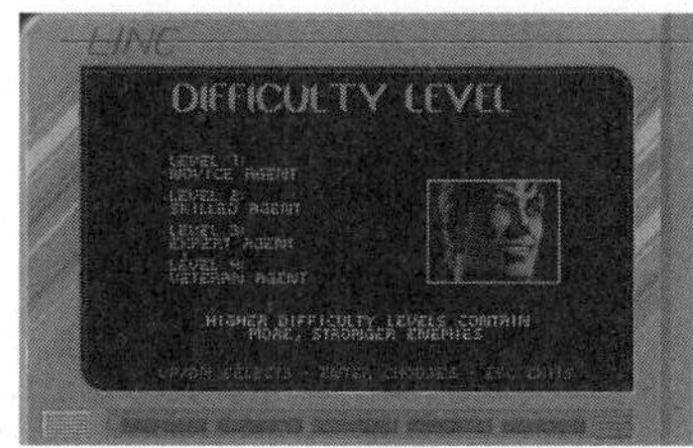

The next two screens are pretty standard stuff, so you can choose a mission and difficulty level. Pretty realistic graphics in the difficulty screen.

Figures 4.38 and 4.39. Initial startup screens of Blake Stone.

The opening screen bears a strong resemblance to DOOM, with the hand-held pistol looking down a corridor. And there are strong similarities between the two games, which reflects id Software's influence on the game. But I consider any contributions from DOOM to be on the plus side.

If you successfully defeat your opponent, you can pick up his weapon. However, if you encounter an informant (dressed in a white lab coat), you can query him and get important information. Of course, you take the risk that he has no information to offer and will shoot you.

Blake Stone has 3D texture mapping in 256 colors and feels like a VR game. You have the ability to maneuver and explore anywhere you have access. Once again,

I found myself bumping into walls trying to round corners or go through doorways. But the main difference between Blake Stone and DOOM is that Blake Stone has bright primary colors. This contributed to the feeling that it was just a game, and the lack of realism gives it less of an adrenalizing effect than DOOM.

There were enough similarities that my experience with DOOM made it easier to play Blake Stone without reading the instructions. Eventually, I read the background story so I could learn more about the game's nuances.

Figures 4.40 through 4.42. Barrier switches, shut-off arcs, and posts.

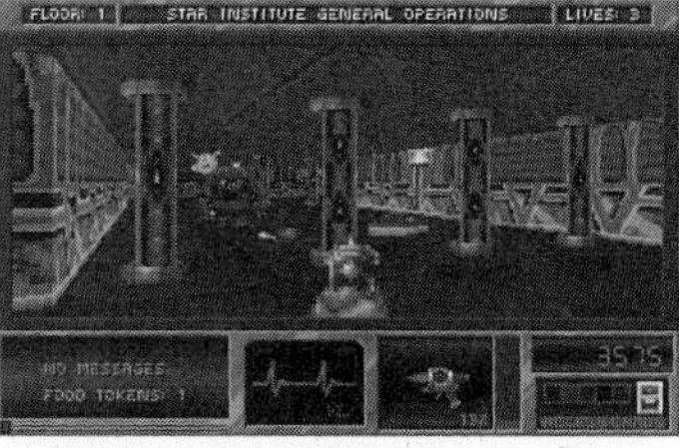

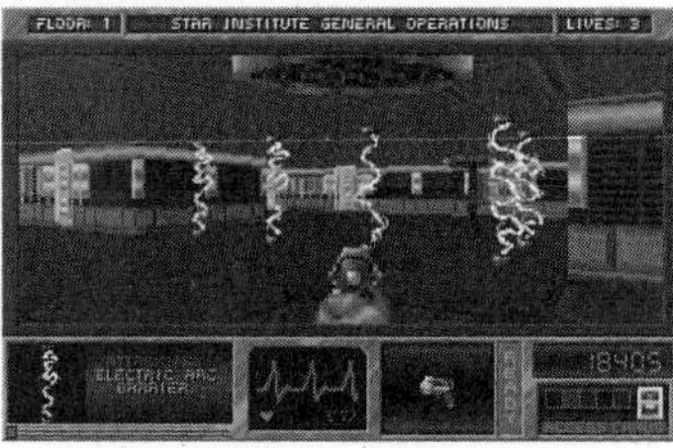

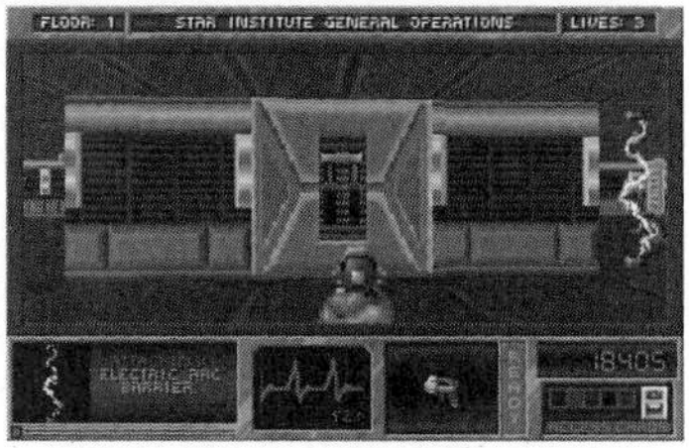

Blake Stone has great graphics, including detailed floors and ceilings. Sometimes, you encounter ugly enemies hidden behind arches and posts. If you find the barrier switch, you can shut these off and gain access.

You can access the automap feature by pressing the Tab key. The automap provides a color-coded map of the current floor. The right side gives you a tally of total points for the game, number of informants alive, and number of enemies destroyed.

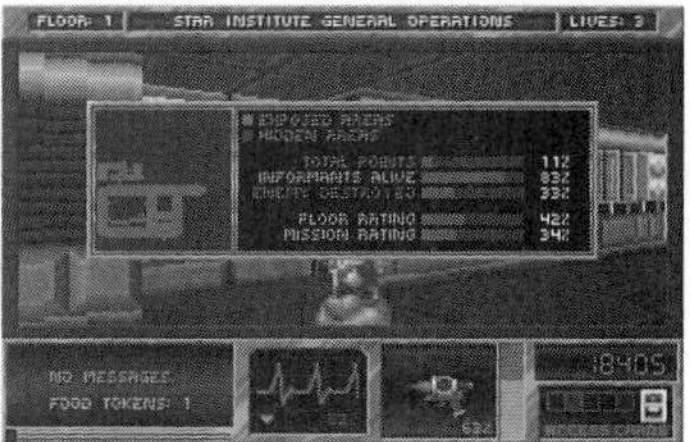

Figure 4.43. The built-in automapping feature from Blake Stone.

You move from one level to another via the elevator, but it will not operate unless you have the red access card—typical game stuff.

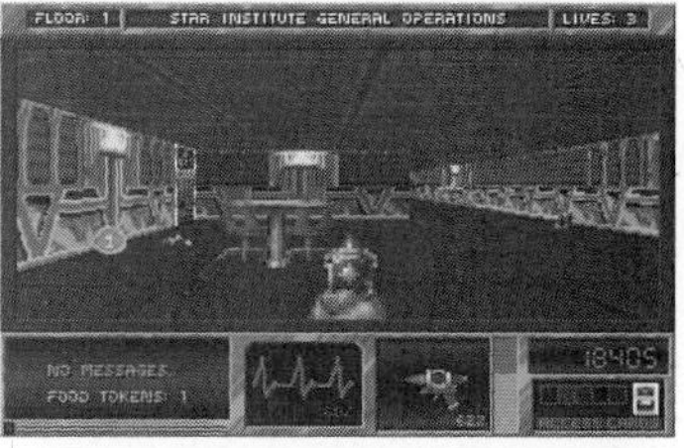

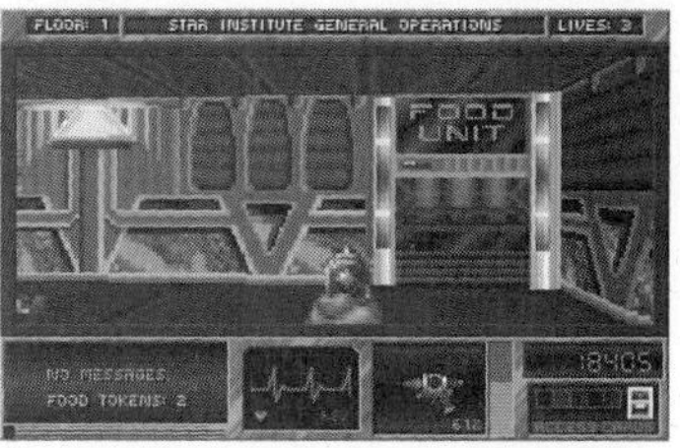

Figures 4.44 and 4.45. Looking at the eating lounge and food unit.

I enjoyed coming upon the eating area. The room is colorful and is complete with tables, chairs, and a food unit. If you have any tokens, you can buy food from the dispenser. This has the additional bonus of increasing your life expectancy.

Figures 4.46 and 4.47. If you successfully defeat the big enemies, you may find them guarding treasure.

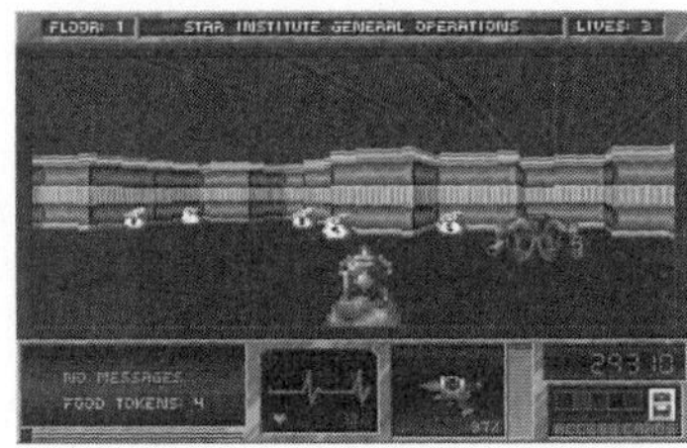

In Blake Stone, you aren't just fighting for your life or the cause—if you can survive the onslaught of Dr. Goldfire's enemies, you may stumble onto some booty.

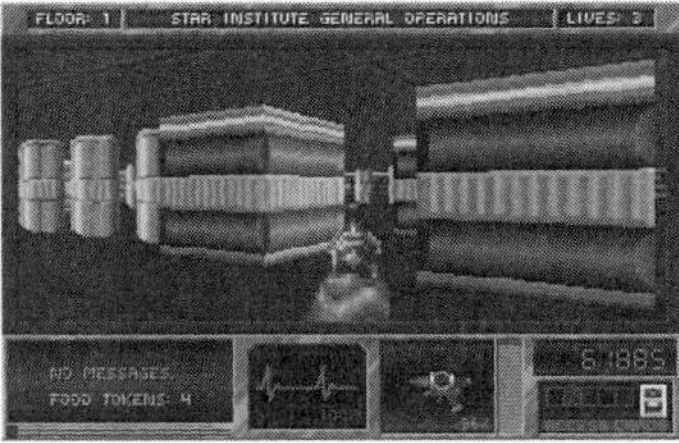

Figure 4.48. Check for hidden passageways.

You can sometimes find hidden passageways if you move along the wall and press the space bar.[30]

Figure 4.49. A blood-spattered maze.

When I came upon the passageway shown in figure 4.49, I realized why the game had a PC-13 rating. This room was pretty graphic and realistic, and could easily put you off if you're sensitive to violence.

---

[30]Sound familiar? If you've played DOOM, you discovered this trick. However, in DOOM you were alerted to a secret passageway by discoloration of the wall or the sound of a door opening and closing. I had no such clues to this movable wall in Blake Stone.

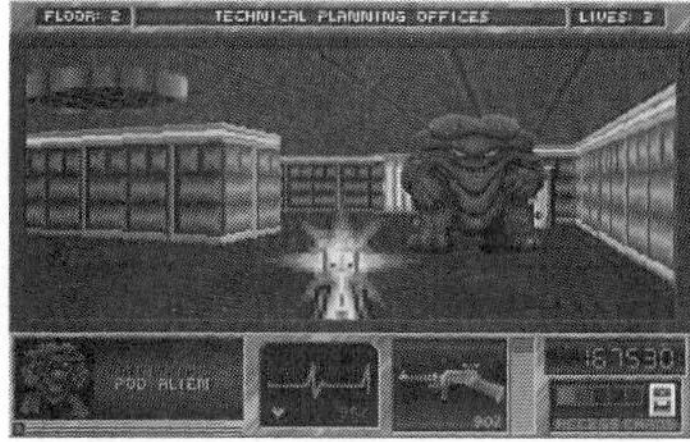

Figure 4.50. One of the slimy "boss" enemies you encounter in Blake Stone.

I enjoy Blake Stone as much as DOOM, but for different reasons. I like the challenge of exploring each of the levels to see what kinds of surprises I might find. And I love the detailed graphics and bright colors of Blake Stone; DOOM is dark and eerie.

The music and sound effects are fun and add a lot to Blake Stone. I really enjoy the ability to maneuver and explore areas without having to point and click. There's nothing that compares to real-time navigation, and Blake Stone offers detailed graphics with true VR-type navigation.[31]

3D Action Games

The following games were sent to us by Apogee Software when we put out the call for VR games, but they are more 3D than VR. They remind me of computerized versions of Nintendo and Sega games. But they're fun and colorful, so here are some samples.

Duke Nukem II

Figure 4.51. Duke Nukem is back!

[31] I can't help myself; I find myself continually comparing Blake Stone to DOOM. DOOM was the first game I played that offered real-time navigation through corridors, up stairs, and so on. And the menacing sounds and feeling of being hunted—as well as the hunted—in DOOM hit me at a guttural level that Blake Stone never touched. Blake Stone has cartoon-like monsters, so you remember it's a game. DOOM has more menacing-looking opponents, which gives a feeling of realism. I find Blake Stone more benign and more playful. But it would be difficult to choose between the two if I had to pick a favorite. Somehow, I can't see Blake Stone ever becoming the cult favorite that DOOM is.

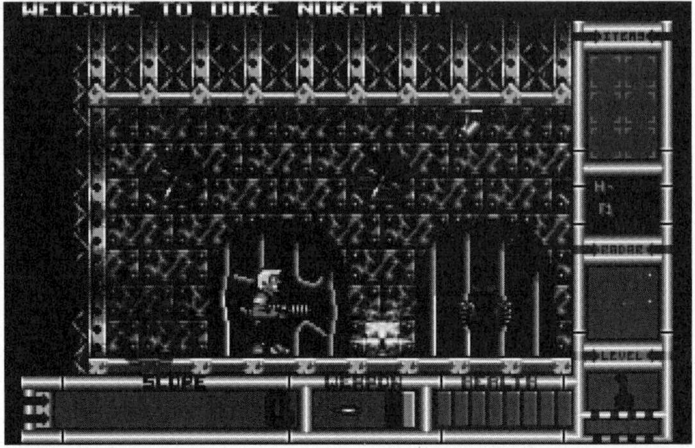

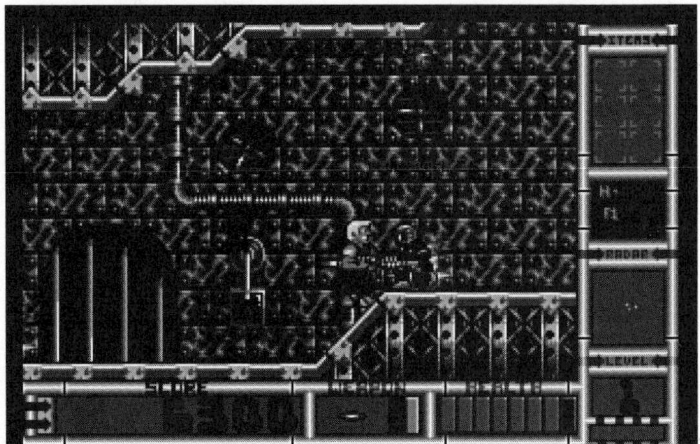

Figures 4.52 and 4.53. Duke goes after the bad guys in a big way.

Duke Nukem II has vivid, parallaxing VGA graphics; music, and digitized sound effects for Sound Blaster or compatible sound cards; and supports keyboard and joystick modes. The game is designed for all skill levels and has 32 levels in four episodes. It includes a Save and Restore feature that can be accessed from the main menu.

Halloween Harry

The All-American values of sex and violence are alive and well in this game, as can be seen from the opening screen.

Figure 4.54. The opening screen of Halloween Harry.

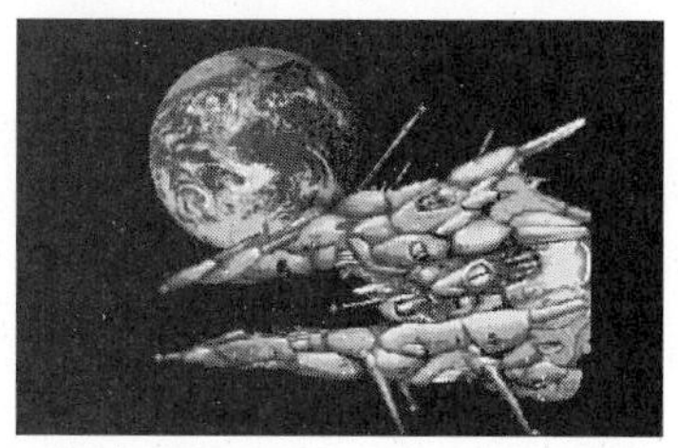

Figures 4.55 through 4.58. Earth is under attack by alien invaders, and Harry is the man for the job.

The story unfolds with a series of images that set the scene. It's the year 2030 A.D. and New York City is under attack by alien invaders. Halloween Harry is the hero of the hour. Duke Nukem fans should find a lot to like in the Halloween Harry game.

Figure 4.59. Halloween Harry encounters a zombie.

Figure 4.59 shows the 256-color scrolling graphics, which are supplemented with sound effects and music. Harry has the ability to fly through levels with his jetpack.

The system requirements for Halloween Harry are a VGA graphics adapter and an 80286 or better IBM-compatible machine. Joystick and Sound Blaster are optional.

Bio Menace

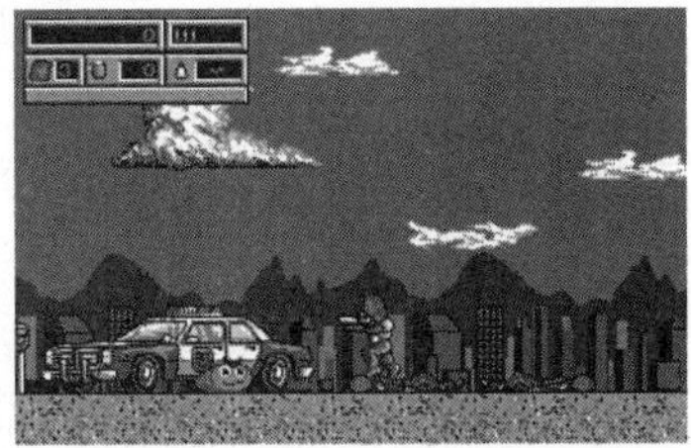

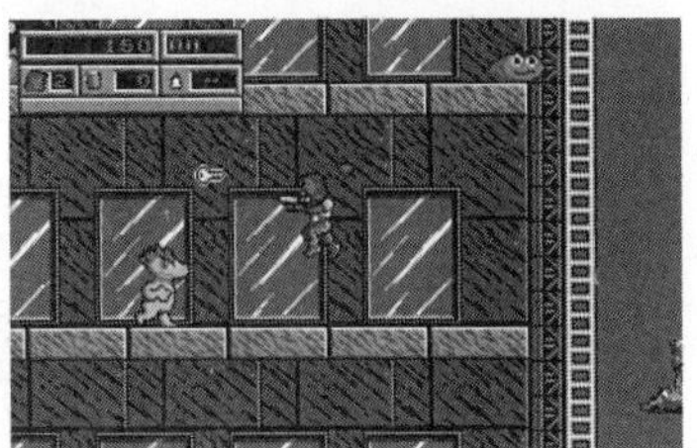

Figures 4.60 and 4.61. Super agent Snake Logan facing some of the mutants created by Dr. Mangle.

Bio Menace has colorful, smooth scrolling graphics that are supplemented with AdLib music and sound effects. The system requirements are an EGA graphics adapter or higher, an IBM or compatible 286 processor or higher; and support for an AdLib music card or compatible.

Adventure and Puzzle Games

This class of games offers some excellent opportunities for virtual environments. However, the classic VR tradeoffs are evident; you often must choose between fluid movement in the environment and good graphics. You will seldom get both with today's technology.

Myst

Myst is an adventurous mystery game that runs under Windows. The game runs from CD-ROM, which makes it possible to have very detailed graphics. Installation is very simple. To install Myst, you must have Windows running. Then simply choose the Run option from File Manager and type ***d:*\INSTALL**, where *d:* is your CD-ROM drive letter. Consult the instructions included with the game for step-by-step instructions.

The System requirements for Myst follow:

- IBM/Tandy personal computer or 100-percent compatible
- 386 DX 33 MHz processor or higher (486 recommended)
- 4M RAM
- Windows 3.1; MS/PC-DOS 5.0 or higher
- Super VGA Graphics Card (640 × 480, 256 Colors)
- MPC-compliant sound card
- Mouse
- Hard disk with 4M of free space
- CD-ROM drive (preferably double-spin)

Myst requires a 256-color palletized display driver, and you will get better results at smaller screen resolutions. If you normally use 1024×768 screen resolution, or 16- or 24-bit graphics, you will need to change to 640×480, 8-bit mode and restart Windows in order to run the game. The payoffs are high resolution graphics and video clips that add a lot of pleasure to the game.

I was quite unprepared for the level of graphic detail I experienced in Myst; it sets new standards for what is possible. The game makes excellent use of music to intensify the experience. The sound is so full, and the sound effects are so well orchestrated that I found the music as pleasurable as the graphics. For instance, down by the water you can hear the ocean lapping on the shore. On top of the island, you can still hear the ocean in the background. There are different sounds for each of the areas on the island. The sounds add a great sense of realism. Metal doors clank, wooden doors squeak, but the overall effect is to enhance the sense of being in a different world.

The tradeoff—there's always a price—is that although Myst provides beautiful graphics and sound, it offers jumpy, point-and-click navigation. In a game like DOOM, you have an opportunity to navigate around corners, proceed forward or go backward, or make a 360-degree turn by moving the mouse. Myst allows limited navigation by clicking the mouse. You can move forward by clicking the mouse in the center of the screen, or turn to the right or left by clicking on the right or left side of the screen. You are cued by a pointing hand on the left and right edges of the screen. Sometimes you can rotate 90 or 180 degrees by clicking, but some portions of the game restrict the places you can go. There is always a pause before you move, and you don't get any sense of the movement. You are in one place before you click, and then you suddenly arrive in a new place. There are some animations that provide transitions, but realistic movement is not what Myst is about.

Once you have visited an area of the island, you can use Zip mode to quickly move between areas. Zip mode is signified by the cursor changing to a lightning bolt. This helps speed up the process of moving, which can be tedious when you want to move quickly between one place and another.

You can save your game, and start it up at a later time by accessing a menu at the top of the screen. To show the menu (it's normally hidden), place the cursor at the top of the screen to see the File and Options menus. The File menu lets you begin a new game, restore a previous game, save your existing game, or exit. The Options menu lets you decide whether to use transitions. If Transitions are on, Myst uses a dissolve effect whenever you move from one screen to another. You can also turn on Zip Mode, which lets you move quickly between places you have already visited. The Options menu also includes information about the game.

I found the level of graphic detail very rewarding, and enjoyed spending time and energy trying to solve the puzzle. Myst is most definitely not an action-oriented game. It is thought-provoking and challenging.[32] The object of the game is to

[32]For those of you using CompuServe, the Gamers Forum has a lot of hints on how to play Myst.

explore an island world and to use various clues to solve puzzles that provide access to unexplored areas. The game is steeped in mystery and keeps you coming back for more.

The story unfolds in a most unusual way. Myst is actually a book describing an island world that you get to explore. As you read the book, you realize you are actually there—exploring the island described in the book.

Figure 4.62. The first page of the book Myst.

The story begins with a page from an open book. If you click on the picture, you are drawn into it and find yourself standing and looking at a mountain with a big gear on top.

Standing on the boardwalk, you can hear the water lapping at the shore. There are several directions you can explore, and it is fun to just choose any direction and begin. I chose not to get a closer look at the gears, but to head up the steps to some buildings.

You must keep a sharp eye out for clues, but this one is pretty obvious, and the first one I happened upon. It is a personal note with a clue. The game provides a nice journal that you can use to keep track of clues. I started out jotting things on yellow post-its, but they kept getting lost or covered up. The journal is much better for keeping notes.

Figure 4.63. The pathway and gears have several colors, with highlights and shade that add to the realism.

Figures 4.64 and 4.65. Notice the shadows falling across the steps, and the scrap of paper on the right side of the boardwalk.

Figures 4.66 and 4.67. Notice the stone pillars on this building, and the level of detail including the brass emblem on the door. Inside the building is a time machine.

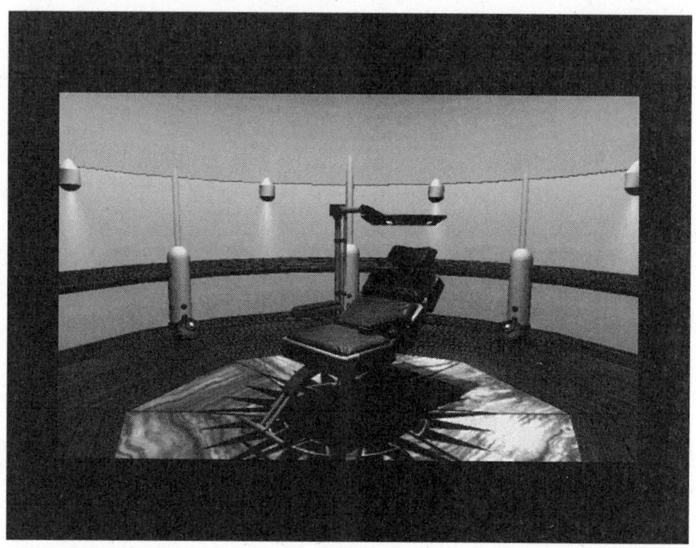

To solve the puzzle, it is important to observe every area carefully. Later, you can use clues to unlock mysteries, like how to use this time machine.

Figures 4.68 through 4.75. A 360-degree view of one of the buildings. The wood is a rich mahogany color, and even the ceiling is ornamented. The paintings on the walls provide important clues, so check them out.

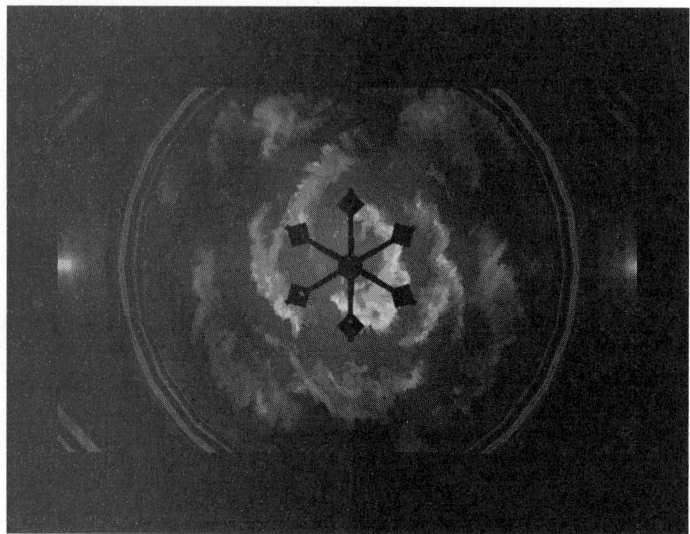

Notice the level of detail inside this building. The wood has a nice texture and reddish color, and the floor has a circular design. Clicking on one of the pictures reveals a hidden staircase.

Figures 4.76 through 4.79. The shadows on the buildings and on the path through the trees add an eerie feeling and enhance the sense of realism.

As you explore the island, you encounter new paths and buildings. And once you have visited an area, you can always use Zip Mode to zip between areas.[33]

Figures 4.80 and 4.81. Solving the puzzle will reveal new areas, or ages, to explore.

[33]Zip Mode is active when your cursor turns to a lightning bolt. You can choose Zip Mode by accessing the menu at the top of the screen.

When you have successfully gathered enough clues to solve portions of the puzzle, you will discover new areas to explore. I had to piece together clues found in four or five locations to discover this building.[34] And I feel like I've barely scratched the surface of the game's potential.

Return to Zork

Return to Zork is a CD-ROM game that runs under DOS. There are two installation options. You can install a minimal set of files to your hard disk, and run everything else from the CD, or you can install about 42M of files and Zork will run much faster. This speeds up performance, but not everyone has that kind of free disk space for a game. The installation program will automatically detect a Sound Blaster sound card and its current settings, although it can't auto-detect other digital audio sound cards. Have your sound card factory defaults handy, because you're going to need them during installation.

---

[34]When I've been working several hours on the book or trying to get software to run, Myst is a nice way to take a break. Sometimes I begin a new game to see if I can find fresh evidence. And sometimes I feel like picking up where I left off to see how much further I can go. The whole family got involved in comparing notes and sharing clues we found. If you get frustrated, it's fun to compare notes with someone else. Each of you may have pieces of the puzzle that will unlock one of the mysteries.

Some suggestions follow for optimizing performance of Return to Zork:

- Set up your system to have as much free conventional RAM as possible. Return to Zork needs a ***lot*** of memory.
- Use the XMS/EMS option. If you have XMS (expanded memory), set up as much free XMS memory as possible.
- Often SMARTDrive and other hard disk caching software can increase performance.
- CD-ROM owners with lots of hard disk space should copy the project file to their hard disks.
- If you don't currently have a CD-ROM drive on your system and are thinking of purchasing one, you should get a double-speed drive capable of sustaining transfers of 300K/second. This will definitely improve performance of Zork and many other CD-ROM based programs.
- Launching Return to Zork from Windows may diminish sound performance.
- Disk-compression software may be incompatible with Return to Zork's program and data compression, which could cause unreliable performance. Install Return to Zork on an uncompressed drive.

This game is extremely entertaining and playful. It offers high-quality graphics and animation that are different from Myst or Iron Helix. When you click on the screen, you invoke an animation that takes you to the next scene. It's similar to an interactive movie.

The accompanying manual is very well written and does a good job of describing how to play the game. It's a quick read, with only 28 pages. I prefer to play games using a mouse, and Zork does a good job of letting you use the mouse to your advantage. The cursors are big, and easy to see and interpret. The game is easy to install and start playing. It has an intuitive interface that invites you to play.

The manual is supplemental rather than required reading. And if you get stuck and need a hint, call the Activision Hint Line at (900) 680-HINT. Of course, you need to be 18 years or older or have your parent's permission to call. Calls are 95 cents per minute, and charges begin after the first 18 seconds.

The game begins with an entertaining sequence that combines video with an overlay of words. Anyone familiar with the original Zork game will enjoy the humorous references to the original game. No doubt about it, sound adds yet another dimension to a game that increases the realism and draws you into a more immersive experience.

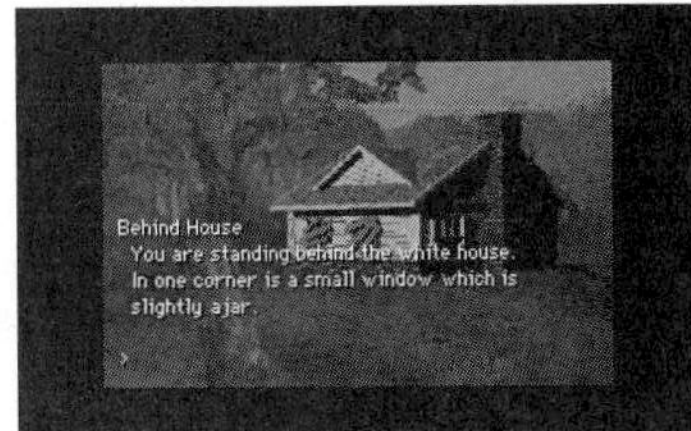

Figure 4.82. The opening video sequence for Return to Zork. Notice the words overlaid on the picture.

Figure 4.83. The Tele-Orb with the Wizard Trembyle, who provides colorful commentary throughout the game.

One of the most colorful characters you meet during the game is the Wizard Trembyle. He offers suggestions and warnings during the game.(35) Take note, because sometimes he warns you against areas that could contribute to your demise.

Figure 4.84. You can pick up and store items in your inventory during the game.

One of the nicer features of the game is that you can interact with the physical environment. If your cursor is over an item with which you can interact, you get action-interface options. You can put the item in your inventory, or combine items with other items in your inventory. Be creative! This combination of items offers the solution to many of the puzzles in the game.

In this picture, you get interface options for the rock. What is the normal reaction to an obnoxious vulture that keeps attacking you? Throw the rock at it, of course.

---

[35]It would be nice to be able to interrupt the video if you've seen it before or don't want to listen to all of it. I find it pretty frustrating to have to listen to the talking crystal ball repeat the same spiel over and over. I would like to be able to click while he's talking, interrupt the animation, and move on.

This opens up other options, such as closer examination of the vulture's roost. The possibilities are endless, which is what makes the game so fun.

Figures 4.85 and 4.86. The lighthouse and its keeper.

If you click on the arrow to follow the path out of the Valley of the Vultures, you end up at the lighthouse. If you knock on the door, you get the keeper. This interaction with characters was unique to Return to Zork. The other CD-ROM games offer interaction with the environment but are devoid of any other human forms. Return to Zork is fun because it lets you visit with other life forms.

Figure 4.87. Inside the lighthouse, you can explore up the stairs.

Once inside, you have an opportunity to visit with the keeper or to travel up the stairs. Navigation is indicated by a bright red arrow.

Figures 4.88 and 4.89. You can interact with most characters in the game.

You can have a conversation with the lighthouse keeper by selecting the Talk To icon from the Action Interface display. Once you select the Talk To icon and engage the keeper in conversation, you'll see a column of icons on the side of the screen. If you click on these icons with the left mouse button, you can direct the tone of the conversation with your body language. What fun!

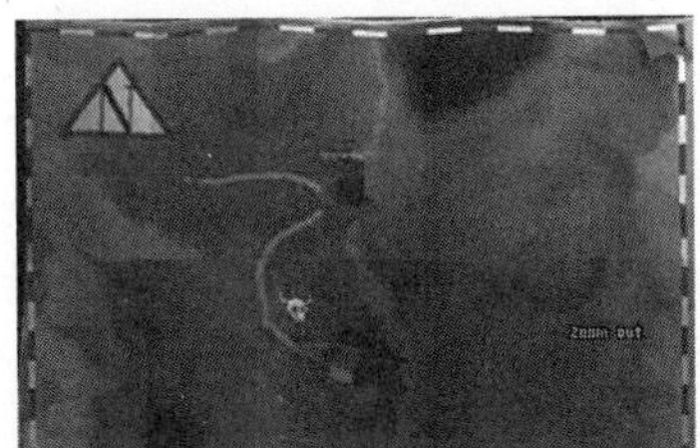

Figure 4.90. The map is one of the few permanent items in your inventory.

The map plots the path taken in your travels. Your current location is indicated by a blinking red dot. The map provides a useful overview for your explorations.

Figure 4.91. Some items located near the lighthouse.

If you get stumped and don't know how to proceed, take a closer look at some of the items in the surrounding area. The combination of some of these items often solves the puzzle of where to go next.

Figures 4.92 and 4.93. Traveling down the water with a brief stop in town.

I floated down the river and came to a cluster of small buildings. I knocked on each of the doors to gather any clues and pick up additional items for my inventory. But be sure to save frequently, in case you suddenly die.

You can access the Zork System menu by placing the cursor in the upper left-hand corner of your screen at any point in the game. You'll know the cursor is in the right location when it changes to a Zork Disk icon. Then just click the left mouse button. Your options are to Save, Quit, Load, Restart, or change some of the effects like visual, music, sounds, or text. You also get the current game score.

Figure 4.94. This screen is accompanied by an evil laugh whenever you explore a dangerous area that proves to be lethal and leads to your early demise.

There are some areas you cannot explore with impunity. If you enter one of them, you die. If you saved your game, you can pick up where you left off.

So, as you can undoubtedly tell, I found Zork really amusing and restful. It was entertaining, and I enjoyed combining different inventory items. Sometimes the combination did nothing, and sometimes it provided an obvious solution to a puzzle.

The navigation isn't as direct as in DOOM, but I enjoyed the graphics and movie-like interaction with the game. And I especially enjoyed the characters I ran into. I would characterize this game as highly entertaining.

Iron Helix

Iron Helix is a CD-ROM game produced by Drew Pictures. It requires Windows to run and, like Myst, requires a 256-color palette. Like Myst, it is a compromise: you get point-and-click navigation and high-quality graphics.

Installation couldn't be simpler, and the program entertains you while you wait. A dinosaur named Timmy eats players who don't send in their registration cards—you'll see a hapless victim who didn't send in his card become Timmy's next meal.

The intent of the game's creators was simple: to keep game play as fast as possible while maintaining high-quality graphics.[36] The game makes good use of background music, which is suitably "spacey."

To play, you must send a probe aboard a heavily armed ship named the *SS Jeremiah Obrian*, and find the ship's cargo—an H-bomb that is armed and ready to be used. You are in the Science Ship *Indiana*, and your goal is to sabotage the deadly mission of the *Obrian* and avert a holocaust. To do this, you must board the renegade ship *Obrian* with your probe and gain security access to the rooms and computers. You must then search the ship for ways to prevent it from deploying its deadly weapons against a peaceful planet. But watch out! The ship has a robotic Defender that is heavily armed and capable of performing all ship functions. You must avoid the Defender and destroy it in order to win.

The interface through which the game is played is the Probe Control panel, which lets you direct the probe through the ship, plug the probe's arm into the *Obrian's* computer, and gather microsamples of organic life.

---

[36]The graphics were certainly creative and well done, but I found the dark corridors and rooms of the game uninspiring and difficult to see. While highly detailed, they were singularly uninspiring.

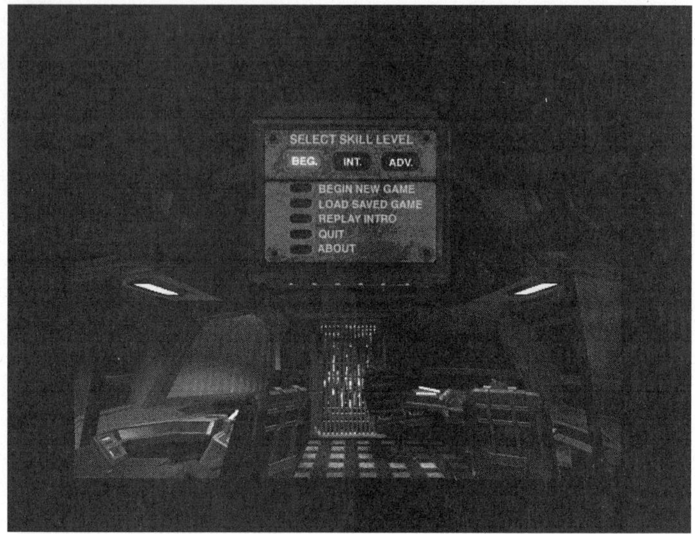

Figures 4.95. The opening sequence of the game begins with a video playing in the monitor at the top of the screen.

Iron Helix takes advantage of a lot of animation and video sequences. The game begins with an introductory video that plays in the monitor at the top center of the screen.[37] When you click the mouse, the video stops and is replaced with a menu. You are given a chance to begin the game, save or load previous games, replay the introductory video, quit, or look at the About box. You can also select the skill level from this menu.

The game takes place through a control panel called the Probe Control Interface. The top left window of the control displays the areas of the ship through which you navigate. The window on the right displays messages about the ship or video displayed in the left window. For instance, if you come to a door (pictured in the top left window), the window at the top right displays a button that says `Open Door`. If you click the button to open the door and do not have clearance, you are informed that you do not have access.

The arrows at the bottom left of the panel are for navigation. You click on the arrows that are highlighted to go up, down, left, right, forward, or backward. The window on the bottom right displays maps of the ship. There are three map modes available.

---

[37]I found this means of introducing you to the game's mission a refreshing break from having to read about it. Most of the other games presented the background information in the manual or in a file on-screen. I enjoyed listening to a character lay out the story in a video.

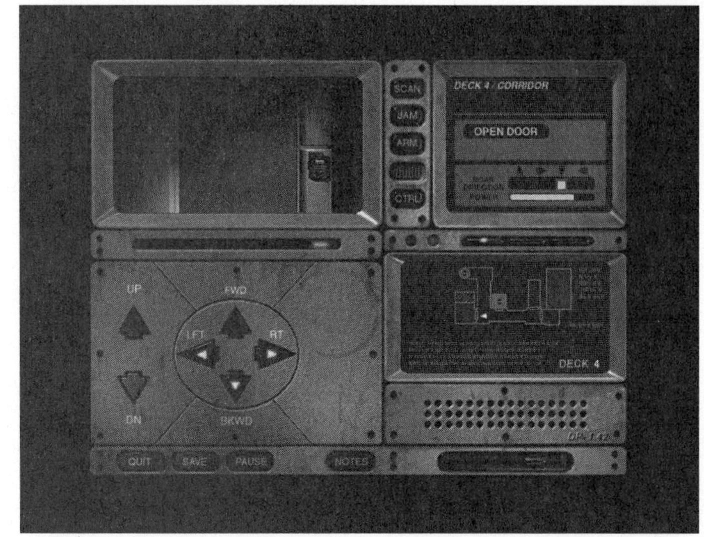

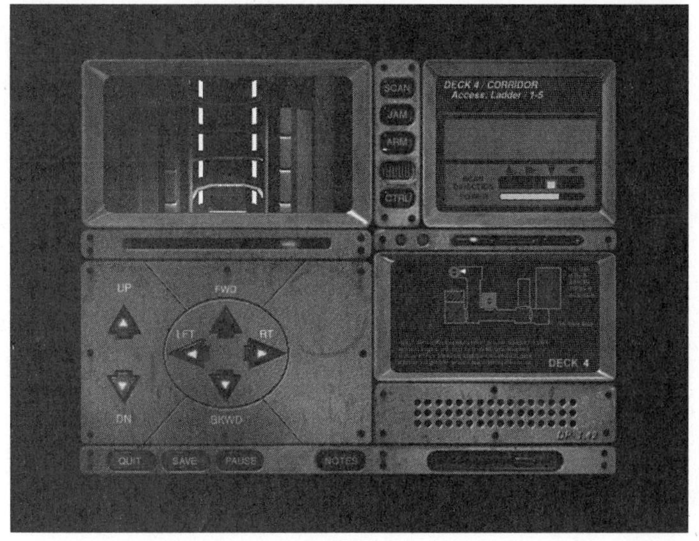

Figures 4.96 through 4.98. The interface for Iron Helix is a control panel.

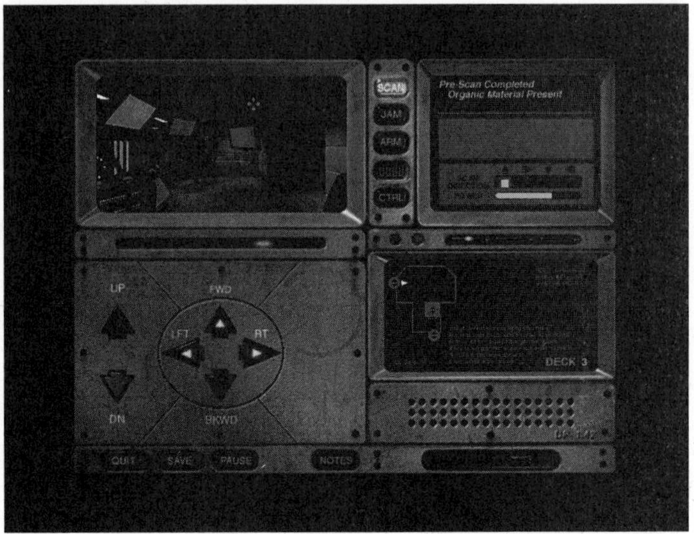

Iron Helix is a game of skill that requires you spend some time reading the manual in order to play. The Operations Manual is 32 pages long, and you would be well advised to look it over. The game offers a Down-and-Dirty Quick Start so you can begin playing Iron Helix immediately, but you probably won't get very far just poking around.(38) The Defender found me, and I died several times while I was just looking around.

System requirements follow:

- IBM 25MHz 80386 compatible or faster
- Microsoft Windows 3.1
- 4M RAM
- Super VGA graphics (256-colors in 640×480 resolution or higher)
- Hard drive required (with 16M of free space)
- CD-ROM drive (150 Kb/sec sustained transfer rate or better recommended)
- Double-speed CD-ROM recommended
- Sound Blaster or compatible required

---

[38] Iron Helix reminds me a lot of my introduction into science fiction. The first science fiction book I read was *Dune*, by Frank Herbert. Reading this book required that I frequently reference the glossary at the back. You can play Iron Helix by just poking around with the probe, and trying doors, but it's a lot more fun if you get into the story and learn the nuances of the ship and its crew.

NOTE

If you don't have one or more of these required features, you will be unable to play Iron Helix.

Stunt Island

Enough preamble. Time to get to the point: virtual reality isn't just part of the game scene. Virtual reality itself can be a game. I'm talking about Stunt Island, from Disney Software. Oh, all the usual game stuff is there, of course—planes you can fly, maps, interesting and cute touches—but this is extremely inexpensive[39] software that you can use to create virtual spaces to play around with. Forget mere flight simulators—how about a virtual space in which the plane crashes into a building and fire trucks scream to the rescue! Crashing your plane isn't necessary, of course. You could also set up a rescue operation at an evil warlord's castle.

I purchased a copy of Stunt Island for less than $40, and if you aren't interested in spending $3,000 for your virtual reality software, it's a heck of an economical start. You give up some things, naturally. You can't create your own objects; all you can do is place pre-existing objects into a scene. The graphics aren't high-resolution; you'll have to settle for MCGA (320×240 and 256 colors). Fortunately, Stunt Island contains a huge number of objects—trees, human figures, animals, machines, buildings, and more—so you won't run out quickly. The image quality is good (especially considering it's only MCGA), especially the navigation screens (see fig. 4.99).

Figure 4.99. A typical navigation screen from Stunt Island.

[39]Ahem. I believe the term is "cheap."

Stunt Island contains 32 predesigned stunts, each of which typically contains a large number of props. If that were all Stunt Island did, it would still be a fun game. The virtual fun starts when you create your own stunts. Before you learn how to do that, however, there are some memory issues to address.

Setting Up Memory

Stunt Island is a DOS program, and it needs a whole lot of memory to run—570K. I had to reconfigure my machine to run Stunt Island with a screen capture program, but if you're using DOS 5 or higher, you shouldn't have a problem. To configure for best use of memory, try the following:

- Make sure that you have a memory manager, such as HIMEM.SYS, loaded in your CONFIG.SYS file.
- Use EMM386.EXE or a similar program to open up the upper memory area for drivers and TSRs. Make sure you load DOS high (`DOS=HIGH,UMB` in CONFIG.SYS) when you do this, of course.
- Load all the drivers and TSRs high that you can using DEVICEHIGH (CONFIG.SYS) or LOADHIGH (AUTOEXEC.BAT), as appropriate.
- Use the MEM command with the /c switch to examine the layout of your machine's memory. This will tell you how much memory each driver or TSR is using, and the size of contiguous memory blocks available for loading high. For best results, type

  mem /c | more

  to avoid information scrolling off the screen. To run Stunt Island, verify that you have at least 570K of conventional memory available.
- Make sure that your mouse driver is loaded, because you'll really want to use it with Stunt Island. You also can use a joystick or a special throttle/yoke device for flight simulators.

Playing with Stunt Island

Stunt Island is software with a sense of humor. It comes with a large number of stock aircraft, and some of them aren't airplanes. There's a hang glider (see fig. 4.100), a duck, and even a pterodactyl. If you decide to try bombing with the duck, you'll find out that the bombs are really, well, eggs.[40]

[40]Yuck! There need to be some limits to virtual messes!

I'm going to skip over a lot of the features of Stunt Island, however, and get right to the virtual meat: the Scene Editor. Figure 4.101 shows the Scene Editor without any elements in the scene. Stunt Island refers to a scene as a stunt, of course. The Scene Editor contains four general areas you need to know about:

Placement Window—This window displays a map of Stunt Island. You can use the View Controls to position the cross hairs, and to zoom in or tilt the point of view.

View Controls—The two boxes on the left side are used to enter coordinates for the cross hairs. (You also can click and drag to move the cross hairs.) The two boxes on the right control the orientation (left/right) and tilt of the Placement Window. The slider is used for zooming.

Prop Display Window—The current prop is displayed in this window.

Prop Controls—These controls allow you to add a prop, place a prop, and make various adjustments. You also can delete a prop if you make a mistake.

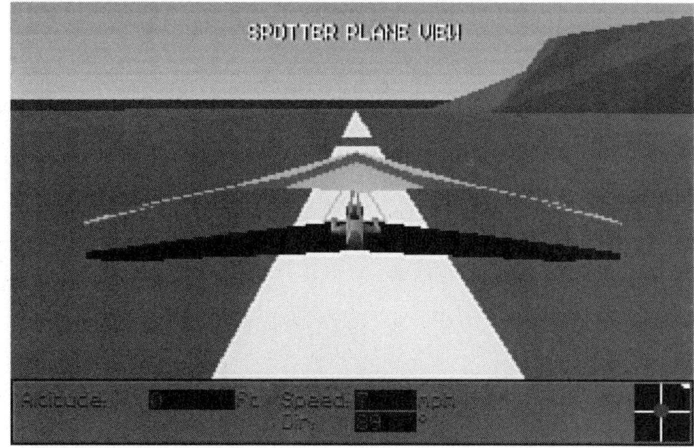

Figure 4.100. A hang glider about to take off from Stunt Island.

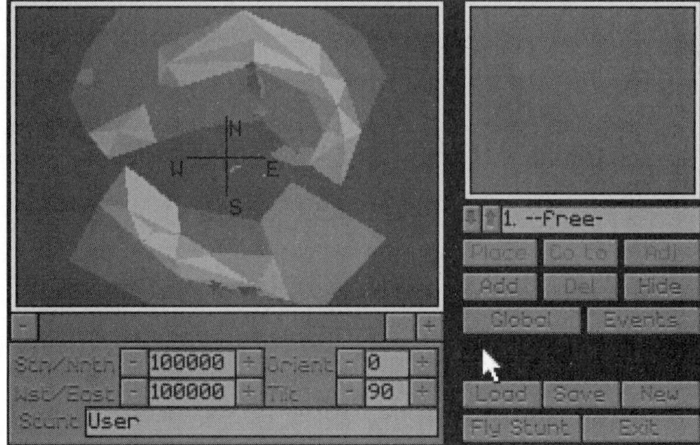

Figure 4.101.
The Stunt Island Scene Editor.

Getting Started

The first task in creating a scene/stunt is to zoom in on the part of the island where you plan to set up. Figure 4.102 shows a small island located in the lagoon in the middle of Stunt Island.

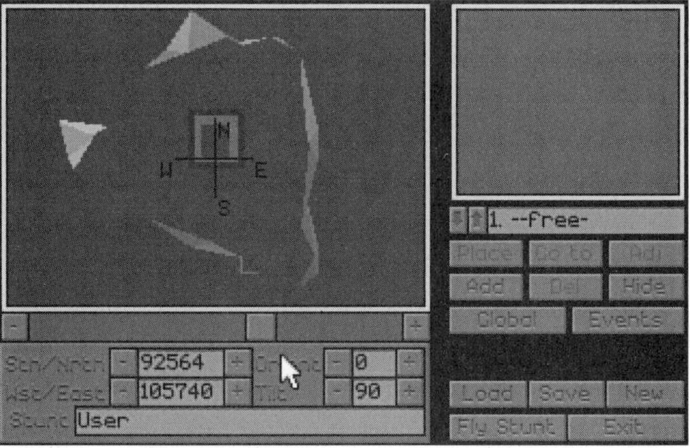

Figure 4.102.
Zooming in to set up a stunt.

We can zoom in even farther, as shown in figure 4.103. This figure shows part of a castle wall, with turrets and crenellations. This progression is typical of Stunt Island—there are lots of interesting details that you will run into as you zoom in.

So far, the views in the Placement Window have been from directly overhead. You can use the tilt box in the view control section to change the tilt angle, as shown in figure 4.104.

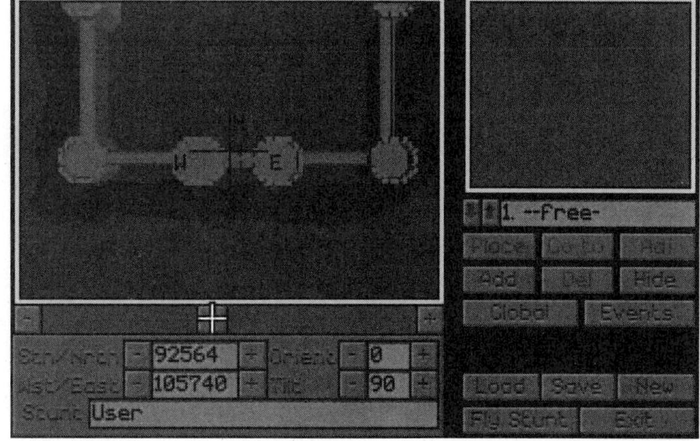

Figure 4.103. Zooming in on a castle on the island.

We'll set up our scene right here at the front of the castle. The first step is to add a prop. Click the Add button (see fig. 4.104) to display the prop categories (see fig. 4.105).

Figure 4.104. A zoomed-in view with a different point of view.

There are nine kinds of props in Stunt Island, and each category has a wide variety of props in it. I do have one criticism of the prop selection: at MCGA resolution, the difference from prop to prop is sometimes pretty minor. For example, it's pretty hard to tell one tree from the next,[41] as you can see in figure 4.106. That's an Ash #3 on top, and a Lime #2 below it.

---

[41]And don't even try to tell the forest from the trees.

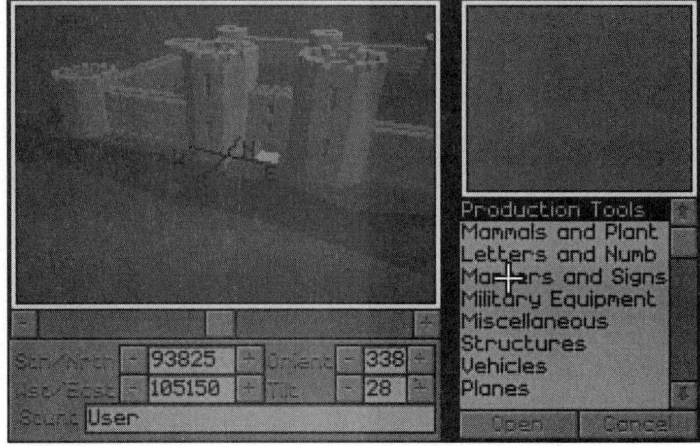

Figure 4.105. Prop categories in Stunt Island.

Props Have Properties[42]

Once you have selected a prop, you can set a variety of properties, as shown in figure 4.107. There are various kinds of props, and you can set different properties for each kind. For example, I've defined an Ash #3 as a free prop. A *free prop* has no dependencies—it does not rely on any other prop to determine its actions (or lack thereof). Other kinds of props include *attached*, which are literally attached to some other prop and act just like a part of that other prop, and *follow* props, which, although not attached, follow another prop wherever it goes.

To position the prop, we'll need to set its altitude. Unfortunately, the Scene Editor doesn't give us any clues about the altitude of the virtual earth at the position of our prop. In the case of the ash tree, I had to experiment to determine that the elevation of the island was about 850 feet.[43] The best technique is to place the prop and then raise the elevation until you can see the prop. Then you can zoom in to position it exactly. If you don't set the correct altitude for a prop, you won't see it (it will be under the virtual ground), or it will be up in the air. Figure 4.108 shows the Ash #3 prop in place at the correct elevation, along with a few other trees.

You also can set the speed of a prop, and set its direction, but that's not much use for the average tree. There are, however, plenty of props that need to move, such as cars and trucks.

---

[42]Don't forget that the word "prop" is actually short for "properties." That means the section title is really "Properties Have Properties," which is pretty dumb.

[43]This is as much of a hassle as you would expect it to be. Some of my guesses about height weren't very good—I wound up with props floating in the air. That cuts the reality part out right there. Are you guys at Disney listening? It would be a Really Neat Idea to be able to position a prop at ground level, not sea level.

*Figure 4.106.
Use the box at the upper right of each figure, with 07 on the left and 11 on the right. Two different kinds of tree props, an Ash (a) and a Lime (b).*

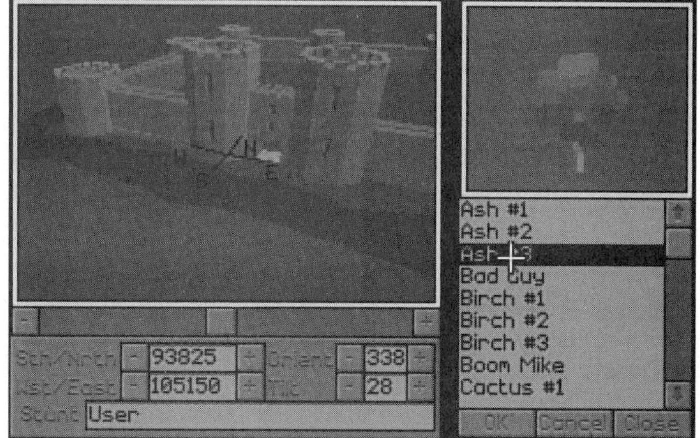

a

b

*Figure 4.107.
Setting a prop's properties.*

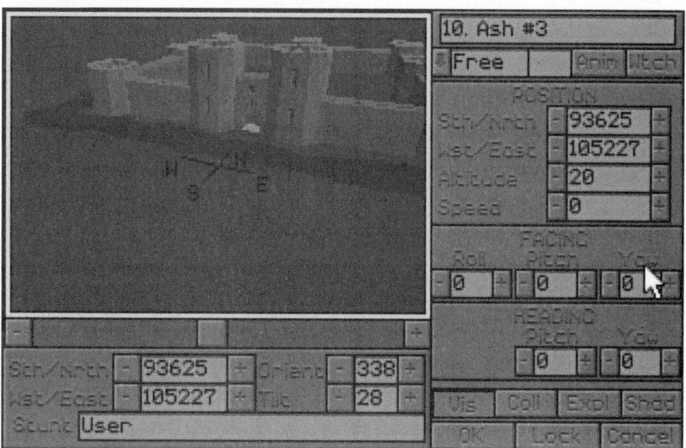

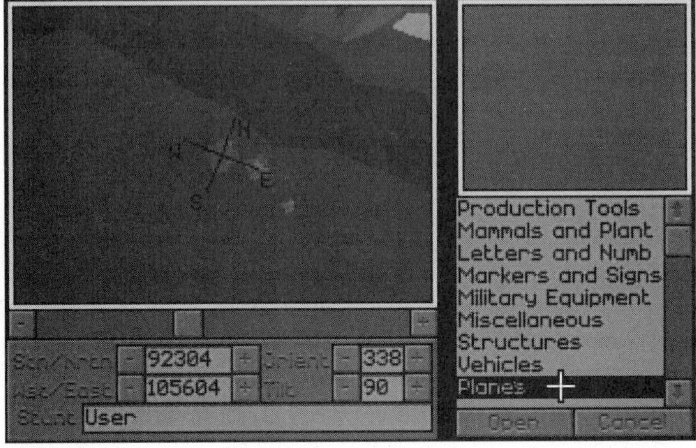

Figure 4.108. A prop has been placed at the location marked by the crosshairs.

Flying Through the Scene

One of the most important props is the aircraft you will fly through the scene. Stunt Island comes with a large collection of aircraft, as you can see in the pull-down list at the right of figure 4.109. One of the more amusing choices—a pterodactyl—is included in the list, as is another favorite of mine, the space shuttle. Stunt Island isn't a fancy flight simulator, however. This game is about stunts, and the flying is pretty simple. You won't, for example, encounter any crosswinds, or be able to adjust trim for precision flying. The flying you'll do will involve fast reaction time and tight turns more than the theory of flight.

Figure 4.109. Selecting an aircraft to fly.[44]

[44]Which begs the question: Is a pterodactyl an aircraft? My editor didn't think so, and I don't either, but as far as Stunt Island is concerned, a pterodactyl is, indeed, an aircraft. Ducks are aircraft, too, if you are curious.

For this example, we'll use a Sopwith Camel as prop number one; you always put the aircraft you'll fly in this prop slot. There are 40 slots for props; you can't use any more than that. It's best to zoom out to place the aircraft, as shown in figure 4.110.

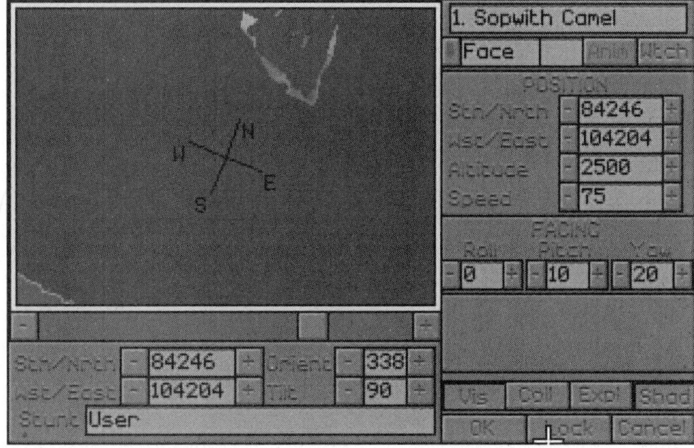

Figure 4.110. Zooming out to place an aircraft.

For this scene, you'll put the plane about a half-mile up and well out from the island. This gives you time to react to the situation as the scene starts. To create a more challenging stunt, you could position the plane lower and closer to the island. You can enter the numbers after clicking the Adjust button; this displays the entry boxes you see in figure 4.110.

The Spotter Plane

Prop number two is always a spotter plane. The spotter always follows the aircraft in slot number one. This is a good time to mention another really neat feature of Stunt Island: cameras. Up to eight props can "carry" a camera; all eight cameras record at the same time. Later, you can edit the clips into a movie. See the section "Editing," near the end of this chapter, for more information. If you don't want to edit, Stunt Island uses a default sequence for editing the take from a stunt, and it's not half bad for the stock stunts.

Whenever you place a prop with a camera, you can display the camera view and set up the view to meet your requirements, as shown in figure 4.111. The Sopwith Camel can be just barely seen at the center of the frame, under the cross hairs. By changing the Pitch, Yaw,[45] and Distance settings at the right in figure 4.111, you can change the view to the one shown in figure 4.112. Once you set the view from the spotter plane, it will follow the stunt plane like a well-trained puppy.[46]

A useful prop for a camera is a balloon, as shown in figure 4.113.

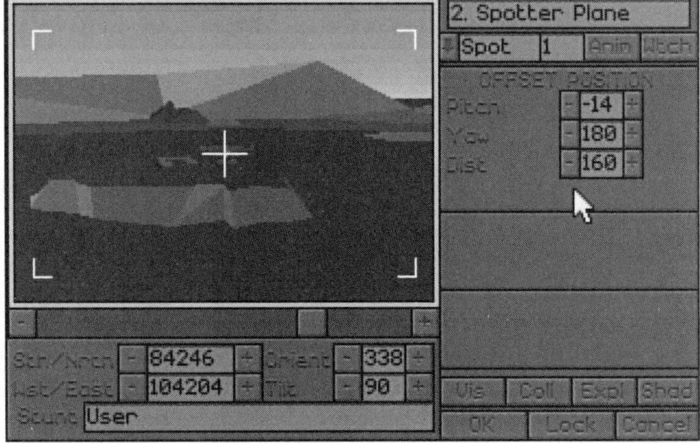

Figure 4.111. Setting the camera view for the spotter plane.

Figure 4.112. Setting the spotter plane position.

---

[45] You had better get used to using such terms if you're going to create your own stunts. Pitch and yaw refer to rotational movement—you change pitch when you rotate something up or down. When you nod your head to say yes, you are changing the *pitch* of your head. *Yaw* refers to side-to-side changes, such as when you shake your head to say no.

[46] Is that why they call it "Spot"?

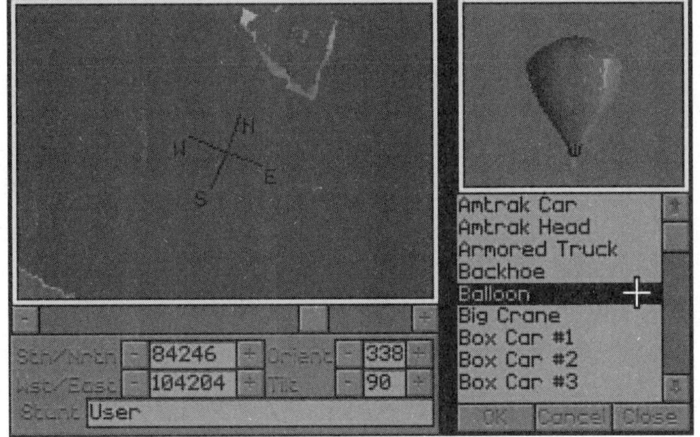

Figure 4.113. Adding a balloon to the scene.

To make this a useful camera, we need to face the balloon in the right direction. You can place the balloon near the castle and then set a compass direction (+263[47] in this case, as shown at the middle right of fig. 4.114) to enable the balloon to face the castle. The facing pitch has been set to -13; this points the camera 13 degrees below true horizontal. If desired, you can put the balloon in motion; I set mine drifting at a lazy 12 miles per hour. This makes the balloon an animated prop.

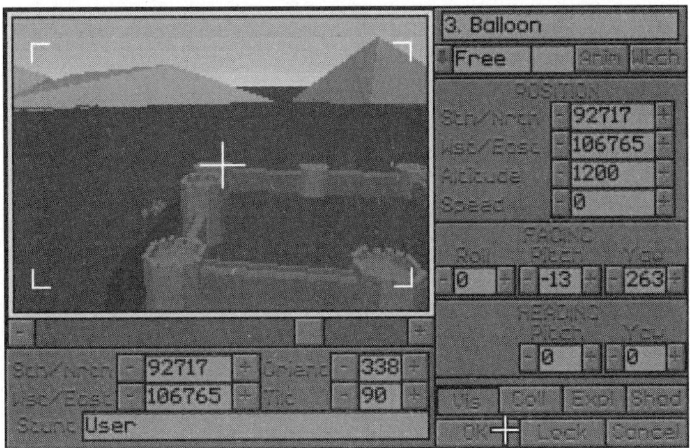

Figure 4.114. Setting the camera view from a balloon.

[47]The number 263 refers to degrees, just like with a compass. Zero degrees is due north.

There are two kinds of animated props: static and dynamic. A *static animated prop* moves for the duration of a scene in the direction and at the speed you set in the Scene Editor. A *dynamic prop* changes direction or speed, or it may explode—it does whatever you tell it to do. For example, you might want a car to explode when it crashes into another object. You edit dynamic props using the Event Editor, a separate tool.

Adding Characters

So far, the scene is pretty tame. Let's add a bad guy, and let's give him a camera to keep him busy because he really can't do anything nasty to our aircraft—he's just a prop. We'll set his camera to view the trees at the castle gate, just in case anything ever crashes into them.[48] I set the bad guy on one of the castle turrets; figure 4.115 shows the view from this location. This figure also shows that, indeed, the official name for this prop is *Bad Guy*.

We don't have a focus for the stunt, so we'll add one: someone to rescue. There's a prop called Hook Man: a man holding a hook, that you can use to pick him up with the airplane.[49] Figure 4.116 shows what the Hook Man looks like, and the crosshairs are located on the turret next to the bad guy. Naturally, we'll set a camera view for this prop as well.

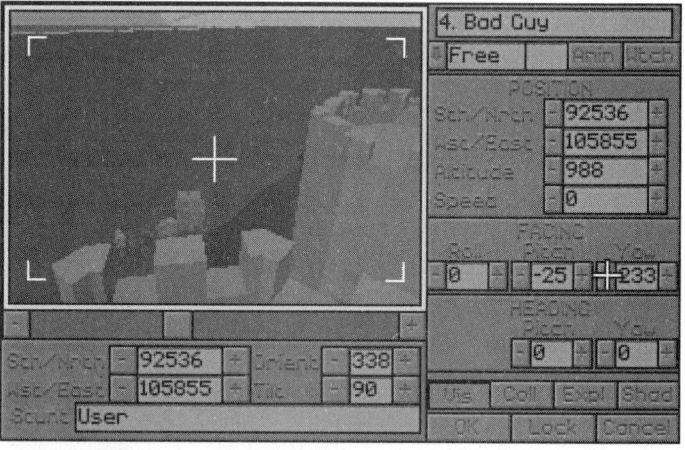

Figure 4.115. Positioning the bad guy's camera.

[48]This author guy seems obsessed with crashing and burning.

[49]Making the pickup is tricky—unless you think to switch the view to the spotter plane. You can easily judge your height correctly with the little expedient. Strictly speaking, it's cheating, but, hey, I'm an alter ego; I can do things like that.

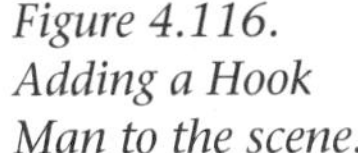

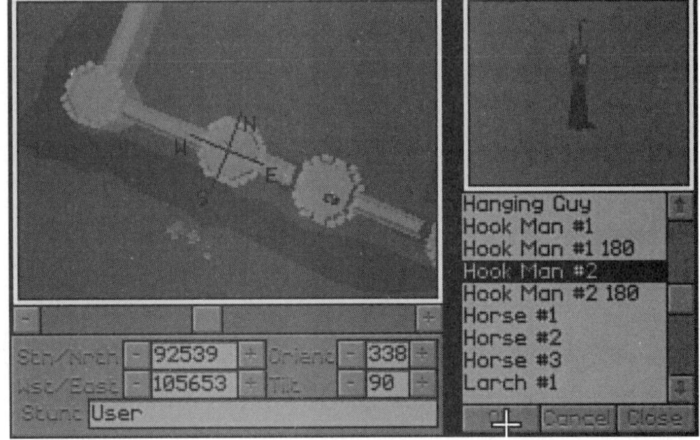

Figure 4.116. Adding a Hook Man to the scene.

This ability to put in a large number of recording cameras is one of the things that makes Stunt Island fun. When the time comes to put together a movie based on your attempts to carry out the stunt, you'll have plenty of footage and numerous camera angles to work with. For any game to be consistently interesting, it has to have a certain depth of features, and Stunt Island goes well beyond that basic point.

You can add additional props, some with and many without cameras, until you have the scene the way you want it. Figure 4.117 shows the final setup for the example scene we've been working on. I added a few goodies, including a large cathedral in the courtyard of the castle. Otherwise, it would be too easy to swoop in and perform the rescue—now you'll have to avoid the cathedral's towers immediately after the pickup.

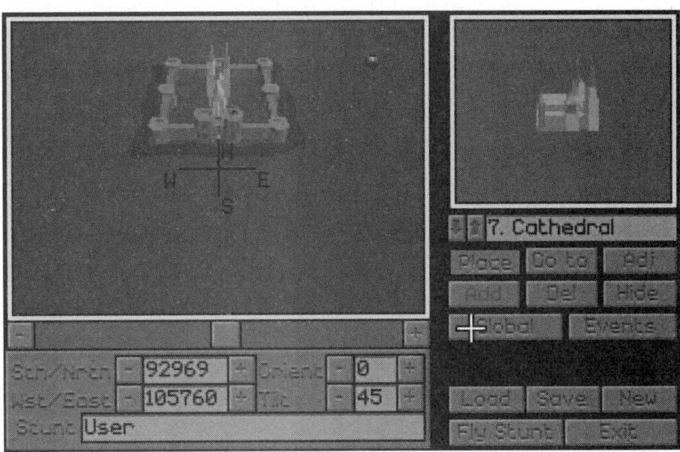

Figure 4.117. The final scene ready to be saved.

Stunt Time!

Once you have set up a scene, you can try it out. The graphic for shooting on location is shown in figure 4.118.

You start a stunt at the controls of prop number one,[(50)] as shown in figure 4.119. This figure shows a complete view, without the cockpit; you also can display a cockpit view by pressing F9. However, the cockpit obscures half or more of the screen.[(51)]

Figure 4.118. Getting set for action!

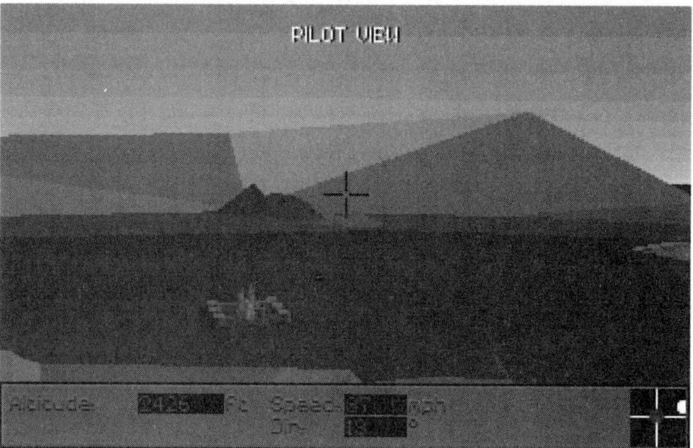

Figure 4.119. The beginning of the stunt.

---

[50]That's your airplane, dummy.

[51]A classic case of over-engineering. All of the cockpit designs are fantastically detailed, but nearly every one of them is so darn big you can't see anything!

Flying the stunt is fun;[52] figures 4.120a through d show four scenes from one attempt to do the stunt. It's no trivial feat to carry out a stunt; you can easily crash and burn if you don't pay attention. That's as it should be; I found that Stunt Island offers a nice balance between challenge and action.

Figure 4.120. Scenes from a stunt in Stunt Island.

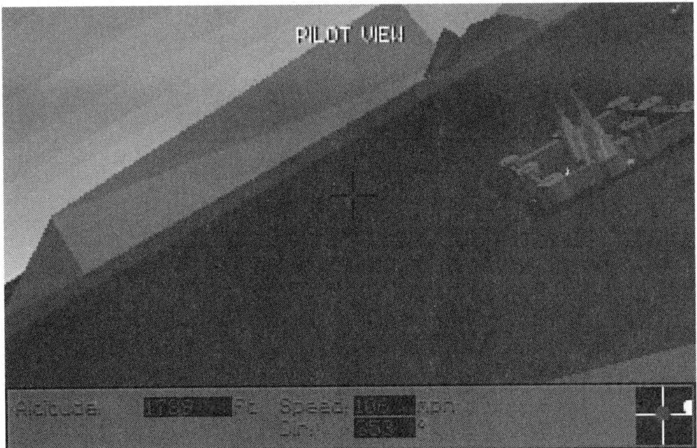

a

b

[52]That's putting it mildly. There may be some things you'll have to put up with along the way, but once you settle into the pilot's seat and go for it, this game really shows where its focus is. The interactivity is great, stunts are well thought out, and they offer quite a challenge.

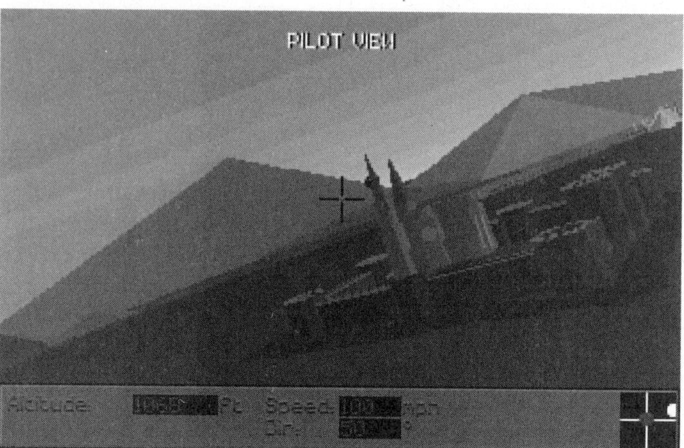

c

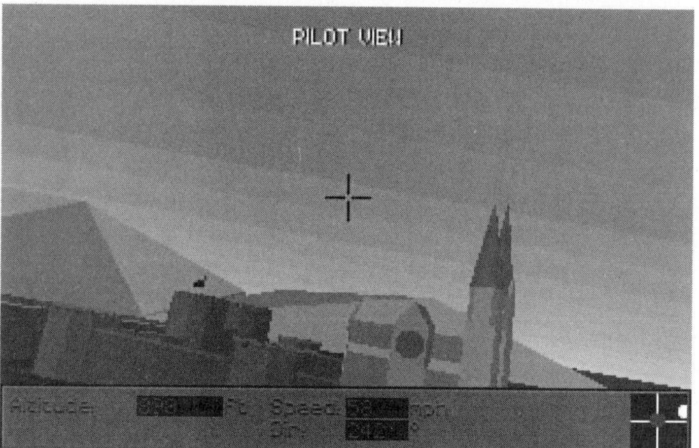

d

Editing

Once you have a stunt completed, you can head for Post Production (see fig. 4.121). This leads to the editing room, where you'll find two editing decks (see fig. 4.122).

In figure 4.122, the deck on the left is the source deck, and the deck on the right is the destination deck. Each deck comes with a complete set of controls for moving forward and backward, as well as markers that allow you to define the segments for editing. The editing process is straightforward.[53]

---

[53]Straightforward, yes; easy to explain, no. Once you get the hang of it, it's a lot of fun to put together a clip based on your stunt work. This was a very clever addition to the program.

Figure 4.121. The Post Production navigation screen.

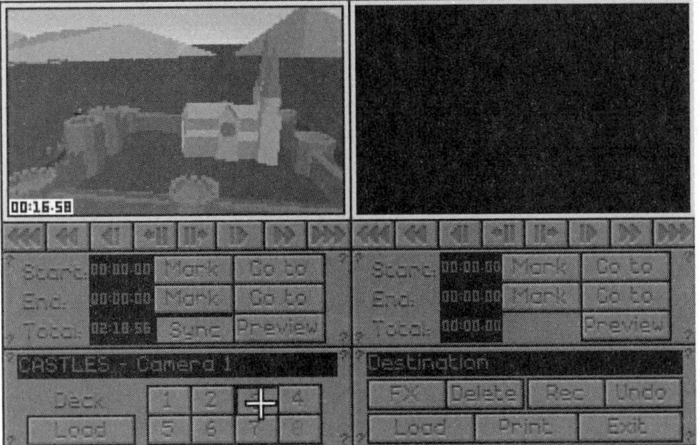

Figure 4.122. The two-deck editing studio of Stunt Island.

1. Load a take into the source deck. A *take* consists of the film from all the cameras during a single stunt attempt.
2. Play the views from the various cameras until you find footage you want to keep. Click the Start/Mark button when you find a good starting point.
3. Continue playing from the starting point (you must stay with one particular camera) until you reach the end of the clip you want; then click the End/Mark button.
4. To copy the clip to the destination deck, simply click the Rec (Record) button.

You can add as many clips, from as many different cameras as you like, to create a movie. You then can save the movie and play it back at your leisure.

Summary

Some folks might say it's stretching a point to call Stunt Island virtual reality, but I don't think so at all. There are important compromises—MCGS resolution is one of the most serious—but all the important ingredients are there: 3D modeling and interactivity. If you can take your virtual reality without a heavy dose of realism, then this program provides an outstanding bang/buck ratio. Of course, it's not a tool for creating just any kind of environment—you're limited to flying your airplane and interacting in predefined ways. But for the money, it's unbeatable.

Educational Games

Apogee Software offers two charming games that help improve math and word skills. The games offer skill levels to challenge any age. My 12-year-old daughter preferred the word game and caught on much faster than I did. As usual, I didn't read directions and it took a while before I figured out you're supposed to match the question mark with a picture. I was more interested in gaining bonus points, and matched the wrong picture and word. The Gruzzles got me immediately!

Word Rescue

This game provides intriguing puzzles to help build children's vocabulary skills. The Gruzzles are stealing all of the world's words, and you have to rescue the world of words while there's still time.

Benny Bookworm asks you to enter your name and select a character. You get to choose whether to use a boy or girl character. If you have already played the game, Word Rescue remembers and tells you how many points you had, and the level you were last on.

The object of the game is to match the correct word and picture. Successful matches are displayed at the top of the screen. When you have successfully completed a level, you are given the key to the next level.

Figures 4.123 and 4.124. Enter your name and select a character.

Figures 4.125 and 4.126. Match the word and picture. If the Gruzzles try to get you, Benny Bookworm will save you.

If you mismatch the picture and word, the Gruzzles try to get you. But you can press a key to get Benny Bookworm to come to your rescue.

Math Rescue

Figures 4.127 and 4.128. Enter your name and select a character.

Math Rescue is fun and educational—it teaches addition, subtraction, multiplication, and division.

In this game, Benny Bookworm has developed into a butterfly, and Benny Butterfly asks you to enter your name and select a character. Once again, you get to choose whether to use a boy or girl character. If you have already played the game, Math Rescue keeps track and tells you how many points you had, and the level you were last on.

Figures 4.129 through 4.132. The screens step you through the selection criteria. Choose the most appropriate level, the type of operations, and whether you want to work on math or word problems.

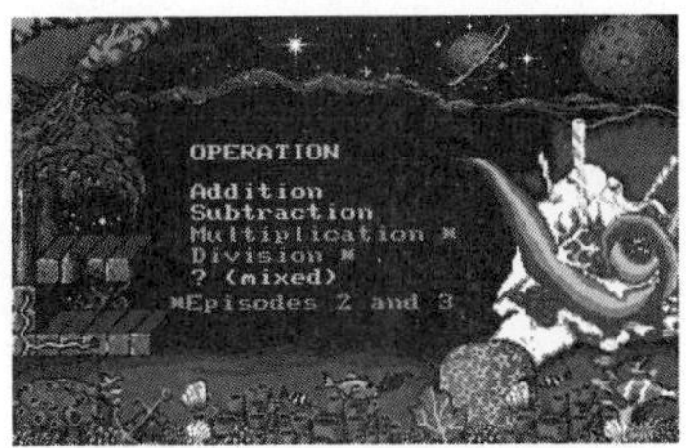

Math Rescue steps you through the selection process. You determine the level of difficulty based on age guidelines. Then you decide what types of operations you want to play with. You can have all math problems, all word problems, or a combination of the two.

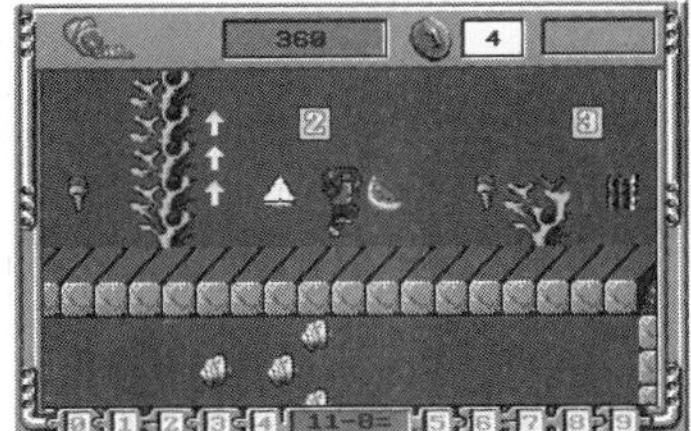

Figures 4.133 and 4.134. Sample screens of math and word problems using subtraction operations.

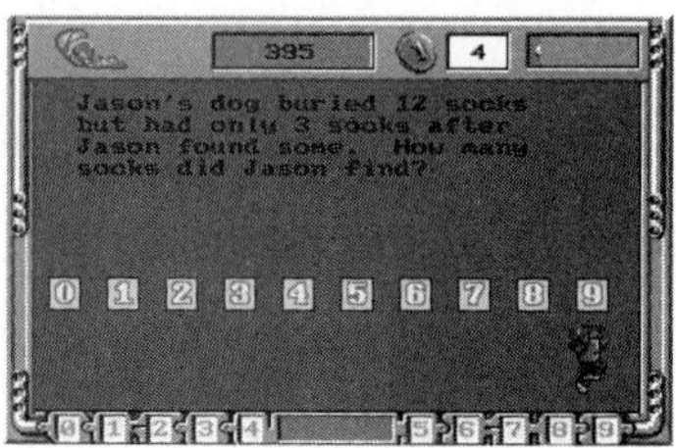

You can solve the math problems by choosing the correct number of items that answer the problem at the bottom of the page. Or you can select the correct number from the series 0-9 in response to the word problem shown at the bottom of the screen. If the answer requires two digits, such as 10, you select a 1 and then a 0.

The games have music and arcade-quality sound effects that supplement the game.(54)

Setting Up Your Sound Card

All sound cards are not created equal. But all sound cards do have certain things in common. Most important, every sound card will require you to set it up before you can use it.(55) There are three steps involved in setting up your sound card:

1. Physical installation
2. Installation of utilities and drivers for DOS
3. Installation of utilities and drivers for Windows

   In many cases, steps 2 and 3 are combined. There is also often a fourth step:

4. Installation of games and other software that may come bundled with the sound card

Let's walk through the process of installing a typical sound card—the Sound Blaster 16. I chose this particular model because many readers will have exactly that card,

---

[54]I could tell by the music when my daughter was playing Word Rescue or Math Rescue. I normally ask the kids to turn down the sound when they play games—the repetitious music drives me crazy! But, I felt like she was doing something educational and had a positive response to the music when I knew she was playing these games. I was pleased she was having fun while she learned.

[55]Of course, if you bought your computer with the sound card already installed, you may find that the software and drivers for the sound card already function just fine. Congratulations if this is the case!

and because it is fairly typical. If you have a different sound card, or a sound card from a different manufacturer, the exact details of your installation will be different. However, the basic ideas will be similar.

Physical Installation of a Sound Card

Adding a sound card to your computer is just like installing any other card. The process involves these basic steps:

1. Remove the cover from your computer.
2. Select an unused slot for the sound card. If the sound card will be connected to an internal CD-ROM drive, be sure to select the slot closest to the CD-ROM drive. Otherwise, the cables connecting the sound card and CD-ROM drive may interfere with other cards in your computer.
3. Remove the small cover for the slot with a Phillips screwdriver.
4. Check the documentation that comes with the sound card to see if you need to set anything on the card itself. There may be jumpers (see fig. 4.135) or switches (see fig. 4.136) to set.

Figure 4.135. Jumpers.

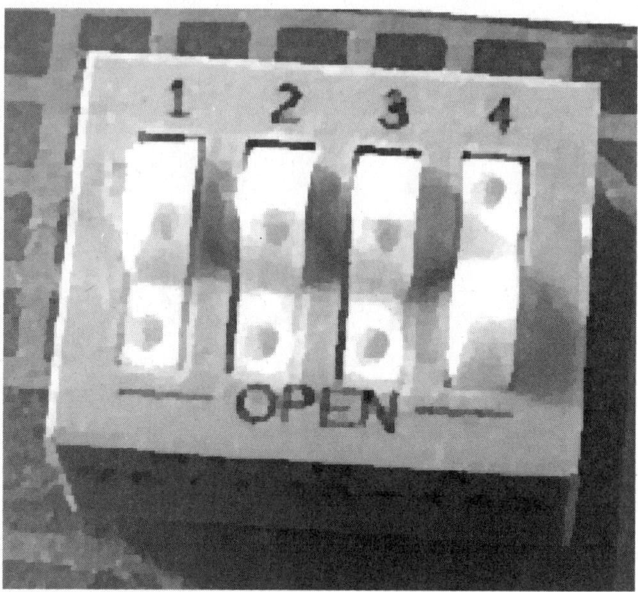

Figure 4.136.
Switches.

5. Carefully insert the sound card into the chosen slot (see fig. 4.137). Don't bend it, don't force it—gently but firmly seat the card into the slot. See figure 4.138 for an example of how far into the slot the card should go. Replace the screw you removed in step 3 to hold the card in place.

Figure 4.137.
A sound card positioned in its slot.

Figure 4.138. This is how far to insert the card.

6. Connect any cables that are required inside the computer. For example, you may need to connect your CD-ROM drive with a flat "ribbon" cable (see fig. 4.139), and an audio cable may also be included if you bought a multimedia upgrade kit that included both a sound card and a CD-ROM drive (see fig. 4.140).[56]

Figure 4.139. A ribbon cable carries data between a CD-ROM drive and your sound card (but not audio!).

---

[56]If you bought these two items separately, you may need to connect the CD-ROM drive's audio outside the computer. Simply buy a 1/8" mini to 1/8" mini cable, and plug it into the CD-ROM drive's headphone output and the sound card's Line In input.

Figure 4.140. Many upgrade kits come with an internal audio cable for CD-quality sound.

7. Replace the cover on your computer.

Interrupts, I/O, and DMA

If it weren't for interrupts, memory I/O, and DMA channels, installing a sound card would be trivially easy. In many cases, you won't need to worry about it, but that's not why books get written! This section is there for those readers who can't use the default settings for their sound card.

First, let's define some terms.

Interrupt—Many of the cards in your computer need to get the attention of the CPU from time to time. To get attention, the card sends an interrupt request[57] to the CPU. There are 16 interrupt lines, but a number of them are used for predefined purposes (such as printer and modem ports; see table 4.2). Your sound card must use an interrupt that isn't already used by some other device in your computer.

I/O Port or I/O Address—A sound card needs a way for the PC to communicate with it. This is done through I/O ports. It must use a port that is not already being used by some other card. For example, if you have a network card, it may also use an I/O port, and must be at a different address to avoid conflict with the sound card.

Memory Address—Many cards need a way to share data with the PC. This is typically done via a memory address. A card using this technique appears as memory to the PC. It must use a memory address that is not already being used by some other card. For example, if you have a network card, it may also use a block of memory, and must be at a different address to avoid conflict with another card that uses a memory address.

DMA channels—When a sound card plays sounds, it is moving very large amounts of data from memory to your sound card (via the I/O port). Most sound cards use Direct Memory Access (hence the acronym, DMA) channels to speed up the movement of this data.[58] DMA channels free the PC's CPU from work by automatically handling the movement of this data. There are only a handful of DMA channels and; as with interrupts, I/O address, and memory addresses, it is critical that only one card use any given channel.

Table 4.2. Interrupts and Their Uses.

Interrupt	*Common usage*
0	Timer
1	Keyboard
2	Access to interrupts 9-15
3	COM 2: and COM 4: (if present)
4	COM 1: and COM 3:
5	LPT2: (if present; can be shared with sound card)

continues

[57]Hence the term IRQ: interrupt request line.

[58]Some high-end sound cards, such as the Turtle Beach cards, use alternative (and faster) methods for moving sound data around inside your computer.

Table 4.2. continued

Interrupt	*Common usage*
6	Floppy disks
7	LPT1: (can be shared with sound card)
8	Real-time clock
9	Redirected IRQ 2
10	Not usually used by system; available for add-on cards
11	Not usually used by system; available for add-on cards
12	Not usually used by system; available for add-on cards
13	Math Coprocessor
14	Hard disk
15	Not usually used by system; available for add-on cards

If your computer has only one COM port, that gives you an extra available interrupt. If you are not using a second printer port (LPT2:), that also gives you an interrupt you can use. Some cards won't use interrupts higher than 8, and having an interrupt or two available in this low range can be important.

Not all cards can be set to any available interrupt. Often, the interrupt is selected by physically altering switches or jumpers on the card, and there may not be a jumper for certain interrupts. You may have to do some juggling to get interrupts for each card in your system.

Every card in your computer doesn't use interrupts; only some of them need an interrupt. For example, your video card probably does not use interrupts. On the other hand, some video cards come with a built-in mouse port—and the mouse port will need an interrupt. You will almost certainly have to check your computer's documentation carefully to determine what cards do and do not need interrupts.

In general, your sound card will almost certainly come with factory settings for interrupts, memory I/O, and DMA channels. You should first try these settings to see if they work—unless you already know that they won't.

Some sound cards will require you to use jumpers and/or switches. Some sound cards will allow you to use software to make these settings. And, naturally, some sound cards will use a combination of methods.

Installing DOS Drivers and Utilities

Let's step through the process of getting your newly installed sound card up and working. Merely putting the sound card into your computer isn't enough; the sound card requires some special software in order to function. This software is called a *driver*. That term may not mean much to you; it comes from the early days of computing. The key fact to know is that the driver is what allows programs to use the sound card to make sounds and music. The driver software sits between other software and the sound card.

One important job the driver does is to keep track of all that information about interrupts, memory I/O, and DMA channels. During installation, you will either tell the driver what settings you set (with jumpers and switches), or what settings should be set by the driver itself using software.[59] Let's see how the Sound Blaster 16 setup program handles these tasks.

Before we start, note that the Sound Blaster 16 uses a combination of jumpers and software settings. The program that performs setup and configuration is **SBCONFIG.EXE.**

The first task is to set the address of the I/O port. Figure 4.141 shows the screen; note that there are four possible addresses that the Sound Blaster 16 can use—220 (default), 240, 260, and 280. You can also choose Auto Scan. Since the I/O address is set by software, Auto Scan will check your computer to see if any other card (such as a network card) is using any of these addresses for an I/O port, and then select an unused address for the sound card's port.

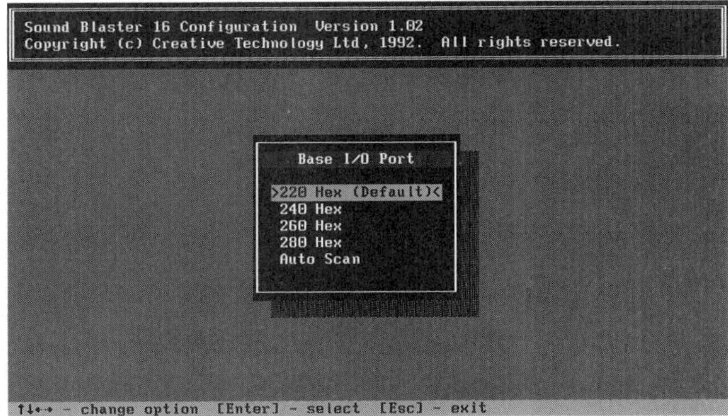

Figure 4.141. Selecting the I/O port address.

[59]There was a time when the only way to set the settings was to physically change a jumper or switch. More and more sound cards are moving over to using software programs to change settings. This is much, much more convenient—you don't have to pop open your computer and pull out the sound card every time you want to make a change. Of course, it is the higher cost sound cards that are using this technology first, so your budget may dictate some compromise.

The setup software will choose whatever address you select to determine if it works properly (see fig. 4.142). It will also test other settings, but those tests aren't shown here to conserve space.

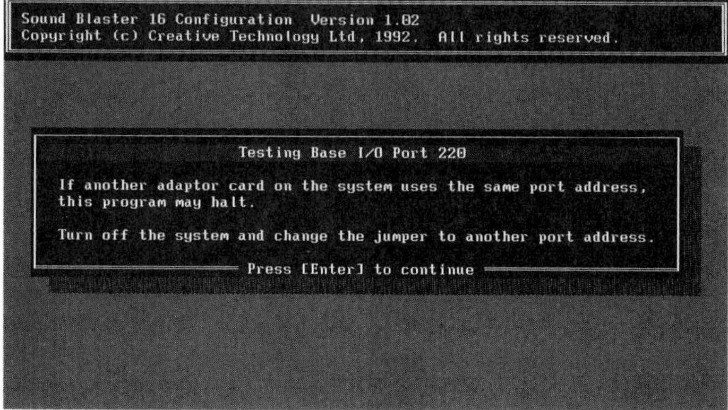

Figure 4.142. Testing the I/O address.

If the address works properly, you will see a confirmation letting you know the port passes testing.

The address you just set was for the portion of the sound card that plays WAV files. Another part of the card is used for playing MIDI files, and it needs a port address as well. Figure 4.143 shows your choices; there are just two: 300 and 330. Both of these are hexadecimal addresses, by the way. That's a base-16 number system used by computers.(60) Note that the MIDI port is set using a jumper on the sound card; if the chosen port does not test OK, you'll need to pop the hood, pull the card, and change the jumper setting. Since you only have two choices, if there is a problem, you may need to change the other card, not the sound blaster.

The next step is to tell the configuration program what interrupt (also known as an IRQ) to use. The interrupt is set in software, so you can either accept the default, or try various settings. There are four choices: 2, 5, 7, and 10 (see fig. 4.144). Try to avoid using IRQ 2—it is used to access IRQs 9 through 15.

60When you and I count, we use the decimal number system—based on our 10 fingers. Computers operate using powers of two—2, 4, 8, 16, 32, 64, and so on. Thus, it makes sense for computers to count from 1 to 16. The numbers from 10 to 15 are represented by the letters A through F. To count from 1 to 10 in base 16: 1, 2, 3, 4, 5, 6, 7, 8, 9, A, B, C, D, E, F, 10. Many scientific calculators do conversions from decimal to hexadecimal and *vice versa*. Of course, you don't need to know any of this to choose a MIDI port; you just have to make sure that the MIDI port is one that nothing else in the computer is using.

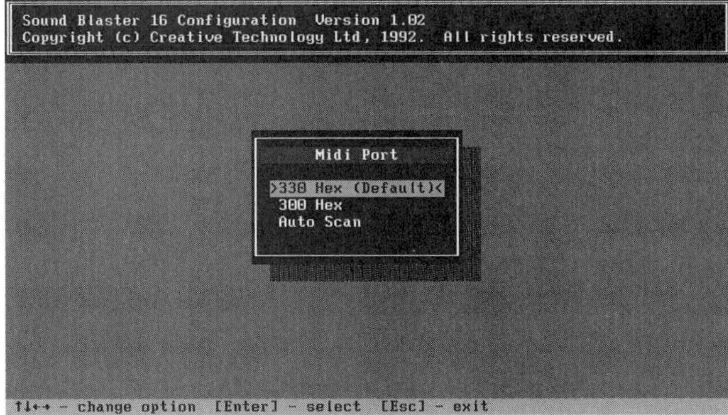

Figure 4.143. Setting the MIDI port address.

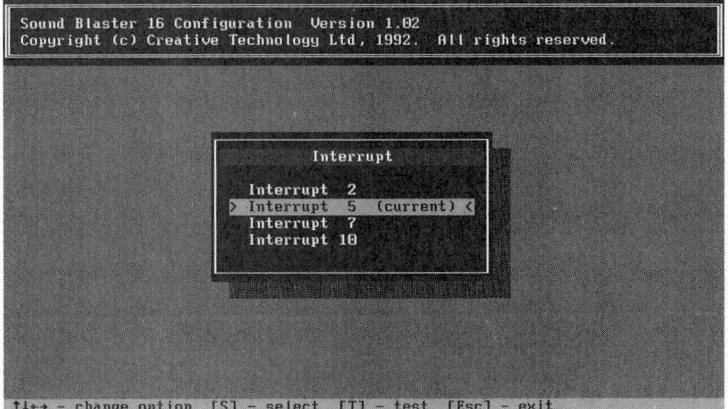

Figure 4.144. Selecting the interrupt for the sound card.

Interrupts 5 and 7 are normally used by printer ports (LPT2 and LPT1, respectively), but this is a case where the sound card and another device can share an interrupt setting.

You'll also need to set an 8-bit DMA channel for the sound card (see fig. 4.145). There are just three choices: 0, 1, and 3. Few devices use DMA channels, so you are unlikely to run into a problem. It's usually safe to accept the default setting.

The Sound Blaster 16 is (as you might guess from the name!) a 16-bit sound card, and you will also be asked to select a DMA channel for 16-bit operation (see fig. 4.146). The choices are 5, 6, 7, or none (that is, use only 8-bit DMA access). Again, accept the default. If there is some reason why your computer cannot use 16-bit DMA, the setting you select will fail during testing. This should not be a problem on new computers.

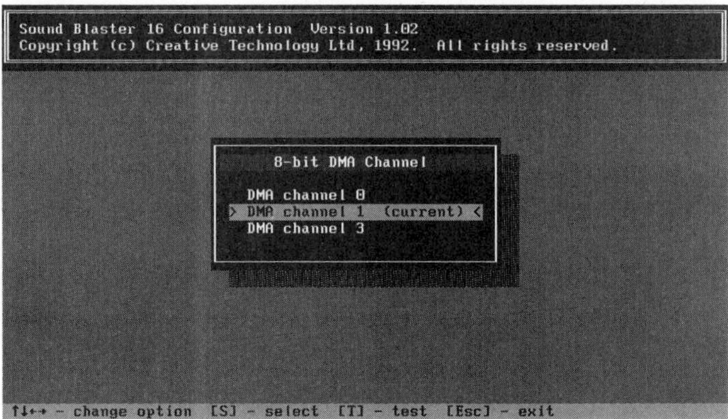

Figure 4.145. Setting the DMA channel.

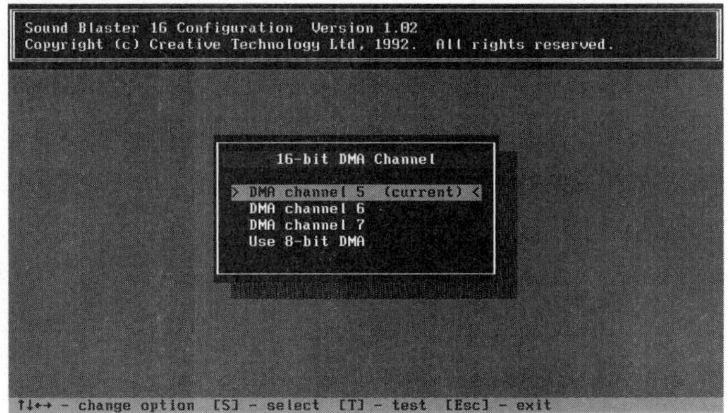

Figure 4.146. Setting the 16-bit DMA channel.

When you have completed the configuration, the setup program will modify your AUTOEXEC.BAT and CONFIG.SYS files. This installs the DOS driver for the sound card every time you reboot your computer.

Installing Windows Drivers and Utilities

You may or may not have to run a separate program to install Windows drivers for your sound card. In the case of the Sound Blaster 16, the configuration program will automatically modify the Windows system files to install the sound card drivers. However, for some sound cards, there may be a separate step for Windows setup. Check your documentation to see if this is necessary for your sound card.

In some rare cases, you may need to install the Windows drivers manually. You may also have to install the driver manually if there is an update, or if your Windows setup is incorrect.

Installing Additional Software

There are all kinds of extra software packages that sometimes are included with sound cards. If you purchased a multimedia upgrade kit, you may also have several software programs bundled with it—games, encyclopedias, clip art, music, and so on. In most cases, you will need to install each included package separately. Each package will have its own requirements and methods, and you'll need to check the documentation to determine how to perform the installations.

Often, bundles do not include the same documentation and packaging that is included with the full retail version of the product. For example, you may get a manual in a plain cover, or no manual at all. This can sometimes make it a bit of a challenge to get the software up and running, and you should be aware of this limitation when you go the bundle route.

II

VIRTUAL FANTASIES

5

CREATING YOUR OWN REALITY

RECIPE

1 VR or 3D editing program
1 large serving imagination

Instructions: This chapter is about space—creating it, modifying it, moving around in it, and having a little fun with it. There will be practice in the art of creating a universe by hand, as well as a tour of the solar system—including a wild ride through an exploding planet.

Don't Fence Me In

The whole idea behind creating your own reality is—what? What is the motivation? What makes it exciting and interesting and worth the time and effort to create your own alternative universe? After all, it's only virtual, right?

Let's face it—reality has its hang-ups. You can only go so far with reality. If you want to go to Paris, you have tickets, luggage, and the language to worry about. The whole idea of virtual reality is that there are no hang-ups, no fences, no limits beyond what's already in the software.

And as the hardware and software advance, those limits will always be farther out than they were yesterday.

Superscape: The Ultimate VR Tool for Your Computer

If money were not an obstacle, this is the tool you would choose for making VR happen. I won't pull the wool over your eyes on this one. When it comes to VR, bigger and more expensive is definitely better.

When I wrote the first edition of this book, the whole point was to give you, the reader, a selection of inexpensive (mostly) tools that you could use on your own PC to work virtual miracles. This time around, with Donna and I both writing the book, a different point of view surfaced. What would it be like, we asked ourselves, to work with software that pushes the envelope of PC-based VR to the limit? In a word, it's cool.

For example, figure 5.1 shows a simple Superscape world. It contains a flashlight and a face. In figure 5.1, the flashlight is off. There are three buttons on the flashlight.[1] You can turn it on, off, or adjust the amount of illumination. Figure 5.2 shows the world with the flashlight turned on. This kind of detailed control is what makes Superscape such a great product.

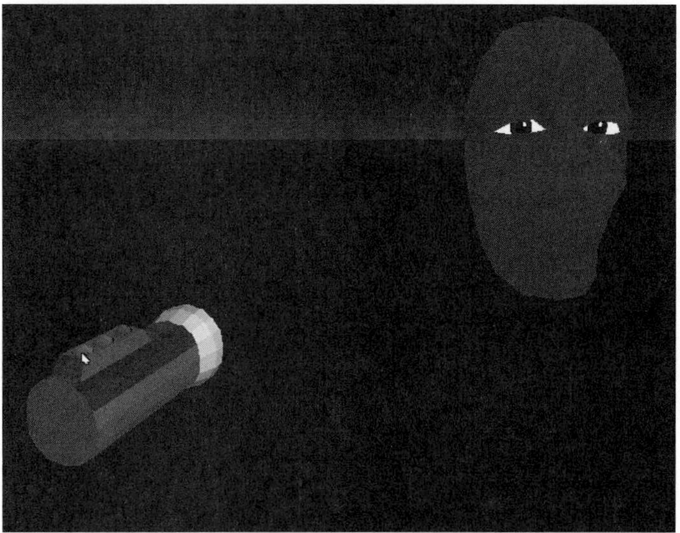

Figure 5.1. A Superscape virtual world with a face and a flashlight.

[1]You can just make them out if you look closely at the figure.

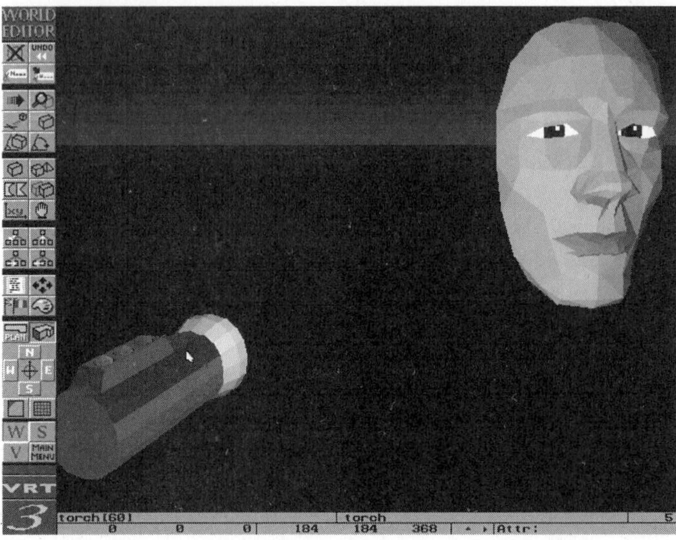

Figure 5.2. The flashlight has been turned on.

Superscape will definitely spoil you. You will get used to the high resolution and the interactive power. You will get used to the tight integration of head-mounted devices and alternate input methods like the Spaceball.

At the same time, Superscape suffers from a mild case of what I call Big Software-itis. All Big Software has one thing in common: a small market. Software written for a small market has two key ingredients: lots of functionality oriented toward that specific market, and a weak user interface. Superscape suffers from this problem—but with a twist: If you've got the bucks for fancy input devices, you'll be fine. If you have to use the keyboard to move around in the virtual space, you will fry your brain before you will memorize all of the cryptic methods you'll use for moving around.

So the answer is obvious: If you have the $10,000 for Superscape, you had better scrape up a few thousand more for a Spaceball. The combination is a killer—it's the only way to virtually fly. Add a good headset with motion tracking and hardware to generate dual stereo outputs for that headset, and you are in VR heaven.[2]

Superscape has two key parts: an editing environment, where you can create, modify, and place objects in your universe; and a viewer, where you can interact with the universe. The editing environment consists of a Shape Editor and a World Editor, and the runtime module is called the Visualizer. Superscape also includes other tools, including a Layout Editor, Texture Editor, Sound Editor, and more.

---

[2]Which raises an interesting point: Does a VR universe have a heaven and/or a hell? I guess it's up to the creator.

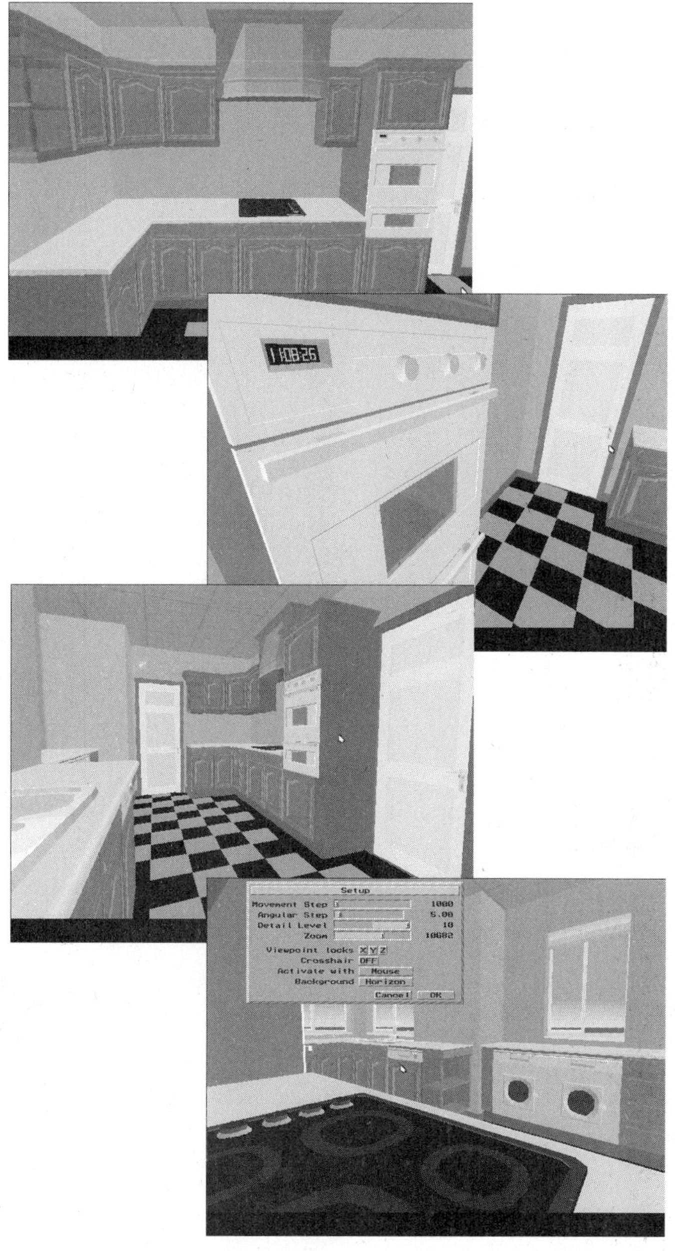

Figure 5.3. Four views of a kitchen created in Superscape. From top: A view of the stove top and range; a close look at the range and a door; looking down the length of the kitchen; a view from the stovetop, showing an interactive menu.[3]

[3]The Visualizer is realistic enough that when you pop up a menu, it's a bit jarring. That's how it should be!

Working in Superscape

Because Superscape supports a range of alternative input devices, we tested it using those devices we had on hand. By far, the niftiest is the Spaceball 2003 (see fig. 5.4). With the Spaceball in one hand and a mouse in the other for selecting icons and menus, you can be extremely efficient navigating the complex tools that Superscape offers. It is significantly more cumbersome to use only the mouse and keyboard.

Figure 5.4. The Spaceball 2003 from Spaceball Technologies, Inc.

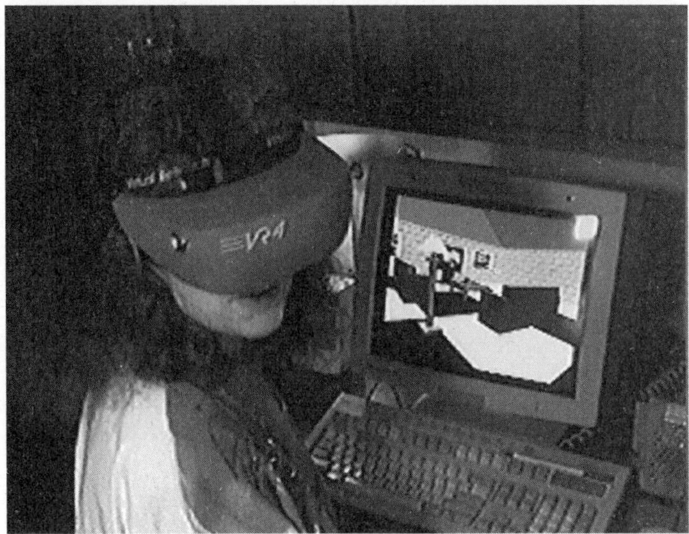

Figure 5.5. A head-mounted device in use by Donna Brown.

We also tried working in Superscape using an HMD (see fig. 5.5). We found that the HMD was great in the Visualizer, but that it did not offer enough resolution for effective development. This is unfortunate, because what the world really and truly needs is a good **and affordable** high-resolution 3D development environment!

If you will be using Superscape for development, I would urge you to look closely into the Spaceball. Superscape is hugely complex, and you can easily double your productivity by investing in the Spaceball.[4] We also tested the Logitech Cyberman (see fig. 5.6), but that device didn't have the same tight control over position that the Spaceball does. At less than one-tenth the cost, of course, that's to be expected. The Cyberman is fun for games, but lacks the sensitivity and repeatability needed for VR development.

Figure 5.6. The Cyberman from Logitech.

[4]Donna found it somewhat harder to use than Ron did. The Spaceball is extremely sensitive, and it also helps if you have a natural ability with maps—you have to think in three dimensions of movement at all times. After several hours of use over several days, however, movement becomes almost second nature. It's very much worth sticking with the Spaceball—movement is very precise.

Superscape World Editor

The main function of the World Editor is to construct a virtual world and the complex objects that furnish it. The building blocks of these objects are the shapes created in the Shape Editor. The World Editor lets you create, position, size, color, bend, rotate, and animate objects. When you finish constructing objects, you can use the Superscape Control Language (SCL) to give additional attributes to objects to control their movement, animation, lighting, distancing, interactivity, and intelligence.

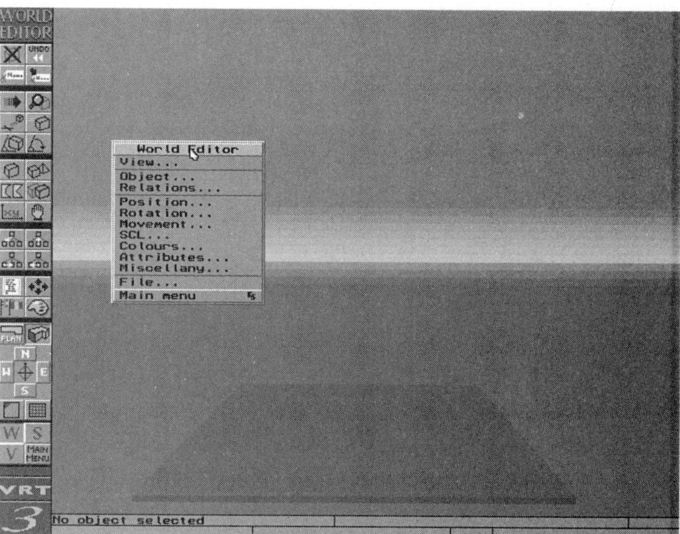

Figure 5.7. The Superscape World Editor.

The icon bar contains seven groups of icons arranged in two columns (see fig. 5.8). They duplicate the functions used most often on the World Editor menus. You can either use the icon bar, or right-click to display the World Editor menu shown in figure 5.7. You can access all features using the menus, while the icon bar only gives you access to the most-used features.[5]

General Object Features

Delete Object—Deletes the current object (and its children).

Rename Object—Renames a selected object.

Undo—The World Editor stores changes made when editing the world, which gives you the chance to undo those changes later in case of error.

[5]Just to be complete, there are also keyboard shortcuts for many features.

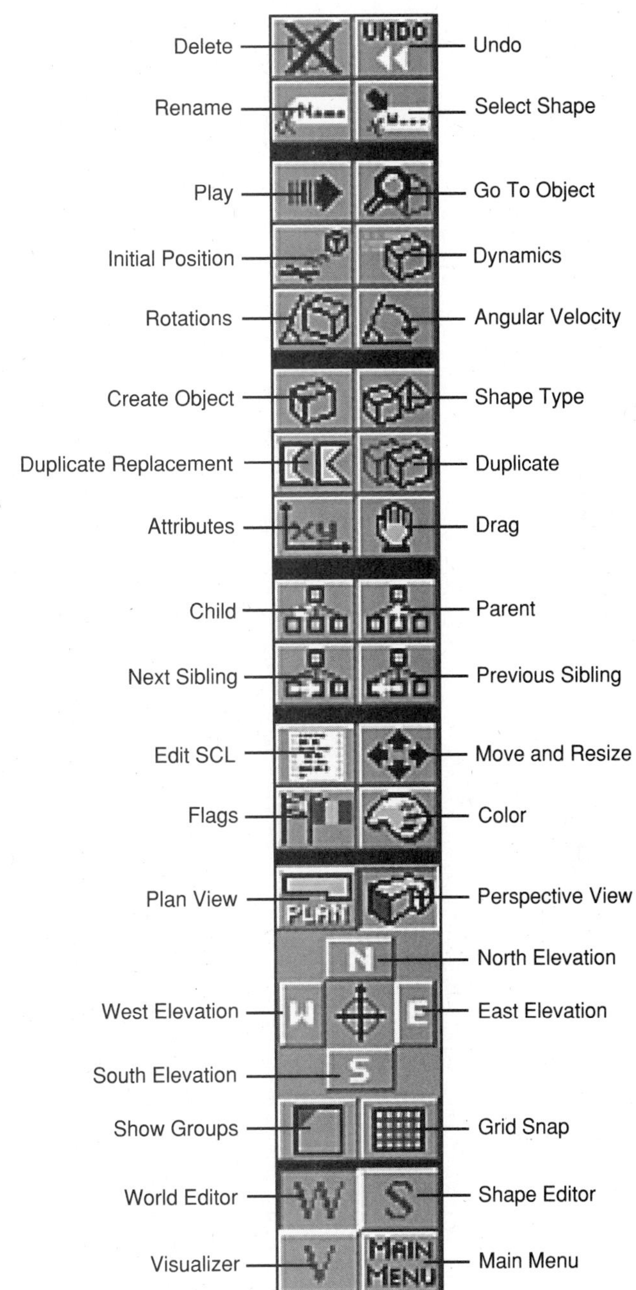

Delete
Undo
UNDO
Rename
Select Shape
Play
Go To Object
Initial Position
Dynamics
Rotations
Angular Velocity
Create Object
Shape Type
Duplicate Replacement
Duplicate
Attributes
Drag
Child
Parent
Next Sibling
Previous Sibling
Edit SCL
Move and Resize
Flags
Color
Plan View
PLAN
Perspective View
N
North Elevation
West Elevation
W
E
East Elevation
South Elevation
S
Show Groups
Grid Snap
World Editor
W
S
Shape Editor
Visualizer
V
MAIN MENU
Main Menu

*Figure 5.8.
The Superscape World Editor icon bar.*

Normally, the World Editor "remembers" several levels of Undo, although more simple functions may be undone than complex ones. By default, 100K of space is reserved for the Undo function. It is possible to change this value by editing the Preferences file, but the default should be enough for most purposes.

If there is not enough memory available to store all the changes being made, you are presented with an alert box warning that the operation cannot be undone. You can choose Cancel to stop the operation or Continue to continue the operation. If you choose to continue, this removes all information about previous Undoes from the World Editor's memory.

Select Object—Lets you select an object by name from an object list. This is useful in large worlds where objects may be out of the viewing area.

Movement

Play—Switches activity on and off in the World Editor so that you can check the directional accuracy of motion attributes, and ensures that objects move and react the way you want. This icon also displays all the objects' motions and executes their SCL and animations, although at a slower speed than the Visualizer.

Initial Position—Sets the initial position of a moving object in the virtual world when the world is first loaded, or when the reset (F12) key is pressed.

Rotations—Rotates an object according to its X, Y, or Z axis.

Find Object—Presents a list of objects from which you can select a specific object.

Dynamics—Lets you apply the following attributes to an object so that it reflects the dynamic features of the real world: gravity, fuel, climbing and falling, friction, restitution, driving velocity, externally modified velocities, maximum velocity, and whether the object can be "pushed."

Angular Velocity—Lets you add angular motion to an object using the angular velocity attribute. This updates an object's rotation attribute, turning the object through a given amount every frame.

Creation and Position

Create Object—Creates a new object with the same dimensions (size) as the shape it uses. The new object can be moved anywhere in the world by using the standard attributes, which contain its position relative to its parent; the Place icon, which allows placement of the object using the mouse in elevation views; or Position in the World Editor menu.

Replacement—Creates a replacement object of the current object in the same position in the world as the original object. The duplicate object will have the same name as the original object, but with a unique numerical suffix, as is the case for normal duplicates. Any children of the original object are not duplicated. This feature is useful for replacing complex objects with progressively simpler replacements to improve processing speed.

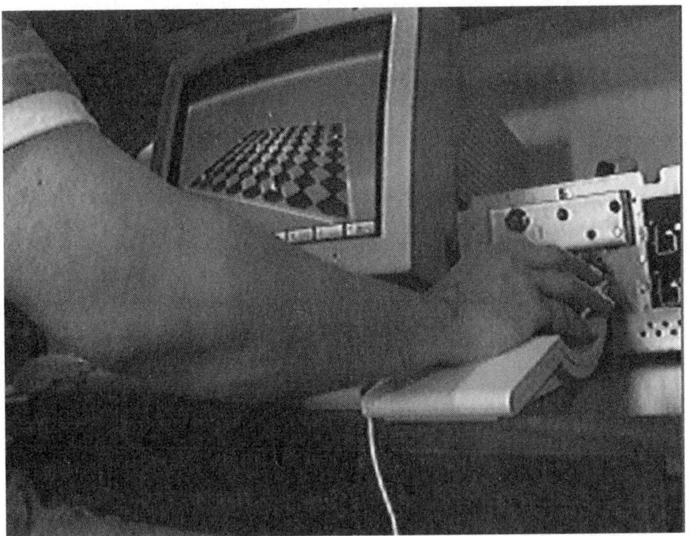

Figure 5.9. A Superscape world in the Visualizer.

Standard Attributes—Each object has standard attributes, which are size, position, and shape type. These specify the minimum amount of information an object can have.

Change Shape Type—Changes a replacement object to use a simplified shape. As an object recedes into the distance, the eye cannot differentiate its separate facets, so it can be replaced by a simpler object that takes less time to process.

Duplicate Object—Duplicates the current object and gives it the current object's name followed by a "duplicate" number in brackets. The duplicate object has all the same attributes as the original object.

Drag—Drags a selected object to a new position. To drag several objects, click on the Drag icon, hold down the Shift key, and click on the required objects. Drag one object to the desired position, and the other objects will follow it.

Tree

The World Editor has facilities that let you step through the object tree structure. Moving up the tree selects the parent of an object; going down selects the first child of the object. Going right selects the next sibling of an object; going left selects the previous sibling of the object.

Select Child—Selects the first child of an object.

Select Next Sibling—Selects the next sibling of an object.

Select Parent—Selects the parent of an object.

Select Previous Sibling—Selects the previous sibling of an object.

Miscellaneous

SCL—Adds an SCL (Superscape Control Language) attribute to an object. SCL can perform some of the actions available through the World and Shape Editors, but offers a wider range of functions. These functions are in the main areas of position, angles and rotations, movement, animation, bending, visibility, color, lighting, and viewpoints. SCL can also be attached to objects to give them a high level of "intelligence" and the ability to react to external events.

Flags—Toggles an object's flag(s) on and off. Flags specify certain simple features of an object, and an object can have several different flags as part of the standard attribute. Some examples of flags are Moveable (makes object moveable), Replace (indicates object is a replacement), Enterable (allows moving objects to enter this object's bounding cube), and so on.

Move and Resize—Alters the position and size of objects in any view.

Color—Changes the color attributes of an object.

Object Viewing

Plan View—Looking down from above.

South Elevation—Looking from the front.

West Elevation—Looking from the left side.

North Elevation—Looking from behind.

East Elevation—Looking from the right.

Show Groups—Displays a visible group of objects.

Perspective View—Restores the object to its original orientation and position.

Grid Snap—Makes objects "snap" to a grid.

VRT Menu

Go to Visualizer—Goes to the Visualizer, which is used primarily as the "playback" software, to display and interact with virtual worlds created in the Shape and World Editors. The stand-alone Visualizer system has only input device configuration options.

Go to Shape Editor—Goes to the Shape Editor, which is used to create points in space and link them together to define two-dimensional faces or facets. These facets are then used to create three-dimensional shapes. Once a shape is created, the Shape Editor lets you color it and add animation features.

Go to Main Menu—Displays the main menu.

The Superscape Shape Editor

The Shape Editor is for creating shapes, not objects. Objects are built from one or more shapes in the World Editor. Shapes are built in the Shape Editor.

The icon bar of the Shape Editor (see fig. 5.10) is similar to that of the World Editor, but it contains some variations.

Shape Management

Clear Shape—Removes the current shape from the current world.

Undo—Clears the most recent action. See World Editor for additional details about Undo.

Rename Shape—Gives the current shape a new name.

Select Shape—Selects the entire shape. Once the shape is selected, you can perform point and facet operations on the entire shape.

Go to Previous Shape—Displays the previous shape for this world. You can edit any of the shapes in the world at any time with the Shape Editor. In general, it's a good idea to store one shape before moving to the next.

Go to Next Shape—Displays the next shape for this world.

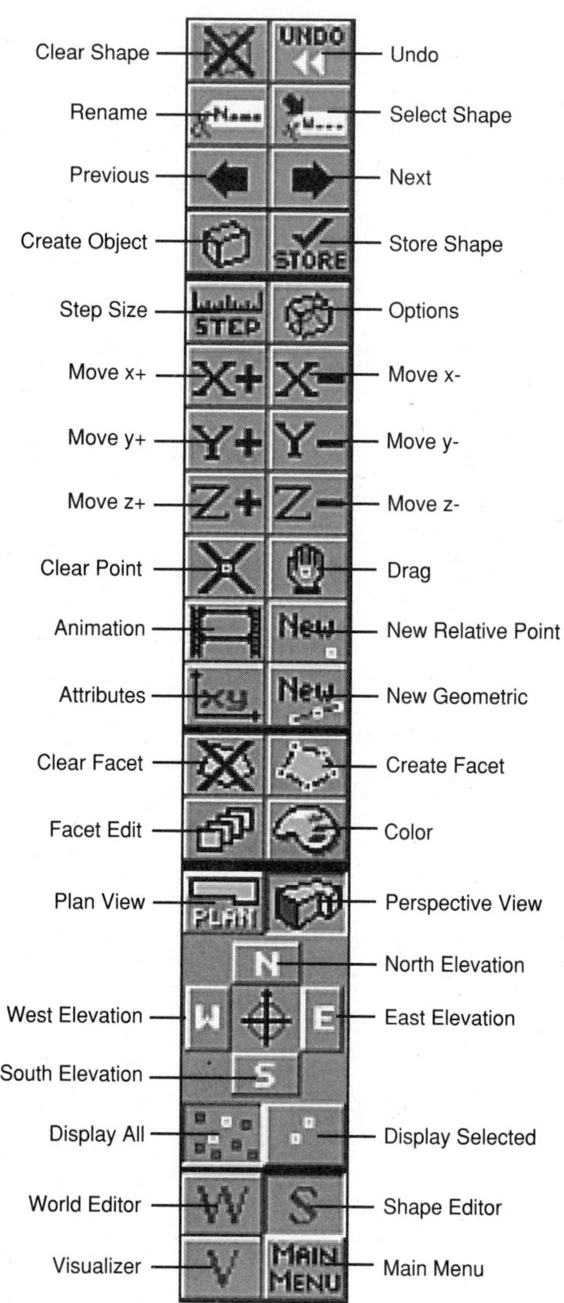

Figure 5.10. The Superscape Shape Editor icon bar.

Create Shape—Creates a bounding box within which you will create a shape. In other words, it adds a new shape to the world. It's up to you to define what that shape is using point and facets.

Store Shape—Saves recent changes to the shape. Many operations will lose changes if they are not stored, but Superscape is friendly about it—it always asks you if you want to store changes before moving on.

Positioning

Change Step Size—The Plus/Minus buttons move the selected point(s) a distance equal to the current step size. By changing the step size, you can increase or decrease fine control over the position of points.

Options Dialog—Allows you to choose which display options are in effect for the current shape. For example, you can turn construction lines on or off, and you can also choose whether to display point numbers, face numbers, and so on.

Plus/Minus Axis Buttons—These buttons are used for moving points in three dimensions—along the X, Y, and Z axes. There is one button for positive motion along each axis and another for negative motion. You can also move points using the arrow keys by pressing the Alt key along with the arrow key(s). Also see the Drag Points button.

Delete Point(s)—Deletes the currently selected point(s).

Drag Points—Allows you to move points by dragging them with the mouse.

Animations—This is a very powerful tool. It allows you to create complex animations by moving the points of a shape to different positions at different points in time. Animation must then be activated in the World Editor. Animations can run by themselves, or can be controlled during interaction with the virtual world in the Visualizer. Animations of complete objects occur in the World Editor; the Shape Editor only handles movement within the bounding box of the shape.

Create Relative Point—Creates a point by specifying its position in X, Y, and Z coordinates.

Set Size—Sets the size of the shape.

Create Geometric Point—Creates a point between two relative points. Geometric points render faster than relative points.

Facets

Delete Facet—Deletes the selected facet(s). A facet is not exactly the same things as a face. In Superscape, a face has two facets—one on each side of the face. You can set different properties and attributes for each facet. For example, a face can be transparent when viewed from one side, and colored when viewed from another.

Create Facet—Creates a facet from the currently selected points. In Superscape, you must be careful to select points in strict clockwise or counter-clockwise order. Otherwise, the facets will not fill the space correctly. The order in which you select the points determines which side of the face the created facet is on.

Edit Facets—Allows you to change the properties of any facet.

Color Facets—Applies a color from the current palette to a facet.

Object Viewing

Plan View—Looking down from above.

Perspective View—Restores the object to its original orientation and position.

South Elevation—Looking from the front.

West Elevation—Looking from the left side.

North Elevation—Looking from behind.

East Elevation—Looking from the right.

Display All Points—Displays all points in the shape.

Display Selected Points—Hides all points that are not currently selected. Points are selected by clicking on them; a second click deselects the point.

VRT Menu

Go to Visualizer—Goes to the Visualizer.

Go to World Editor—Goes to the World Editor.

Go to Main Menu—Displays the main menu.

The Superscape Visualizer

The Visualizer is the simplest part of the Superscape—there is no icon bar, there are no tools. The Visualizer has just one job: To help you interact with the virtual environment.

Figure 5.11. The Visualizer and its menu, showing a simple VR world.

As I mentioned previously, the Spaceball is by far the coolest way to move around. The intuitive capabilities of the Spaceball make it easy to move around, even in complex ways, such as turning and rising simultaneously. This is a very satisfying way to interact with a virtual environment.

Working with Superscape

Superscape comes with a bunch of manuals, and it looks pretty intimidating as you try to get started with it. I got a little worried when I first tried to use it—the interface looks to be quite different from other things I had tried to use.

That kind of a difference is often a warning sign, telling you that a product is funky. In this case, however, the differences were often improvements. You can't just sit down and immediately use Superscape, but as you learn how to work with it, it quickly begins to make sense. Even after my early fears, I give the interface a real A+ for workability.

However, that doesn't mean it's simple. The Superscape interface gets a good grade specifically because it makes a huge amount of power available to you. That means it's still going to take some time to get used to it.

The Superscape main menu is extremely nonintimidating,[6] as shown in figure 5.12. It's really just a list of the major tools available to you. The three most important tools—the World Editor, the Shape Editor, and the Visualizer—are listed first, and then other tools are listed. We'll focus mainly on the Big Three in this tutorial.

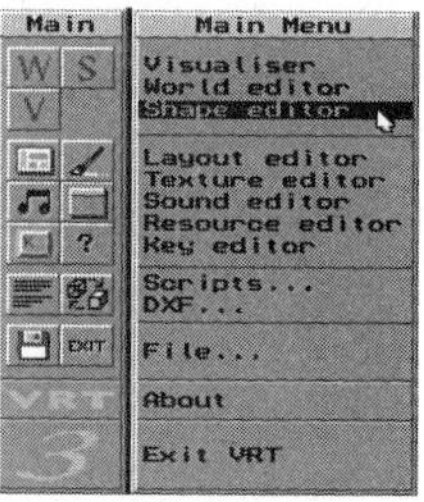

Figure 5.12. The Superscape main menu.

Creating a Shape

We'll begin with the Shape Editor. Before we create our first shape, let's look at some of the key features of the Shape Editor. When you first start it, you see a default shape: a cube (see fig. 5.13). Because the facets of the cube are colored, and because the cube is the same size as its bounding box, it's not clear yet which is which. You'll see the difference when we create a shape later in this tutorial.

Accessing menus in the Shape Editor is easy—just click with the right mouse button to display the Shape Editor menu (see fig. 5.14).

---

[6]Unless you look at how small it is, and remember that you just paid around $10,000 for this product! But have no fear—the main menu is just an entry point. There's enough functionality here to keep you busy for years.

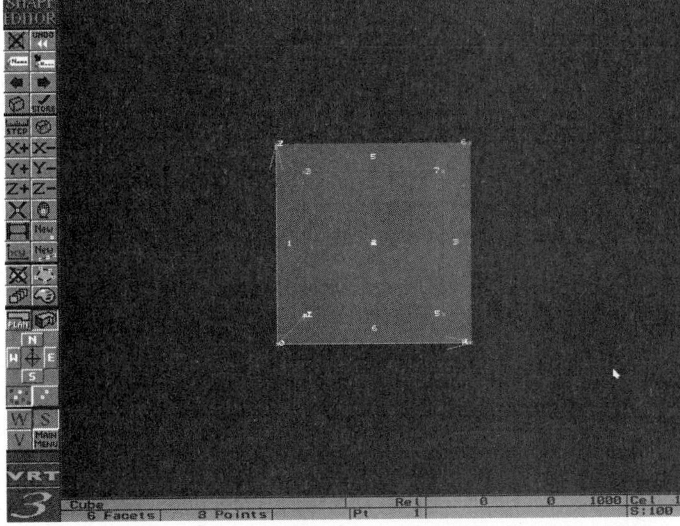

Figure 5.13.
The default cube shape.

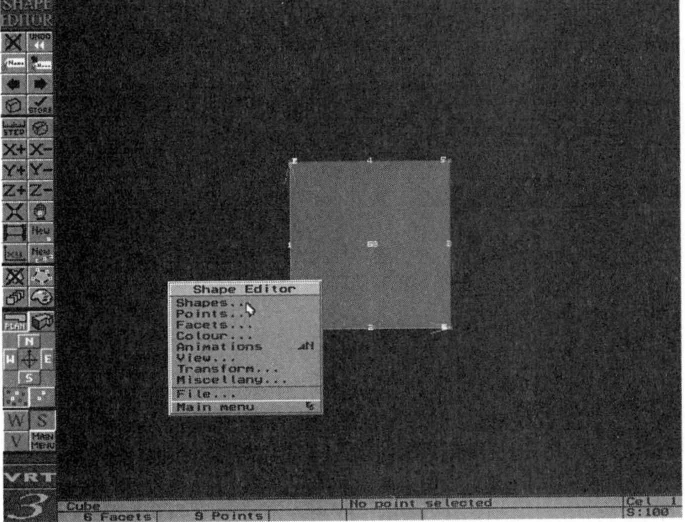

Figure 5.14.
All menus are just a right-click away.

You can easily change your point of view by using the arrow keys. Figure 5.15 shows a view of our cube from slightly below and to the right.

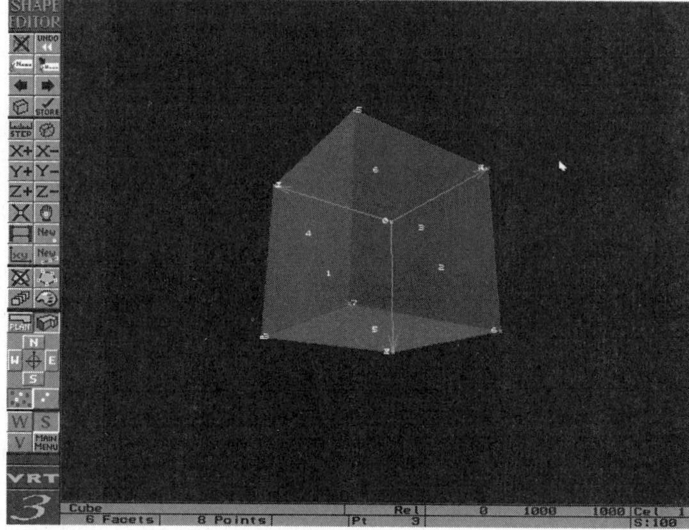

Figure 5.15. The point of view has been changed using the arrow keys.

You can also add a background[7] for the shape (see fig. 5.16). The background will not appear when you place the shape into an object. It is used to guide your work. For example, you could load a digitized view of an object, and then create on top of that to get the most realistic results.

Figure 5.16. You can use a background for tracing.

[7]Use the File menu option, Load Backdrop, after right-clicking.

You can also change the color of individual facets on the shape, as shown in figure 5.17. Clicking on the icon that looks like a painter's palette displays the Color pick list shown in figure 5.17. The color you pick will be applied to the currently selected facet(s).

Figure 5.17. Changing the color of a facet.

Enough theory! Let's get down and dirty, and create a shape of our own. Simply click the Create Shape icon in the icon bar. You'll see the outline of a cube. This isn't a cube like the last example—it's just the bounding box for our shape. To begin, click the New Relative Point icon, which displays the dialog box shown in figure 5.18.(8) You are being asked to supply the X, Y, and Z coordinates for the new point. Look ahead to figure 5.19, and note that the origin of the coordinate system is at the lower, front left of the bounding box. Creating a point at 250,250,250, as shown in figure 5.18, creates a point relatively close the origin because the bounding box is, by default, 1,000 × 1,000 × 1,000.

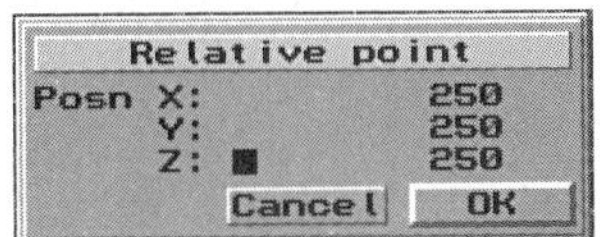

Figure 5.18. Creating a new relative point.

[8] Relative points must be created first—geometric points can only be created when you have two or more relative points to start from.

One point makes exactly nothing in 3D, so we'll need at least one more relative point to make a line. By changing just one coordinate to 500, we get the results shown in figure 5.19.

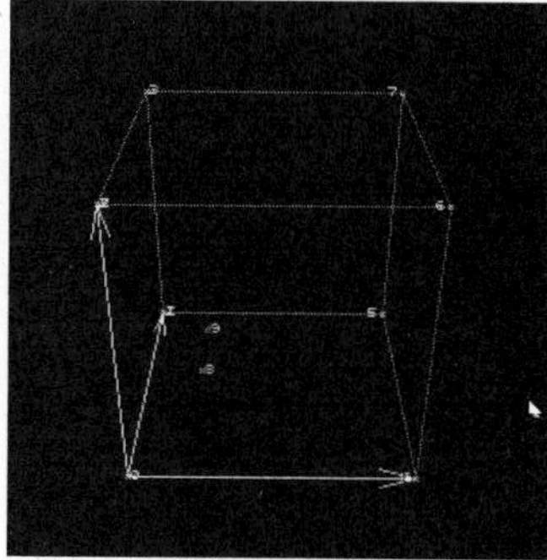

Figure 5.19. Two relative points have been created.

Note that each of the points is marked by a small x and a number. By default, each point displays as an x, and every point has a unique number.[9] To select a point, click on it once, and the x changes to a tiny square. I have selected both points (numbers 8 and 9) in figure 5.20.

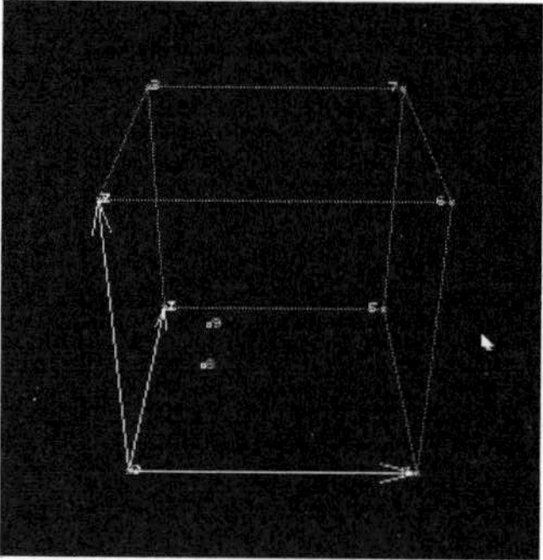

Figure 5.20. A selected point is marked by a tiny square instead of an x.

With these two relative points selected, we can easily create a geometric point—just click on the New Geometric Point button. The new point, number 10, is created between the two relative points (see fig. 5.21).

---

[9]Facets also have numbers, and you can display them using the Options button in the icon bar.

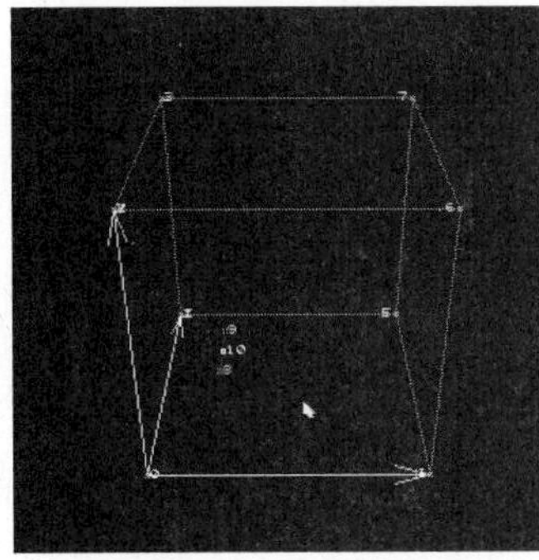

Figure 5.21. The new geometric point is midway between the two relative points used to create it.

By adjusting the coordinates in the New Relative Point dialog box, you can easily create two more relative points at the corners of a square (see fig. 5.22). The new points are numbered 11 and 12. In the figure, the mouse has been dragged around the two new relative points to select them. Once they are selected, you can create a geometric point between them, point number 13. I then continued to create two more geometric points on the other two sides of the square.[10]

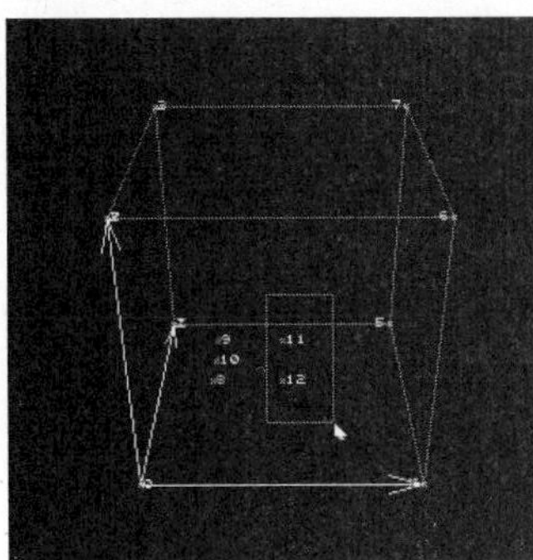

Figure 5.22. Two additional points have been created.

Now we have a whole lot of points, and it's time to create some facets. This is also easy to do. Look ahead to figure 5.23, which shows that we're going to create small triangular facets at the corners of the square. Clicking in counterclockwise order,[11] we click points 14, 8, and 9 to select them. Then click on the Create Facet button to create the facet. That's all there is to it! Figure 5.23 shows three facets already created. Each facet, like each point, has a unique number.

[10]For perfectionists and detail freaks, that means I created point 14 between points 8 and 12, and point 15 between points 9 and 11.

[11]If you click in clockwise order, the facet will be created on the other side of the face, and you won't be able to see it unless you rotate the shape. Remember: All faces have two sides! To create a facet on the side facing you, click counterclockwise.

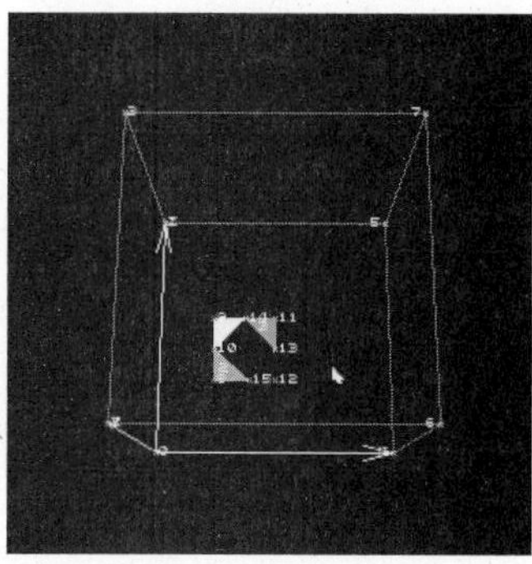

Figure 5.23. Three facets have been added to the shape.

All those numbers can get in the way of seeing your shape clearly, so you can turn them off. Select the Options button, and click on the buttons for face numbering and point numbering to turn them off. The result in shown in figure 5.24—the shape and the bounding box are now much less cluttered-looking.

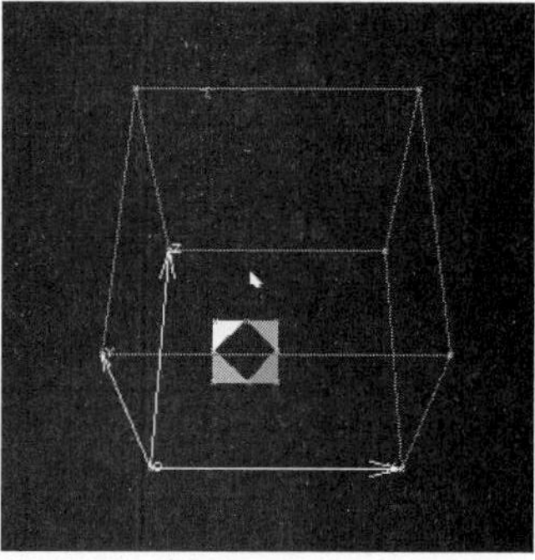

Figure 5.24. Point and facet numbering have been turned off.

We've done a lot so far, but our shape is not yet 3D—and that's what we're here for! It's easy to add points in the third dimension—just use the Z coordinate to create a new relative point above the existing points. You can use the X+, X-, Y+, Y-, Z+, and Z- buttons on the icon bar to position the new point exactly at the center of the existing shape (see fig. 5.25).

By selecting the appropriate points (in counterclockwise order, of course), you can easily create new facets that connect the existing facets to the new point. Figure 5.26 shows the first such facet, while figure 5.27 shows the object with all four new facets in place.

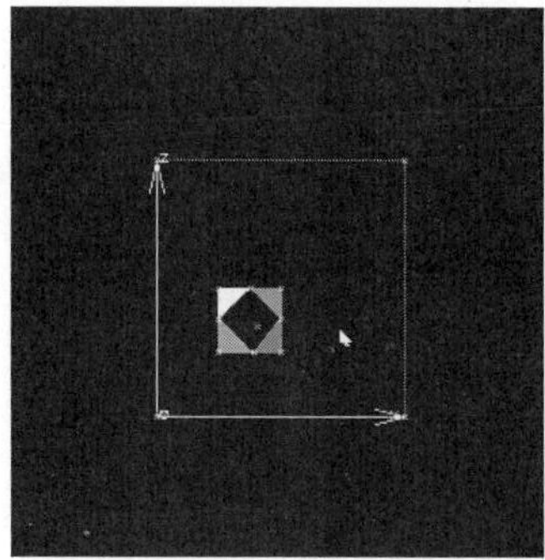

Figure 5.25. Creating a new point above the existing points.

Figure 5.26. Adding a facet.

Figure 5.27. All four new facets are in place.

We have one small remaining problem—the shape is much smaller than the bounding box that contains it. Ideally, the bounding box should be just big enough to contain the shape. This is easy to do—the Wrap Shape menu selection takes care of it in one step. The result is shown in figure 5.28. The shape is really too small, however, and what we really want to do is to set its size. As shown in figure 5.28, the Set Size button allows you to set the size of the object in each dimension.

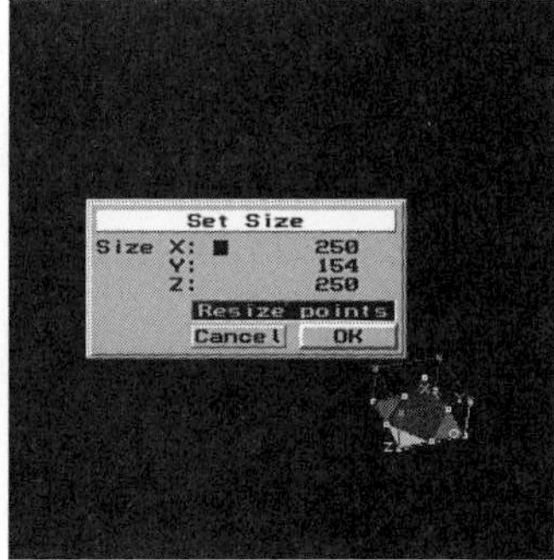

Figure 5.28. Wrapping the bounding box to the shape and setting a new size.

The result of resizing is shown in figure 5.29. I changed each dimension by multiplying the previous length by 4, but you could also distort the shape by changing different dimensions by different multipliers.

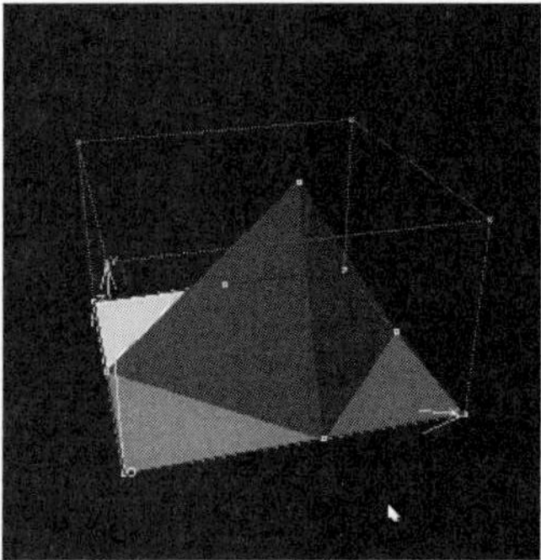

Figure 5.29. The shape has been resized.

There are lots of other things you can do to a shape, but we'll explore just one more—animation. Shape animation is an extremely powerful tool, but it's super easy to use. You start by creating new frames using the Animation Controller (see fig. 5.30). The Insert button will insert new cels[12] in the animation; 15-25 should be good for what I've got in mind.

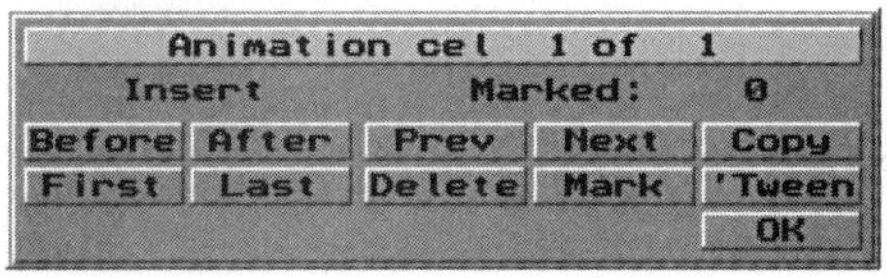

Figure 5.30. The Animation Controller.

---

[12]An animation cel is a single image. It is not the same as a frame, however; a frame can have several cels in it. Each cel is a single image of one or more objects. For example, if you have an animation of a bouncing ball and a waving stick, each frame could have one cel for the ball and another for the stick.

Animation consists of nothing more than moving around the points of the object. Be default, all points are static; you must define which points are to become dynamic using the Points menu (see fig. 5.31). To make a point dynamic, select the point and then click on Convert stat-dyn (static to dynamic).

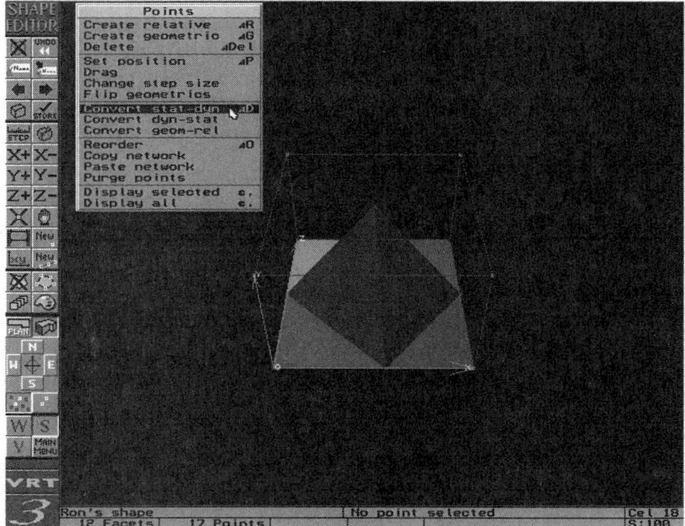

Figure 5.31. Defining dynamic points.

With the animation controller active, you now go to the first cel (click the First button in the controller), and move the dynamic points to their starting position.[13] Now select all points that will move in the animation, and click the Mark button. This tells the Animation Controller which points are involved. Not all dynamic points will be involved in all animations—you can, after all, have several different animations for the same shape!

Now click the Last button in the controller to move to the last cel. Move the dynamic points to their final location (see fig. 5.32).

To create the intermediate cels, click the Tween button. This displays the various types of tweening, as shown in figure 5.33.

[13]If they are already where you want them, of course, you do nothing!

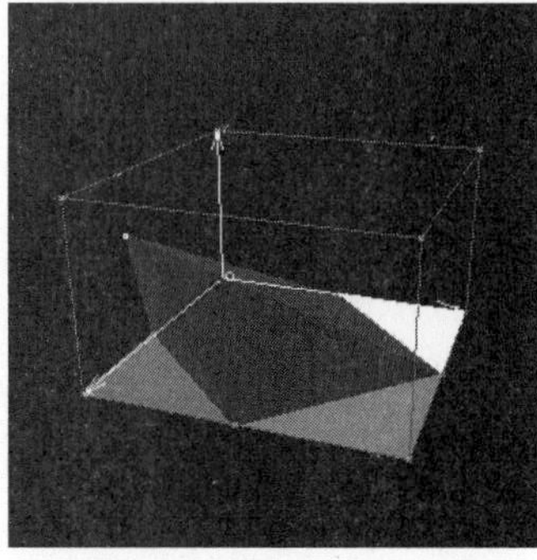

Figure 5.32.
The end point of the animation.

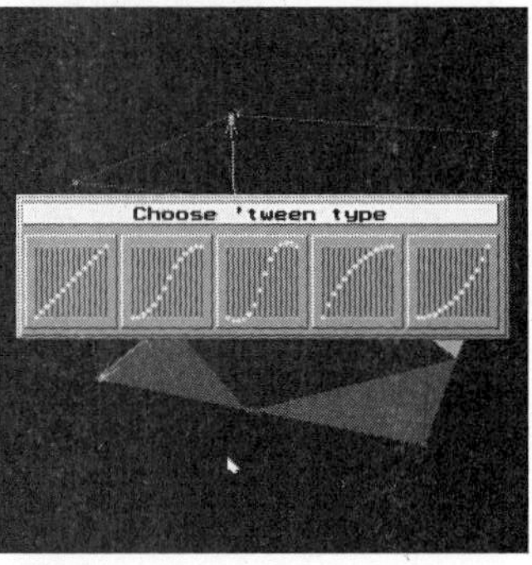

Figure 5.33.
Choosing the Tween type.

There are five different kinds of tweening shown in figure 5.32 (from left to right):

Linear	Points move at a constant speed and then stop.
Cosine	Points accelerate and decelerate at the start and finish of the animation.
Exaggerated	Points overshoot slightly at both ends.
Accelerate	Points accelerate and then stop.
Decelerate	Points decelerate to a stop.

These types of tweens allow you to create life-like motion for your animation. Figure 5.34 shows an intermediate cel in the animation. Figure 5.35 shows the animation in the World Editor.

The Shape in the World

You can move to the World Editor by clicking the W icon in the icon bar. The world will be pretty dull—no objects to speak of. The first order of business is to create an object based on our shape. It couldn't be easier: Click on the Create Object button in the icon bar to display the dialog box shown in figure 5.35. Then pick the shape of your choice, and click the OK button. As you can see at the right of figure 5.35, you can preview each shape. This is convenient if you have a large library of shapes for your world.

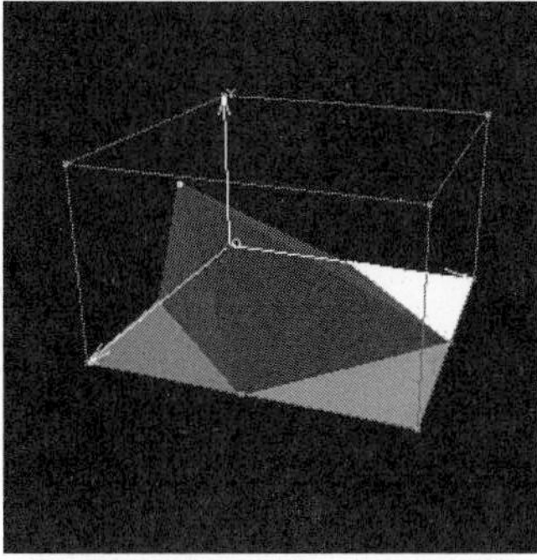

Figure 5.34. An intermediate point in the animation.

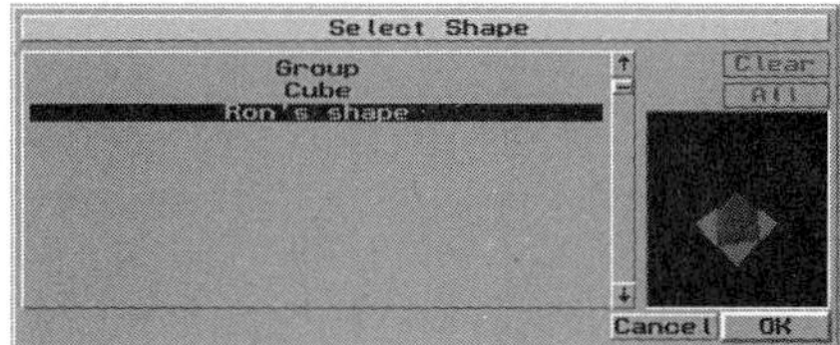

Figure 5.35. Selecting a shape in the World Editor.

The shape will attaches itself to the cursor, and the view switches to the Plan View (see fig. 5.36). Position the shape where you would like it to be, and click to place it.

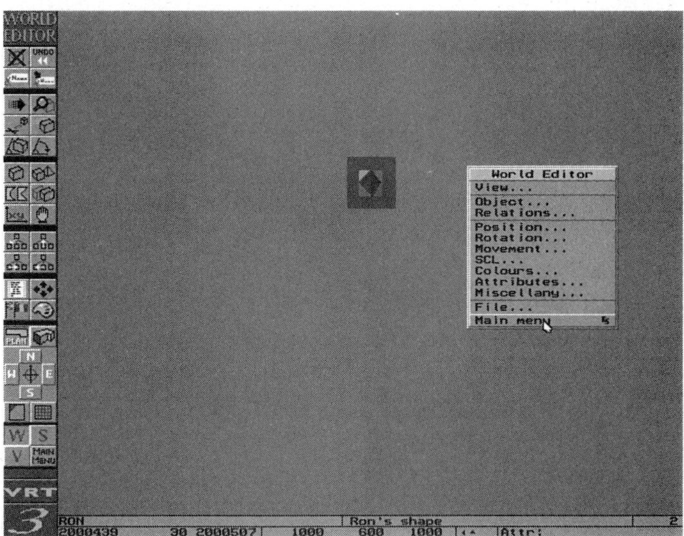

Figure 5.36. Placing a new object.

To activate the animation, use the Movement submenu. You will create an animation (number 1; everything has a number in Superscape). You must then choose the Animation mode. The mode determines if the animation runs at all, loops, operates interactively, and so on. You can also set the speed of the animation, starting and ending frames, and so on. As usual, Superscape offers complete control.

Virtual Is as Virtual Does

To interact with the simple world, go to the Visualizer by clicking the V icon. Figure 5.37 shows four views of the animation in progress in the Visualizer.

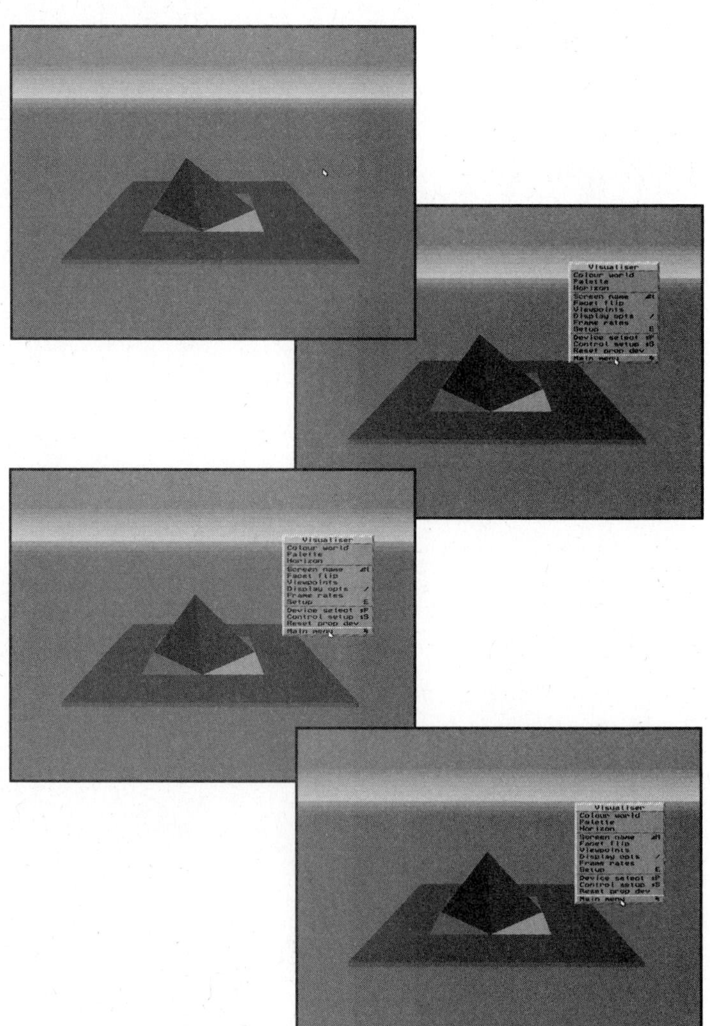

Figure 5.37.
Four views of the animation.

You can easily add textures to the object instead of the flat colors is has now. Access the Texture Editor from the main menu; you'll see something like figure 5.38.

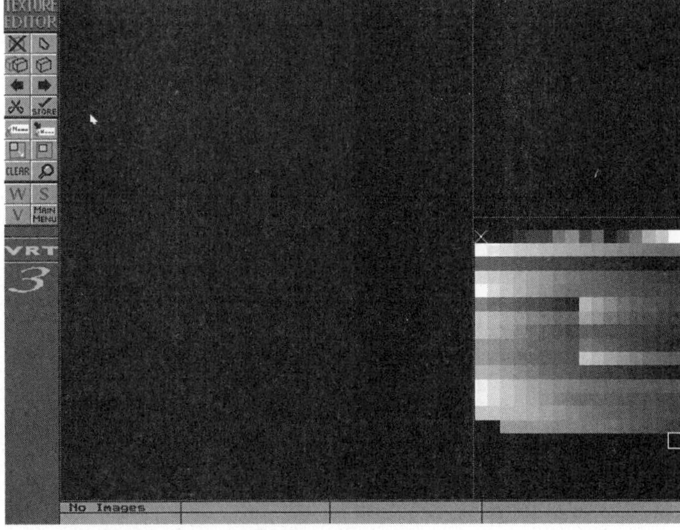

Figure 5.38. The Texture Editor.

You can load a PCX file into the Texture Editor and build a library of textures. Figure 5.39 shows one of the texture files supplied with Superscape. There are only a few, so count on creating your own textures.

Figure 5.39. A texture from a Texture library.

A scanner is the ideal way to collect textures. Or, you can use PhotoCD discs and convert the PCD files to PCX using any competent image-editing software. I use Photoshop from Adobe, but Corel supplies a simple PhotoCD with its converted Corel Professional Photos on CD-ROM—and it works really well! Plus, you get a ton of useful images, and several of the CD-ROMs contain texture images.

Figure 5.40 shows the dialog box for applying a texture in the World Editor, and figure 5.41 shows the result.

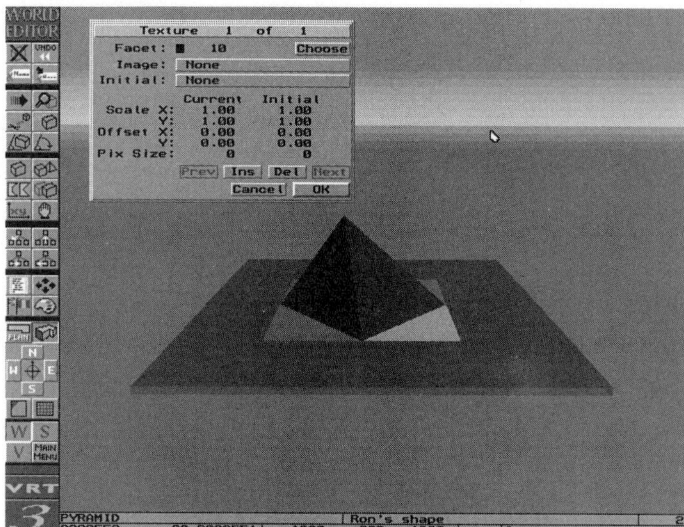

Figure 5.40. Setting a texture for a facet.

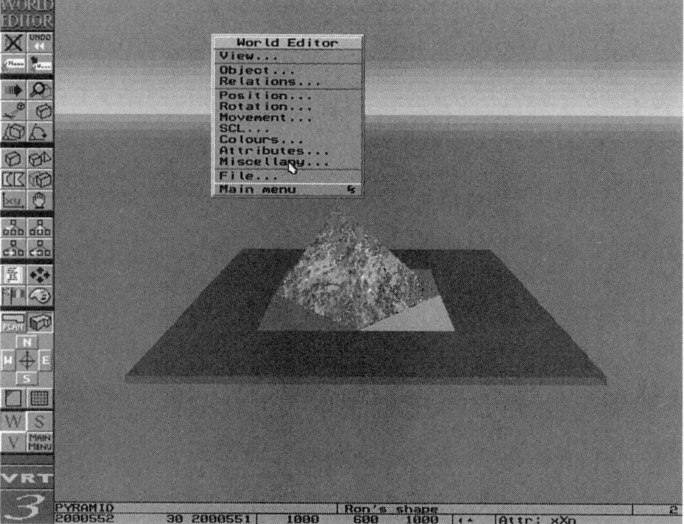

Figure 5.41. A texture has been applied to several facets.

All in all, Superscape was a pleasure to work with. It's awfully darn deep, however, so if you go this route, plan to take a few weeks to learn the ins and outs of the product. It's definitely a solid, professional effort. It's expensive, but if you need the best, this is it!

Give Me Some Space!

Virtual reality is very convenient. It doesn't have the same limitations as regular reality. Gravity, for example, is actually a serious bother when it comes to programming for VR. Friction is another real hassle. Sometimes, of course, these are highly desirable. If you are an industrial engineer designing parts for a new jet, things like friction and gravity are the point of the VR process—you want to learn about the performance of your designs in the real world by messing around with them in a virtual world. If the correspondence between real and virtual is not accurate, and that jet crashes...

For the rest of us, the stakes are so low as to be negligible. Fun is the order of the day. And when it comes to fun, things like gravity and friction can get in the way or be part of the game—rules become arbitrary. You can omit the rules, make up new rules, or give the rules a new twist. For example, if you would like to fly through the solar system, the distance between the planets in the real universe is inconveniently large. Things like the mass of propellant required to accelerate quickly, the effects of acceleration, and the speed of light all contribute to making a real-time simulation not much fun. But if we were to conveniently ignore such details, the solar system could be as accessible as an amusement park ride.(14)

14Time to discuss the moral side of virtual reality. I recently read an editorial regarding the existence of nature shows on television. Surely, the author suggested, if there were an unmitigated good on television, it would be nature shows. He then shot down that argument by pointing out that nature shows are actually quite artificial, and are giving people an incomplete—and often a staged—picture of reality. For example, nature shows are dramatic, while nature itself consists of vast stretches of very undramatic time punctuated by short, intense dramas. Only the latter are presented to the television viewer, and the result, the author suggested, is a twisted, inaccurate, and sometimes dangerous view of nature.

Can the same be said of virtual reality? Does the twisting and altering of the rules of the nature of reality carry some kind of price tag? I won't pretend to have an answer, and the whole issue is so uncertain that I almost don't have an opinion on the matter. If pressed, I would mention that overuse of carrots can lead to serious trouble, too. I can't buy the idea that adults are credulous enough to buy that nature shows represent reality. If we have become so civilized that we can be fooled extensively about the nature of reality itself, then, yes, we ought to back up a little and reconsider. Heck, a walk in the woods will disabuse just about anyone of false views of nature, and an occasional slip on a banana peel ought to be enough of a reminder of the effects of gravity for even the most jaded VR fanatic.

The Solar System

Speaking of the solar system, why don't we create one of our own? This is a big project, and I'm going to pull out the big guns to do it "right"—3D Studio, to be exact. This does not mean that you couldn't use such software as REND 386 or Imagine to create your universe, but 3D Studio has some advantages that I like for this project. The first of those is space itself. 3D Studio is quite expansive about its use of space. The scale of objects within a 3D space can be anything you want it to be. If we want to work at a scale of millions or billions of miles, that's OK with 3D Studio.

I'm going to introduce some inaccuracies into this version of the solar system for the sake of simplicity. If you are following along at home, check the footnotes to see how to add more "reality" to the project.[15] For this demonstration, I'll take you as far as the Earth. That leaves Mars and the gas giants for an extra-credit project.

In the beginning, there was the opening screen of 3D Studio (see fig. 5.42). Into this reality came the cursor, and the cursor said to the menu, Create/GSphere.[16] And the result was good (see fig. 5.43). This is going to be the sun. When you are asked to provide a name, use "Sun." Before it acts like the a sun, however, you'll need to set some attributes.

---

[15]What is reality, anyway, in these days of quantum mechanics, wave-particle duality, and string theory? Not to mention the uncertainty principle. At the subatomic level, we're living in an "unpredictable, many-dimensioned world that isn't even continuous, or even consistently solid." If these terms are unfamiliar, they are part of the lingo of nuclear physics. Here's a rough translation into ordinary English: the universe is made up of little bitty particles that jump from here to there, even when there's no actual connection between here and there. How they do that, when they do that, and whether they stay as little bitty particles while they do it is all open to question. There. Doesn't that give you a nice, cozy feeling about the nature of reality?

[16]3D Studio lets you create two kinds of spheres. One kind is constructed of faces that are oriented to lines of latitude and longitude (LSphere). The other kind is more like a geodesic sphere (GSphere). For our purposes, there isn't much need to distinguish between the two. If you planned to deform the sphere into a different shape, then the way that the sphere is constructed would be more important. In our case, I'm not planning anything worse than a planetary explosion. Either kind of sphere will be fine, although there are subtle differences in how they explode.

RECIPE

4T 3D Studio
1 Astronomy book
1 CompuServe account
A dash of Photoshop
1 part disdain for pure celestial mechanics

Instructions: Create a series of spheres in 3D Studio, then apply texture maps corresponding at least roughly to planetary features. Consult a book on astronomy for things like relative sizes of the planets. For a gourmet touch, download planetary images from CompuServe, or create your own in Photoshop or another photo-realistic paint program. Unless you want to spend an enormous amount of time on the recipe, leave out exact details of celestial mechanics.

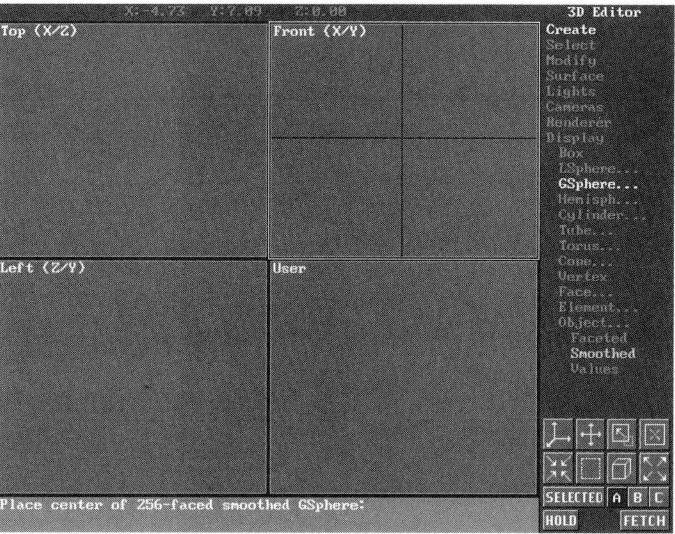

Figure 5.42. The 3D Studio opening screen.

The first step is to put a light inside the sun. Place the light at the center of the sphere. Make it an *omni light,* which does not cast shadows and will therefore illuminate the scene even though it is inside an object. Set the brightness of the light to 255.

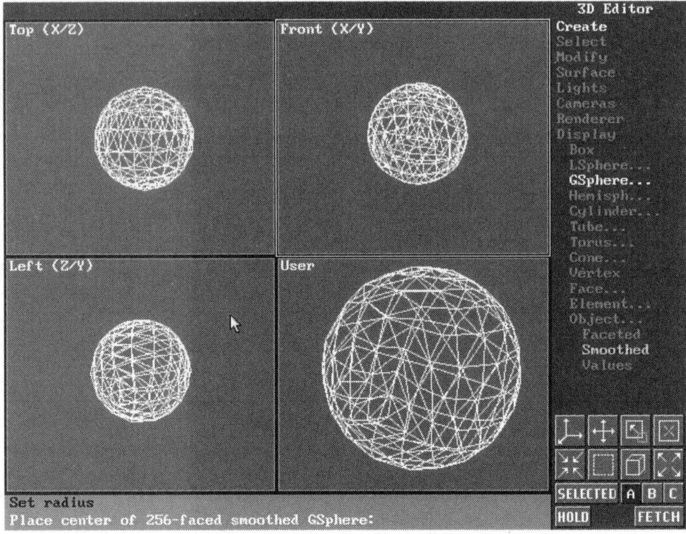

Figure 5.43. A geodesic sphere.

Use the Surface/Material/Choose menu to access the Material Selector (see fig. 5.44). This is a list of the materials available in the current library. Believe it or not, Yellow Glass will make a good start—you'll need to modify it a bit in the Materials Editor, however. For now, choose Yellow Glass as the current material, and then assign it to the sphere. You'll be adding some surface texture to the sun in the Materials Editor, so you will also need to apply mapping coordinates to the sphere. Set the mapping type as Spherical, scale the coordinates to be just slightly smaller than the sun, and then locate the center of the mapping coordinates coincident with the center of the sun sphere. Check both the Front and Left viewports to make sure that the mapping coordinates are located properly, and then assign them to the sun sphere.

To check your work, render the User view at a small size, such as 320×200.[17]

You'll need to modify the settings for Yellow Glass in the Materials Editor. Press the F5 key to change to the Materials Editor now. To modify the Yellow Glass material, load it using the Material/Get Material option from the Scene menu (see fig. 5.45).

---

[17] You can set the rendering size using the Render/Setup/Configuration dialog box.

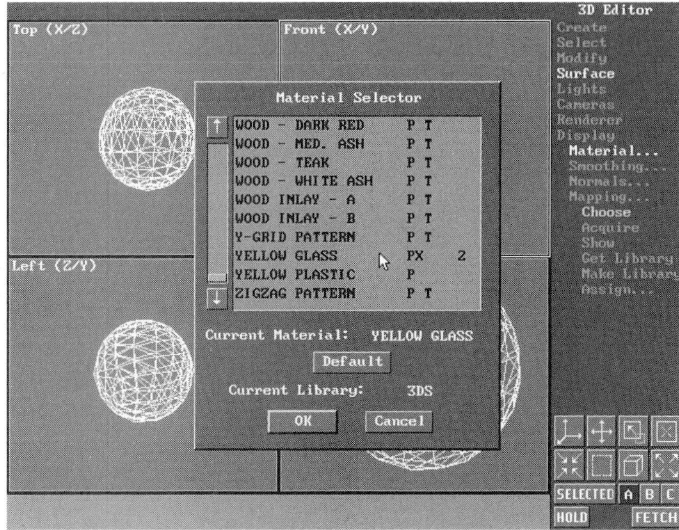

Figure 5.44.
The Material Selector.

Figure 5.45.
Getting a material from the current scene.

Make the following changes to the Yellow Glass material:

- Reduce the shininess to 0.
- Add a texture map using the Texture button at the bottom of the screen. Choose one that seems appropriate for a sun. I would suggest using the file GRANITE.CEL, which is about as close as you can come without using a sun-specific image. You can create a texture map from scratch using a

paint program, or download an image of the sun from one of the CompuServe graphics forums.[18]

- Add a bump map using the Bump button at the bottom of the screen. In most cases, you'll want to use the same image you used for the texture map or a variation of it. GRANITE.CEL works great.
- Click the Self-Illum button to make the sun a self-illuminating object. This is the only way to create a sun that is at all realistic. Putting multiple lights inside the sun and making it partially transparent does not give you a bright enough result.

To see the results of your tinkering, click the Render button. When you have the material just the way you want it, use the menu at the top of the screen to put the material into the current library. Give it an appropriate name, such as Sun Texture. You must put a material into the library in order to be able to use it in the 3D Editor. You could also put the revised material Yellow Glass back into the scene, but only do this if you do not need the original material for other objects.

"Let there be light" is only the beginning—it's on to Mercury. Create another GSphere (see fig. 5.46). In the real solar system, the size difference between Mercury and the sun is enormous. In fact, the real solar system is made up mostly of empty space. This makes for a challenging simulation, and the easiest way to solve it is to make the planets larger. The goal of this simulation is to tour the inner solar system. Since a realistic model would spend most of its time on the way to the next planet, a model with enlarged planets makes more sense for this example. If your goal is to show the empty space instead of the planets, a realistic model would do a better job.

For example, I initially tried creating Mercury at the size shown in figure 5.47. The object representing Mercury is so small, I thought it might be hard to find, so I put the mouse cursor next to it—Mercury is the tiny little dot just in front of the mouse cursor.

The material Orange Plastic makes a reasonable starting point for Mercury. I made some modifications in the Materials Editor (see fig. 5.48). I set the shininess down a bit to 7, and added a texture map and a bump map. I used the same file for both: TILE009.TGA. This is a standard texture file that comes with 3D Studio. It gives a nice planetary look to the surface of Mercury. As with the sun, you can explore

[18]There are a number of NASA images in various forums on CompuServe. You can also check the Astronomy forum for possibilities.

CompuServe for interesting planetary images. The Astronomy Forum (ASTROFORUM) would be a good place to look; you can find many NASA images there.

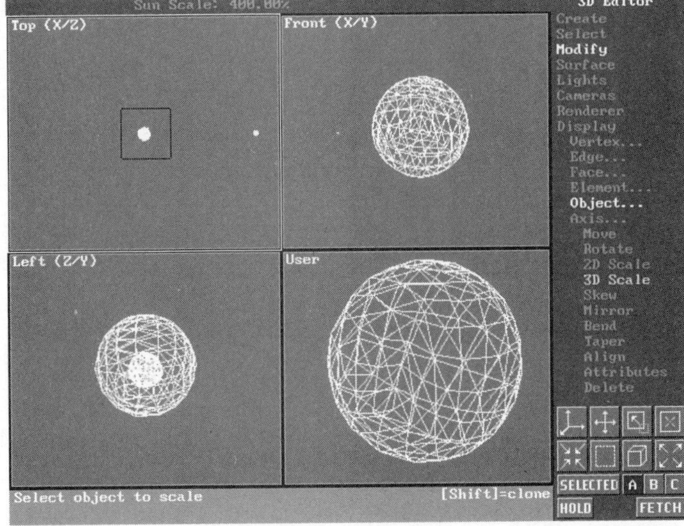

Figure 5.46. Creating Mercury as another GShpere.

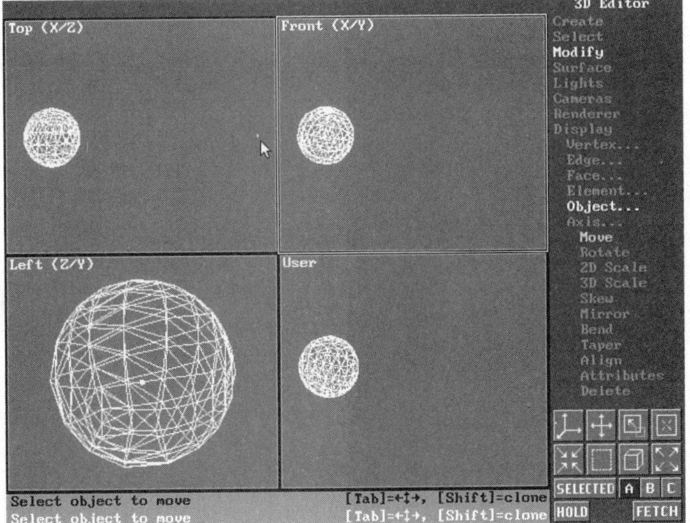

Figure 5.47. A smaller version of Mercury.

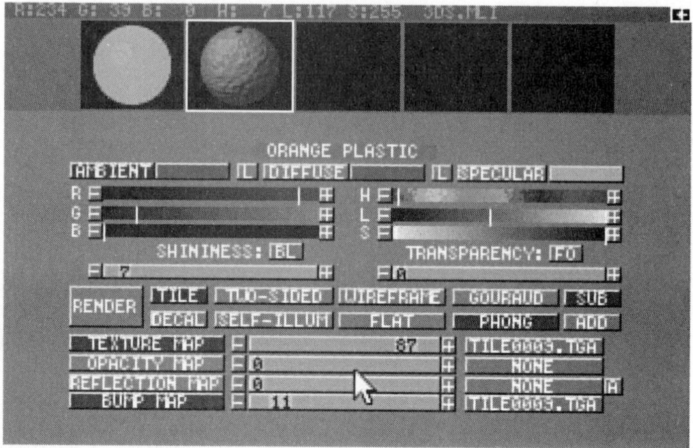

Figure 5.48. Setting material attributes for Mercury.

The solar system model is very large, and rendering can be a pain if you don't add a camera or three. I would suggest adding a camera for each object you want to test during development. Figure 5.49 shows a camera set up for viewing Mercury. The Top and Front viewports show the camera in relation to the planet. The Left viewport shows the extreme difference in size between the sun and Mercury. The lower right viewport, labeled Camera01, shows the view through the camera.

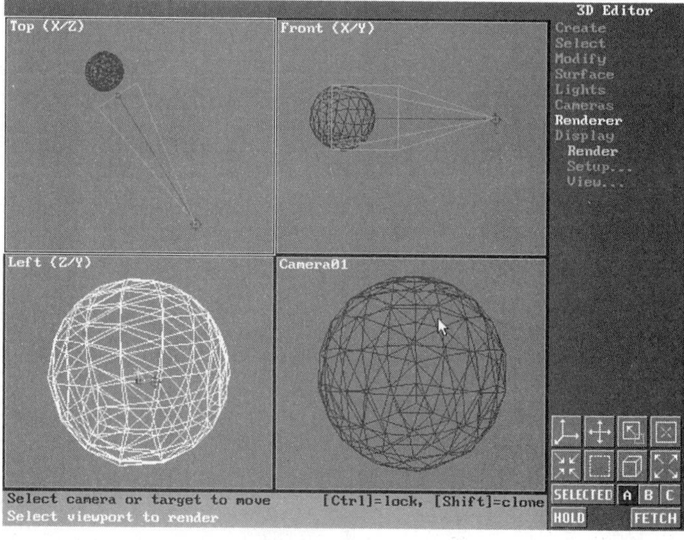

Figure 5.49. Setting up a camera for test renderings of the planets.

Once you have a camera set up, you can render to see how well the choice of materials works. Figure 5.50 shows an artfully arranged camera view, with both Mercury and the sun in the camera frame. The only problem with viewing Mercury from the back is that it is lit from the front by the sun—all you will see from this angle is a dark disk.

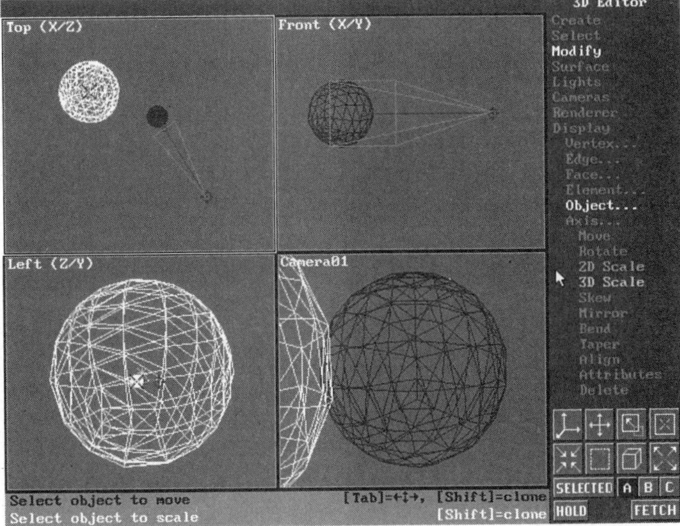

Figure 5.50. Composing a view for the camera.

To apply the revised material to Mercury, you will need to follow the same steps you used for the sun. Don't forget to set the mapping coordinates. While we are on the subject of mapping coordinates, I'd like to point out a common source of frustration in renderings. Figure 5.51 shows the wrong way to set up spherical mapping coordinates for an object in 3D Studio—the coordinates are trying to be exactly the same as the object they will be assigned to. It is better to make the mapping coordinates a little larger or a little smaller than the object. If the size difference is too small, part of the mapping coordinates will wind up on the inside of the object, and part on the outside. This results in a fractured appearance during rendering. Using different sizes avoids the problem.

The next step, of course, is to create Venus. Venus is larger than Mercury, so size the GSphere accordingly. There is a useful material, Blue Planet, that makes an excellent starting point for Venus (see fig. 5.52).

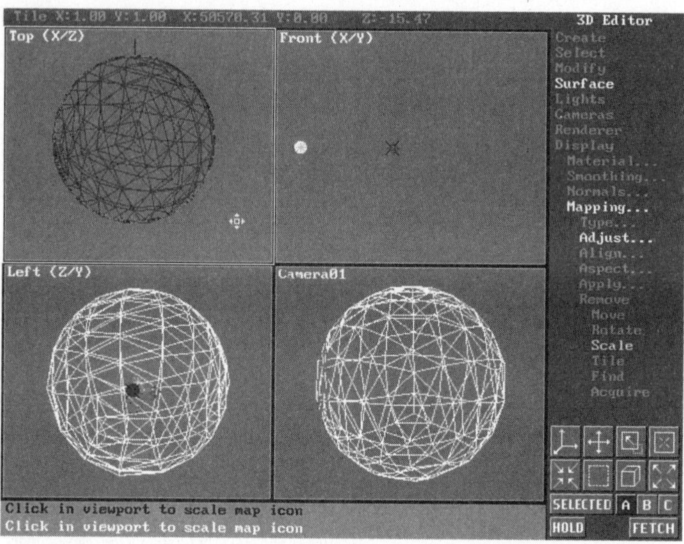

Figure 5.51. Incorrect setting of mapping coordinates.

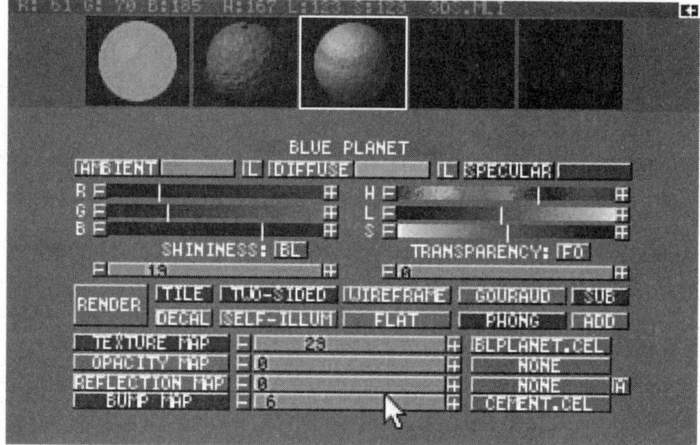

Figure 5.52. Setting material attributes for Venus.

I suggest a few changes to Blue Planet to make it look more like Venus:

- Reduce the shininess to 19.
- Reduce the texture map percentage to 29.
- Use CEMENT.CEL as a bump map, with a percentage setting of 6.
- Set the Ambient and Diffuse lighting to a light bluish cyan.

As with the sun and Mercury, you will need to put the revised material back into the library or the scene, and you'll need to set appropriate mapping coordinates for Venus. Check your work by creating a camera for Venus and rendering. To set the camera viewport, use the Camera Selector shown in figure 5.53. You can access the Camera Selector by pressing Ctrl-V, clicking the Camera button, and then clicking on the viewport to be used for a camera view.

Finally, create the planet Earth as yet another GSphere. Figure 5.54 shows the Earth before a camera has been created for Earth. Earth is the tiny dot at the right of the Top viewport. 3D Studio comes with a map of Earth that you can apply as a spherical texture map in the Materials Editor (see fig. 5.55).

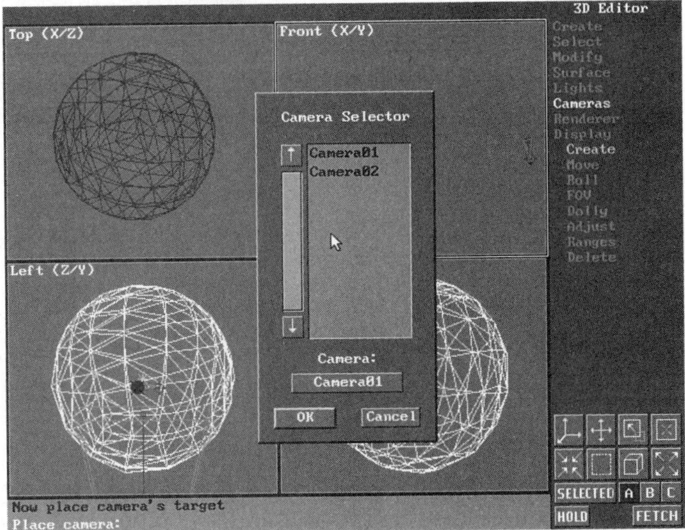

Figure 5.53. Selecting the camera to use for the camera viewport.

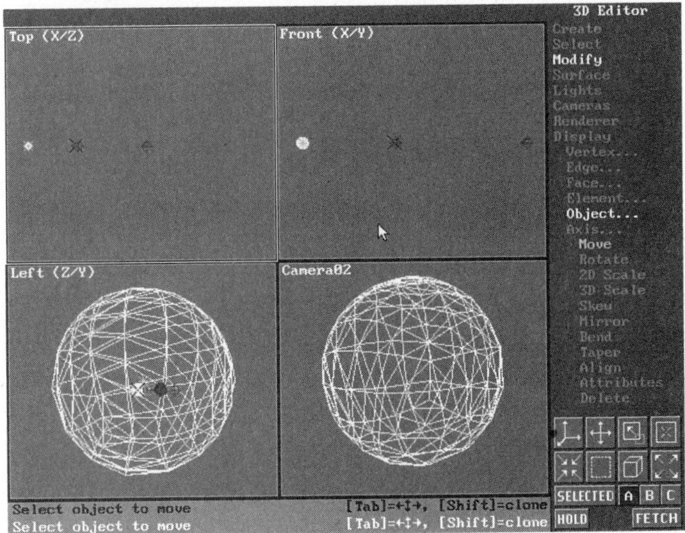

Figure 5.54. Creating Earth.

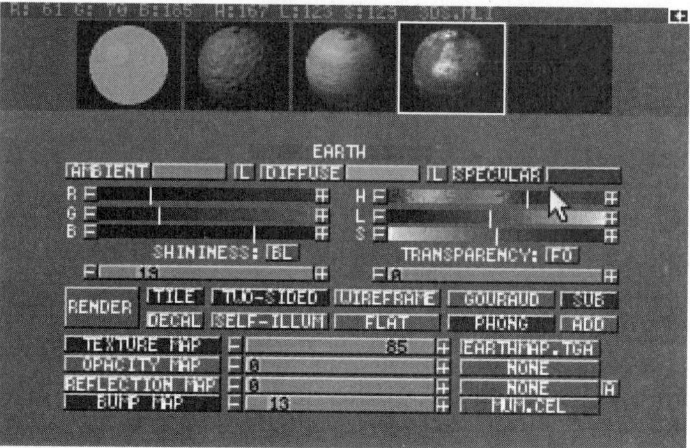

Figure 5.55. Creating an Earth material in the Materials Editor.

Set the texture map to the file EARTHMAP.TGA, using a texture map setting of 85 and bluish colors for the Ambient and Diffuse attributes. You may also want to add a bump map for visual interest; I used MUM.CEL, which has the humorous effect of making the Earth look like a slightly under-inflated beach ball. You can see all four materials in small-scale renderings in figure 5.55.

As with the other objects, I would suggest creating a camera to test the rendering of the Earth before moving on. You can continue to create the additional planets in the same manner shown for the inner solar system. For this example, the Earth is the last planet you'll create. Once you have enough planets to satisfy your cravings for creative power, add a camera a little farther out than the Earth (see fig. 5.56). You'll use the Keyframer to fly this camera through the model of the solar system in the Keyframer.

Figure 5.57 shows the camera attached to a dummy object,(19) and a path that takes it past the Earth. The current frame number is 120 out of 480(20) total frames. This view is from above, and shows the first stage of creating the camera path.(21) I have

---

[19]Dummy objects can be created in the Keyframer using the Hierarchy menu. A dummy object is required because you cannot create a unified path for the camera and its target, but you can create one for a dummy object. You only need to use the Hierarchy/Link menu option to link both the camera and the target to the dummy object. Wherever the dummy goes, the camera/target will follow.

[20]I later adjusted the animation to use 600 frames. 480 frames wasn't enough to provide a smooth trip over more than 100 million miles. The Earth is only 93 million miles from the sun, but I took the long way around.

[21]I will call it the camera path for the sake of clarity, but keep in mind that it is actually the dummy object's path that is being adjusted.

labeled the various objects in the view to make it easier to follow along. Note the small squares along the path. They are key frames that I created using the Paths/Add Key menu option. I added the key frames at approximately even intervals along the path, and they can be used to adjust the path.

Figure 5.56. Adding a camera for the fly-through.

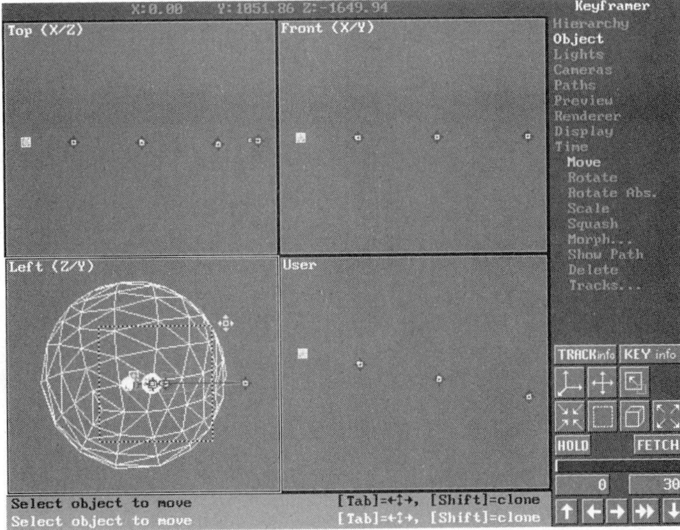

Figure 5.57. Setting up the camera for a flight through the solar system.

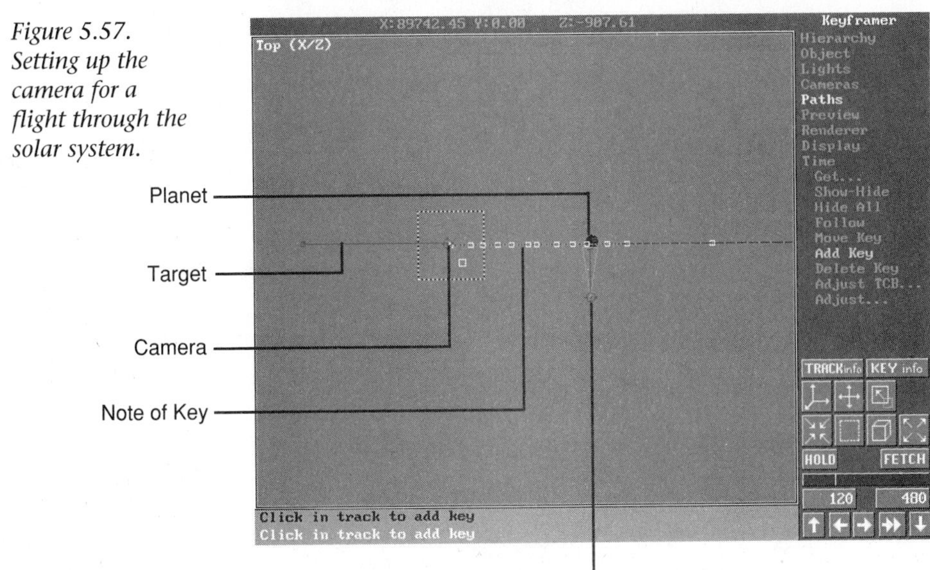

Not only would this straight path be boring, but it happens to go right through the Earth—not good. There are several approaches you can use in this situation. One is to orbit the Earth and then fly away again, as shown in figure 5.58. This was done by simply clicking and dragging the various key frame indicators to new positions.

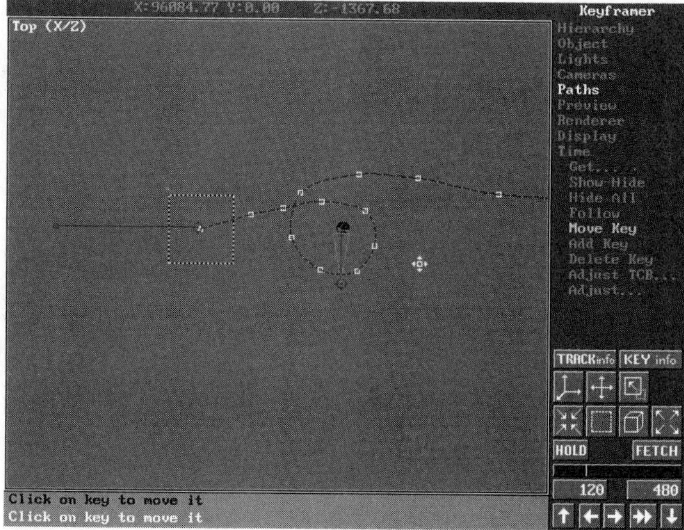

Figure 5.58. Orbiting the Earth.

This isn't enough, however, because the camera angle remains the same—that is, pointing toward the sun. To face the camera toward the Earth, use the Object/Rotate menu option to rotate the dummy object so the camera faces the Earth at each of the key frames.[22] Figure 5.59 shows the camera angle properly adjusted.

You can also make changes to the camera to make life easier. Figure 5.60 shows the Camera Definition dialog box, which allows you to set various camera parameters. If the orbit is too close to the planet, for example, you can use a wider lens angle. The Stock Lenses listed correspond in their behavior to typical lenses for a 35mm camera. That is, the lenses with focal lengths ranging from 15mm to 35mm are considered wide-angle lenses, the 50mm lens is a "normal" lens, and the remaining lenses are considered telephoto lenses.

---

[22]For an added dimension of realism, you can tilt the Earth's axis by 22.5 degrees in the Front view before you add the rotation. You can also add appropriate axial tilts for the other planets if you want.

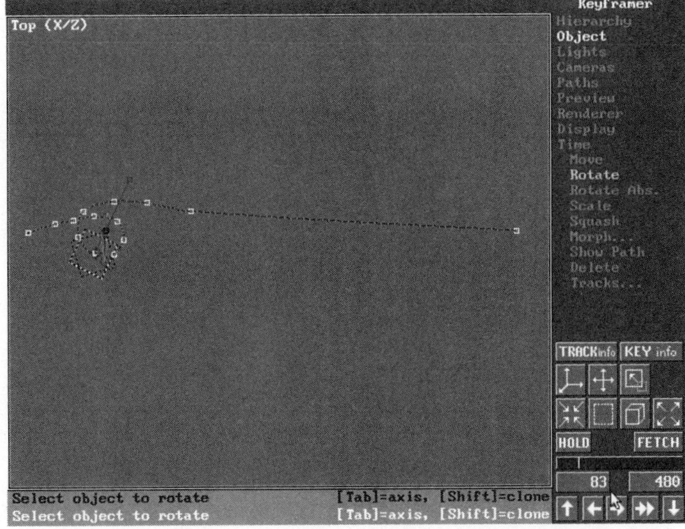

Figure 5.59. Adjusting the camera angle while in orbit.

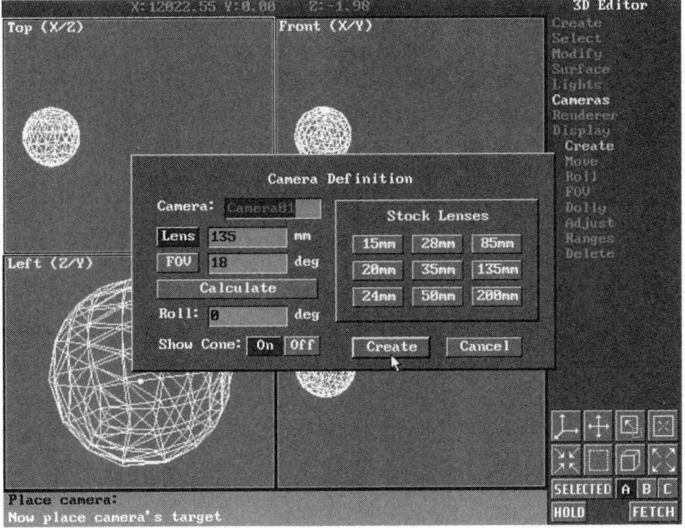

Figure 5.60. Adjusting the camera.

Another possible approach for a fly-through is to create a path that weaves from planet to planet. To create such a path, move to the last frame and position the dummy object (and therefore the attached camera) between Mercury and the sun using the Object/Move menu option (see fig. 5.61).

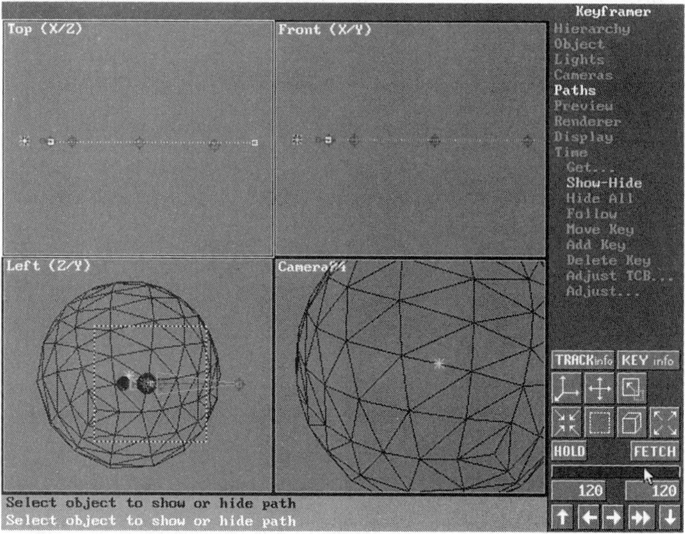

Figure 5.61. Setting the camera position for the final frame.

Add a series of new key frames using the Paths/Add Key menu option as shown in figure 5.62. These should be spaces at approximately equal intervals.

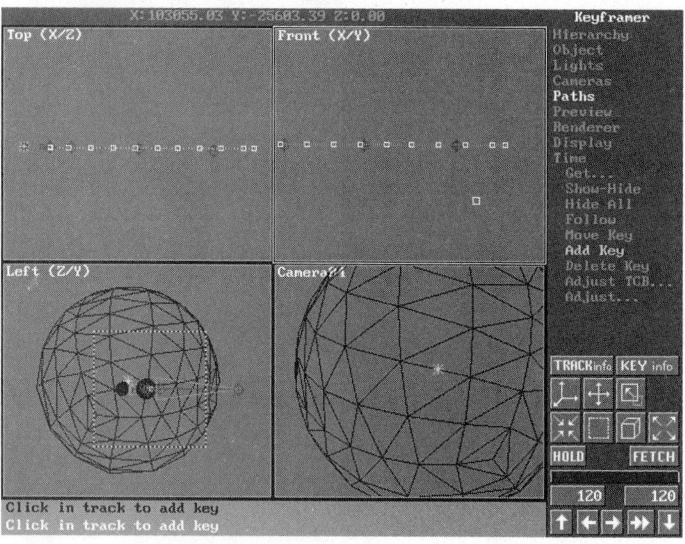

Figure 5.62. Adding additional key frames.

You can now enlarge the Top view to adjust the position of the camera in the corresponding key frames. Press Ctrl-V to access the Viewport dialog box shown in figure 5.63. You can choose from any of the viewport arrangements shown in the top two rows of the dialog box. To determine which view shows up in a port, choose a view from the list at the bottom, and then click in a viewport in the diagram at the bottom left. If you choose Camera and there is more than one camera, you will see a dialog box asking you to specify which camera to use for that viewport.

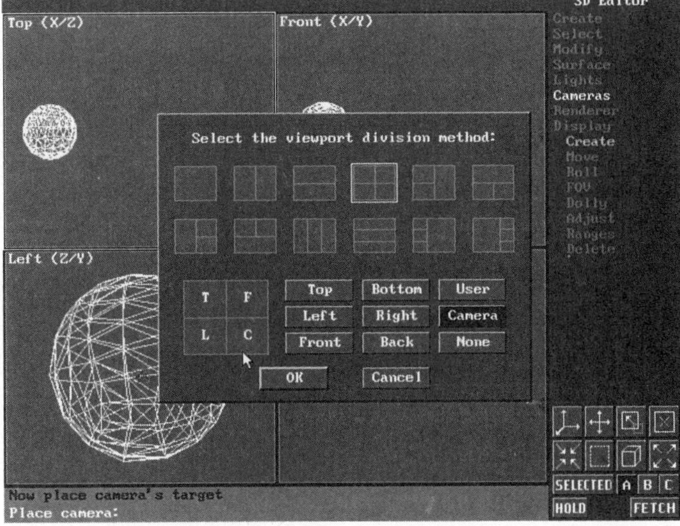

Figure 5.63. Adjust viewport configuration.

Figure 5.64 shows an enlarged Top view with the key frames adjusted to take the camera on a weaving path through the inner solar system. You can enlarge the view to show just a portion of the path, as shown in figure 5.64. This allows you to adjust the relative positions of the camera and planets very precisely.

Using this technique, you may not need to adjust the camera angle at all. If you adjust the angle of approach correctly, the approaching planet will be framed nicely in the Camera view. If necessary, of course, you can change the camera angle or lens focal length to get the views you want.

The two methods for moving the camera through the solar system mentioned so far do not animate the planets in any way. There are two kinds of planetary animation that you can add: rotation on an axis, and an orbit around the sun.

Axial rotation is easy to add. Use the Top view and zoom in on each planet in turn. Determine an appropriate number of frames to use for one rotation, and then move to that frame. Use the Object/Rotate menu option to rotate the planet 360 degrees in the Top viewport. Click the Key Info button, and then click the planet you just rotated. Click the Repeat button in the dialog box that appears, and then click OK. I used a 50-frame repeating rotation for the Earth, and 100 days and 25 days for Venus and Mercury, respectively.[23]

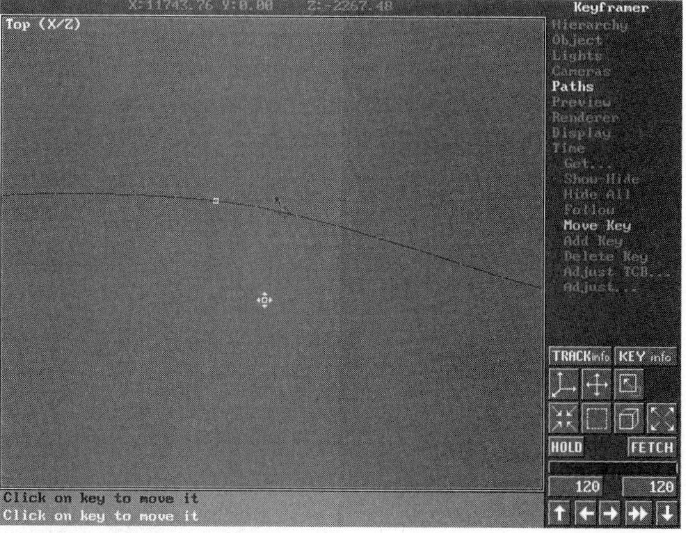

Figure 5.64. Zooming in to adjust camera position.

To create an orbital revolution, I first create a very thin torus (doughnut) shape (see fig. 5.65). I used the 3D Editor to scale the torus so that it corresponded to the size of Earth's orbit.[24] This will serve as a guide shape for placing the orbital path. I used a total of 600 frames, and set that as a full orbital period for Venus. Because the Earth moves more slowly in its orbit, you can have the Earth move through 75 percent of its orbit. Because Earth is starting at the 3 o'clock position (seen in the Top viewport), that would take it to the 6 o'clock position if we rotate it counter-clockwise. To place the Earth along the path correctly, move to the one-third point (frame 200) and move the Earth to the 12 o'clock position, using the torus as a guide for placement. Move to frame 400 and place the Earth at the 9 o'clock position, and then move to frame 600 and place the Earth at the 6 o'clock position.

---

[23]In real life, the Earth's orbit is slightly elliptical.

[24]Unless you have managed to lay out the key frames in a perfect circle, you may also need to adjust the camera position in additional frames. Step through this portion of the animation one frame at a time to check the camera angle. If the camera angle isn't consistent with respect to the Earth, the Earth will appear to jump from frame to frame.

To view the path, use the Paths/Show-Hide Path menu option. Click on the Earth to display its path. You will probably need to add additional key frames to make the path into a rough circle. Repeat this process for the other planets, changing the positions in frames 200 and 400 according to the speed at which each planet will move. For example, I moved Mercury through one and one-third revolutions over the 600 frames. You can scale the torus prior to adjusting each path to give yourself a guideline.

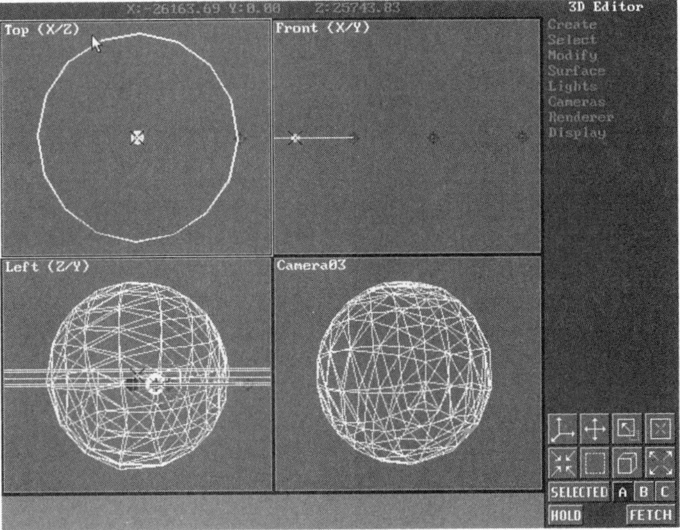

Figure 5.65. Using a torus to guide placement of a path.

Figure 5.66 shows the orbital paths for all three planets. Note that all the paths are in the same plane (check the Front viewport). Note also that the path for the Earth does not close. You can't see it in this view, but the path for Mercury overlaps itself from the 3 o'clock position to the 12 o'clock position. Delete the torus when you are done.

The final task is to create a path for the dummy object/camera. The process is similar to that used for the planets, with one important difference. Instead of following a circular path, the camera should follow a spiral path from one planet's orbit to the next. Figure 5.67 shows the complete path for all objects—three planets and the camera—in an expanded Top viewport.

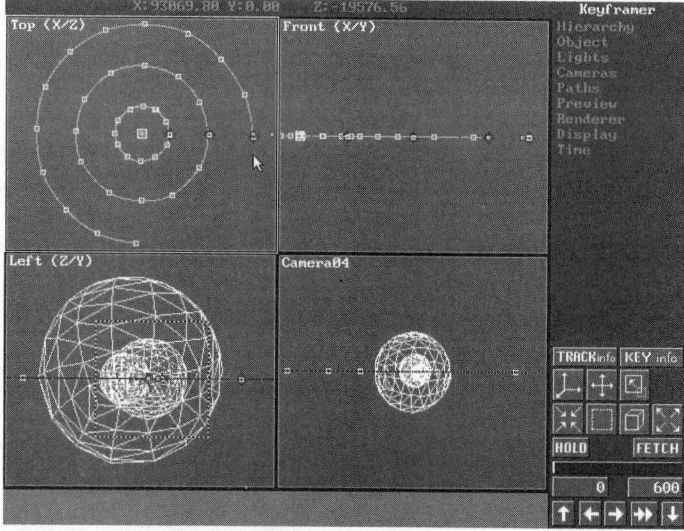

Figure 5.66. Orbital paths in place.

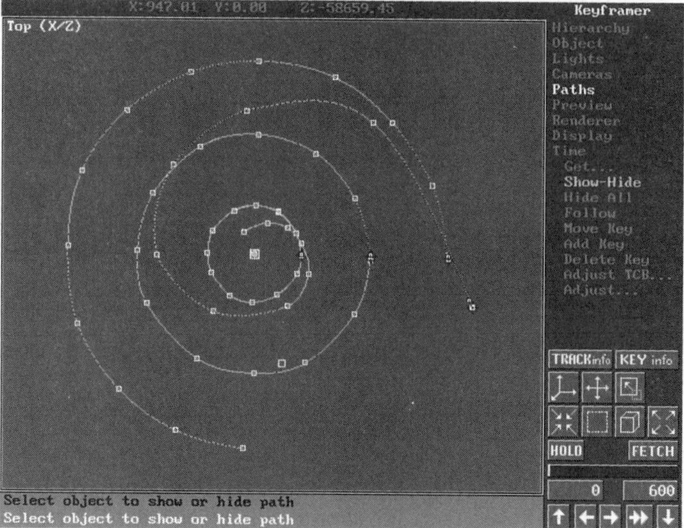

Figure 5.67. The paths of all objects in the scene.

To make sure the camera makes a close approach to each planet, set the dummy object's position every 100 frames. For example, move to frame 100 so you can see the positions of the planets, and then place the dummy object near the Earth. Move to frame 200, and now move the dummy object past the Earth and inside the Earth's orbit. Move to frame 300, and move the dummy object near Venus. Continue this until you have a rough spiral path to frame 600. You can then add additional key frames to smooth out the spiral.

For a final touch, I created a star map in Adobe Photoshop.[25] I then created a material using it as a texture map. You can add a GSphere a little bigger than Earth's orbit, and apply the material (make it two-sided, of course, since you'll be seeing the inside of the sphere) to it. If you make sure to apply spherical mapping coordinates, you'll see stars in the background of your animation. This adds a nifty touch of realism. However, if you get too close to the star background, the stars get bigger, which isn't very realistic at all—be careful where you aim that camera!

The Gallery Tour

Figures 5.68 through 5.73 show various scenes from the resulting animation. The walnut-like appearance of Mercury was accidental, but since we're going to learn how to blow it up in the next section, I thought that it fit right in, so I left it that way.

Figure 5.68. A frame from the solar system animation. This is a view of the Earth from the beginning of the animation.

[25]Nothing fancy, just some white dots on a black background, 1024×768, and saved as a 24-bit Targa file.

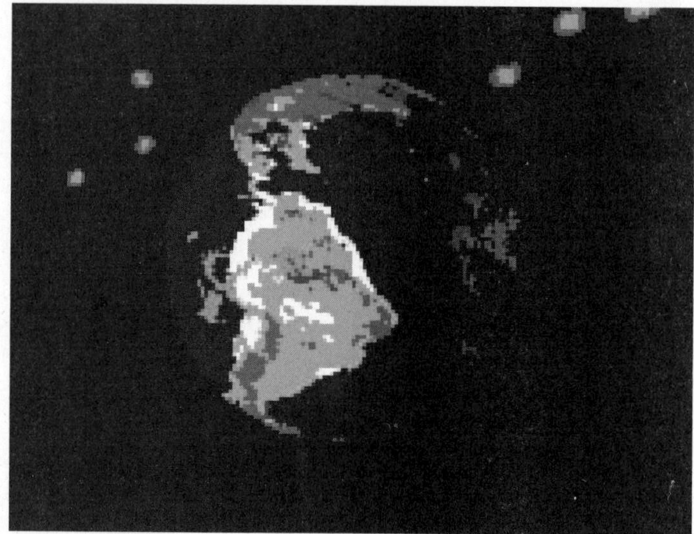

Figure 5.69.
A frame from the solar system animation. Another view of Earth. The camera has moved closer on its trip to the sun.

Figure 5.70.
A frame from the solar system animation. A distant view of Venus after the camera turns away after passing Earth.

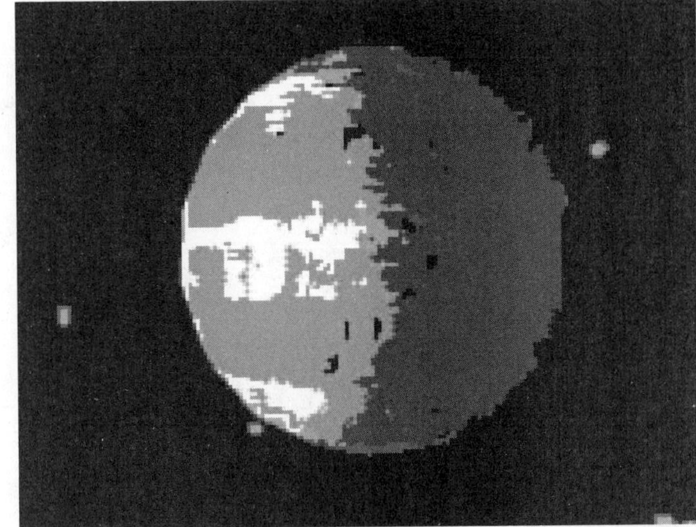

Figure 5.71.
A frame from the solar system animation. A close view of Venus.

Figure 5.72.
A frame from the solar system animation. This is a view of the sun while passing between Venus and Mercury.

Figure 5.73. A frame from the solar system animation. A view of the planet Mercury from near the end of the animation.

A Solar Overview

There is another way to view the solar system that is quite interesting to look at, particularly if you have any fascination with astronomy. It uses a modified version of the solar system you just created.

Begin with the final animation of the preceding section of this chapter. Delete the sphere with the stars, and create instead a flat plane to use as a background.(26) Use the Top viewport, and the Create/Box menu option. The flat plane should be quite large, in order to make sure that it will be visible from all angles, as shown in figure 5.74. About three to four times the size of the solar system is about right.

You will also need to create a camera located above the solar system. The best place to create it is in the Front viewport. Place it directly above the sun, and place the target on the sun (see the Front viewport in fig. 5.74). Finally, create a "rocket" parallel to the camera that travels along the spiral path (see the Left viewport in fig. 5.74). I used a simple cylinder. Looking from high above the solar system, a cylinder is fine. If you plan to zoom in for a close look, you can take some time to create a fancier-looking rocket or spacecraft.

---

26 3D Studio also allows you to specify a background, but such backgrounds don't move with the camera. Although this exercise doesn't move the camera, it would be a simple thing to animate the camera and zoom in on the planets.

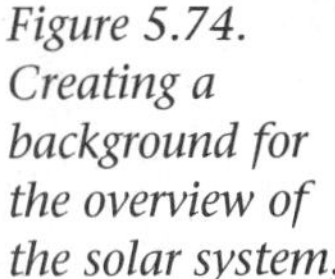

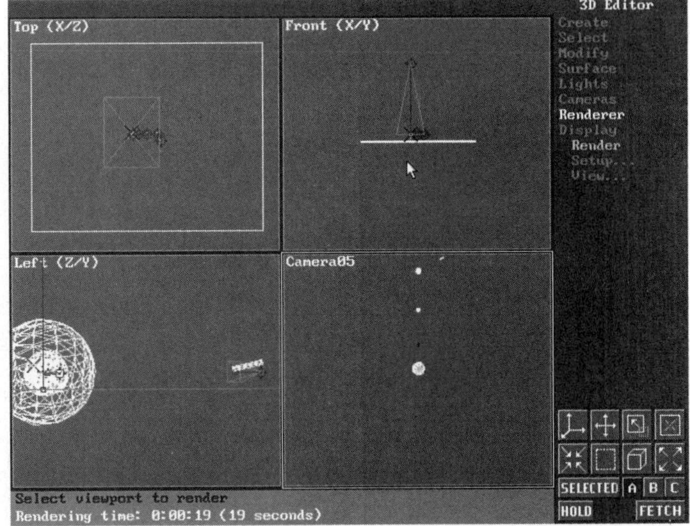

Figure 5.74. Creating a background for the overview of the solar system.

The Camera05 viewport in figure 5.74 shows the view from the camera that you placed above the plane of the solar system. The sun is at the center, and the planets above it are Mercury, Venus, and Earth. The little line above and to the right of the Earth is the spacecraft that matches the original camera's position. To make the rocket follow the camera, use the Hierarchy/Link menu option in the Keyframer.

To render from this new point of view, simply choose Renderer/Render from the menu. That's all there is to it! Figure 5.75 shows a frame from the resulting animation. It's not much to look at, but in the actual animation, you can make out the phases of the planets as they circle about the sun, as well as the movement of the camera/rocket.

Other variations you can try from this vantage point include

- Zooming in on the spacecraft as it approaches Mercury.
- Viewing the solar system from a lower angle than 90 degrees.
- Starting out with a view close to Earth, and then moving above to show the entire solar system. You could link the camera target to the spacecraft with good results.

There is actually no end of interesting approaches to working with the model of the solar system. Comets, asteroids, alien spacecraft, or runaway planets are all interesting possibilities to explore.

Figure 5.75.
An overview of the solar system.

A Wild Ride

And now for something completely different: a wild ride through an exploding planet.

RECIPE

1T 3D Studio
1t Particle Systems IPAS routines from the Yost Group (explosion)
1 Solar system (choose planet)

Instructions: Start with the solar system from the previous recipe in this chapter. Adjust camera orbit to pass through Mercury just about the time it is set to explode. Render and serve.

The software for the explosion uses a special feature of 3D Studio. During rendering, 3D Studio can call an external process to modify the object or its properties. There are four kinds of callable external processes:

Image Processing—Adds 2D effects to rendered scenes. Examples include halos, contrast enhancement, motion blur, and so on.

Procedural Modeling—Changes a 3D object in some way. Used to implement fractal mountain generators, object builders, object-deforming tools such as rippling, and so on.

Animated Stand-In—Creates an animation based on an object in a 3D scene. That is, the object is a "stand-in," or substitute, for the animation. The animation will appear only in the rendering, not in the 3D Editor or Keyframer. Useful for such things as snow, fireworks, explosions, and so on.

Solid Texture—These are static or animated 3D patterns. You can assign them to materials in the Materials Editor. Examples include wood, marble, variable color, and so on.

As a group, these external processes are called IPAS routines. The name is taken from the initial letter of the four kinds of processes. An explosion is an AXP (Animated stand-in eXternal Process).

The explosion AXP will break the object into pieces that will move outward from the origin of the explosion. The smallest possible piece of an object will be a single face. There are a number of parameters you can set for the explosion. To create a large number of faces, you can *tessellate* an object. Use the Create/Object/Tessellate menu option (see fig. 5.76). Then click on the Mercury sphere to break each face into three faces. Accept the default values. Tessellation triples the number of pieces that an explosion can create from an object.

As you can see in figure 5.76, after the tessellation, Mercury has many more faces than the other spheres. In fact, there are so many you can't really tell one face from another.

To apply the explosion AXP to Mercury, use the Modify/Object/Attributes menu option. Figure 5.77 shows the Object Attributes dialog box. The bottom third of the dialog box contains information about the external process. To add an external process, click the button next to the word `Name`.[27]

---

[27] 3D Studio comes with a number of sample IPAS routines, but the explosion routine is not one of them. I obtained mine from the Yost Group. You can obtain a complete catalog of IPAS routines by writing to them at 3739 Balboa St. #230, San Francisco, CA 94121.

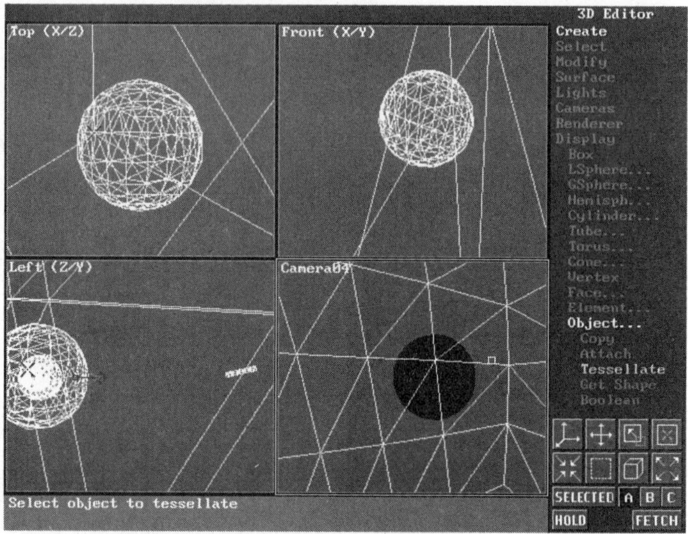

Figure 5.76. Tessellating the Mercury sphere.

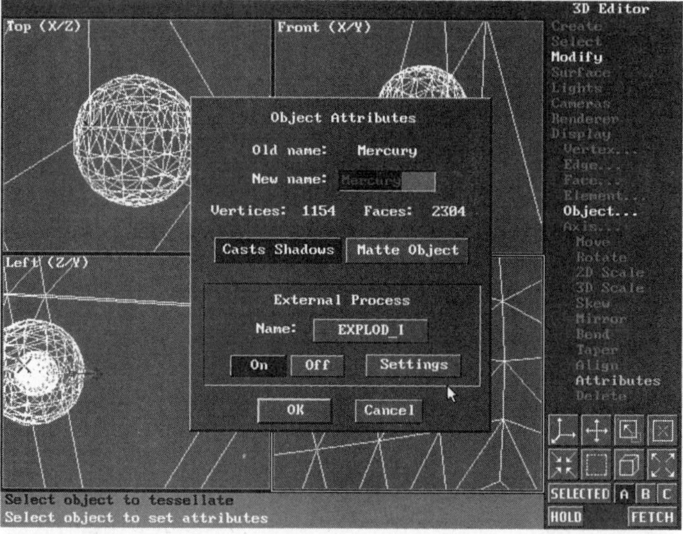

Figure 5.77. Setting object attributes to an external process.

To change the settings for the explosion, click the Settings button. This displays the dialog box shown in figure 5.78. The purpose of each setting is explained in table 5.1.

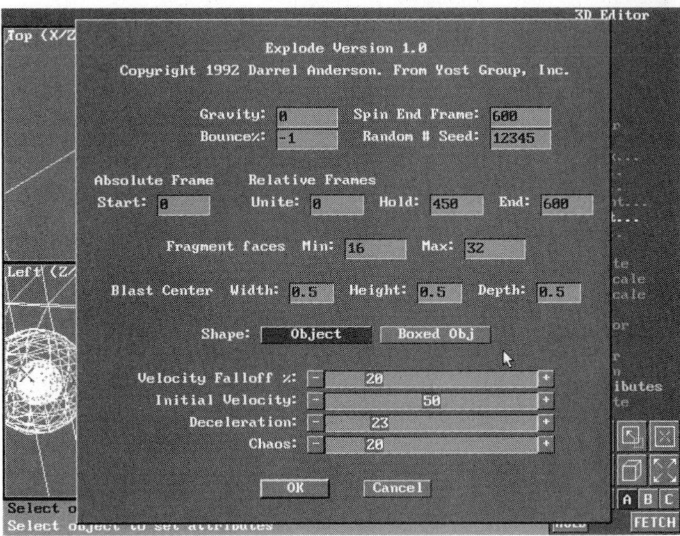

Figure 5.78. Settings for an explosion.

Table 5.1. Explosion Settings.

Setting	*Description*
Gravity	After the initial explosion, the pieces will be affected by gravity. If you want the pieces to fall quickly, set gravity to a large number. Normal gravity is 1. To eliminate gravity, enter a value of zero.
Bounce %	Controls bounce characteristics. A setting of -1 eliminates bouncing entirely; pieces will continue to move indefinitely in the direction they start with.[28] A setting of zero causes the pieces to stop when they reach the ground, defined as the portion of the original object's bounding rectangle with the lowest Y axis value. Positive values cause increasingly larger bounce. A setting of 50%, for example, means that the piece will bounce to 50% of the height it fell from.

continues

[28] If deceleration exists, the objects will eventually come to rest, however.

Table 5.1. continued

Setting	*Description*
Spin End Frame	The pieces spin off from the original object. The rate of spin decreases from the explosion frame to the spin end frame.
Random # Seed	If you have multiple objects using the same AXP external process, you can vary the initial conditions by using a different random seed number.
Absolute Frame Start	Specifies the Keyframer frame number where the effect will start. Until this frame, the object will be hidden.[29]
Relative Frames Unite	This and the next two settings are relative to the Absolute Frame Start setting. If Unite is set to 50, for example, the object will start in pieces at the absolute frame, and then come together over the next 50 frames.[30] A setting of zero will avoid any kind of Unite action.
Relative Frames Hold	Determines the number of frames that the object will stay intact after the Unite frame. For example, if absolute frame start is zero and Unite is zero, a setting of 100 for Hold means that the object will start to explode at frame 100.
Relative Frames End	The object explodes to nothing during the interval between the Hold frame and the End frame. Expanding on the example cited earlier for Relative Frames Hold, an End setting of 200 would result in the object beginning to explode in frame 100 and finishing in frame 200.
Fragment Faces Min/Max	Allows you to control the size of the pieces. Each piece will have at least the number of faces specified in the Min setting, and no more faces than the

[29]The start of the effect and the start of the explosion can easily be two different frames. Unless you want the object in question hidden, use zero for this setting.

[30]The position of the pieces, and therefore the appearance of the object, is exactly the same 50 frames before coming together as it is 50 frames after blowing apart. This means that if you use these settings to pull an object together and then explode it, the two actions will be mirror images of each other. This is not very natural looking, so keep that fact in mind when you design your animation.

Setting	*Description*
	number specified in the Max setting. In the case of an exploding Mercury, with its many tessellated faces, good numbers would be 10 for Minimum and 100 for Maximum.
Blast Center Width/ Height/Depth	These settings control the center of the explosion. They are relative to the bounding box of the object. A setting of .5 in each item places you at the center of the object.
Shape	For certain situations, you can add a special boxed object that will control the parameters of the blast rather than a real object. These buttons tell the AXP process which of the two to use. In this example, you would select Object to allow the Mercury sphere to control the explosion.
Velocity Falloff %	Each fragment starts with an initial velocity based on the Initial Velocity setting. If a falloff percent greater than zero is used, a fragment's initial velocity is less if it is farther from the blast center. A setting of zero gives all fragments the same initial velocity.
Initial Velocity	Determines how fast each fragment moves as the explosion starts. A setting of 100 means that a fragment will move 1/10th of the object's size per frame.
Deceleration	Controls the rate at which fragments slow down over time. If you enter a value of 100, fragments will lose 10% of their speed per frame.
Chaos	Introduces random variation in several of the settings, including initial velocity, tumbling and spinning, and gravity.

A starting set of values for the Mercury explosion is shown in figure 5.78. Some different settings to try include the following:

- Change the origin of the blast to be on the surface of the planet. For example, change the Blast Center Depth setting to 0. Experiment with different settings for Velocity falloff if you try this.

- Lower the deceleration value and increase the initial velocity to cause the fragments to fly off into space.
- Change the size limits (Min and Max) to see what kinds of fragment shapes result.

To add a little zest, you can add a light inside Mercury. This will reflect off the object fragments, resulting in a more realistic explosion. The easiest way to do this is to add an omni light at the center of the planet. This will affect the appearance of other objects since omni lights shine "through" objects. You would need to turn the light off until the Hold frame to avoid unwanted light on other objects.

For a more realistic effect, you can put one or more spotlights inside the planet. Spotlights are capable of casting shadows. This takes longer, but yields a more realistic result. Figure 5.79 shows what it's like to add spotlights to the scene—all those lines make it difficult. The circles in the Top viewport are the cones showing where the spotlights will illuminate the scene. The lines in the other views are simply other objects in the scenes.

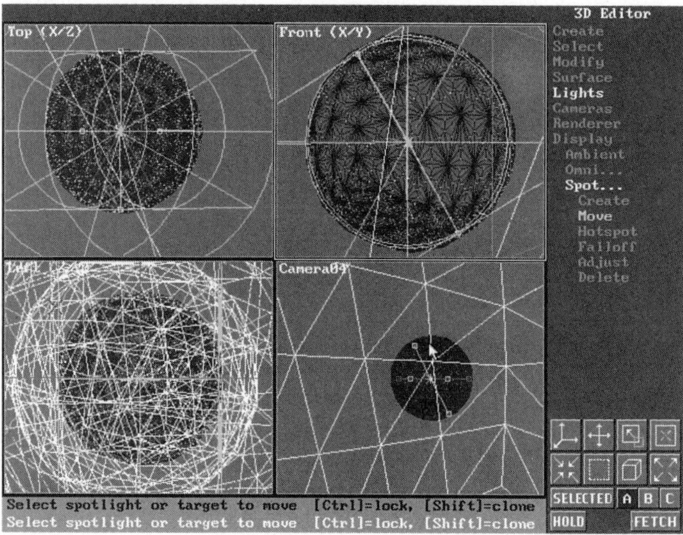

Figure 5.79. Adding lights to the inside of Mercury.

The reason for zooming in so far in figure 5.80 is to locate the lights for making adjustments. You should set the lights to a light level of zero in frames 0 and 449, and to 255 in frame 450 (that's the frame in which the explosion takes place). That way, the lights won't interfere with other objects.

When you are dealing with masses of lines from multiple complex objects, there are two solutions. One, you can change the display geometry of individual objects to Box mode. Two, you can simply zoom in—way in, as shown in figure 5.80—until you can find what you are looking for. The lights are the four small square objects in the Front viewport at the upper right.

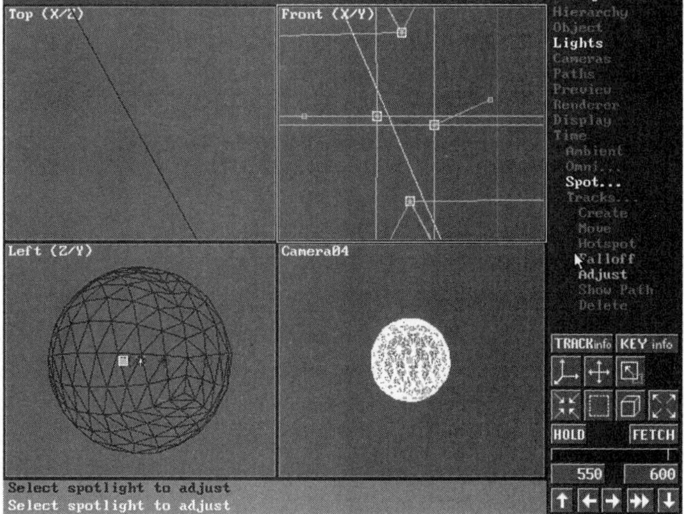

Figure 5.80. Zooming in to find objects (lights, in this case) amid the maze of lines.

Yet another option is to create a self-illuminated object inside the planet Mercury. This might provide some of the justification for the planet exploding. See figure 5.81 for an example of such an object inside the planet.[31]

[31]That spiked object is created in an interesting way that is worth an explanation. I first created a GSphere, and then selected it (Select/Object/Single). I then used Create/Object/Tessellate, and clicked the Edge button in the resulting dialog box. The appearance of the sphere won't change much—apart from the new faces, that is—but if you look carefully, you will see that the vertices are selected. Click the Modify/Object/3D Scale menu option, and then click the Selected button at the bottom right. Click in a viewport, and then drag the mouse to the right to enlarge only the selected vertices—the result is a nice set of spikes.

Figure 5.81. A self-illuminated object inside an exploding planet.

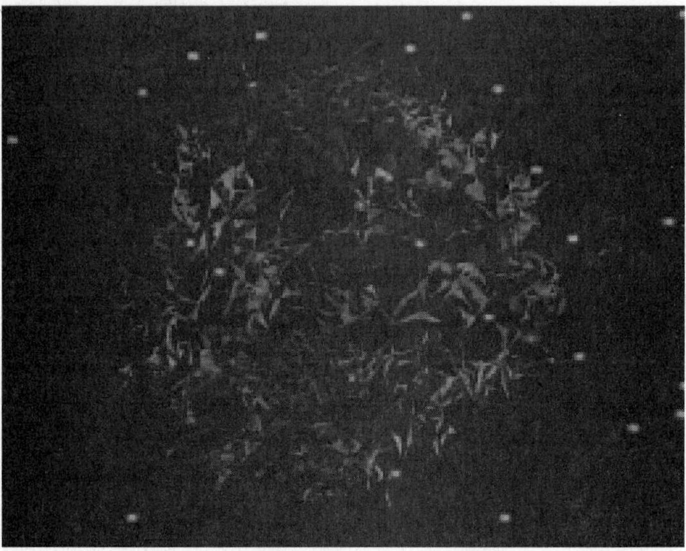

Figures 5.82 through 5.85 show four frames from the animation of the explosion of Mercury. Figure 5.82 shows the planet in the frame immediately preceding the breakup, and the subsequent figures were taken at eight-frame intervals thereafter.[32] The most important things to notice about the explosion are

- That the fragments are made up of triangles[33]
- That the larger fragments sometimes take on an accordion-like shape

---

[32]These frames were taken from a "trial run" of the explosion animation and do not include the object inside the planet.

[33]Why? Because faces are triangles, and fragments are made of faces.

The only way to reduce such effects is to edit the object by hand, creating the fragments yourself by welding pieces together and making groups of faces into elements, and by creating your own faces out of larger faces.

Figure 5.82. The frame immediately preceding the beginning of the explosion.

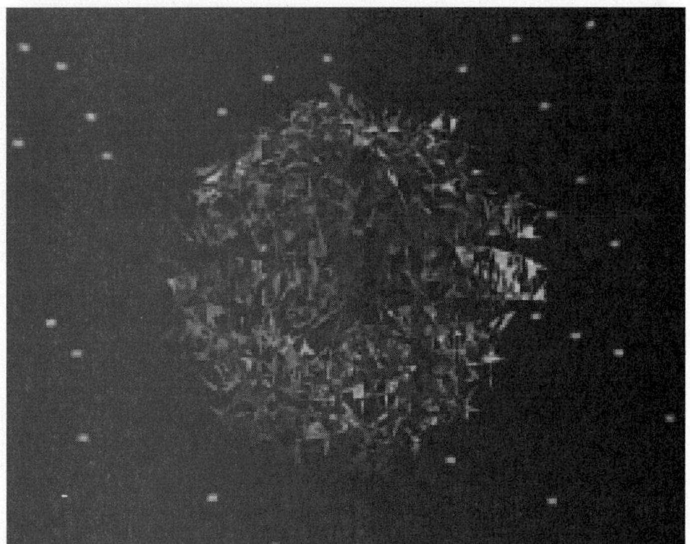

Figure 5.83. Seven frames after the explosion.

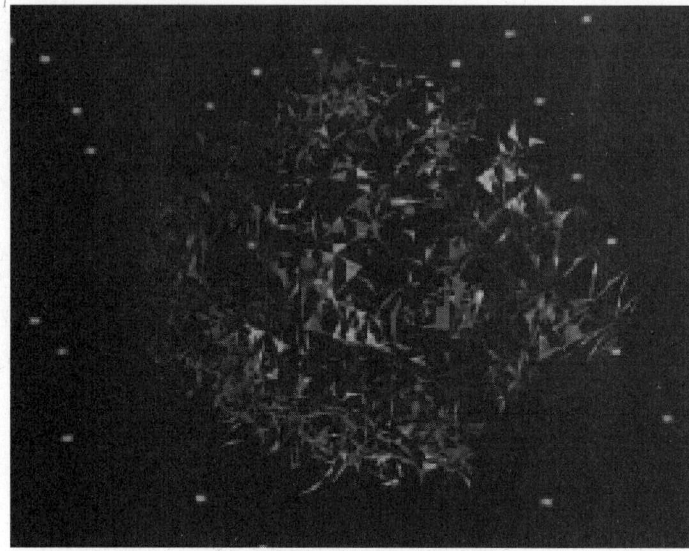

Figure 5.84. Fifteen frames after the explosion.

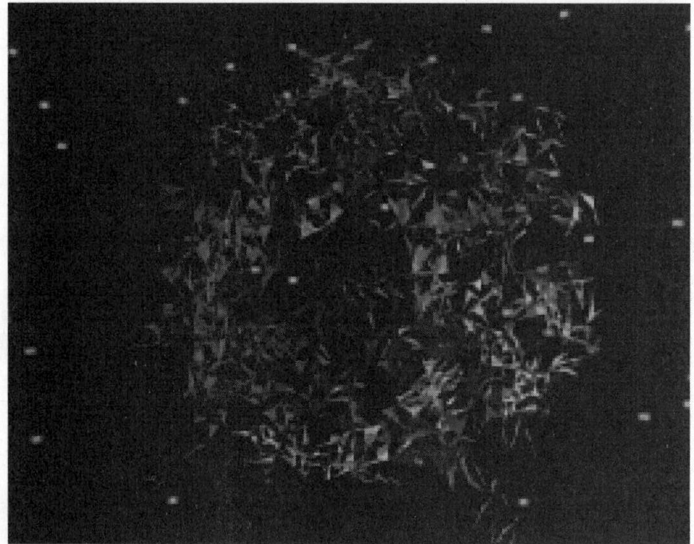

Figure 5.85. Twenty-three frames after the explosion.

The Solar System Gallery

During the development of the solar system model, there were many wrong turns and many interesting ones. I have collected some of the interesting images, and a few instructive ones, here for your enjoyment.

Figure 5.86. A rendering of the Earth from an early fly-through.

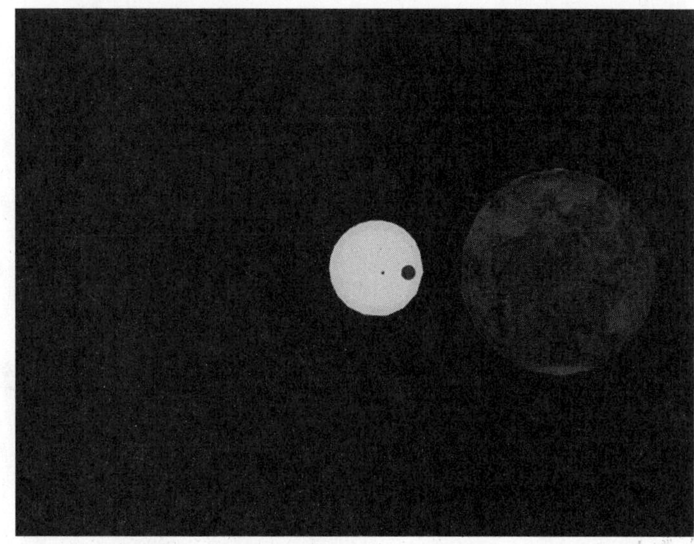

Figure 5.87. A view of all three inner solar system planets. From left to right: the sun, Mercury (the small dot in front of the sun), Venus (the larger dot in front of the sun), and the Earth.

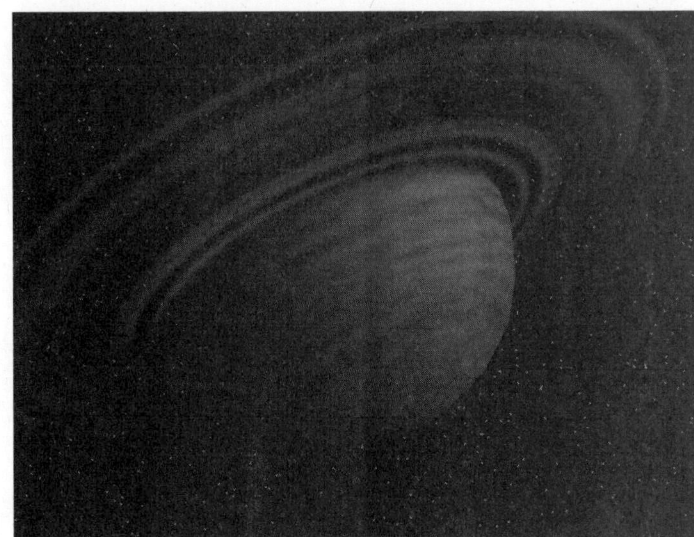

Figure 5.88. A rendering of a planet based on Saturn. The rings are merely a flat, circular object that was created with Object/ Create/Boolean. Object one was a very thin, square box, and object two was a sphere. The Boolean operation Intersection results in a flat, round object that you can apply a map to.

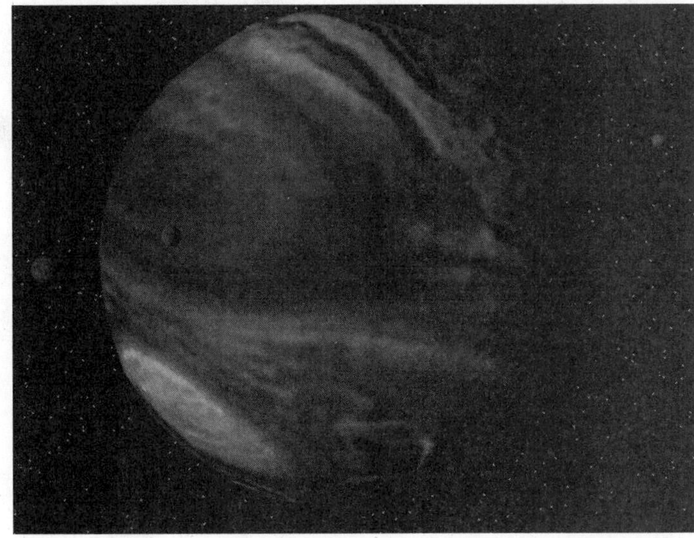

Figure 5.89. A rendering of a planet that uses a portion of the surface of Jupiter as a texture map (with a Bump setting of 1% to give some sense of height to the surface). The moons use the Bumpy Camouflage material, with the color revised toward brown to be more "planetary."

6

I CAN FLY!

Flights of Fancy

I love to fly.[1] And I know I'm not alone. So despite the fact that I've used up lots of superlatives describing various aspects of virtual reality, virtual flight is at the top of my list of Cool Stuff. As you learned in Chapter 1, it's not even hard to do. A fly-through is really an animation. This is not the same as an interactive virtual flight, where the visuals are recalculated for every frame. Because a fly-through is just an animation, it is relatively easy to play it back. You don't need hot hardware to play a fly-through, though a decent graphics subsystem doesn't hurt.

The holy grail of near-term virtual reality, however, is real-time, interactive movement, whether it be simulated flight, or walking, or driving, or whatever. On a personal computer—even one sporting a souped-up Pentium and all the hardware you can load into a single case—there just isn't enough horsepower to do all the processing that's required to move within a virtual space in real time and still handle such mundane tasks as updating the screen. Some systems come close, but the closer they come, the more they cost. Thus the value of the fly-through. If you insist on interactivity, you'll have to settle for lower quality graphics. If you insist on high-quality graphics, you'll have to settle for a fly-through.[2]

Even if a fly-through isn't the holy grail of virtual reality, it is one of the most interesting and challenging aspects of virtual reality. It takes patience and a willingness to learn a huge number of details if you want to create a sophisticated fly-through, but you can also have fun with products like Vistapro. In this chapter, I'll show you how to fly with Virtus VR and 3D Studio. Then, for some really complicated excitement, you'll learn how to use Vistapro and 3D Studio together for some interesting effects. For other examples of fly-throughs, see Chapters 1 and 8.

---

[1]And I'm not talking about airplanes! Maybe I should say, "I'd love to fly." But after spending so much time virtually flying, "I love to fly" is more accurate.

[2]You can simulate real-time interactivity using fly-through technology. Create an animation for every possible interactive choice, and then play the appropriate animation based on the interactive input. For example, if the user wants to enter a room, you would play an animation that moves through a door and forward into the room. If the user signals turn right, you play an animation of the viewpoint turning to the right. If the user signals turn left, you play that animation. I've included a sample of this kind of fly-through with the sample files for this chapter.

Virtus VR Takes Off

Simply using Virtus VR, as you learned in Chapter 2, is like doing a fly-through. As a Windows product, Virtus VR is limited to the standard mouse for flying, but its clever interface makes flight simple, if not necessarily easy.(3)

Figure 6.1 shows the key to using Virtus VR: the instruction cube. It comes right in the Virtus VR package, is easy to assemble, and conveniently tells you all the important stuff about both world creation and flight.

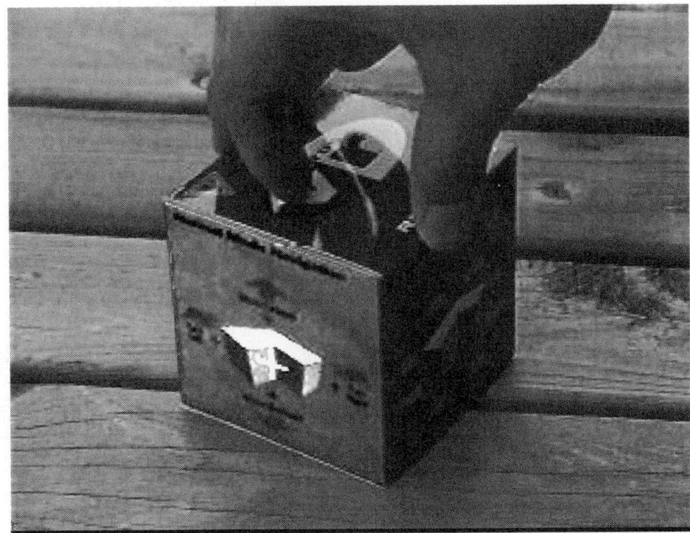

Figure 6.1. The key to understanding fly-throughs in Virtus VR is this little cardboard cube.

Each face of the cube gives you pertinent information about using Virtus VR. Well, almost every face is useful; the top face is little more than the product logo. The two most important faces are shown in figure 6.1. They tell you how to use the mouse and the keyboard to fly through the universe.

There are two mouse modes, and each mode gets one face of the cube. Mode one is the mouse alone. Mode two is the mouse and the keyboard used together. In both modes, you move by clicking with the mouse in the Walk window. A crosshair marks the center of the window, as shown in figure 6.2.(4) The following mode-one mouse clicks are used to move in the environment:

---

[3]Virtus WalkThrough shares the same interface.

[4]It's been a while, but I wonder if you can place the scene shown in the figure. Hint: It's located in Waco, Texas. Another hint: That tank is about to roll through the walls. If the theme seems morbid, other famous (or should I say infamous) scenes are also included, such as Dealy Plaza in Dallas, Texas. VR and 3D technology are often used to reconstruct crime scenes for after-the-fact analysis.

Click above crosshair	Move forward
Click below crosshair	Move backward
Click right of crosshair	Turn right
Click left of crosshair	Turn left

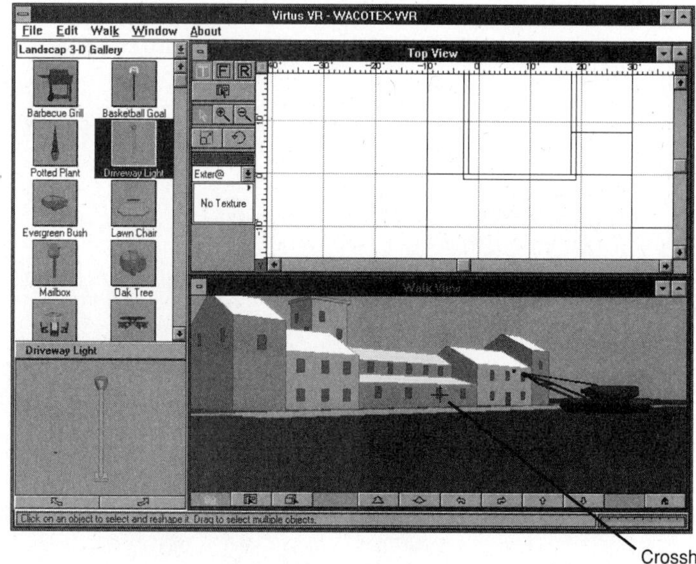

Figure 6.2. The Virtus VR environment, including the Walk window (lower right) used for fly-throughs.

You can move around quite a bit with just these clicks, but there are times when you want to move up or down, or tilt forward or backward, and so on. The Shift and Control keys come to your rescue. In mode two, holding down one key or the other opens up new possibilities. For example, when you hold down the Shift key, the mouse clicks have different results:

Click above crosshair	Look up (pitch up)
Click below crosshair	Look down (pitch down)
Click right of crosshair	Roll right
Click left of crosshair	Roll left

When you hold down the Control key, these movements become possible:

Click above crosshair	Rise up
Click below crosshair	Sink down
Click right of crosshair	Slide left
Click left of crosshair	Slide right

Clicking in other areas of the Walk window yields a combination of moves. For example, clicking above and to the left would result in a rotation to the left and a move forward. Very important fact: **the farther away from the crosshairs you click, the larger the motion.**

You can also click on the small buttons at the bottom of the Walk window to move in basic ways. You can refer to the detailed information about Virtus VR and Virtus WalkThrough in Chapter 2 before continuing with the fly-through exercise if you haven't done so already.

Many of the scenes included as sample worlds with Virtus VR and Virtus WalkThrough contain prerecorded fly-throughs. You can play the prerecorded version, or you can create your own. Figure 6.3 shows the Walk menu, where the secret to fly-throughs is found: the Rewind, Play, and Record selections. It's not as fancy as a 3D VCR-style controller, but it gets the job done. You not only can use the mouse and the Shift/Control keys to move around, you can record your movements for later playback. When you save a file, the recorded fly-through is saved with the file.

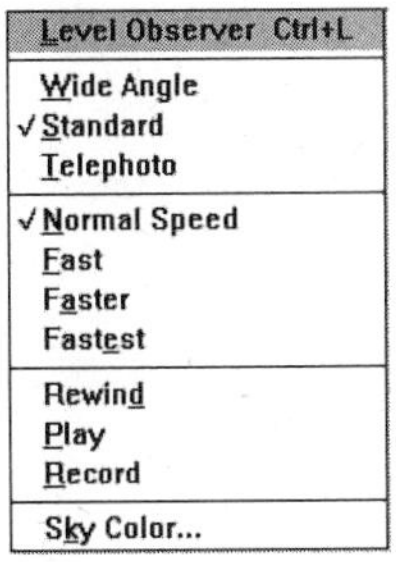

Figure 6.3. Control the Walk environment, including Play/Record capabilities, by using the Walk menu.

Level Observer Ctrl+L
Wide Angle
✓Standard
Telephoto
✓Normal Speed
Fast
Faster
Fastest
Rewind
Play
Record
Sky Color...

To record a fly-through, you must click the Record button first. If you make a mistake, there is no way to edit the fly-through; you'll have to start over. To restart, just click the Walk/Stop menu option,[(5)] and then click Walk/Record again.

Let's take a look at what you can accomplish during a fly-through. Figure 6.4 shows the starting point of a short fly-through I created.

To begin the fly-through, I clicked several times in the area above the crosshairs, and slightly to the right. This moved me closer to the tank, as shown in figure 6.5.

[5]The Rewind menu option changes to Stop when you are recording.

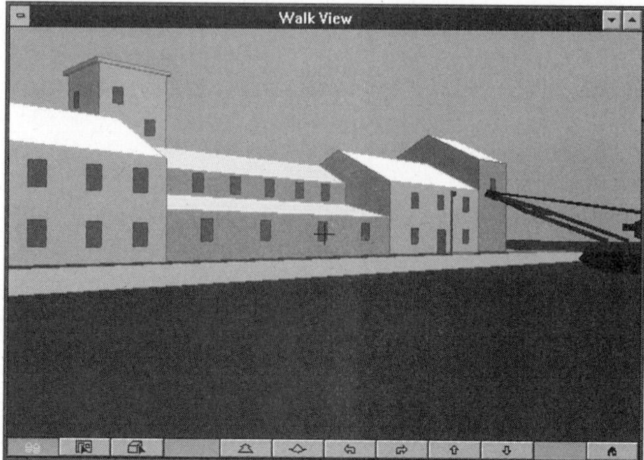

Figure 6.4. The beginning of a fly-through.

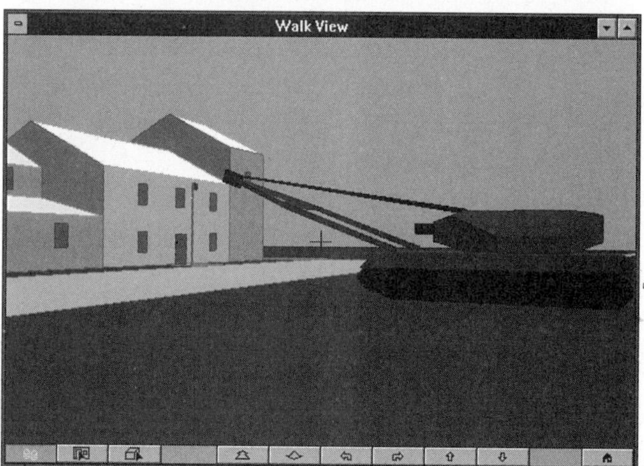

Figure 6.5. Moving forward into the scene.

If you continue to move forward, you can get as close to objects as you want. Unless the object has texture, however, you won't get any additional details (see fig. 6.6).

You can also use the Shift and Control keys to move to true flight positions, as shown in figure 6.7. You can move to almost any position; the virtual universe is a big place inside Virtus VR. You only need the patience to keep clicking the mouse to move as far as you want. The models can be quite complex, as you can see by looking at figure 6.8.

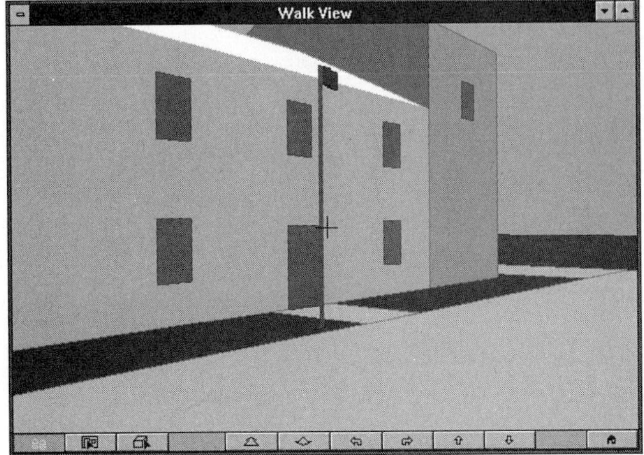

Figure 6.6. Object detail does not increase beyond a certain level, no matter how close you get.

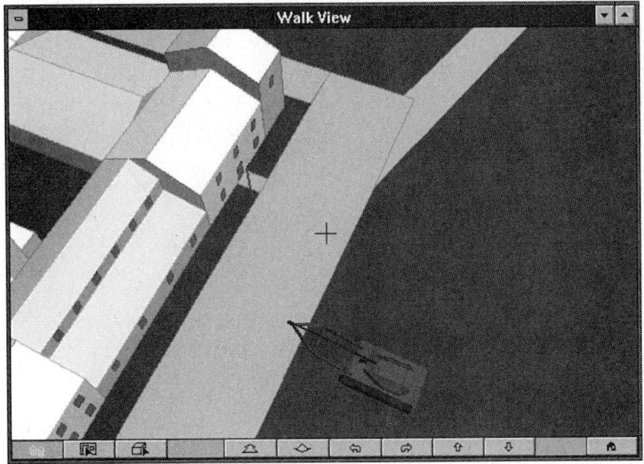

Figure 6.7. Looking at the scene from above.

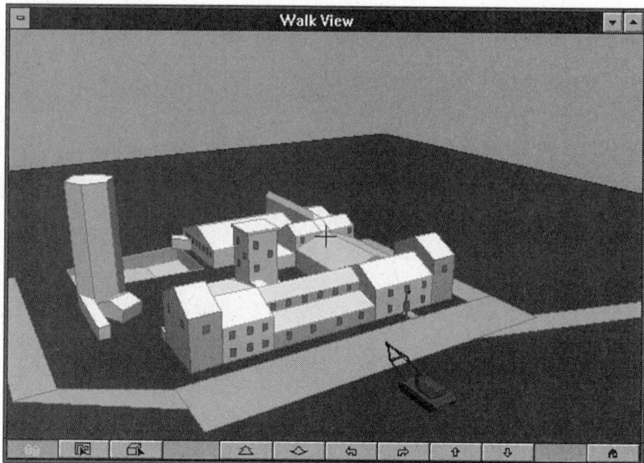

Figure 6.8.
Virtus VR models can be complex.

You can also explore interior spaces. The Waco, Texas model doesn't contain any interior objects (see fig. 6.9).

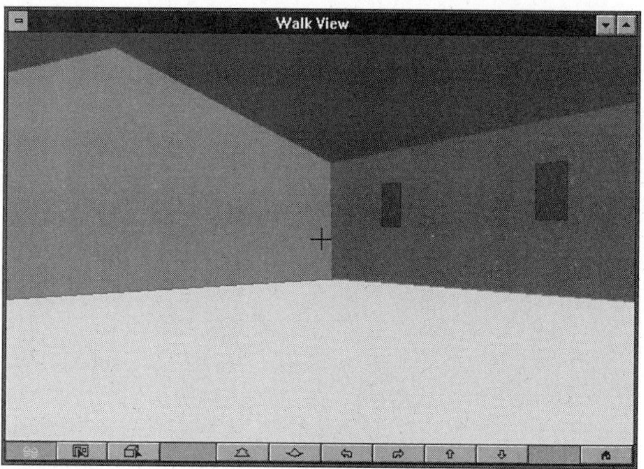

Figure 6.9.
The beginning of a fly-through.

You can, of course, use the libraries to add objects or people to interior spaces. Figure 6.10 shows a conference table added to the room shown in figure 6.9.

When you have completed the fly-through, you can save it to disk with the rest of the file, or you can record it as an FLC file.[6] Look for the Snapshot option on the File menu (see fig. 6.11). This allows you to save the current Walk view as a bitmap file, or the current recorded fly-through as an FLC file (see fig. 6.12).

If there is not a recorded fly-through, the Animator Pro menu option will be blank.

---

[6]That's Autodesk's animation file format.

Figure 6.10. Adding a conference table gives the room some scale.

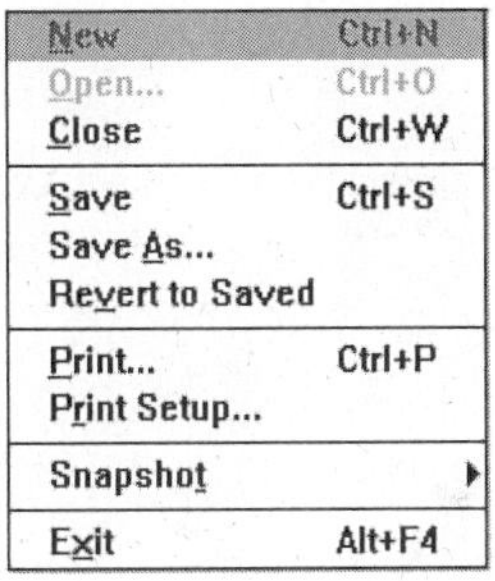

New Ctrl+N
Open... Ctrl+O
Close Ctrl+W
Save Ctrl+S
Save As...
Revert to Saved
Print... Ctrl+P
Print Setup...
Snapshot
Exit Alt+F4

Figure 6.11. The Snapshot menu option.

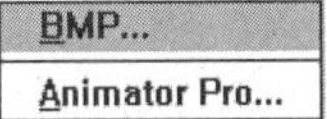

Figure 6.12. You can save bitmaps or animations.

If you choose to save the animation, the dialog box shown in figure 6.13 appears. You can set the size of the animation to any of the preset options, or use a custom size. Remember that larger animations require faster computers to play back smoothly. The animation can be in color or grayscale, and you have the option of specifying which portion of the animation to save to disk.

If you click on Smooth Path, the program adds frames to make the animation smoother.

If desired, you can import the FLC file into a Video for Windows-compatible editor, add sound to the animation, and save it as an AVI clip.

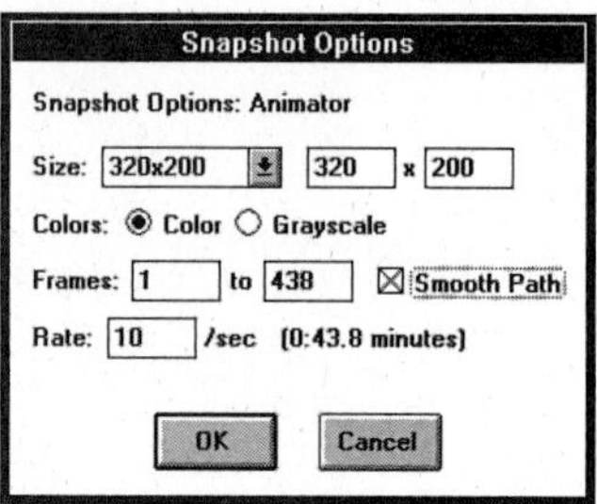

Figure 6.13. Options for saving an animation to disk.

Setting Up a 3D Studio Fly-Through

You can create a complete virtual space in 3D Studio,[7] but there are easier ways of going about the process. You can import DXF files[8] created with other software, such as AutoCAD, and many other engineering and architectural programs. Many low-end programs also export 3D images in DXF format, such as 3D Concepts and Generic CADD. For this example, I chose the 3D image file from Chapter 3—the house and yard. This image has quite a genealogy. It started as a floor plan in the Home Design series from AutoDesk, and was turned into a 3D file (with a 3DD extension) in 3D Plan. It was then loaded into 3D Concepts, and saved as a DXF file. Now it can be loaded into 3D Studio.

3D Studio can load DXF files directly, using the File/Load menu option (see fig. 6.14). If you accept the default values, the file will be loaded with many of the image characteristics intact. For example, objects will still be objects—the refrigerator will not decompose into its separate parts.

Figure 6.15 shows the house file loaded into 3D Studio. All of the pieces are there, though not always in ways that you might expect. The walls, for example, are constructed of many, many tiles. Unfortunately, this creates a lot of visual clutter, as you can see in figure 6.15. You can get some relief from this by setting Display/ Geometry to hide *backfaces* (faces on the hidden side of objects). 3D Studio also allows you to set individual objects for box display. The object is displayed as, yes, a box, which is very fast, but there are no details. If you aren't working on a particular object, this is a convenience.

---

[7]Note: This fly-through was created with Release 2 of 3D Studio, which is one release behind the current version. However, this does not affect the situation at all. Most of what you need to pull off a good fly-through isn't built into 3D Studio—whether you use Release 2 or Release 3, most of what you need to do involves concepts, not version-specific tools.

[8]DXF files are the standard of the 3D universe. They are most commonly used by AutoCAD, but are now supported by a wide variety of software packages. Like most file format standards, DXF owes its standardization to nothing more than the success of the program.

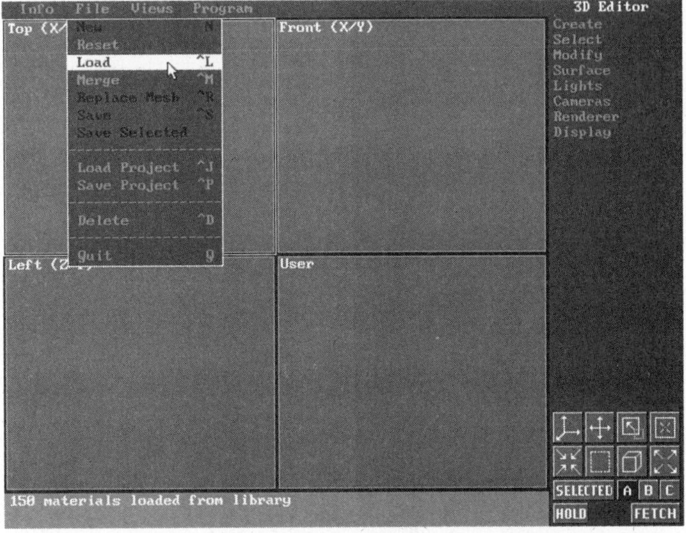

Figure 6.14. Loading a DXF file into 3D Studio.

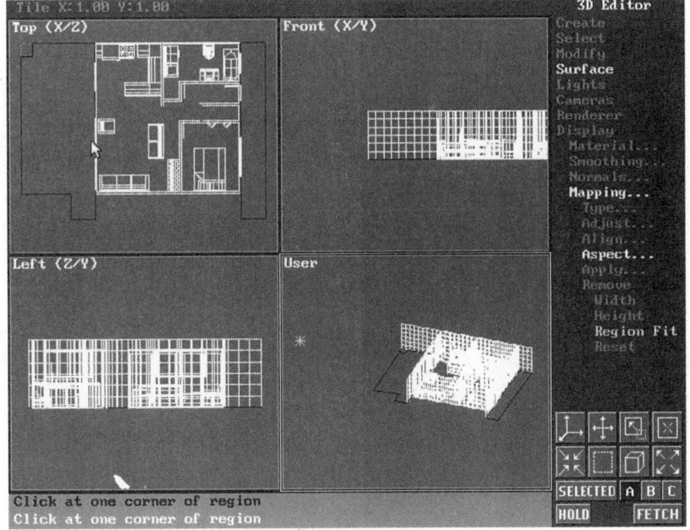

Figure 6.15. The DXF file has been loaded into 3D Studio.

Although the file is largely intact,[9] one key element of virtual reality is missing at this point. There are no surface colors or textures on any of the objects. 3D Studio allows you to associate specific materials to objects. In fact, it has a Materials Editor you can use to specify the characteristics of a wide variety of materials. The Materials Editor is sophisticated, and only the basic features are discussed in this chapter. See Chapter 8 for more on materials engineering in a virtual space.

3D Studio comes with a large number of ready-to-use materials, and for the most part you can use them for this example. Specifying existing materials is easy. Choose Surface/Material/Choose to select a material, and then use Surface/Material/Assign/Object to apply it to an object.[10]

3D Studio supports extended objects. That is, you can group objects together. 3D Studio calls the component objects elements. In the file used for this example, objects with similar characteristics are grouped together.[11] Grouped objects don't have to be "physically" together—they can be anywhere in the virtual space. Figure 6.16 shows that doors, door frames, and window frames are actually one object. The floor plan in the Top view shows this clearly, even including the bifold doors in the bedroom at the lower right. You can assign the material Teak to all of these at one time using the menu choice Surface/Material/Assign/Object, or you can assign specific materials to any one element using Surface/Material/Assign/Element.[12]

You must repeat this process for every group of objects in the virtual space.[13] You can draw on the extensive library of material included with 3D Studio, or you can make up your own.

---

[9]There were a few bugs in the loaded image. For example, several faces on the bathtub object were missing, and had to be corrected by hand. In other cases, the "face normal" of an object was set incorrectly. The *face normal* is the direction that a face faces. If it faces away from the camera, then you won't see anything there unless the material you chose for that face or object is two-sided. If you ever see missing objects, or missing parts of objects, it's a safe bet that some face normals are facing the wrong way. You can easily set all of an object's faces to normal by using the Unify Normals command.

[10]You can apply materials to portions of an object as well. 3D Studio is extremely flexible about such things once you learn the ins and outs of the menus.

[11]This was done in the original floor plan software when groups of objects were given similar physical characteristics, such as color.

[12]This is typical of the depth (and complexity) of 3D Studio. The menu structure is not something you can learn in a day or a week; knowledge of the pathways and byways comes with experience over several months.

[13]Perhaps you could try some Blue Marble for the bathroom fixtures, or a nice Almond for the appliances in the kitchen. If you don't find the color, texture, or material you want, you can probably create it using the various tools in the Materials Editor.

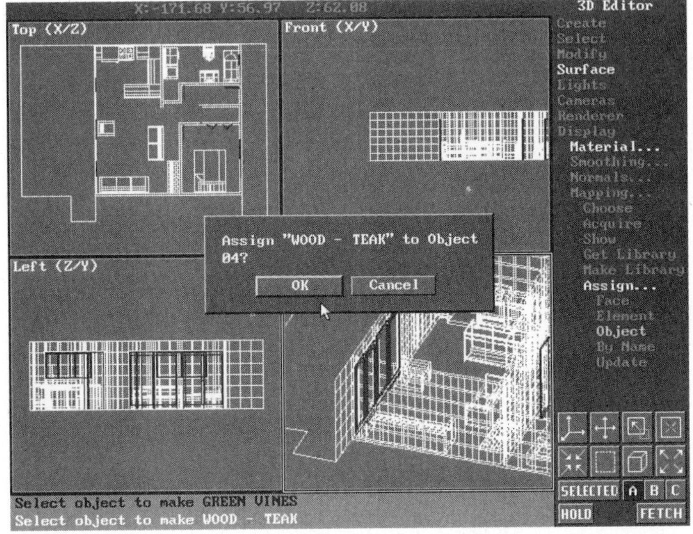

Figure 6.16. Assigning the material Wood - Teak to a 3D Studio object.

Once you have added materials, the next task is to create lighting. 3D Studio offers a range of lighting options, but the most interesting is Spotlights, since it casts shadows. You can place a spotlight in the same locations that you would find in many homes—near the ceiling, or in the center of a room. Figure 6.17 shows the dialog box for setting the attributes of a typical spotlight.

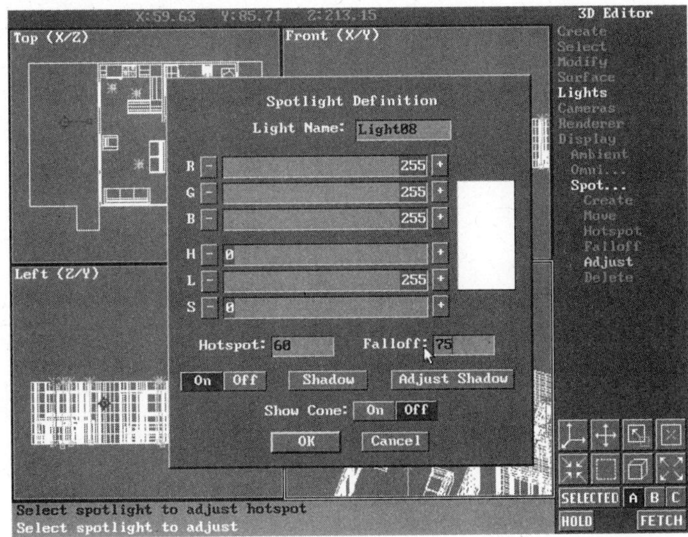

Figure 6.17. Setting the attributes for a spotlight.

The *hotspot* refers to the portion of the light cone that is the brightest, while *falloff* refers to the zone where the light fades from bright to dark. To simulate a typical room light, the values for both should be large—large enough to brighten just about the entire room the light is in. Figure 6.18 shows the lights in place. Each light is connected to a target that determines the direction in which the light shines. For this example, the target is the floor directly underneath the light. The Top view at the upper left shows the lights in Plan View, while the User view at the bottom right shows the lights (and their targets) in a 3D perspective view.

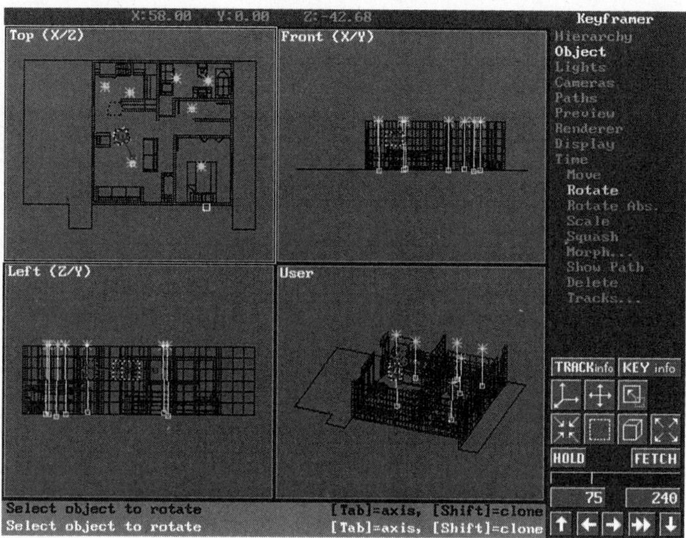

Figure 6.18. Adding lights to a virtual space.

We have the set, we have the lights—the next step is a camera.

Flying the Camera

Before you can fly the camera, you need to create one with the Camera/Create menu choice. As with lights, you place both the camera and the target at which it is aimed.[14] Figure 6.19 shows a camera and a target. I set the camera for the beginning of the fly-through, on the patio outside the doors. It is at approximately eye height. The target is only a short distance away. This was a deliberate choice—it wouldn't work very well to have the target very far away, since the camera will be

---

[14] 3D Studio has some interesting support for camera features. One of my favorite features is the ability to set the focal length of the lens, using the same values you would use for a standard 35mm lens. For example, for interior shooting, you would typically use a wide-angle lens. For this example, I used a 28mm lens. A wider lens would show more of the room, but it also would add distortion—just like a real lens.

moving about in a relatively cramped space. You may, however, set the target arbitrarily far from the camera. For example, you could move the camera a large distance away and use a zoom-lens setting to bring the subject closer in the camera view.

Once the camera has been created, you have all the ingredients needed for the fly-through. Move now to the Keyframer by pressing the F4 key. In the Keyframer, you can create animation frames for the fly-through.

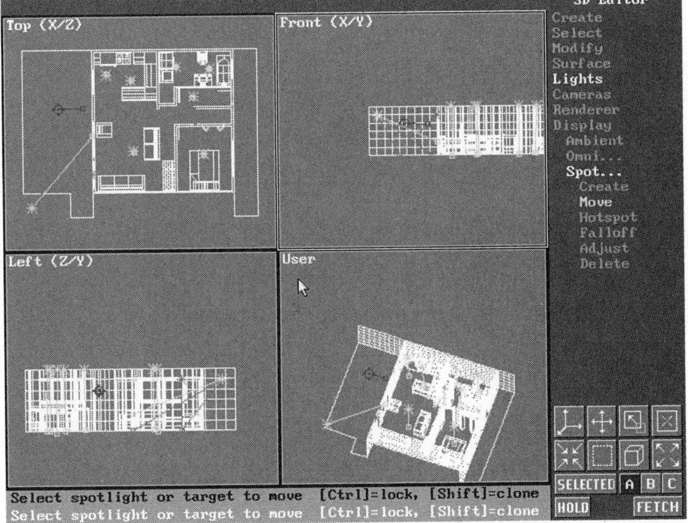

Figure 6.19. Adding a camera and target to the virtual space.

Strictly speaking, 3D Studio does not allow you to fly cameras as part of an animation. Nor can you move or fly a camera target. The trick is to create a dummy object using the Hierarchy menu. A dummy object has many of the characteristics of a real object—you can move it, scale it, rotate it, and so on—but it is invisible when the scene or animation is rendered. Figure 6.20 shows the Keyframer screen, and a dummy object has been created. It is marked by a dotted outline to make it stand out from normal objects.(15)

[15]It is obvious that the dummy object was created in the Top view. That is the only view where the dummy object and the camera line up. This is a hazard of using a 2D interface to create 3D objects: you can only work in one plane at a time. If you look at the Front or Left view, you can see that the dummy object was created at the default zero level in the 3D space. It's a simple matter to move the object in, say, the Front view to put it in the same position as the camera. In fact, since it is invisible, you can put it right over the camera with no ill effects.

Once you have created the dummy object, link the camera and the target to it using the Hierarchy/Link menu option. Do this once for the camera and once for the target. Once you have created the links, be careful to move only the dummy object, not the camera or target individually.

It is very easy to create the path the camera will follow for the fly-through. There are at least two useful ways to do it, and I will explain both of them. The first method involves setting specific camera positions at regular frame intervals. In this example, I set a new camera position every 15 frames. The second method involves setting the initial camera position in frame 1 and the final camera position in the last frame, and then creating camera positions along the default path and moving them into position. The second technique requires a deeper knowledge of the way the 3D Studio works, but it can be very useful as a first draft for a path.

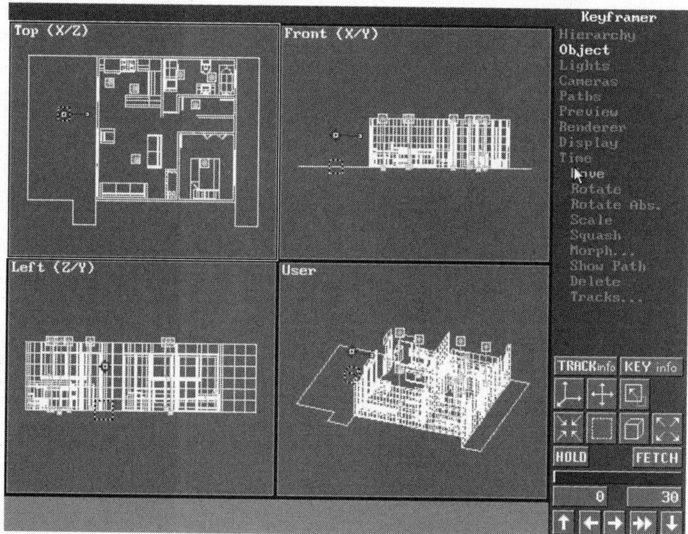

Figure 6.20. Adding a dummy object to the scene.

You can use the Time menu or the buttons at the bottom right of the Keyframer screen to move to specific frame numbers. You can also set the total number of frames to be used for the animation. A typical animation uses 15 frames per second. To make the fly-through move at a natural speed, you need to calculate the distance of the total flight and decide how long it should take. In this example, it should take about eight seconds to move from the patio to the bathroom, which will require 240 frames. The final version of this fly-through, which you can find on the CD-ROMs, is somewhat longer and uses 360 frames.

At each camera position (every 15 frames in this example), there are two camera settings to adjust: position and rotation. For example, after the camera "walks" in through the patio door, it must turn left. If you do not rotate the camera to follow the change in direction, it will give the appearance of facing sideways. Sometimes this will be the effect you want, but it is often awkward for the viewer.

To change the camera position, use the Object/Move menu option. Then click on the dummy object and move it to the new location. Fifteen frames is just one second, so you shouldn't move it too far. In fact, sometimes you may want to leave the position of the dummy object unchanged and simply change the rotation. This mimics a person turning in place. As a general rule, if you move fast, don't use rotation. If you use a fast rotation, don't use much other movement.

To change the camera rotation, use the Object/Rotate menu option. You then can click on the dummy object to rotate it. There are three axes of rotation available; press the Tab key to change from one to the next. Use the Top view for best results and control. Most rotation will be from side to side, either to match changes in the camera path, or to look at interesting objects in the virtual space. You can simulate looking up and down by applying rotations in the Left or Front views, depending on which direction the camera is facing at the time.

Figure 6.21 shows a set of views in the Keyframer that have been set up for working with a camera path. The view at the upper left shows the patio, and the camera is inside the dummy object at the upper left. The Front view shows the entire home, with the camera located just to the left of the house. The lower left view is a Plan View that shows the entire camera path,[16] starting at the top left center of the view, and moving toward the bottom of the view. The view at the bottom right is a view through the camera lens from the current camera position on the patio.[17]

You can use the Paths/Move Key menu option to adjust the camera position at key frames. 3D Studio will automatically alter the intervening points between the key frames.[18] To see a very rough approximation of your animation, make the Camera view the active view by clicking in it, and then click the double-arrow icon at the bottom right to play the animation. For a complex scene, playback may be delayed in order to draw all the objects in the scene. If this is the case, playback speed may vary, depending on how many objects are in the scene at any given frame.

---

[16] To see the camera path, you must use the Paths or Camera menu and click on Show Path. Normally, an object's path is hidden.

[17] This view is of frame 4, so the camera hasn't really begun to move yet. It is still very close to its starting position.

[18] A key frame is any frame in which you have established a position for the object. In this example, that would be 15, 30, 45, ... and so on.

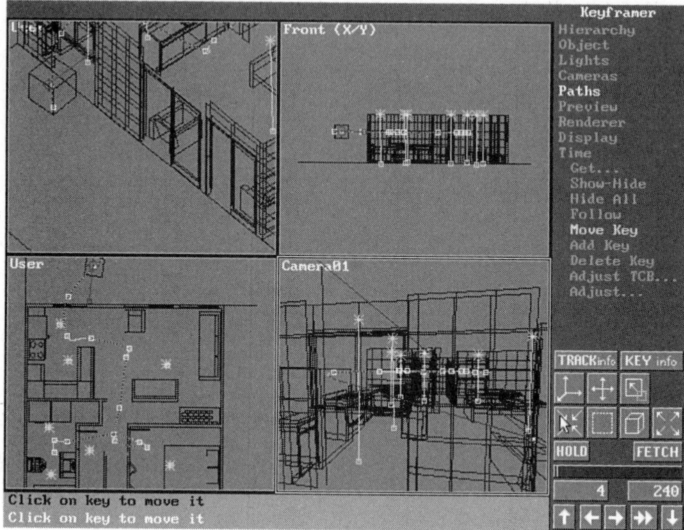

Figure 6.21. The Keyframer set up for working with a camera path. Note the existence of a path in the lower left view, marked User.

To see a rough, but real-time preview, click the Preview/Make menu option. This will take some time to create, but not nearly as long as it takes to render the scene.

You also can have a little fun with a fly-through. Before you render the animation, find places in the scene where you can personalize the virtual space. For example, you might want to hang a painting, or display a vase full of flowers. Adding details to just a few objects can transform a dull, dreary scene into one that is interesting.

For example, I couldn't resist adding a painting to this particular fly-through. Despite the presence of furniture and appliances, the walls were inescapably bare. Figure 6.22 shows how it is done.

The view at the bottom right shows the painting selected; these are the darkest lines in the viewport. The object that will be the painting itself is the only object selected, but there is also a frame around it. You can see one corner of the frame in the Top viewport. Note that the painting is recessed inside the frame to help yield a 3D appearance. In addition to this painting, I added a wall mirror to the bathroom.

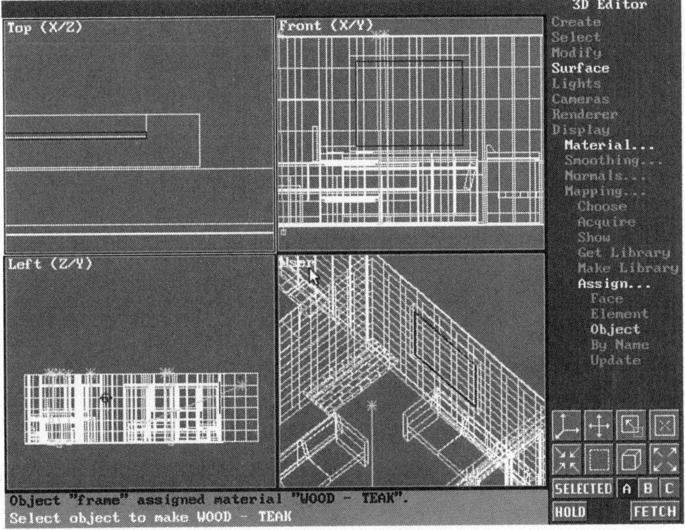

Figure 6.22. Adding a painting to a scene.

But these are just objects, created in the 3D Editor and modified slightly until they are just the right size.[19] The Materials Editor is where the magic takes place. Figure 6.23 shows a Materials Editor screen.[20] The currently selected material is called "Painting of Me." This is the material that gets applied to the thin rectangle inside the frame (see fig. 6.22). It has the following characteristics:

- The shininess factor is set to 82 out of 100. This ensures that the painting will reflect the scene around it, just as you would expect of a real painting behind glass. You also could create a glass object, but this is easier.
- For safety's sake, I made this a two-sided material. That means that no matter which way the face normals point, you will see the painting. This is a cheap but common trick.
- Two of the four buttons at the bottom of the image are highlighted: Texture Map and Reflection Map. The Texture Map is set to a file, RON.TGA, which is an image of me taken from a video file that accompanied an earlier book. The Texture Map slider is set to 100, which means that only the image file will be used to cover the surface of the object. If

---

[19]All these added objects started out with the Create/Box command. I did a little nipping and tucking with the Create/Object/Boolean command to make everything fit properly.

[20]Please excuse the appearance of the scroll bars near the center of the image, and of the samples at the top of the image. They don't actually look like that. In order to capture the screen, I had to use a 16-color VGA graphics mode. Normally, you would use the Materials Editor in a 256-color mode.

the slider were set to a lower number, the colors set above for Ambient, Diffuse, and Specular would show through to some degree.

- The Reflection Map is set to Automatic. This tells 3D Studio to handle reflections of the surrounding space automatically. The Reflection Map slider is set to 25, which means that only a partial reflection will occur—this is intended to imitate the behavior of real glass, which only reflects a similar small percentage of the light that strikes it.

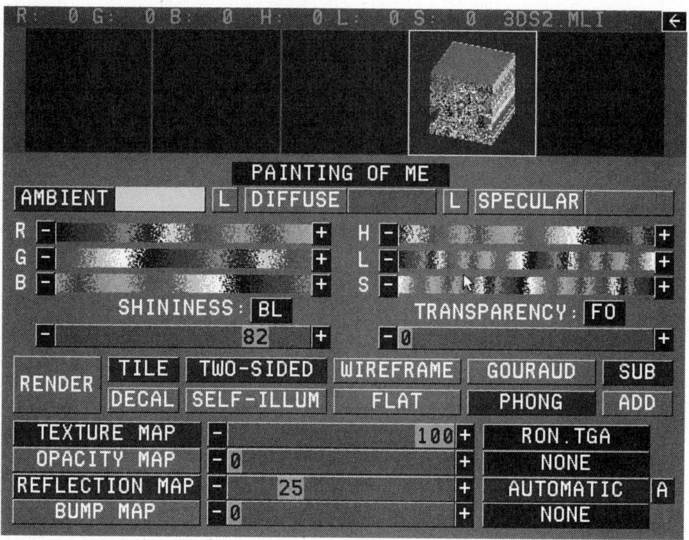

Figure 6.23. Creating a material with texture and reflection maps.

To save this material in the Materials library, use the Materials menu at the top of the screen. Choose Put Material from the drop-down menu. You must re-put a material if you change it in any way after creating it.

If you create a reflection map for a flat object, there are special rules to follow when you assign the material to an object. The most important rule is to make sure that you attach the material with a reflection map only to the actual faces that will do the reflecting. If you apply it to the whole object, 3D Studio will decide which face to apply reflections to, and it may not be the one you want!

Figure 6.24 shows the dialog box that appears if you click the Automatic button. For most reflection maps, you can use an Anti-aliasing setting of Low—objects in a reflection map are usually small, and don't require much anti-aliasing. However, for objects that are flat, you must click Yes for Flat Mirror, or you will not get acceptable results. 3D Studio uses a different reflection algorithm for flat objects.

If the object with the reflection map will be stationary, then click the First Frame Only button to activate it. This instructs 3D Studio to create the maps used for reflections only once, which avoids a lot of unnecessary rendering time.

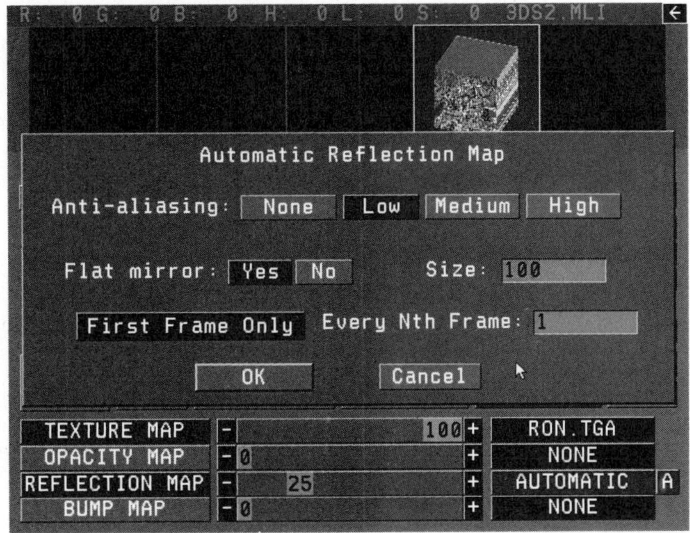

Figure 6.24. Automatic reflection map settings for a material used with flat objects.

For the mirror in the bathroom, I modified an existing 3D Studio material called Chrome Sky. The settings are similar to that for the painting, but there is no texture map, and the reflection map is set to 100 percent. This material is also two-sided,[(21)] and the settings for Automatic Reflection Map are the same as shown in figure 6.24.

The fly-through animation file is on the CD-ROMs with the files for this chapter. Figures 6.25 through 6.28 show various scenes from the animation.

[21]More out of laziness than necessity.

Figure 6.25. Frame 5 from the 360-frame animation of the house fly-through.

Figure 6.26. Frame 83 from the 360-frame animation of the house fly-through.

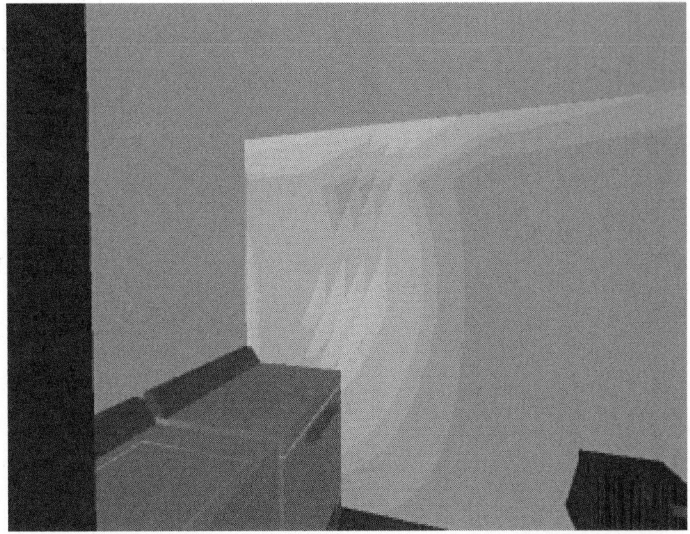

Figure 6.27. Frame 283 from the 360-frame animation of the house fly-through.

Figure 6.28. Frame 360 from the 360-frame animation of the house fly-through.

Fly-Through via Helicopter

The last section was more of a walk-through than a fly-through, but this section will more than make up for that with an exciting helicopter fly-through of Crater Lake, Oregon. It will take the combined resources of both Vistapro and 3D Studio, but it's worth it.

RECIPE

1 copy Vistapro 3.0
1 fly-through animation
1 copy 3D Studio
1 or more objects to animate
1 large dose patience[22]

Instructions: This is a complex, gourmet-level recipe, and all the instructions won't fit here on the card. See the accompanying text for details of preparation. This recipe is a real crowd pleaser, and is excellent for large parties such as demonstrations and presentations.

Chapter 1 covered the details of creating an animation with Vistapro, and you'll build on that in this section. The basic steps in the complete process follow:

- Create the fly-through animation using Vistapro and Flight Director.
- Analyze the data in Flight Director to determine the lighting angles on the helicopter at various points in the animation.
- Record the relative positions of the sun and the helicopter in a table for reference in 3D Studio.
- Create a helicopter as an object in 3D Studio, as well as a screen and a camera. Position the helicopter between the camera and the box.
- Create a material that uses the fly-through animation as a texture map.[23]

---

22 This is a frequently needed ingredient in VR recipes—keep plenty on hand in the cupboard.

23 Yes, you can use an animation as a texture map. You can save the animation as an FLC file, or you can use a series of bitmaps by providing a list of the bitmaps in a text file.

- Apply the material to a box the same relative size as the animation (320×240 and 320×200 are the two most common sizes).
- Create a light and position it according to the table you created from studying Flight Director for frame 1.
- Animate the helicopter to create realistic lighting and motion.
- Render!

Admittedly, this is a long list of tasks, but the results are well worth it. The entire process isn't as tedious as it sounds; some of these steps are easy. Others, of course, will tax your patience heavily.

Analyze the Data

Figure 6.29 shows the map portion of the Flight Director screen after the path has already been created. Since the goal is to track the relationship between the helicopter and the sun, I have taken the liberty of putting icons into the map image to indicate their relative positions at the start of the animation. The sun is located to the east (north is at the top of the map), and stays there throughout the animation.

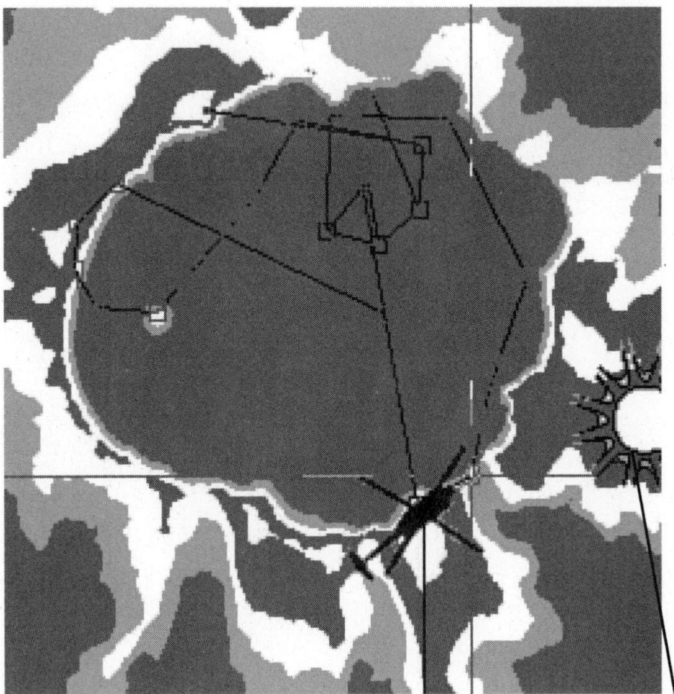

Figure 6.29.
A path in Flight Director.

The helicopter, however, twists and turns as it follows its path. If you don't add a light that moves, the helicopter won't look very realistic. The lighting on the scene will be coming from one direction, and the lighting on the helicopter will be coming from a different direction. This is subtle, but it is an important consideration if realism is your goal.

It would be more precise to consider the sun angle for each and every frame, but that's not realistic—there are 615 frames in the animation! Instead, you only need to identify key points along the path where the sun angle on the helicopter changes. Figure 6.30 shows the key points along the path, with the frame numbers for those points.[24]

There's a second level of analysis that you may also want to perform: banking. The Flight Director will bank the virtual aircraft during turns. This causes an apparent tilt of the landscape. If you

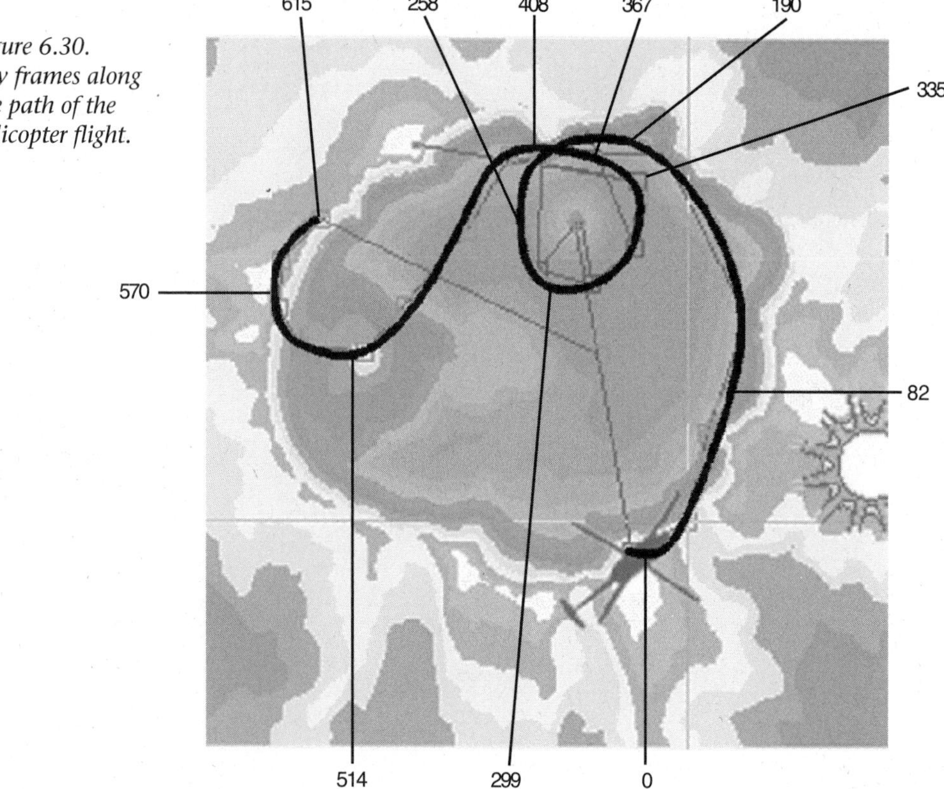

Figure 6.30. Key frames along the path of the helicopter flight.

[24]Finding the frame numbers is easy. As you move along the path in Flight Director, it displays the frame number on the screen.

want the last touch of realism, you can record the bank angles for various frames and then use that list to adjust the bank angle of the helicopter in 3D Studio.

Record Relative Positions

The easiest way to record the sun angle is to create a chart. Figure 6.31 shows the kind of chart I use, although the pretty helicopter and sun pictures are replaced with an arrow and a small circle, drawn by hand. In figure 6.32, the far left column is a frame number. In the middle column, the sun is held constant on the east side of the box, and the position of the helicopter at each frame changes.[25] These positions are easy to determine—the process doesn't require much thinking. With so many variables to keep track of, a minimum of thinking is a good thing.

The next step is to normalize[26] for the helicopter; the reason for this will be evident in a moment. To normalize, use your imagination to rotate the helicopter and the sun together until the helicopter is facing straight up. This keeps the angle between the helicopter and the sun constant, resulting in a nice, neat, normalized column of figures (the right column).

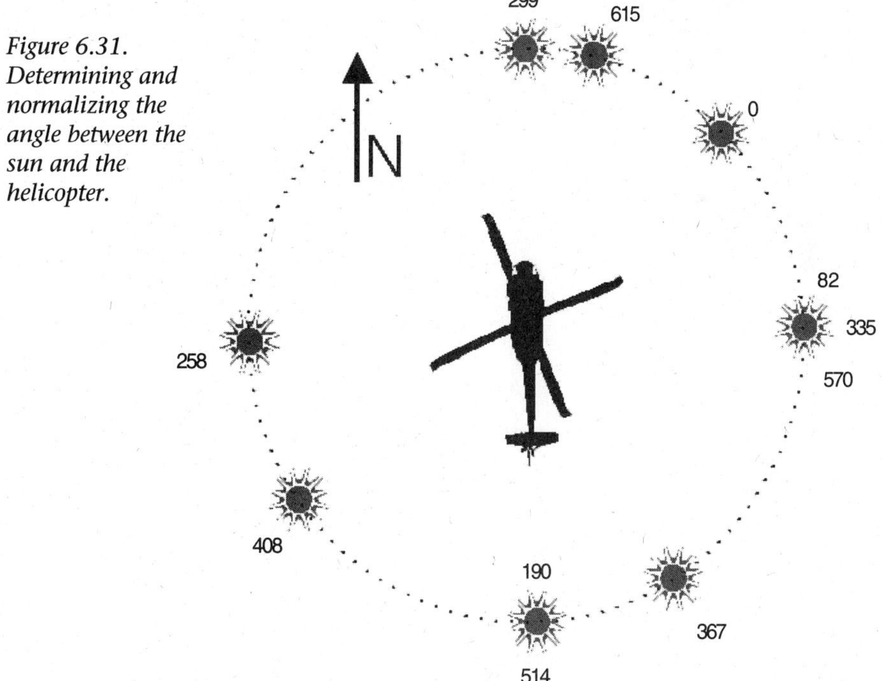

Figure 6.31. Determining and normalizing the angle between the sun and the helicopter.

---

[25]The position of the helicopter is assumed to be tangent to the direction of motion for this example. If you set targets for nodes, this will change the situation. The direction the helicopter is facing, toward the target, is used as the position instead of the tangent.

[26]Normalizing is a common mathematical operation. Normally, it means keeping one variable constant and adjusting all the other variables appropriately.

You're almost done now. The final step is to combine all the images from the right column into a single image, as shown in figure 6.32. I added the frame numbers to the diagram to make it easier to work with the illustration in 3D Studio. If you want to look ahead, figure 6.36 shows how this drawing corresponds to the location of the light in various frames.

If you want to also add bank angles for that extra touch of realism, you'll need to step through the frames in Flight Director and record the frames in which the bank angle changes. Table 6.1 shows the variation of the bank angle for the first 100 frames of the animation.

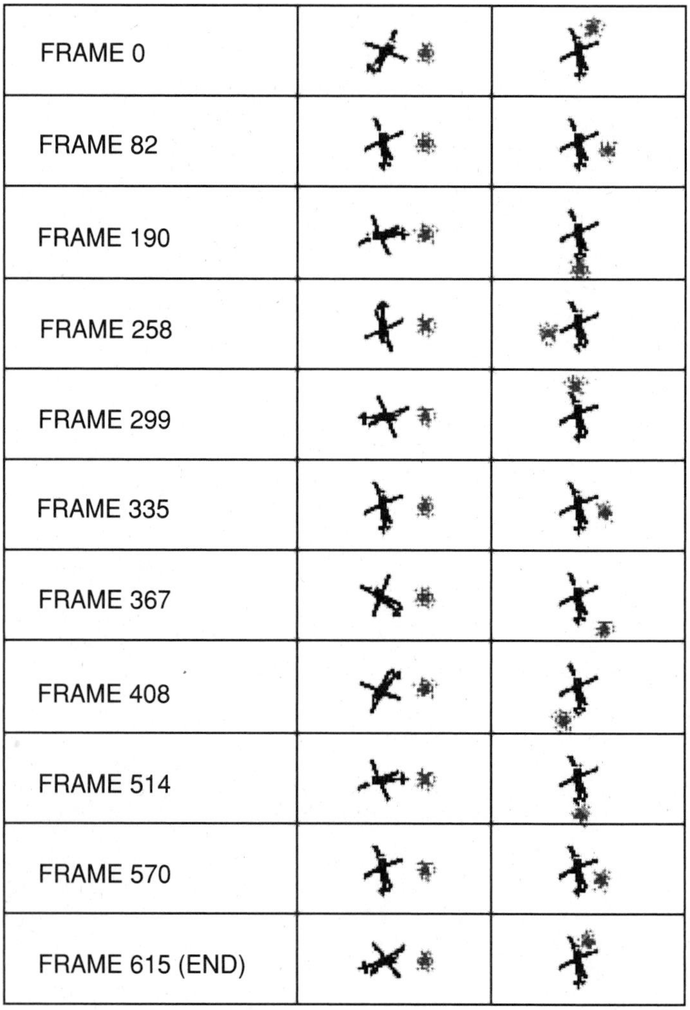

Figure 6.32. Illustration to keep at hand while working in 3D Studio.

FRAME 0		
FRAME 82		
FRAME 190		
FRAME 258		
FRAME 299		
FRAME 335		
FRAME 367		
FRAME 408		
FRAME 514		
FRAME 570		
FRAME 615 (END)		

Table 6.1. Bank-Angle Changes in an Animation.

Frame	*Bank Angle*
0	-8
2	-7
4	-6
7	-5
12	-4
14	-3
16	-2
19	-1
21	0
28	1
31	2
48	1
53	0
62	-1
65	-2
70	-3
72	-4
92	-3
96	-2

Use the slider at the bottom right of the Flight Director screen to step through the frames and examine the bank angle. The bank angle is displayed at the right center of the screen.

Create a Helicopter and Other Objects

There are two ways to create a helicopter in 3D Studio: from scratch, or out of the box. Fortunately, 3D Studio includes a sample file with a helicopter already in it, which you can use for this demonstration. Figure 6.33 shows the helicopter loaded into the 3D Editor. The "screen" that will be used for the animation also is evident, particularly in the Top and Left views—it's right there in front of the helicopter. It's a simple box, but a very thin one. The animation image size is 320×200, so you should use the same proportion for the screen. Create it in the Front viewport to make life easy.

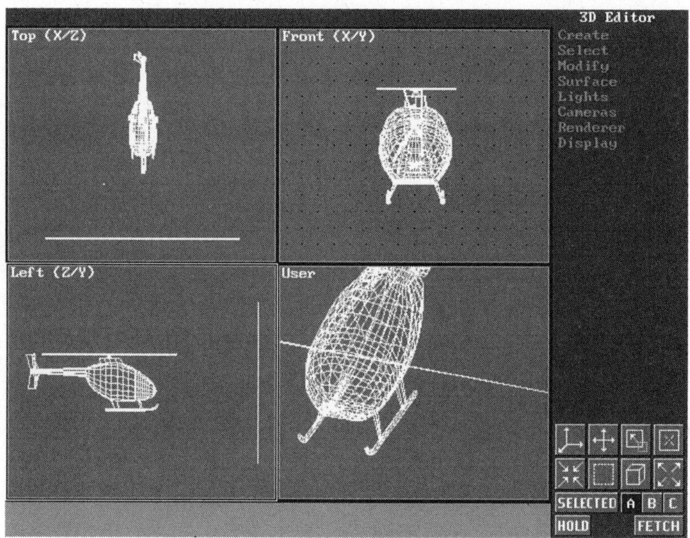

Figure 6.33.
A helicopter and a screen in 3D Studio's 3D Editor.

The helicopter is made of three separate objects:(27) the main rotor, the tail rotor, and the helicopter body. There are two levels of animation involved. The rotors, naturally, must rotate in relation to the body. The body then must move up and down, and bank left and right to make realistic movements as determined by the analysis of the animation path.

The rotor animation should be considered part of the process of creating the helicopter. That way, it will be there when you need it. To create the rotor animations, determine the number of frames to use for one revolution; I used a setting of 30 frames, but you may prefer a faster or slower rotor. I chose 30 frames because that

---

[27]Each of the objects has some individual elements, but they can be ignored for the purposes of this description. For example, the main rotor and the rotor shaft were created as separate objects, but they are joined together during all phases of the animation and thus can be considered as one object.

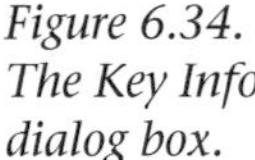

Figure 6.34.
The Key Info dialog box.

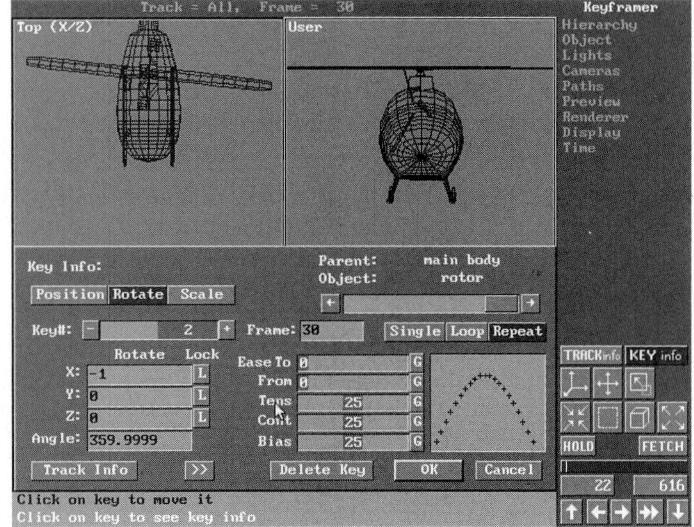

seemed to provide a sense of rotor motion. After moving to frame 30, I rotated each of the rotors through 360 degrees. That would only result in one rotation. To create a repeating rotation, click the Key Info button at the bottom right of the screen and then on the rotor. This displays the Key Info dialog box (see fig. 6.34).

Click the Repeat button to make this a repeating animation. That's all there is to it. Do the same for the rear rotor. Then use the Hierarchy/Link menu option to link each of the rotors to the helicopter body. Now you have a helicopter, complete with rotors that rotate without any further fuss.

There are two more objects to create: a camera and a spotlight.[28] The camera requires only a little care to set up:

- Create the camera with the Camera/Create menu option. Place the camera directly behind the helicopter body. A longer lens setting works best; try something in the range of 85mm to 135mm. Adjust the camera position with the Dolly command until the right and left edges of the screen are just outside the camera viewport.[29] Ignore the extra space at the top and bottom—the screen is matched to the image size, and if you also set 320×200 as the output size, the extra space will not appear in the rendered frame even though you can see it in the viewport. See figure 6.35 to see what the camera viewport should look like at frame zero.

[28] It doesn't have to be a spotlight, but a spotlight creates shadows that add interest to the scene.

[29] You did remember to press Ctrl-V to bring up the viewport dialog box and make one of the views a camera view, right?

Figure 6.35 also shows the correct position of the spotlight for the beginning of the animation. In the Top view, it is located at the right of the helicopter and slightly forward. In the Front view, you can see that the light is also located slightly above the helicopter. This angle, too, is derived from the sun position in the original file.

Just for fun, I have tilted the helicopter aggressively forward. This is not necessary, but it gives the opening frame a sense of action and urgency. As a final touch, also link the spotlight target to the helicopter body. This will ensure that the helicopter is always illuminated.

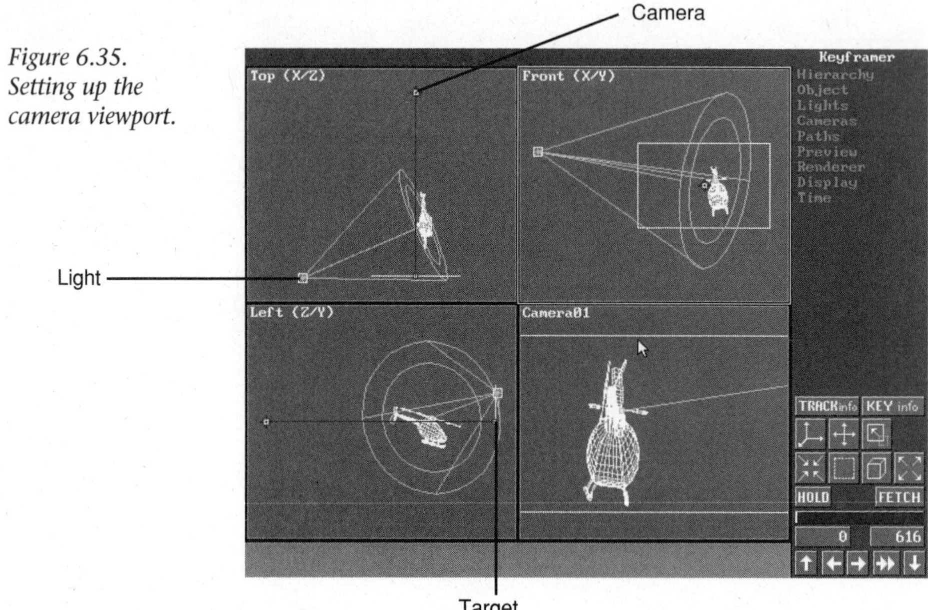

Figure 6.35. Setting up the camera viewport.

Animation as Texture Map

You can use an animation as a texture map using the same procedures as described earlier for bitmaps. Use the Materials Editor to create a new material, and select the FLC file created with the PCX2FLC utility (it comes with Vistapro) as the texture map. Set the Texture Map slider to 100 percent. During rendering, each frame of the animation will use the corresponding frame from the fly-through animation in the FLC file. It's all automatic.

All you need to do is use the Material/Object/Assign menu option to apply the material to the screen. If you want to avoid checking face normals, make the material two-sided.

Virtual Reality Gallery

Right and bottom:
two mountain landscapes
rendered with Vistapro

Olympus Mons rendered in Vistapro
(vertical scale exaggerated).

Virtual Gallery

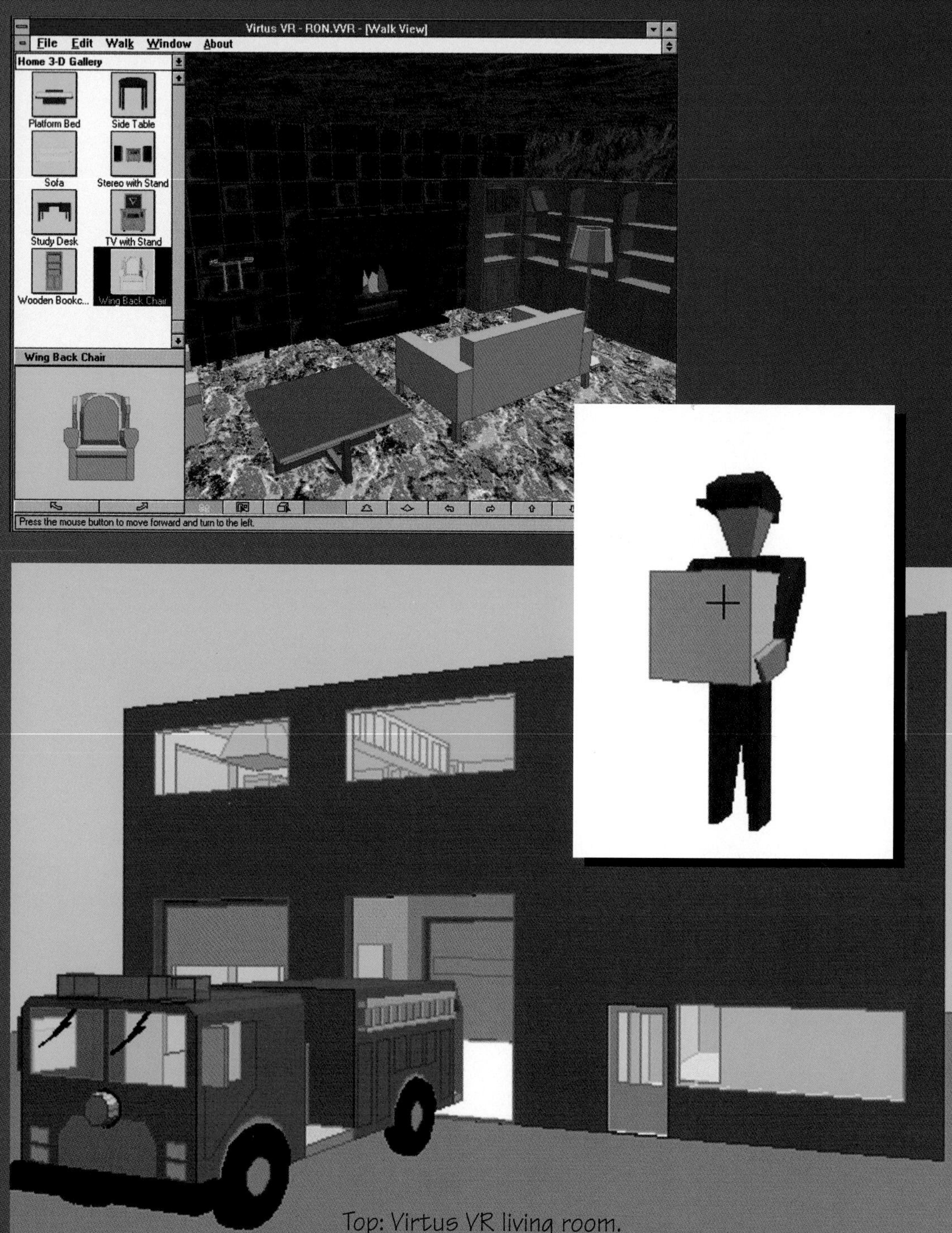

Top: Virtus VR living room.
Center: It's Brutus, inhabitant of Virtus virtual worlds.
Bottom: A Virtus WalkThrough firehouse.

Top: A fanciful creation courtesy of 3D Studio.
Middle/bottom: A magical spaceship created with trueSpace.

3D Studio creations
Top right: A jumping man.
Top left: A virtual building in a photograph of a city street.
Bottom: 3D objects.

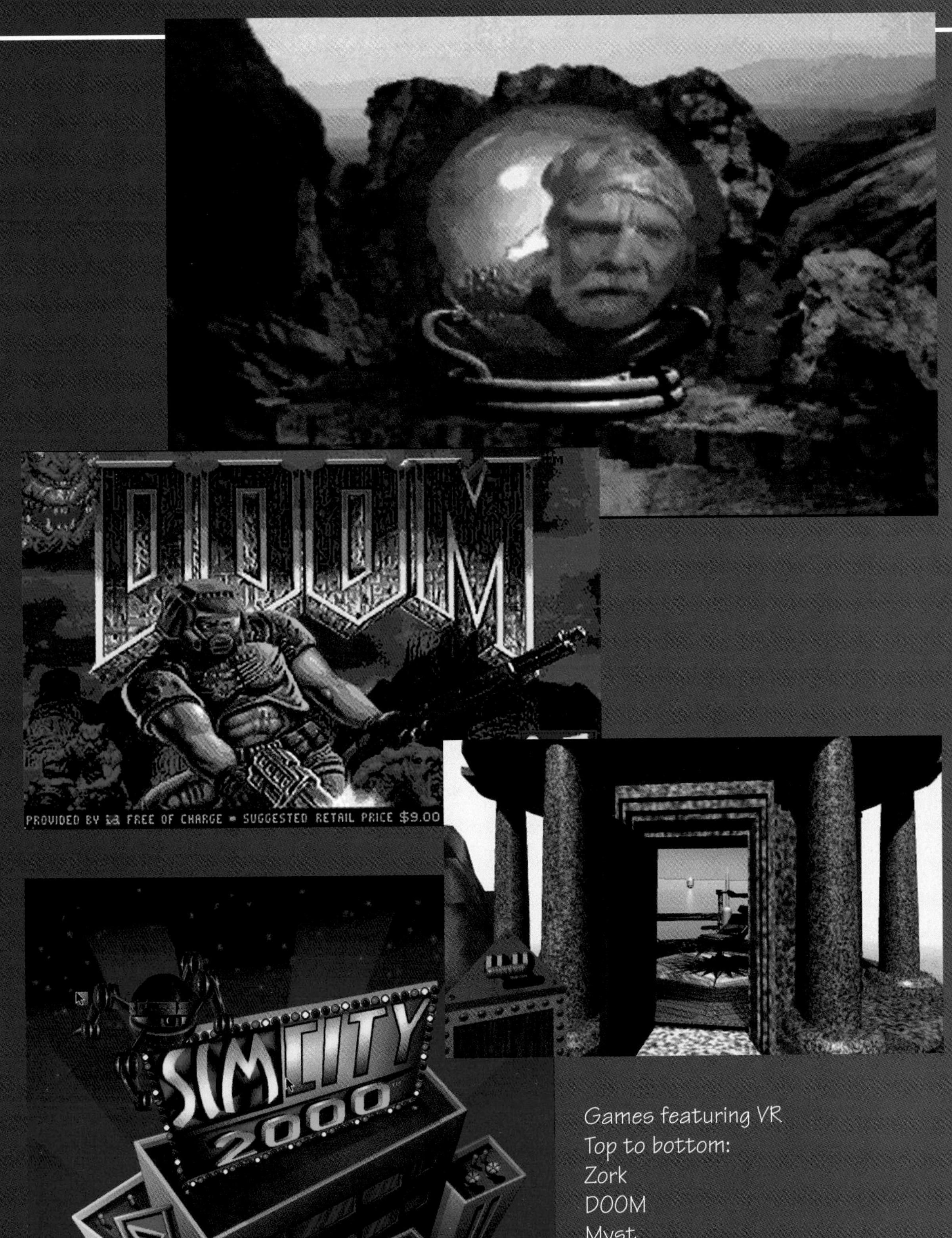

Games featuring VR
Top to bottom:
Zork
DOOM
Myst
Sim City 2000

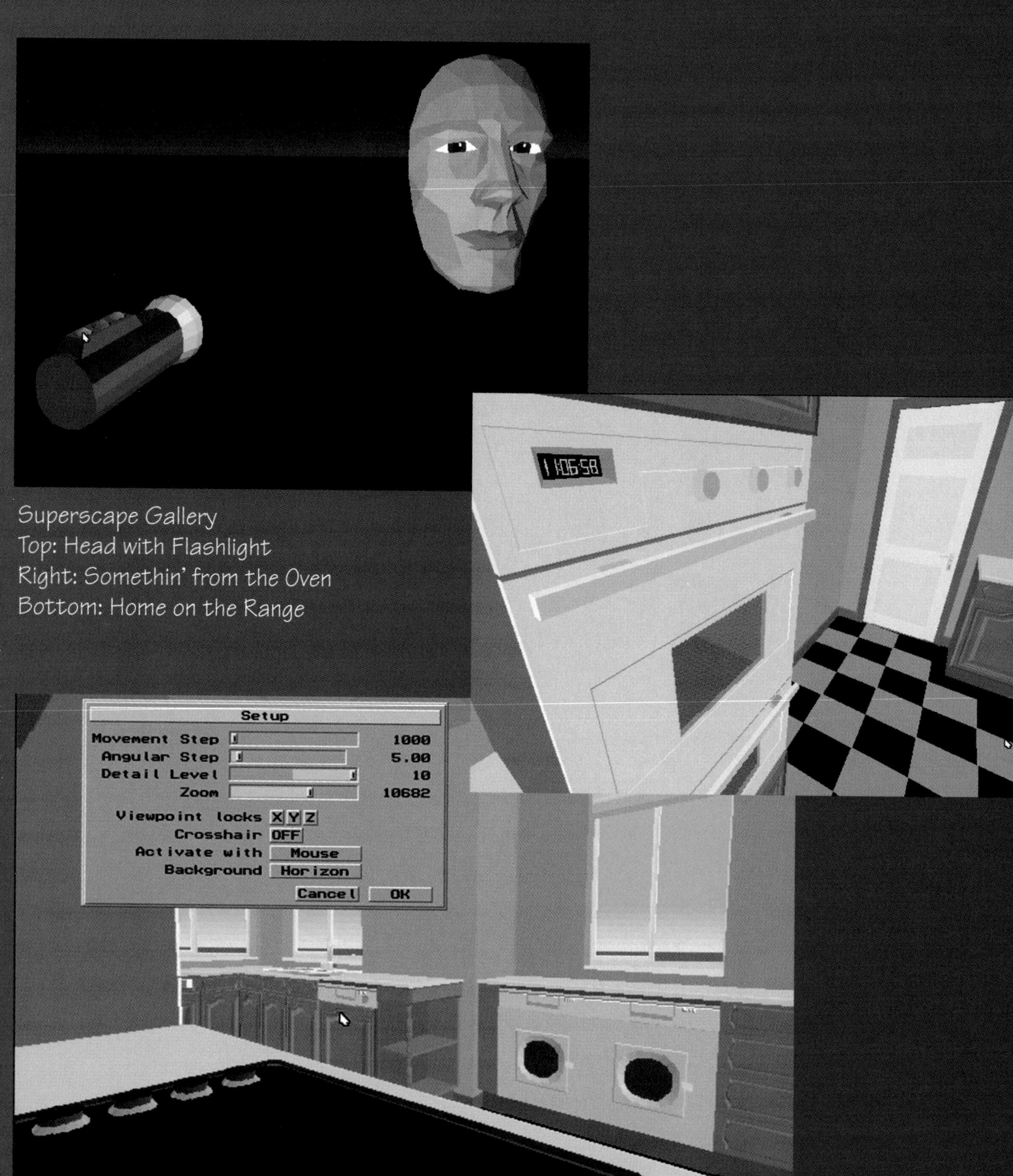

Superscape Gallery
Top: Head with Flashlight
Right: Somethin' from the Oven
Bottom: Home on the Range

Virtus Walking
1: move forward
2: move backward
3: move right
4: move left
5: up and to the right
6: left and down

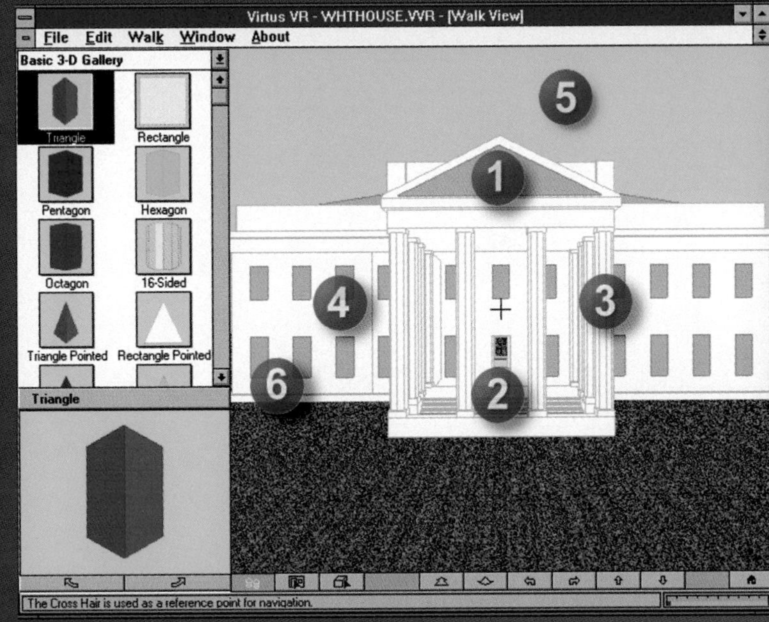

Left: A fanciful planet.
Below: A 3D Studio helicopter flies through a landscape animation created in Vistapro.

A Vistapro landscape--Mars, perhaps? -- enhanced with a Lens Flare effect in Photoshop.

Left: A 3D red/blue image created with Vistapro 3.0. When viewed through red/blue 3D glasses, the 3D shape (Mt. St. Helens) is evident.

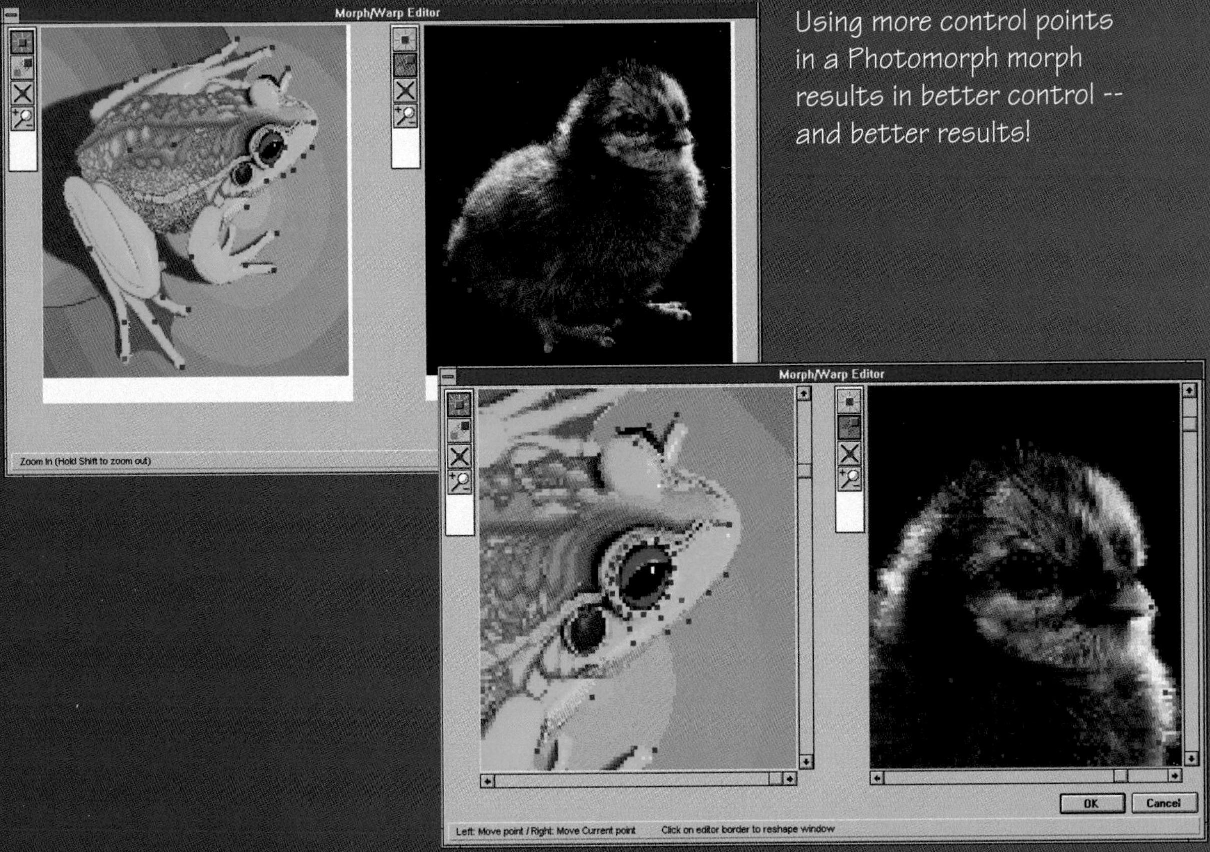

Morph/Warp Editor

Zoom In (Hold Shift to zoom out)

Morph/Warp Editor

OK

Cancel

Left: Move point / Right: Move Current point

Click on editor border to reshape window

Using more control points in a Photomorph morph results in better control -- and better results!

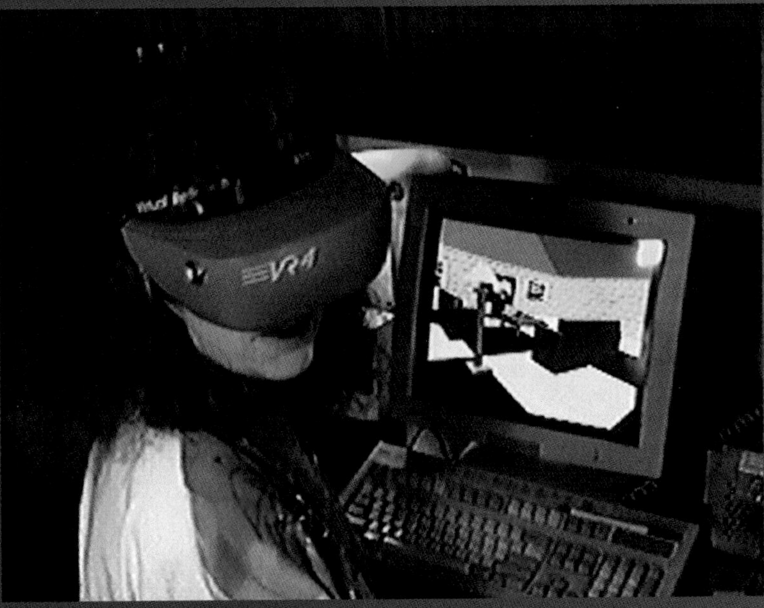

Right: Donna in action with Vream and an HMD.

A fanciful application of VR Studio. These could be a pair of space cadets in a miniature flying saucer investigating your home!

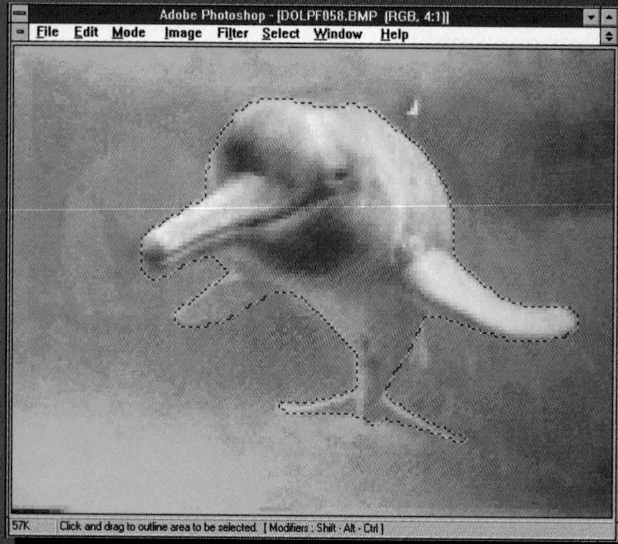

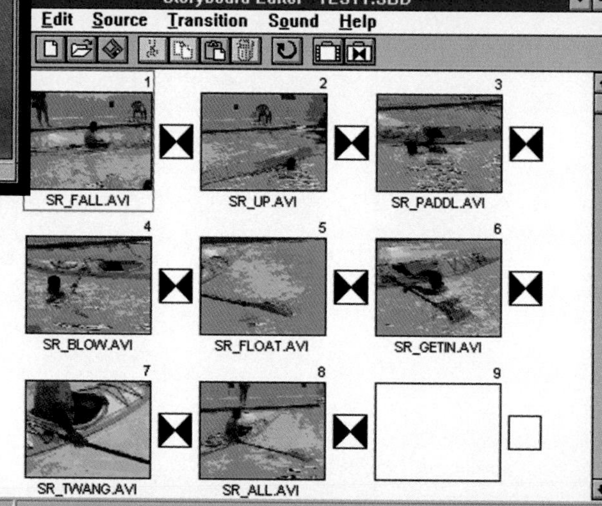

Above: Using Photoshop to alter a frame from a video clip.
Right: A sample view of a Media Merge Story Board session, showing eight video clips loaded.

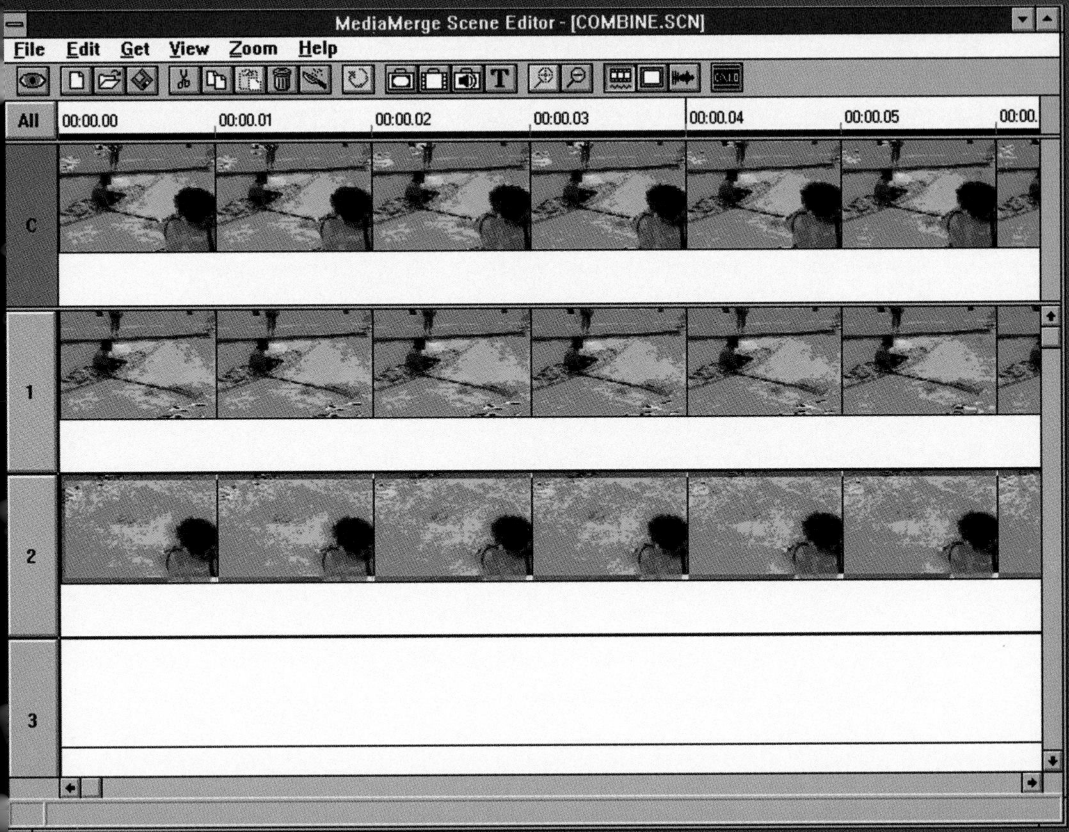

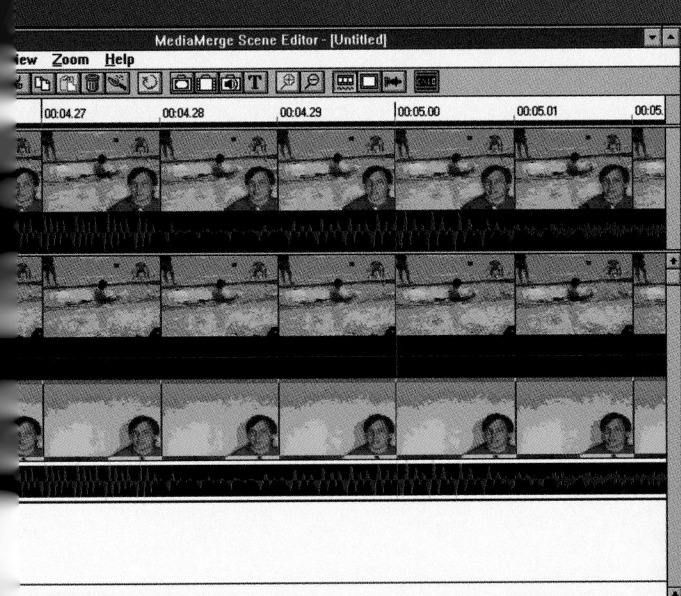

Above: A composite of two video clips in the Media Merge Scene Editor.
Left: The lower video clip was taken in front of a blue screen so the talking head (that's author Ron) could be superimposed easily over the kayak clip. See text of chapter 8 for details.

Right: A sample frame from a 3D Studio animation that uses morphing.
Below: A sample 3D Studio screen. Note use of color to differentiate lines -- yellow for lights, blue for a camera, and black for the model.

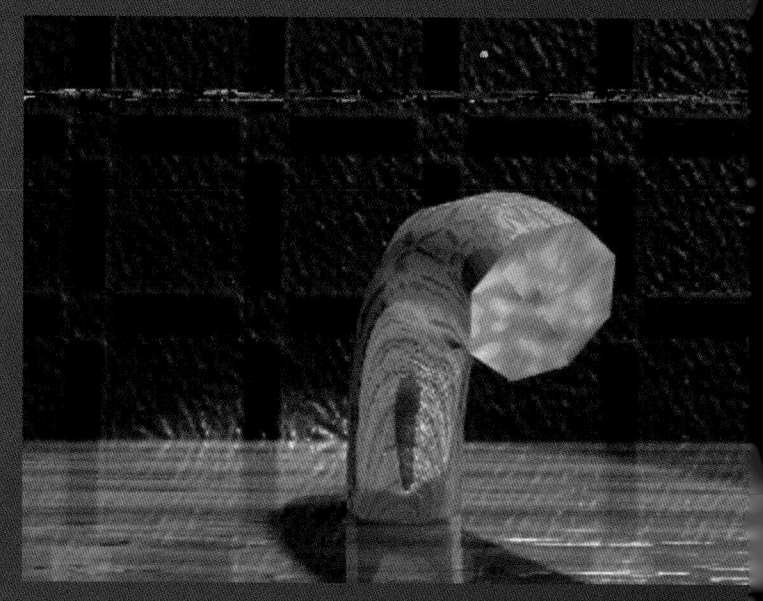

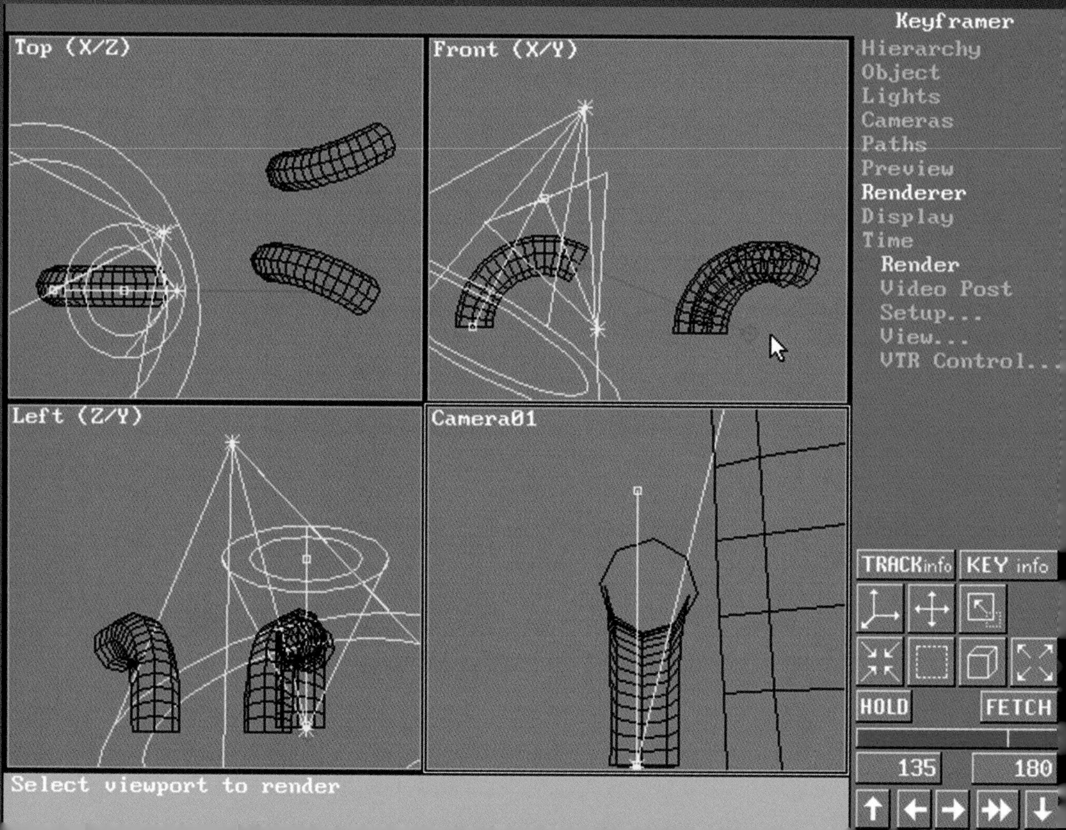

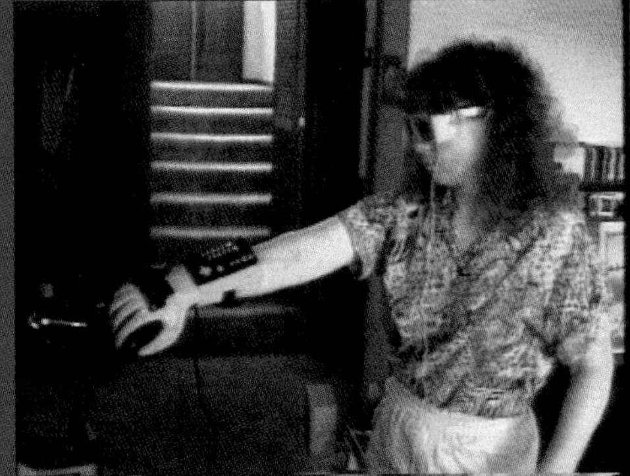

Above left: The Mattel Powerglove in use with Rend 386. Note how the physical and virtual gloves display the same gesture.
Above right: Donna tries out the Power Glove and LCD glasses, both from #DTV.

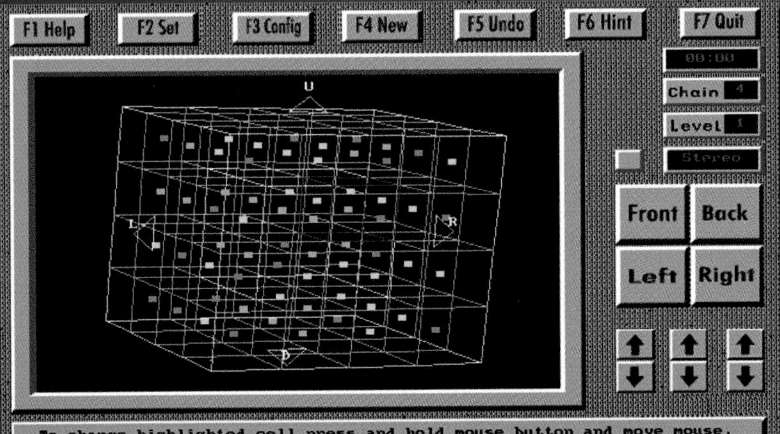

Left: A 3D Go game -- a classic example of how hard it can be to visualize a third dimension on a two-dimensional surface!

Right: A sense of humor is essential for any work in a virtual space -- as this interactive example from The Return of Zork proves.

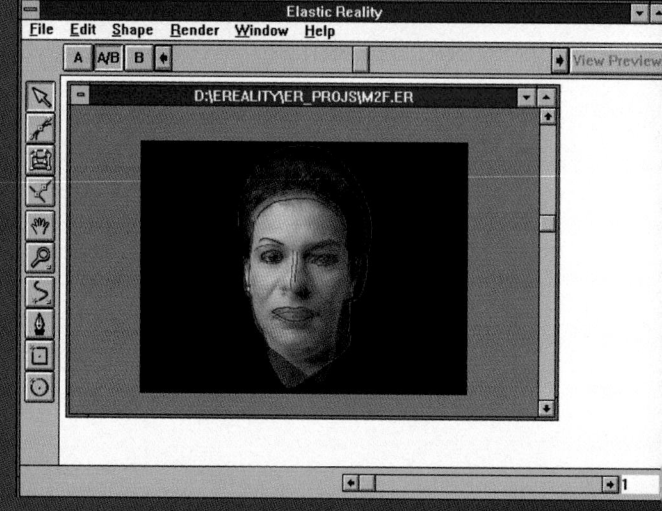

Left: Five frames from a morph created with Elastic Reality. Note how smooth and lifelike the transition is.
Above: The combined A/B roll image (see text for details).
Below: Adjusting the edge density of a morph.

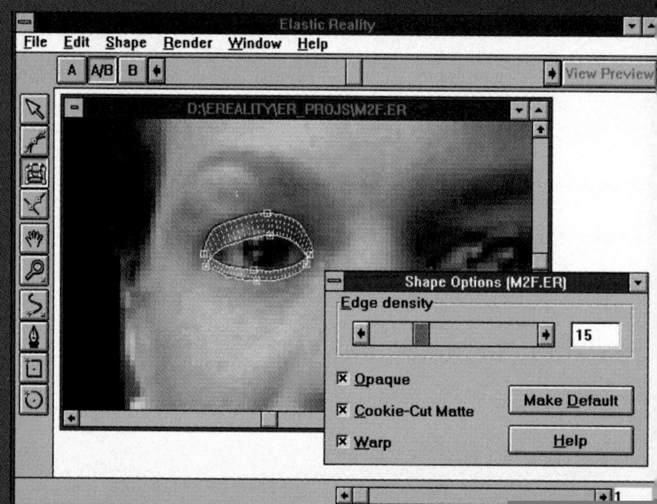

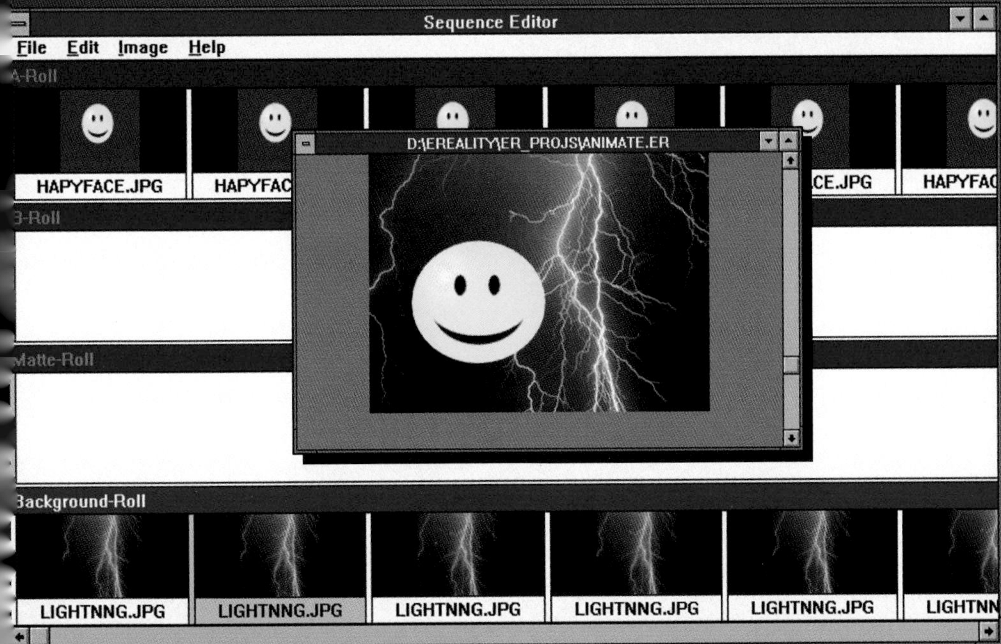

bove: The Elastic Reality Sequence Editor, with A-roll and background clips loaded.
set: The resulting composite.

bove: A living room created
ith Vream.
ight: The kitchen of the
ame house.

Virtual Gallery

Right: Vream display for Cybereyes.
Below: Vream display for Cyberscope.

The left and right halves of a stereo image superimposed. Stereo pair created with 3D Studio; superimposed in Photoshop.

Lighting

The light is the key to a realistic final result. With all of the analysis already performed, it's easy to animate the light correctly. With a worksheet similar to figure 6.32 at hand, you can easily animate the light correctly. Look at figure 6.36—it shows the desired result. If you look closely, you'll see that the key points along the light's path correspond to the points in figure 6.32. To arrive at this happy conclusion, move to each frame listed in figure 6.32 and move the light to a point corresponding to the orientation shown in the right column of figure 6.32. When this is complete, display the path for the light. It should look like figure 6.36. You may need to add key points, or move a few around, to get the best results.

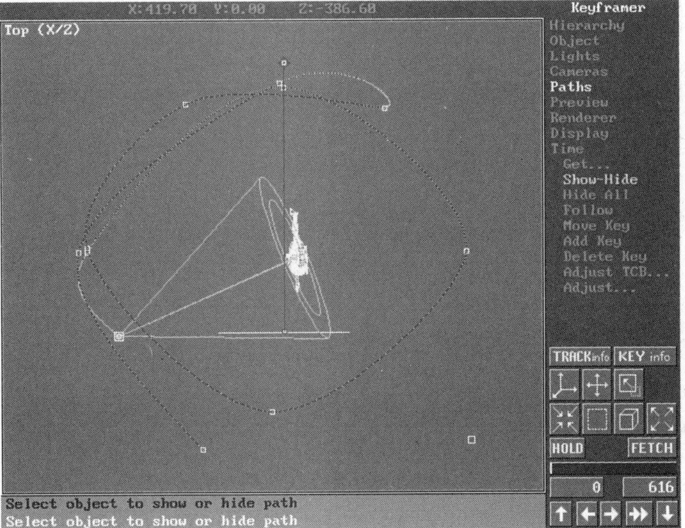

Figure 6.36. The fully animated spotlight.

Animate Helicopter

There are two kinds of movement that you can apply to the helicopter. One is simple bobs and weaves based on the animation. The other is bank adjustments to adjust for turns. If you plan to add the bank adjustments, you should make them first. These are simple adjustments—move to the frames where the bank angle changes, and adjust the bank angle one degree plus or minus as needed. Once this is done, you can add all the bobs and weaves you want.

To change the bank angle, work in the Front viewport. Use the Rotate command to make the changes; press Tab to change the axis of rotation to the correct one. For bobbing and weaving, you can tilt forward and backward, or move the helicopter around. Figure 6.37 shows the path for the helicopter. The path doesn't show the numerous rotational changes, only the bobbing and weaving.

NOTE

If you only make position changes in the Front view, you will keep the helicopter in the correct relationship to the screen—no closer, and no farther.

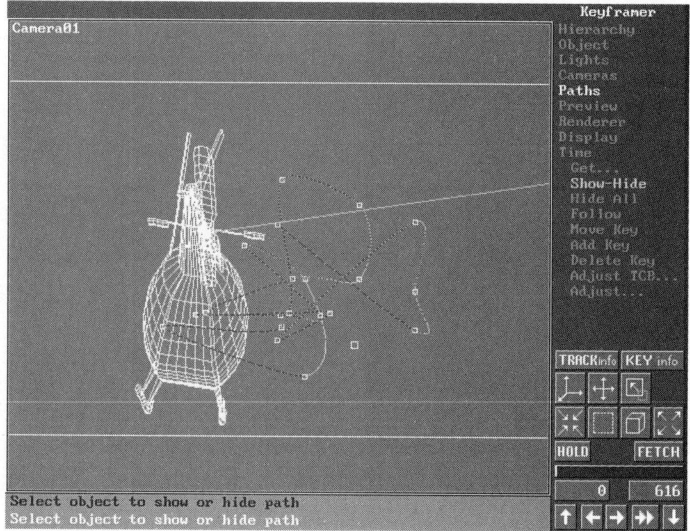

Figure 6.37. The path for the helicopter body.

Render

Figure 6.38 shows four views of the helicopter at frame 503, near the end of the animation. Figure 6.39 shows a rendering (at 640×480, instead of the smaller 320×200 used for the animation) of the image for this frame. You also can render the animation at 160×100 if you want to have a much shorter rendering time and can settle for a lower resolution.

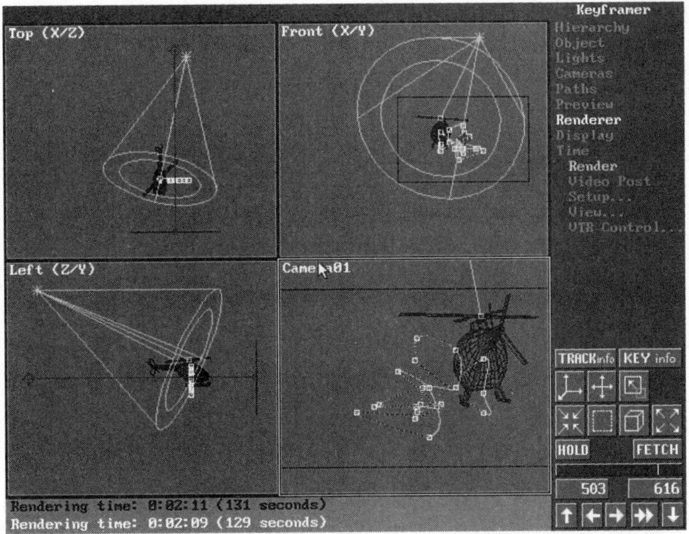

Figure 6.38.
Frame 503 in the Keyframer.

Figure 6.39.
A rendering of frame 503.

Gallery

Figures 6.40 through 6.50 show the "key frames" identified for the lighting changes. Even if you aren't able to play the animation from the CD, you can see from these figures how the lighting angle, banking angle, and position changes are used to provide a realistic-looking helicopter addition to the fly-through.

Figure 6.40. Frame 0 of the animation. The light is coming from forward and to the right of the helicopter.

Figure 6.41. Frame 82 of the animation. This figure shows a bank of -4 degrees.

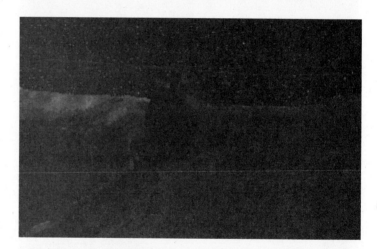

Figure 6.42. Frame 190 of the animation. This figure shows a bank of -5 degrees, and the helicopter has been moved to a low position in the frame. The lighting is now coming from behind the camera.

Figure 6.43. Frame 258 of the animation. The light is now on the opposite side of the helicopter from where it started.

Figure 6.44. Frame 299 of the animation. In this frame, the light is directly ahead of and slightly above, the helicopter.

Figure 6.45. Frame 335 of the animation. The helicopter has come full circle, 360 degrees. The lighting is now back at the right side of the helicopter. The bank angle is zero.

Figure 6.46. Frame 367 of the animation. The light is nearly behind the camera again.

Figure 6.47. Frame 408 of the animation. A minor shift from the previous figure: the light is now behind and to the left. The bank angle is-6. This frame is a good example of how a correct bank angle adds to the realism of animation.

Figure 6.48. Frame 514 of the animation. I added some spice at this point in the animation—the camera has begun to zoom in on the helicopter. The light is nearly exactly behind the camera.

Figure 6.49. Frame 570 of the animation. The zoom is complete. I moved the helicopter to the lower right corner of the frame more to keep it out of the way during the zoom than for any other reason.

Figure 6.50. Frame 615 of the animation. To conclude the animation, the helicopter jumps quickly to the center top of the frame, and looks over the entire lake after coming over the crest of the ridge. This was an attempt to add a touch of breathlessness to the animation, a feeling of swooping into the overview.

7

HARDWARE FOR VIRTUAL WORLDS

The Hardware Universe

Playing with virtual reality on your computer falls into two very distinct categories: doing it with special VR hardware and doing it without.

Most VR hardware is expensive, and if we weren't writing this book there's absolutely no way we would have been able to afford many of the devices you are going to read about in this chapter. So far, the main explanation we have offered for the current state of VR has been that CPU power hasn't caught up to the requirements of serious VR. In this chapter, we encounter another big reason: the cost of hardware for serious VR.

There are some cheap alternatives, many of them from a pioneering VR company called 3DTV. I have combined all the products from 3DTV into Chapter 13, "The Virtual Future," where you can find out what is possible with affordable (mostly) VR hardware. There are, as you would expect, some compromises that you must make in the name of affordability. In this chapter, we'll be looking at (mostly) expensive but powerful VR hardware—the kind you can't afford just for fun, but that is ideal for specific VR tasks. The focus here is based on our experiences with the hardware on special features of key hardware. For complete information, including prices and how to contact the manufacturer, see Chapter 14, "VR Hardware."

The Party Line

I have a bone to pick with traditional VR, and this is the perfect place to discuss the issues. The traditional definition of virtual reality goes something like this:

> **Virtual Reality provides an interactive environment that simulates a real environment.**

However, this little definition usually carries a lot of baggage with it that isn't spelled out. If you and I were to talk down the hallowed halls of just about any institution doing VR research, we'd find the following assumptions tagging along in any discussion of VR:

- Helmet devices are required for VR
- Body suits are desirable for VR
- Head tracking is required for VR
- Alternate input devices should be as natural as possible

I hate to spoil the party, but this is a pile of virtual hogwash. Such narrow definitions of VR may work in the narrow hallways of research, but out here in the real world where you and I want to use VR and VR-related stuff in meaningful ways, different rules and assumptions have to apply. This is never more true than when it comes to hardware. Here's Ron's Rule about VR hardware:

If it costs too much, it's irrelevant (for now).

In other words—go ahead, spend your big bucks on military and research VR hardware. But don't make me wait until that $100,000 headset comes down to $199 to have some fun!

What Really Matters

What really matters is what you and I can do. Pure VR makes no more sense than pure multimedia or a pure sports car. There will always be purists, of course, and may they always have the money they need for the pursuit of purity. I'm talking here about the rest of us. What matters is being able to use this stuff, either for fun or in meaningful—***and affordable***—ways.

I know I've just made a few enemies, but, darn it—VR isn't just some high and mighty technology. Pure VR is just a small part of the entire technology related to VR, and the ways that you and I will use VR probably won't be foreseen by the purists. We will be striking out in new directions, finding new uses, and integrating the technology into our lives. So we're the ones who should have the control, right?

Now that we have that little business squared away, let's consider the possibilities.

Where Is the Hardware Going?

At the high end, the hardware is going where the money is pointing, as is the case with all "high technology." If the military has the money to pay for fancy head-mounted systems, then the hardware is going toward goals that the military sets. However you might feel about the military and its goals, what this means for VR in general is that there is a force driving the leading edge of development ahead. A given technology might have just one or two examples in development, and price tags in the millions—even the mega millions—aren't uncommon.

The direction of high-end hardware is not always evident; military implies security and secrecy. However, much of the research is being done at colleges and universities, and enough is out in the open to suggest some amazing possibilities. For example, there is research into the use of low-power lasers to "write" a VR environment right into your eyes from a small, lightweight face unit. Currently, researchers would be happy to get a monochrome heads-up display working, but the possibilities are striking for VR.

At the middle level, VR (much of it fairly traditional) is feeding off the needs of industry. There are chemists using headsets to visualize molecular structure, for example. There's also an entertainment angle—headsets and VR arcades for trade shows, for example. Where the high end might see just a handful of prototypes, the middle level is about numbers—hundreds or thousands of units make for a successful technology at the middle level. To buy your VR toys, you need relatively serious money—from $5,000 to $100,000.

The middle level is where you will find primitive body suits, data gloves, stereo HMDs, and all the other stuff that was fantasy just a few years ago.

At the lower level—mostly under $1,000, to be considered affordable—there are actually only a few VR devices that will make you say, "Wow!" Most of the affordable technology is still making very serious compromises. Of course, most of this stuff didn't even exist at these prices last year, so we are making progress. But you shouldn't expect a really fantastic VR experience with affordable hardware. Interesting, yes; stimulating, yes—but true VR, no.

What you will find in the affordable range are VR alternatives to the mouse, and simple 3D head-mounted hardware.

How Much Does Hardware Matter?

I'm of two opinions on this. On the one hand, as part of writing this book, I've had the chance to play with some of the high-end hardware. On the other hand, there's a lot you can do without any special hardware at all.

I set some limits, which means that I didn't get to try as much as I would have liked. Our rules for hardware were simple: We had to try it out on our own PCs. Special-purpose VR hardware is great for its intended audience, but we wanted to stick to stuff that you or I could connect to a PC and *use*.

If you are on a budget and want to play with VR, there are some very good software-only products that will give you both enjoyment and a learning experience. You won't meet the purists' definition of VR—immersion in an environment. But, if you are like me, you will be fascinated by what you find and by what you can do.

If you have the money to explore hardware, there are some good options. VR hardware is quite sophisticated, and for most of us, that means that building your own is out of the question. You need to know a fair amount about computers and electronics to pull off creating your own VR hardware—it's not for the average garage mechanic. What this means is that if you just want toys, you can get them relatively cheaply—certainly for less than $1,000, and occasionally for less than $100.

If you want stuff that works really well, you will occasionally find it for less than $1,000, but usually between $1,000 and $5,000. That's serious money for any hobby, so anyone without a business purpose for VR should be forewarned: It's going to cost.

A good example is alternative input technology. A Logitech Cyberman, which costs less than $100, is fun but hardly something to build entire virtual worlds with. A Spaceball 2003, on the other hand,[1] costs about $2,000 and is something you can really use and control during development.

Where you fit into the hardware universe will be a combination of desire and funds—there's no way around that until two things happen:

- The market for VR hardware gets bigger, bringing economies that follow from increased production.
- The technology advances to the point where cheaper components can be used.

Until then, I can only tell you that there is some seriously fun hardware out there, but it's gonna cost you serious money in most cases. Only you can decide if the thrill is worth the cost.

Throughout this chapter, where I have found a technology that really does the job well, I've identified it with this icon.

This icon identifies hardware that, whatever its cost, does the job so well that I'd buy it for my own use. That's a pretty strict criterion; I don't spend money for stuff unless it's awfully darn good.

Input Devices

The line between input and output devices isn't always clear, because a good VR system has to handle both seamlessly, and input and output are often tied together in feedback loops. So I will sometimes draw arbitrary lines between the two, just for the sake of keeping things neatly organized.

One only has to look at the wide variety of alternate mouse devices to understand that no one input device will work for everyone. In the not too distant future, when VR input is as common as mouse input, we'll no doubt see a bewildering array of interesting input devices. Until then, there are a few basic designs from which to choose.

[1]Quite literally on the other hand, actually.

Freedom and 3D

The job of a VR input device is to allow you to work fluidly in three dimensions. There are many different tasks that an input device is called on to perform, such as

- Changing the point of view
- Selecting or picking up objects
- Moving objects
- Rotating objects
- "Throwing" and dropping objects
- Interacting with menus, toolbars, icons, buttons, and so on

You are probably used to thinking and talking in terms of 3D by now. The three dimensions are usually described as coordinates in space, with the axes called X, Y, and Z. However, there are actually six things to consider, and they are called the *six degrees of freedom*. The first three are the familiar directions of 3D space:

Up/down

Left/right

Forward/backward

The second three will be familiar to anyone who has played with a flight simulator or flown a plane:

Roll	Rotation about an axis along the length of the "airplane."
Pitch	Raising or lowering the nose of the airplane.
Yaw	Rotating about an axis that goes vertically through the airplane.

An input device must do all six jobs well, and there are very few that pull it off.

Mouse and Keyboard: Dead?

One can only hope that these two instruments of VR torture will be dead soon, but they are still alive and well. From a designer's point of view, the mouse and keyboard have their place—the input requirements during the design phase are complex. At runtime, however, these arcane input devices have no place. Stumbling through 3D space with 2D input devices is a situation whose days are numbered.

However, as you learn in this chapter, that number is still pretty big—it still costs a few thousand dollars to get first-class VR-level input. There are some good toys, like the Logitech Cyberman, to see us through.

Cyberman: Budget Input

The Cyberman is one of those quiet little surprises known only to folks who've been around VR for a while—there is just about zero effort to market the Cyberman to the mainstream computer/multimedia community. Although the Cyberman supports all six degrees of freedom, it is most often used with games. It lacks the fine degree of control required for serious VR, but for games like DOOM, it can be a lot of fun.

Figure 7.1 shows the Cyberman out on our back porch—not, I assure you, where we use it. Its *real* home is next to the kids' computer, where it gets used occasionally for DOOM and other games. Because the Cyberman doesn't make for a very good mouse, it only gets used in those situations where it's the best choice.

Figure 7.1. The Logitech Cyberman.

The primary limitation of the Cyberman is that it's hard to control. Figure 7.2 shows how you hold the Cyberman while using it. Although the wrist is supported on the base, the weight of your hand can't really rest on the Cyberman's control handle. If you do put the weight of your hand down, that's the same as moving down—and you can't control your position or direction if you do that. This means that there is always some tension in your hand.

A second problem is the looseness of the control handle. It offers little or no resistance, so it's hard to judge how far you are moving it.

These problems, however, are not fatal flaws—they just relegate the Cyberman to the toy category. But toys are fun, and the Cyberman is fun. When matched to the right software, in fact, it's a blast. Having one control for every direction of motion is a great convenience.

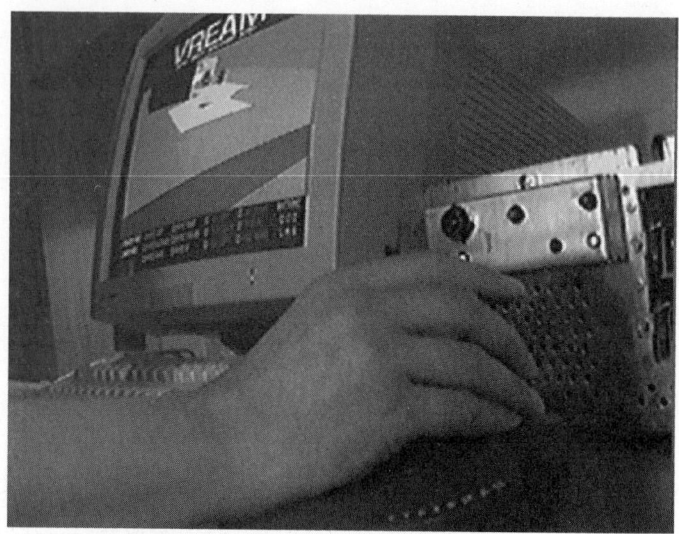

Figure 7.2. The Cyberman in use.

Spaceball 2003

Simply put, the Spaceball 2003 is the input device of choice for VR development. You can spend more, you can spend less, but both of us agree that it's hard to beat the smooth, intuitive performance of the Spaceball.

The Spaceball is very futuristic-looking, as you can see in figure 7.3. The ball itself doesn't actually move; it responds to the pressure of your fingertips in the six degrees of freedom described earlier in this chapter.

Figure 7.3. The Spaceball 2003.

Figure 7.4 shows the Spaceball sitting at our test computer; that's it at the right side of the monitor. The scene on the monitor is from the runtime of Superscape. It's a platform with bumper cars, into which falls a soccer ball that the cars then bop around.

Figure 7.4. The Spaceball ready to use.

Figures 7.5 and 7.6 show the Spaceball in use. The sloped platform provides great support for your hand and wrist, so the Spaceball is much more stable to use than the Cyberman. You do not hold the Spaceball like a joystick; light finger pressure is all that is required for input. This makes it very easy to control movement in all six directions.

The row of buttons, shown most clearly in figure 7.6, allows applications that support the Spaceball to provide easy access to key features.

The normal way to use the Spaceball is to have both it and the mouse connected to your computer, with the keyboard between them. The manual suggests that you use your customary hand for the mouse, and the other hand for the Spaceball. However, I did just the opposite and liked it.

Using the Spaceball is a lot like being able to reach into the screen and move the objects there directly, but that's not an exact analogy. As I became more familiar with using the ball, I had a sense of having a vehicle within the virtual space that I could control somewhat like you probably control a helicopter. Since you can use the Spaceball to move simultaneously in several different directions—rotation and tilt while dropping and moving forward—it's really just not like anything else you've ever tried on a computer.

To start with, however, you may want to stick to one degree of freedom at a time—multi-degree movement is a lot easier *after* you develop an intuitive sense of the ball.

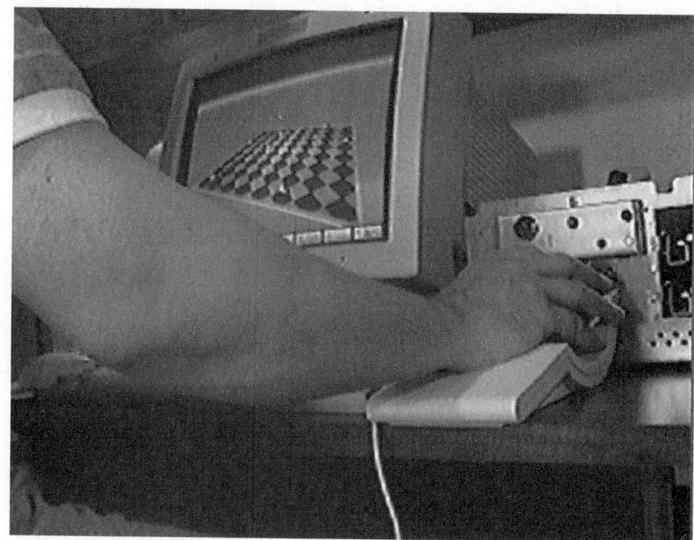

Figure 7.5. The Spaceball provides full support for your hand.

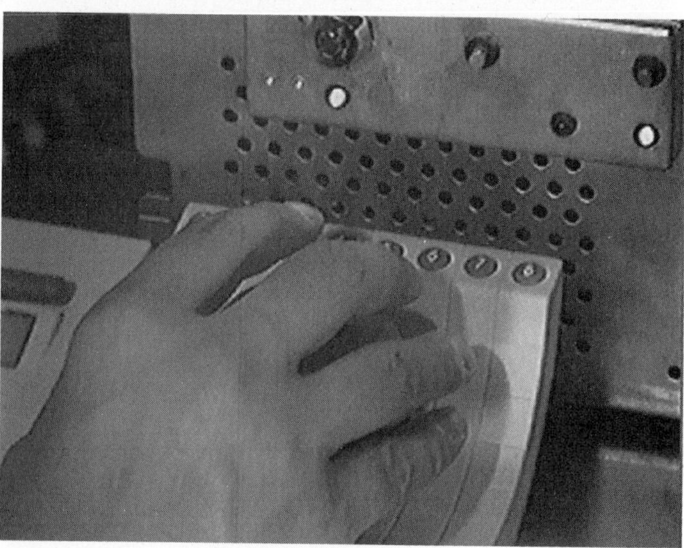

Figure 7.6. This close-up shows the function buttons on the spaceball.

Glove Input

We use our hands for lots of things, from driving to writing and typing. It would seem only natural to use them for virtual reality using gloves with built-in sensors. It's a great idea, of course, but it has turned out to be very costly to implement. As a result, there are only a few glove-based input devices. And all but one are very expensive.

The low end of glove technology is very low priced: the Mattel Powerglove. This former toy has developed a second life as a VR input device. The Powerglove isn't high tech, of course, but it is an interesting and fun input device. It allows crude interaction with a VR environment. A number of devices and software products that support the Powerglove are offered by the 3DTV company, and you can find information in Chapter 13 on how these items work together.

There isn't much of a mid-level when it comes to glove input. Unlike the Powerglove, which has a few simple sensors that detect when you bend your fingers, real glove technology requires dozens of accurate, miniature sensors. The human hand is a marvelously complex instrument, and merely keeping track of all the things it does requires a very high degree of technical sophistication.

For example, the CyberGlove from Virtual Technologies contains up to 22 sensors. There are three flex sensors and one finger-angle sensor for each finger, plus sensors for thumb crossover, palm arch, wrist flex, and wrist angle. All of this has to be packaged into a lightweight glove that still allows you to use your hand.

Even so, all that a glove does is track the relative movement of the parts of your hand. The movement of the hand in space is another issue entirely. For example, to pick up an object in a virtual world, you can't just close your hand; you have to position your hand next to the object. That involves keeping track of the hand's position in space. That requires more sensors.[(2)] Given that individual sensors can cost $2,000, this is not technology you're going to find on your PC tomorrow.

The Rest of the Story

Creative solutions for VR development and exploration are underway, and some of the devices that have been developed for input are quite interesting.

---

[2]VR is a sensor-intensive process. The whole issue of sensing position, velocity, and other variables is a big part of the research going on at the cutting edge of VR. The weight, resistance, cost, bulkiness, and electrical requirements of sensors will become a more and more important part of making VR a success.

For example, consider the Immersion Probe. It's part pen, part robot, and completely off-beat. We did not have one available for testing, but it is an interesting alternative for anyone working in a CAD environment.

The key to proper use of the Immersion Probe: the tip. Rotation, position, tilt—all of this movement information is relative to the tip of the unit. It's like having a cursor in 3D space.

But there are plenty of other alternative input devices out there; the Immersion Probe is just one clever idea, and time alone will tell us which ideas are the best.

For the Birds?

With a name like Flock of Birds, you might expect something fanciful or magical, but this product is simply a high-quality sensor—or, more precisely, multiple sensors. That multiplicity is the key ingredient in Flock of Birds—getting a bunch of sensors to work together is quite a challenge.

Flock of Birds is position-sensing technology. That means that there are two pieces involved: a transmitter and a receiver. The transmitter goes on the object to be tracked, and the receiver keeps track of it. Transmitters and receivers are shown in figure 7.7.

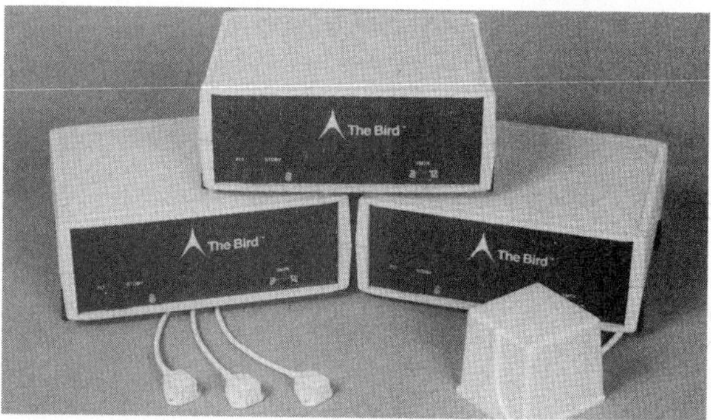

Figure 7.7. Transmitters (front) and receivers for Flock of Birds position trackers.

There are many issues involved in sensor tracking, and just about all of them conspire to make the job hard and complicated. Consider the following facts:

- Each sensor must transmit in such a way that it can be identified reliably. It wouldn't do if the receiver(s) gets confused about which sensor is which.
- Sensor sample rate is critical to success. However, the more sensors you have, the harder it is to check in with each one of them. For example, if

you sample 100 times per second for one sense, you can only sample each of two sensors 50 times per second. Every new sensor adds to the overhead.

- The environment can interfere with sensor accuracy. For example, metals and magnetized materials can throw sensors out of whack.
- The range at which sensors can be tracked accurately can be surprisingly small. Until recently, distances over 2 to 3 feet were about the maximum extent for safe tracking.

The bottom line: Keeping track of sensors is a big job, and that's what accounts for the high cost. Flock of Birds is one of the more successful technologies. The product employs DC, not AC fields, so it is less sensitive to metals and magnetized materials. Flock of Birds also handles sample rates in a unique way to ensure that sampling rates are not decreased as new sensors are added—thus the name Flock of Birds. The accurate range is also quite large—up to 8 feet.

Besides its uses in VR, Flock of Birds is often used for character animation. You simply attach a bunch of sensors to a person at key points, and then use the output as input to an animation program. For example, if you want to animate a 3D model of a person to make it dance, simply attach sensors to an accomplished dancer, record the movements, and then input them to your animation program.[3]

But Flock of Birds isn't the only sensor game in town. Polhemus offers 3Space Insidetrack, which is billed as a "PC insertable tracking system." It uses a board inside your computer, an external receiver, and multiple tracking devices. Figure 7.8 shows the various components that make up the system.

You can also use sensor products with software such as VREAM, Sense8, 3D Studio, Superscape, and many special purpose packages. Contact the manufacturer of a given software package to determine if it supports Flock of Birds or Polhemus 3Space Insidetrack.

Computing for the Handicapped

One area in which virtual reality research shows some great promise is in alternative computing tools for the handicapped. For example, head-tracking, an important capability for high-end VR, has useful applications for handicapped

[3]We aren't talking about just any animation program here. You'll need special-purpose software, such as Alias Power Animator (416-362-9181) or Kinemation from Wavefront (805-962-8117).

computer users. Origin Instruments, for example, offers the HeadMouse (see fig. 7.9), a Microsoft-Mouse compatible box that allows you to use your head movements to control the mouse cursor.[4]

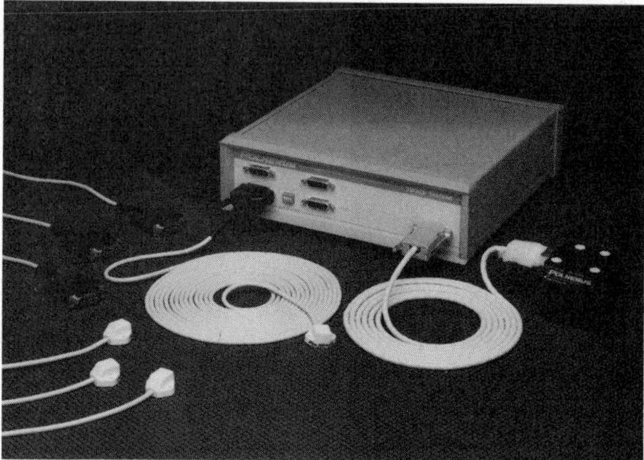

Figure 7.8. Polhemus' 3Space Insidetrack, 3D tracking hardware for the PC.

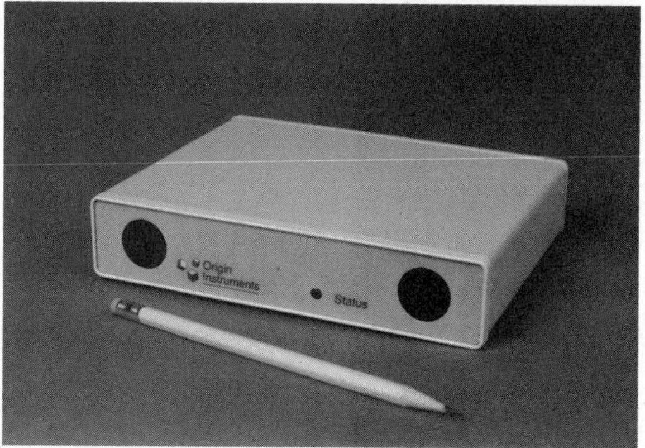

Figure 7.9. The HeadMouse, a head-controlled pointing device.

The HeadMouse is a wireless optical sensor that tracks a tiny, disposable target that is placed on the user's head or glasses. The unit can be combined with an on-screen keyboard to allow input without any use of the hands. As with most systems for the severely handicapped, a mouse click is achieved by lingering in one position for a set period of time or by using an external switch. A wireless transmitter is available for such a switch.

---

[4]The HeadMouse is also compatible with the Apple Macintosh mouse and the IBM OS/2 mouse.

Origin Instruments also sells the Dynasight sensor that measures the 3D position of a target. In most cases, it is used to track head movement and is coupled to interactive stereo displays. This offers simple but effective head tracking for applications that support response to head movement.

GAMS: Unique 3D Input

GAMS stands for Gesture And Media System, and it's the magic wand of VR interactivity. A system of ultrasonic speakers is arranged around a room-sized space, and the operator is free to move around in the space with one or more wands. GAMS tracks the movement of the wand, and the wireless receiver can respond to clicks on the wand.

Figure 7.10. The GAMS unit in use.

GAMS has a wide variety of potential uses, from performance artists controlling MIDI devices by moving a wand in 3D space to immersive data visualization. Speaking of visualization, the best way to understand GAMS is to see it in use. I've included an AVI file on the CD-ROMs that shows GAMS in action as part of an alternative musical experience.[5]

[5]Yes, it's as strange as it sounds. Check it out.

Output Devices

If input is the overlooked part of the VR hardware story, then output is the exact opposite: That's where most of the world's attention is focused. The reason: the glamour and allure of expensive headsets and 3D environments.

But let's face it—there's something to be said for glamour and allure. After all, that's what puts the coolness in cool, right? The more flash and pizzazz we get out of these PCs of ours, the better. As virtual reality moves forward, it does so with thrill after thrill, not unlike a carnival ride. There's plenty of time to settle in and get serious when VR becomes a mature technology.

Head-Mounted Devices (HMDs) and Goggles

Figure 7.11. A just slightly over-hyped but amusing display of a VR headset from Kaiser Electro-Optics.

If only there were a set of 3D stereoscopic goggles you could pick up for $100, everybody would be doing VR. Unfortunately, the arrival of low-cost goggles and HMDs is somewhere off in the indefinite future. At the top end, the military can spend $80,000 and more for HMDs that include full head-tracking, stereo inputs, and crystal-clear resolution.

Head tracking is really an input issue, as the computer must receive data from sensors on the HMD that provides precise information about head angle, distance, rotation, and so on. With individual sensors running into the thousands of dollars, this is not consumer technology. We tested the VR4 HMD, from Virtual Research Systems (408-748-8712), for one week. At more than $6,000 per unit, even without head tracking, the VR4 isn't exactly consumer-level equipment. Figure 7.12 shows the VR4 in use by Donna while working with VREAM. The unit includes stereo headphones, and the large cable at the back of Donna's head is the connection at the base unit. The base has two audio and two video inputs, but of course, you need a source to provide true 3D input.

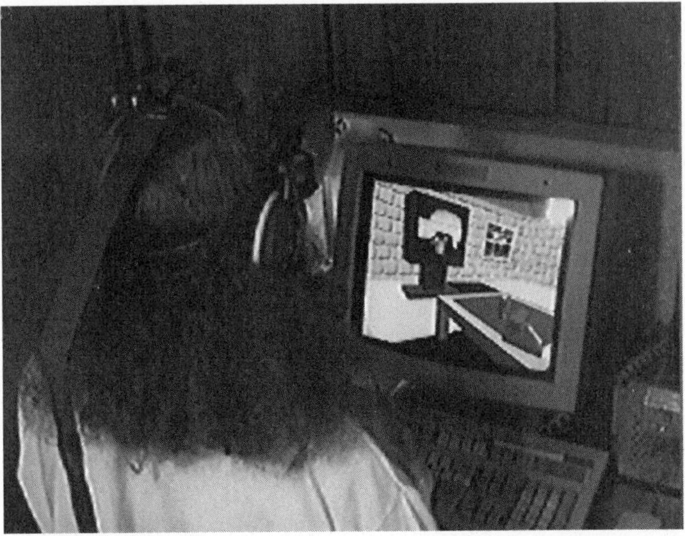

Figure 7.12. The VR4 headset in use.

Figure 7.13 shows the headset from the front. It looks big, and you might be wondering how comfortable is it to wear and use. That cable at the back acts as a counterweight to the front of the unit. It isn't exactly heavy, but the careful balancing of the unit makes it much more comfortable. As long as you keep the cable behind you, the unit balances very comfortably.

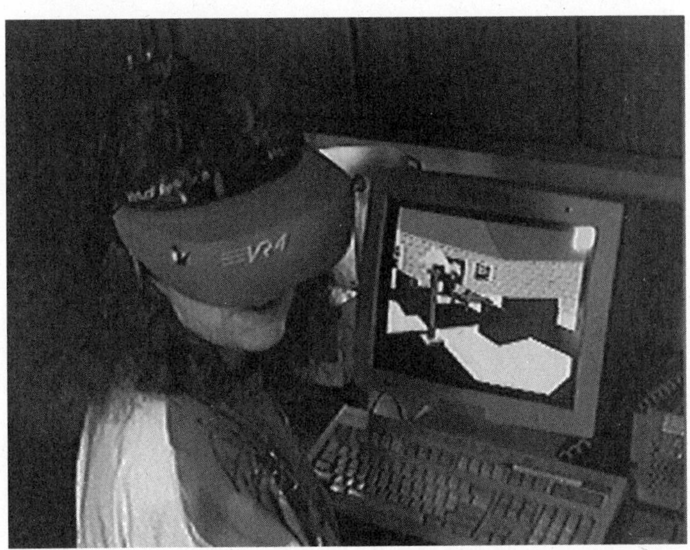

Figure 7.13. The VR4 headset from the front.

To understand how the VR4 functions, it helps to know what's inside. Figure 7.16 shows the unit upside down, and you can see the two video units nestled inside the front of the unit. There are small controls at the sides of the unit that allow you to adjust the distance between the two videos. You can also slide the front back and forth to adjust for comfort.

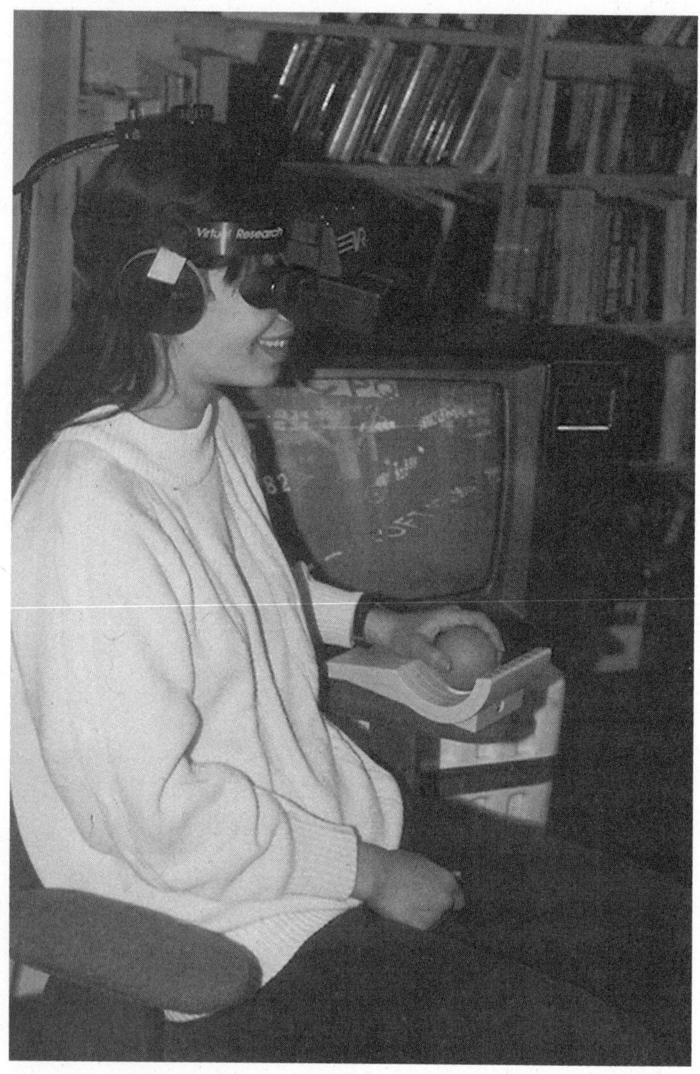

Figure 7.14. The VR4 and the Spaceball 2003 being used to control vrTrader, a virtual reality stock trading program from Avatar.

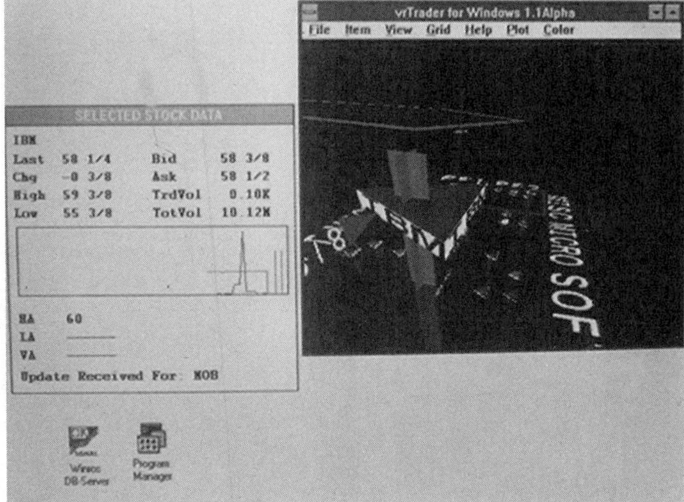

Figure 7.15.
A screen view of vrTrader.

Figure 7.16.
A look at the inside of the VR4.

Figure 7.17 shows an even closer look at the two video units. There is a thick lens on each to allow you to see the video image clearly at close range.

There is good news and bad news about VR at this level. $6,000 is considered a great price for a unit like the VR4 these days. The unit is lightweight, inexpensive, and sturdy when compared to much of the competition. It's still a bit much for household use in terms of cost, weight, resolution, and just about any other key parameter. If you really need a helmet, the tradeoffs are certainly worthwhile. But we have a way to go yet before we have the HMD equivalent of the Sony Walkman.(6) Of course, now that we no longer have the VR4 around, we miss it. Clearly, the presence of a low-cost HMD in the marketplace will bring a radical transformation in the VR universe!

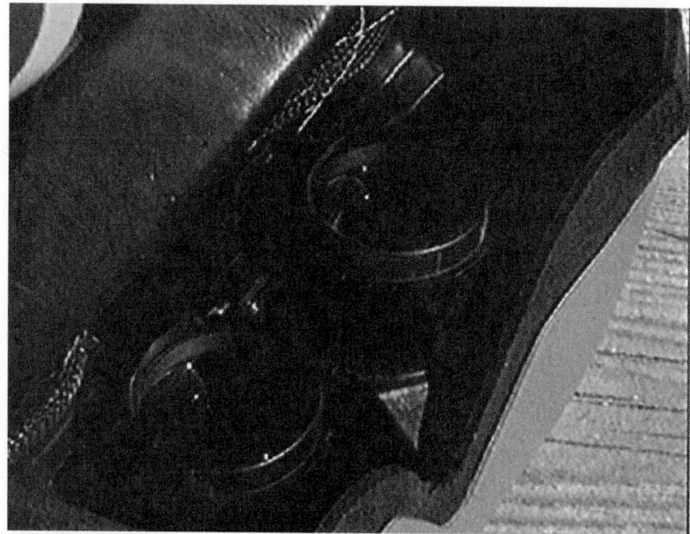

Figure 7.17. A close look at the video units inside the VR4.

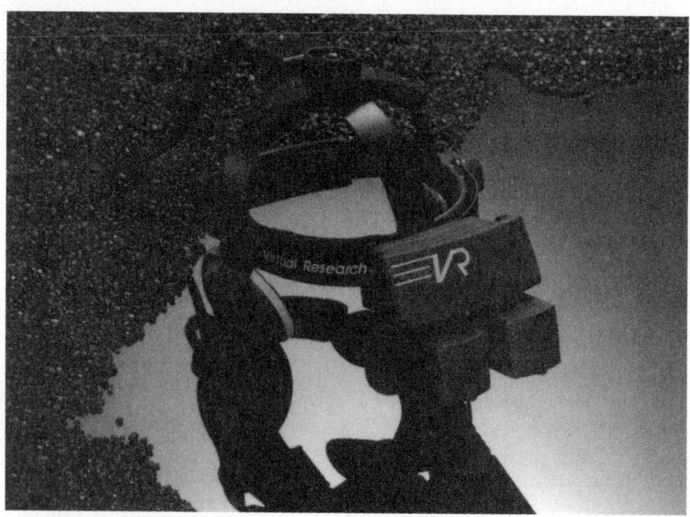

Figure 7.18. Another HMD model from Virtual Research.

[6]Unless you are willing to count the Virtual Vison Sport (see fig. 7.19), which gives you a set of goggles that provides TV reception for one eye, and is coupled to a belt pack, which is the tuner.

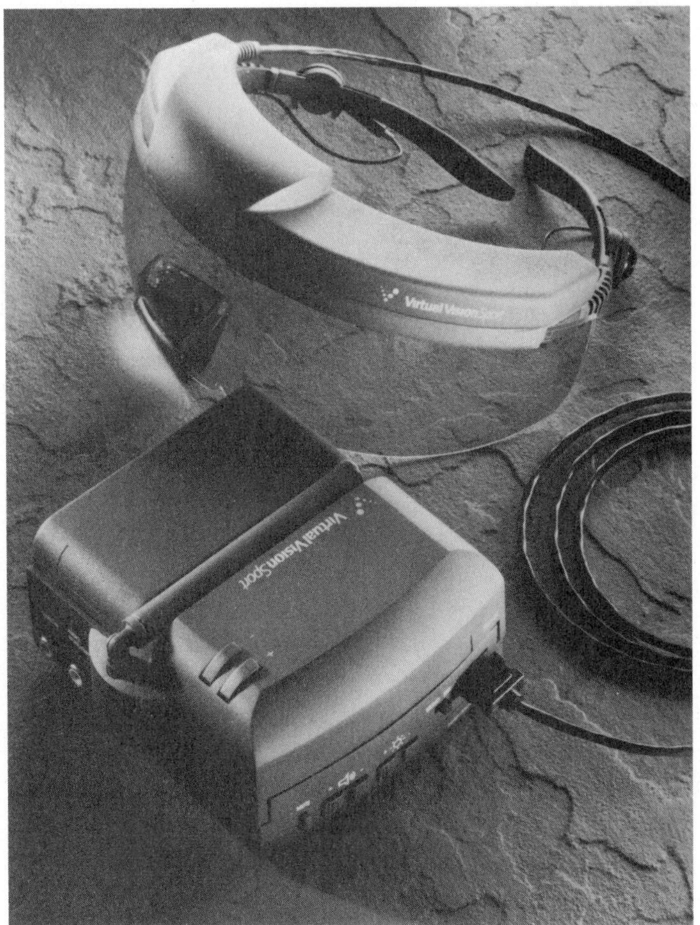

Figure 7.19. The Virtual Vision Sport, featuring a TV view for one eye.

There are less expensive units than the VR4, of course, such as the CyberEye from General Reality.[7] The CyberEye sacrifices wide-angle view for higher resolution in a smaller area and costs around $2,000. To see what the CyberEye looks like, see the entry in Chapter 14, "VR Hardware."

Goggles are a possible alternative to HMDs. The most common kind use LCD in the eyepieces. A cable is attached, which causes the LCD for each eyepiece to go black alternately. If the image source—a TV or your computer monitor—is synchronized to the goggles, separate images for each eye can be obtained. This allows you to see a useful but very flickery form of 3D.

---

[7]Don't you just love the names that VR companies come up with? I suppose this is a pun on General Electric.

Figure 7.20. Our all-time favorite (tongues are firmly in our cheeks) promotional photo for a VR headset: the Liquid Image.

As we were going to press, 3DTV Corporation announced an improved method of using 3D goggles that provides less flicker. See Chapter 13 for details. For information about additional HMDs and goggles that we did not test ourselves, see Chapter 14, "VR Hardware."

Cyberscope

On the other hand, there is an affordable way to get stereo VR. It's called the Cyberscope, and it's a clever and functional solution to the problem of inexpensive stereo. Figure 7.21 shows the Cyberscope in use on a 17-inch monitor.[8]

Figure 7.21. The Cyberscope attached to a monitor.

Unlike goggles and HMDs, the Cyberscope is stationary. You attach it to your monitor and must look through the eye pieces for a 3D effect. Before you start thinking that this is just plain weird, I have to tell you the most important part: It works, and it works well. And at about $150, you can't beat the price for flicker-free VR/3D.

Figure 7.22 shows the inside of the unit. There is a light baffle running down the center (whose purpose will be clear in a moment), and a series of mirrors at the back near the eye pieces.

Figure 7.23 shows the screen without the Cyberscope attached. The view shows a VREAM runtime session, and the screen is divided into left and right halves. The image of each half is rotated 90 degrees. The light baffle keeps the two images from interfering with each other, and the mirrors rotate the view back to horizontal and

---

[8]You may also have noted that the top is not on our computer, to the right of the monitor. We have to install so many different pieces of hardware that we gave up keeping the lid on ages ago.

present the correct image to each eye. *Voila*—instant 3D. Not all VR software supports the Cyberscope, but for software that does, such as VREAM, the 3D is quite easy to achieve.

Figure 7.22. The interior of the Cyberscope.

Figure 7.23. A view of a VREAM screen set up for the Cyberscope.

You look into the eye pieces of the Cyberscope from above. In figure 7.24, you can see the light from the screen, but the camera has the screen out of focus. I have included a video clip on the CD-ROMs that shows this entire sequence, and it makes the process very clear.

Figure 7.24.
The Cyberscope from above.

The Cyberscope, in our opinion, provides the best 3D value for the money.

Feedback

99.99999% of computer output goes to the eyes, but that does leave approximately .00001% for other senses, such as touch. TiNi Alloy offers *tactors*, small fingertip devices that provide tactile feedback. Figure 7.25 shows a single tactor and control unit.

The tactor strip can be attached to a mouse button, a key on the keyboard, or any physical device. The feedback consists of a kind of "buzz" provided by small actuators in the tactor. You cannot feel actual objects; you just get your fingertip stimulated when the software triggers the tactor.

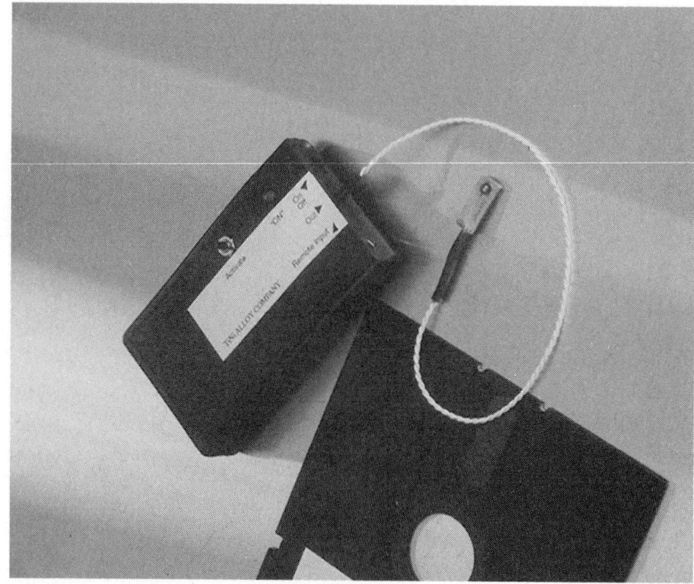

Figure 7.25. A tactile feedback device from TiNi Alloy and distributed by Mondo-tronics.

We did not find any software that supports the tactor directly, so it is of interest primarily to researchers and hobbyists who want to experiment with tactile feedback. The physical interface is simple—just plug the control unit into a serial port. As a programmer, all you need to be able to do to activate the tactor is to send any kind of data through the serial port. Programs such as Visual Basic make this very easy to do.

Summary

We had a lot of fun with almost every aspect of VR, but it was very clear that the hardware toys were the most fun. Whether it was Donna, Ron, or the kids, there was a heightened sense of excitement every time we tested a new piece of hardware. The helmet was clearly the Big News but wasn't much of a surprise. Probably the biggest surprise was how much we liked the innovative Cyberscope; we kind of expected it to be funky, not functional, but it was very useful and easy to set up and use.

But there was also a note of caution behind the excitement. As exciting as 3D is initially, it fades to normal pretty quickly. I would like to see 3D visual technology overtake what we have now the same way that stereo sound technology wiped out mono. The cost of stereo versus mono sound, however, wasn't large. The current cost of 3D visuals—at least the really fancy stuff—is so large that one must wonder if it will ever arrive in the consumer marketplace.

There are now several products on the edge of consumer acceptance. The Cyberscope is probably a little too awkward for popular use, however, and LCD glasses must overcome the flicker problem if they are going to make it. But both these technologies are very affordable, and it only takes a small amount of enthusiasm to overcome the minor problems and awkwardness, and have some fun.

On the other hand, if you can get your hands on an HMD, go for it!

8

SEEING IS BELIEVING

The human visual system is mostly an electromechanical device.[1] We seldom think of it that way, of course; we just know that we can see, and we take that pretty much for granted. Each aspect of our visual system has some interesting flaws and loopholes. The eye itself, being mostly mechanical, has the most weaknesses. These can be exploited to fool the eye into thinking that what it sees is real when it is not. This means that a visual virtual reality need not be perfect to be perceived as real, which makes the job a lot easier.[2]

There are numerous examples of optical illusions; figure 8.1 shows an example. The two horizontal lines don't look like they are parallel, but they are. If you doubt it, just lay a ruler against the lines to verify it.

Figure 8.1. An example of an optical illusion. The lines are parallel but don't appear to be so.

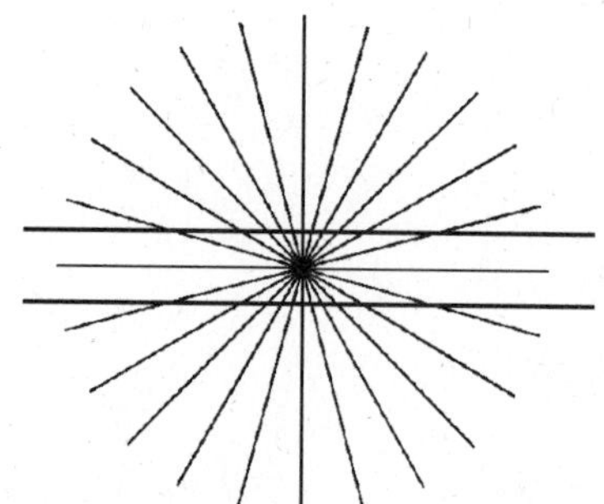

There is actually a wide variety of ways in which the eye can be fooled. By taking advantage of these flaws, the eye can be made to see color where there is none,[3] or to not see objects that are really there,[4] or to see the same object in completely different ways. For example, figure 8.2 shows a drawing of a cube. Depending on how your eyes perceive the cube, you can see it from either the bottom or the top.[5]

---

[1]I know; you think I should say "biological" in there somewhere. Strictly speaking, perhaps I should. However, biology is just a short way of saying "an amazingly tiny, sophisticated, and self-repairing electromechanical device," right?

[2]Perhaps someday we'll even bypass the eye entirely—see William Gibson's book, *Virtual Light,* for speculation along that front.

[3]The most common example involves spinning disks with concentric semicircles on them. The disk is white, and the circles are black.

[4]The most common reason to not see things that are there is the development of an afterimage. Try staring at a tile floor sometime—the lines between the tiles will come and go, as the afterimage tends to cancel them out. This works best when the tiles and the lines between them are of contrasting colors or values.

[5]If you don't see both forms, just stare at the image for a while—the image will usually flip by itself without you having to do anything.

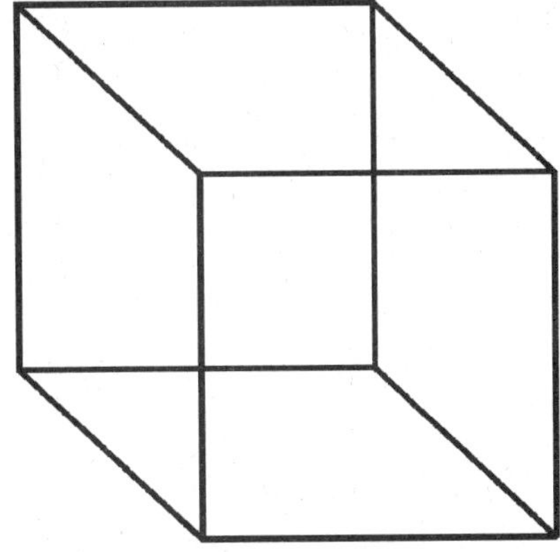

Figure 8.2. Another example of an optical illusion. The cube will sometimes appear to have its top toward you, and sometimes its bottom.

Figure 8.3 shows one of the most famous optical illusions, and one that is purely psychological in origin. What do you see when you look at figure 8.3: the pedestal of a table (white) or two faces (black)?

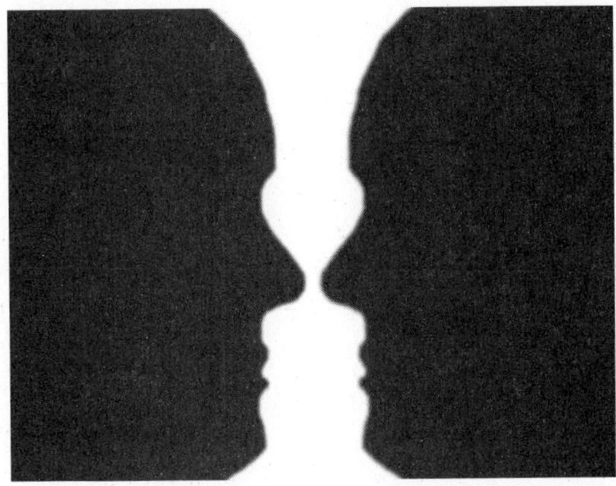

Figure 8.3. What do you see? A table pedestal or faces?

In this chapter, you'll learn how the eye can be fooled into thinking things are real, and you'll also learn about *morphing*, the art and science of making it appear as though one object were being turned into another.

Seeing Is Not Believing

There are two elements of perception involved in seeing an object in a virtual reality. The first element, the physical and electrical systems, has been analyzed by various branches of science so that it is reasonably well understood. The second element, our attitudes—the willingness to believe—is perhaps an even more important consideration.

The folks who analyze literature for a living use the term *suspension of disbelief* to describe the process of becoming involved in a story. When you open a book, sit in a movie theater, or observe a play, you know for a fact that what you are observing does not reflect reality. The book is just words on a page; the movie is just flickering light on a screen, and the actors are not who they seem to be. When you sit down at your computer to create or interact with a virtual space, you must likewise willingly suspend your disbelief. You must allow yourself to be deceived.[6]

However, it is impossible to quantify such things. The mechanics of seeing, however, being better understood than attitudes, suffer from no such limitation.

Motion

The first trick that is used to fool the eye is sequential imaging. You know the technique by the more common names in use: animation, movies, and video. All these media use the same basic method to convince your eye that motion is occurring—putting a series of images in front of your eye so fast that your eye is fooled. The rate at which the images are presented is critical to the process. Movies and animation normally use a rate of 24 images per second, whereas video uses 30 frames per second.[7]

Digital video—video that has been converted to digital form and stored on a CD-ROM or a hard disk—is an emerging technology that has an increasing role in virtual reality. Digital video, however, must move from its current limitations—15 frames per second—to play a larger role. The wide acceptance of digital video (thanks in large part to Video for Windows technology) is leading to rapid advances.

The frame rate is critical to the success of this trick. However, not all parts of the eye respond to the trick equally well—and this has some important ramifications for virtual reality technology. To simulate reality more effectively, a VR display

---

[6]I like the phrase "allow yourself to be deceived" better than "suspension of disbelief" for several reasons. One, it is more accurate. Two, it avoids indirection. (That's an indirect way of saying, "it is direct." Get the point?) Three, I like going against the grain.

[7]Strictly speaking, this is not exact. Video is an interlaced technology. This means that half of the image is put onto the screen first—every other horizontal line of pixels. This is called a *scan*, and the horizontal lines are called *scan lines*. In the second scan, the rest of the image is put onto the screen. These two scans constitute a single frame; each of the scans is commonly referred to as a *field*. Thus, each frame has two fields. The process is called *interlacing*, and if you have ever tried to work with a 1024×768 video card using an interlaced signal, you know that the result of interlacing is flickering.

Thus, while video technology is the easiest to extend into virtual reality, it brings with it some potential flickering problems. Recent advances in television technology, such as HDTV, look more like the displays normally used on computers, which do not use interlacing and are thus much more stable.

system should wrap around the user's head. This adds peripheral vision to the simulation. But peripheral vision uses a different part of your eye, and that part doesn't work like the part that you use to see directly in front of you.

The eye has two kinds of light receptors: rods and cones. Cones are located mostly in the center of your eye, and they are very good at distinguishing colors. Rods are located mostly around the edges of the eye, and they are very good at distinguishing differences in brightness. Therein lies the problem. The most noticeable defect when using frames to simulate motion is the change in brightness that occurs when you change from one frame to the next. The sequence goes like this:

- Frame 1 is displayed.
- Nothing is displayed.
- Frame 2 is displayed.

The problem is that nothing is in the middle. Depending on the medium, it will be more or less obvious. A movie uses a shutter to block the light while the frame is advanced, whereas video intermixes the frames somewhat. In either case, the rods at the outer part of the eye are particularly susceptible to the change in brightness that is associated with frame changes. This means that your peripheral vision is most likely to be affected by a visual system with excess flicker. It also means that a wraparound display must be better at flicker reduction than the typical computer monitor.

The Third Dimension

Once the object and the virtual world are in motion, the next consideration is to convince the eye that the world exists in three dimensions. This is easier said than done. The history of motion 3D can be summed up in a few lines:

- Red/blue glasses
- Polarized glasses
- Shutter glasses

Each of these techniques relies on a simple aspect of two-eyed stereo vision: each eye sees the scene from a slightly different point of view. The change in viewpoint, although small, is easy to see. Place your finger in front of your face, and put your other hand in front of one eye. You will see your finger against whatever background is behind it (see fig. 8.4 for the camera equivalent of this exercise).

Now, without moving your finger, shift the hand to the other eye. Note that the position of the vertical line against the background has shifted (see fig. 8.5).[8]

---

[8]The technical term for this is *parallax*.

Figure 8.4. The view through the left "eye."

Combined-Image 3D

Your brain combines any two images it receives in separate eyes and creates the 3D effect right there in your head. This means that if we can:

- Capture two sets of images, one for each eye, and each from a different viewpoint, and
- Find a way to present the separate images to the correct eyes

we can engage the brain to create a 3D image. Most 3D systems that use this method actually combine the two images into one image, and then use special glasses to send only the correct half of each image to the correct eye. The three kinds of glasses listed earlier use different techniques to achieve this result. The mechanism used to create images for each kind of glasses also differs.

Red/Blue Glasses

This is the easiest form of 3D technology, but it is also the least effective. To view the 3D image, you must wear glasses that use a blue film in one eye and a red film in the other. The source image contains overlapping blue and red versions of the scene. Figure 8.6 shows such an image in black and white, but you can make out the two images easily.

To create the image, all that is needed is something called a *stereo pair*. This is just a fancy term for two images that represent what your own eyes would see if they had been there instead of the camera that took the pictures.(9) One image is

---

[9]This is not always exactly true. To enhance the 3D effect, you can increase the distance between the two cameras. Instead of using a few inches between the cameras to mimic the distance between our eyes, you can move the cameras several feet—or even more—apart. If the cameras are moved too far apart, this can destroy the 3D effect, however.

encoded using blue colors only, and the other image is encoded using only red colors. When you view the image, the red image goes to one eye, and the blue image goes to the other eye—thanks to the colored filters in the glasses. The result is a so-so 3D image.

Figure 8.5. The view through the right "eye." Note the shift of the vertical line against background.

Figure 8.6. A red/blue stereo image.

Polarized Glasses

Polarized glasses also put both images into a single image, but instead of using color, this technique relies on the capability to polarize light.[10] It is most commonly used with movie projection. When the image for one eye is projected onto the screen, light polarized at a specific angle is used. The corresponding lens on the glasses has a filter on it that will only allow light polarized at that angle to enter. The image for the other eye uses a polarization angle that is different by 90 degrees. The corresponding lens on the glasses also has a matching polarizing angle. The result is that each eye sees only the image intended for it.

A significant advantage of the polarized technique is that you can use real colors in each image, so the resulting 3D view is much better than with red/blue glasses. The disadvantage, of course, is the need for equipment to polarize the light.

Shutter Glasses

Shutter glasses take a kind of brute-force approach to the problem. Each lens contains a shutter that simply blocks the view of the eye on that side when the shutter is closed. This method works well with video sources—if you recall, a video frame is actually made up of two fields. If we put the image for one eye in one field, and for the other eye in the other field, the shutter can be used to block the "wrong" field for each eye. The result is that each eye sees only the information that is intended for it.

The downside to shutter glasses is that they effectively cut the vertical resolution in half. This method also requires heavier, more complicated, and costlier glasses than either of the other methods. This is offset by the fact that little or no special equipment is needed to encode the images.

Options

As a general rule, there are two points in the 3D process where costs and technology get in the way: creating the image and decoding the image. The best balance of quality, cost, and convenience is probably shutter glasses. Red/blue glasses are easy to use, but image quality is inferior. Polarizing is effective but requires a projection system. Shutter glasses cost more than other kinds of 3D glasses, but they provide the ability to create images at a minimal cost.

---

[10]If you are not familiar with polarization of light, here is a simple explanation. Light behaves like a wave. Normally, light waves vibrate every which way. A polarizer restricts the vibrations to one direction—for example, up and down. A beam thus polarized can be used for one image, and one polarized to a side-to-side vibration can be used for the other image. Each side of the glasses has a set of ultra-tiny, parallel slits that only allow light matching the polarization to enter the slits.

Multiple Images

The ideal VR system would put a separate image in front of each eye. Wraparound, head-mounted displays will make this possible. Currently, this technology is going through a process that laptop LCD screens went through several years ago. The manufacturing capacity of the industry is waiting for demand, and demand is waiting for manufacturing capacity to increase and bring down prices.

Until there is an advance that will move this stalemate off dead center, the cost of even modest-quality, head-mounted displays will be high—more than $1,000. There are some head displays at lower prices, but they are basically just televisions that hang in front of your eyes.

Bending Reality to Fit

Let's back away from 3D a bit to look at a fascinating technology that has only recently moved from the realm of the super computer to the desktop: morphing. *Morphing* is the art of appearing to transform one object or picture into another. You'll learn about two products in this chapter: Elastic Reality—quite possibly the coolest piece of desktop software anywhere—and PhotoMorph.

RECIPE

1 copy Elastic Reality
1 starting image or video clip
1 ending image or video clip
Dash of flash and panache
1 Media Player, VidEdit, or Adobe Premiere

Instructions: This is gourmet cooking at its best—easy to whip up, but your guests will inevitably be stunned by the subtle flavors of this dish. Served in all the best video studios and a Hollywood favorite for years, this scrumptious product is now available for home use.

There are a number of commercial and shareware morphing products on the market. My favorite,[11] hands down, is Elastic Reality. In the first edition, the Best in Class was another excellent product: PhotoMorph. This is still a wonderful product—see the next section of this chapter for the details—but Elastic Reality marks an important watershed in desktop morphing. Formerly available for the SGI (Silicon Graphics) platform, Elastic Reality has been used for many of the special effects you see on TV and at the movies. Whether Elastic Reality is busy morphing Dracula into a bat in an Energizer Bunny commercial, or creating the amazing morphs in the movie *Wolf*, it is one powerful piece of software.

This presented a problem while I was testing the software and writing about it. There are levels of cool when it comes to software. Some software is mildly cool and quite enjoyable. Other software is very cool and hard to put down—Vistapro is a good example. Rarely, a product comes along that I can only call mega cool—so hot, so exciting, that you simply cannot put it away. To shut it down becomes an offense against one's inner child. One can only be dragged kicking and screaming from such fun. I'm a bit jaded—after all, I have access to just about everything in VR—but I still fell head over heels in love with Elastic Reality. There was no way I wanted to stop playing with it and start writing about it. There was always one more special effect to try, one more feature to explore. Therefore, be warned: this is addictive stuff. If you bought the first edition of this book and became hooked on Vistapro, that was nothing. Elastic Reality bends and twists reality so cleanly that you'll find yourself always wanting just one more morph.

If you somehow manage to satisfy your cravings for the ultimate morph, you are still not home free. Elastic Reality does much more than mere morphs. It is a real studio in a box; you can create mattes or traveling mattes, create composites, do A/B rolls, and incorporate backgrounds. This is a powerful, flexible, and versatile package.

Figure 8.7 shows two images taken from a professionally done morph created with Elastic Reality.

As clean and impressive as the morphs you create with Elastic Reality are, they are not that hard to do. Follow along as I show you how it's done.

Elastic Reality runs under Windows. If you are familiar with typical Windows programs, it will be easy to use Elastic Reality. Figure 8.8 shows the opening window for the program.

---

[11]This is Ron speaking.

Figure 8.7. Even Ulysses S. Grant can be made to smile with Elastic Reality.

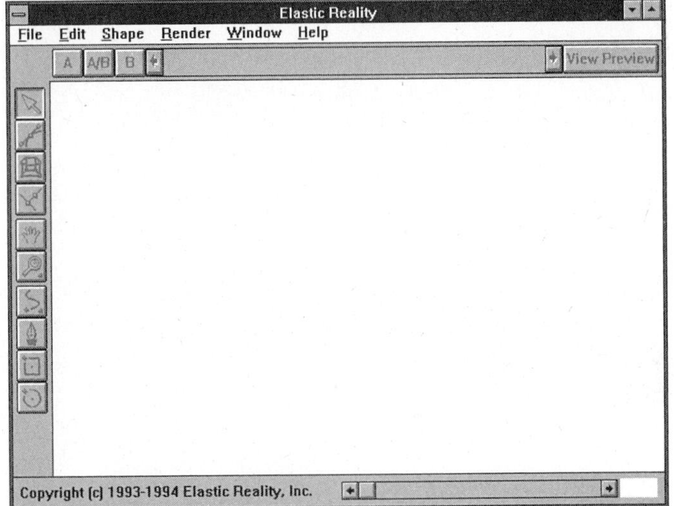

Figure 8.8. The opening window of Elastic Reality.

All the tools above and to the left of the main window are gray—you can't use the tools until you load one or more images. If you load one image, you can use Elastic Reality to warp the image—enlarge eyes, puff out cheeks, or otherwise animate a still image. If you load two images, you can morph from one image to the other. In this example, you will learn how to morph from one image to another.

Figure 8.9 shows a completed project loaded into Elastic Reality. Note that you can see both images at the same time, as well as the control lines that define the morph. Look in the color section of this book to see how the program uses color to distinguish the morphing lines for each image. In black and white, you can't tell which of the lines over the faces belongs to which image.

I have created control lines for each image. Figure 8.10 shows the starting image of a man, including the control lines. Figure 8.11 shows the image without the control lines.

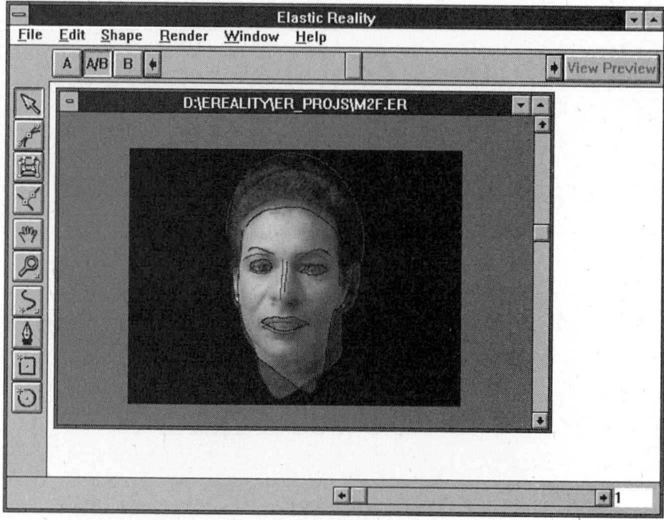

Figure 8.9. A completed Elastic Reality project, showing both images at the same time.

Figure 8.10. The starting image for the morph, with control lines.

Figure 8.11. The starting image for the morph.

There are probably an infinite number of ways you can arrange control lines for any given morph. Learning what kinds of lines to use and where to put them gives you a great deal of power and control. In figure 8.10, I have added control lines for all the major features and outlines involved:

- A line down the middle of the nose
- A line outlining the top of the head
- A line outlining the hairline
- A line outlining the lips
- A line outlining each ear
- A line down the middle of each eyebrow
- A line around each eye

For every control line in the starting image, you'll need a corresponding line in the ending image. Figure 8.12 shows the ending image with control lines, and figure 8.13 shows just the image. Note how the lines in figure 8.12 are on or near the same physical features used in figure 8.10.

Figure 8.12. The ending image for the morph, including control points.

Figure 8.13. The ending image for the morph.

Let's look at how a single pair of control lines was created for this morph. Figure 8.14 shows a close-up of the man's eye. I used the Freehand tool to roughly outline the eye. I then used the Reshape tool to carefully align the control line with the outline of the eye. A control line is made up of segments, with control points where the segments join. You can use the same techniques to adjust and reshape a control line that you would use on a Bezier curve in a typical desktop publishing illustration package like Corel or Illustrator.

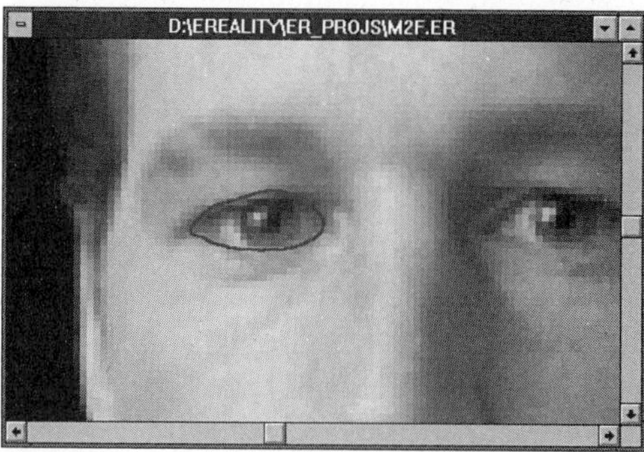

Figure 8.14. Using the Freehand and Reshape tools to add a control line.

This control line defines the starting image of the eye. It will control the position and size of the eye during the morph. If the morph occurs over 30 frames, the eye will move 1/30th of the distance toward its final position in the final image for each frame.

Starting and ending control lines must have the same number of segments. The easiest way to make sure that this is so is to use the Clipboard. Click the control line to select it, and then copy it to the Clipboard (Edit/Copy menu selection). Click the B button at the top left to see the ending image, and then choose Edit/Paste to insert a copy of the control line. You can then use the Reshape tool to change the size and shape of the control line to match the eye in the ending image. Figure 8.15 shows the result.

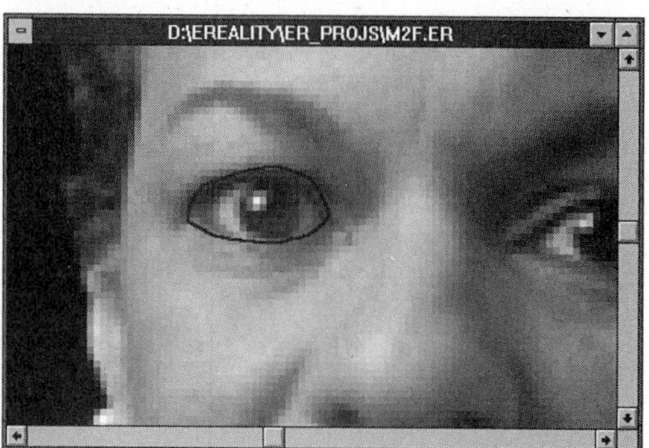

Figure 8.15. The control line has been copied to the ending image and reshaped to fit.

By pressing the A/B button, you can view both images at the same time (see fig. 8.16). You can see both images overlapped, as well as both of the control lines. When the images are overlapped, the differences between the two control lines are easy to see. One is lower than the other, and one is taller than the other.

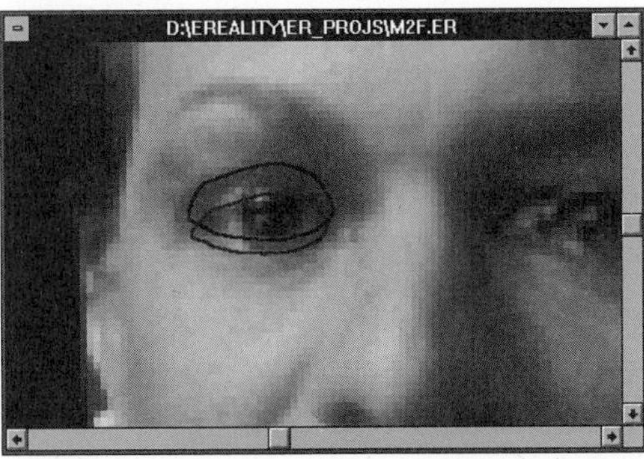

Figure 8.16. Viewing both images with the A/B button pressed.

We have now created the starting and ending control lines for the morph, but there is more to do. Click on the smaller of the two control lines (the one from the starting male image) to select it. This displays a bounding box around the control line (see fig. 8.17).

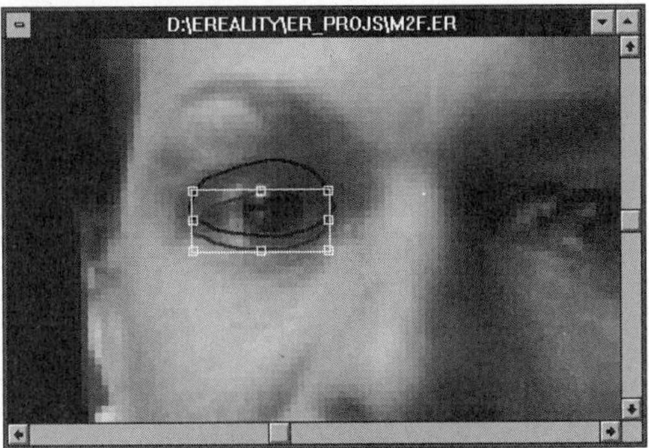

Figure 8.17. Selecting a control line displays its bounding box.

While holding down the Shift key, click on the second (ending) control line. Now both control lines display their bounding boxes (see fig. 8.18).

Now comes the magic part—while both control lines are selected, press the J key (for Join). This tells Elastic Reality to join the two control lines for morphing purposes. The line you select first is always the starting control line, and the line you click second is always the ending line.

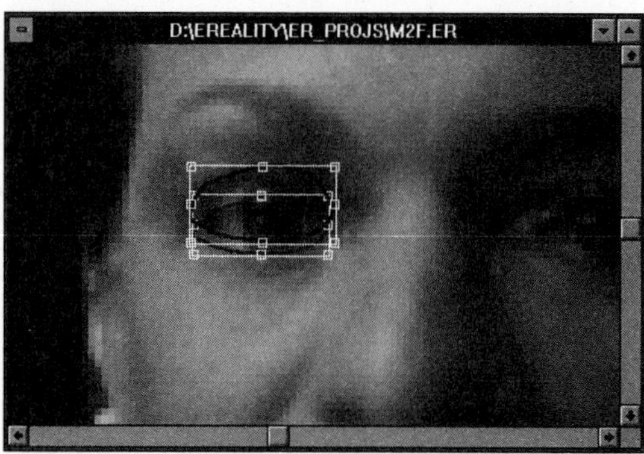

Figure 8.18. Both control lines are selected.

Figure 8.19 shows the result. The bounding boxes are now made up of dashed lines. The starting box has long dashed lines, and the ending box has shorter dashed lines. This allows you to keep track of which is which.

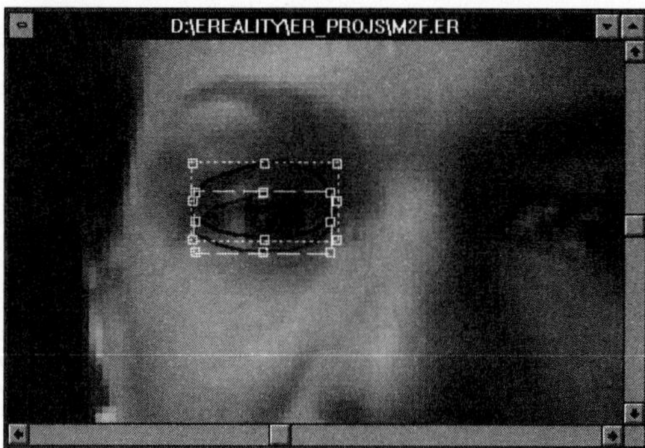

Figure 8.19. The control lines are now part of a morph.

You can control the level of fine detail during the morph by setting the edge density. Click on the Correspondence tool (see fig. 8.20) to display the current edge density. This shows up as yellow dashed lines between the two control lines. To change the edge density, click the Window/Shape Options menu selection. This displays the dialog box shown in figure 8.21. Use the slider bar at the top to increase or decrease edge density. Increasing edge density will improve the way that Elastic Reality controls the morph from one frame to the next.

Earlier, I mentioned the Reshape tool. Let's look at how you can use this tool to easily change the shape of a control line.(12) Figure 8.22 shows a close-up of the control line for the woman's lips. Note that the control line is defined by a series of points shown as small white squares.

---

[12]Control lines aren't the only way you can control morphing. You can also use the Ellipse and Rectangle tools to add closed control shapes. Control lines can be open, as for the nose; or closed, as for the eyes. Ellipses and rectangles are always closed.

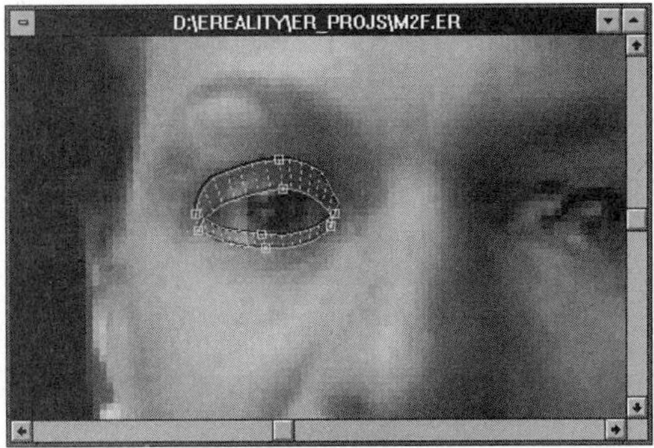

Figure 8.20. Displaying edge density.

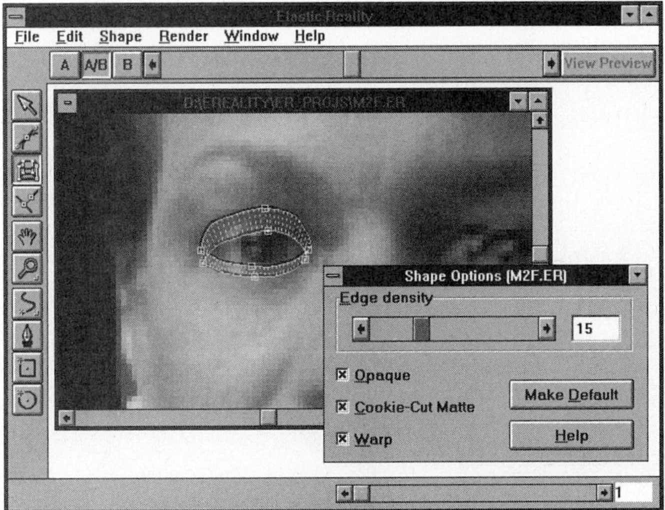

Figure 8.21. Changing edge density.

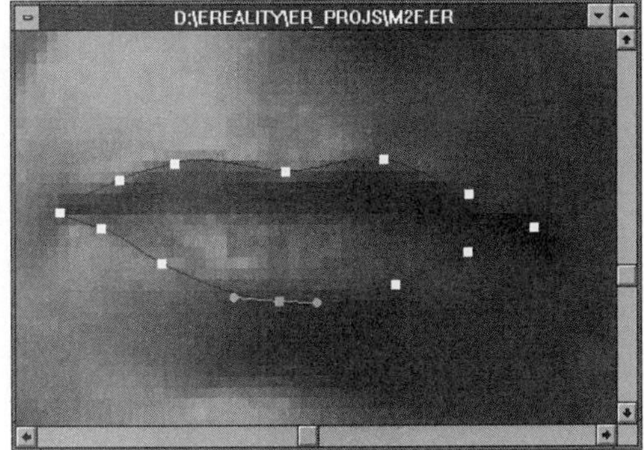

Figure 8.22. A close-up view of another control line.

In figure 8.22, one of the points has two small circles next to it, connected by lines (look at the bottom of the lower lip). You can change the shape of a control line in two ways. You can move the points themselves, or you can use those two little circles to change the way that the shape curves. These curves are called *Bezier curves.*[13] Figure 8.23 shows the result of dragging out the little circles (called *handles*).

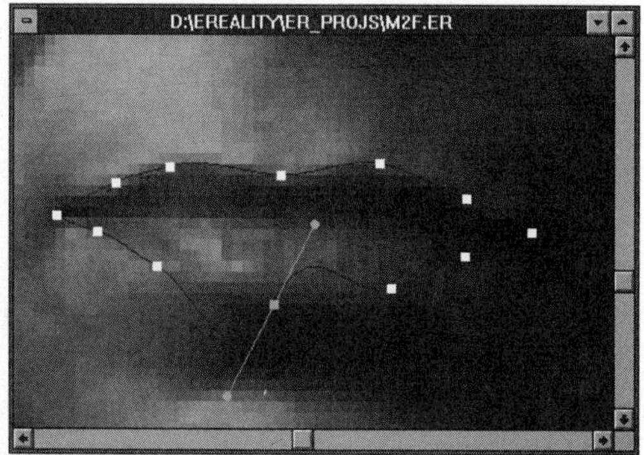

Figure 8.23. Changing the shape of a control line using handles on a point.

When you have created control lines for all the main features in your images, you are ready to create your morph. Figure 8.24 shows a close-up view of the two images and the control points using the A/B button. I created morphing pairs using the J key for each corresponding pair of control lines.

Figure 8.24. A close-up view of the control lines for both images.

[13]Named after a Frenchman; approximate pronunciation is Bezz-ee-ay curves.

Note that in figure 8.24 there is a slider control at the bottom right. The slider is all the way to the left, indicating frame 1 of the morph. To see a wireframe preview of the morph, drag the slider slowly from left to right.[14]

To create a single-frame preview, position the slider in the middle of the control at frame 15 (by default, a morph consists of 30 frames, but it's easy to change this number using the Window/Output options dialog box). Press Ctrl-P (or use the Render/Render Preview menu selection) to activate preview mode, and wait a few seconds for the preview to complete. Figure 8.25 shows what frame 15 looks like. To create the final morph, use the Window/Output options to set the type of output you want—bitmaps, AVI files, and many popular (and many obscure!) other file formats. Use the Render/Render Final menu selection to output to disk. Look in the color section to see a series of frames from the morph.

Figure 8.25. The middle frame of the morph.

As pleasing as these results are, this is just a small part of what you can accomplish with Elastic Reality. You can also create many different kinds of special effects. Let's look at just one quick example.

Figure 8.26 shows the Sequence Editor. This is used to load multiple images. The top line is for the A image or sequence, the next for the B image or sequence, the third for a matte, and the last for the background. You can have one or more lines with an image or sequence, depending on the effect you want to create.[15]

---

[14]You can also play the wireframe animation automatically. Use the Window/Wireframe controller menu selection to display the wireframe controller dialog box.

[15]For the previous example, in which we morphed a man's face into a woman's, the man's face was loaded into the A Roll sequence, and the woman's face was loaded into the B Roll sequence. Now you know why we pressed the A, A/B, and B buttons to view the images!

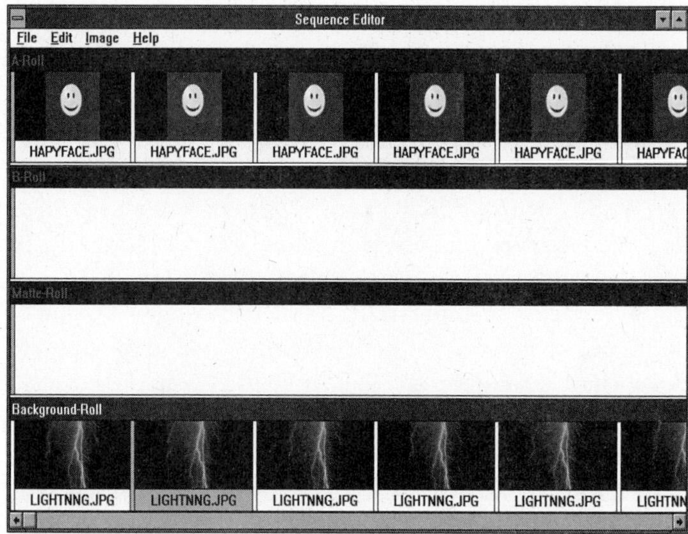

Figure 8.26. Using the Sequence Editor.

In figure 8.26, an A image and a background image have been added using the Insert menu selection on the menu bar. The A image will appear over the background image of a lightning flash.

Figure 8.27 shows the A image in the Elastic Reality window. I have added a circle around the smiley face, and there is a second circle partially visible at the upper left. These are a morphing pair; note the dashed lines that make up their bounding boxes. By setting the background as a cookie-cutter matte, only the portion of the A image within the starting bounding box will appear over the background. I also used the Window/Render options dialog box to change the relationship of the two control lines—the ending control line at the upper left will control the position of the starting image rather than provide a morph. I created a simple 30-frame animation of the ending circle; figure 8.28 shows an intermediate frame of the animation with the ending circle just below and to the left of the starting circle.

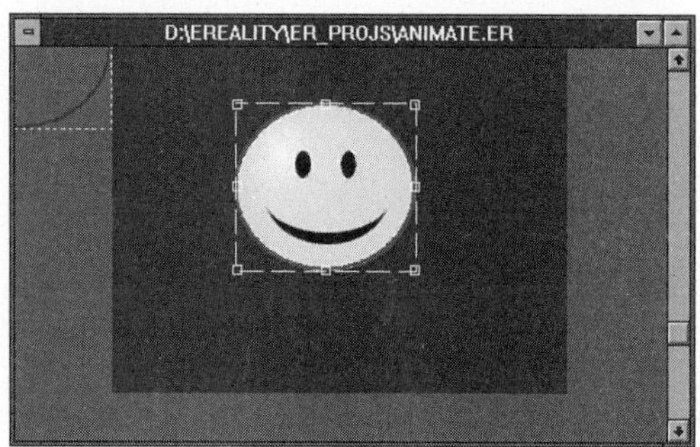

Figure 8.27. Starting and ending control shapes are in place.

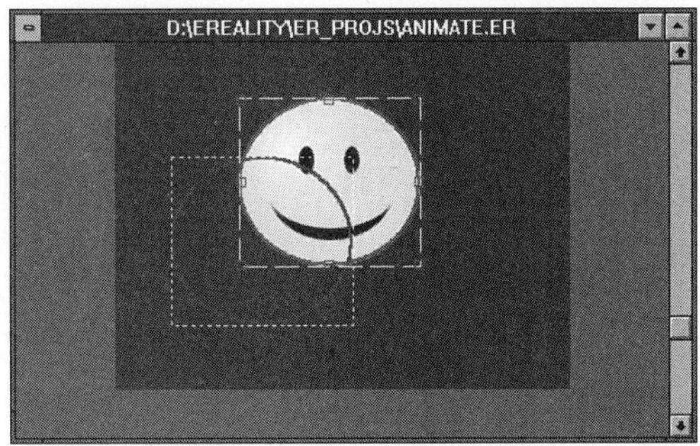

Figure 8.28. The ending control shape has been moved in frame 13.

Pressing Ctrl-P to render frame 13 results in the image shown in figure 8.29. This image retains the control shapes for your reference. Figure 8.30 shows the actual image with the control shapes removed.

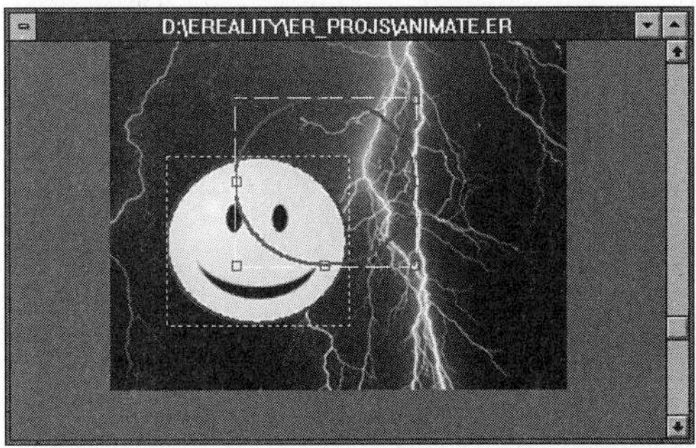

Figure 8.29. A preview of frame 13 of the animation.

Figure 8.30. A rendering of frame 13.

Using this technique, you can easily overlay objects from one image, animation, or video clip onto another image, animation, or video clip.

If you *really* want to explore Elastic Reality—and there is plenty to explore that I don't have room to even touch on here—there is only one way to do it: cold, hard cash. But if there was ever one program that you might want to buy instead of lunch, this is it.

The Morph the Merrier

Good morphing software must not only follow the basic rules for morphing but must be sensitive to various nuances of the morphing process. PhotoMorph does an excellent job of balancing all these requirements, and the newest edition adds a host of extra features that create some exciting possibilities.

RECIPE

1 copy PhotoMorph
1 starting image
1 final image
10-100 little square dots
1 Media Player or VidEdit

Instructions: This is a real taste treat. However, the recipe calls for a light touch—sort of like working up a soufflé or a puff pastry. Take two images, roughly similar in outline if possible, then dot lightly with square-dot sprinkles. Careful positioning is a must! Serve the AVI output in Windows, or slice into DIBs for Animator Pro.

I have included a number of PhotoMorph examples on the CD-ROM. One of the neatest features of PhotoMorph is that it outputs AVI files. You can view these easily using Windows Media Player. I also have included a demo version of PhotoMorph on the CD-ROMs. You are limited to using just a few files, but it is otherwise a full-featured version of the software. This gives you a chance to test-drive PhotoMorph before you decide whether you want to buy it. Along with Vistapro, PhotoMorph is very high on my personal must-have software list.

Figure 8.31 shows the basic PhotoMorph program windows. The main window has nothing in it, and there is a separate window called the Project Editor.

PhotoMorph is a bit like two programs in one. You can load bitmaps into the main window, where you can perform various operations on them as needed. You can add borders, change the contrast of an image, and so on. You will probably still use your favorite photo-paint software for major image manipulation, but you can always perform simple adjustments at the last minute in PhotoMorph.

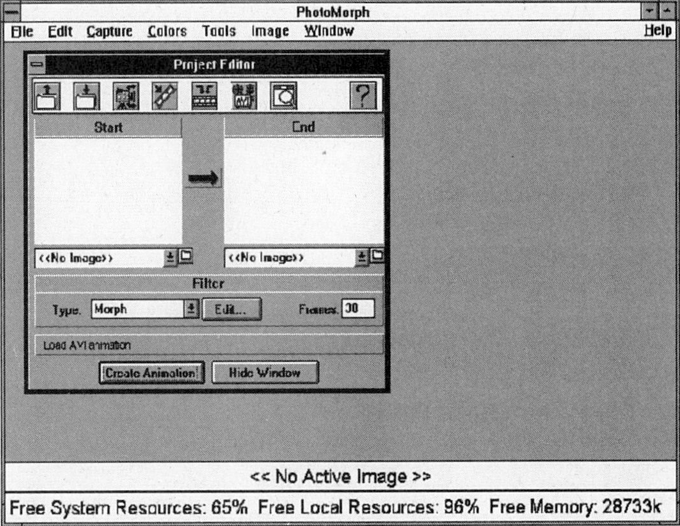

Figure 8.31. The basic PhotoMorph windows.

Morphing is simple, and morphing is complex. The simple side involves the method used for morphing. You simply place a point on an image and then tell the morph program where that point should wind up in the final image. After entering a series of points, you let the software perform the morph. The complex side involves the art of placing those points where they will do the most good.

Let's look at an example. There are two files on the CD-ROMs that you can use for this example. They are DOLPHIN.BMP and EYE1.BMP. To load these images into the Project Editor, use the File/Project/Open menu option to open the file D2EYE.BMP. This loads the two image files into the main window and into the Project Editor (see fig. 8.32).

There are numerous controls in the Project Editor window, and you'll learn about those in the next section. For now, simply click the Edit button at the bottom center. This displays the editing screen (see fig. 8.33). I used the Magnification icon to enlarge the eye portions of both images—this is where most of the morphing takes place. Note that there are square dots in both images. Only one dot in each image is active at a time, however. These are illustrated in figure 8.33.

I carefully adjusted the position of each key dot in both images. If a dot was at the corner of the eye in the dolphin image, I made sure that the corresponding key dot in the other image was also exactly at the corner of the eye. Because the sizes of the eyes are different in the two images, this involved a lot of moving around of the dots.

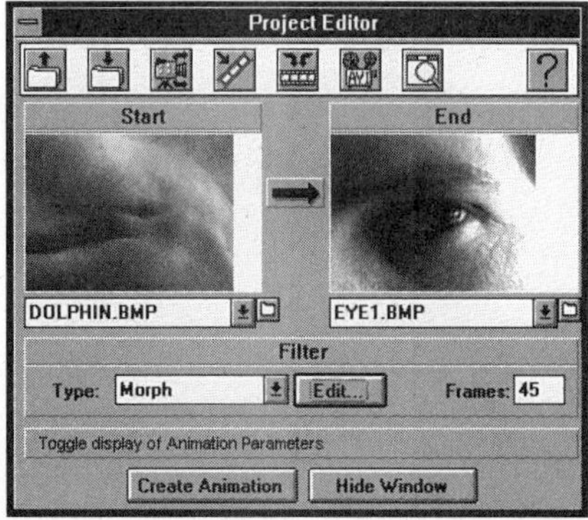

Figure 8.32. Two images loaded into the Project Editor.

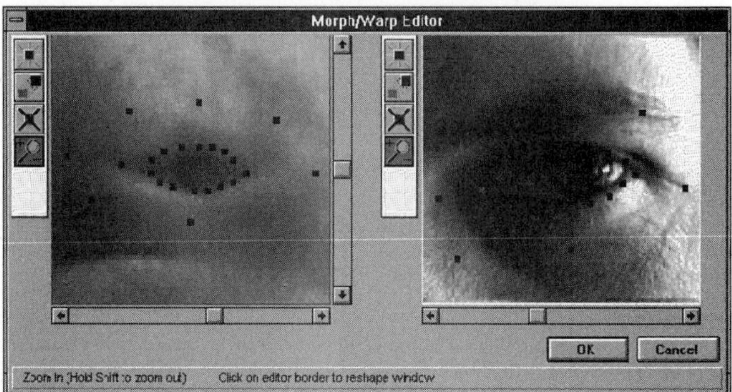

Figure 8.33. The edit window.

When I had the dots where I wanted them,[16] I saved the changes and returned to the Project Editor. I clicked the Create Animation button, and it took a few seconds for the AVI file to be generated.[17] This file (D2EYE.AVI) is on the CD-ROMs; see Appendix A for information on accessing files. Figures 8.34 and 8.35 show two frames from the morph. As you can see, the images blend smoothly.[18]

---

[16]Where to put the dots is the subject of much of this chapter—don't expect to just lay down a few dots and get a world-class morph right away. By the end of this chapter, you will learn enough skills to allow you to have a good idea of where to put those dots for your own morph. However, you will probably find that there is a certain irreducible amount of trial and error in the morphing process.

[17]One of the nice features of PhotoMorph is the speed with which it creates the morph output.

[18]This is much clearer if you play the AVI file itself. Still black-and-white images cannot convey the subtlety of the morph.

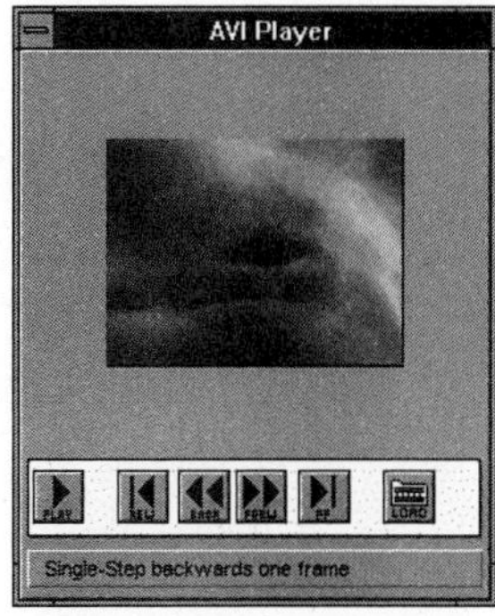

Figure 8.34. A frame from the morph animation.

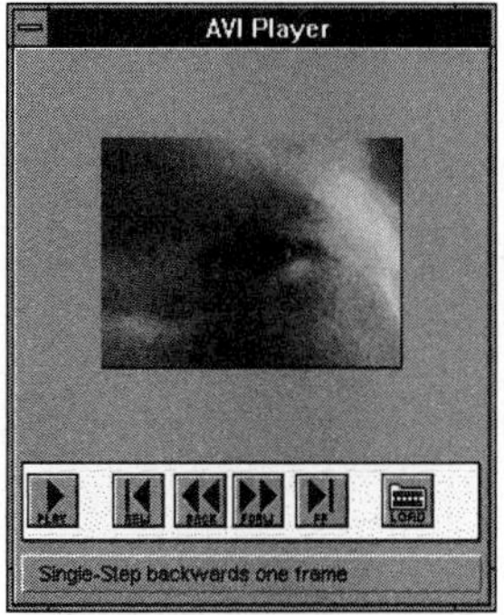

Figure 8.35. Another frame from the morph animation.

Video + Video = Video

Morphing still images, while fun and exciting, is just one step along the way to getting the most out of morphing. The really cool morphs, the ones you see at the movies and on TV, involve motion. If we are going to use morphing to create alternate reality, motion is required. The impact is much more dramatic than it is for still images.

PhotoMorph allows you to use two AVI video clips for input, and will produce a morph AVI as output. To pull this off, you are going to have to follow the same rules (and tedious procedures) that the Big Guys in Hollywood have to follow:

> **Rule #1**—All motion must be planned for and controlled.
>
> **Rule #2**—Careful attention to detail is the only way to ensure a smooth morph.
>
> **Rule #3**—If at first you don't succeed, modify, modify, and then modify again.

Let's look at a motion morph. The following example is taken from the sample images that come with the PhotoMorph demo on the CDs, so you can follow along at home. To begin, of course, you must have installed the demo from the CDs to your hard disk.

Run PhotoMorph by double-clicking. In the Project Editor, load two AVI clips: one into the Start image and one into the End image. Figure 8.36 shows the file CHRIS26.AVI as the starting image and EDIE26.AVI as the ending image. You load video clips in the same way that you load a single image. The direct approach is simplest: click on the small folder icon just below the right bottom corner of the image window. This displays a File Open dialog box, and you can select any valid AVI file.

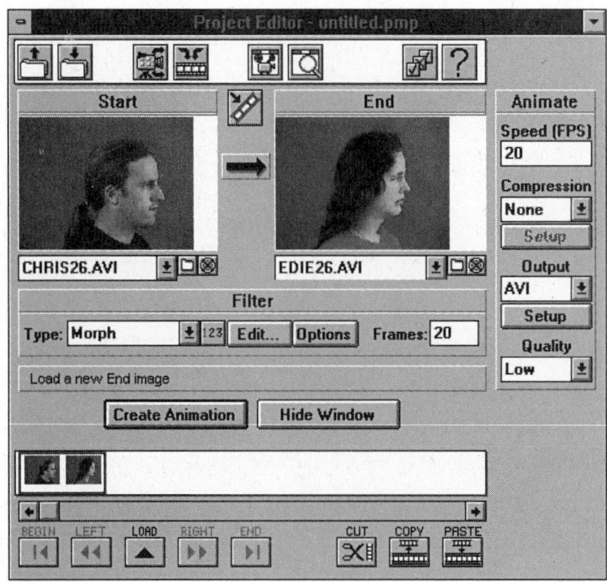

Figure 8.36. Loading AVI files for morphing is as easy as loading single image files.

In this example, both video clips contain extremely similar motion and framing. In both cases, the person's head rotates slowly, and each is a head-and-shoulders shot. This is in keeping with Rules #1 and #2—control and detail are what make a morph successful. Even so, there are some problems evident in the beginning frame match-up. The man has long hair, but it's arranged in a ponytail, while the woman's hair is fuller and has nothing to tie it down. In addition, the man's ear is exposed, while the woman's is not. These are issues that must be dealt with during the morph, plus any additional issues that appear in later frames.

When you have loaded both images, the process of adding morph points can begin. When you perform a morph on a pair of images, you create only one set of control points. You might imagine that you'll need a separate set of control points for each matching pair of frames in the video clips. Fortunately, PhotoMorph uses Smart Points to make the job simpler.

You can also perform a "morph" without setting any control points at all. However, that's nothing more than a fade from one image to another; it's not really a morph at all. Almost any video editor will do that much for you. As you'll see shortly, morphing can be much more effective than a simple fade.

When you click on the Edit button to enter control points, the Morph/Warp Editor window looks very familiar (see fig. 8.37). There's one important difference, however: the scroll bar below the images. The scroll bar is used to move from frame to frame in both video clips.

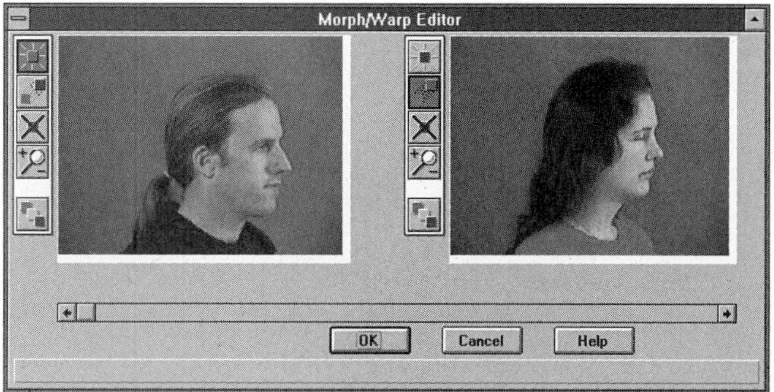

Figure 8.37. Editing a video clip morph.

As you can see in figure 8.37, the scroll bar starts out at the far left, which means you begin with frame 1 of each video clip—a very good place to start. Your job is to place control points as you would for any morph, paying special attention to boundaries and features. Figure 8.38 shows the first point: right on the nose. However, because a motion morph only keeps each frame on-screen for a fraction of a second, you do not need to control the points, or place as many points, as you might for a simple morph. Figure 8.39 shows a good starting set of points.[19]

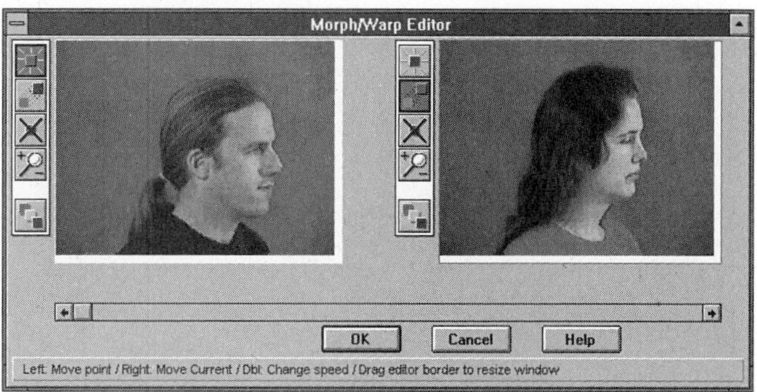

Figure 8.38. Placing the first control point.

[19]It might even be too many, but I'm conservative.

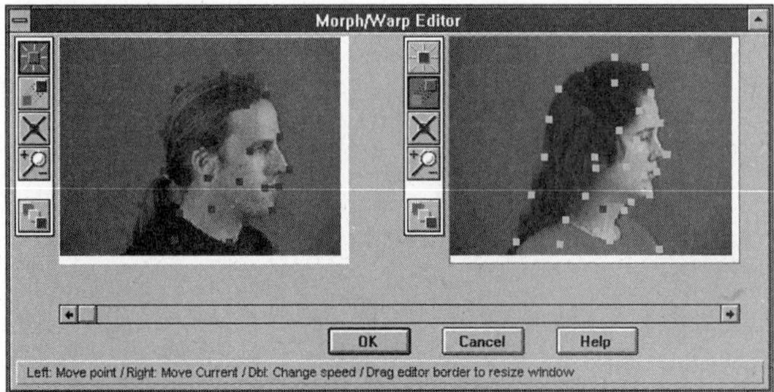

Figure 8.39. A starting set of control points.

There are a few things worth noting about the placement of the control points. First, there are two points used to define the man's ear. Normally, I would probably use at least six, because quite a bit of movement would occur during the morph between the ears in both images. However, as the head turns, the ear will disappear, so I only have to control it for a limited number of frames.[20] There are two corresponding points defining the woman's ear (or as much of it as is visible through her hair). They are much closer together. That means that, during the morph frames where ears are visible, there will be a size change based on the location of the control points in both images.

The next step is to move forward through the video clips as far as you can without losing track of what the points are for. Figure 8.40 shows frame 4 of both clips. The heads have started to turn, so the control points no longer line up with the features in the images. The next task, therefore, is to move the control points so they match up with the proper features and boundaries in the images.

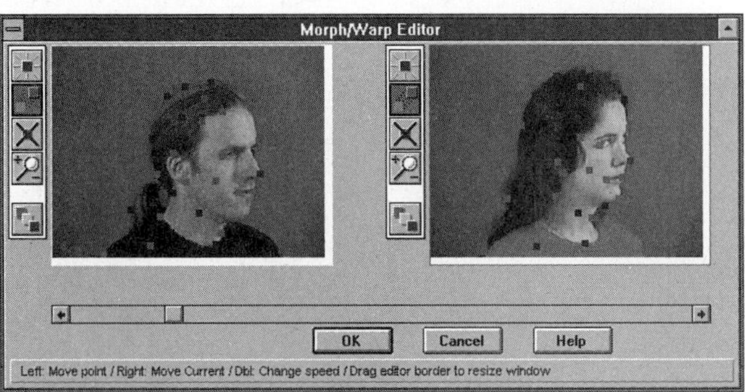

Figure 8.40. Moving to a new set of frames in the clips causes misalignment of the control points.

---

[20]You can delete control points later in the morph if they are no longer needed. The points will still remain in the earlier frames.

Figure 8.41 shows the control points adjusted for frame 4. There are still two points for the ears, and I have realigned all points to correspond to relevant features. A second eye has begun to reveal itself in both images, so I have shifted one of the control points to take over the job of tracking that eye. The important thing is that the control points for any frame correspond to similar features in both images.

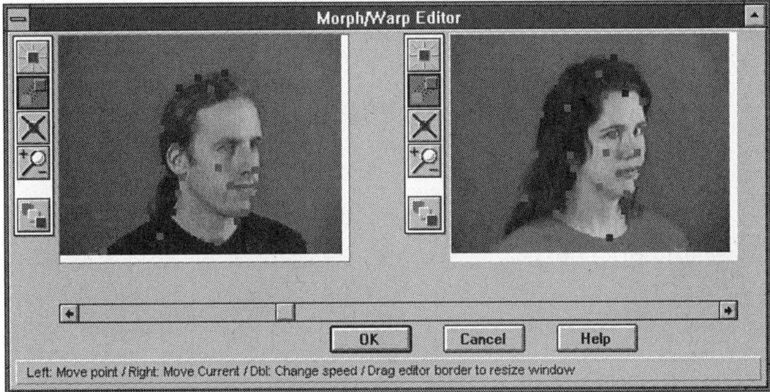

Figure 8.41. The control points have been adjusted for the new position of features in both images.

If you were now to look at frames 2 and 3, you will see that the control points for these frames are in positions between those of frames 1 and 4. The control points in frames 1 and 4 act as keys, and PhotoMorph will calculate intermediate control points for frames that you do not edit manually. In fact, if you only move some points on a given frame, only those points you actually change or create will be key points. PhotoMorph will add Smart Points on all frames between key points.

This process continues until you reach the end of the video clip. The number of key points you will have to create or adjust depends completely on the nature of the morph. For example, if there is little change in position or rotation, you may set key points every 15 frames, every 5 frames, or some other number. You'll have to determine the best interval yourself—Rule #3 in action.

Figures 8.42 through 8.45 show the rest of the key points I set for this example.

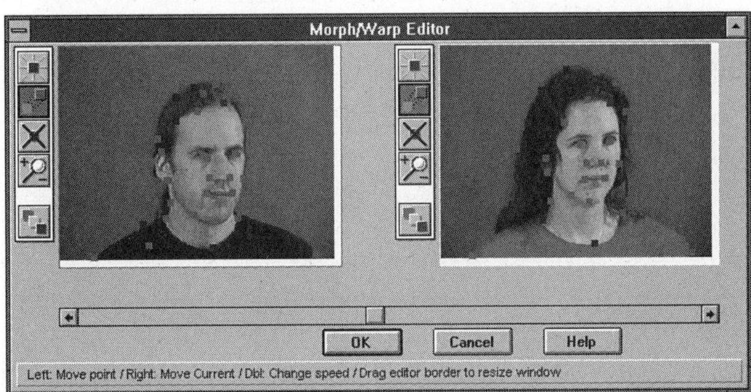

Figure 8.42. Control points for frame 7.

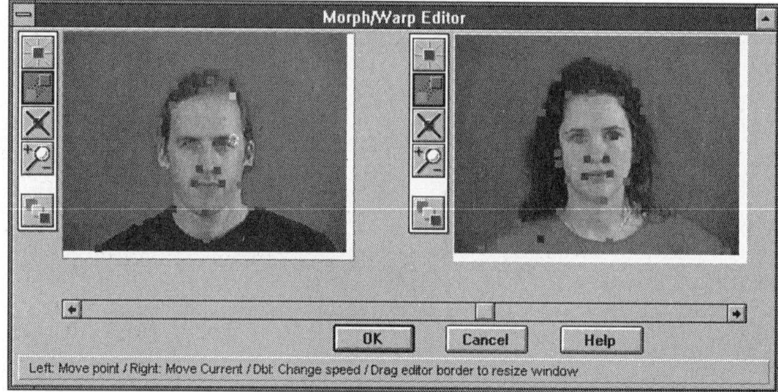

Figure 8.43. Control points for frame 10.

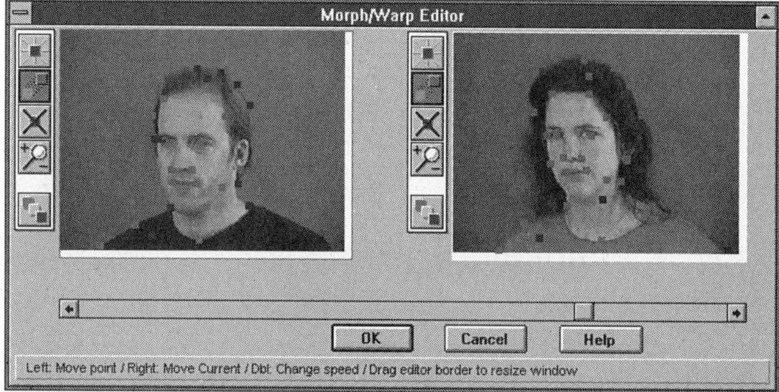

Figure 8.44. Control points for frame 13.

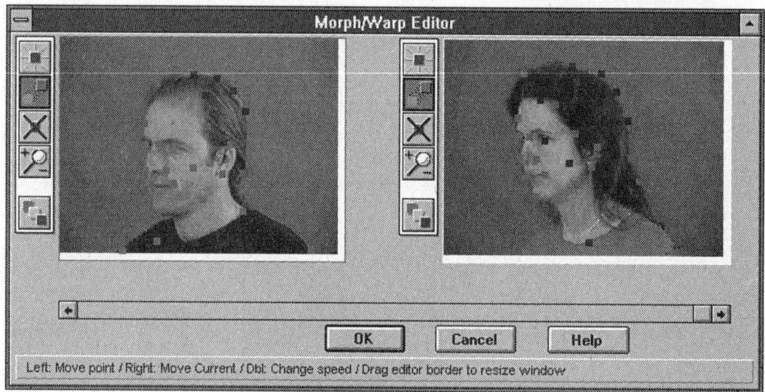

Figure 8.45. Control points for frame 16.

When you have set control points at all of the key frames you need, click the OK button in the Morph/Warp editor. This returns you to the Project Editor, where you can click the Create Animation button. You can view the completed animation using either Media Player or PhotoMorph's built-in viewer.

To see the advantages of a morph over a simple fade, let's look at some sample frames from both kinds of transition. Figure 8.46 shows two frames. The image on the left is taken from a simple motion fade. Note that there is a distinct shadow of the woman's hair at the left of the neck and to the right of the face. The image on the right is taken from a morph. Note that the hairline has been adjusted outward from the face, a proper morph between the two different hairlines. There is still some ghosting, and that can be solved by adding a few additional control points.[21]

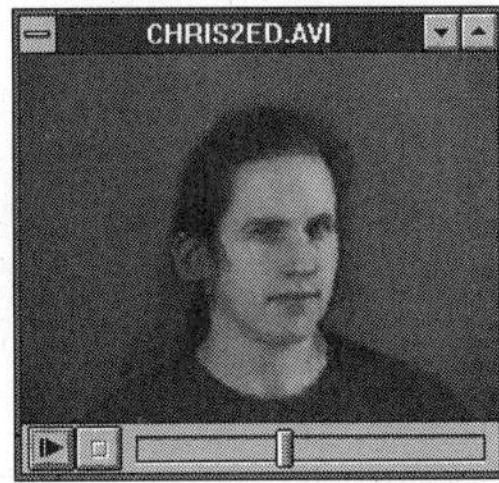

Figure 8.46. Left: Simple fade. Right: Morph using control points. Note that morph controls change more tightly.

Similar advantages of the morph over the fade are clear in figure 8.47. The hair is again more clearly defined and less ghostly. More important, the face outline is much clearer, and more truly intermediate between the two faces.

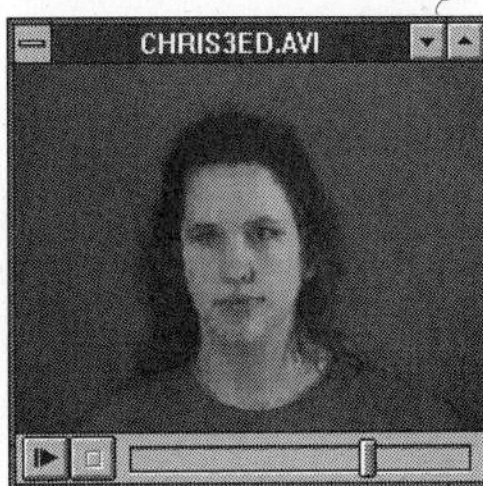

Figure 8.47. Left: Simple fade. Right: Morph using control points. Note that hair is much better defined using a morph, and that the face outline is clearer.

Figure 8.48 shows an even clearer example of why a morph does a better job. The crispness of the morph image compared to the fade makes the best case yet for taking the time to create control points.

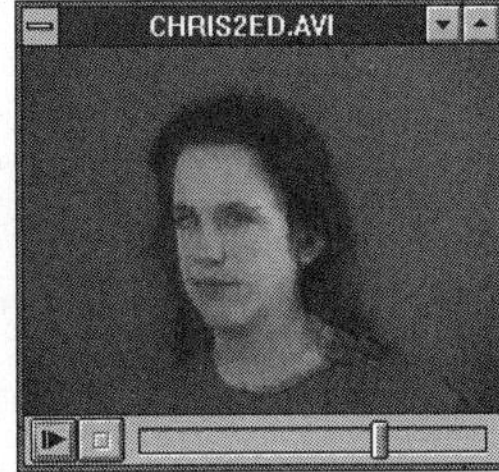

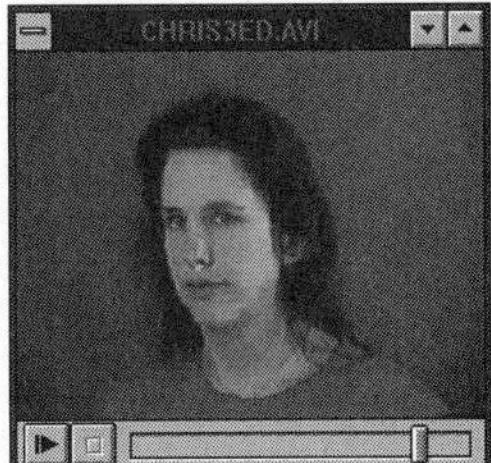

Figure 8.48. Left: Simple fade. Right: Morph using control points. Note that details are much clearer in the morph.

---

[21]Rule #3 in action again.

This is just one small example of what you can accomplish with the advanced features of PhotoMorph 2. Here's just a *sample* of the features you'll find in PhotoMorph 2:

- Change image bit depths.
- Change image file formats.
- Flip, mirror, invert, crop, scale, and rotate images.
- Apply filters to images, such as sharpen, blur, de-speckle, emboss, median, trace edges, noise, maximum, minimum, and (my favorite!) Old Movie.
- Have up to three filters/morphs/warps/transitions going on at one time.
- Create a sequence of morphs in one animation.
- Preview the morph without having to create the entire file.
- Motion warping.
- Colorizing.
- Distortions, such as ripple and wave.
- Create overlay using alpha channel or chroma/luma keys.
- Create transitions such as fade, melt, and random.

I'm excited about PhotoMorph, as you can probably tell. The program design, engineering, and features are all excellent, and it's even easy to use. It's high on my list of recommended software.

The Square and the Circle

That's enough razzle-dazzle for now. Time for a little hard reality: Morphing is at least as much an art as a science. PhotoMorph does a better job at controlling the smoothness and realism of the morph, but there are things you can do to get absolutely perfect morphs. It's worth some time and effort to see exactly how morphing works before you try anything too fancy. A clear understanding of what the software does with all those control points will give you a good start to successful morphing.

Figure 8.49 shows a simple project file loaded into PhotoMorph. Note that the image files that make up the project are not only loaded into the Project Editor, but into the workspace of the main window as well. You can make changes to the bitmaps using the Image menu option before morphing, should that be necessary.

Before discussing the details of the dots, let's take a moment to list and describe the basic features of PhotoMorph. Most of the morphing work is done in the Project Editor (see fig. 8.49). There is a row of buttons across the top of the window (see table 8.1), and two image windows marked Start and End. The currently open images are listed under both of these windows for easy access. The little folder icon next to the file names enables you to easily add more image files to the list.

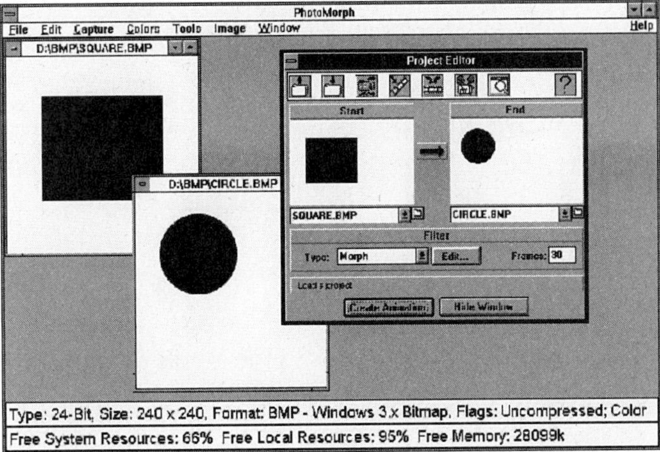

Figure 8.49. PhotoMorph with a project loaded.

Below the images is a section of the window called Filter. There are three controls here: the type of the filter (warp or morph), an Edit button, and a Frames control. A warp simply alters the pixel positions in an image, whereas a morph both alters the pixel positions and fades to a second image. The Edit button takes you to the editing screen where you place and move those little square dots. The Frames control tells PhotoMorph how many frames to create in the AVI file. More frames means a smoother but slower morph.

At the bottom of the window are two buttons: Create Animation and Hide Window. The former creates the AVI file, and the latter hides the project window.

Table 8.1. The PhotoMorph Project Editor Toolbar (left to right).

Icon	*Description*
Load Project	Loads a project file from the disk.
Save Project	Saves the current project to disk.
View/Hide AVI Controls	Displays additional controls related to AVI file creation, such as compression method. This is a toggle control.*
View/Hide All	Alternately hides and displays the animation and AVI controls.*

continues

Table 8.1. continued

Icon	*Description*
View/Hide Animation Controls	Displays additional animation controls. This is a toggle control.*
Play AVI file	Opens the AVI player.
Enlarge window	Enlarges the project window.
Help	Access to Help files.

***Note:** The AVI and Animation controls are explained near the end of this section.

Now for the fun part: the dots. To place dots, click the Edit button in the Project Editor window. This displays the Morph/Warp Editor (see fig. 8.50).

There are four buttons at the left of each of the images. From top to bottom, these buttons

- Create a new dot
- Move a dot
- Delete a dot
- Enlarge/reduce the image

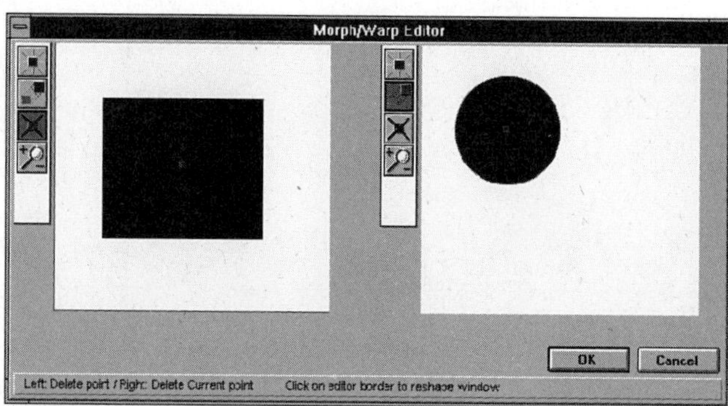

Figure 8.50. The Morph/Warp Editor window.

Clicking a button changes the operating mode of the window. For example, when you click the top button (Create a New Dot), any time you click in that image, a new dot will be created.[22] If you click the Enlarge/Reduce button, the cursor changes

[22]As a general rule, you should create one dot at a time. Adjust that dot's position in both images before you create another dot. If you create too many dots at once, you will lose track of which dot is which.

to a magnifying glass and will alter the scale of that image until you click a new icon.

The editing window is resizeable, but you must use the Enlarge/Reduce icons to change the scale of an image.

In figure 8.50, there is a single dot in each image.[23] The dots are located at the center of each object. Note that the image of the square has been enlarged and the image of the circle has not. You can adjust the scale of each image independently.

Your first experiment is to find out what kind of morph takes place when you put dots in the center of corresponding objects. This is a simple example, but I have made it more interesting by using two completely different shapes. In a real morph, not only will the shapes have different characteristics, but there will also be many different shapes. The circle and the square are mere teaching devices, sort of like using training wheels when you learn to ride a two-wheel bike.

To create the morph, click OK in the Morph/Warp Editor, and then click the Create Animation button in the Project Editor. A slider will appear in a small window showing you the progress of the morph operation, and you'll see a polite little window informing you when the operation is complete. To view the AVI file, you can simply click the Play AVI button in the toolbar. This displays the first frame of the AVI file (see fig. 8.51).

Figure 8.51. The first frame of a morph animation.

[23]When you create a new dot in an image, the corresponding new dot in the other image is created automatically.

This is, as you would expect, simply the square that the morph is supposed to start with. Click the FORW button to step forward through the morph. Several frames in, you will see something like figure 8.52.

There are two obvious things going on here:

- The image of the square is fading out, and the image of the circle is fading in.
- Both of the images are slightly deformed. The circle is somewhat more deformed than the square.

The deformation of the two objects requires some explanation. During a morph, there are actually two morphs going on at the same time. The square is being morphed into the circle and, behind the scene, the circle is being morphed into the square. For example, if the morph takes 10 frames, at frame 1, the image of the square has been deformed 10 percent toward the shape of the circle. In addition, the circle has been deformed 90 percent toward the shape of the square. In this case, we have only used one point to define the morph, and that doesn't give the program much information about the shape of either object.

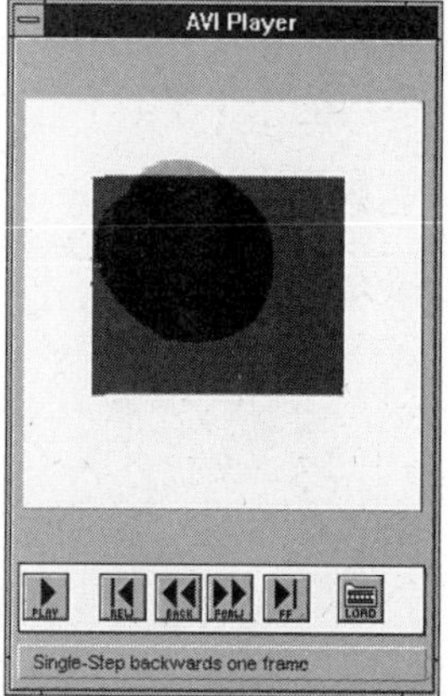

Figure 8.52.
A frame from the middle of the morph.

You see, the software doesn't look for the boundary of the square or the circle. The purpose of the dots is to tell the software where key points are—such as boundaries.[24] Because we have only defined one key point, the changes from frame to frame are not well controlled. This is the source of the odd deformation of the circle in figure 8.52.

---

[24]There are other kinds of key points, but it would only muddy the waters to talk about that here. Stay tuned.

If you continue to step forward in the animation, you will get to a frame near the end that looks something like figure 8.53. This frame also shows signs of an under-controlled morph. The circle is nearly right, but the edges of the square are going squiggly on us.

By the time we get to the next-to-last frame (see fig. 8.54), the square has all but faded away, and the circle is in good shape.

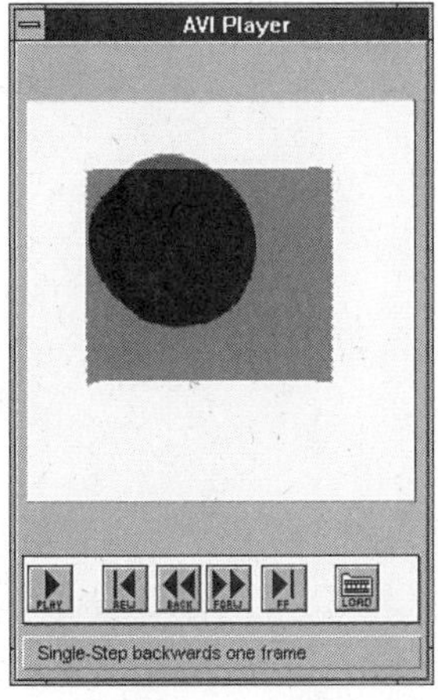

Figure 8.53. A frame near the end of the animation.

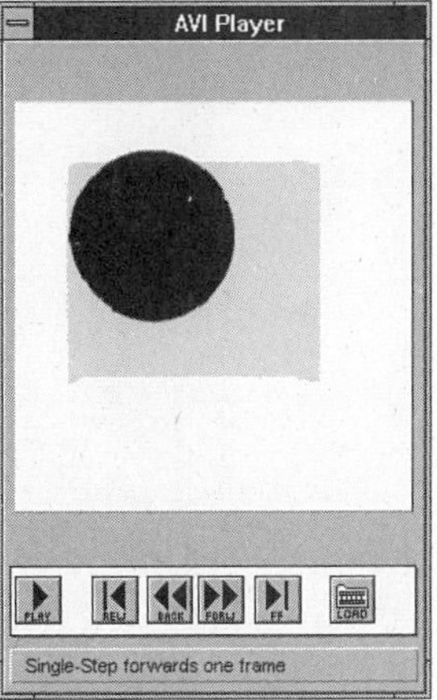

Figure 8.54. The next-to-last frame of the animation.

Clearly, if we want better control of the morphing process, we'll need more dots. This is a good time to rename the dots for what they really are: control points. The trick to creating a good-looking morph that will fool the eye is to place the control points where they need to go. The purpose of the rest of this section, where we will explore a seemingly endless succession of ways to place control points on these simple figures, is to show the effects of various placements on the resulting morph. So hang in there; all will be made clear.

Figure 8.55 shows a different setup in the Morph/Warp Editor. This time, instead of a single control point at the center of each object, there are four control points. There is one each at the corners of the square, and one each at corresponding points on the circle. The control points may be hard to make out, but they are there.

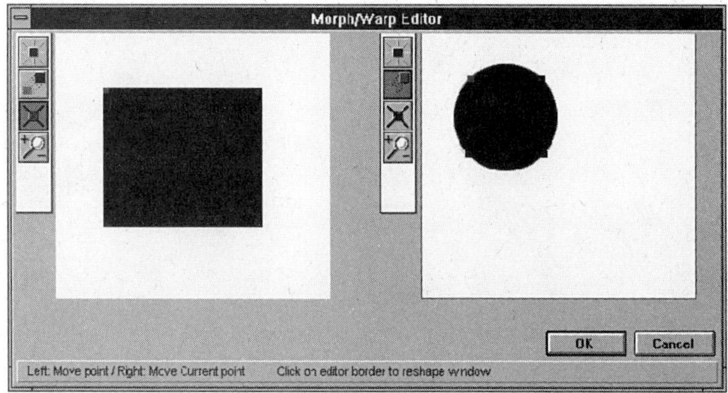

Figure 8.55. Using four control points.

To see the results of this arrangement, click OK and then Create Animation. A check of the AVI file shows a frame like the one in figure 8.56.

Figure 8.56. A frame from the new morph animation.

This is very different from figure 8.52. Now there is a much better correspondence between the circle and the square. Still not perfect, but significantly better. The control points at the corners of the square are doing their job—the two objects are fairly well aligned at these points.

Still, the effect is not satisfactory. Let's try a slightly different arrangement of control points (see fig. 8.57). This time, the control points are located just outside the square and the circle. (Compare with figure 8.55.)

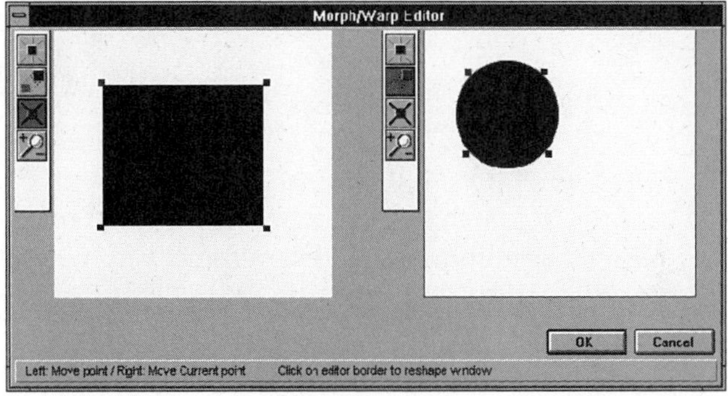

Figure 8.57.
A different arrangement of control points.

The result of the new placement is shown in figure 8.58.

Figure 8.58.
A frame from the new morph animation.

The alignment at the corners is now very firm. However, the points along the edges of the square do not line up at all with the edges of the circle. Let's try more control points (see fig. 8.59).

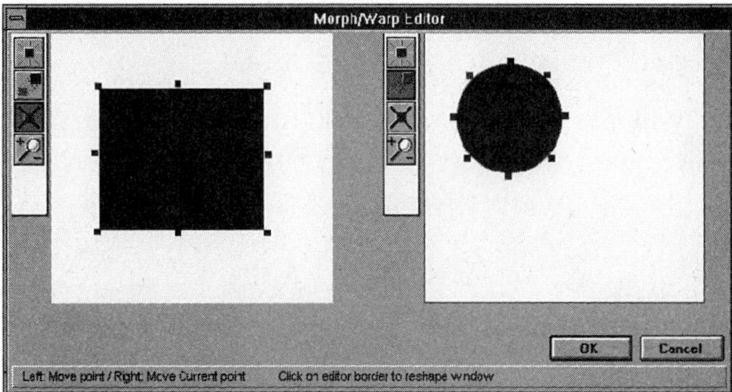

Figure 8.59. Adding control points along the edges of the objects.

The result of the additional control points is shown in figure 8.60. The morph is now much, much better—in fact, you could make a case for stopping here and calling it a morph. A close examination, however, shows a few minor flaws that may be worth some further attention.[25]

The lower left of the morph object shows a minor misalignment—there's a bit of black hanging out to the side that shouldn't be there. In addition, by adding the control points along the edges, we have lost some of the control we had at the corners of the square—these now extend beyond the circle.

> **TIP** New control points affect the action of existing control points. Be prepared to rearrange control points after adding new ones.

With this tip comes a side tip: check your work before you add too many new control points, so you can see what the effect of the new points is. You could wind up with a muddled mess if you try to do too much without checking your work.

You might try simply adding more control points (see fig. 8.61).

The result is shown in figure 8.62. This is not good—the result is worse than it was before!

On a hunch, I tried the same number of control points but arranged them a little differently, as shown in figure 8.63. The extra control points have been moved much closer to the corners.

The result of this attempt at a fix is shown in figure 8.64.

---

[25] If this morph were not so demanding, we probably could, indeed, stop here. However, you will sometimes find just such a high-contrast situation (black next to white, in this case), and it will be useful to know how to handle it.

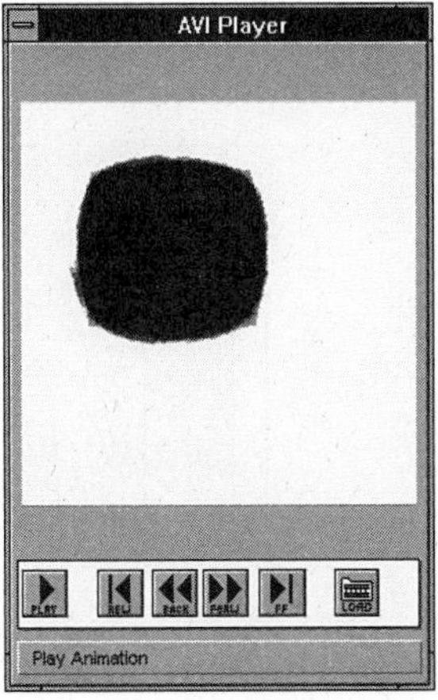

Figure 8.60.
A frame from the morph with edge control points.

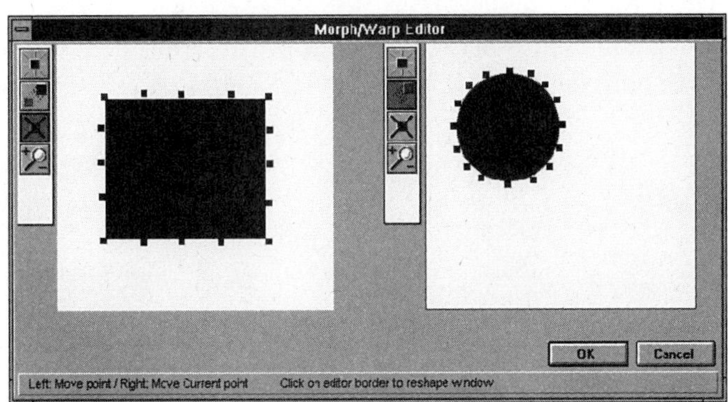

Figure 8.61.
Adding yet more control points.

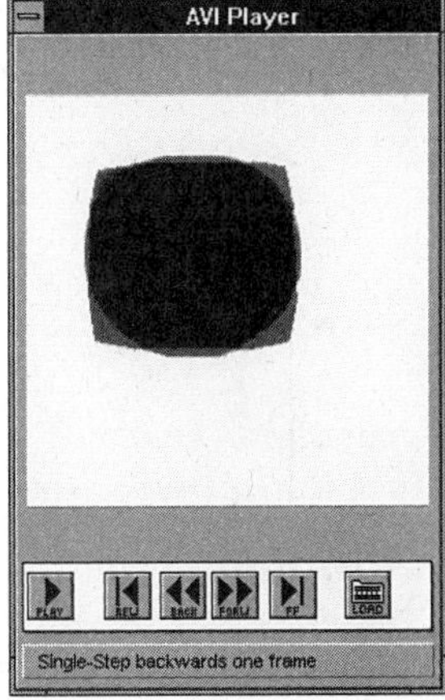

Figure 8.62.
The result of adding more control points.

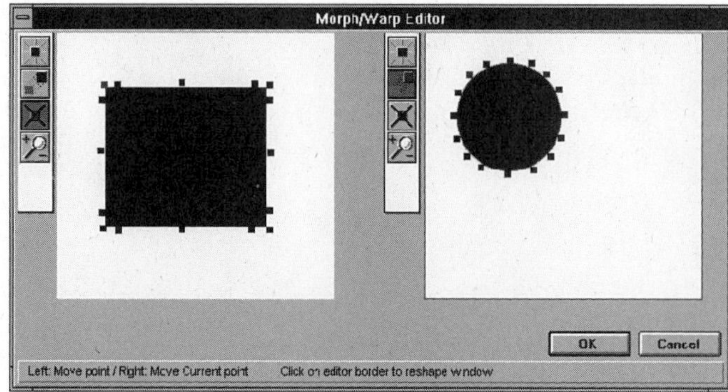

Figure 8.63. Moving the control points around.

This offers some advantages that are worthwhile, but there is still some misalignment—the two figures are simply too different. The improvement comes in the form of straighter lines along the edges of the square, which will make for a more gradual and therefore more pleasing morph. To see the difference more clearly, compare figures 8.62 and 8.64.

Figure 8.64. The result of shifting the control points closer to the corners.

There are many lessons to be learned from this extended example. The following list summarizes them. However, the most important lesson to learn is that it is difficult and challenging to try to morph dissimilar objects. Ultimately, you can never do a perfect morph between objects that vary by too large a factor:

- Objects with corners need control points just beyond the corners.
- Straight lines need control points near their ends to preserve the straightness.(26)

26This assumes, of course, that the situation requires such preservation. By all means, locate control points away from the corners to speed up the transition to a curve when that is desirable.

- Odd morphing can usually be remedied by adding more control points.
- Check the effects resulting from the addition of new control points. These may change the effects of existing control points.
- When in doubt, more control points are usually better than too few.

One thing that was not covered in this example was the effect of having control points at very different locations on the start and end images. Such positioning required large-scale morphs. Here's another general rule: the farther apart matching control points are in the two images, the greater the risk of some fatal flaw that will spoil the morph.

The Frog and the Chick

Let's have a little fun with morphing: how about turning a frog into a chick? Figure 8.65 shows two images loaded into the Project Editor. The starting image is a frog and the ending image is a chick.

Figure 8.65. A more complex morph in the Project Editor.

This morph presents some interesting challenges. The first step is to find areas in the images that correspond to one another—and there are more of them than you might expect. For example, look at the frog's two right feet. They match nicely with the chick's two feet. It would be a good idea to set up corresponding control points for each of the toes.

Other good places for control points would be eye-to-eye, and the overall outline of the animals. Figure 8.66 shows a good first attempt at control points. Some of the control points on the chick may be hard to see because of the black background, but they are there.

Figure 8.66.
Adding control points in the Morph/Warp Editor.

However, these control points have at least one important problem: the frog's eye is not sufficiently controlled. Figure 8.67 shows a frame from the morph animation—the frog's eye has split. Part of it is migrating down to the chest, while the rest of it heads where it should: toward the chick's left eye.

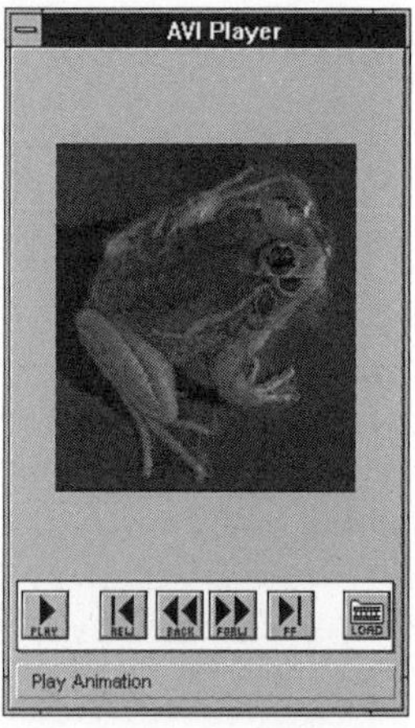

Figure 8.67.
A frame from the frog-to-chick morph.

Figure 8.68 shows why this is occurring. Look at the control points around the frog's eye. There is only one control point for the lower third of the eye. This would often be enough to give adequate control, but in this case the eye is very close to the control points along the lower jaw. The control points along the jaw have a long way to go to morph to the corresponding control points on the chick's chest. When you have this combination—control points moving in opposite directions and moving over large distances—you often will need more control points to avoid problems.

You also can divide and conquer. By adding an additional row of control points in the area between the eye and the jawline, you establish a boundary that reduces the impact of the eye/jaw control points on each other. Any given control point has the greatest influence on the control points immediately adjacent to it. If there is at least one control point between them, points will have much less impact on each other.

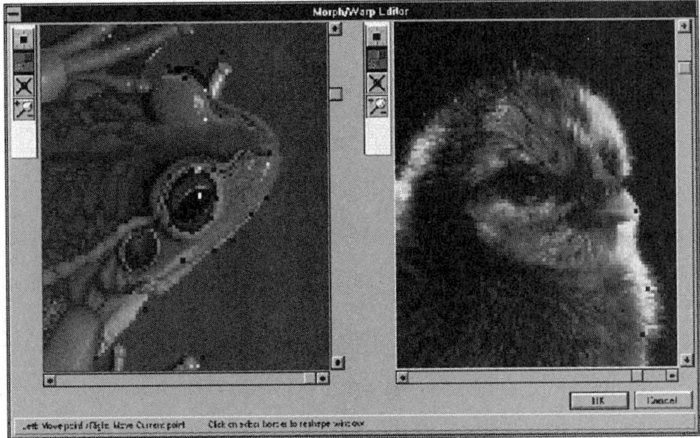

Figure 8.68. A close-up of the eye portion of the morph.

Now look at figure 8.69. I have made both of the changes I suggested. There are twice as many control points around the frog's eye.[27] There are also three new points between the eye and the jawline.

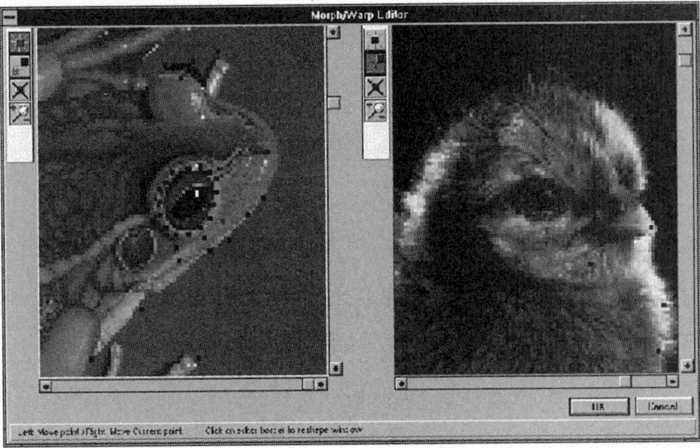

Figure 8.69. Revised control points around the frog's eye.

---

[27]Remember: Too many control points is seldom a problem, while too few almost always is a problem.

Figure 8.70 shows the result of adding the control points. The eye of the frog is now intact during the morph. Because the eye is red, it stands out and thus is a very important morph object. The human eye will follow the brightest or most colorful object in a scene. If you can identify the most prominent object in a morph and control it carefully, the observer will be satisfied even if certain other aspects of the morph aren't quite perfect. This is especially true in the frog/chick morph because there are those extra frog legs at the top of the frog picture. As you can see in figure 8.70, if you do not control them too tightly, they conveniently disappear.

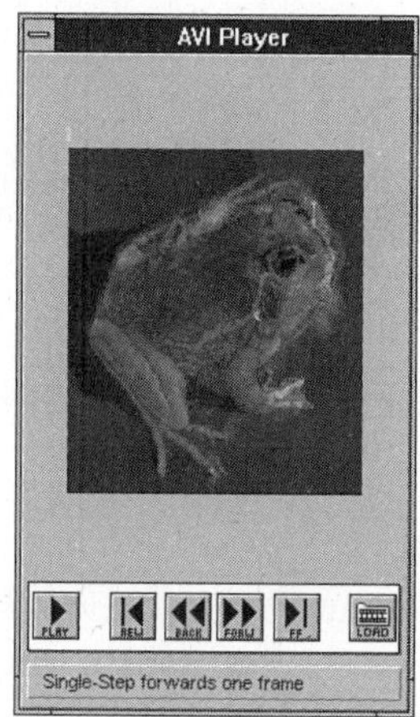

Figure 8.70. The frog's eye now morphs correctly.

The Circle and the Circle

The frog's eye was challenging to morph properly because it moves a large distance. Let's look at a more controlled situation. Figure 8.71 shows a morphing project with two circles, one at the upper left (start) and one at the lower right (end).

There is no shape-changing involved in this morph. The starting object is a circle and the ending object is a circle. Movement, however, is a critical consideration when morphing. To see the kinds of problems inherent in movement, let's add a single control point to each object (see fig. 8.72). This won't create a successful morph, but it will illustrate the kinds of problems encountered during a move.

Figure 8.73 shows a frame from the morph, about halfway through the animation. As you can see, the two objects are trying to move toward each other's initial position. This leaves a distorted trail of garbage behind.

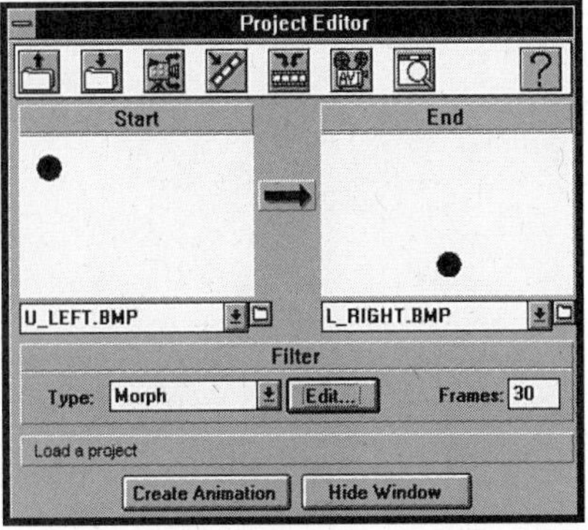

Figure 8.71.
A morph that changes location, not shape.

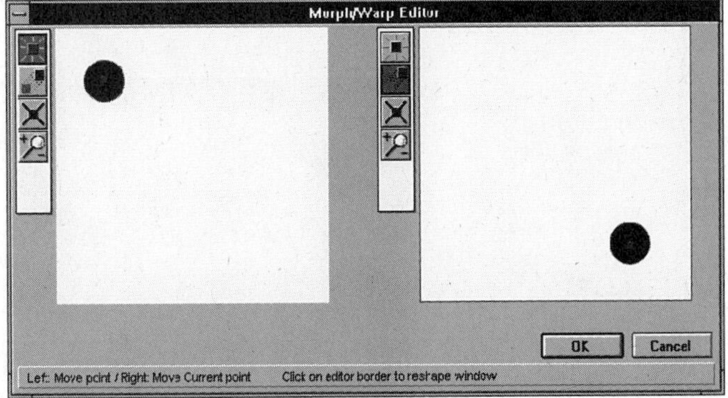

Figure 8.72.
A morph with only a single control point in each object.

To get better control of the move, your first instinct would be to add more control points. A minimum of eight is likely to be needed, based on our observations in the preceding examples (see fig. 8.74).

However, as you can see in figure 8.75, the result isn't quite right. There are two little "rocket jets" coming out of the end of the circle as it moves.

In figure 8.76, I have zoomed in on the circles to show a slight change that I made to the control points. Because a bit of the object was getting left behind, so to speak, I added some white space to the area within the control points.

The result of what I'll call over-controlling is shown in figure 8.77.

As you can see, we have reached the point of diminishing returns. The rocket jet is mostly gone, but now the object outlines do not coincide. This is a case where your own judgment must prevail—depending on the nature of the image, you can choose to under- or over-control for the best overall result.

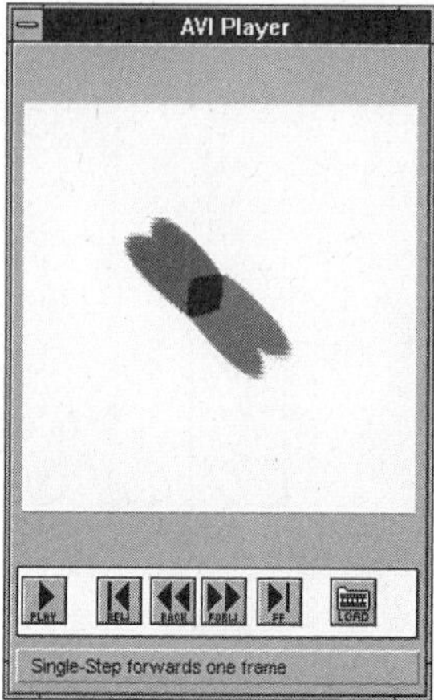

Figure 8.73.
The hazards of an under-controlled move.

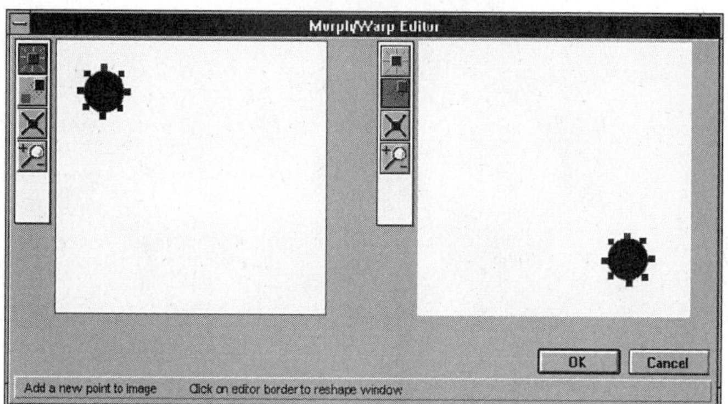

Figure 8.74.
Using eight control points.

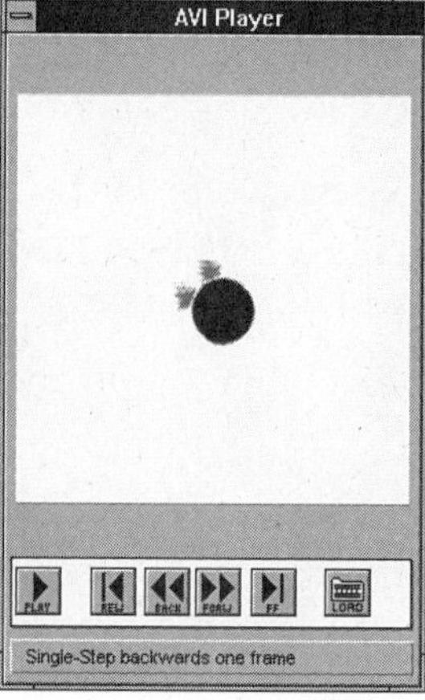

Figure 8.75.
Some artifacts of the move remain under-controlled.

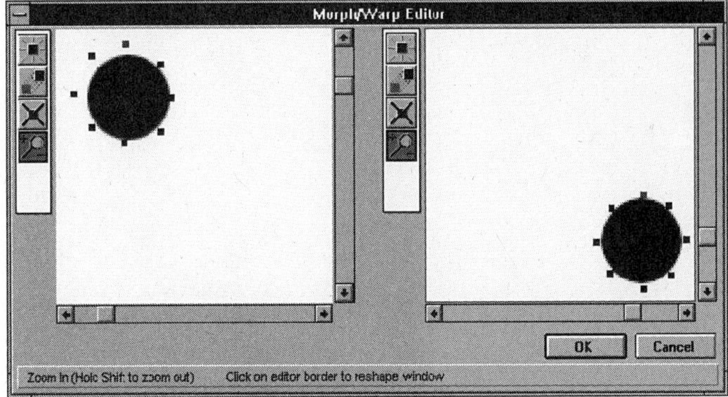

Figure 8.76. Shifting the location of a few control points.

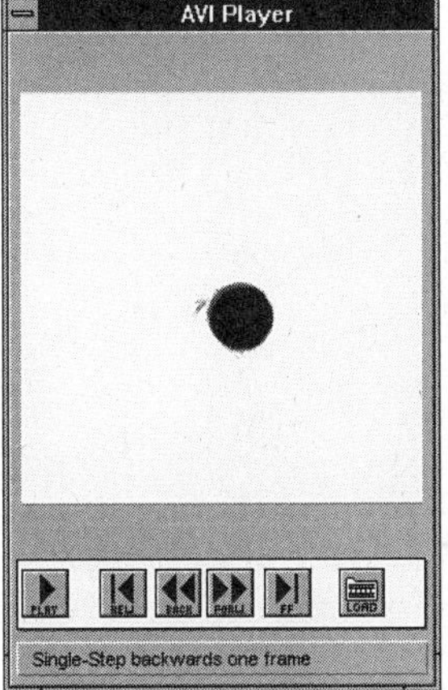

Figure 8.77. An over-controlled morph can also cause problems.

Summary

In this chapter, you learned about how the eye can be deceived into believing that images are more or less real. However, tricks and techniques are only part of the story—the eye's owner must be willing to be deceived. As demonstrated by morphing, the extra time it takes to smooth out the unreality of artifice can be well worth your while.

Just as the eye has a hard time accepting the transformation of a frog into a chick, it is equally happy to be amazed if it sees nothing inherently wrong visually; if the motion is smooth, if there are no jumps, if the transformation is at least plausible, then the impossible can be made to seem real.

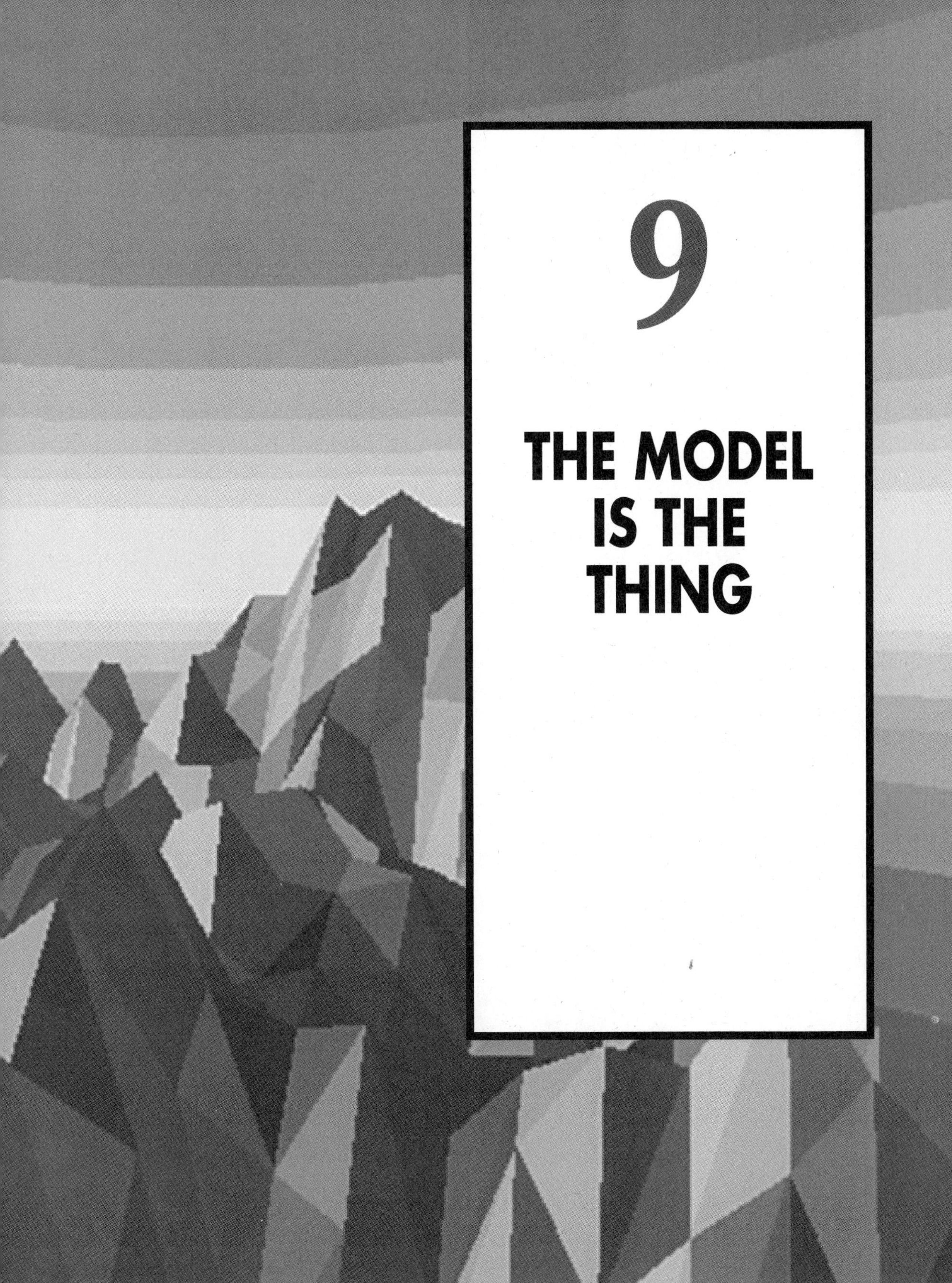

9

THE MODEL IS THE THING

Today's virtual reality hardware and software are really just models of reality. This takes me back to Chapter 2, where the subject was artificial reality instead of virtual reality. In many ways, the phrase *artificial reality* is much more appropriate for the technology available. The original idea of virtual reality was of an electronic (or otherwise) simulation that was, at its best, indistinguishable from reality. The reality of virtual reality is quite different. An analogy will serve to illustrate the differences.

Granularity

Weather forecasters use models to simulate the earth's weather systems. These models are extremely complex, and run on some of the fastest and largest computers in use today. These models are modeling reality, but not only are they not reality, they aren't even very close to reality. The reality of weather is that it is complex, chaotic, and, in truth, pretty much unpredictable. A model necessarily leaves out details. The term used to describe the accuracy of a model is *granularity*. This term comes from the concept of graininess. For example, photographs use grains of silver compounds to create an image. Some grains are dark and others are light. The smaller the grains are, the more closely the image will resemble the original. Figure 9.1 shows an image constructed of very large grains, and figure 9.2 shows an image constructed of very small grains.

Figure 9.1. An image constructed of large grains.

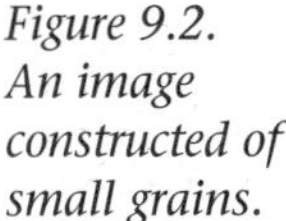

Figure 9.2. An image constructed of small grains.

Granularity is easy to spot in a picture, but it is not always so easy to see in a model of something. Back to the weather simulation: granularity here involves the distance between the sensors used to record weather information. If the sensors are 100 miles apart, that means that aspects of weather smaller than 100 miles or so will not be part of the model—a grain is 100 miles in size.

The granularity of time is also a consideration when you create a model. If those weather stations sample the weather once a day, the model will have large "time grains." If the weather stations sample the weather every hour, that's a much higher granularity and a much more accurate model.

Both kinds of granularity are crucial factors when modeling any aspect of reality. Reducing the size of the grains in a model costs money, however. There is a general rule at work here: more grains means more CPU power, more bits of data, more time, and more money.[1]

A 486/66 computer, with a cutting-edge video display and the fastest hard disk available, isn't going to be able to create a simulation of reality that will fool anyone. The emphasis is on virtual and artificial, not on reality. Even if you spend $10,000 or more, the hardware can only do so much. This chapter,[2] therefore, will be about what you and I can do on a reasonably fast computer, on our own, and not about what you could do "if only."

[1]It doesn't always cost more money, however. Today's computers are a hundred or more times faster than the original IBM PC, but they cost about the same. It has always cost about $2,500 for a decent computer—we just keep getting better computers at that same price.

[2]And, in many ways, most of this book, too!

What If...

What if virtual reality were really that close to the "real" reality? What would it mean? I've been wondering that for years—and there are a ton of science fiction writers and futurists who have been wondering, too. Even screenwriters and the folks who create commercials have been speculating. Thanks to TV, there's more VR in our lives than if we really had it available!

There are, for example, the beer ads that feature futuristic environments in which sports contests are held. There are all those headsets to be seen in all those ads—unconstrained by the realities of weight and bandwidth, among other things.

It's fun to conceive of the future before it arrives, but the future has a funny way of ending up quite unlike what anyone expected. Just look back at the concept of "future" that was current in the '50s and '60s (let's not forget the Jetsons!), and you'll see what I mean. All the advances in all the sciences haven't changed the fundamental unpredictability of the future.

Even so, what ***would*** it be like to have VR—really good VR? I think in some ways, we already know. You might not realize it, but you have been exposed to some cutting-edge VR already, in your neighborhood movie theater. Not every time you go, mind you, but sometimes, yes, it's virtually real in that dark room, full of flickering lights and magic.

It's the magic, you see, that makes the difference between virtual reality and artificial reality. Having HMDs, data gloves, 3D stereo, head tracking—that's all just the mechanics of VR, and constitutes mere artificial reality. It's like a plastic apple—it's interesting until you pick it up and try to bite into it.

Without the magic—what the literature instructor in college calls a "willing suspension of disbelief"—VR is all mechanics and no soul. True, good mechanics make it easier, just as *Star Wars'* special effects made that movie so much more fun. But without the spookiness of Darth Vader, the boyish charm of Luke, and the mystery of Obi Wan, it would have been just another pile of nuts and bolts.

The purpose of art—and VR is no less an art than any other—is to stir the imagination, and the model is just one piece of the puzzle.

VREAM and Modeling

In Chapter 5, we took a look at one of the premiere VR development packages: Superscape. At $10,000 or thereabouts per copy, it is not what you would call mainstream VR software. But it is powerful and flexible. Let's take a few steps down toward reality and discuss an affordable package: VREAM. The version of VREAM covered in this chapter isn't the one you'll see on the store shelves, however; a new version was due out just as we were going to press. It should be available as you read this chapter.

VREAM as it is covered here is a mid-level product in almost every regard. It isn't as sophisticated as Superscape, but it has more features than the low-end products like Virtual Reality Studio (discussed later in this chapter). VREAM strikes a balance between price and features, and is a good product for getting started with VR modeling.

The interface is a bit awkward, but it can be mastered with a little persistence. The big problem—as with any VR tool—is moving around in 3D space while working on a 2D device: your computer screen. The Logitech Cyberman helps, of course, but the keyboard is laid out logically and need only be memorized. The keystrokes for moving around will be revealed shortly.

First, figure 9.3 shows a scene rendered in VREAM. The first thing to notice is that the resolution is low—320×200. This is true only of the version of VREAM current at the time I am writing—by the time you are reading this, a higher-resolution version will be available.

Figure 9.3. A city scene created with VREAM.

Even at low resolution, however, the results look good. It's easy to tell that the house is a house, the tree is a tree, and so on. This is because VREAM does a great job of handling scene lighting—a real plus, as it gives you excellent 3D cues. The only time you may get disoriented is when you get very close to an object.

VREAM supports texture mapping, which allows you to add realistic surface features to objects. You can have brick walls, signs, fabrics, and so on just by creating a PCX image.

Figure 9.3 is an exterior scene. You can move around in the scene and look at the various objects. You can even go inside certain objects, such as the house, where you will encounter yet another level of detail. Figure 9.4 shows a scene in the interior of the house—there's a box of cereal on the counter, a picture on the wall, and so on. There are plenty of cues to help you recognize the 3D nature of the space.

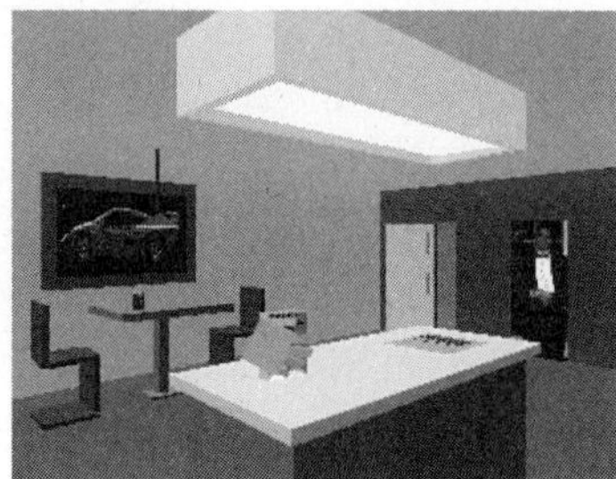

Figure 9.4. An interior space created with VREAM.

If you look closely at the box of cereal, you will note that there is a hand grasping it. VREAM allows you to grab objects in the 3D space and manipulate them. This can be done with the mouse or by using a Mattel Powerglove.

VREAM also allows you to establish some realistic parameters for your universe, such as gravity and light. This means that objects will fall when dropped, for example. This level of realism makes up for the lack of high resolution in VREAM—and the next version, which will add higher resolution, should make VREAM a great package.

That said, I found VREAM more awkward to use than Superscape. I'll discuss some of the problems I had in the next section.

Working with VREAM

When you first run VREAM, you'll see the screen shown in figure 9.5. It gives you three choices:

- Run the VREAM 3D World Editor
- Invoke the VREAM runtime system
- Exit

Simply put, you use the 3D World Editor to create your VR world, and the runtime system to explore it.

The World Editor is shown in figure 9.6. It consists of a menu bar at the top, with a couple of status bars below it. The work area occupies most of the screen, and there are two rows of tools at the bottom.

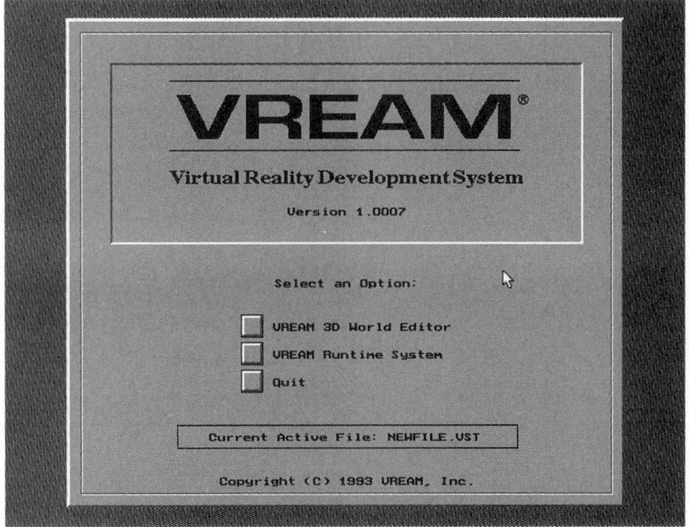

Figure 9.5. The VREAM opening screen.

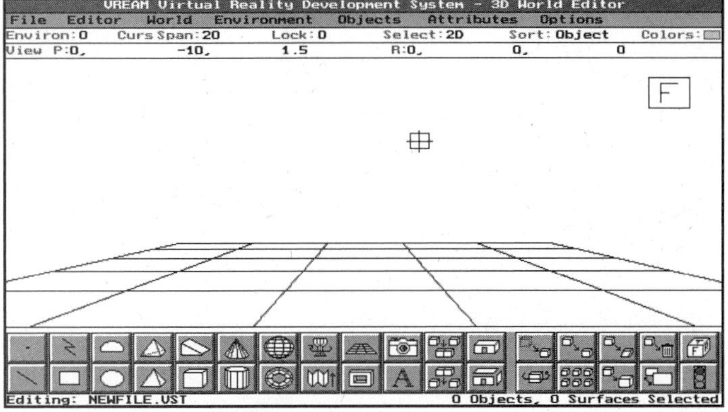

Figure 9.6. The VREAM 3D World Editor, ready to create a fresh new world.

VREAM isn't exactly intuitive—at least it wasn't for me. The first time I ran it, I was totally confused, and couldn't figure out how to do anything at all! I always worry when this happens, because I think that software should be so logical that you just *know* how to use it.

That's also pretty unrealistic, especially when it comes to 3D software. Fortunately, VREAM comes with a detailed tutorial that will help you learn what all the menu choices and icons can do for you. I'll cover a subset of the operations available to you in a tutorial of my own and provide a complete reference to the icons.

However, I think it's a good idea to review the VREAM manuals[3] to learn the fine points of many of the tools. They aren't as sophisticated as Superscape's tools, but there are nuances to their use that you'll have to know to avoid mistakes. For example, it's critical to always create in a counterclockwise direction if you want stuff to be on the correct side of a face.

VREAM 3D World Editor Tools

One of the major components of the World Editor is the toolbar, which lets you create and edit objects to be included in your virtual world. The toolbar is displayed at the bottom of the screen, and is composed of a series of buttons. Figure 9.7 shows you the name of the various tools. Refer to these names on the next few pages as we discuss what each tool can do for you.

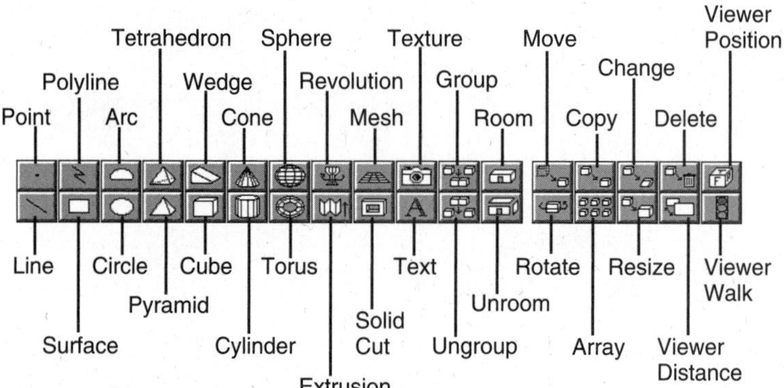

Figure 9.7. The VREAM 3D World Editor's toolbar revealed.

The toolbar contains two kinds of tools: Drawing/Creating tools and Editing tools. To select a tool, just use your basic button-pushing skills: Position the cursor over the button and click with the left mouse button. You will then have to watch the bottom of the screen for instructions specific to each tool. For example, when you create a cube, you'll be asked for the width, depth, and height in sequence. You provide these measurements, of course, by clicking and dragging.

Drawing/Creating Tools

The left side of the toolbar is composed of Object Draw tools that are used to create object primitives, groups, and rooms.[4]

---

[3]Yes, there's more than one—VREAM comes in a ***big*** black box.

[4]I like this idea of creating an entire room. VREAM was the first product we encountered that had such a logical feature. The implementation is a bit weird if you like things like windows and doors, but it works great.

POINT TOOL

The Point tool creates a single-point object or multiple-point objects by defining each point individually. Each point is defined by a single point in space, and is displayed on the screen as a single pixel. This tool is intended to be used as a reference object in the Environment Editor rather than as a finished object in worlds. For instance, points may be placed throughout the environment, and then locked on to with the Point-Tracker feature when drawing other object primitives.

LINE TOOL

The Line tool lets you create a single-line object or multiple-line objects by defining the two endpoints for each line. You can draw a series of line endpoints by using the second endpoint for the current line as the first endpoint for the next line.

POLYLINE TOOL

The Polyline tool lets you create a single polyline object that contains multiple line segments by defining the endpoints for each line segment in the polyline. The Polyline tool is similar to the Line tool in that you use the second endpoint for the current line segment as the first endpoint for the next line segment. The main difference between the two is that the Line tool enables you to create multiple single-line objects, whereas the Polyline tool enables you to create a single polyline object consisting of multiple line segments.

SURFACE TOOL (3-SIDED SURFACE)

The Three-Sided Surface tool lets you create a single surface (polygon) object that contains exactly three sides, by defining the three points that define the surface. The VREAM Environment Editor also contains a Four-Sided and an N-Sided Surface tool, but the Three-Sided Surface tool is more efficient for defining three-sided objects.

Each individual surface object must be a *convex* surface—that is, a surface that contains interior angles at each of its vertices that are less than 180 degrees. In order to create a *concave* surface (one containing an interior angle greater than 180 degrees), you can group together two or more convex surfaces.

SURFACE TOOL (4-SIDED SURFACE)

The Four-Sided Surface tool lets you create a single surface (polygon) object that contains exactly four sides by defining the four points that define the surface.

Like the Three-Sided Surface tool, each individual surface object must be a convex surface (a surface that contains interior angles at each of its vertices that are less than 180 degrees). In order to create a concave surface, you can group together two or more convex surfaces.

SURFACE TOOL (N-SIDED SURFACE)

The N-Sided Surface tool lets you create a single surface (polygon) object that contains from 3 to 256 sides. The number of sides of the polygon, along with the positions of the N points in space that comprise the polygon, are defined by you. If you exit from the N-Sided Surface tool before setting at least 3 points, no surface object will be created.

ARC TOOL

The Arc tool lets you create an arc object based on the definition of a center point for the arc, the radius arc, the start and stop angles for the arc, and the number of segments along the circumference of the arc. The arc objects will have varying resolutions based on the number of segments used along the circumference of the arc. A high-resolution arc containing many sides along its circumference will appear more rounded, but will also require more processing.

CIRCLE TOOL

The Circle tool lets you create a circle object by defining the center point of the circle, the radius circle, and the number of segments along the circumference of the circle. By letting you define the number of segments along the circumference of the circle, this tool gives you the option of creating circle objects of varying resolutions. For instance, a high-resolution circle (one containing many sides along its circumference) will appear more rounded, but will also require more processing.

One of the features of the Circle tool is that you can draw perfect polygons containing a number of sides equal to the number of segments specified for the circle. Say, for instance, that you enter a value of 16 or more for the number of segments; you will create a rounded polygon approaching a circle. However, if you enter a smaller value for the number of segments, the Circle tool can be used to create perfect polygon surfaces of varying sides. For example, a perfect pentagon will be generated if you create a five-sided circle, and a perfect hexagon will be generated if you create a six-sided circle.

TETRAHEDRON TOOL

The Tetrahedron tool lets you create a tetrahedron object based on the definition of a base point for the tetrahedron, along with the height, width, and depth of the tetrahedron. You are prompted to set each of these values.

PYRAMID TOOL

The Pyramid tool lets you create a pyramid object based on the definition of a base point for the pyramid, along with the height, width, and depth of the pyramid. You are prompted to set each of these values.

WEDGE TOOL

The Wedge tool lets you create a wedge object based on the definition of a base point for the wedge, along with the height, width, and depth of the wedge. You are prompted to set each of these values.

CUBE TOOL

The Cube tool lets you create a cube object based on the definition of a base point for the cube, along with the height, width, and depth of the cube. You are prompted to set each of these values.

CONE TOOL

The Cone tool lets you create a cone object based on the definition of a center point for the base of the cone, the radius of the base of the cone, the height of the cone, and the number of sides along the circumference of the cone. You can select a number from 3 to 256 for the number of sides of the cone; the default value is 16. You are prompted to set each of these values.

You can define the number of sides along the circumference of the cone, which lets you create cone objects of varying resolutions. A high-resolution cone (one containing many sides along its circumference) will appear more rounded, but will also require more processing.

CYLINDER TOOL

The Cylinder tool lets you create a cylinder object based on the definition of a center point for the base of the cylinder, the radius of the base of the cylinder, the height of the cylinder, and the number of sides along the circumference of the cylinder (an integer value from 3 to 256; the default is 16). You are prompted to set each of these values.

You can define the number of sides on the circumference of the cylinder, to create cylinder objects of varying resolutions. A high-resolution cylinder (one containing many sides along its circumference) will appear more rounded, but will require more processing.

SPHERE TOOL

The Sphere tool lets you create a sphere object based on the definition of the center of the sphere, the radius of the sphere, and the number of longitudinal and latitudinal segments of the sphere. You are prompted to set each of these values.

You can create sphere objects of varying resolutions by defining the number of longitudinal and latitudinal segments of the sphere. A high-resolution sphere (one containing many longitudinal and latitudinal segments) will appear more rounded, but will also require more processing.

TORUS TOOL

The Torus tool lets you create a torus object based on the definition of the center of the torus, the radius of the torus, the radius of the tube comprising the torus, the number of tube segments, and the number of torus segments. You are prompted to set each of these values.

You can create torus objects of varying resolutions by defining the number of torus and tube segments. A high-resolution torus (one containing many sides and tube segments) will appear more rounded, but will also require more processing.

REVOLUTION TOOL

The Revolution tool lets you create a surface-of-revolution object based on the definition of a polyline object (to serve as the object to be revolved), the center of the surface of revolution (around which the polyline will be revolved), the angles through which the revolution will take place, and the number of sides that will comprise the circumference of the surface revolution. You are prompted to set each of these values.

In order to use this tool, you must have already created a single polyline object using the Polyline tool. You can create partially revolved objects by specifying start and stop angles that cover less than a 360-degree rotational area.

You can create revolution objects of varying resolutions by defining the number of revolution sides. A high-resolution revolution (one containing many sides along its circumference) appears more rounded, but also requires more processing.

EXTRUSION TOOL

The Extrusion tool lets you create a surface-of-extrusion object based on the definition of a polyline object (to serve as the object to be extruded), the direction and magnitude of the extrusion, and the number of levels that will comprise the surface of the extrusion. You are prompted to set each of these values.

In order to use this tool, a single polyline object must have been previously created using the Polyline tool. The Extrusion tool will extrude the selected polyline into 3D space based on a direction and magnitude defined by you.

You can create extrusion objects of varying resolutions by defining the number of extrusion levels. A high-resolution extrusion (one containing many levels) will contain more component polygon surfaces along its extruded length, but will also require more processing.

MESH TOOL

The Mesh tool lets you create a general polygon mesh object that is bounded on four sides by straight lines. The mesh object consists of multiple four-sided polygons that are interconnected to form a meshed surface. You are prompted to define the mesh by entering the four bounding corners of the mesh, along with the number of rows and columns of lines that will be used to comprise the polygons of the mesh.

The mesh object primarily consists of rows and columns of lines in 3D space joined together to form a surface of multiple four-sided polygons. If, for example, a mesh object is created having 5 rows and 4 columns, then a mesh is created having 20 vertex points ($5 \times 4 = 20$) bounding 12 internal polygons. Each of the 20 points within the mesh can be individually manipulated. This lets you form a flat mesh surface into a bumpy terrain by individually changing the position of the vertex points along the mesh surface. Additionally, the individual polygons within the mesh object can be set to different colors using the Surface Color option from within the Attribute menu.

You can create mesh objects of varying resolutions by defining the number of rows and columns within the mesh. A high-resolution mesh (containing many rows and columns) will contain more component polygon surfaces, but will also require more processing.

SOLID CUT TOOL

The Solid Cut tool lets you cut a hole in a currently existing surface object. The Solid Cut tool is capable of cutting a four-sided rectangular hole in a four-sided surface object primitive. You will be prompted to set the four solid cut points.

You can use the Solid Cut tool to create multiple types of effects when building virtual worlds with the VREAM system. It is especially useful for cutting holes for windows and doors out of surfaces that are used to build room objects. This lets the viewer easily see inside a room from the outside, or view the area outside a room from the inside.

TEXTURE TOOL

The Texture tool lets you create a single texture object that is bounded by exactly four sides, by defining the four points that define the texture and by selecting the PCX image file that will be displayed as the texture. You are prompted to set the four texture points.

You can use the Texture tool to incorporate photorealistic textures into virtual-reality worlds. *Textures* are digitized representations of real-life images such as a picture of a person or the wooden grain of a table. Texture information usually represents two-dimensional (flat) data, but within the VREAM system, two-dimensional texture information can be applied to a polygonal surface residing in three-dimensional space.

You can create a texture object by defining a four-sided polygon in space and by selecting a PCX bitmap image file to be applied to the surface area comprising the four-sided polygon. A PCX bitmap file must be created that contains the desired image to be displayed as the texture. The PCX file format is a standard graphics file format supported by a wide variety of graphics paint programs. The PCX file can be created in many ways: by scanning a picture using a digital scanner, by drawing an image from scratch using a paint program, or by converting an image from another file format into a PCX file using a graphics-conversion program.

TEXT TOOL

The Text tool lets you create a text object by defining the characters to be contained in the text object, the position of the text in space, the font style to be used in creating the text, and the font size to be used in the text. You can set the font style and font size prior to selecting the Text Tool button. Do this by selecting the Font Style and Font Size options from the Editor menu. You will be prompted to define the actual characters to be displayed in the text object and the position of the text object. Use the keyboard to enter the text characters and the 3D cursor to define the position of the text.

The text object can contain any text passage you want, up to 80 characters (including spaces). VREAM uses a set of standard-stroked[(5)] font files to provide the information required to generate text characters in different font formats. The Text tool internally constructs the specified text passage using standard lines to create the words in 3D space. Even though the text object is actually a two-dimensional (flat) object, it can be used as detail lettering on all types of objects such as signs,

[5]A standard-stroked font is one that has no crossing lines or other elements that would prevent it from being projected into the third dimension cleanly.

billboards, books, and so on. And because the text object is an actual object primitive within VREAM, it can be given attributes like all other objects. This means that a text object can be given motion so that it rotates and moves, its size and color can be altered, it can be picked up and moved around with the 3D Hand, and it can be used as the condition or response object of a dynamic link. Additionally, certain font styles can be extruded into 3D space to easily create three-dimensional text. This can be done with the Extrusion tool.

GROUP TOOL

The Group tool lets you create a group object consisting of one or more previously created objects. To use the Group tool, select one or more objects that were previously created within the active environment. Define a group object by clicking the Group Tool button once the desired objects have been selected, and then enter a name for the group object in response to Group tool prompts.

The Grouping feature lets you combine multiple objects (3D primitives, groups, and rooms) and create a group of object primitives that can be treated by the system as a single object. For example, four elongated cube objects can be grouped with one flattened cube object to create a table with four legs. This single group object can be assigned attributes, resized, moved, and used to serve as the condition or response object for a dynamic link, just like any other standard object.

UNGROUP TOOL

The Ungroup tool lets you break a group object down into its component objects. To use the Ungroup tool, one or more group objects must have been previously created and selected within the active environment. To ungroup a group object, select the desired group object(s) and click the Ungroup Tool button.

The Ungrouping feature lets you break down group objects into their next level of hierarchical object components. For example, a group named MAINGROUP may be comprised of a cube object primitive and a group object named SUBGROUP. When the group MAINGROUP is ungrouped, it will be broken down into the cube object primitive and the group SUBGROUP. Note that the group SUBGROUP will not be broken down because it is one hierarchical level removed from the affected group. Select the group SUBGROUP to break it down into its component parts.

ROOM TOOL (CUSTOM ROOM)

The Custom Room tool lets you create a room object consisting of one or more previously created 2D surface object primitives. The 2D surface object primitives that can be used to create a custom room using the Custom Room tool are the three-sided surface, four-sided surface, N-sided surface, arc, and circle. One or more 2D surface objects must have been previously created and selected within the active environment in order to use the Custom Room tool.

The Room feature combines multiple 2D surface objects, thereby creating a room of 2D surface object primitives that can be treated by the system as a single object. For example, six four-sided surfaces can be roomed together to form an enclosed rectangular room. This single room object can be assigned attributes, resized, moved, and used to serve as the condition or response object for a dynamic link, just like any other standard object.

Room objects are special objects within the VREAM system. They are created as a single entity (constructed from surface objects), but they can hold other objects inside them that can be independently manipulated. Rooms can be constructed with doors and windows, which allows the viewer to see inside the room from the outside, or to look outside the room from the inside.

You create room objects by combining 2D surface objects (as the walls of the room) so they collectively enclose a common space that is defined as the inside of the room. These 2D surface objects that comprise the walls of the room can be combined in a variety of ways to create a room. Rooms can be created in the shape of rectangular boxes, pyramids, cylinders, spheres, and many other shapes.

ROOM TOOL (ROOM FROM OBJECT PRIMITIVE)

The Room from Object Primitive tool lets you create a room object from a previously created 3D object primitive. The room object will be formed in the exact shape of the 3D object primitive. The 3D object primitives that can be used to create a room with this tool are the tetrahedron, pyramid, wedge, cube, cone, cylinder, and sphere. To use this tool, exactly one 3D object primitive must have been previously selected within the active environment. Define the room object by clicking the Room Tool button once you have selected the desired object, and then enter a name for the room object when prompted by the Room tool.

The Room from Object Primitive feature lets you automatically convert a single 3D object primitive to a single room object containing multiple 2D surface objects that serve as walls for the room. For example, a single cube object can be converted to a room object that contains six four-sided surface objects defining the walls of the enclosed, rectangular room. This single room object can be assigned attributes, resized, moved, and used to serve as the condition or response object for a dynamic link, just like any other standard object.

Room objects are special objects within the VREAM system. They are created as a single entity (constructed from surface objects serving as walls of the room), but can hold other objects inside them that can be independently manipulated. Rooms can be constructed with doors and windows, which lets the viewer see inside the room from the outside or view outside the room from the inside.

There are generally two ways of creating room objects with the VREAM system: Use the Custom Room tool, which requires that the surfaces that define each wall be individually created and formed into the shape of an enclosed room; or use the Room from Object Primitive tool, which allows you to easily create room objects from a single 3D object primitive. This is possible because the VREAM system internally breaks the selected 3D object primitive down into its component surfaces and then reconstructs those surfaces in the form of a room object.

UNROOM TOOL

The Unroom tool lets you break a room object down into its component surface object primitives. To use the Unroom tool, select one or more room objects that were previously created and are within the active environment. To unroom a room object, select the desired room object(s) and click the Unroom Tool button.

The Unroom feature breaks down room objects into their next level of hierarchical object components. In the case of a room object, this next level of components will always consist of surface object primitives (three-sided surfaces, four-sided surfaces, N-sided surfaces, arcs, and circles). So, when a room is unroomed, the resultant objects in the environment will always be surface object primitives. However, unlike a group object that can contain other groups, a room is limited in the kind of objects it can contain. For example, a room cannot contain another room or a group, but a room can be contained by a group. This lets you break down a group into one or more rooms, but does not let you break down a room into one or more groups.

Editing Tools

The right side of the toolbar is composed of the Object Edit tools that are used to edit existing objects and to change the current viewer's position in space.

MOVE TOOL

The Move tool lets you move objects from one position in space to another within the same environment. You must have previously created and selected one or more objects within the active environment in order to use the Move tool. You define the distance and direction in which the object(s) are to be moved by drawing a vector in 3D space. The direction and magnitude from the beginning point of the vector to the ending point of the vector will define the change in distance and direction for the object(s). You are prompted to set each of these values.

ROTATE TOOL

The Rotate tool lets you rotate objects from one orientation in space to another. In order to use the Rotate tool, you must have previously created and selected one or more objects within the active environment. You define the desired rotation for selected objects by entering values into a dialog box defining the yaw, pitch, and roll of the object(s). You are prompted to set each of these values.

The values used to define yaw, pitch, and roll offsets of the selected object(s) are indicated in degrees. These values represent the amount that the objects are to be rotated (around their natural centers) in each of the respective directions. Note that the values entered in the Rotate dialog box define relative offset values for the yaw, pitch, and roll of the selected object(s), based on their current orientation in space. So if you enter a yaw value of 10 degrees, the current orientation of the selected object will be updated by 10 degrees in the yaw direction. If you again enter a yaw value of 10 degrees for the same object, it will be rotated another 10 degrees in the yaw direction, making the total offset from the original orientation a total of 20 degrees.

COPY TOOL

The Copy tool lets you copy objects within the active environment and define the precise location in space of the newly copied objects. The Copy tool performs a similar function to the Move tool, except that the Copy tool generates an exact duplicate of a selected object in addition to moving it in the specified direction and distance.

To use the Copy tool, you must have previously created and selected one or more objects within the active environment. You then select the objects to be copied and define the distance and direction in which the object(s) are to be moved by drawing a vector in 3D space. The difference in direction and magnitude from the beginning point of the vector to the ending point of the vector will define the change in distance and direction for the object(s). You are prompted to set each of these values.

Note that when an object is copied, most of its attributes are copied along with it. However, certain attributes, such as the name of the object, must be updated so that links and other references that affect the initial object will not be confused by the existence of the copy.

RECTANGULAR ARRAY TOOL

The Rectangular Array tool lets you create multiple copies of objects within the active environment. These copies are arranged in a uniform pattern of rows and columns called a *rectangular array*. You define the number of copies to be made by entering the number of rows and columns of objects to be created. The Rectangular Array tool performs a similar function to the Copy tool, except the Rectangular Array tool generates multiple copies of a selected object with one operation, evenly spacing the resultant objects to your specifications.

To use the Rectangular Array tool, you must have previously created and selected one or more objects within the active environment. You first select the objects to be copied, and then are prompted to specify the number of object copies to be created and their locations. You will also be prompted to enter the number of rows of objects to be created, the number of columns of objects to be created, the distance between objects within each row, and the distance between objects within each column.

Note than when an object is copied (using either the Rectangular Array tool or the Copy tool), most of its attributes are copied along with it. However, certain attributes must be updated, such as the name of the object, so links and other references that affect the initial object will not be confused by the existence of the copy.

CHANGE TOOL (SINGLE POINT)

The Single Point Change tool lets you change the position of a single point within the environment. This single point may be contained by one or more than one object. You can alter the shapes of objects in the environment by changing the position of the points that comprise them. To use the Single Point Change tool, you must have previously created and selected one or more objects within the active environment. After you select the Single Point Change tool, you select the object point to be changed (from one of the selected objects) by selecting it with the 3D cursor in Point-Tracker mode. You then define the distance and direction in which the point is to be moved by drawing a vector in 3D space. The difference in direction and magnitude from the beginning point of the vector to the ending point of the vector will define the distance and direction of the change for the object point. You are prompted to set each of these values.

There are two Change functions available from within the VREAM World Editor Change tool. The Single Point Change tool (which we are currently discussing) lets you change the position of a single point in the environment, whether it belongs to one or multiple objects. The Surface Point Change tool lets you change the positions of multiple points in the environment by selecting one or more object surfaces that contain the desired points. Both Change Tool functions are useful when building VREAM worlds.

CHANGE TOOL (SURFACE POINTS)

The Change Surface Points tool lets you change the positions of multiple points within the environment by selecting the surfaces that contain the desired points, and then by defining a vector to describe the position change. You are prompted to set each of these values.

RESIZE TOOL

The Resize tool lets you change the size of one or more objects within the active environment. The Resize tool will expand or contract a selected object from the natural center of the object outward. Thus, the center of the object will remain in the same position in space, but the position of the points surrounding the center of the object will be updated.

DELETE TOOL

The Delete tool lets you delete one or more objects from the active environment. It provides a mechanism for verification and confirmation of the selected objects prior to deleting them. You will be prompted to verify the Delete operation, at which time you may choose to continue or to cancel the deletion. If the deletion is performed, a confirmation prompt is displayed showing the number of objects that were successfully deleted.

VIEWER DISTANCE TOOL

The Viewer Distance tool lets you move immediately to a specified distance from the current location while maintaining the same orientation in space. This may have the effect of moving the viewer forward or backward, left or right, or up or down within the scene, providing a new view of the current environment.

VIEWER POSITION TOOL (PREDEFINED POSITION)

The predefined Viewer Position tool lets you move immediately to a new, predefined position and orientation in space, so you can view the current scene from a new perspective. When you select the Viewer Position Tool button from the toolbar, VREAM displays a dialog box containing 16 viewer-position options. Fifteen of the options allow the viewer to jump immediately to a new, predefined position and orientation in space. One of the options lets you define a new, unique viewer position and orientation in space.

The Viewer Position tool complements the Viewer Walk tool, which lets you walk through the environment in real time using a variety of interface devices such as a joystick or keyboard. The Viewer Position tool lets you immediately jump to an exact location in space, and is useful in obtaining a new perspective of a scene without taking the time to walk to that new position.

The Viewer Position tool can also be used with the Viewer Distance tool to quickly gain new perspectives of the environment from varying distances. The Viewer Position tool lets you position and orient the viewer in space; the Viewer Distance tool lets you move the viewer into or out of the scene while maintaining the same orientation in space.

VIEWER POSITION TOOL (UNIQUE POSITION)

The Unique Viewer Position tool lets you move immediately to a new unique position and orientation in space, viewing the current scene from a new perspective. After selecting the Viewer Position Tool button, you are prompted to select one of 16 viewer-position options from the dialog box. Fifteen of the options let you jump immediately to a new predefined position and orientation in space, and one of the options lets you define a new, unique viewer position and orientation in space.

VIEWER WALK TOOL

The Viewer Walk tool lets you walk through the current active environment. This feature gives you virtual-reality capabilities within the VREAM 3D World Editor, and lets you walk through environments as they are being built.

The VREAM 3D World Editor lets you operate within two modes: Edit mode and Walk mode. Edit mode is used to perform editing functions, such as drawing objects, assigning attributes, or assigning links. While in Edit mode, you remain primarily stationary in space. You have the ability to jump to a new location in space using the Viewer Position and Viewer Distance tools, but you cannot work through the environment in real time.

When you select the Viewer Walk button, you activate Walk mode in the VREAM 3D World Editor. The viewer lets you walk through the environment using any active interface devices that have been enabled to control the viewer, such as a joystick or the keyboard. While in Walk mode, any active interface device used to control the viewer will let you control all three degrees of translational and rotational freedom of the viewer, which lets you move or rotate in any direction in space. However, you do not have access to the World Editing functions while in Walk mode. To continue editing the current environment, you must exit Walk mode and return to Edit mode.

Note that in order to use interface devices in Walk mode, you must have previously defined and enabled their script commands within the VRMCFIG.SYS file. Some devices are supported by VREAM, and you can use them simply by making the appropriate menu selections. The step-by-step instructions for each device are covered in detail in the VREAM documentation.

The Interface Device commands that control the viewer and the hand for a particular world are stored as World Attribute commands within the script file for that particular world. This configuration lets VREAM maintain active interface devices for the 3D World Editor (stored in VRMCFIG.SYS) separately from the active interface devices for a particular world (stored in the script file for that world). This enables the 3D World Editor to utilize a different set of hardware interface devices than the actual virtual world being developed. Thus, you can freely set and change runtime interface devices while building a virtual world within the 3D World Editor without having to connect them to the system.

At a minimum, you will need a keyboard (for viewer control) and a mouse (for cursor control) while building worlds within the 3D World Editor. The keyboard provides access to the complete range of viewer movement and rotation functions.

Creating with VREAM

That's a lot of preamble, but now it's time to get down to business.(6) Let's create something! Return with me now to the VREAM 3D World Editor's screen. In figure 9.8, I have clicked on the Polyline tool, and then clicked out a multiline path. To end creation, I clicked the left and right mouse buttons simultaneously.

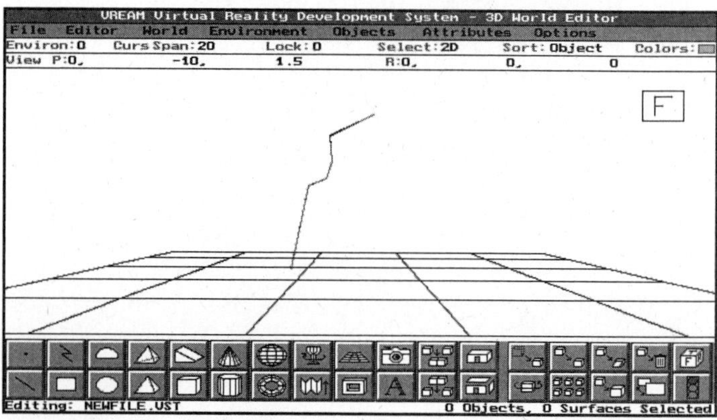

Figure 9.8. Creating a polyline.

---

(6)Our main intention here is to give you as clear a picture of VREAM as we can so you can make an informed purchase decision. If we make a mistake, we'd rather provide too much information, not too little!

The Rotate tool is a splendid tool for dramatic transformation, so we'll use that to create a complex shape from the polyline. To do so, you must click on the polyline to select it, and it must be the ***only*** object selected. To make sure it is the only object, use the Object/Clear All menu selection first. Then click on the polyline. You know an object is selected when you can see little black rectangles at the end points of its lines, as shown in figure 9.9.

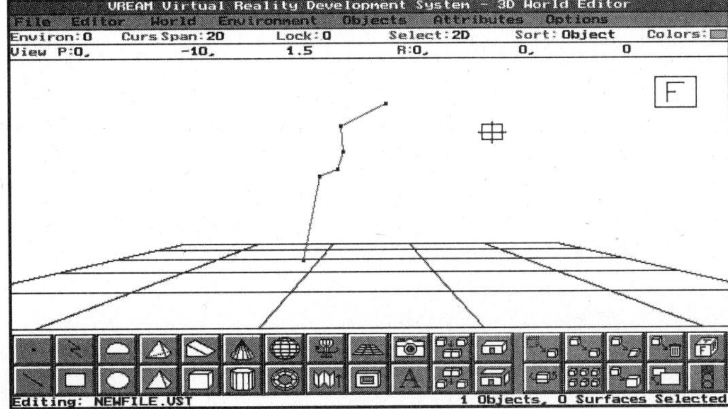

Figure 9.9. The polyline is now selected.

You can have more than one object selected at a time, but some operations require that you have only one object selected. Rotation is one of those operations. Once you have selected the polyline,[7] click on the Rotation tool. It will prompt you for several values, including the starting angle for rotation (I used zero), an ending angle (I used 360, for a complete circle), and a center of rotation. Figure 9.10 shows the results—a 3D shape that was created by rotating the polyline in space.

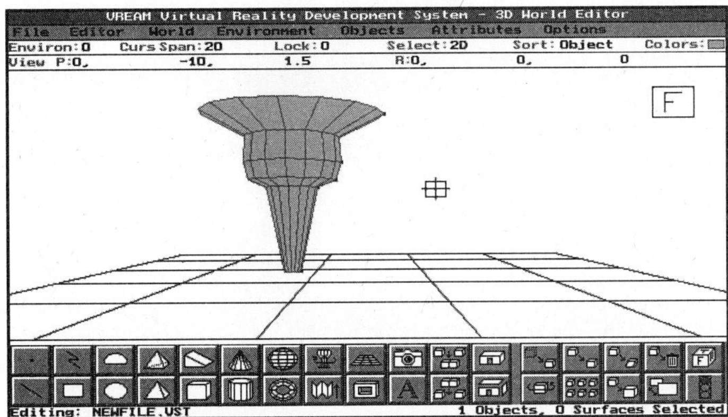

Figure 9.10. The completed rotation.

[7]And only the polyline...

If you specify less than a 360-degree rotation, the beginning and ending polylines will be joined. You can make the join transparent by setting appropriate surface values for those faces.

You can create all kinds of primitive shapes with the various Drawing/Creation tools. Figure 9.11 shows a variety of different objects, including a wedge, a torus, and a sphere.

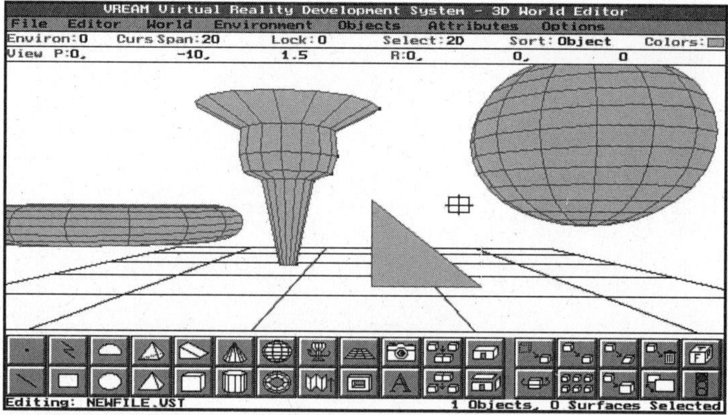

Figure 9.11. A variety of 3D objects created with the World Editor.

As you have been working, you have been creating a script for your world—you just aren't aware of it—and, in many cases, you don't need to be aware. Figure 9.12 shows the script behind the simple world we've created so far. It looks pretty scary, and it is. Most of the time—and especially while you are getting started—you can ignore the existence of the script. Once you become proficient and start thinking up cool things for your world to do, you'll find that sometimes the only way to get the job done is to edit the script.

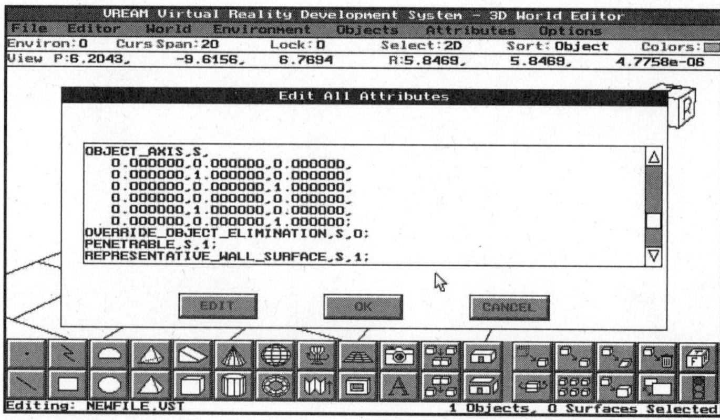

Figure 9.12. Viewing and editing the script for your world.

Fortunately, most of the attributes of an object can be set with the menus. Figure 9.13 shows the choices available on the Attributes menu. You can define an object's touch distance, rotation, and many other characteristics.

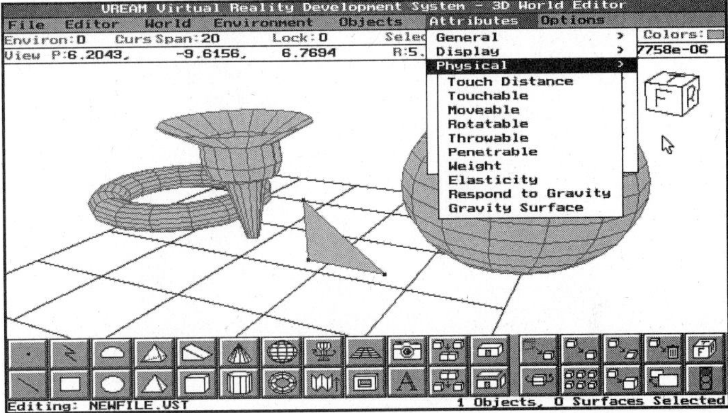

Figure 9.13. Setting object attributes with the menu.

Another thing to note about figure 9.12 is that the point from which we are viewing the world has changed. The button at the bottom right, the Walk tool, allows you to use the keyboard to change your point of view. The mouse affects the hand (if present), which is used for grabbing, pointing, and pushing. The following keystrokes and mouse moves are worth knowing:[8]

System Control

Key	*Action*
F5	Hand on/off
F6	Wireframe on/off
F7	Solid on/off
F8	Hide wireframe on/off
F10	Quit
Alt-X	Quit
Shift	Move and rotate faster (with movement keys)

[8]In fact, if you work with VREAM, you'll probably want to copy this list and paste it on the wall next to your screen.

Clicking the left and right mouse buttons simultaneously will terminate the current drawing or editing action, and is also used to terminate walking.[9]

Movement

Key	*Action*
q	View moves left
w	View moves right
a	View moves backward
s	View moves forward
z	View moves down
x	View moves up

Rotation

Key	*Action*
e	View yaws left
r	View yaws right
d	View pitches down
f	View pitches up
c	View rolls left
v	View rolls right

[9]Not knowing this simple fact can make it very frustrating for a new user. Imagine entering Walk mode and then finding no intuitive way to get back out. You can't click on the Walk tool because the mouse has other work to do (moving the hand). It would be nicer if there were screen zones and moving the mouse out of the work area would turn it back into a pointer, so you could click the Walk button to turn it off.

Hand Movement

Mouse Move	*Action*
Left move	Hand moves left
Right move	Hand moves right
Up move	Hand moves up
Down move	Hand moves down
Right Click + Up move	Hand moves forward
Right Click + Down move	Hand moves backward

Hand Rotation

Mouse Move	*Action*
Middle Click + Right move	Hand yaws left
Middle Click + Left move	Hand yaws right
Middle Click + Down move	Hand pitches down
Middle Click + Up move	Hand pitches up
Right Click + Left move	Hand rolls left
Right Click + Right move	Hand rolls right

Hand-Finger Movement

Mouse move	*Action*
Left Click	Make fist (grab)
Right Click + Left move	Index finger in (push)
Right Click + Middle Click	Thumb in (point)

These controls are awkward at best, but they do work if you practice them. And it will take some practice! If you have access to a 3D-input device, such as a Cyberman, you'll find it easier to move around. The best thing about a 3D-input device, though, is using it to operate the hand—the operation becomes much, much more intuitive with a 3D-input device. I found myself needing to "walk" about the world frequently, to check my work, or to gain access to a particular face on a particular object.

To return to a standard view of your world after walking about, click the Position tool (immediately above the Walk tool, at the right). This allows you to choose from a variety of views: Front, Top, Right, Right-Front, and many more.

Once you have created the objects in your world, you can set global parameters for the world. For example, if you want the world to work with a Cyberman during runtime, you can click on the World menu, shown in figure 9.14. One of the selections is Interface Devices, which will open a dialog box allowing you to choose an alternate input device for the world.[10] Advanced users can write scripts to process incoming events from the input device. This allows you to have the device control objects in the world. For example, you might want to have the user control a car using the Cyberman.

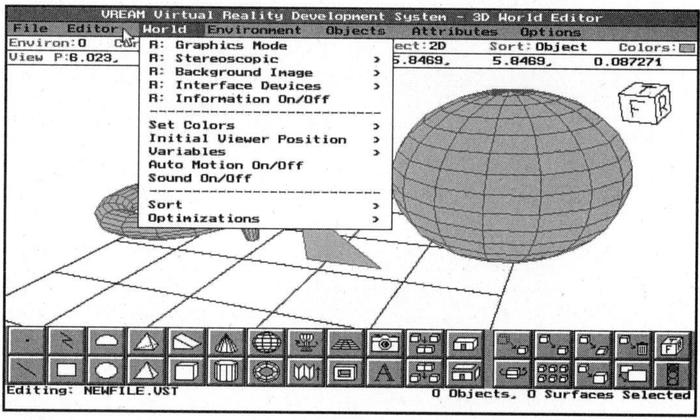

Figure 9.14. Setting global values for your world.

To view your world with the runtime module, simply exit the 3D World Editor and return to the main screen. Select the runtime system, and VREAM will put you right into your world. Figure 9.15 shows the runtime view of the sample world I've created so far.[11]

---

[10]This makes it easy, but it also means that you'll have to save a different version of your world for each input device.

[11]Note that the index finger on the glove is bent. This was unintentional; it's normally all fingers up unless you click the mouse buttons. In this case, the screen capture program required me to press both the right and left buttons to capture a screen. This causes the hand's index finger to close, as you'll see in many of the figures.

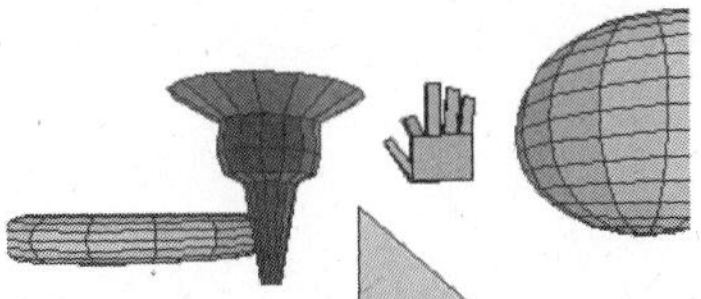

Figure 9.15. Using the VREAM runtime system.

You can use the same keys to move around during runtime that you use with the Walk tool during development. Figure 9.16 shows another point of view after moving around a bit. It also shows the hand closed around the object we created with the Rotate tool—I grabbed the object by clicking the left button and, while keeping the left button down, I moved the mouse, and the object moved with the hand. This is the basic VREAM grab.

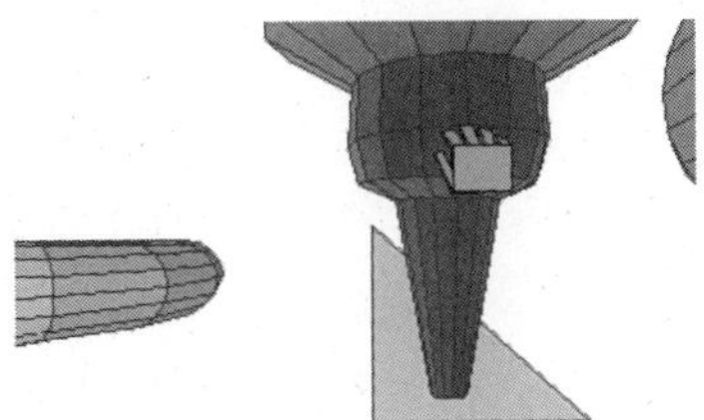

Figure 9.16. Grabbing an object with the hand.

You can modify the appearance of the runtime model with the function keys. In figure 9.17, I have turned off the wireframe lines, which gives a more realistic look to the world.

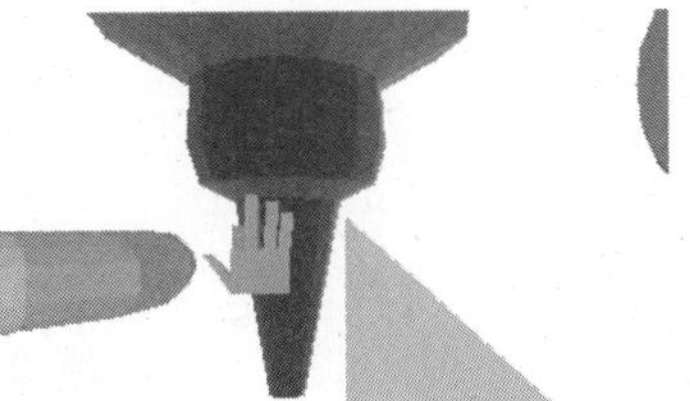

Figure 9.17. Wireframes are now off.

You can also rotate your point of view, as shown in figure 9.18. Rotation takes a bit longer than other forms of navigation, because it is a significant change in your point of view and takes some additional calculating on VREAM's part.

Figure 9.18. Rotating the point of view.

I can't overemphasize what I've said before: when it comes to navigating with the keyboard, practice, practice, practice.

Alternate Output Devices

One of the areas in which VREAM really shines is in the use of alternate output devices, including Crystal Eyes, the Cyberscope, and HMDs. As with input devices, you must use the World menu to set a specific output device for your world. Figure 9.19 shows the output VREAM uses for a Cyberscope, while figure 9.20 shows the output for Crystal Eyes. As you can see, VREAM creates two images—one for each eye. In each case, the device takes care of making sure that only one image goes to each eye.

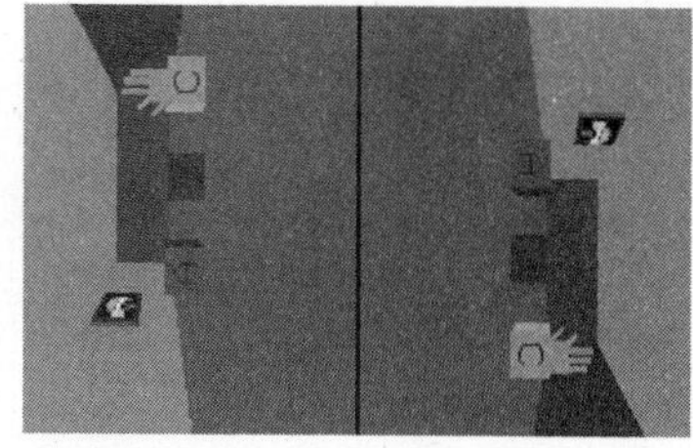

Figure 9.19. VREAM output for a Cyberscope.

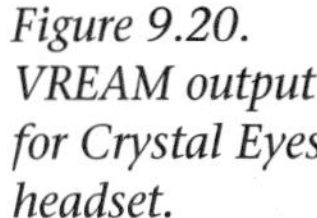

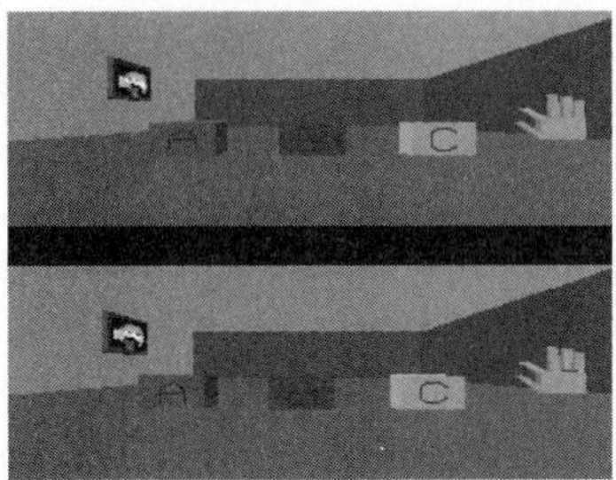

Figure 9.20. VREAM output for Crystal Eyes headset.

See Chapter 13 for a low-cost method of using the Crystal Eyes output with LCD shutter glasses, courtesy of 3DTV Corporation. See Chapter 7 for information about many different kinds of input and output hardware.

Creating a Room with VREAM

We've covered a lot of territory about VREAM, but we have one more step to take: using VREAM to create a virtual room. This is the basic process of creating spaces with VREAM, and you can easily move on to add furniture or other objects to a room once you understand the basic concepts.

We begin as we did in the first example: with the VREAM 3D World Editor. We'll create our room from a cubic shape. The first step: click the Cube tool and follow the prompts to lay out a slightly flattened cube (see fig. 9.21). You will be asked to use the mouse to mark the width, depth, and height of the cube.

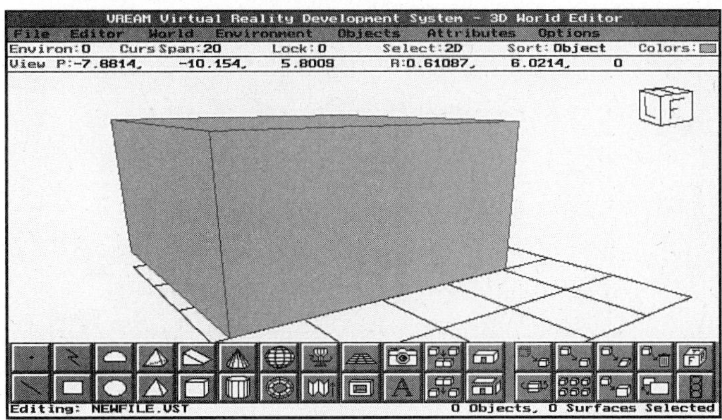

Figure 9.21. The VREAM World Editor, with a cubic shape created.

As when we rotated the polyline to create an object, the first step is to select the cube, and only the cube. To select the cube, click anywhere on it with the cursor. Figure 9.22 shows what the cube should look like when it is selected—there will be small black rectangles at the vertices.

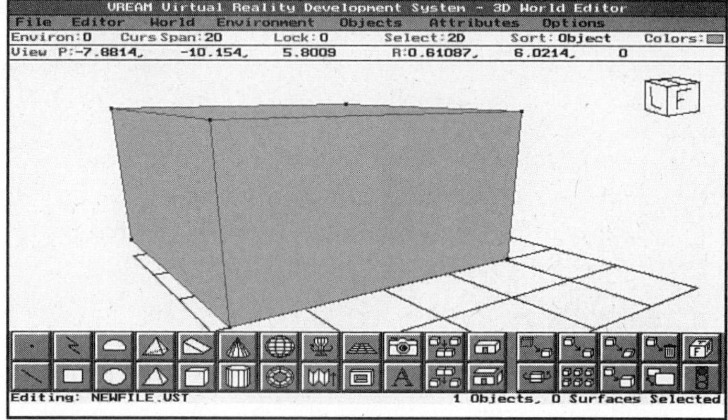

Figure 9.22. Selecting the cube.

Now click on the Room tool. This displays the dialog box shown in figure 9.23, which asks you if you want to create a room from a primitive shape (yes) or create a custom room (not right now). Click and respond to the prompts at the bottom of the screen.

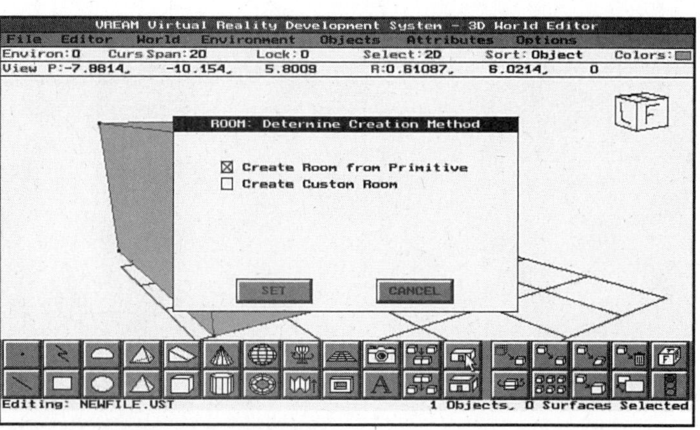

Figure 9.23. Creating a room.

The most notable effect of this process is that there is no noticeable effect. The cube looks just like it did before we started, as shown in figure 9.24. Let's take a moment to look at what has actually happened here.

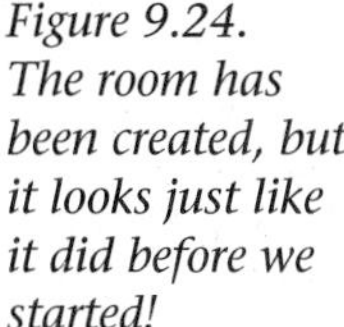

Figure 9.24. The room has been created, but it looks just like it did before we started!

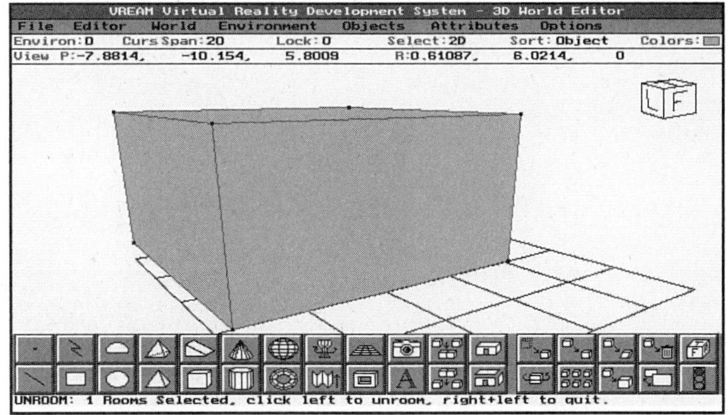

The cube we created was all one object. It had six sides, and if you tried to move any part of it, you moved the whole cube. When we turned the cube into a room, we made each of the sides into its own object—we now have six objects. These objects don't look any different, because they are positioned in exactly the same place as the cube's sides.

To verify the nature of the change, use the Unroom tool to take the room apart. It won't be turned back into a cube; it will turn into six separate objects. You can then use the Move tool to move one of the sides to reveal the interior (see fig. 9.25). Use the same basic maneuvers for any VREAM tool: Select the object, click the tool, and follow the dialog box at the bottom of the screen.

Figure 9.25. One of the sides has been moved.

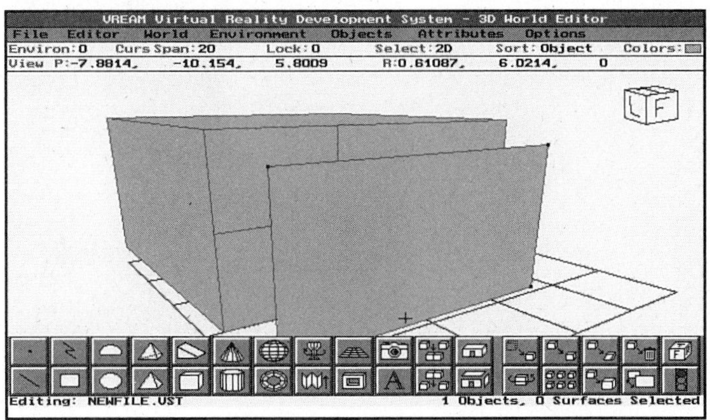

So far, we have a pretty boring room—there are no windows or doors. These are easy to create with the Cut tool. To cut out a portion of a wall for a door, for example, select the wall, click the Cut tool, and then click on the points that define the opening. Figure 9.26 shows a door cut into a wall with the Cut tool.

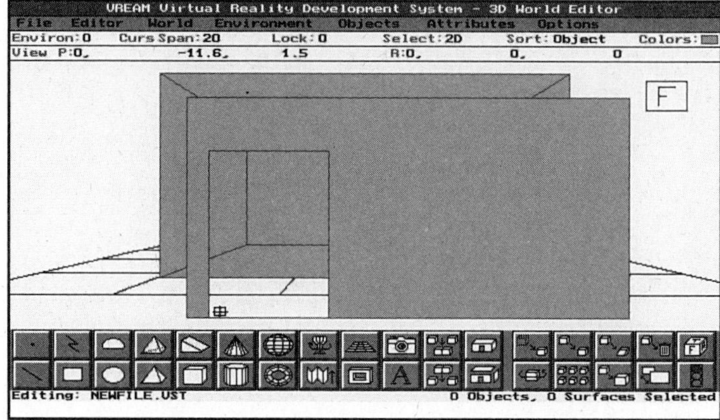

Figure 9.26. Creating a door with the Cut tool.

It will be easier to make the door exactly rectangular if you use the status bars to note the position of the cursor. Figure 9.27 shows the dialog box for selecting one of the three status display modes. You can also change modes by pressing the F3 key.

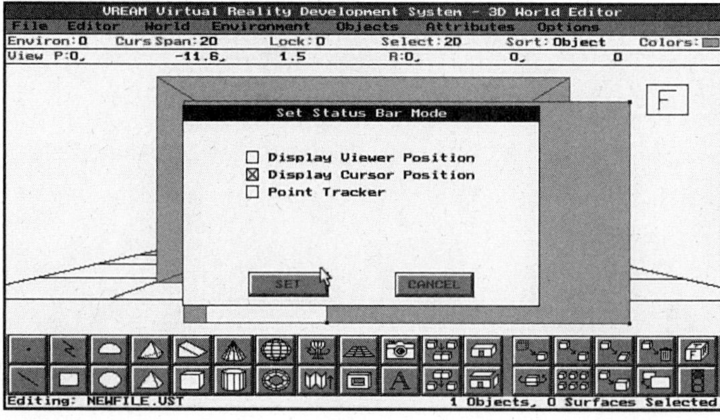

Figure 9.27. Selecting a status display mode.

The three modes available are

Display Viewer Position—The coordinates displayed on the status bar are those of the Viewer—your point of view.

Display Cursor Position—The coordinates reflect the current 3D position of the cursor.

Point Tracker—The coordinates reflect the position of the point nearest the cursor. This is useful when you want to create or move objects at specific existing locations.

Set Display Cursor Position before you use the Cut tool, and you can easily make sure that you use rectangular coordinates for your door opening.

After you have added any openings that you require, you must use the Create Room tool to put the room back together. This is as easy as selecting the various faces that make up the room and clicking the Room tool. Figure 9.28 shows a room I created without moving one wall out of the way. It has a single door, but you could easily create windows as well.

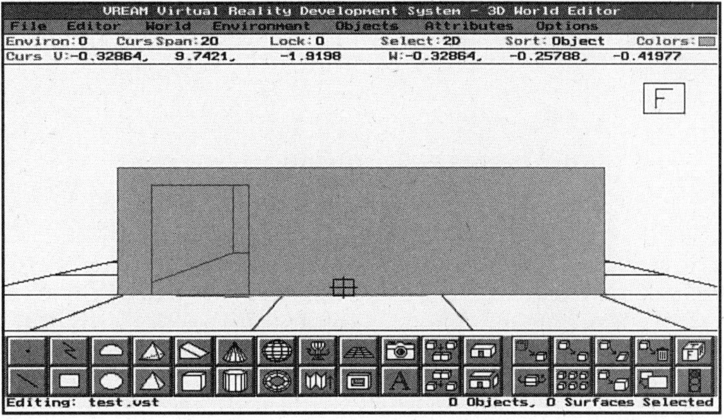

Figure 9.28.
A room with a view.

Figure 9.29 shows the same room, but this time the point of view is inside the room, and you are looking out through the doorway.

Once you have created one or more rooms, you can proceed to apply textures to the walls, build furniture, add knick knacks, and so on. VREAM comes with plenty of power for creating all kinds of objects, and creation is straightforward using the primitive tools. For more complex objects, you can move individual points to create subtle shapes.

This concludes the VREAM tutorial. VREAM is powerful, if a bit awkward to use. The price is right, however, and with a little effort, you can create some very sophisticated models.

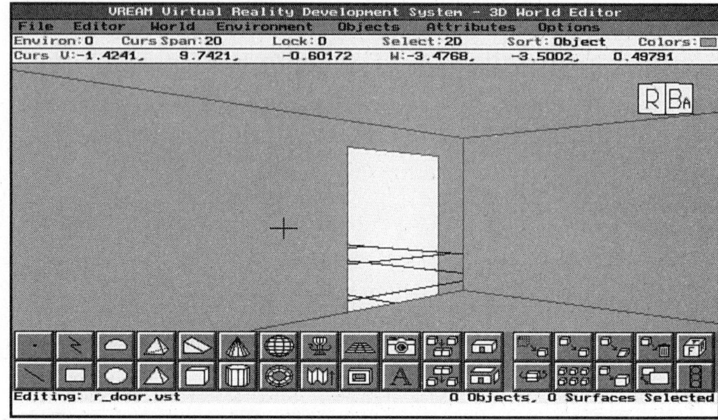

Figure 9.29. Enjoying the view from the room.

Rules and Conditions: the Heart of the Model

Modeling goes beyond the Imagine 2.0 nuts and bolts of VR—it is not just about putting images on a computer screen or a head-mounted helmet display. Modeling is also about ***rules.*** The virtual objects in the model must obey rules that correspond to reality.(12)

In the rest of this chapter, you will learn how to use Virtual Reality Studio to create a simple model of reality. In keeping with the title of the book and my general tendency to look for the fun side of anything, it will be a slightly twisted reality.

Virtual Reality Studio uses rules, but it calls them *conditions*. Whatever the name, a rule is a rule: it specifies how an object responds or behaves. There are many levels of conditions in Virtual Reality Studio. You can associate conditions with an object, and you can create conditions that apply all the time to all objects—and there are also levels in between:

General conditions—These conditions apply everywhere in the artificial universe. They are useful for tracking purposes, such as timers and counters.

Local conditions—These conditions apply to one area.(13)

---

12 Assuming, of course, that it is reality that you intend to model. If your intention is to model a fantasy world, then the rules can be whatever you like.

13 VR Studio allows you to switch from one area to another. Each area has its own objects. For more information about areas, see Chapter 2.

Object conditions—These conditions apply only to a single object.

Initial conditions—These conditions are applied when a session starts, or when a session is reset.

Procedures—You can create a library of procedures that can be used in conditions at all levels. For example, if the initial conditions make a certain object invisible, and the object itself becomes invisible under certain conditions, you could create a procedure that could be called from the Initial Conditions and the Object Conditions.

Figure 9.30 shows the Conditions menu. It includes access to the conditions just listed, as well as several other features, including animation. Animation is described in the Animation section of this chapter.

Let's begin by looking at object conditions. Use the Conditions/Object Conditions/Edit menu selection to access the Condition Editor (see fig. 9.31). This is a simple text editor into which you can type commands. The example in figure 9.31 shows a condition that responds to a "shot." If the object is shot, then it will fade. This condition is associated with object 118,[14] which is the roof of the house.

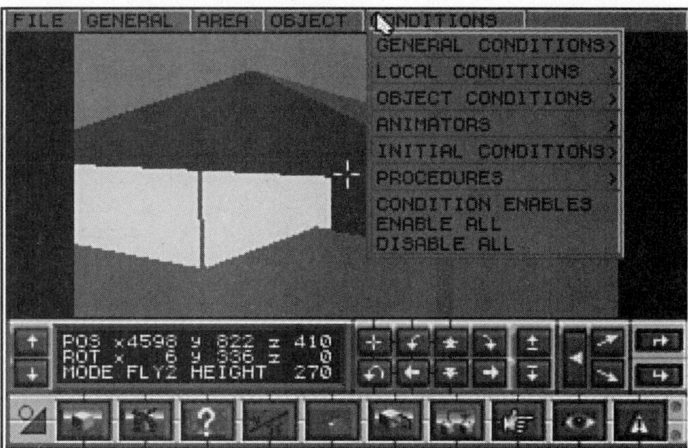

Figure 9.30. The Conditions menu.

The idea of a "shot" requires some explanation. There are a total of three things that can happen to an object:

Shoot—To shoot an object, click it with the left mouse button.

---

[14]Yes, there are 118 objects in this scene! This is the same scene that was created in Chapter 2. The large number of objects needed to create an interesting VR Studio scene required some patience and a good memory. A notepad is extremely handy for keeping track of things.

Activate—To activate an object, click it with the right mouse button.

Collide with—A collision occurs when your point of view runs into an object.

The terminology reflects Virtual Reality Studio's origins as software designed to create 3D games. This makes for a fun combination. You not only get to create virtual worlds—you get to play in them!

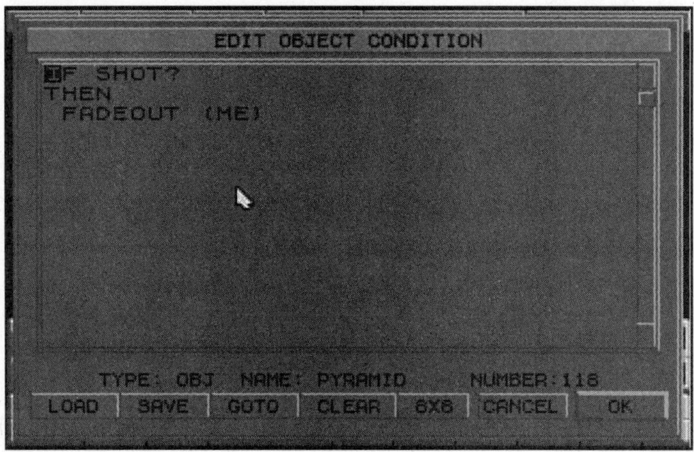

Figure 9.31. Object Condition Editor.

Return now to figure 9.31. There are three lines of program code in the example. The first line is a test:

```
IF SHOT?
```

The `IF` command is a conditional command, and it is used like an `IF` statement in any other programming language. The word `SHOT` is followed by a question mark. Some VR Studio commands can be used with or without the question mark. For example, the command `VISIT` means to set a flag saying that an area has been visited. The command `VISITED?` tests the value of the flag to see whether the area was visited.

The next part of the command, `THEN`, is simply an announcement to VR Studio that the following command is to be executed if the `SHOT?` statement is true. The statement

```
FADEOUT (ME)
```

is the action to carry out. Fadeout is one of many functions provided with VR Studio that changes the state, location, or appearance of an object. For example, you can move an object, turn it into a wireframe, and so on.

Once the condition exists, you can test it in VR Studio. Click on the roof with the left mouse button, and it will slowly fade to invisible. Of course, there's not much use in having an invisible roof if you can't put it back the way it was. Figure 9.32 shows an object condition I added to the vertical column that supports the roof.

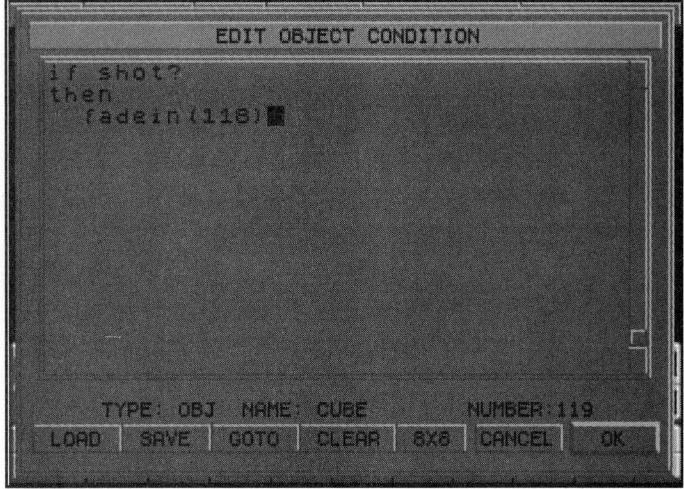

Figure 9.32. A second object condition.

The statements in this condition are similar to the statements in the roof condition. However, this time the action to be carried out is

```
fadein(118)
```

The `fadein` will bring the object (the roof) back. There's another difference to note as well. In the first example, the fadeout was applied to `me`. This is a special variable that always refers to the object that the condition is attached to. Because we are clicking the column, it won't help much to have the column fade in. You can find the number of an object in many ways—the number is shown, for example, when you select an object, and is also shown in many operations (such as the Object Editor). You cannot use object names in conditions—hence my earlier suggestion that you keep a notepad handy to keep track of the details of your world.[15]

Thus, the statement

```
fadein(118)
```

[15] You can also take the time to name your objects, but this can be just as tedious as using a notepad. If you plan to develop a very complex scene and to modify it over a long stretch of time, it will certainly be worth your while to create unique names for each object.

will cause the roof to fade back into the scene. Figure 9.33 shows the pointer on the roof, and the roof fading out of the scene. Figure 9.34 shows the mouse pointer on the column, and the roof fading back into the scene.

Figure 9.33. The roof fading out after being "shot."

Figure 9.34. The roof fading back in after "shooting" the column.

Fading in and out are only two of the things you can do with conditions. Virtual Reality Studio 2.0 comes with a large number of commands and statements you can use. Table 9.1 lists some of the more interesting ones. There are many more in addition to these examples. Collectively, these commands and statements are known as the *Freescape Command Language (FCL).*(16)

16Have you ever noticed that almost all computer-related acronyms use three letters? We're getting awfully close to adding a new part of speech: nouns, pronouns, verbs, adverbs, three-letter acronyms, prepositions...

Table 9.1. Freescape Command Language: Sample Commands.

Command	*Description*
activated?	Tests to see if the object was clicked with the right mouse button
addvar	Adds a value to a variable
loop/again	Loops through a set of commands a specified number of times
border	Displays a specified border on the screen
box	Draws a box of the specified size on the screen
collided?	Checks to see if the current object has collided with anything
defarray	Creates an array
destroy	Destroys the specified object[17]
for/next	Works like a for/next loop in BASIC
if/then/else/endif	The familiar "if" control structure
include	Includes an object in an animation
goto	Moves the player to a specified entrance
lockonto	Moves the player so that a specified object is centered on the screen
moveto	Moves animation to a specified position
pause	Pauses execution and waits for a specified key press
setground	Sets a new ground color
sound	Plays a sound file
startanim	Starts playing an animated sequence
time	Gets system time—usually used for displaying time in instruments

So far, you have learned about three ways that you can interact with an object and cause the condition to execute: shooting, activating, and colliding. You also can make an object into a sensor. To experiment with sensors, create two cubes and shape them as flattened, floating buttons as shown in figure 9.35. Both objects are

[17]This command also points to the roots of VR Studio as a game-creation product. This is a good thing—not only can you use VR Studio to create nifty virtual spaces, you can then turn them into games and have some fun as a reward for the effort you put into their creation.

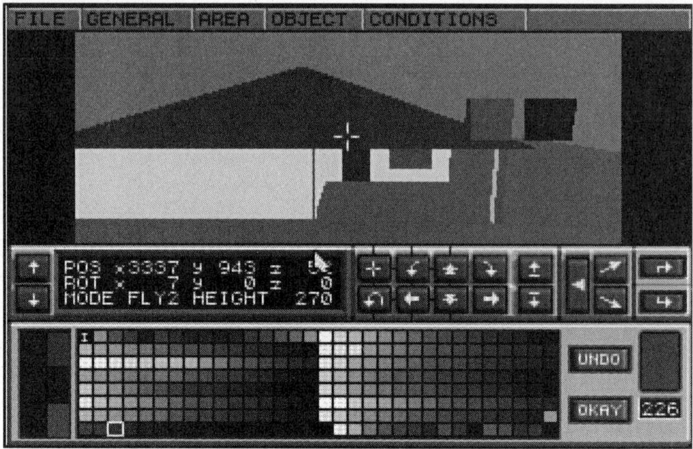

Figure 9.35. Creating objects to use as sensors.

poised over the entry to the house. They should be placed so that you will pass under one object or the other when you try to enter the house.

Use the Object/Attributes menu selection to display the dialog box shown in figure 9.36. There is a group of buttons on the right side of the dialog box.[18] Click the SNS button at the top right. This stands for *Sensor*. The button will turn dark, and the Sensor button at the bottom center of the dialog box will be activated. Click the Sensor button, which will display the dialog box shown in figure 9.37.

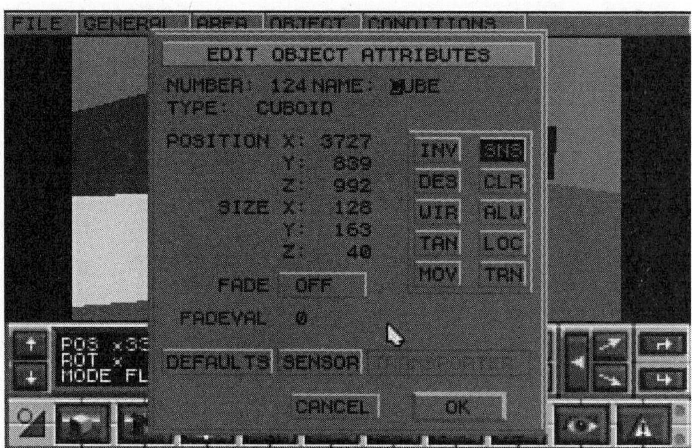

Figure 9.36. The Object Attributes dialog box.

[18]If you are curious about the function of these various buttons, all will be explained shortly.

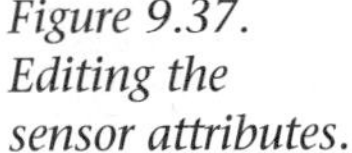

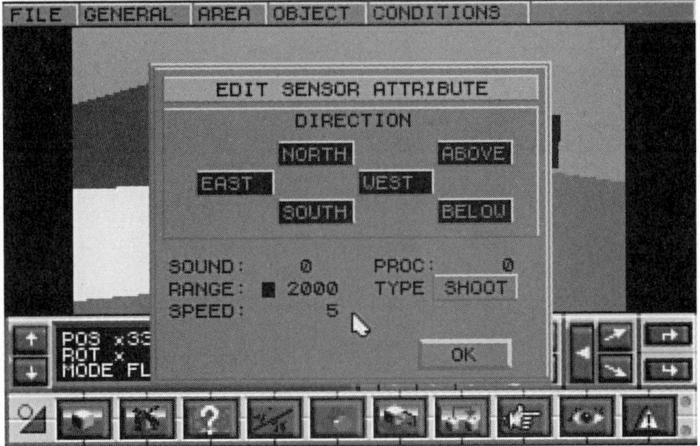

Figure 9.37. Editing the sensor attributes.

A sensor does what its *Star Trek*-like name implies: it senses your movements. The top half of the dialog box allows you to specify the directions in which the object will sense, and the lower half of the dialog box allows you to define the characteristics of the sensor. By default, all the directional buttons are in black, meaning that they are activated. To select one or more active directions, make sure only the directions you want to use are darkened. For example, to specify that the example sensor will only sense when the player moves below it, click all the buttons but the Below button to turn off sensing in those unneeded directions (see fig. 9.38).

The remaining entries in the dialog box control the characteristics of the sensor:

Sound—Determines which sound, if any, is to be played when the sensor is activated.

Range—The distance over which the sensor operates. The sensor will not detect anything until the player moves within this distance in a direction that is "on."

Speed—How quickly the sensor will react, in 50ths of a second. For example, a setting of 5 indicates that the sensor should respond in 1/10th of a second.

Proc—Which procedure is to be called when the sensor is activated.

Type—There are two types of sensor: detect and shoot. A shoot sensor gives a visual indication when it is activated, and a detect sensor does not. In all other respects, they are identical.

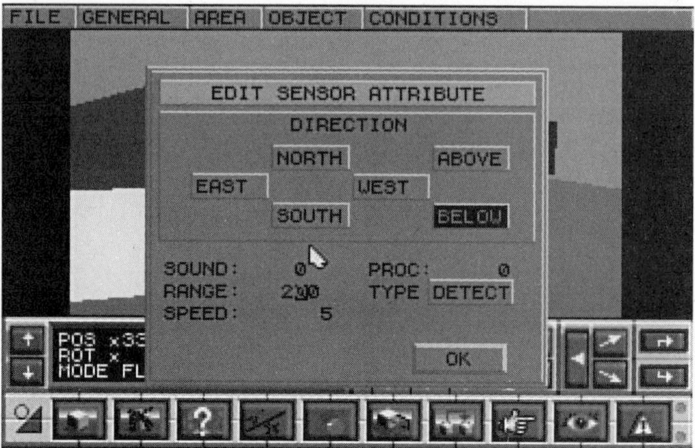

Figure 9.38. Adjusting the directions for sensing.

You can use sensors simply to play sounds, but the best way to use sensors is to have them call procedures. As explained earlier in this chapter, a *procedure* is a small, independent program that can be called from anywhere in a condition or from a sensor. To create a procedure, use the Conditions/Procedures/Create menu selection. To edit the procedure, use the Conditions/Procedures/Edit menu selection (see fig. 9.39).

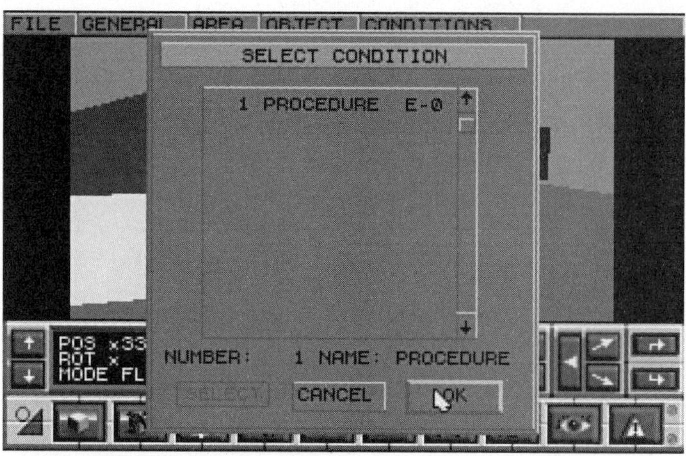

Figure 9.39. Editing a procedure.

This displays a list of available procedures—in this case, just the one we created. You must create new procedures before you can edit them. Procedures are referred to by number—another good use for that notepad I keep telling you to have handy. To edit the procedure, click on the line in the list box. (There is only one line in this case.) Then click the OK button. This displays a dialog box just like the Condition Editor (see fig. 9.40). You can enter commands and statements just as you did in the Condition Editor.

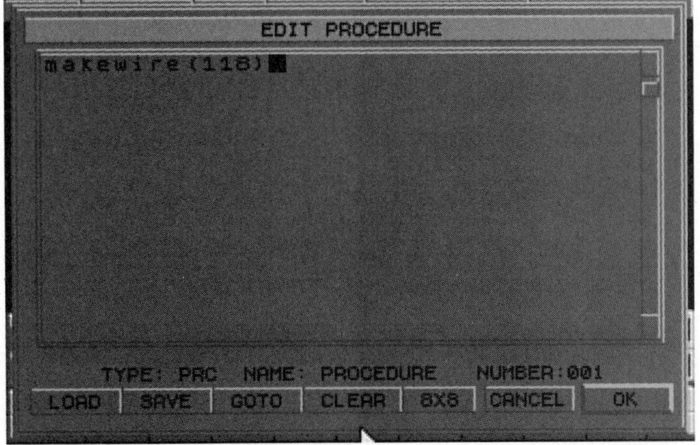

Figure 9.40. Entering a command into a procedure using the Procedure Editor.

This procedure contains just one statement, but you could enter multiple statements just as easily. The statement is

```
makewire(118)
```

The number is an object number, and it is the roof again. Moving under the sensor will cause the roof to be displayed as a wireframe object instead of a solid object. Figure 9.41 shows a cube in both solid and wireframe modes.

To complete the example, you can add the statement

```
makesolid(118)
```

to a second procedure. You then can change the sensor attributes for each object to point to the appropriate procedure number (see fig. 9.42, which shows procedure number 2 being set as the active procedure for a sensor).

Figure 9.41. Examples of a cube in solid (a) and wireframe (b) modes.

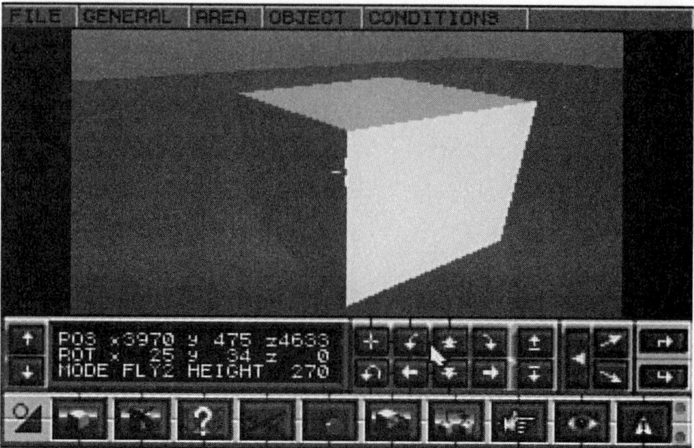

a

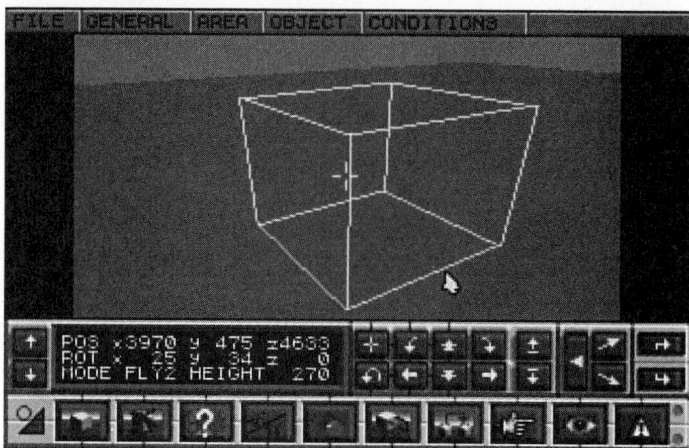

b

In the previous examples, we have put opposite statements in different objects, which allows the player to reverse actions. You can put the reversal action in a single object condition. To do this, you must first test to find out the current state of the object. Figure 9.43 shows a condition that tests to see if an object is invisible. First, the condition checks to see if the object has been shot.[19] If it has, the rest of the code is executed. If not, nothing happens. If the object is invisible, it is faded in. If the object is not invisible, it is faded out.

---

[19] If you recall, a shot consists of a click with the left mouse button.

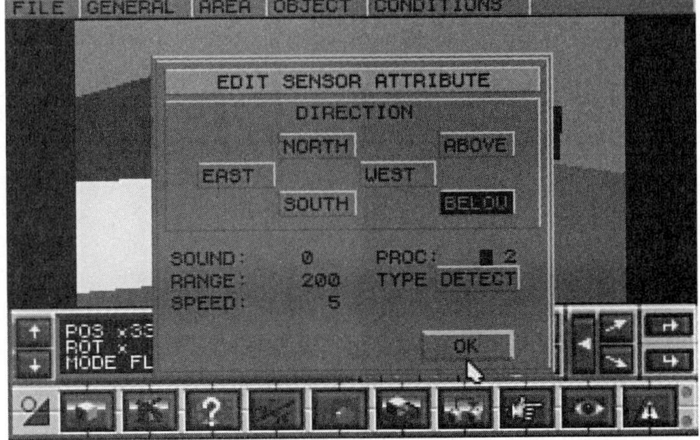

Figure 9.42. Setting the procedure number for a sensor.

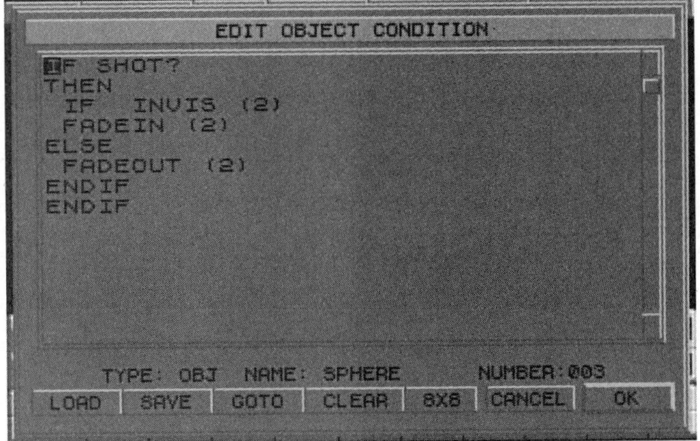

Figure 9.43. Testing the state of an object before acting on it.

Backgrounds and Borders

To recap, you have learned about two important aspects of Virtual Reality Studio so far. One, you can use it to build 3D virtual environments. Two, you can create rules that the object must obey while a "player"[20] moves through the space. Now you will learn about a third way that you can control the virtual space: backgrounds and borders.

[20]This term, like many in VR Studio, is derived from its origins as a game-creation tool.

Don't be deceived by those simple terms. As it happens, a VR Studio background/border[21] is actually quite an active place. For starters, you can have a whole collection of borders in your world and switch from one to the next using conditions. Typically, you would use a background with a specific area. For example, if you were creating a space journey, you might have one background represent a launch-control center, and another background represent the inside of the space vessel. You can use the Border command in FCL to change the border at any time.[22]

A border also can have controls placed on it, just like the controls in VR Studio itself. You'll learn how to create such controls in this section. Before you do, however, let's look at one of the borders that comes with VR Studio to see how everything works together.

Start by adding a border. This is a rather round-about process, unfortunately. Begin with the menu selection File/Borders/Locate. This is where you tell VR Studio where the borders are located.[23] Now you can use File/Borders/Add to actually add the border. This displays a modified file dialog box (see fig. 9.44). The buttons for navigating to other drives and directories are disabled. Unfortunately, you can't preview the border to see what it looks like until after you have added it.[24]

For this example, choose the file SPACEVGA.LBM and click OK. This displays the dialog box in figure 9.45, which allows you to set various attributes of the border. The most important one to note is the one labeled Freescape Window. Set it to Off. This tells the program to ignore the current 3D window and to load the entire background. If it is set to On, the portion of the screen covered by the 3D window will be black when you load the file.

---

[21]Backgrounds and borders are really the same thing in VR Studio. The menu uses the name *border*, but it's really a *background*. All will become clear shortly.

[22]If all you want to do is display an image, you also can use the Loadscreen command. It will load an image file, and you can optionally display the 3D window on top of it.

[23]Oddly enough, they are located in the BORDERS subdirectory. Why this is not the default, I'll never know. Every other operation that accesses files does fine with the usual methods for loading files, so this unique method for handling borders is completely mysterious.

[24]Yet another odd and frustrating aspect of using borders. It's a good thing that, once I had a border loaded and set up, I liked the result. A clear case of the end justifying the (oddly designed) means.

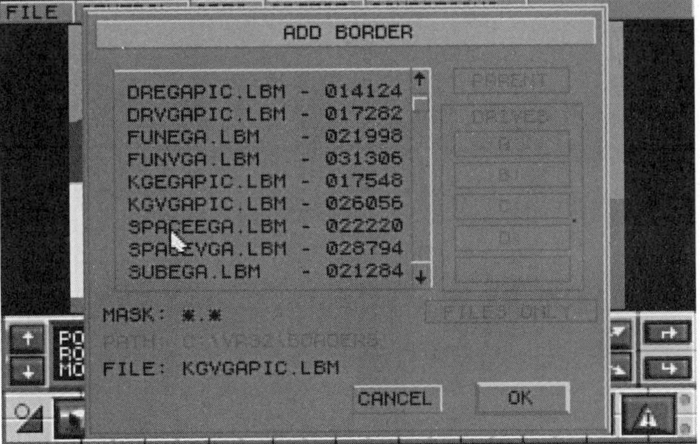

Figure 9.44. Adding a border file.

Figure 9.45. Setting border attributes.

You may have noticed that the border number of the example in figure 9.45 is 2. That happened because I wound up creating two borders without realizing it. The way that borders are handled is, no question about it, confusing. If you get lost, you are not the first person to have that happen. I do think that borders add a lot to the finished product, however, so it is well worth your time to persevere.

To view the border, use the File/Borders/View menu selection. This displays the dialog box shown in figure 9.46.[25] Click the border you want to view, and then click OK.

[25] The user interface of VR Studio is a bit quirky, and I have tried to include as many illustrations as possible to make your use of the product easier. The documentation leaves too much to one's imagination.

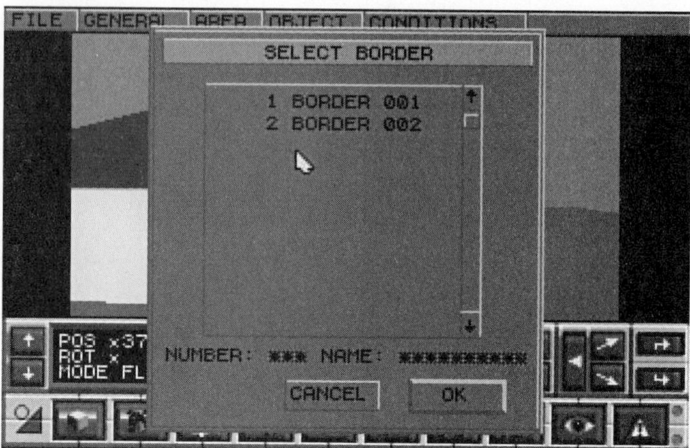

Figure 9.46. Selecting a border.

The border should now be displayed on your screen (see fig. 9.47).[26] As you can see, the "border" occupies most of the screen real estate. The black area in the center of the screen is where the 3D world will be displayed.

The next step is to tell VR Studio where that black part of the image is so it can use it as the equivalent of a view screen. Use the General/Set View Window menu selection to display the dialog box shown in figure 9.48.

Figure 9.47. A sample VR Studio border image.

[26]The image is of a space-control center. The 3D space you will be viewing is of the house created in Chapter 2. If you find this an odd mixture, imagine if you will that a space probe has just landed on a strange planet where the entire land surface is covered with suburban tract houses, and that the folks in the control center are about to launch a remote robot probe to explore the area. Now everything makes perfect sense.

There are four numbers in this dialog box: the X and Y coordinates for the upper left corner of the window, and the width and height of the view window. Despair not. You do not have to enter these numbers by hand. Click the Set button, which will give you the display shown in figure 9.48.

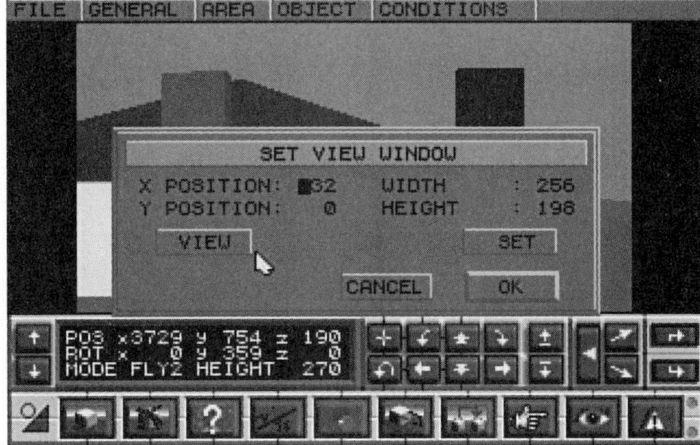

Figure 9.48. Setting the view window.

The numbers from the dialog box shown in figure 9.48 are repeated at the bottom-right corner of figure 9.49. The thin lines indicate the size and position of the view window corresponding to these numbers.

Figure 9.49. Setting the view window visually.

It would be much easier to adjust the view window if you could see the background. Click on the gray box at the bottom right to open the Select Border dialog box, and select SPACEVGA.LBM again. It is displayed along with the outline of the view window (see fig. 9.50). This allows you to match the outline of the view window to the background. To move the window, click and drag it. To change its size, click carefully in the little box at the bottom right of the outline.

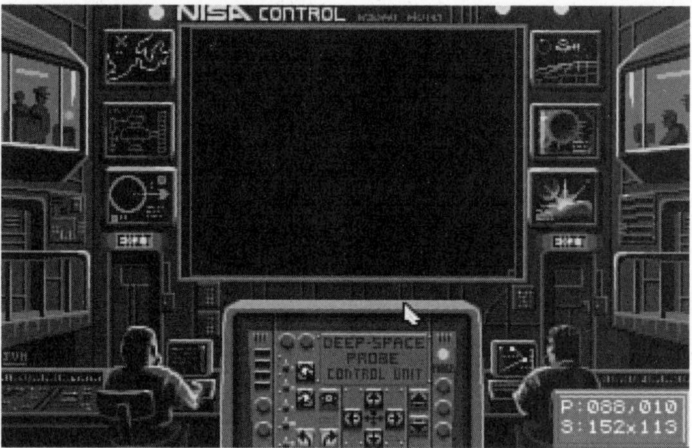

Figure 9.50. Adjusting the view window over the background.

Right-click on the screen to return to the Set View Window dialog box, and click OK to accept the new values. To test your handiwork, click the Eye icon at the lower right of the main VR Studio screen. The view window appears (see fig. 9.51).

Oops—there's no border! This is by design. You can test features of your virtual environment without wasting time loading a border. To see the border, you'll have to get back to the VR Studio screen. Press F1 to do so.

Use the General/Defaults menu selection to open the dialog box shown in figure 9.52. This dialog box is used to set up the state of your world when it is loaded or reset. There are two areas to pay attention to. At the bottom, enter the number of the border you want to be displayed at startup. Just above that, you can set the default mode. I prefer Fly2 for its flexibility, but you can set any appropriate mode here. Note also that you can set a default entrance and area. This is important for establishing the initial position in your world. You can accept the default of area 1, entrance 1, or change these values to anything you want.

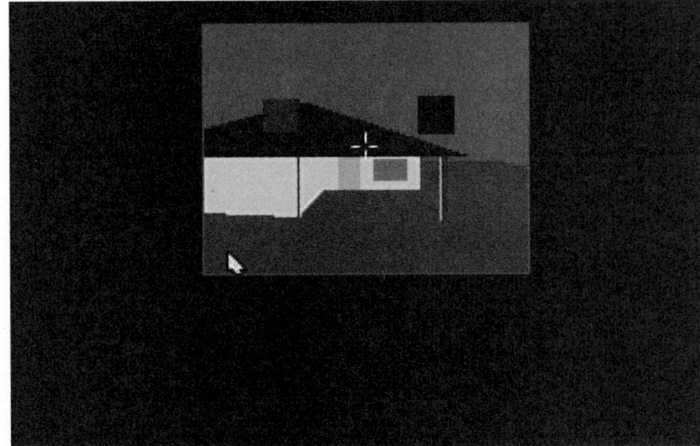

Figure 9.51. Testing the size and position of the view window.

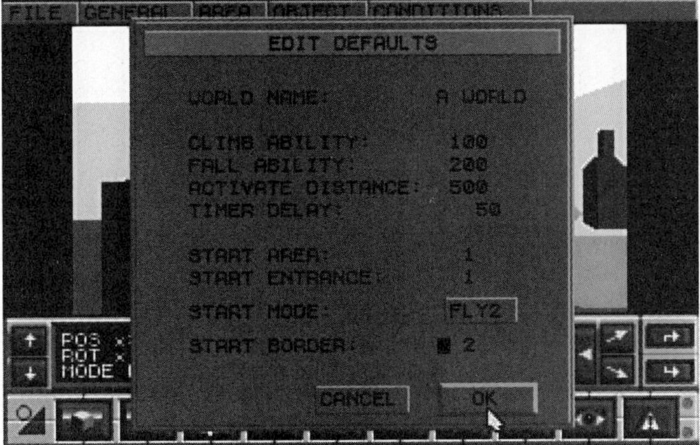

Figure 9.52. Setting the defaults for your virtual world.

Let's test the view window again. Click the Eye icon, and then press the Esc key to reset your world. The following should happen:

- The border is displayed.
- You are positioned at the area and entrance numbers you set.

The result is shown in figure 9.53.

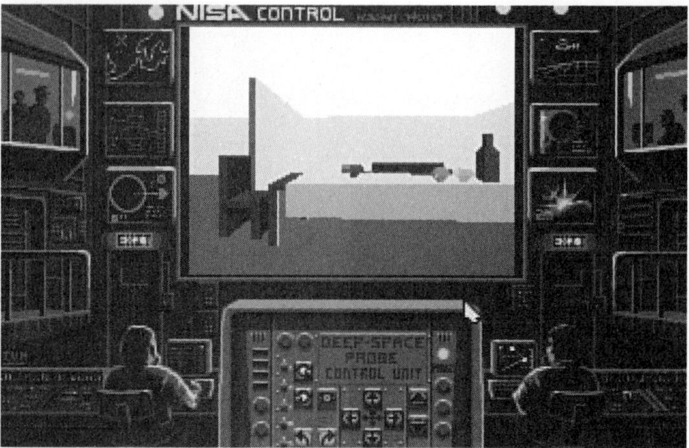

Figure 9.53.
The border and view window working together.

Controls

Now you can see the benefit of being able to locate your own controls on the border. As things stand, there is no way for you to move around in the 3D world you have created. There are controls included at the bottom-center of the border, but they don't do anything—they are just pretty pixels with no powers. You need to tell VR Studio where to put the controls using the General/Controls menu selection. This displays the Edit Controls dialog box (see fig. 9.54).

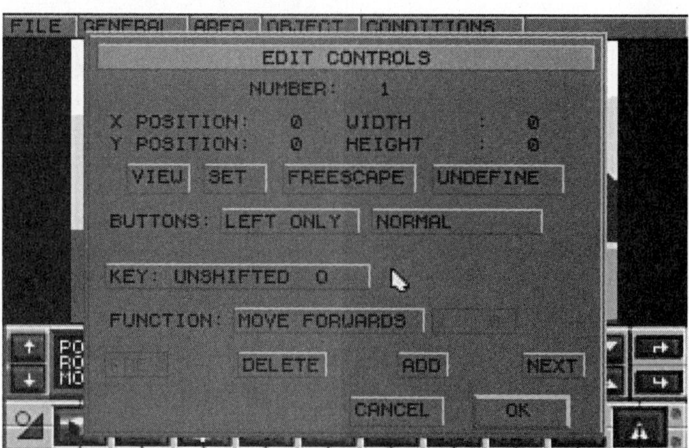

Figure 9.54.
The dialog box for editing controls.

There is a lot going on in this dialog box. Table 9.2 lists the various controls in the dialog box and explains what they do.

Table 9.2. The Edit Controls Dialog Box.

Control	*Description*
X/Y Position	The upper left corner of the control.
Width	Width of the control.
Height	Height of the control.
View	Works like the View button for borders.
Set	Works like the Set button for borders. It takes you to a screen where you can set the size and location of the control area visually.
Freescape	Sets the size of the control to be the same as the 3D view window.
Undefine	Returns the values of the control to the state they were in originally.
Buttons	Establishes which mouse buttons are used for the control.
Key	Indicates whether there is a keystroke associated with the control and, if so, which one.
Function	Specifies what the button does. There are a number of built-in functions, or you can add your own.
Prev	Moves to the previous control.
Delete	Removes the control.
Add	Adds a new control. You will be asked to specify a procedure to be called when the control is activated.
Next	Moves to the next control.

Most of the actions you need already exist as predefined controls. Figure 9.54 shows the Move Forwards control. To tell VR Studio where this control is located, click the Set button. This will display the screen you used to set the view window. Click on the gray box at the lower right to select and view the border, and then move or change the size of the control outline. Figure 9.55 shows the control outline where it doesn't belong. It is just like the outline for the view window. To move the control around, click and drag. To change the size, click and drag in the little box at the lower right of the box outline.

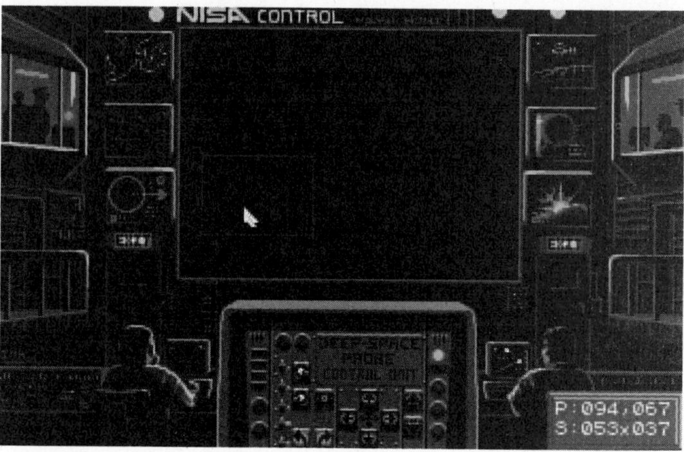

Figure 9.55. Adjusting the size and position of a control.

Drag and size the outline until it exactly covers the small arrow pointing up (the Move Forward control) on the control panel at the bottom center of the screen. Then repeat this process to set the Move Backward control.(27) With these two controls, you now have primitive movement capabilities: forward and back. Figure 9.56 shows the initial entrance point for the world, and figure 9.57 shows the change in viewpoint that results from a few clicks on the Move Forward control.

Figure 9.56. The initial view of the world.

[27] To access this control, just click the Next button in the Edit Controls dialog box.

Figure 9.57. A changed view after pressing Move Forward a few times.

Instruments

In addition to controls, you can create instruments that use dials, numbers, or text to display information. For example, you could create a control to display the time. To create a control, use the General/Instruments/Create menu selection, and then use General/Instruments/Edit to change the settings. Figure 9.58 shows the Edit Instrument dialog box.

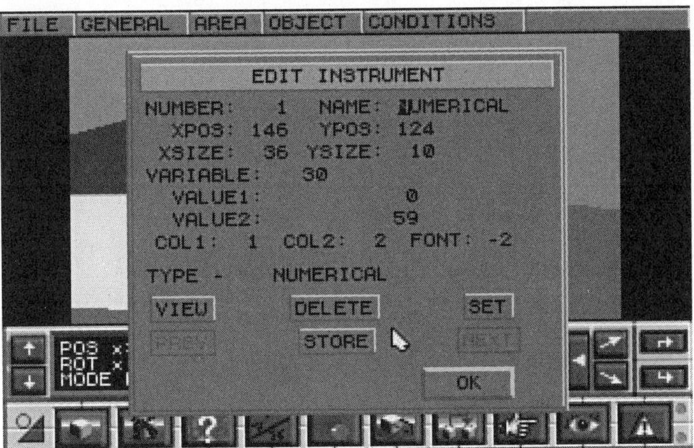

Figure 9.58. The Edit Instrument dialog box.

Table 9.3 describes the function of the various controls in the dialog box.

Table 9.3. The Edit Instrument Dialog Box.

Control	*Description*
Number	The sequential number for the instrument. Like most things in VR Studio, each instrument has a unique number.
Name	Unlike many things in VR Studio, each instrument can have a name.
XPOS	The X coordinate for the instrument's upper left corner.
YPOS	The Y coordinate for the instrument's upper left corner.
Variable	The numeric variable that will contain the data to be displayed in the instrument.[28]
Value1	The minimum value the instrument's variable can have.
Value2	The maximum value the instrument's variable can have.
Col1	Foreground color.
Col2	Background color.
Font	Font to use.
Type	The kind of instrument. Examples include numbers, text, or a dial.
View	Views the instrument.
Delete	Removes the instrument from the list of instruments.
Set the	Works like the View button for borders. It takes you to a screen in which you can set the size and location of instrument visually.
Prev	Edits the previous instrument.

[28]This is the first mention of variables in VR Studio. You will note that even variables have numbers. To refer to a variable, append the letter V to the number. In this example, V30 would be used. If you are not familiar with programming, a *variable* is like a container. It holds a value, and that value can be changed in the program. The opposite of a variable is a *constant*—a value that doesn't change. The number 5, for example, is a constant.

Control	*Description*
Store	You must click this button to store the changes you make to an instrument.
Next	Edits the next instrument.

In this example, because we plan to use the instrument to display time (specifically, seconds), the minimum value should be set to 0, and the maximum to 59. The other values can stay as they are. To position the instrument, click the Set button and use the same techniques you used for controls. Position it just above the control console at the bottom center of the border.

The key to controlling the instrument is the variable, in this case V30.[29] The value of the variable will be displayed in the control. All we need is some method to update the variable with the current time while the program runs.

Fortunately, VR Studio provides just that opportunity in the General conditions. If you think of a VR Studio session as a kind of live, interactive movie, the General conditions are executed between frames. First, create a new General condition using the Conditions/General Conditions/Create menu selection. Then edit it using the Conditions/General Conditions/Edit menu selection. Select the condition you just created, and click OK. This displays the dialog box shown in figure 9.59.

Yes, it is the familiar Condition Editor. I have taken the liberty of adding the time function. It takes three variables—one each for hours, minutes, and seconds. We don't care about the hours and minutes, so I have used dummy variables (V31 and V32) for them. The variable defined for this instrument, V30, is in the seconds position of the function.

When this condition is executed—and thanks to the frame orientation of VR Studio, that will be frequently—it will update the instrument we created with the current time. If you wanted to display hours, minutes, and seconds, you would use three variables. Figure 9.60 shows the clock instrument in place, displaying a value of 32.

[29]The first 30 variables, from V0 to V29, are system variables with special meaning. They are explained in the documentation for VR Studio, and need not concern us here.

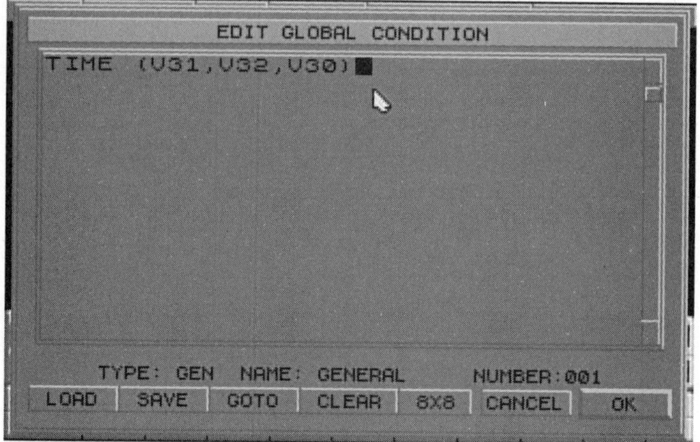

Figure 9.59. Editing a Global condition.

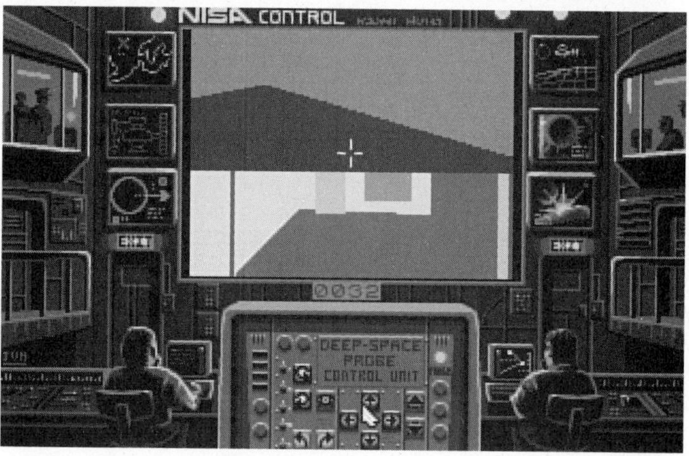

Figure 9.60. An operating instrument.

In addition to numbers, you also can display text in instruments. If you were to truly create your world as a game, you could display comments to the player as well as a score.

Animation

Virtual Reality Studio supports two kinds of animations. You can animate objects (or groups of objects), and you can place small 2D animations on the border, and they will play automatically. The former are referred to simply as *animations*, whereas the latter are called *brush animations*.

Object Animations

Object animations are based on conditions. In fact, there is a special set of conditions for animations. To access them, use the Conditions/Animators/Create and Conditions/Animators/Edit menu selections. The basic structure of an animator follows:

- Include the objects for the animation.[30]
- Start command.
- Enter the commands for the animation.
- End command.

For example, the following set of commands would move a single object continuously, 10 units at a time:

```
Include(2)
Start
Loop (30)
Move (0,0,10)
Again
End
```

To play the animation—for example, from a sensor or object—create a condition and add a set of commands like this:

```
if shot?
then
startanim(1)
endif
```

Substitute the actual number of the animation for the value of `1`.

That's all there is to creating and using an animation. The key, of course, lies in using the various FCL commands to create the appropriate movements. However, these animations open up a whole range of possibilities for the worlds you create.

Brush Animations

Now let's take a look at brush animations. These apply only to the border, not to the 3D space.

The process of creating a brush animation is awkward, with a lot of details. You begin by using the General/Brushes/Cut Brush menu selection to load an image. The file WORLDVGA.LBM is a good example. Once you have selected the file, you'll see the screen shown in figure 9.61.

---

[30]These can be any objects or groups on the 3D space you created.

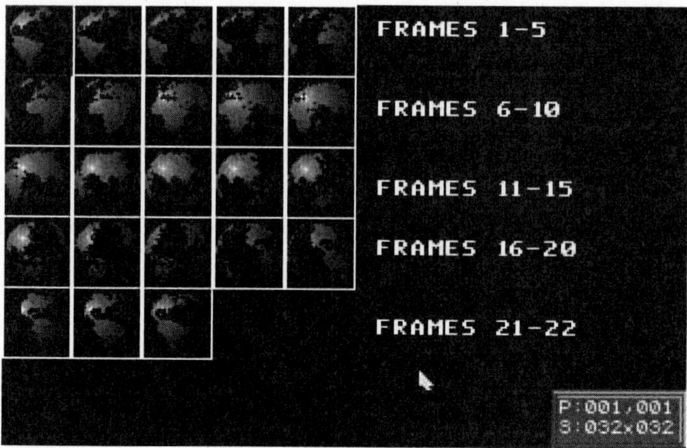

Figure 9.61. Cutting a brush for an animation.

You'll see a thin outline around the first image in the animation. Make sure that it corresponds to the exact outline of the image, and then click the right button to complete the cut. Add the brush to the list of brushes, and then go back to the cut screen to cut the next frame. Repeat this process until all frames have been cut.

What you now have is a set of brushes. The next step is to create a brush animation, and then add the brushes to the animation. Use General/Brush Animation/Create to create the animation and then General/Brush Animation/Edit to work with it. The dialog box shown in figure 9.62 is used to build the animation brush out of the brushes you cut.

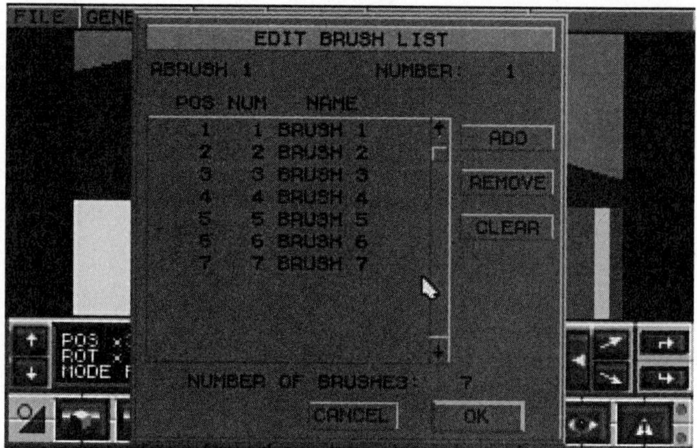

Figure 9.62. Editing an animation brush.

To add the individual brushes, click the Add button and select them from the list of brushes, one at a time. When you have loaded all the brushes, click OK. You can preview the animation (as shown in fig. 9.63) by clicking the Preview button.

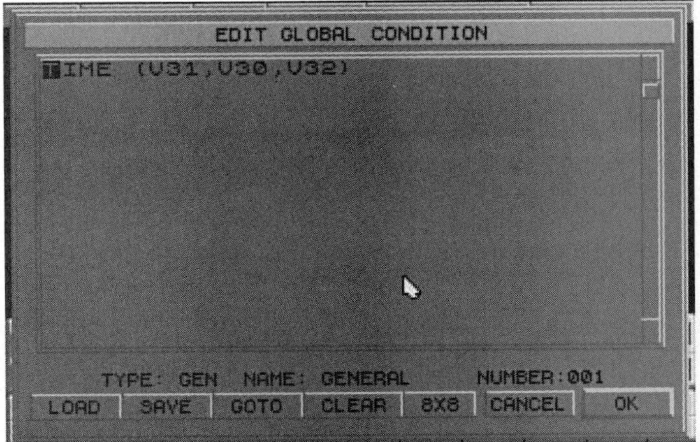

Figure 9.63. Previewing a brush animation.

You can then place the brush animation using the same techniques that you used for the view window and the controls/instruments. To access the dialog box for adjusting the position and size of the animation, use the General/Brush Animation/Edit menu selection, and click the Set button. The animation will play automatically: single, repeat, or random, depending on the setting in the Edit dialog box (see fig. 9.64).

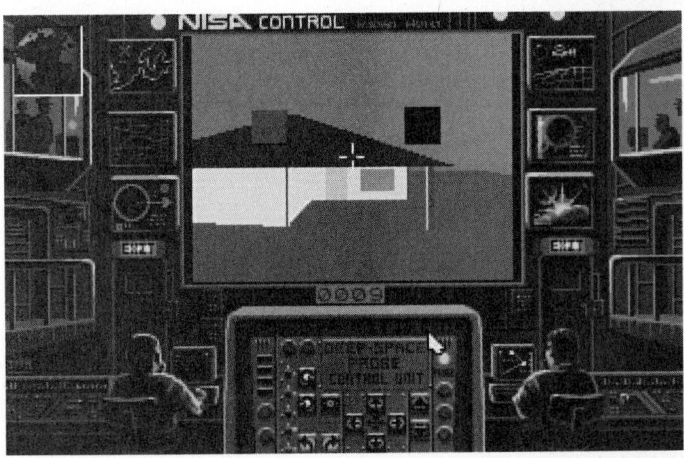

Figure 9.64. An animation playing automatically (that's it at the upper left).

Summary

Virtual Reality Studio has many features of the bigger VR programs. In fact, it was created by a company in England that has developed high-end, sophisticated VR simulations. I have a love/hate relationship with VR Studio. On the plus side, it offers an inexpensive way to explore virtual spaces. On the negative side, there are some bugs that need to be resolved, and the interface is, at best, awkward. On the whole, however, and considering the cost, VR Studio offers a decent value and an easy entry into virtual reality.

III

VIRTUAL REALITIES

10

YOU ARE THE STAR

This chapter will show you how to combine video with virtual reality.[1] This involves putting real objects into a virtual space.[2] For example, in this chapter you'll learn how to put a video of yourself into a landscape created with Vistapro, or into a 3D Studio animation. You'll also learn how to do the opposite: add a VR/3D object to a digital video clip. The road to these objectives winds around a bit, but the end result makes the journey well worthwhile. You'll start with an introduction to Media Merge and Adobe Premiere—two powerful video-editing programs. After learning how to work with Media Merge and Premiere, you will learn how to set up a simple video studio.[3] Finally, in the last section of this chapter, you'll find out how to put all the pieces together to create your own VVRs (Video Virtual Realities).

Video Basics

Everyone agrees about one thing when it comes to using video on a computer:

> **Video allows you to *show* what you mean, instead of just describing it.**

If you have a new product, you can show your customers how it works, and how it will benefit them. If you supply technical equipment, now you can show your users how to perform maintenance. In both cases, using video to get your message across is smart, because it's almost impossible to describe something that the reader hasn't seen before. In the case of virtual reality, the virtual spaces you create may never have been seen by anyone before.

These advantages of video led to Stage One of video on a PC: the video clip. A *video clip* is a self-contained bit of video that shows one thing and one thing only. This is good, but it's not enough.

Media Merge is Stage Two: the video production. With Media Merge, you can now show not only what you mean, you can tell a story—and you have the tools to tell it very well.

---

[1]Which raises a question: What does one call such a hybrid? *Virtual Video* springs to mind but isn't terribly accurate. I lean toward *VVR—Video Virtual Reality*. Let's face it: Just about everything else has a three-letter acronym.

[2]"Objection, your honor! Video objects are not real objects," the defense attorney says, jumping from his seat. "Overruled," the judge says, adding, "Everyone knows that video is real. Don't you watch reality TV?"

[3]That's an interesting concept: Setting up your own video studio. Be honest now: Did you ever think you would be reading a book, thinking to yourself, "Hmmm...should I set up a video studio this weekend?" The fact that one can now rationally consider such possibilities points out how far we've already gone toward virtual reality.

For example, some folks have complained that the size of a PC video window is small—usually somewhere between 160×120 and 320×240. At most, this covers one quarter of the screen. If what you have in mind is watching the latest Indiana Jones movie, this argument has some merit. But if the video window is sharing the screen with such things as interactive menus and buttons, text blocks, and bitmaps; video in a window suddenly becomes even better than full-screen video. For example, you could create a virtual space, add video elements to it, and then place it within the context of a text story line, or combine it with still images, add music or narration, and so on.

Learning to work with video is like any other skill: A little time and repetition will go a long way toward making you good at it. This chapter will show you the basics of putting together a real video production, and then how to apply those skills to virtual reality.[4] The title of the video is *Kayak Self Rescue*. The video footage comes from a demonstration of one of the popular sports in my hometown. I chose this subject for several reasons:

- The subject is not widely known, so it will be a good proof of the concept that video is useful for communicating about new ideas.
- The subject is graphic: boats, paddles, water, and the paddler are all easily seen and comprehended—even in a small, 160×120 format video.
- The subject is inherently interesting: If you are planning on kayaking in the ocean, knowing how to rescue yourself is pretty important stuff.

I will take you step by step through the process of creating a video using video files included on the CD-ROMs that come with Media Merge. They are all located in the tutorial directory—feel free to peek at them ahead of time. The files are described individually in the section "Working with Media Merge" in this chapter.

Video Concepts

In one sense, all of us are video experts. Think about how much television you've seen over the years: every commercial, every sitcom, every movie you have ever seen has been part of your education for working with video on a computer. Like most of us, the only thing lacking is a framework of knowledge that will help you decide what video techniques to use in your own productions. That will come with time, of course, but this section will give you a jump start.

---

[4]This chapter started out as a "guest chapter" in the documentation for Media Merge. I was very impressed with the capabilities of Media Merge, as well as it's potential for combining virtual reality and video. I've added a lot of additional material to the portions of the chapter that cover Media Merge, including some tricks and tips that are not covered in the Media Merge documentation.

There are five key areas that you should think about before you begin to produce video:

> **Moving Images**—Video shows movement. Use that movement to your advantage. Don't rely on static, boring subjects in your video clips—when was the last time you saw a commercial that didn't jump and dance and dazzle you? With Media Merge, you can mix and match static and dynamic content.
>
> **Transitions**—A video production is made up of several video clips. How you make the transition from one clip to the next is important.
>
> **Content**—Video moves and is therefore interesting in its own right. Don't use that as an excuse to use boring material. Seek out subjects that are interesting—that will double the impact of your final production.
>
> **Timing**—Unlike a book or a document, a video production rolls along in real time. Timing of various events—music, narration, dramatic moments, and so on—is critical.
>
> **Pace**—Finding the right pace for your video is important. Short clips that whiz by will confuse, and long, similar clips risk boredom.

Each of these topics is described in detail in this section.[5]

Moving Images

Video is movement. Unlike static images, video allows you to show life in action. To create videos with impact, you'll want to put as much action in your videos as possible.[6] The key to using movement is simple: Tell your story with actions, not words, whenever possible.

For example, there will be times when you simply must use a video clip of a *talking head*. That's any video that simply shows someone talking. Instead of sitting that person behind a desk, why not have him look up as he starts speaking, or perhaps he could be walking or pointing at the subject he is talking about. Even adding an interesting background—a seacoast, a factory floor, a busy workplace—adds visual interest.

---

[5]My earlier book, *PC Video Madness*, includes an extended treatment of a variety of video issues, including how to use a camera, how to light a scene, and other topics.

[6]That is not strictly true, although if you will only be doing television commercials, you can assume that it is always true. Action is a good thing; too much action is usually confusing. In general, it is easier to err on the side of too little action.

Another important aspect of movement involves movement within the frame from one scene to the next. One scene can contain a subject at the upper left; the next can use a subject at the lower right. Use such motion to add interest—but be careful not to overdo it with stuff coming from all directions. For example, you could have a series of three subjects move into the frame from the left, and then have one subject come in from the right to offer a summary.

Finally, movement is not the ultimate answer for every video clip. You may want to emphasize something by allowing it to be perfectly still during a clip.

Transitions

The best videos are made up of a number of video clips. The example video in this chapter, for example, uses eight clips. Normally, you won't just chop from one video clip to the next; you'll add transitions between clips. Transitions include such effects as wipes and fades,[7] and Media Merge makes it very easy to add transitions to your video productions.

There are three major types of transitions:

- Same-subject transitions
- New-subject transitions
- Breaking transitions

You should use different kinds of wipes and fades for each type of transition.

A same-subject transition occurs when you have two clips that are very closely related. For example, the first clip might show a complete picture of a product, while the next clip shows a close-up of a particular part of the product. Generally, you should use soft, unassuming effects for same-subject transitions. A dissolve is a good technique to use in these situations.

A new-subject transition occurs when you have two clips that do not relate closely but have some relationship to each other. For example, the first clip might show how to load paper into a new printer, while the second clip might show how to attach a fax device to the printer. Both clips are about the printer, but they are also about different topics. This is a more abrupt change, and you can signal the abruptness of the change by using an appropriate transitional effect. In this example, a wipe would be a good choice.

---

[7] *Wipes* and *fades* are transition effects used between scenes in video production. You see them all the time on your TV, especially during commercials.

A breaking transition occurs when two clips are about very different subjects. For example, if you have a series of six clips that show different aspects of a printer, and then have five clips that show different aspects of a copier, you should use a transitional effect to make it clear that a major break is occurring. You may also want to add a title sequence to alert the viewer to what is going on. In this example, the Media Merge Boxes effect (the new video clip fades in using small, random boxes) would work well—especially if you use color between the videos. You could easily put title text on a solid color.

Content

There is sometimes a temptation to rely on the movement in a video image to keep the viewer's interest. It's true that video alone is interesting simply because it moves. But if you want your productions to stand out, keep a sharp eye out for interesting content as well.

People make particularly interesting video subjects, but not if they are nervous about the experience. Help the subject of the video relax by minimizing the impact of the videotaping process—don't constantly start and stop recording. Set everything up in advance, and let your subject act naturally.

For inanimate objects, get as close as you can to the object. Fill the frame! PC video sizes are small, and you don't want to lose detail if you can avoid it. If the subject is large—like the kayaks in the tutorial later in this chapter—keep the background simple so the outline of the subject is clear.

Take some close-up shots of various details. You can use some of them later during production to emphasize these details.

Timing

As you work with video, you will automatically develop a sense of timing. It is one of the most important assets you can have for creating video productions that are strong and effective. Knowing when to end a video clip and start the next one is something of an art. However, there are a few basic rules that will get you started.

- A good starting point usually involves action. You don't need a lot of tape prior to the beginning of the action. In fact, the only reason to use any slack time at the beginning or end of a clip is to use it as part of a transition, such as a fade from black.

- Every clip has a start and an end; you just have to find out where they are. Don't settle for just any ending point. Here's a trick: Count the action beats in a clip. A *beat* is anything that happens—he picks up a pen, he touches his hat, he pauses for effect, he points at the audience. Everything that happens is a beat. End a clip on a strong beat.[8]
- Good things come in threes. A three-beat clip is often perfect. Or try two clips to set up the idea, and then hit hard with a third clip. Use same-subject transitions between the three clips and follow the third clip with a new-subject transition.

Pace

It's very important to find the right pace for each video production you create. I am speaking here of the overall video, not individual clips. If the video moves too slowly—if the story is being told too slowly—your viewers will lose interest. If the video is too fast, your viewers will miss important information.

Keeping a video at a useful pace can be difficult if you don't have experience with video production. Fortunately, there's a simple cure. Find someone you trust to view your material and give you feedback about the pacing. Here are some questions you can ask yourself to get started:

- Does each video clip move the story along?
- Is each video clip part of the same story?
- Is there any part of a clip that seems to be just hanging out, serving no useful purpose?
- Is each video clip long enough to make a clear point? Is it short enough to hold interest?

The Viewer over Your Shoulder

With experience, you will learn to be your own best viewer. Until then, sit down to look at your video in progress with an imaginary viewer looking over your shoulder at your work. Ask yourself if the video you are creating will be interesting and useful to that viewer.

---

[8]Sometimes, the clip must serve other masters. For example, a clip may have a natural ending, but the script requires that you hold that subject for more time. Perhaps the narration is complex at that point, and the clip has to last at least long enough to explain the subject. If the clip is truly boring, you might be able to use one of those detail shots I mentioned earlier. While you are in the field videotaping, it's always a good idea to collect more shots than you think you'll need.

Working with Media Merge

Media Merge provides two tools for working with video files: the Storyboard and the Scene Editor. The Storyboard is used to arrange your video clips in the right order and to put transitions between clips. The Scene Editor is used to merge multiple audio and video clips into a single clip. You can create some very interesting effects using the Scene Editor.

RECIPE

1 Storyboard Editor
1 Scene Editor
1 sound-editing program
1 video-capture card
1 Video camcorder or VCR
1 solid color background
1 tripod

Instructions: Toss images into camcorder (use a tripod for best results) and blend well. Select best chunks and capture to hard disk. Merge clips using Scene Editor, and create sequence using the Storyboard. Serve and watch your guests smile. For a gourmet touch, add virtual animation instead of one or more video files.

Let's start with the Storyboard. It's very easy to use, and all by itself it gives you a lot of power.

The Storyboard

The concept behind the Storyboard is simple. There are two kinds of slots, as you can see in figure 10.1. The big boxes are slots for video clips, and the little boxes are slots for transition effects. To create a video production, you just put all of your video clips into slots and then select transitions to use between the clips.

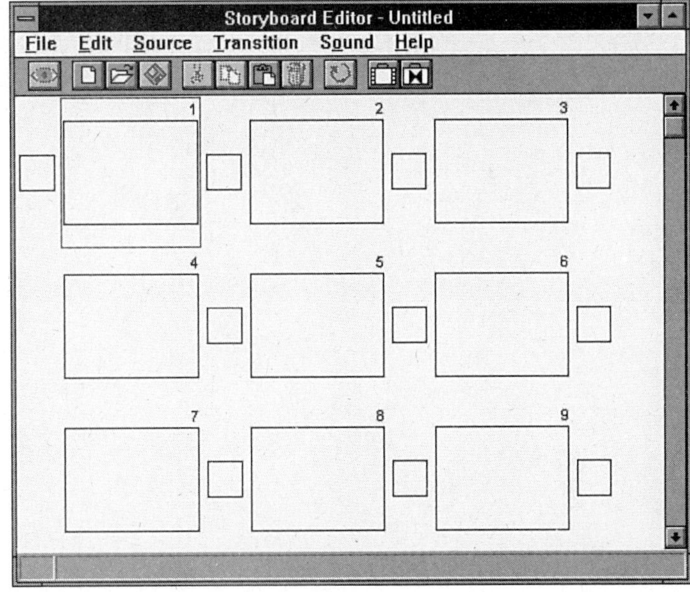

Figure 10.1. The Storyboard window.

Let's add a video to the first large box (it has the number 1 at the upper right corner). Double-click the box to display the dialog box shown in figure 10.2.

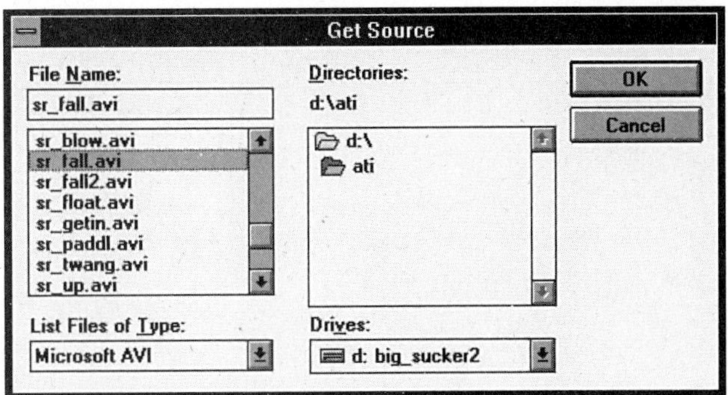

Figure 10.2. Selecting a source video to add.

This is a standard Windows Open File dialog box; you can use it to locate and load a video clip. To follow along, find the file \TUTORIAL\SR_FALL.AVI on the CD-ROMs that come with Media Merge. Click on the file name, and then click the OK button to load it. A small image of the first frame will appear in the box, as shown in figure 10.3.

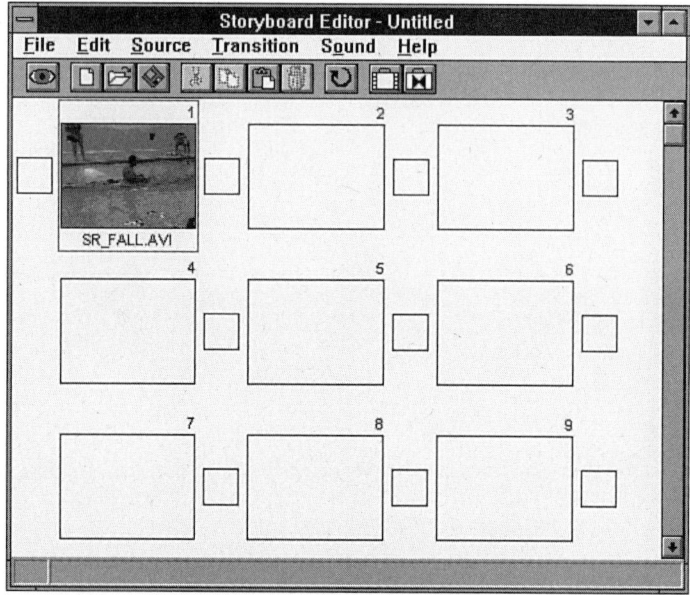

Figure 10.3. A file has been added to the Storyboard.

You can edit the clip easily. If you have not already done so, use File Manager to create a file association between AVI files and VIDEDIT.EXE. Then, when you want to edit the clip, just double-click it to launch VidEdit.

Even though you only have one clip so far, you can add a transition effect. You'll put it in the small box to the left of the file you just loaded. To create a transition, double-click the small box now. This will display the Transition Browser dialog box (see fig. 10.4).

There are nine kinds of transitions you can use. Each transition has options that you can set to vary the effect. Table 10.1 lists all the transitions and suggests ideas for using them effectively.

A dissolve is often a good choice for an opening transition. Double-click the Dissolve icon to display the dialog box shown in figure 10.5. The top half of the dialog box is used to set the parameters for the transition, and the lower half is used for setting the style of a transition. A dissolve doesn't have any style settings.

The top half of the dialog box is divided into three sections. The preceding video clip is controlled in the left section, the next video clip is controlled in the right section, and the length of the transition is controlled in the middle section.

Unlike most transitions, an opening transition has no video on the incoming side. The Storyboard supplies a solid color in place of the missing video clip. (Note that the Use Color check box is checked in fig. 10.5.) To change the color, just double-click on the black box. Use Color means that when the AVI file is created, you will see the color shown for the time indicated in the Duration box. In this case, the duration of the solid color is two seconds. You can change this value by typing a new value or by using the up/down arrows at the right.

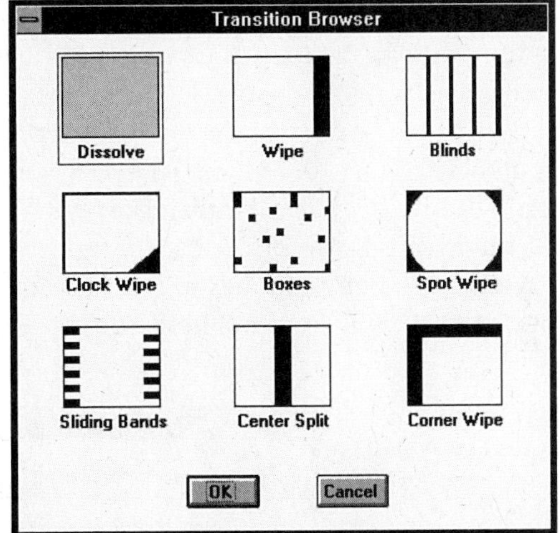

Figure 10.4. Using the Transition Browser.

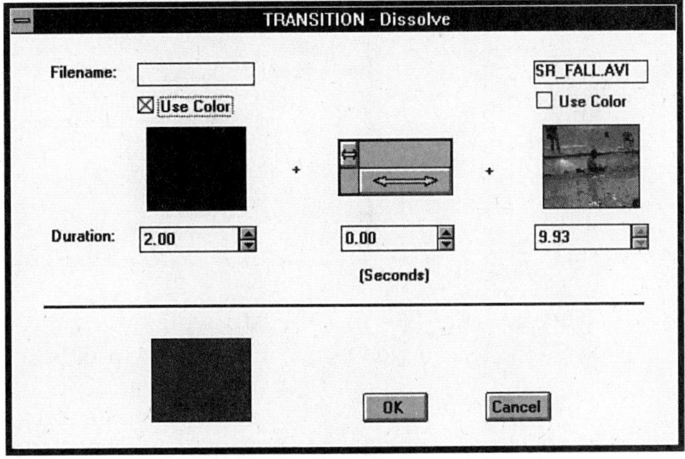

Figure 10.5. Setting options for the Dissolve transition.

The video clip that will follow the transition is shown at the right in the dialog box. Under the image is the length of the video clip (9.93 seconds in this example). The file name appears above the image.

In the center of the dialog box is a little contraption that controls the duration of the transition. The top half shows the preceding video clip, and the bottom half shows the next video clip. The duration is initially set to zero, so the blocks representing the two video clips do not overlap. The time you enter as a duration is the time that the two video clips will overlap. During the overlap time, the transition will be in progress. This means different things for different transitions.

In the case of a dissolve, the image on the left—solid black—will dissolve to the image on the right—the video clip. For example, if you enter a value of 1.5 seconds into the box below the duration contraption, it will change its appearance, as shown in figure 10.6. Figure 10.7 shows frame 13 from the transition—the image is still dark, and we are slightly more than halfway through the transition. Because the duration is 1.5 seconds, and the video was created with 15 frames per second, there is a total of 22 frames in the transition. Frame 1 will be completely black, and frame 22 will be completely from the video file.

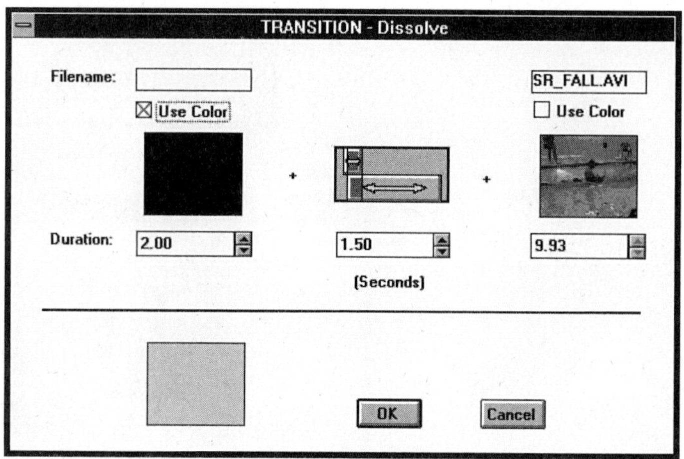

Figure 10.6. A dissolve with a duration of 1.5 seconds.

Note in figure 10.6 that the bars representing the two videos now overlap. If we were to create a video file right now, we would see

- .5 seconds of black
- 1.5 seconds with the video clip SR_FALL.AVI fading in from the black
- 8.43 seconds of the rest of the video clip SR_FALL.AVI.

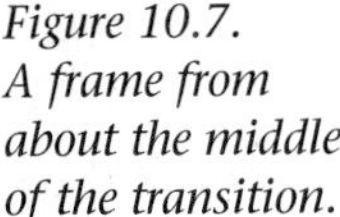

Figure 10.7.
A frame from about the middle of the transition.

The duration contraption is designed to help you visualize the relationship of the three pieces: the preceding video clip, the transition, and the next video clip.

Adding a transition to a video production does not add additional video to the production. A transition is applied during the time that two video clips overlap.

Click the OK button when you have all the durations set correctly. The Storyboard screen now looks like what you see in figure 10.8. The appearance of the small box has changed to show that a transition exists. To edit the transition, just double-click the small box.

This is a good time to look at table 10.1, which explains the various transitions and how to use them effectively. Although the terms *video 1* and *video 2* are used to refer to the video clips, either or both can also be a solid color for any of the transitions.

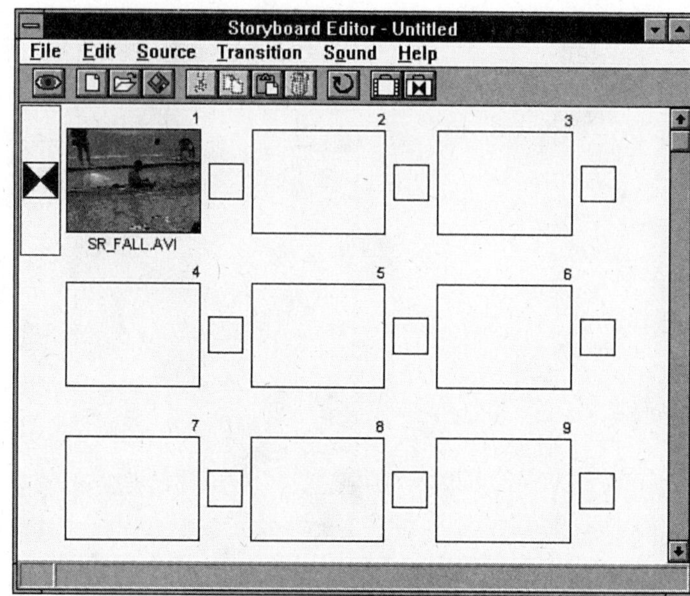

Figure 10.8. The Storyboard with one video clip and an opening transition.

Table 10.1. Transition Effects in the Storyboard.

Icon	*Transition*	*Description*
	Dissolve	Fades from video 1 to video 2 over the time specified. Useful for same-subject breaks between clips, but it also functions well in breaking transitions if you use a solid color as one part of the fade.
	Wipe	Moves one video over another. Different style settings allow you to control which video moves. You can slide the next video over the preceding video, or you can push one video clip with the other. Useful for new-subject transitions. You can wipe from eight directions: top/bottom, left/right, or the four corners (diagonal wipe).
	Blinds	The transition looks just like Venetian blinds and can be done horizontally or vertically. This is a fairly dramatic transition and is best for new-subject and breaking transitions.

Icon	Transition	Description
	Clock Wipe	A radial wipe.
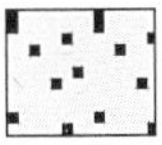	Boxes	Random boxes appear to create the transition from one clip to the next. Can be used almost anywhere, but don't overuse it because it is a very noticeable effect.
	Spot Wipe	Video 2 appears over video 1 in a growing spot; the spot can have several different shapes. This is a useful transition for video clips that have the subject located in the center of the frame. Best for breaking transitions, but in the right situation (*dramatic* is the key word here), it can be effective as a new-subject transition.
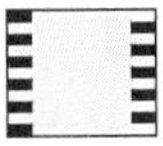	Sliding Bands	Numerous bands interlock like the teeth of a comb, with video 2 sliding over the top of video 1. A good new-subject transition, although it is sometimes effective as a same-subject transition, too.
	Center Split	A very good breaking transition. Video 2 (or, often, a solid color) comes in from both sides like a closing door.
	Corner Wipe	Video 2 slides over video 1 from one of the corners. This is an effective new-subject or breaking transition. You also can use it to create a shuffle effect with a sequence of same-subject videos.

Each of these transitions has its own individual style settings. For example, you may be able to select the direction the effect moves from, or how one video clip replaces another during the transition.

There are seven more files used for the complete *Kayak Self Rescue* video, as shown in figure 10.9. I also have added transitions for each of the video clips, as indicated by the shading of the small boxes.

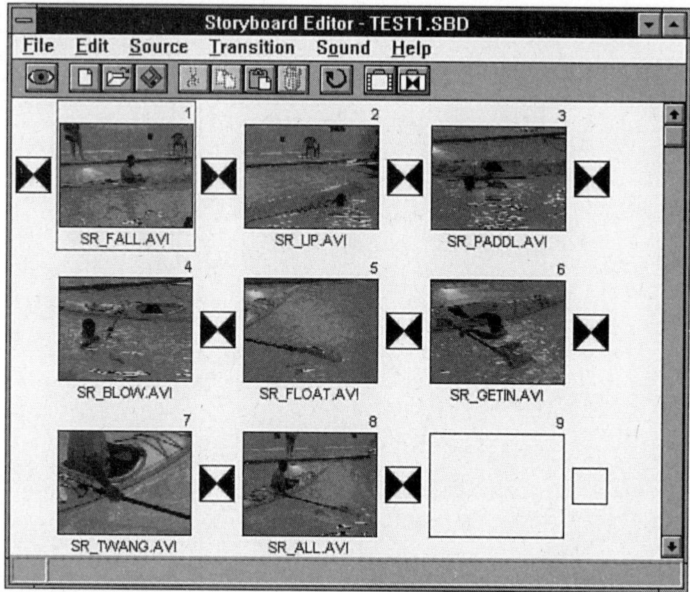

Figure 10.9. The complete Kayak Self Rescue video in the Storyboard.

Let's take a look at how I arrived at the choices for some of these transitions. This will give you some insight into the factors that will play a role in your own selection process when you create your own video productions with the Storyboard.

You often can determine what transition to use simply by examining the ending and beginning segments of the adjoining video clips. For example, figure 10.10 shows the ending frame of the video clip SR_FALL.AVI. Figure 10.11 shows the starting frame of the video clip SR_UP.AVI.

These images are very similar. Both show the kayak upside down, and the position of the paddler is similar, although we can't see much of him in figure 10.10. I chose to use the Sliding Bands transition because it adds some texture during the transition, which would otherwise be a very boring transition. Blinds also might be a good choice—there are no hard-and-fast rules about which transition is best. A dissolve wouldn't be effective, however, because it would look like the person in figure 10.11 was appearing out of nowhere. In some situations, of course, this would be exactly the right effect, but not here: this is a serious subject!

Figure 10.12 shows a frame from the midpoint of this transition. The textural quality of this transition is evident. It adds interest to an otherwise mundane transition.

Figure 10.10. The ending frame of SR_FALL.AVI.

Figure 10.11. The starting frame of SR_UP.AVI.

Figure 10.12. A Sliding Bands transition at the midpoint.

Let's look at another transition. There is a same-subject transition between the clips SR_BLOW.AVI and SR_FLOAT.AVI. Figure 10.13 shows the last frame of SR_BLOW.AVI. The paddler is inflating a small flotation device that he attached to his paddle. Figure 10.14 shows the first frame of SR_FLOAT.AVI, which is a close-up of the float on the paddle. I chose a dissolve to make the transition as smooth and unobtrusive as possible.

Figure 10.13. The last frame of the file SR_BLOW.AVI.

Figure 10.14. The first frame of SR_FLOAT.AVI.

Figure 10.15 shows the middle frame of the transition, with the two images superimposed. The paddle image is gradually fading in.

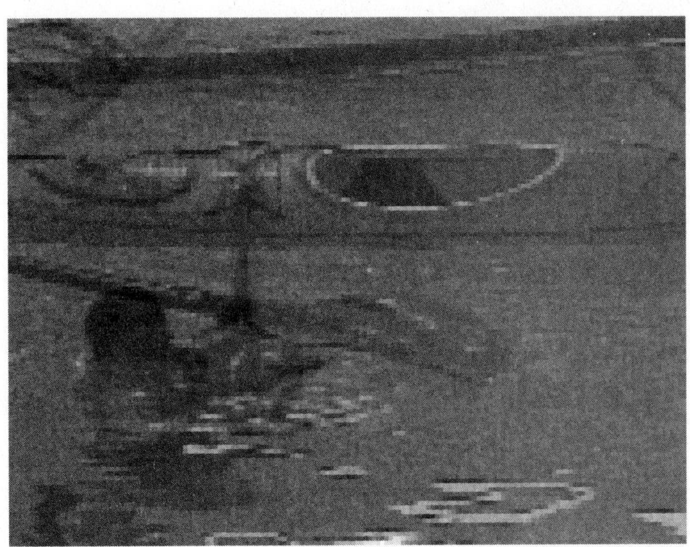

Figure 10.15. The last frame of the file SR_BLOW.AVI.

> Use longer duration (1 to 2 seconds) for same-subject transitions, and shorter duration for new-subject and breaking transitions (.5 to 1.5 seconds or less).

And remember: As with all rules, there are times when you will need to break the rules. Only you can decide when the time is right!

The Scene Editor

The Scene Editor is an extremely powerful tool. If you haven't worked in a video studio (and that includes just about everyone), the concepts may be completely new.

There are two important concepts used in the Scene Editor: time line and keying.

A *time line* is a method of representing a video project on your screen. The starting time (zero) is at the left of the screen (see fig. 10.16). *Keying* allows you to selectively add or remove portions of the video image. It is the process used to place the weatherman in front of the weather map on the evening news. You'll learn how to use keying later in this section.

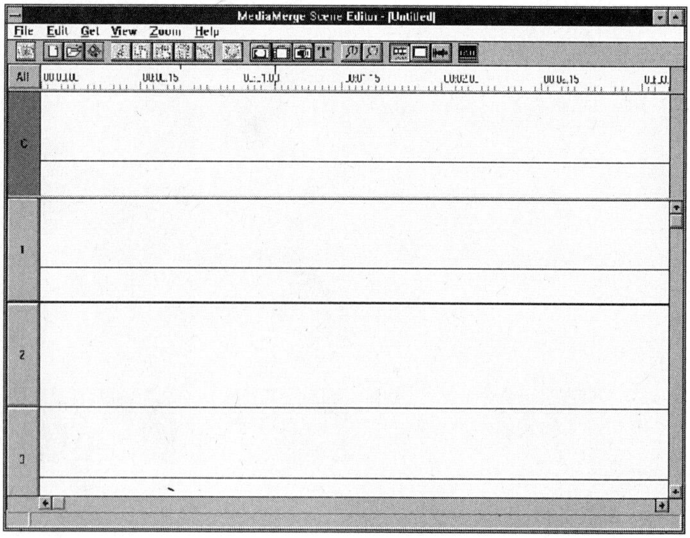

Figure 10.16. The Scene Editor screen. The time markers are at the top, beneath the toolbar.

The Scene Editor consists of the time markers and time lines. The time markers are located at the top of the screen, just below the toolbar. These mark time as explained in the section "Time Lines Explained" that follows. The time lines are the horizontal bars below the time markers. The top time line is labeled with a C at the left edge. This is the composite time line, and it shows how the final video will look. The other time lines are slots that can hold video clips, audio, bitmaps, or text.

When you produce a video using the Scene Editor, the various objects in their various time lines will be combined into the final video production.

Time Lines Explained

The individual frames are marked with tic marks at the top of the window, just beneath the toolbar. The starting time is marked as 00:00.00. This is a special form of time-keeping. The first two digits are minutes, and the second two digits are seconds. The last two digits are frames. An expanded version of this time format can include hours at the leftmost position: 00:00:00.00.

There are 30 frames in one second. That means that time is represented like this in the Scene Editor:

00:00.00—Starting time

00:00.15—Halfway through the first second

00:01.00—The first second

00:01.15—Halfway through the second second

00:02.00—The second second

To represent each frame, time is shown like this (see fig. 10.17):

00:00.00—The first frame

00:00.01—The second frame

00:00.02—The third frame

...

00:00.29—The 30th frame

00:01.00—The 31st frame

The kind of video you see on your television uses 30 frames per second. Most of the time, on your computer, you won't work with a full 30 frames per second, but because that is the maximum number of frames per second, that's what the Scene Editor must use. The most common rate you will work with is 15 frames per second. In that case, each frame will occupy two ticks on the time line.

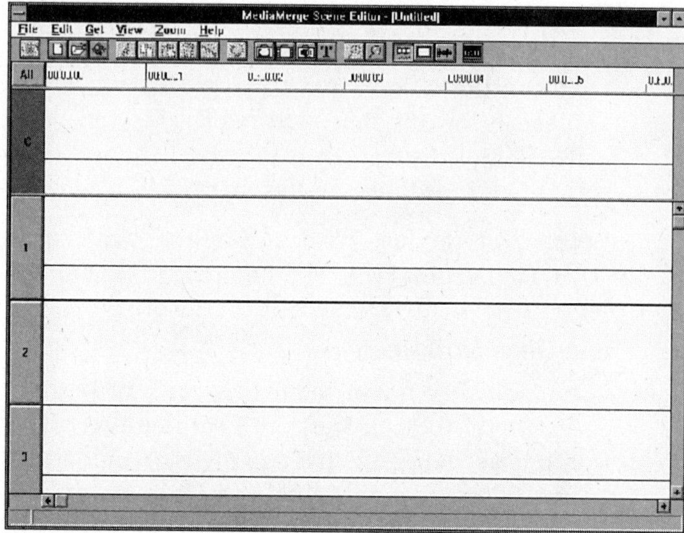

Figure 10.17. A time line expanded to show every frame.

You can adjust the scale of the time line easily in the Scene Editor. You can zoom in to see every frame, or you can zoom out to see the entire scene at a glance. Each tick on the time line can represent a single frame or many frames. The Zoom menu lets you choose how many frames you will see at one time. During this tutorial, you will learn how to adjust the scale of the time line.

The time line comes into play when you load one or more video files into the Scene Editor. It will show you how long each video is. You can use the time line to set the starting time of a video or to check the ending time of a video. The time line gives you precise control over the composition of a video scene.

A video scene can be made up of any of the kinds of resources shown in table 10.2. You'll learn how to use each of them in this section.

Table 10.2. Scene Editor Resources.

Resource	*Description*
Video Clip	Any AVI file. The video clip may or may not have any audio in it.
Audio Clip	Any WAV file.
Still Image	A bitmapped image. Valid file formats include BMP, PCX, GIF, TIF, TGA, EPS, and WMF.
Text	The Scene Editor allows you to create a moving or scrolling text object.

Video Clips

You can use the Scene Editor to combine video clips using overlay techniques. The first step is to load in the base video clip using the Get/Video menu selection. The cursor will change to a little hand—click at the left edge of time line #1 to place the video file. The result is shown in figure 10.18. The loaded clip is SR_ALL.AVI, from the tutorial directory of the CD-ROM disc. It is one of the clips used in the Storyboard example.

Figure 10.18. A single clip loaded into the Scene Editor.

The top half of time line #1 contains the video clip, and the bottom half of time line #1 contains the audio portion of the AVI file. The composite time line shows the same images as time line #1 because there is only one clip loaded. Now load a second video clip: SR_STROK.AVI. Place it in time line #2, as shown in figure 10.19.

Now look at the composite time line. It contains the same images as time line #2. The images from time line #1 have been completely lost. This is temporary. The important point to notice is that the images in each successive time line are placed on top of the images in the preceding time lines.

Here is where you learn to use keying techniques. Click on time line #2 to select it (if it is not already highlighted). Use the Edit/Set Overlay Option menu choice to display the dialog box shown in figure 10.20.

This dialog box is the heart of the Scene Editor. You'll learn about all of its capabilities elsewhere in this documentation. Right now, you'll learn how to use it to create a *Chroma key*. This uses color to select which portions of the video image will stay and which will be dropped.

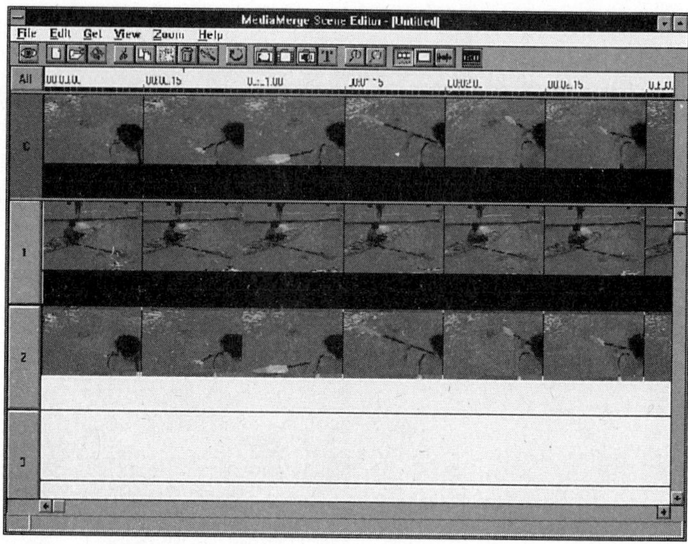

Figure 10.19. Two clips loaded into the Scene Editor.

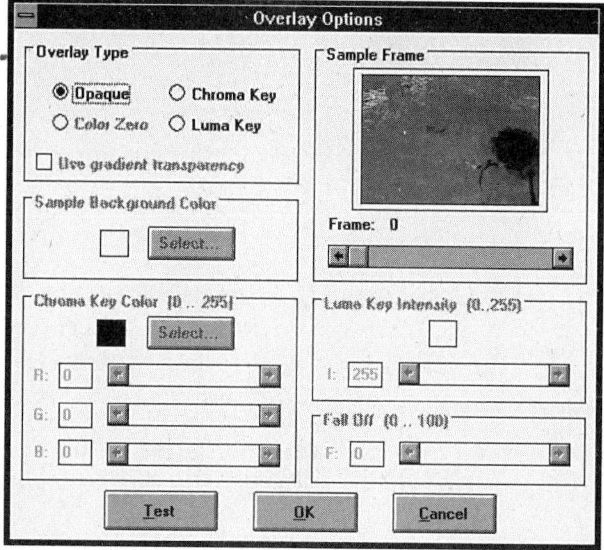

Figure 10.20. Setting overlay options for a video clip.

Click the Chroma key radio button. It's in the Overlay Type box at the upper left of the dialog box. Now move the mouse to the small image in the sample frame box. The cursor changes to a small dropper, which you can use to select the key color. Click in the large green area just above the paddle. The values for the Red, Green, and Blue portions of the color should match those shown in the Chroma Key Color box (see fig. 10.21). If they do not, click again on a slightly green shade, or enter the values using the keyboard.

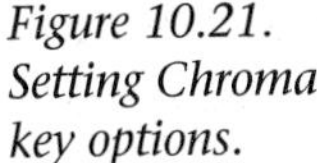

Figure 10.21. Setting Chroma key options.

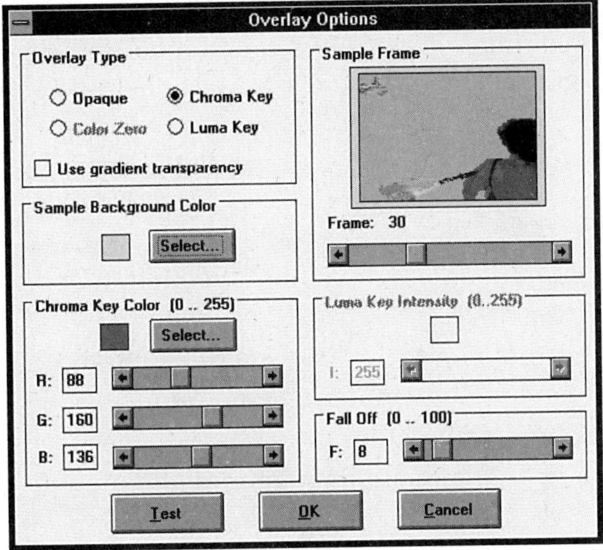

When you select a Chroma key color, that color is used to select the portion of the video image to drop. Try clicking on various colors. You'll see that all portions of the video image matching that color seem to disappear. Here's the trick: *Any video image in another time line will show through wherever the Chroma key color exists.* This is true only for time lines with lower numbers than this time line. In this example, setting a Chroma key color in time line #2 allows us to see the image in time line #1 wherever the Chroma key color exists.

Selecting only one color value to use as a Chroma key won't actually give you useful results in most cases. The Fall Off box at the lower right of the dialog box allows you to expand the Chroma key effect to similar colors. In this example, there is a range of green colors that need to "disappear." A Fall Off setting of 8 is about right.

When you have all the settings—Overlay Type, Chroma key Color, and Fall Off—set correctly, the sample frame should look like the example in figure 10.21. Click OK to save the settings. The Scene Editor now looks like figure 10.22.

The Composite time line looks completely different. The video clip in time line #1 now shows through the areas that contain the Chroma key colors. As objects move from frame to frame, only those areas that contain the Chroma key colors will allow the first video clip to show through.

Because this is a time line, you may want to set the starting point of the overlay video clip in time line #2 so that it ends at the same time as the first video clip. To do this, you will need to change the zoom factor. In figure 10.22, the time line has been zoomed all the way in to show each individual frame. To zoom out, select the Zoom/1 second (30 frames) menu selection. This will show the full video clips in the time lines. You can click and drag the clip in time line #2 until its ending point matches that of the video in time line #1, as shown in figure 10.23.

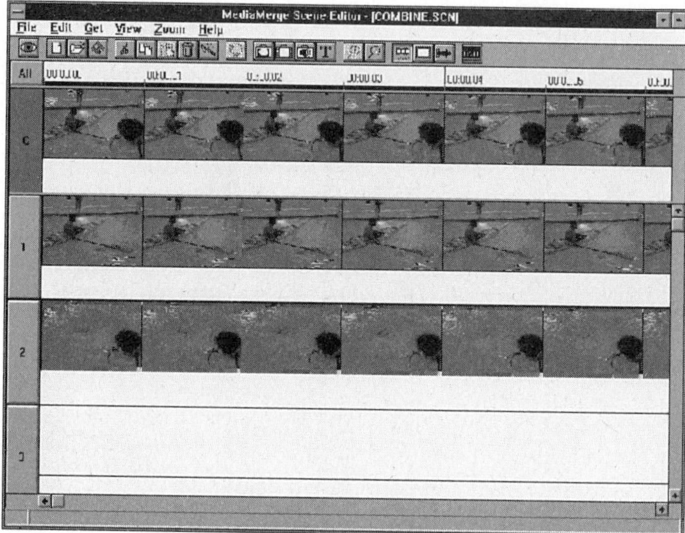

Figure 10.22. The Composite time line has been altered by the use of Chroma key.

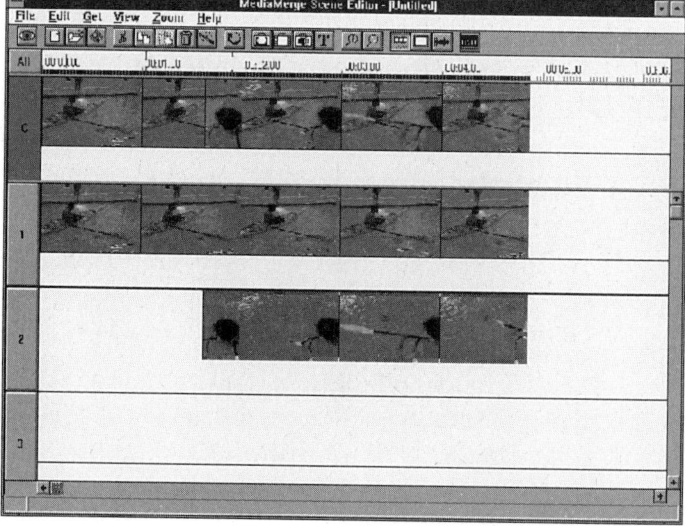

Figure 10.23. Adjusting video clip timing in the Scene Editor.

You can use multiple video clips to create multilayered effects. Figure 10.24 shows three video clips loaded, and key colors have been created for two of them, allowing the underlying video clips to show through.

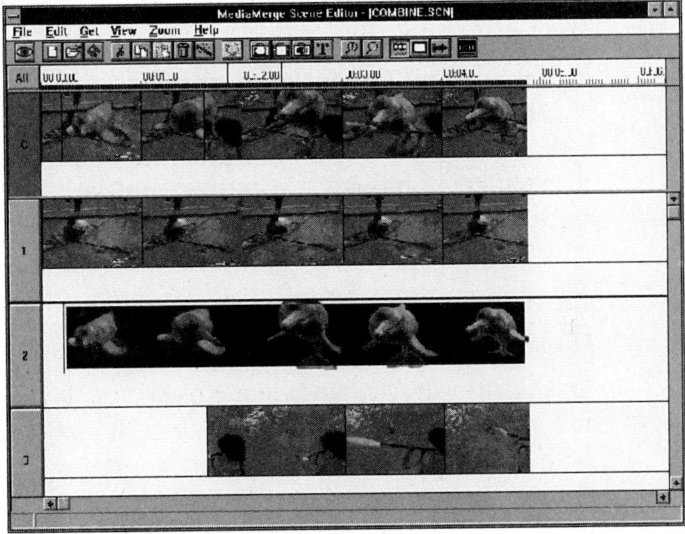

Figure 10.24. Using three video clips to create multilayered effects.

TIP You can adjust the starting or ending point of a video clip (or audio clip, for that matter) by clicking and dragging the beginning or ending edge of the clip in its time line.

Note that the video in time line #2 has a black background behind the dolphin. There is a story behind this video that explains how to work with videos that do not work well with conventional keying. The dolphin was swimming in a huge tank at the Pittsburgh Zoo when I shot the video. The water and the dolphin are nearly the same color. Chroma key not only made the water disappear—it took most of the dolphin with it. But the dolphin was such a nice clip that I took some extra time to create a black background for each frame. The process is time-consuming but well worth it if you have an image you really need to use with keying.

My favorite program for this process is Adobe Photoshop. The Windows version includes a number of tools that make the process much easier. To modify the individual frames, use VidEdit to save the frames as bitmaps first. Then, you can load each bitmap into Photoshop, make the changes, and then load all the revised bitmaps back into VidEdit.

To save the video sequence as a series of bitmaps, use the File/Extract menu selection in VidEdit. Choose DIB Sequence from the list of options at the lower left of the dialog box. Enter a base file name for the sequence, such as DOLPH001.BMP. It will take a few moments for VidEdit to create all the bitmap files. They will have sequential names—DOLPH001.BMP, DOLPH002.BMP, and so on. Figure 10.25 shows one of the bitmaps (frame 57) loaded into Photoshop.

Although the goal is to select the background and fill it with black, I find it easier to select the dolphin, and then invert the selection. Because the color of the dolphin and the color of the background are so similar, you cannot use the magic wand in Photoshop for this purpose. Instead, choose the Lasso tool. Hold down the Alt key while you click along the dolphin's outline, and then double-click to create the selection. The dolphin will be outlined by a dotted line (see fig. 10.26).

Use the Select/Invert menu selection to invert the selection. This causes only the background to be part of the selection (see fig. 10.27).

Make sure the background color is black, and then use the Edit/Fill menu selection to fill the selected area. Use the settings shown in figure 10.28.

Figure 10.25. A frame converted to a bitmap and loaded into Photoshop.

Figure 10.26. The dolphin has been made into a selection.

Figure 10.27. Inverting the selection.

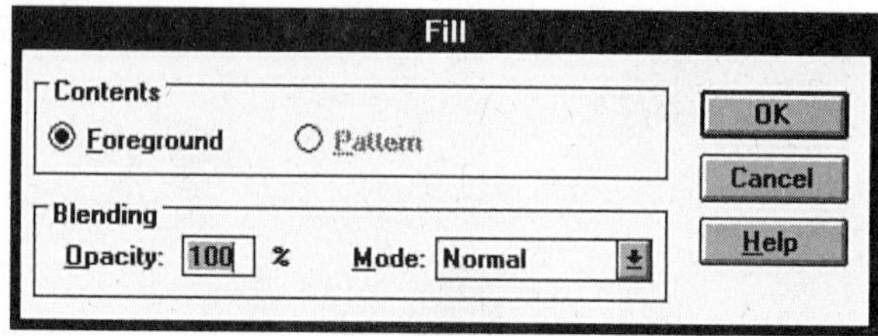

Figure 10.28. Fill settings for a solid black background.

The result of the fill operation is shown in figure 10.29.

Because there is usually only a small difference in the position of an object from frame to frame, you can use Photoshop's ability to copy a selection to your advantage in this situation. Rather than go through the tedious process of outlining the dolphin by hand in the next frame, you can use the Image/Calculate/Duplicate menu selection to copy the selection. Figure 10.30 shows the dialog box that you will work with.

Figure 10.29. The filled selection.

To copy the selection boundaries without copying its contents, you must use the settings shown in figure 10.30. The source document should be the bitmap you just worked with; the selection must still be active. The channel must be Selection—otherwise you will wind up copying the image or a single color channel. The destination document—which must already be open, by the way—should be the bitmap for the next frame. The channel for the destination should also be the selection. I highly recommend using the Invert option, located at the bottom of the dialog box. The current selection is the background. You will almost certainly have to make minor edits to the selection in the new bitmap, and edits are much easier when you are working with a selection area that matches an object. Inverting the selection should make it nearly match the outline of the dolphin in the new bitmap. The result of the operation is shown in figure 10.31.

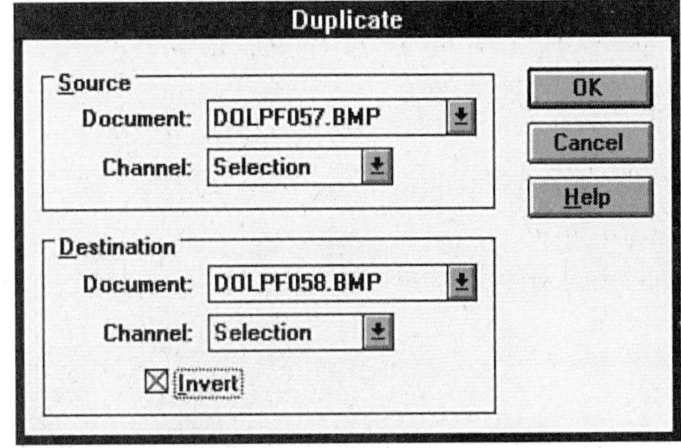

Figure 10.30. The Image/ Calculate/ Duplicate dialog box.

Figure 10.31. A selection mask copied to a new bitmap.

Note that the outline is offset quite a bit from the new image. However, this was due to camera shake (the camera was hand-held). Grabbing and moving the selection to cover the position of the dolphin makes a nearly complete match. A few minor edits, and the selection mask is complete, as shown in figure 10.32. You can now proceed to invert, fill the background, and copy the mask to the next frame.

Occasionally, the difference from frame to frame will be large, and you will have to re-create the selection mask from scratch. Even so, this is far less tedious than re-creating the mask for every frame.

When you have completed the process and have filled the background for every frame, you can use VidEdit to File/Insert the DIB Sequence and save it as an AVI file. Figure 10.33 shows a sequence of frames from the modified video sequence.

Figure 10.32. The copied and modified selection mask.

When used in Media Merge, the modified sequence will look something like figure 10.34.

Figure 10.33. The modified video sequence.

Figure 10.35 shows yet another use for video overlay. The first video sequence (in time line #1) is the finished production from the section "The Storyboard" of this chapter. Time line #2 contains a talking head. Instead of just using a narration, I used the talking head to give the piece a focus and a little personality. The audio track is in time line #2.

The result of this scene is shown in figure 10.36. The entire video from the section "The Storyboard" appears to play in the background. Figure 10.37 shows this more dramatically. Even the transition effects are located completely behind the head.[9]

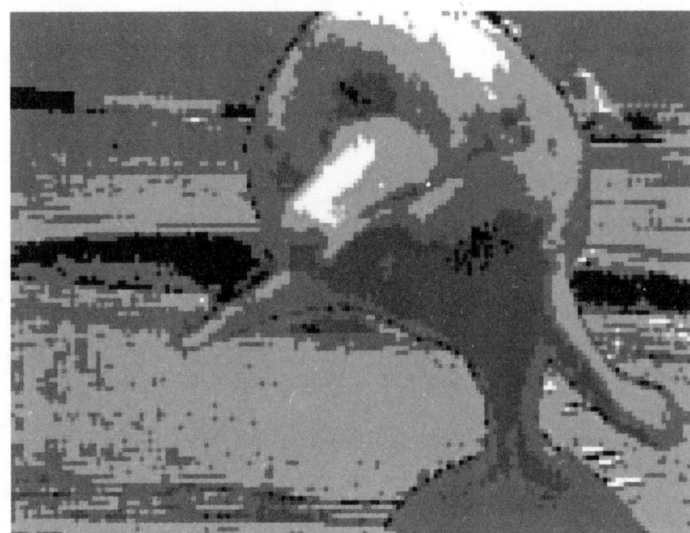

Figure 10.34. An example of a modified frame in use.

[9]That's my head, of course.

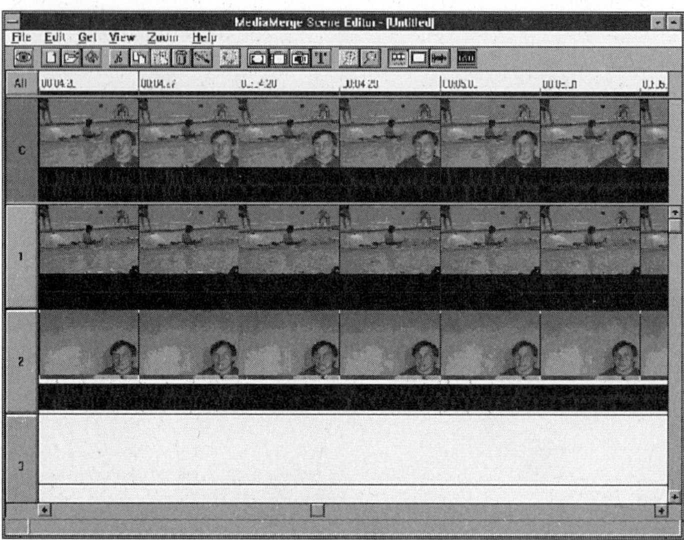

Figure 10.35. Integrating a "talking head" into a video clip.

Figure 10.36. A frame from the combined video.

If you must use talking heads, this gives you a powerful tool for making them much more interesting!

Audio Clips

Audio clips are very easy to use in the Scene Editor. In fact, you can use the Scene Editor to mix multiple audio sources. To add an audio source, use the Get/Audio menu selection. As with a video clip, the cursor will change to a little hand. Click in the audio portion of a time line to place the audio clip.

Figure 10.37. Another frame from the combined video. Note that the effect is completely in the background of the "talking head."

Figure 10.38 shows an audio clip placed in time line #2, where a video clip was already placed. Because the video clip did not have an audio track, there was an open spot for adding audio. Note that the audio track shows up in the composite track. The Scene Editor will mix the various audio tracks into a single track for you when you File/Produce the video.

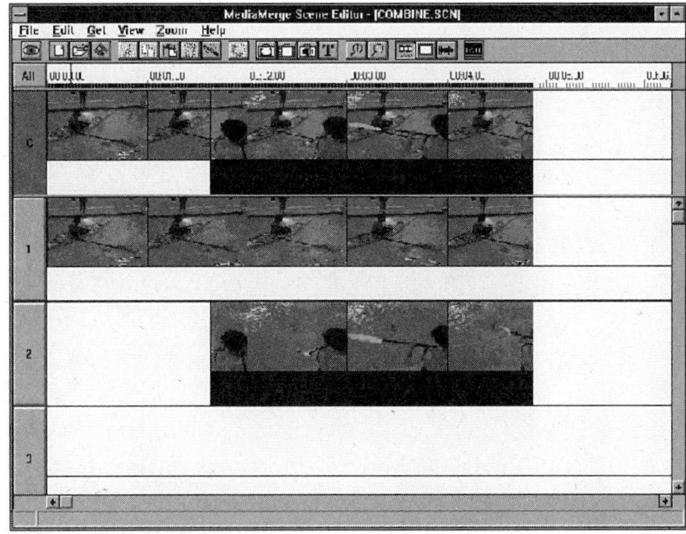

Figure 10.38. Adding an audio clip to the Scene Editor.

Still Images

Still images are also easy to use. Use the Get/Still menu selection to load a still image. As with video and audio clips, the cursor will change to a little hand, and you can then drop the still image into a time line. It will initially occupy a single frame, as shown in figure 10.39. (I have used Chroma key to allow the kayak frames to show through the new frame. That's me, Mr. Author, in the still.)

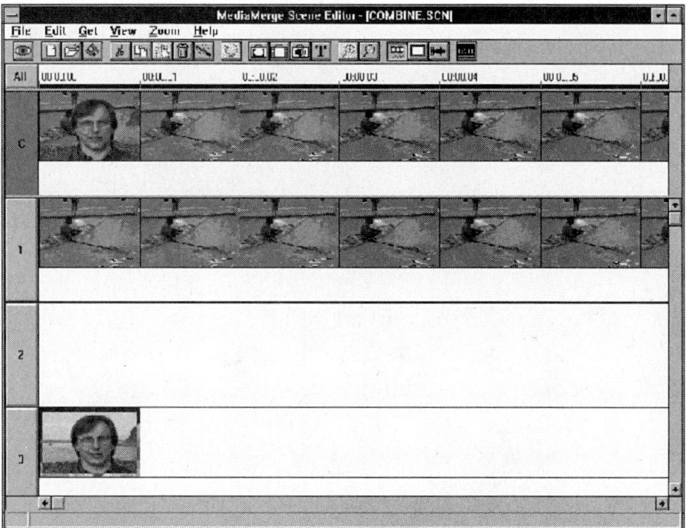

Figure 10.39. Adding a still image to a frame.

You can expand the duration of the still image by simply clicking and dragging the right edge of the image in the time line. This adds the still image to additional frames, as shown in figure 10.40.

Text

Text has many uses in a video production—titles, credits, explanations, identifiers, and more. For example, you can use text in a video to

- Identify a speaker
- Identify a product
- Explain an action

Traditional titles and credits can be created in the Scene Editor. For example, you can create a title for the *Kayak Self Rescue* video by using the Get/Text menu selection. This displays the dialog box shown in figure 10.41.

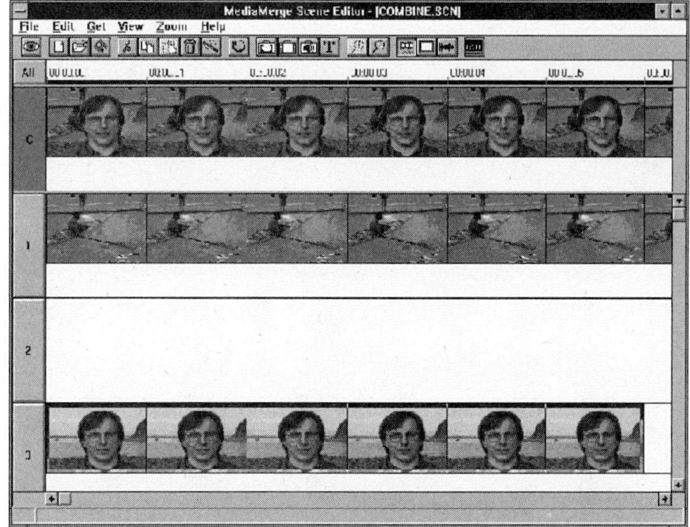

Figure 10.40. Extending the duration of a still image.

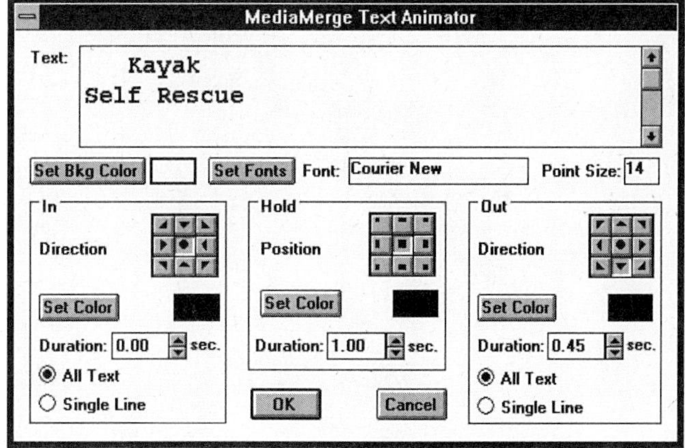

Figure 10.41. Adding text to a scene.

The top portion of the dialog box allows you to enter text and choose fonts (including style and size). The lower portion of the dialog box contains three boxed areas that can animate your text.

The In box lets you choose in which direction the text will enter (or use the center dot to create stationary text). You can choose the **text** color and the duration of the entry. This is useful for such text as scrolling credits.

The Hold box allows you to define a position where the text will stay put, and you can set a color and duration. This is useful for titles. You can also combine In and Hold—slide the text in from any direction and then hold it in place.

The Out box is similar to the In box. You can determine what direction the text will take to exit the screen, set color, and set duration. You can combine the Out settings with In and/or Hold.

Let's look at an example of animated text. In figure 10.41, there is no In setting, so the text will appear within the frame in the position marked by the Hold setting (the center of the frame). The duration of the hold is 1 second. After 1 second, the Out setting will be used. It calls for the text to scroll downward over the course of .45 second.

Figure 10.42 shows several frames from the Scene Editor, showing the result of these text-animation settings.

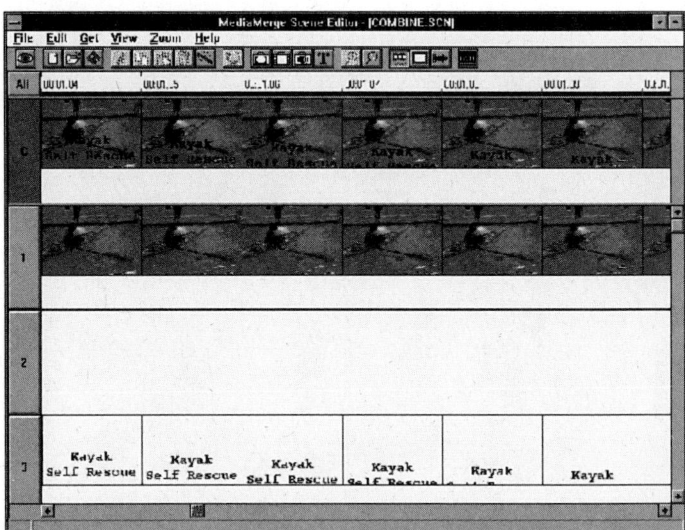

Figure 10.42. Text animation in the Scene Editor.

Working with Adobe Premiere

Premiere provides a single environment for working with all aspects of video production. Control of video clips, overlays, transitions, effects, and audio is combined into a single window. As you can see in figure 10.43, however, that one window contains a lot of smaller ones.

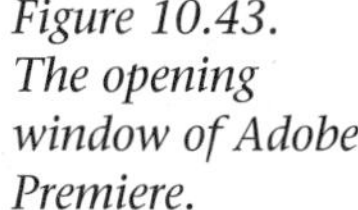

Figure 10.43. The opening window of Adobe Premiere.

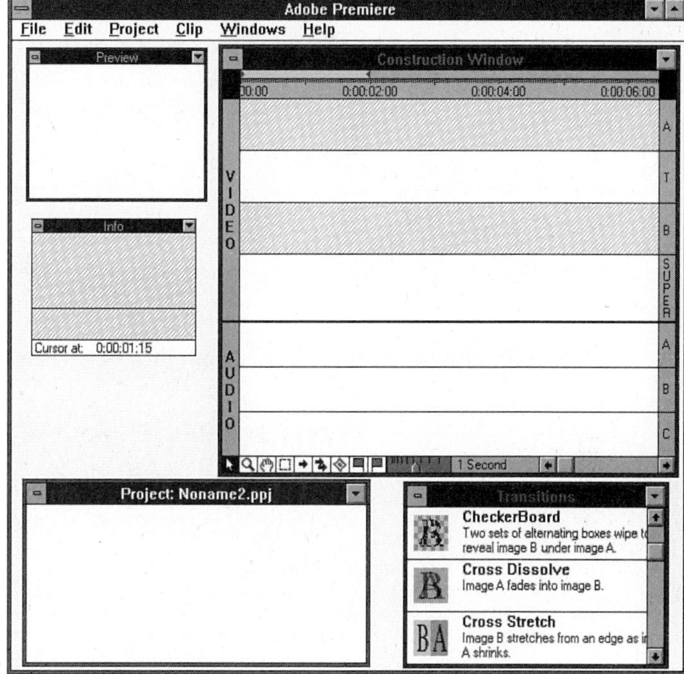

Working clockwise from the upper left, those windows are

Preview—You can preview all or part of the production at any time by pressing the Enter key. The preview plays in this window.

Construction—This is where you build your video production from a variety of sources, including video clips, bitmaps, audio files, animation, transitions, effects, and so on.

Transitions—Clip-to-clip transitions are stored here. To use one, just drag it to the Construction window.

Project—Contains the files for the project.

Info—Provides information about the current file in the Construction window.

There are also a number of temporary windows you will use from time to time. Most of them are viewers for various kinds of files—video clips, bitmaps, sound files, and so on.

One of the most important windows is the *Transitions* window, shown in more detail in figure 10.44. Premiere comes with a wide variety of transitions, some of them quite dramatic. However, in most cases, you'll use a small subset of the transitions. If you try to use a fancy transition every time, you'll overwhelm your audience. Discretion is the better part of creativity as well as of valor.

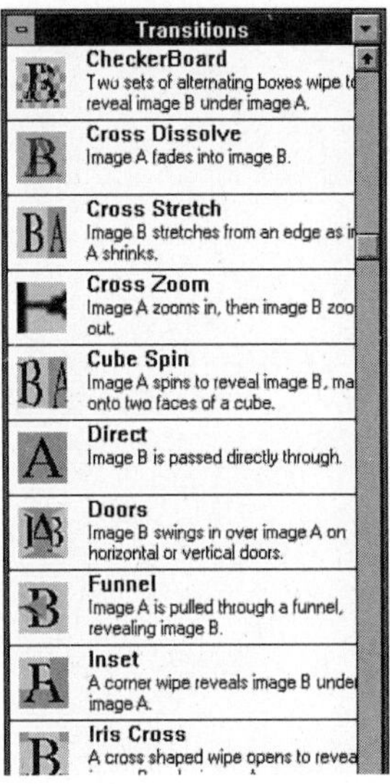

Figure 10.44. Premiere comes with about 30 transitions of various kinds; only a subset is shown here in the Transitions window.

The first step in any video production using Premiere is to load the various files you plan to use into the Project Editor. As you can see in figure 10.45, you can select more than one file at a time for adding.

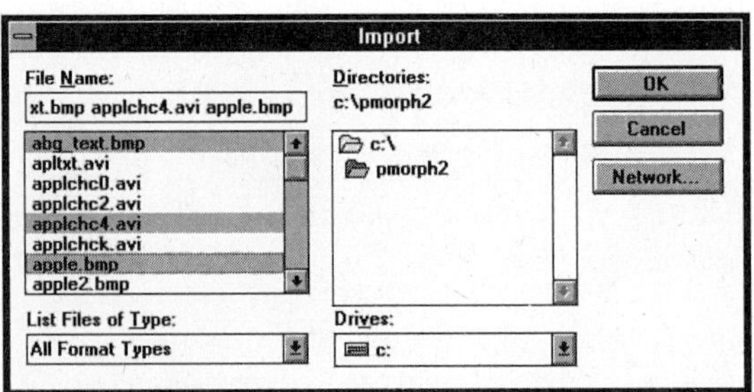

Figure 10.45. Adding multiple files at one time.

When you load files into the project, they are visible in the Project window (see fig. 10.46). If the file contains an image (AVI, FLC, BMP, and so on) you will see a small representation on the left side of the Project window. Details about the file—type, duration, instance, size, and so on—appear at the right.

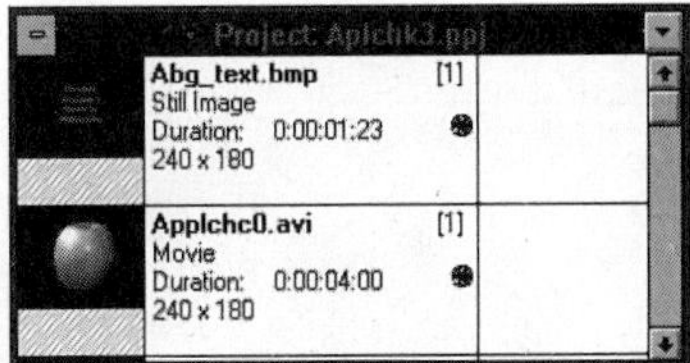

Figure 10.46. Detail of the Project window.

In this example, I will show you how to use the basic features of Premiere to build a video production out of video clips, bitmaps, and transitions. We'll go over the process in some detail, because Premiere has a lot of power. You may not realize how powerful if you don't dig behind the surface a bit.[10] The finished production will include the following:

- Text fades in from black
- Image of apple fades in under text
- Text fades out
- Apple morphs to image of chick
- Hold briefly on image of chick
- Chick morphs back to apple
- Apple fades to black

That's just the video portion. We will add to that a simple animation created in 3D Studio. The animation shows a ball bouncing randomly in 3D space, and we'll overlay that on top of the video just described.[11]

Figure 10.47 shows the text bitmap, and figure 10.48 shows the apple-plus-text bitmap. You'll note that the text says *Absolute Beginner's Guide to Multimedia.* That's the title of another book I wrote, and the video production was intended as the "theme video" for the CD that accompanies that book.[12]

---

[10]If you purchase Premiere, be sure to read the manual. You really will learn things that will surprise you, because the key to the best use of Premiere is learning cool ways to combine features. Unlike many software packages, where you learn specific procedures, Premiere is extremely open-ended in its possibilities. In particular, the back of the manual has some amazing tricks you can do only if you know the secrets.

[11]This is a simple example of what can be done with video overlay; you'll see detailed interaction between video and animation later in this chapter. If you want very tight integration between the video and the animation, you should complete the video first, and then build the animation to match the video exactly. For example, I could have created a 3D animation of a worm, which starts out in a hole in the apple, and winds up in the chick's beak as breakfast (hmmm...do chicks eat worms?). Unfortunately, the idea came along after I had already written the chapter—now you have something to try at home.

[12]The final video, as an AVI file, is also included on the CD that comes with this book.

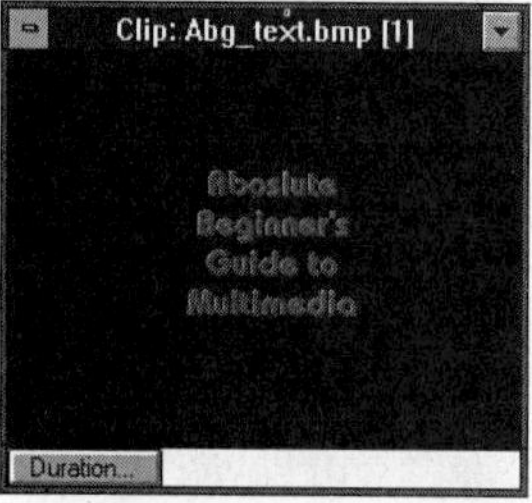

Figure 10.47.
The text bitmap.

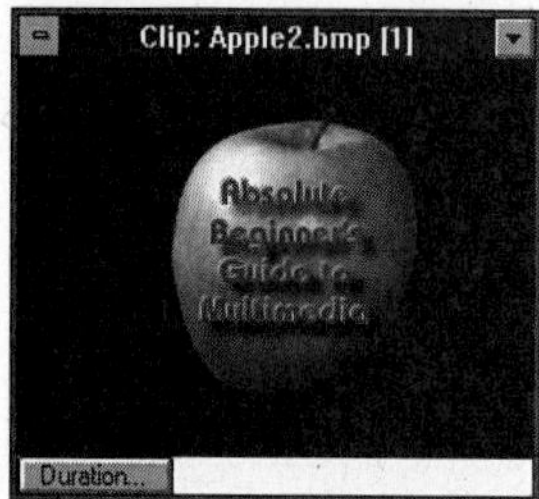

Figure 10.48.
The apple-plus-text bitmap.

The apple is shown in figure 10.49, and the chick bitmap is in figure 10.50. These two images were morphed using PhotoMorph; see Chapter 8 for information about PhotoMorph.[13]

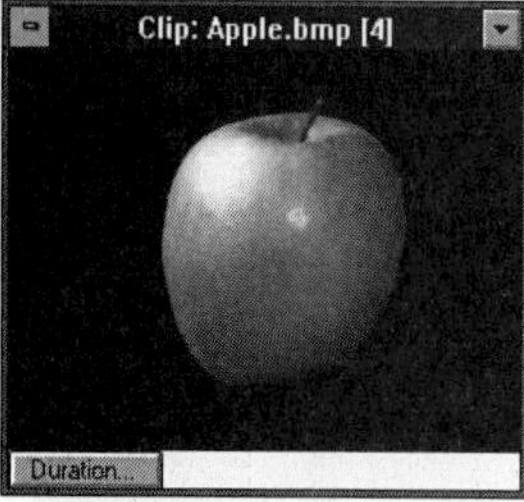

Figure 10.49.
The apple bitmap.

Figure 10.50.
The chick bitmap.

[13]Note also that there is a demo version of PhotoMorph on the CDs.

Once all the files have been loaded into the Project window, you can start dragging them one at a time into the Construction window. There are two tracks for videos in the Construction window: A and B. The names of each track are found at the right edge of the window. From top to bottom, the tracks in the Construction window are

Video A	One of the two video tracks.
Transitions	Transitions between clips go here.
Video B	The other video track.
Super	Video clips for overlay go here.
Audio A	One of three audio tracks.
Audio B	Another audio track.
Audio C	Yet another audio track.

To put any clip (audio or video or bitmap or whatever) or transition into a track, just drag it from its window to the track. You can only drag onto valid tracks—you can't put a WAV file in a video track, for example.

Figure 10.51 shows the first video clip on video track B—there is no need to start with track A. This clip is the bitmap with just text. When you drag a bitmap onto a video track, you must adjust the duration. Note that the right edge of the bitmap corresponds to the 2-second mark in the timeline at the top of the Construction window.

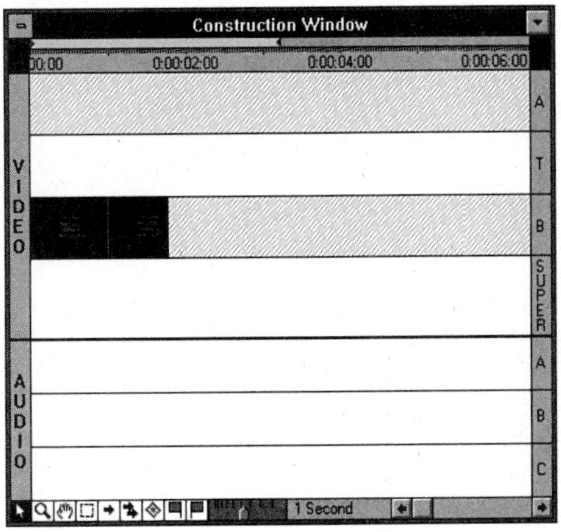

Figure 10.51. Adding the first video clip.

To add the second clip, you simply drag it from the Project window to track A in the Construction window (see fig. 10.52). Since the script calls for a fade between the clips, the clips must overlap. The fade will occur during the overlap.

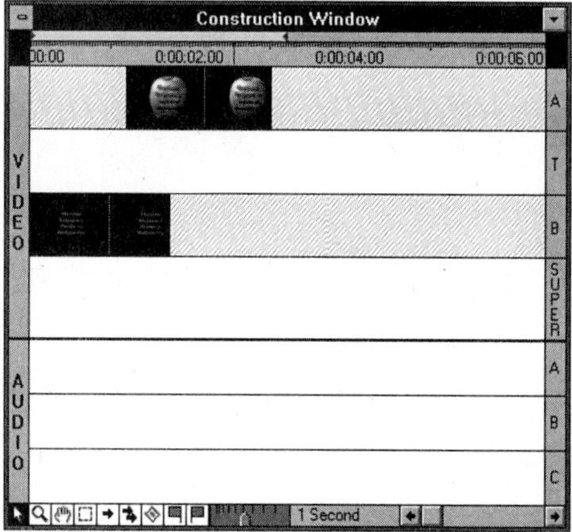

Figure 10.52. Adding the second video clip.

But the fade is not automatic. By default, any video on track A will show on top of any video in track B. To create a fade, we must add a transition from the Transition window. For a simple fade, the Cross Dissolve transition is the best choice. You can drag the transition to the Transition track in the Construction window the same way as you drag a clip from the Project window. Figure 10.53 shows the Cross Dissolve in place. If the starting and ending points of the transition do not match the starting and ending points of the two clips after dragging, simply click and drag the left and/or right edge of the transition to the correct position. Note that when you move the edge of the transition near the edge of a clip, it more or less "jumps" to a matching time point.

If we were to stop here, we'd have a very simple but perfectly functional video. You don't have to add any video clips at all to a Premiere project to get video output.

You should double-click the transition to verify that it is set up properly. By default, the transition probably is set up for a fade from track A to track B, and we want the opposite result. A double-click will display the dialog box shown in figure 10.54.

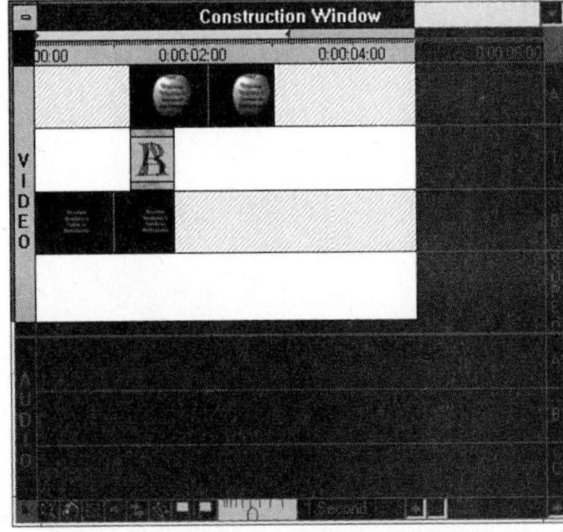

Figure 10.53. A transition has been added to the Construction window.

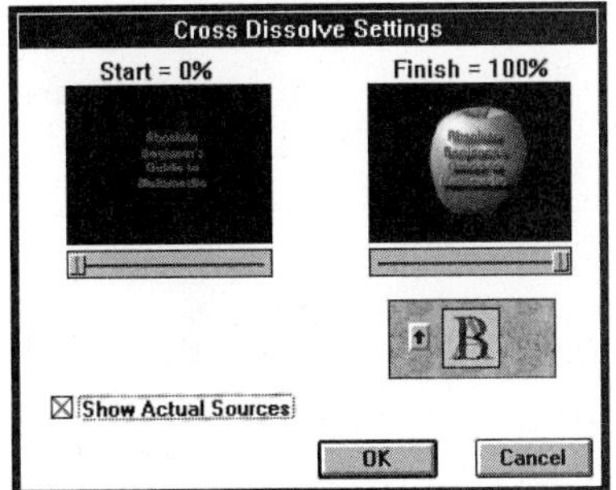

Figure 10.54. Editing a Cross Dissolve.

Note that I have clicked the Show Actual Sources check box. Otherwise, all you get is a big letter A on the left, and a B on the right, or vice versa. Looking at the actual source clips eliminates any possibility of a mistake.

The box on the left is marked Start, and that's how the transition will look when it begins. The start percentage is 0%, which is good for a Cross Dissolve. For some transitions, you may want to start in the middle to get the right effect; just move the slider below the image to select a different start percentage. If you do not see the text image on the left, and the text-plus-apple image on the right, click the arrow in the small image of the transition at the lower right to reverse the direction of the transition.

To preview the dissolve, drag the slider below the left image slowly from left to right. Don't forget to put it back to 0% when you are done. I've forgotten to do that a zillion times, and you usually don't notice the problem until you create the final video production. Since it can take an hour to compress a minute of video, that's a lot of wasted time! Always verify your transitions before you take the time to create the output file.

Let's continue with adding the various pieces of the production. Figure 10.55 shows the next clip to add—the apple image. The script calls for a fade from the apple-plus-text to just the apple. The apple is the starting point of the morph. If we simply did a fade to the morph, we'd wind up fading over the first portion of the morph, and that wouldn't be at all smooth.

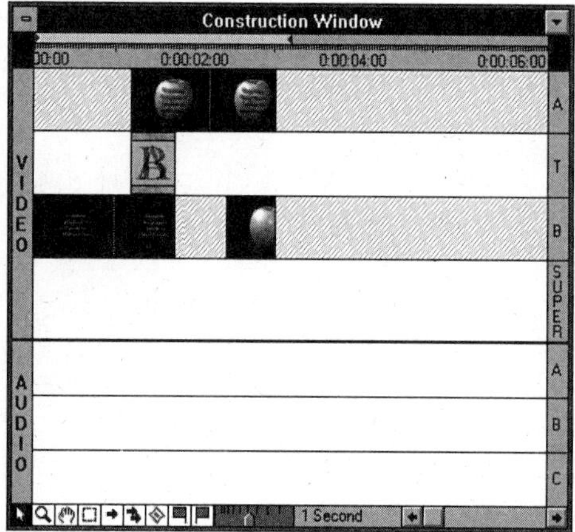

Figure 10.55. Adding another bitmap to track B.

This transition is also a fade, so we'll use the Cross Dissolve again. Figure 10.56 shows the dialog box for the transition. Verify that the right image is on the right side of the transition.

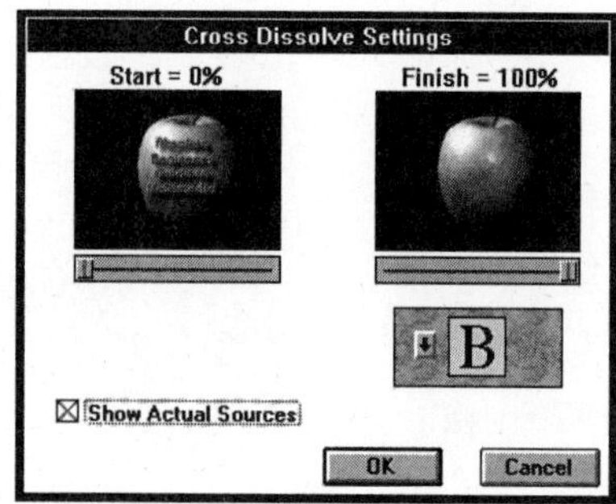

Figure 10.56. Verify that the transition proceeds in the correct direction.

The next step is to load the apple-to-chick morph that was created in PhotoMorph. This clip is about 5 seconds long—too long to display properly at the time scale we've been using. It would disappear out the right side of the Construction window. To change the time scale, click on the bottom edge of the Construction window where you see the small pointer, just to the left of the time scale indication of 1 second. Click just a short distance to the right of the pointer to zoom out; a time scale of 2 seconds is about right. We'll now see twice as much as we did before; compare figure 10.57 to figure 10.55.

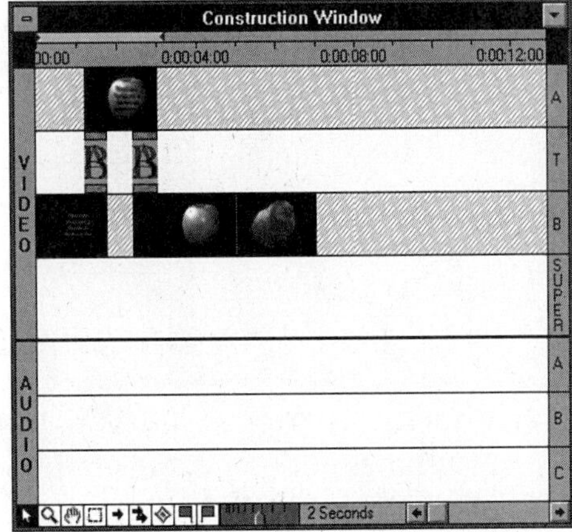

Figure 10.57. Adding the morph clip and changing the time scale.

Note that we now have three bitmaps, two transitions, and one video clip (the morph is an AVI file). Next, the script calls for a hold on the image of the chick. We'll use a bitmap for that, as shown in figure 10.58. The bitmap itself is shown in figure 10.50.

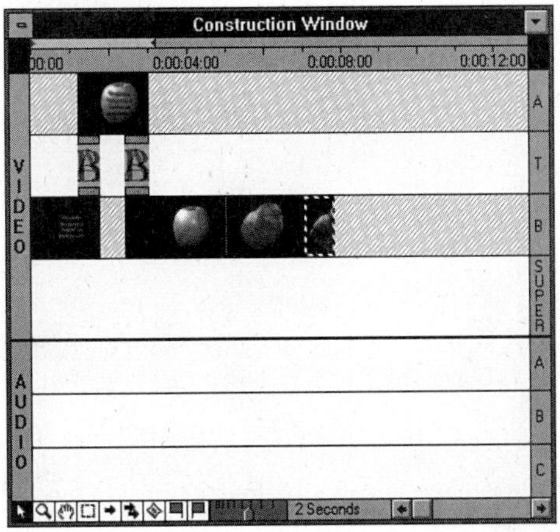

Figure 10.58. Adding a bitmap of the chick.

Now we want to reverse the morph. I could have created a reverse morph, of course, but there's an easier way to handle this. Drag the morph clip a second time from the Project window, but this time drag it up to track A, with a start point matching the end point of the chick bitmap (see fig. 10.59).[14]

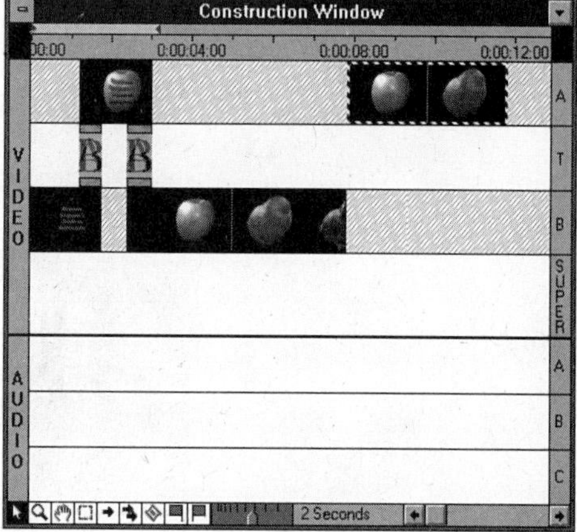

Figure 10.59. Adding the same clip a second time.

This time, there is no overlap and no transition. This is called a *cut* in video lingo. However, as things now stand, the morph will simply repeat itself from the beginning—and that's not at all what we want here. Click on the second version of the morph, in track A, and then use the Options/Filters menu selection to display the dialog box shown in figure 10.60. Select the Filter Backwards (video) from the Available list, and then click the Add button to move it to the Current list.[15]

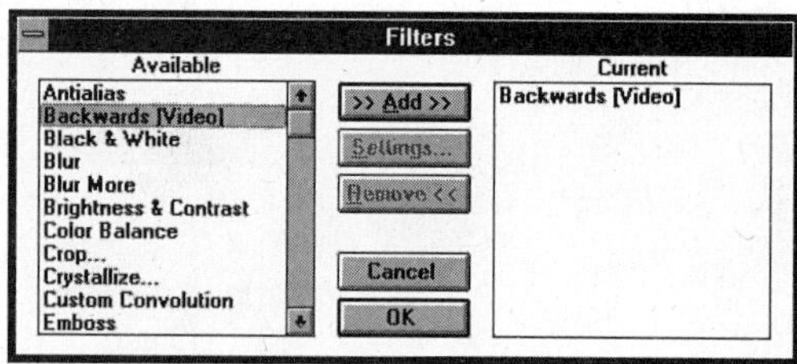

Figure 10.60. Adding a filter to a clip.

[14] If you look in the Project window, you'll see that you now have a second copy of the morph clip there, with a small 2 at the upper right. This indicates that it is a second instance of an existing clip.

[15] You can add more than one effect to a video clip. However, each filter adds significant processing time, and you can easily double or triple production time if you add extra filters.

Now, when we create the final production, Premiere will give us an exact reverse of the morph. You will not see the morph backward in the Construction window, however.

The script now calls for a fade from the ending apple image of the morph to black. We'll need to add a bitmap of the apple for the fade, as shown in figure 10.61. Figure 10.62 shows the dialog box for the Cross Dissolve; note that the apple is on the left, and the color black is on the right. This is the default color for any transition if there is no video clip on the other track.

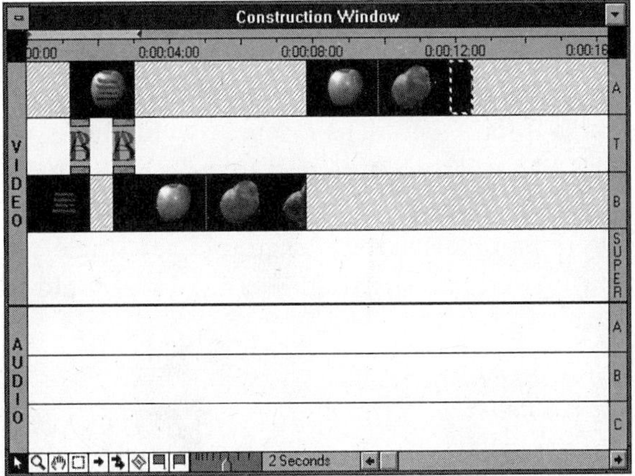

Figure 10.61. Adding another bitmap.

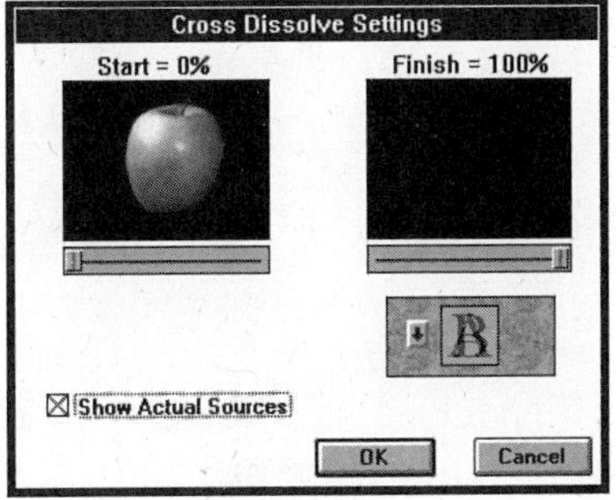

Figure 10.62. Cross dissolve for end of the production.

We can use this to create a fade from black at the beginning of the project. Just drag a Cross Dissolve to the Transition track at the beginning of the project. Peek ahead to figure 10.65 to see what this looks like. Figure 10.63 shows the dialog box for the Cross Dissolve at the beginning of the project.

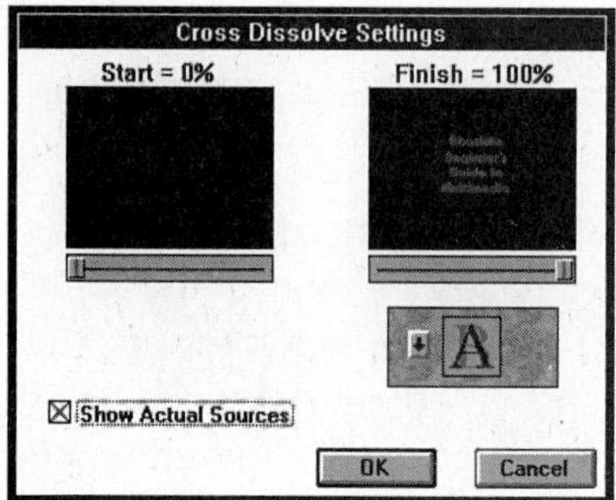

Figure 10.63. Setting a cross dissolve for the beginning of the project.

We have now added all the features and effects needed for the video clip; it's time to add the 3D object. I used 3D studio to create a simple bouncing ball. Since the impact of the comet with Jupiter was all the rage at the time of writing, I gave the ball a surface texture using a map of Jupiter as a base. I output the animation as an FLC file, and then imported that file into the Project window. Figure 10.64 shows a sample frame from the animation. The ball moves against a black background. It's important that the background be a single, uniform color. Black is OK, but since the ball uses mostly shades of red, blue would have been better.

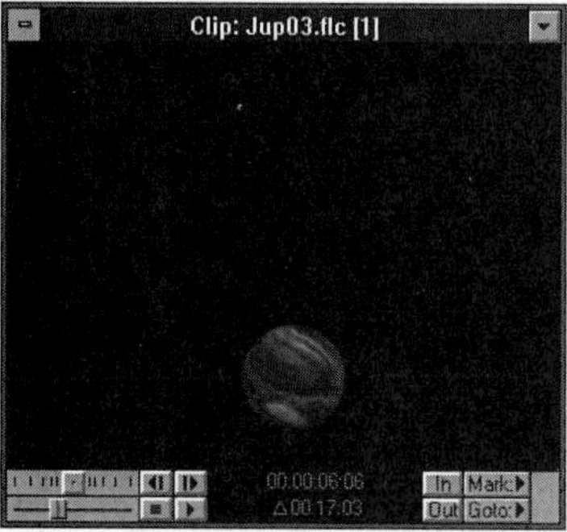

Figure 10.64. An animation created in 3D Studio.

Figure 10.65 shows the appearance of the Construction window when the animation has been added. It is longer than the space we've been working in, and you can drag the right edge to match the right edge of the video production using the mouse.

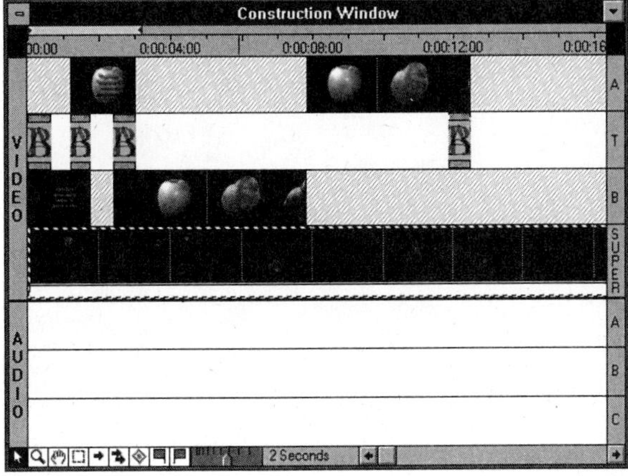

Figure 10.65. Adding an FLC file to the project.

The intention here is to use the ball as an overlay above the video clip; that's why I placed it in the Super[16] track. However, overlay is not automatic. You must tell Premiere how to overlay. Figure 10.66 shows the dialog box for transparency settings. By default, there is no transparency. The small Key Type box is the heart of the matter. Clicking on the small arrow to the right displays a list of possible techniques you can use to tell Premiere what portion of the video clip should be transparent. In this case, a Chroma key is one good choice; we can use the color black. You could also use a Luma (brightness) key and have all very dark portions of the clip become transparent.

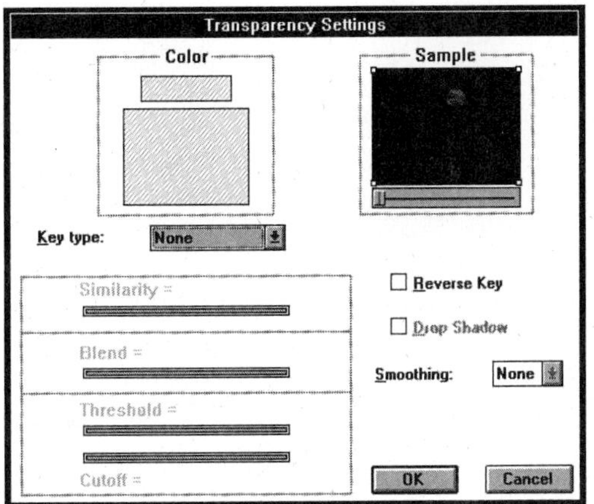

Figure 10.66. The Transparency Settings dialog box.

[16]*Super*, of course, is short for *superimpose*.

Let's use Chroma key. This places an image from one frame in the window at the top left. The cursor changes to a small eye dropper, and you can simply click on the color you want to use for Chroma key. In figure 10.67, the color black is selected, and the image at the upper right now shows transparent wherever the color black exists in the frame.[17]

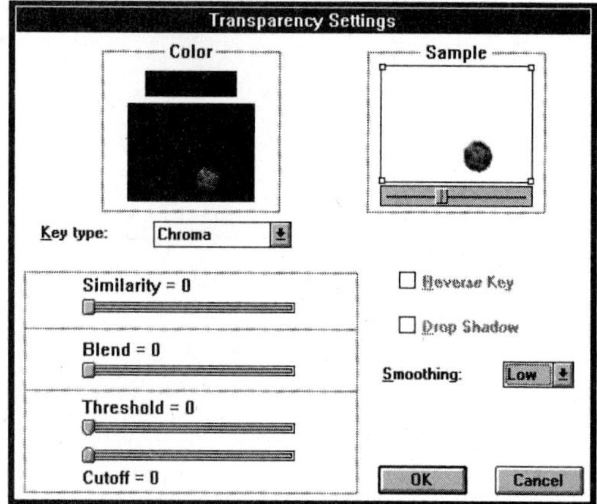

Figure 10.67. Setting transparency parameters.

Figure 10.68 shows the appearance of the Construction window after these changes. Note that the white bar below the Super clip is now dark, indicating that a transparency setting exists. Note also that there is a thin light line above the backward morph clip, indicating that a filter exists for this clip.[18] For my part, I widened the Construction window to reveal the far right end of the Super clip. I did that to make it easy to change the length of the clip by dragging the right edge toward the left.

Figure 10.69 shows the Project completed and ready for output to an AVI file.

Before outputting a file, click on the Movie menu selection Output Options (see fig. 10.70). This displays the Project Output Options dialog box (see fig. 10.71). If you are following along with your own copy of Premiere, make sure your settings match those shown. If you are familiar with video production, you may want to make changes to the video size, codec used for compression, data rate, and so on.

---

[17]There are a number of different subtle changes you can make that I'm not covering here; be sure to check the documentation for Premiere for suggestions on how to tune overlays and transparencies.

[18]Premiere is good at little bits of communication like this. It uses subtle but effective techniques to let you know what is going on.

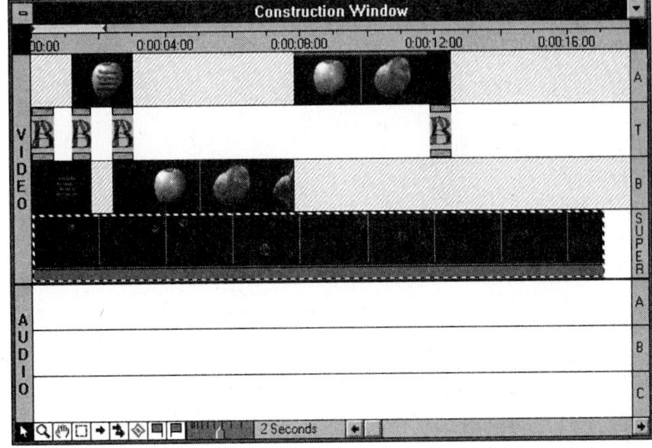

Figure 10.68. Widening the Construction window to reveal the end of the Super clip.

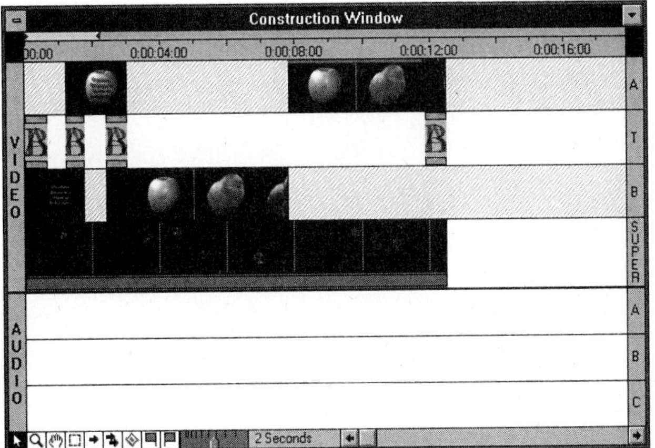

Figure 10.69. The completed project.

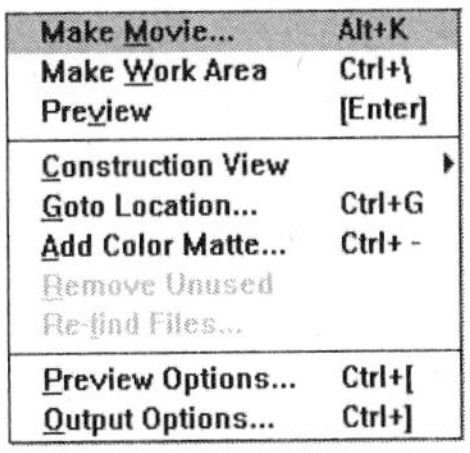

Make Movie...	Alt+K
Make Work Area	Ctrl+\
Preview	[Enter]
Construction View	▸
Goto Location...	Ctrl+G
Add Color Matte...	Ctrl+ -
Remove Unused	
Re-find Files...	
Preview Options...	Ctrl+[
Output Options...	Ctrl+]

Figure 10.70. The Movie menu.

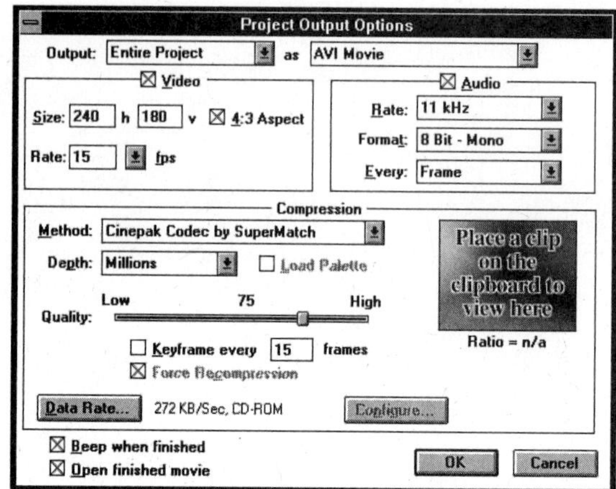

Figure 10.71. Setting Output options.

When everything is ready, you can use the Movie/Make Movie menu selection to output an AVI file. Figure 10.72 shows the Make Movie dialog box. You can verify Output options at the bottom of the dialog box, or you can change Output options by clicking the Options button at the lower left. To output the completed production, enter a file name and click OK. Figure 10.73 shows a sample frame from the final file.

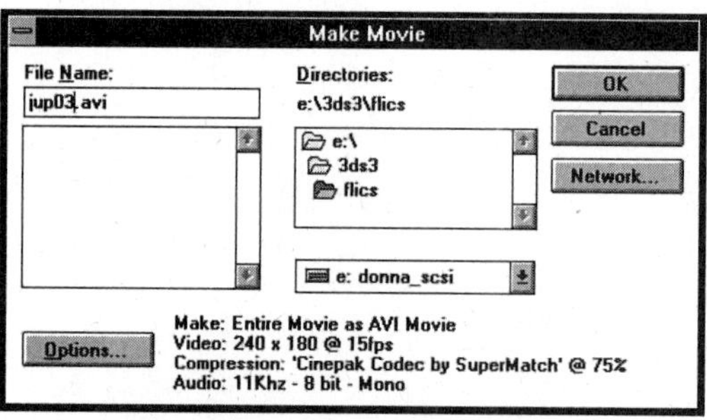

Figure 10.72. The Make Movie dialog box.

Figure 10.73. A sample frame from the finished production.

Your Own Video Studio

If you already own a video camera of any description, you now have half of what you need to put yourself in a virtual space. The other (and less costly) half is a card for your computer that will capture video. Setting up the physical studio is the easiest part of all.

Video Camera

I have yet to meet a video camera (camcorder) that isn't up to the task. Whether you have a large, VHS camera or one of those miniature 8mm or VHS-C cameras, there are only two output signals that you will encounter in North America: composite and S-Video.[19] Most video capture cards will handle either, and all of them will handle a composite signal. There's no need to understand the technical nature of these signals.[20] All you need to know is that S-Video uses a higher resolution than composite, and that either one is fine for video capture, because at 160×120 or 320×240 you're hardly pushing the capabilities of either kind of signal.

Video Capture Card

There are two video capture cards available that I use and like: the Video Spigot[21] and the Smart Video Recorder.[22] Each has specific advantages and disadvantages.

The Video Spigot is the best of its class. It is one of several cards that captures incoming video signals without compressing them. After the video is captured, you compress it using a codec.[23] Compression is essential for working with video. Uncompressed video creates huge data files that are just too much for most computers to handle. Compression allows you to shrink video file size enormously. This does affect image quality, but the better codecs minimize the damage.

---

[19]Neither of these has anything to do with RF signals. Radio Frequency signals are used for broadcast television. Newer televisions have the usual RF input as well as composite and sometimes, S-Video inputs.

[20]For example, I don't.

[21]From Creative Labs.

[22]From Intel.

[23]*Codec* stands for either *encode/decode* or *compress/decompress*—depends on who you ask.

The image quality of the Spigot (as it is affectionately known) is very good, and installation and ease of use are also very good.[24] The board has also proven itself to be reliable in heavy use. Perhaps the best part of owning a Spigot is the Cinepak codec that comes with it. This codec is one of the best when you have to squeeze the data rates really low. However, be warned: Cinepak tends to have a somewhat digital appearance. It yields very sharp images, which means that the individual pixels stand out well. This is great when you have things like text or buildings in a video, and not so great for faces.

The Smart Video Recorder is also the best of its class. It is one of a few cards that capture and compress in one step. Like the Spigot, the SVR (as it is affectionately known) is easy to install and use, and it has excellent image quality. It is also very reliable, and comes with the Indeo codec—another excellent choice for compression. Indeo tends to generate a softer image, with less sharpness. This is great for faces and not so great for text.

I tend to favor the SVR for much of my own work, as the real-time compression from the on-board i750r chip saves a lot of time. For example, compressing with the Cinepak codec after capture can add 30 to 60 minutes of compression time for each minute of video. Cinepak is a great codec, however, and there are times when the wait is well worth your while. You won't regret owning either of these capture cards.[25]

The Studio

Once you have a video camera and a video capture card, it's time to set up your studio. I set up mine in my garage, but you can use any space that has at least one blank wall. One advantage of the garage is that I can often just open the garage door to get plenty of natural light. Figure 10.74 shows my basic setup.

---

[24]The bane of video capture cards is that they must use things like IRQs and memory addresses. Unfortunately, it is up to you to find unused IRQs and memory addresses. The Spigot installation software tries to help, but it can only go so far. You may have to check your installed hardware to determine what IRQs and memory addresses are available. If you can't solve the problem, some of the engineers who designed the Spigot have been known to hang out in the Multimedia Forum on CompuServe.

[25]Of course, that only means that one of my readers will get the proverbial bad apple and complain. No one, least of all a hardware manufacturing company, is perfect. One other point: Neither of these cards does video overlay, which is a completely different ball game. Video overlay involves adding the video signal to your existing video display, rather than capturing the video to a hard disk. Completely different hardware is used for capture and for overlay. If you require both, look into the Bravado 16 from Truevision. I've used it, and it does a great job. Also a completely different process is outputting your VGA display to videotape. If that's your bag, try the Video VGA from Truevision or the VGA Producer from Magni Systems.

The only critical piece is that square thing in the middle of the picture. It's a piece of bright blue fabric used for Chroma key. With the solid color in the background, it's easy to use Media Merge to blend in any object I can videotape. I added weights to the bottom of the cloth to keep it from fluttering (especially when the garage door is open!), and you might also want to add a long, thin strip of wood to the bottom edge. This adds weight and helps keep the cloth from showing fold marks.

I added a few other bits and pieces to complete my simple studio. I invested in a simple color monitor (a Panasonic 1379 is a good and inexpensive choice) that I use to preview the video image, a microphone, and a video tripod.[26] The tripod is a critical piece of equipment. Without it, camera jitters can ruin your video footage and make it useless.

Figure 10.74. A simple video studio setup in a garage.

This setup is easy to use. Place the object—yourself, for example—in front of the blue screen, and turn on the camera. That's all there is to it. If you want to have the object appear to move within the virtual landscape, you can move the camera instead of the object. For example, if you want the object to start out at the lower left of the video frame, and then move to the upper left, tilt the camera instead of moving the object. This gives you very tight control over the location within the video frame.

---

[26]Don't settle for just any old tripod. A video tripod uses a fluid head that makes for smooth panning and tilting. Regular tripods don't have this feature.

Going Virtual with Media Merge

You now have everything you need to go virtual: the software, the hardware, and a studio to create the video. It's time to do some serious virtual video. There are four steps involved:

- Create the virtual space
- Make the videotape
- Capture the video
- Merge it!

Create the Virtual Space

There are a variety of ways to create a virtual space, but not all of them will work with the methods described in this chapter. File formats are the backbone of the process of combining video and virtual reality.

The video file doesn't present any problems. It can be loaded directly into Media Merge. The problems, if any, crop up when you try to use the animation output from the software you use to create the virtual space. That animation must be converted ultimately to an AVI file. That's not a problem if the software can output using the FLI or FLC file formats. For example, Vistapro outputs single frames as PCX files, but it comes with a utility program that will convert the PCX files into an FLC file. If you don't already know what file formats your software supports, check the documentation.

It's easy to use Media Merge's Scene Editor to combine the video file with the animation file, but it's not so easy to make the blend look realistic. For example, as you learned in Chapter 6, the lighting in the virtual space must be matched when you videotape the real object that you plan to include. If you don't do that, the difference in lighting angle can be jarring to the viewer. If the lighting angles are too complex, you can minimize the effect by using an overhead light in both the virtual space and for the videotaping. Such lighting casts minimal shadows, and movement of objects causes only minor changes to shadows.

If the animation of the virtual space uses a camera, and you change the camera angle, you'll need to duplicate the camera angle when you videotape.

All of this may sound like a lot of bother, but it's really just basic bookkeeping. A little time taken to jot down frame numbers and camera or light angles, for example, can add a real sense of reality to your creation. The techniques you use can be based on the examples in Chapter 6.

Make the Videotape

There are several levels of camera technique that you can use when you are photographing a real object that will be added to a virtual space. These range from the simple to the complex:

- Stationary camera, stationary target
- Stationary camera, moving target
- Moving camera, stationary target
- Moving camera, moving target

Each of these has different uses and applications, and a different level of difficulty.

Stationary Camera, Stationary Target

This is the easiest way to get started. Because neither the camera nor the target is moving, the logistics are very simple: position the object/target, aim the camera, make the tape. If you need to move the lighting during filming, that adds a bit of complexity, but once you start the camera, you've got two hands free.

Stationary Camera, Moving Target

There are different ways of moving an object, and each of them creates different challenges. If the object is moving in the same place—that is, it does not change its distance from the camera—the only question is the mechanism for moving the object. You do not want any of the support system showing up in the video. If you must have a visible support, make sure that the support is covered with the same color and kind of fabric you used for the background. You can, for example, make a glove for your hand, drape cloth across your arm or shoulder, and move the object the old-fashioned way: by hand.

If the distance between the camera and object changes, the issues become more complex. The biggest priority is to keep the object in focus. If your camera has auto focus, that will keep the object in focus in most situations. However, there are several special situations where auto focus may not be adequate. For example, some auto-focus systems use the center of the frame for focusing. If the object is at the edge of the frame, the camera may try to focus on the background cloth—a hopeless task, since the cloth is uniform in color and lighting.

Moving an object away from the camera also presents special problems. The further away you are from the object, the bigger the background must be. This can create a practical limit to how large an object you can videotape. For example, putting all of your body into the frame requires a very large background—most likely from floor to ceiling. If possible, use a continuous strip of background material and curve it to cover part of the floor and ceiling—this will avoid any creases that may be difficult to remove in Media Merge. Most fabric is only 60 inches wide, and this can cause problems, too.

If you are serious about using large objects, you have two choices: build a larger studio, or remove the background in each frame using a program like Photoshop.

Moving Camera, Stationary Target

Instead of moving the object, you can move the camera in such a way that it looks like the object is moving. This is the technique that was used to animate the various star fighters in the movie *Star Wars*. The movie studios rely on computers and motorized camera transports to work their magic. If you try this technique, you will have to think through the necessary camera motions very carefully, and you will probably need to move the camera by hand. This can be very unsteady, and you would need to create tracks to even out the camera movement. Some motions can be done using a tripod, but they aren't the useful ones. Panning and tilting will seldom give you the effect you want.

There is another type of moving-camera shot, however, that is easy to take. This involves just the opposite of what I have been describing so far. Instead of adding video to a virtual space, you can add virtual objects to a video. In this case, you are free to do whatever you want to do with the camera. When you have the tape you want, you can add the virtual object. For example, if you create a bizarre space alien in Imagine, and then animate it in the foreground,[27] you can use Media Merge to put the alien into any video. Or, you might hold the camera while walking along a path, and then add a floating spacecraft or a pair of robot arms to the foreground. Let your imagination run wild.

Moving Camera, Moving Target

There should seldom, if ever, be a need for this combination. Almost any movement can be accomplished using either a moving camera or a moving target.

Capture the Video

Once you have your video tape, the next step is to capture the video sequence to your hard disk. You'll need a pretty fast computer to handle video capture. I recommend at least a 486/33, although the Intel Smart Video Recorder may work

---

[27] With an appropriate single-color background, of course.

satisfactorily with slower hardware because it offloads some of the work to its on-board video compression chip. A fast hard drive is critical. I use a disk with an average seek time of 10ms.[28] Any disk under 15ms is acceptable, but 12ms or less is better. A fast video display card is very desirable for playback, but it won't have much impact on capture.

Here are some hints on video capture from my book *PC Video Madness*:

- Test the capabilities of your system before you try to capture for any real projects. Start easy—try to capture at 160×120 using 256 colors and 15 frames per second as a beginning. If that works, try 24 and then 30 frames per second. Verify that you are getting reliable performance. Then you can try such things as 24-bit color codecs like Indeo and Cinepak. You won't get the benefits of 24-bit color, of course, unless you have a video display adapter than can handle it.
- If you use the Intel Smart Video Recorder, set the following options in VidCap for capture: Indeo codec, highest quality setting, and key frames set to 1. This almost always gives you the best results. The key frame setting is critical for the Indeo codec Version 2.12 to correct a potential problem with ghosting when the frame contents change dramatically from one frame to the next. After capture, use VidEdit to save the file using No Change as a compression option and using the data rate of your choice.
- Use a permanent capture file. To create a permanent file, start by defragmenting your hard disk with a utility like Speed Disk from The Norton Utilities.[29] Then run VidCap, and from the File menu choose Set Capture File. The dialog box allows you to set the size of the capture file. Allow from 10 to 25 megabytes per minute of capture, depending on such things as image size, frame rate, and bit depth. If you will be using the Intel Smart Video Recorder or another board that compresses in real time, you'll need less space—usually at least one-third less than for uncompressed (also called *raw*) capture. After you capture a video sequence to the permanent capture file (which will now always stay defragmented until you erase it), use Save As in VidEdit to save the file with an appropriate name after you have made any necessary changes. This preserves the capture file for future use.

---

[28]The *ms* stands for *milliseconds* and refers to average seek time. I use a Micropolis 2112A, with a 1.05 gigabyte IDE drive. The SCSI version, the 2112, is also a good choice.

[29]Having a fragmented hard disk slows down access times because files wind up being in several pieces. In the case of a large video file—say 50 megabytes or so—a fragmented hard drive can mean that the file is cut into hundreds of pieces.

- Unless you need to play the video files from a CD-ROM, don't use the Pad for CD-ROM feature in the Compression options. However, the 150K data rate is a good target if you want the file to be playable on a variety of machines. Any file with a data rate over 300K per second may not play well on the majority of machines—such high data rates demand the fastest computers, hard disks, and video systems. In general, don't compress until you create the final video—use uncompressed files throughout development to preserve image quality.

Merge It!

Once you have the two files, you can merge them with Media Merge's Scene Editor. The process is exactly like the example earlier in this chapter. To refresh your memory, I'll list the steps again:

1. Load the file with the virtual space animation in time line #1. In this case, it is a Vistapro landscape animation.
2. Load the file with the video object in time line #2. I am the object in this example.
3. Load any additional video objects into the appropriate time lines. In this case, I wanted a dashboard effect; I used a bitmap between the video of me and the landscape animation.
4. Set the overlay properties for each video object. Select the background color as the Chroma key color, and then adjust the fall off until the background disappears completely. You may want to experiment with the Feathering options located in the upper portion of the dialog box.
5. Check the appearance of the results in the Composite time line. Figure 10.75 shows the kind of results you can expect. The Composite only uses 8-bit color, so don't be alarmed if the images there don't look as detailed as you were expecting. If what you see is what you want, use the File/Produce menu selection to create the final product. In figure 10.75, the video in track 1 is already a composite video: I added a still image of a cockpit as an overlay using Chroma key. I then loaded the resulting video in for a second overlay. I could have overlaid all three videos in one step, of course. In this case, I wanted to do several versions using the same cockpit. The dashboard bitmap is shown in figure 10.76.

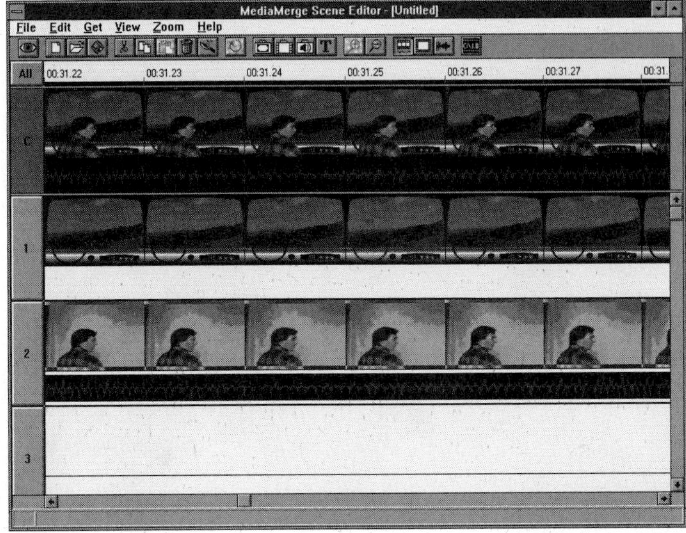

Figure 10.75. Several video files loaded into the Scene Editor.

Figure 10.76. A bitmap used to create a dashboard for the composite video.

Figures 10.77 and 10.78 show single frames from the video produced using the files loaded into the Scene Editor for figure 10.76. These images have been compressed, so the detail is not as crisp as in the original. Note that all three elements of the composite are integrated into the images: the Vistapro landscape, the dashboard, and the video of me, Mr. Author (or, in this case, tour guide—play the file MEETME.AVI on the CD-ROMs in the VRMAD directory).

Figure 10.77.
A single frame from the produced video.

Figure 10.79 shows a frame from the original video I made in my garage studio. The surface behind me is the blue cloth I used as a backdrop. It is not quite exactly uniform in color, but Media Merge allows you to make adjustments for this using the Falloff slider.

Figure 10.78.
Another single frame from the produced video.

Summary

The list of possibilities for working with a combination of virtual-space animation and video files is endless. The ability to layer multiple images with Media Merge gives you a powerful tool for creating never-before-seen images. Whether you add video to a virtual space or enhance a video by adding virtual objects, you will likely find yourself on the cutting edge of computer technology for quite some time.

Figure 10.79.
A frame from the original video, before making the composite.

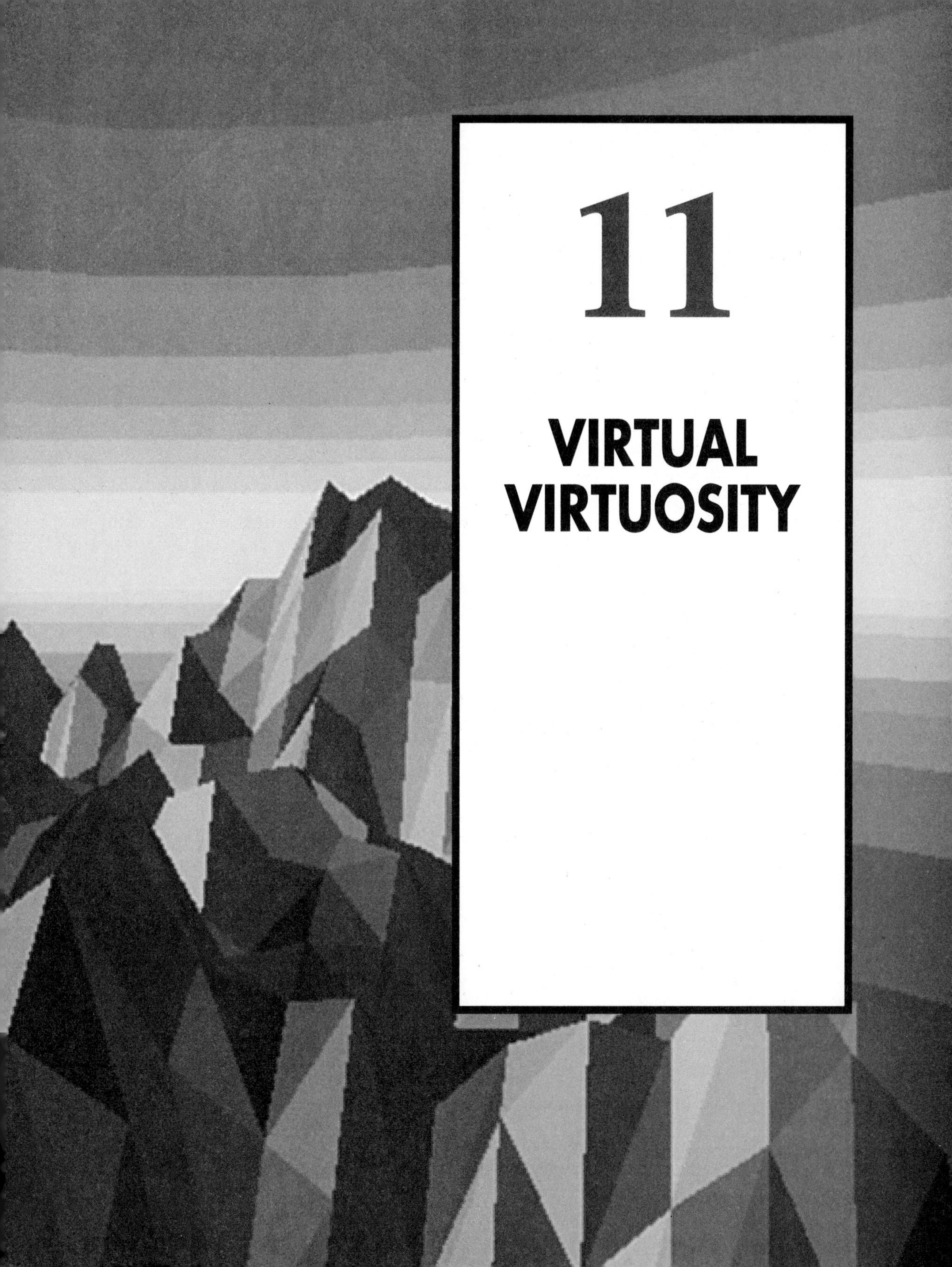

11

VIRTUAL VIRTUOSITY

From total immersion to 3D morphing, from flights of fancy to detailed pseudo-realities, virtual reality is as much an art as a science. Life on the cutting edge has always been that way. There are few prefabricated solutions on the cutting edge. Virtual reality is completely different from humdrum, everyday programs like spreadsheets and word processors.

Once upon a time, of course, spreadsheets and word processors were new, fun, and exciting. But as the various programs from the various vendors look more and more alike with each new version, virtual reality is a mere babe in the woods. Like multimedia, virtual reality still has room for the home-grown product, for the enthusiast to go places no one has ever gone before.

Today's VR tools, as limited and experimental—and sometimes costly—as they are, still offer enormous possibilities to anyone who is willing to put in the time and effort to stretch the limits. Out there, in the trenches, the Cezannes, Van Goghs, and Picassos of virtual reality are sweating out the details in front of their computers, trying to find a sense of style, a way of doing things that breaks completely new ground.

These are the virtual virtuosos. These are the people who aren't willing to wait until someone else gives them the tools to build new worlds—they'll build them now, either by finding new ways to use the tools available or by creating their own tools out of their impatience.

In this chapter, you'll learn about stretching and bending tools to get what you want, when you want it. This chapter features the high end of 3D-modeling software: 3D Studio from Autodesk. A morph here, a reflection there, and pretty soon you can have your own virtual creatures.

For this example, you will build a cylinder in a sparklingly technological-looking environment, and then make it come to life. It will bend down toward you, and then shake its "head" threateningly at you. After the example, I'll show you some possibilities for adding even more pizzazz to the animation.

The results will be first-class, because 3D Studio is used by many professionals to create the artificial realities you see on television, in commercials, and in movies.

The Column that Ate the Animator

You will create just a handful of objects in this scene, but the results will make it look like it took forever to do. Begin by setting the values for a cylinder using the Create/Cylinder/Values menu selection, as shown in figure 11.1.

RECIPE

1 copy 3D Studio 2.01
1 highly developed sense of imagination
1 conception of a virtual space and its inhabitants

Instructions: The recipe can only suggest where to go with this gourmet item. Begin by visualizing a scene that has some impact—something that hits you in the gut. For example, pretend you have been hired to create a scene in a movie where an inanimate object comes to life. What would it look like? How would it move? Then work at it and work at it until it appears to come to life in an animation. Serve only when really, really ready.

To create the cylinder itself, use the Create/Cylinder/Smoothed menu selection. When asked, use the name Cyl01. Make the cylinder tall and thin, as shown in figure 11.2. Apply the material Blue Glass(1) to the object.

Let's cover a little background information before proceeding. To animate the column, you're going to use a little trick. You will actually use a morph(2) to transform the column into various versions of itself. Instead of animating a single column, you will create different versions of the column, and then morph from one to the next.

---

[1]These are just suggestions; feel free to adjust the mapping and materials to suit your own concept of a column that will come to life. By the way, you need not specify the same material for the object copies—morphing has no effect on the surface characteristics of an object.

[2]See Chapter 8 for more information about morphing.

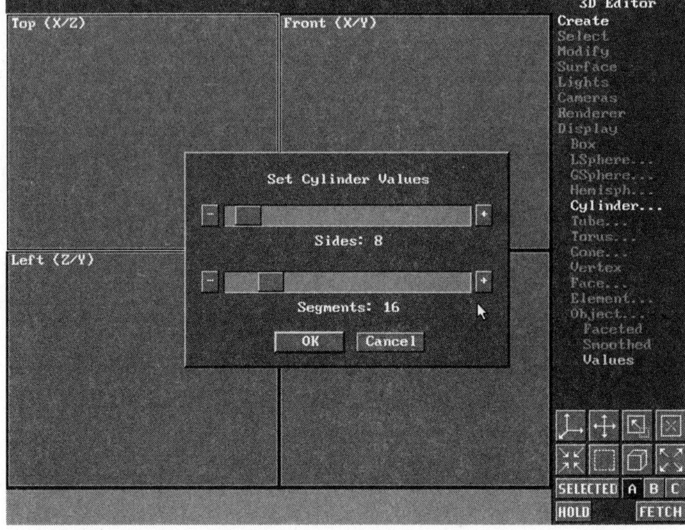

Figure 11.1. Setting values for a new cylinder.

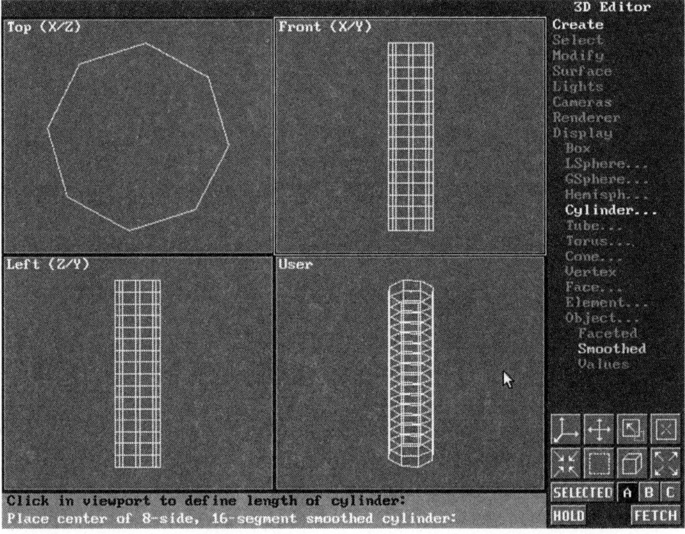

Figure 11.2. Creating a tall, thin cylinder.

Create four copies of the column. The easiest way to do this is by cloning. Use the Modify/Object/Move menu selection, but hold down the Shift key when you select the column for moving. This creates an exact copy of the column, including the surface material. Name each of the cylinders appropriately, such as Cy102, Cy103, and so on. You can use any of the viewports for the moving and cloning operations, as shown in figure 11.3.

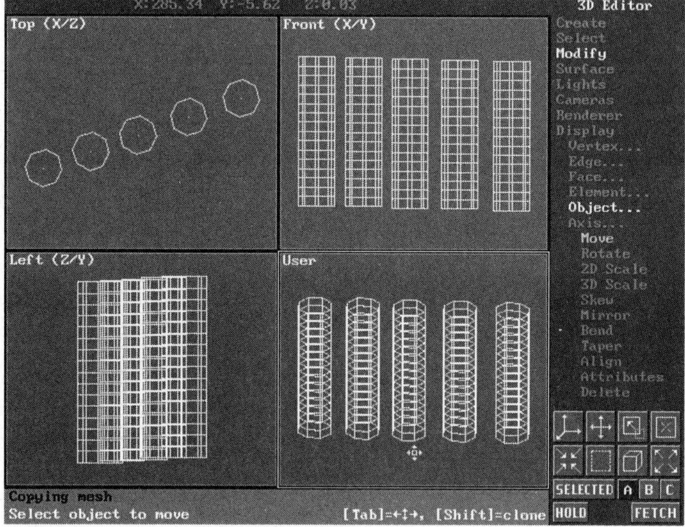

Figure 11.3. Five identical cylinders.

Now use the Modify/Object/Bend menu selection to bend cylinder #2 30 degrees. Make sure that the cursor that appears has a little arrow pointing up. If the arrow points in a different direction, press the Tab key until it points up. Figure 11.4 shows the cylinder as it looks during the bend operation. A shadow cylinder shows the degree of bending. Check for the exact degree of bending in the status line at the top of the screen.

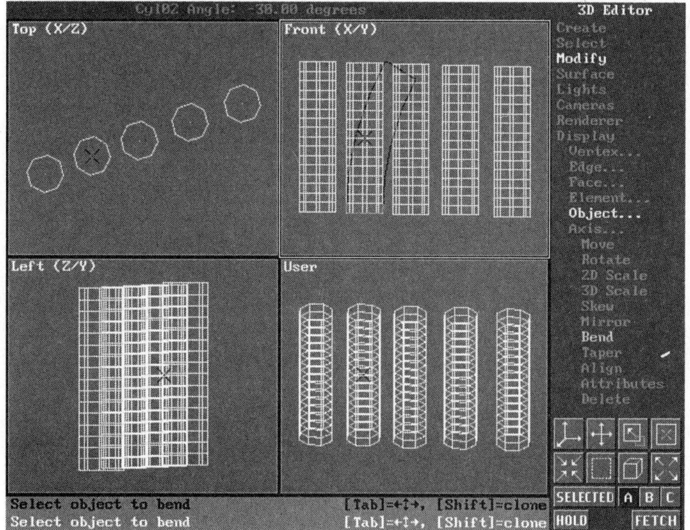

Figure 11.4. Bending a cylinder.

Now move to cylinder #3, and bend it to 60 degrees. Bend cylinder #4 to 90 degrees and cylinder #5 to 120 degrees. Once you have bent all the cylinders, the screen should look something like figure 11.5.

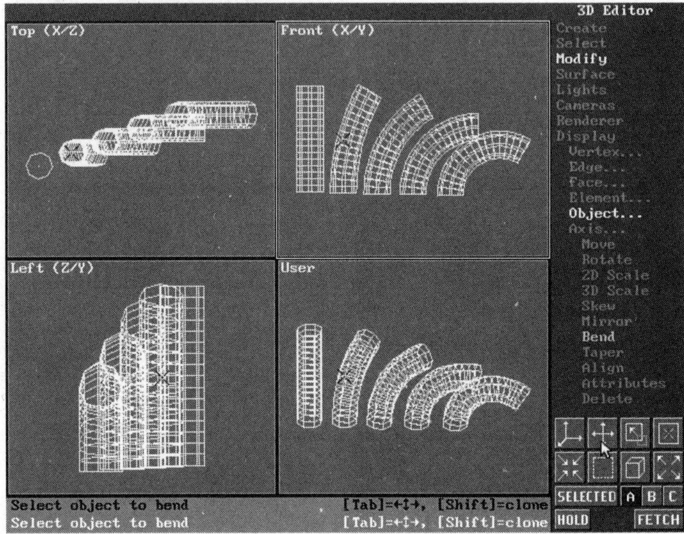

Figure 11.5. Different degrees of bending on the cylinders.

Press the F5 key to go to the Keyframer, 3D Studio's animation tool. Use the Display/Hide/Object menu selection to hide each of the bent cylinders.[3] The only remaining object is the original cylinder, as shown in figure 11.6.

This is the point where you apply the morphing. Move to frame 30, and then go to the Object/Morph/Assign menu selection. Click on Cy101, which will display the dialog box shown in figure 11.7. This is a list of the objects in the scene that are valid morph objects for Cyl01.

Click on Cyl02, and then click OK. The cylinder now appears bent, as shown in figure 11.8.

Move to frames 60, 60, and 120, and morph the cylinder to cylinders 3, 4, and 5. In frame 120, the cylinder appears nearly bent over (see fig. 11.9).

---

[3]Simply click on each cylinder to hide it.

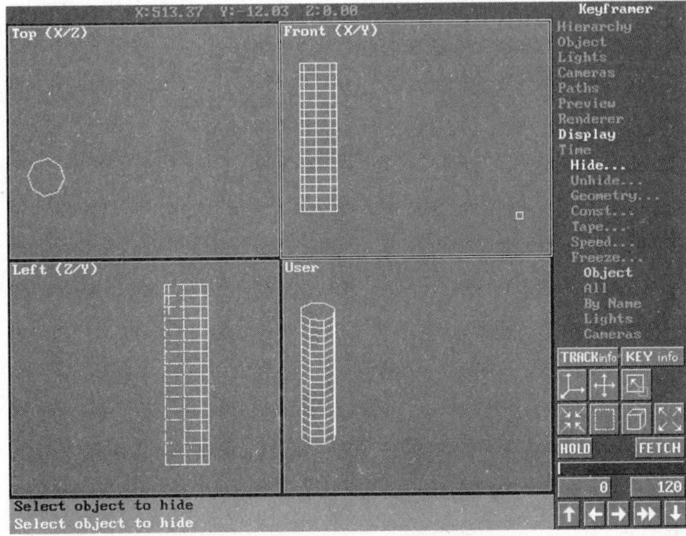

Figure 11.6. The bent cylinders have been hidden.

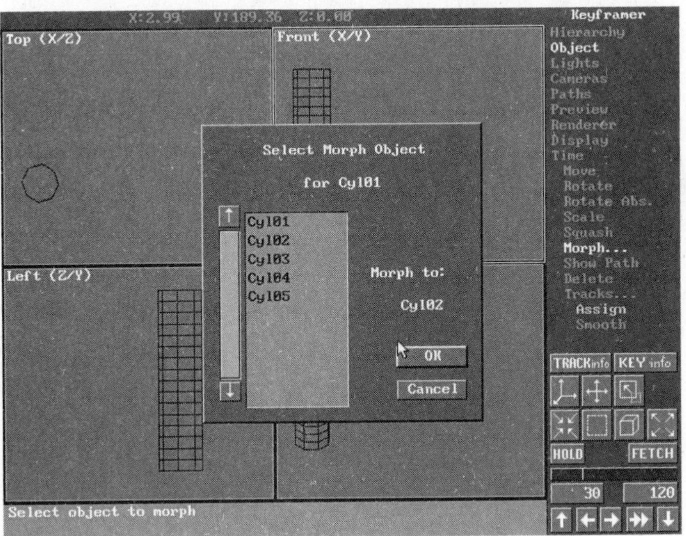

Figure 11.7. Selecting an object to morph to.

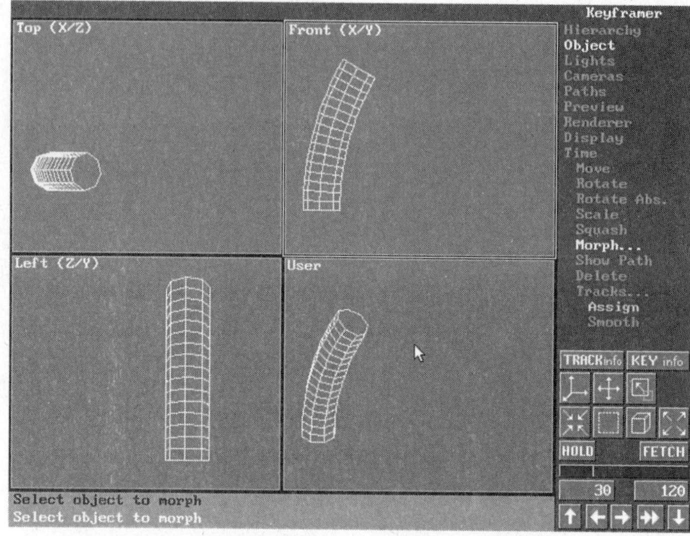

Figure 11.8. The cylinder appears bent in frame 30.

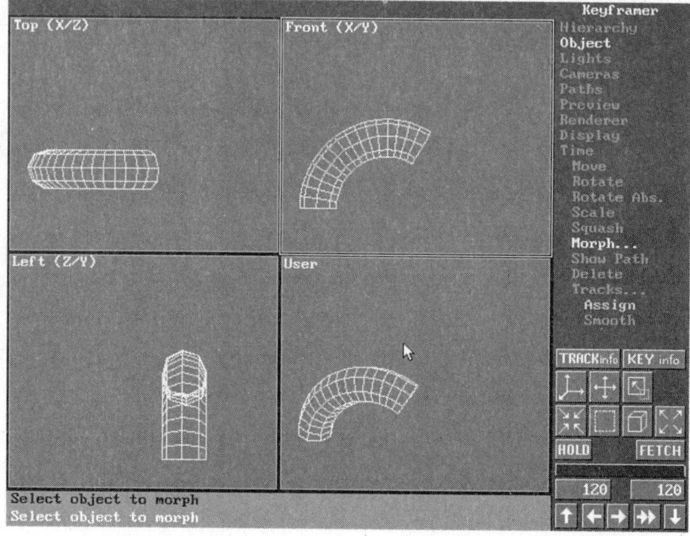

Figure 11.9. The completed morph.

Throughout the morph, the cylinder did not move. It did not, for example, move to the location of cylinder #2 when morphed to that cylinder. Morphing is actually a limited action. It does not affect the surface properties of an object, nor does it affect position. In fact, morphing does only one thing. A morph merely moves the vertices of one object to the (relative) positions of the vertices in the second object. In other words, all that a morph does is change the shape of an object to match the shape of a second object.

One side effect is that you can only morph objects that have the same number of vertices. When you click on an object to morph it, you are presented with a list of the objects in the scene that have the same number of vertices. If you want to morph, say, a sphere into a cube, you will first have to add vertices to the cube—lots of them, as a matter of fact, because the typical sphere may have hundreds, while a stock cube has but eight.

One of the best ways to create objects with the same number of vertices is to copy them, as we have done here, and then make changes to the copy. Another method is to use the 3D Lofter (another 3D Studio tool) to create the two shapes, and then loft them into 3D objects. This offers more flexibility, but can take much more time.

Now you can set about getting the most out of the morph. Return to the 3D Editor by pressing the F3 key. Use the Cameras/Create menu selection to open the dialog box shown in figure 11.10.

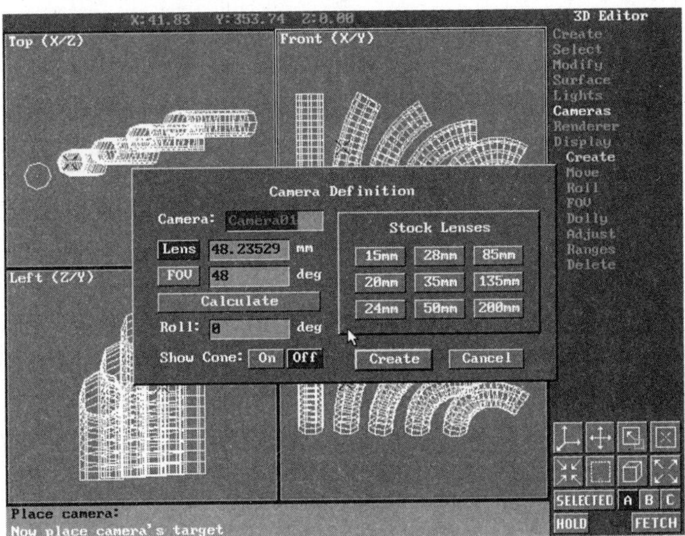

Figure 11.10. Adding a camera to the scene.

There are a number of lenses to choose from, and the lens you select will affect the appearance of the bending column. A wide-angle lens[4] will make the column look far away—it won't show the effect to its best advantage. A telephoto lens[5] will show the column close up, but if we get too close, the morphing will not be seen

[4]The lens focal lengths from 15mm to 35mm are considered wide angle.

[5]The lens focal lengths from 85mm to 200m are considered telephoto.

in its entirety. In this case, the so-called normal lens is best—50mm. Select this lens by clicking on it.

To make one of the viewports show what the camera sees, press Ctrl-V to display the dialog box shown in figure 11.11. Click the Camera button, and then click in one of the viewports at the lower left of the dialog box. The viewport marked with a U would be a good choice, because the User point of view isn't needed when you have a camera viewport.

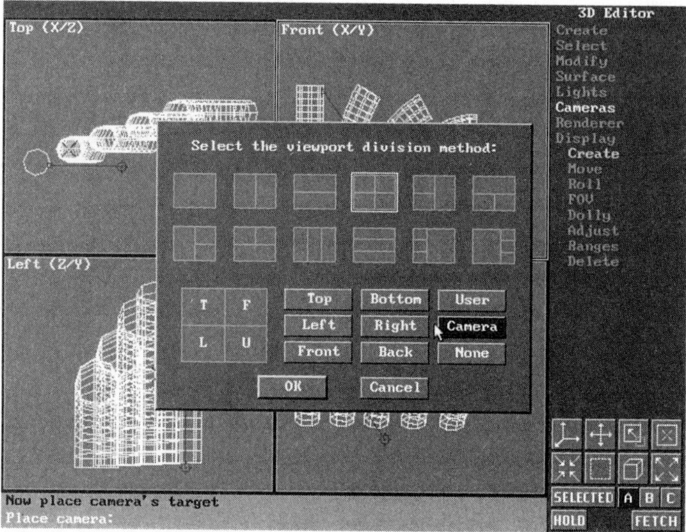

Figure 11.11. Changing the contents of a viewport.

Place the camera at a low level, looking up at the column. You should also add a light to the scene. A spotlight would be nice because it casts shadows, which will add depth to the scene. Figure 11.12 shows the light and the camera in position in the 3D Editor.[6]

The light from above, however, may not be enough. This leaves the underside of the column in shadow as it bends. Because the camera sees mostly the underside of the column, it would be a very boring animation—not at all appropriate for a movie scene. You can add a second spotlight below the bending column, as shown in figure 11.13. Note that this illuminates the area right in front of the camera at the end of the sequence.

---

[6]You may need to change the position of both objects, depending on exactly where and how the column moves during the morph.

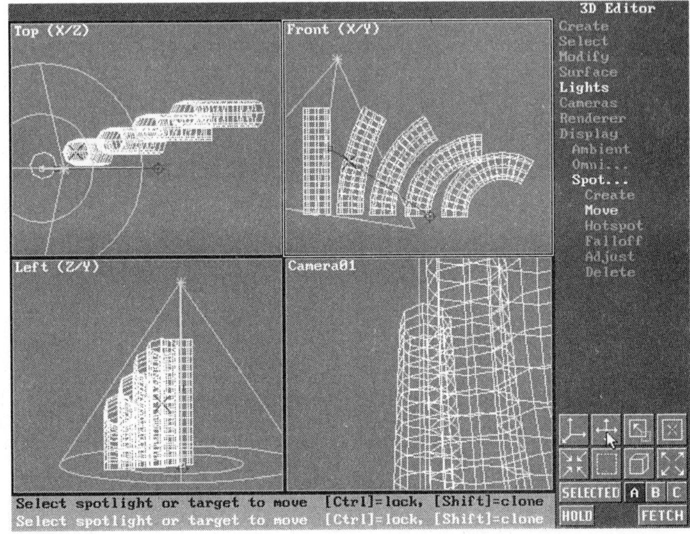

Figure 11.12. The scene with a light and camera added.

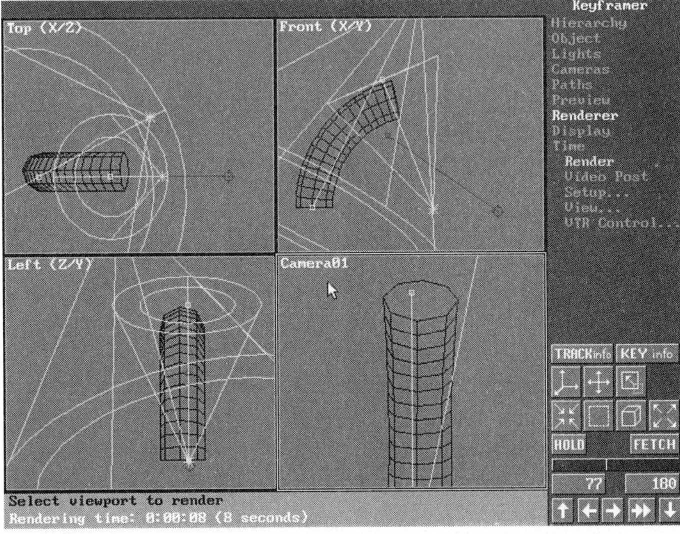

Figure 11.13. Adding a second spotlight under the column.

The animation as it now stands is OK, but it lacks punch. A bending column, after all, doesn't have much personality. If we want this column to really look like it is coming alive (and we'll have to if we ever want to see our payment from the movie's producer), we'll have to add more motion. Time to head back to the 3D Editor.

Create two copies of cylinder #5—the one that is bent farthest. Figure 11.14 shows the two additional objects (best seen in the Top viewport) after they have been bent a second time, this time sideways.

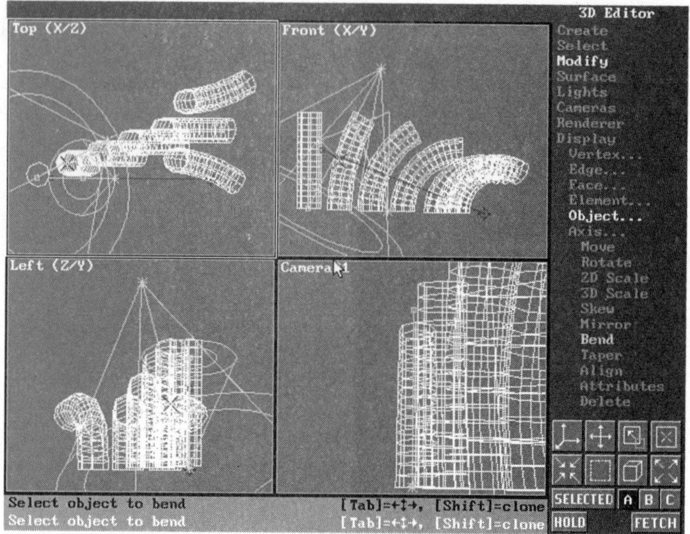

Figure 11.14. Adding two more bent cylinders.

These two new cylinders can be used to add some rather interesting morphs. Return to the Keyframer and add 60 additional frames (for a total of 180). Move to frame 135 (see fig. 11.15) and add a morph to one of the new objects.

Move to frame 165 and add a morph to the other object, and then move to frame 180 and morph to cylinder #5. Now hide the two new objects using the Display/Hide/Object menu selection. Figure 11.16 shows how the cylinder looks in wireframe view in frame 165.

If there is anything about the animation that you are not satisfied with, the easiest way to make adjustments is with the Track editor. To use the Track editor, click the Track Info button at the lower right, and then click on the cylinder. This displays the Track Info dialog box (see fig. 11.17).

Note that there is a dot at each frame where you created a morph. To edit a morph, simply click the Key Info button at the lower left of the dialog box, which will display the Key Info dialog box (see fig. 11.18).

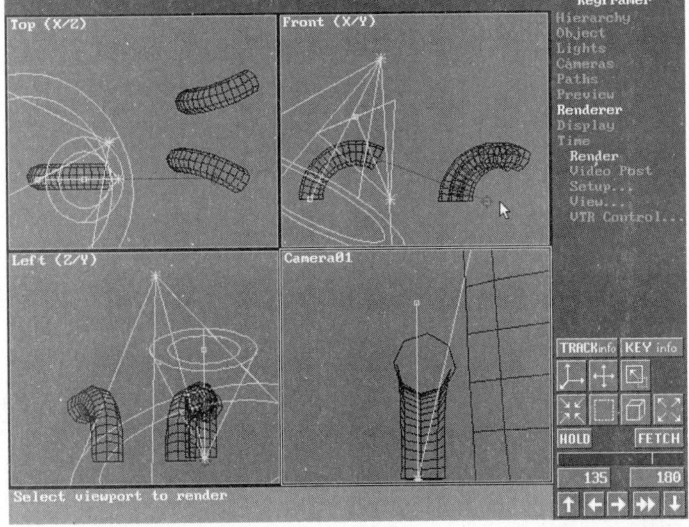

Figure 11.15. The view in the Keyframer before hiding the new objects.

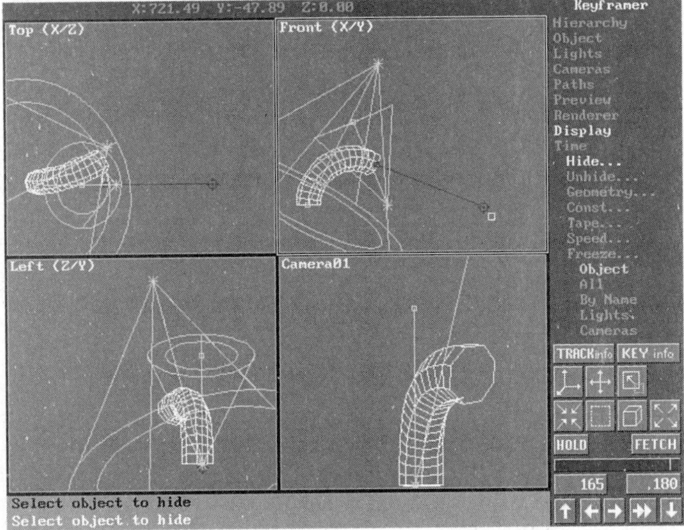

Figure 11.16. A view of the cylinder bending both down and to the side.

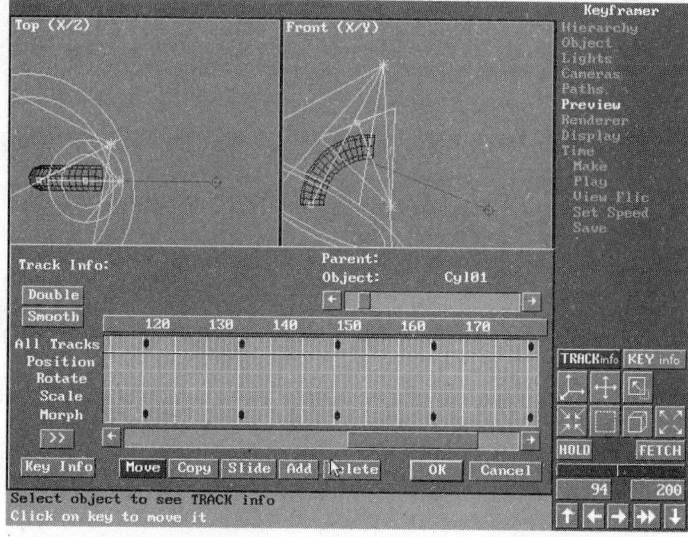

Figure 11.17.
The Track info for the cylinder.

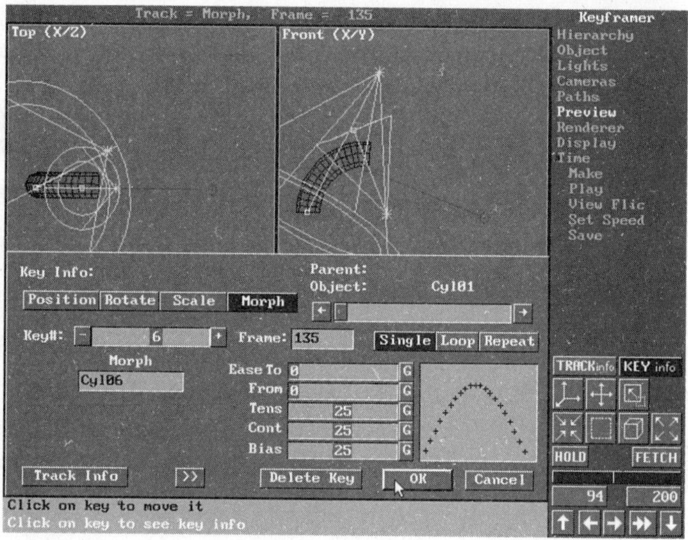

Figure 11.18.
The Key Info dialog box.

Using the Key Info dialog box, you can change the object you are morphing to, and you can also change the Ease To settings. This can give you a high degree of control over the pace of motion during the morph. The Ease To value affects the velocity with which an object (or, in this case, a morph) approaches a key frame. If the value is zero, there is no change in velocity. If the value is 50 (the maximum), the change in velocity will be as high as possible.

The Ease From setting also affects velocity. A high setting (50 is also the maximum here) will increase velocity, leaving the key frame.

In other words, if you increase the Ease To setting, the pace of the morph will speed up as it reaches the key frame. If you increase the Ease From setting, the pace of the morph will be fast as it leaves the key frame and then slows down. You can use these controls to change a boring, same-speed morph into a dynamic, unpredictable virtuoso performance.

There are three other settings in the same area of the Key Info box that can be useful:

> **Tension**—This control determines how abruptly a transition occurs. A setting of 50 means the transition is very abrupt; 25 is average; and 0 means that motion will even go in reverse, if necessary, to make the transition as smooth as possible.
>
> **Continuity**—This control determines how smooth the changes will be at the key frame. A setting of zero means the change will be abrupt—all in one frame. A setting of 25 means the change will be smooth, and a setting of 50 forces an overshoot prior to and after the key frame.
>
> **Bias**—This control determines whether the settings that apply to a given key frame will apply equally to entry and exit, or favor one or the other. A value of 50 emphasizes entry, a setting of 25 is neutral, and a setting of 0 favors exit.

These settings, which were designed primarily to control motion, can have either interesting or ruinous effects on a morph— experimentation is the only useful guide.

As interesting as we have managed to make the morph so far—a snake-like column wobbling dangerously from side to side—we are not done. We can add substantial mood to the morph by creating a suitable background. If you recall, the specifications called for a "sparklingly technological-looking" background. The first order of business is to create the background object. I opted for a simple background, consisting of a floor and one wall (see fig. 11.19).

The objects are simply boxes created in the 3D Editor using the Create/Box menu selection. I adjusted the size and position of the boxes to make sure that they filled the camera view. I then assigned suitable materials to each of them—Blue Marble to the floor, and a material I created for the wall using pattern #150 as a texture map. Figure 11.20 shows a rendering of the scene.

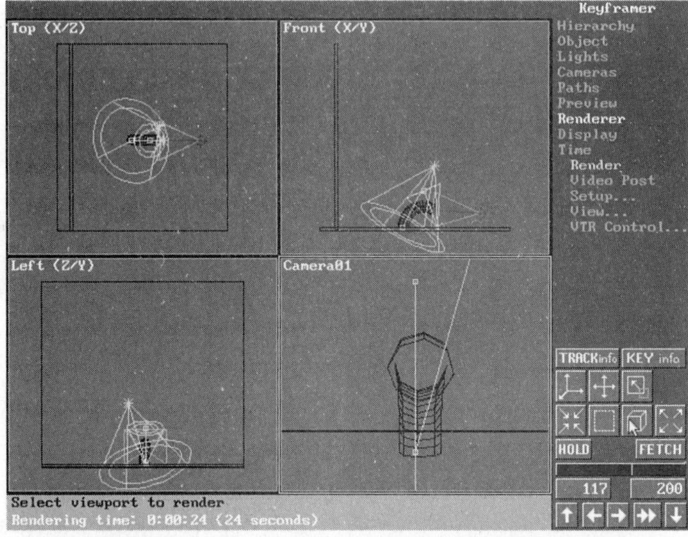

Figure 11.19. Adding objects for a background.

Figure 11.20. A rendering of the first frame in the morph.

All three objects can be seen in this rendering. The blue glass is nearly transparent, however, and may not be an ideal choice. We'll return to this subject in a moment. For now, see figure 11.21, frame 107 of the animation. The cylinder is bent at a little bit more than 90 degrees.

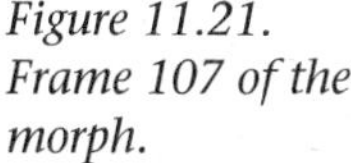

Figure 11.21. Frame 107 of the morph.

In figure 11.22, the cylinder is bent completely to one side.

Figure 11.22. Frame 134 of the morph.

There are some things you can do to improve the appearance of the animation. I made the following changes, and then rendered the image in figure 11.23.

- Added an automatic reflection map to the blue glass material and increased its shininess.

- Added a bump map to the blue marble to create some highlights and shadows in the surface and added automatic reflection mapping.
- Added shininess to the pattern of the wall and added a bump map.

Figure 11.23. Frame 135 with changes to the characteristics of the materials.

As you can see, this adds quite a bit of atmosphere to the scene. We are almost there, but not quite. For a final touch, add a spotlight that illuminates the wall in the background. Place the light so it is above and nearly in the same plane as the wall—this will cause harsh shadows that emphasize the texture of the wall. The final result is shown in figure 11.24, and can be found on the disk as BEND.AVI.

What's Next?

This scene is really just a basic morph in 3D Studio. I have added a few extra touches to give the animation more impact. But there are more things that you could do. For example, you could join a face to the top of the cylinder using the Create/Object/Boolean menu selection. 3D Studio comes with a large number of sample files, several of which contain heads or faces that would be useful in this situation, or you could create your own from scratch.

You could also add other objects to the scene and have the cylinder interact with them. For example, a ball could roll in from the side, and then get eaten by the cylinder when it bends down.

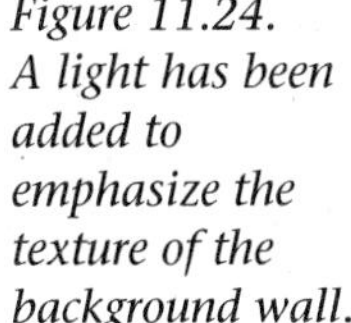

Figure 11.24. A light has been added to emphasize the texture of the background wall.

You can also replace the simple patterning of the back wall with a rock wall that looks like a dungeon, or a sparkling, futuristic metallic look. You can add objects—lights, paintings, decorations, and architectural details—to the back wall or the floor.

The bottom line is this: The more you put into a scene, the more you are going to get out of it. Of course, knowing when you are done—when adding even one more detail would be too much—is just as important!

trueSpace Virtuosity: Virtual Planets

In Chapter 5, you learned how to create your own solar system using 3D Studio. Let's take a different approach to the problem, and use trueSpace to create an Alternate Solar System just for us.

Before we start, however, a few words about the differences in the two products are in order. 3D Studio packs a tremendous amount of power under the hood. That means that it has layer upon layer of features—which translates into layer upon layer of menus. trueSpace is less ambitious, so it has less to navigate through. Caligari, the maker of trueSpace, has taken full advantage of this. It has made the interface simpler, and that means it's easier to maneuver around and get things done.

In this exercise, we'll create a bunch of planets, give at least one planet some moons, and put them all into orbit around a sun. Along the way, you'll learn more about creating surfaces in trueSpace.

Figure 11.25 shows the starting point: an empty virtual universe in trueSpace. I have taken the liberty of creating a new perspective window using the Window tools at the bottom right. If you haven't already been through the trueSpace tutorial in Chapter 3, you might want to use it to get familiar with the basics. There is a demo version of trueSpace on the CDs at the back of this book, which you can use to follow along with the tutorial.

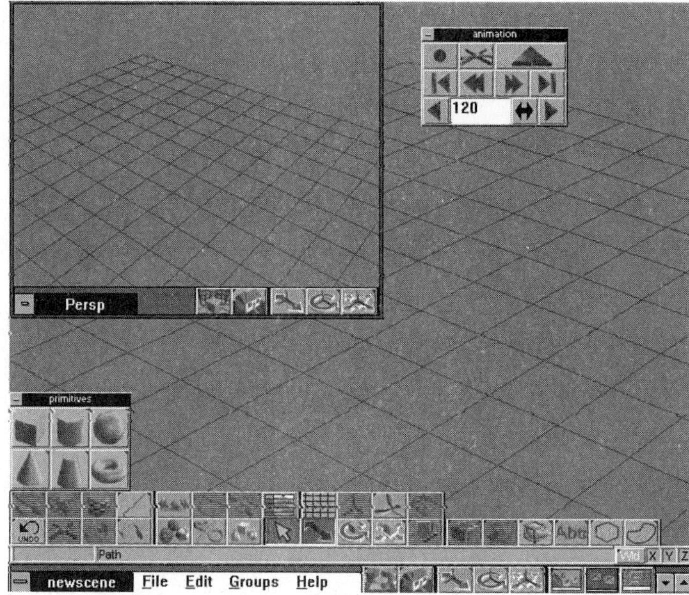

Figure 11.25. trueSpace's main window and toolbars.

The first step is to use the Primitives Panel (see fig. 11.26) to add a sphere roughly at the center of the small Perspective window (see fig. 11.27). To add the sphere, simply click on the Sphere tool in the Primitives Panel; you'll get a sphere of default size and orientation.

If the sphere isn't in the location you want, you can use the tools shown in figure 11.28 to (from left to right) select it, move it, rotate it, or scale it.[7]

---

[7] The last tool is for navigating hierarchies; remember it for later.

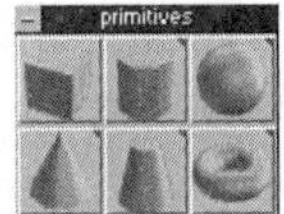

Figure 11.26. The Primitives Panel, used for creating simple 3D objects.

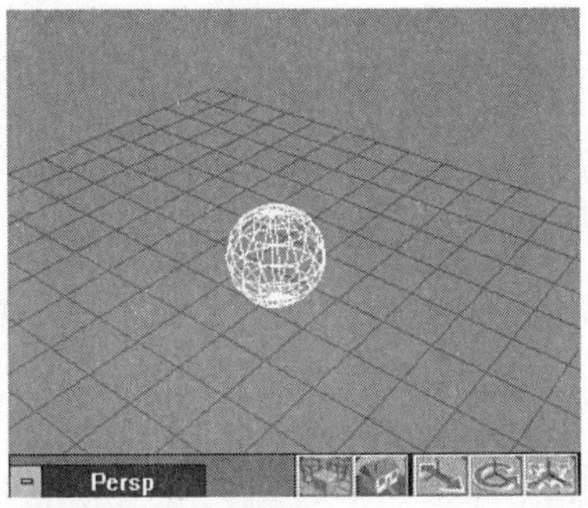

Figure 11.27. A single sphere has been added.

Figure 11.28. Tools for manipulating objects.

A single sphere doesn't make for much of a universe. The next step is to add a smattering of planetary objects—spheres of different sizes. To change the size uniformly, hold down both left and right mouse buttons while you drag to resize. Figure 11.29 shows the central "sun" sphere and two smaller "planetary" spheres.

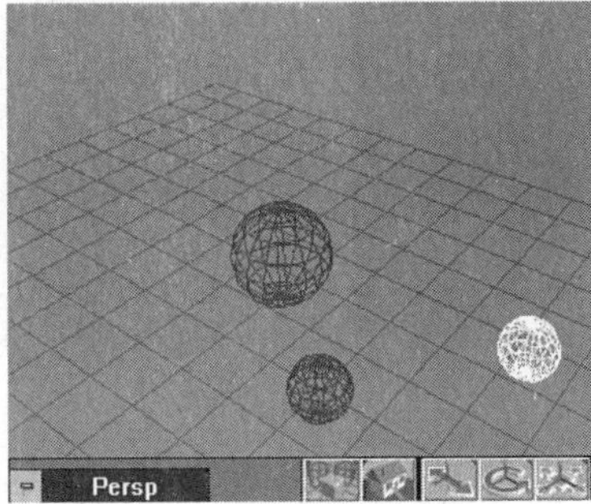

Figure 11.29. Three spheres added to the universe.

If you make a mistake, there are two easy ways to back out. You can use the Undo selection on the Edit menu (see fig. 11.30), or you can click the Undo button (see fig. 11.31).

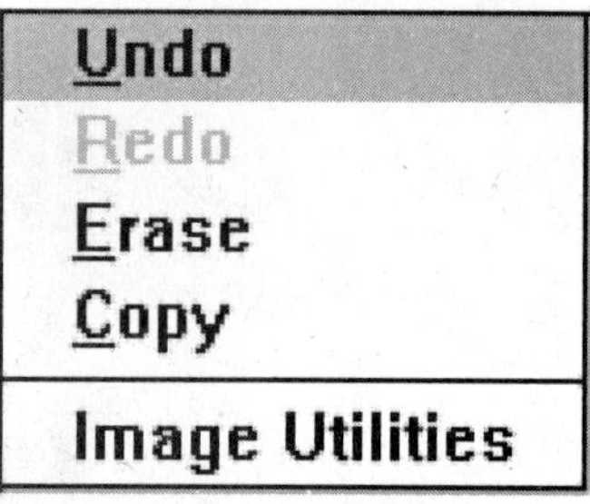

Figure 11.30. The Edit menu.

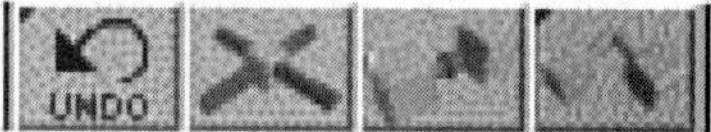

Figure 11.31. The Undo button, left, is a quick way to back out of a mistake.

Continue adding spheres, moving farther out from the "sun" as you go. You may want to adjust the sizes of the spheres, as I have done in figure 11.32. In figure 11.32, there is a central sun, two small inner planets, and several larger planets. The last planet out (lower right) has two small moons. Remember that you are seeing in 3D; the nearer objects appear larger than they really are.

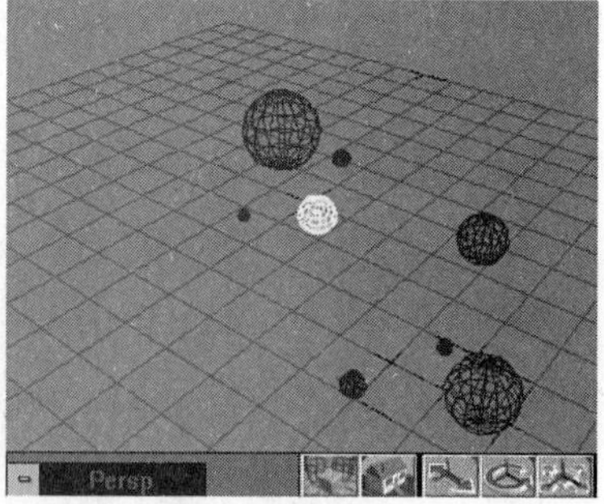

Figure 11.32. All the objects are present for the solar system.

Figure 11.33 shows the system from above, and you can see the relative sizes and positions of the objects more clearly. To change to this view, you can either create a new Top View window, or change the view temporarily using the second button from the left in the Perspective window.

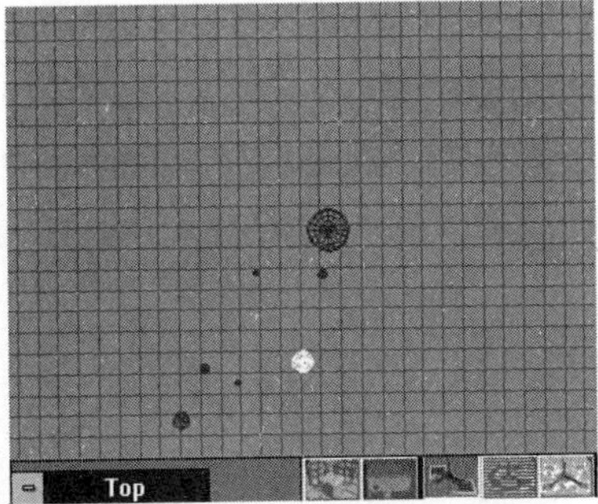

Figure 11.33. The view from above.

Our little solar system is static so far—there is no movement, no animation. Clicking on the Path tool[8] opens the small dialog box shown in figure 11.34. From left to right, the three buttons at the top are

- Move points
- Create points
- Remove selected point(s)

The number next to the word `Segments` refers to the number of frames that will be created between the path points you create. This means you don't have to click for every frame and every point; you can let trueSpace handle the intervening points and frames.

To create a path for the selected object (the object in white is the selected object), simply select the object, click the Path tool, and then click on the middle top button. Now, every time you click in the workspace, trueSpace creates a new Path point, plus 10 intervening frames. Figure 11.35 shows a partially drawn path for one of the planets. Since these are orbits, they will be circular or elliptical.[9]

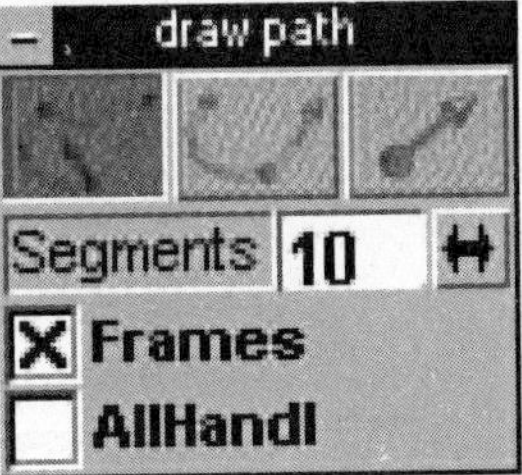

Figure 11.34. The dialog box for creating and editing paths.

[8]See Chapter 3 if you are unsure about which tools are which.

[9]You can also create paths of certain basic shapes such as a circle.

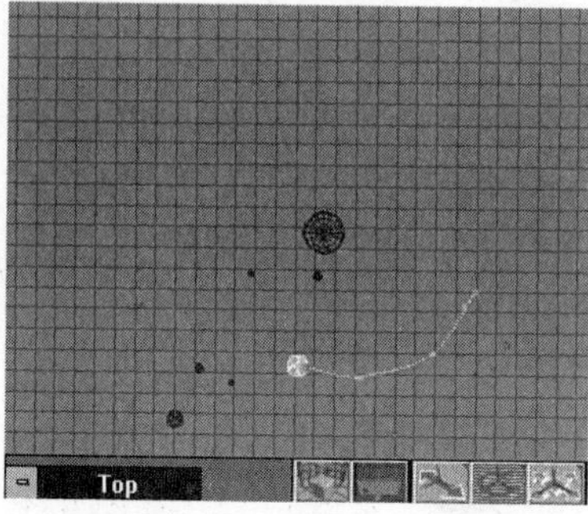

Figure 11.35.
A partially drawn path.

Figure 11.36 shows the completed path, and figure 11.37 shows the path for one of the inner planets. As you can see in figure 11.38, the path can be anything you want it to be, including the highly elliptical orbit shown.

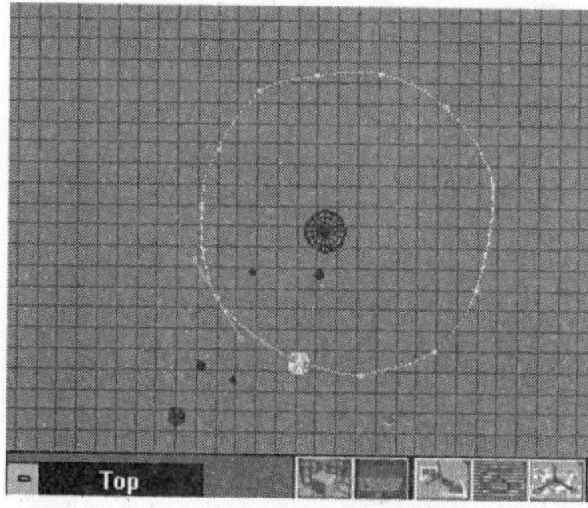

Figure 11.36.
A completed path.

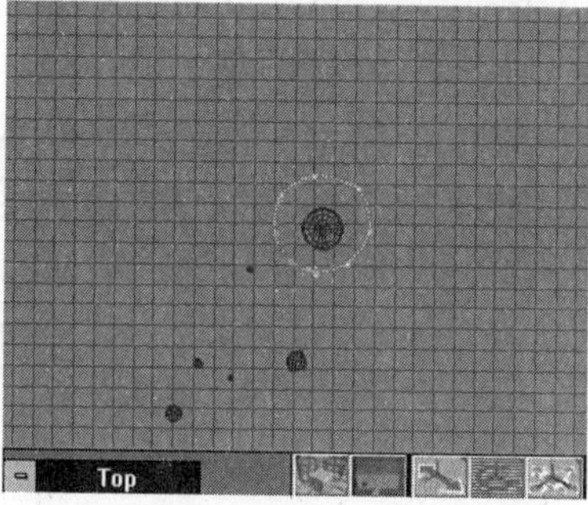

Figure 11.37.
A path for an inner planet.

Figure 11.39 shows a path in the Perspective window. Because the view is 3D, you are seeing the path in perspective. In general, I prefer to modify a path in a "regular," non-perspective view, such as Top or Front.

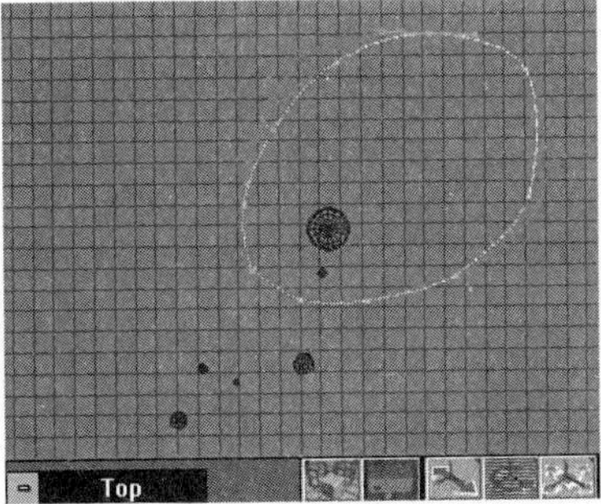

Figure 11.38.
A highly elliptical path.

Figure 11.40 shows a rendering of the scene. The 3D nature of the objects is much clearer in a rendering. The materials that are used for the object surfaces and the background color are default values; we'll be changing them to get a more realistic[10] appearance.

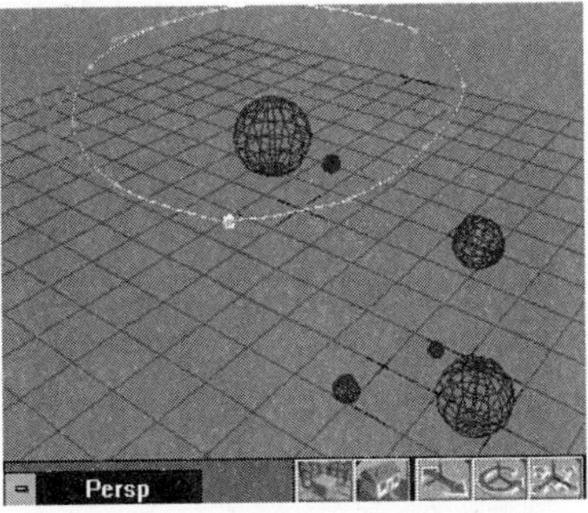

Figure 11.39.
A path in the Perspective window.

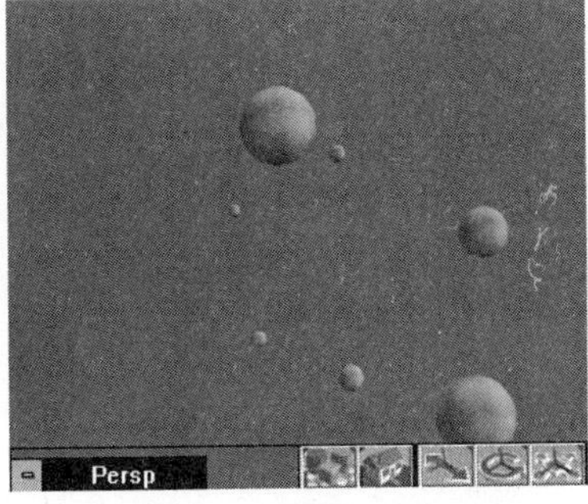

Figure 11.40.
A rendering of the scene so far.

---

[10]Or at least more interesting!

To see the animation in action as a wireframe model, click the Animation tool. This displays the Animation controller (see fig. 11.41). You can also right-click on the same tool to display the Animation Parameters dialog box (see fig. 11.42).

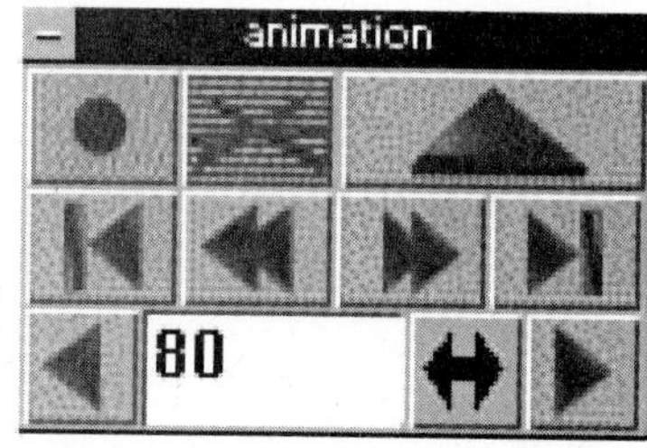

Figure 11.41. Use the Animation Controller to control playback and position.

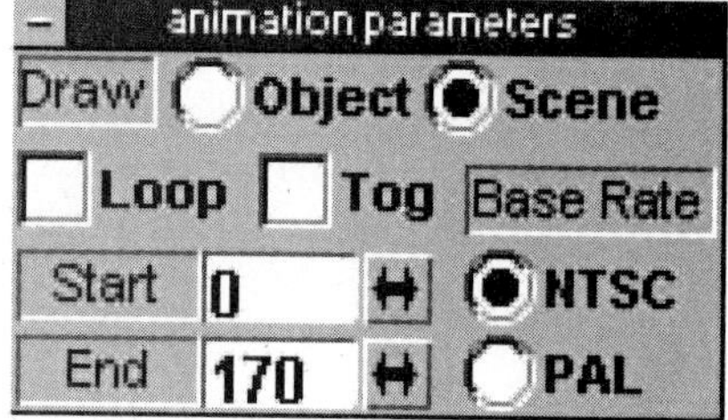

Figure 11.42. The Animation Parameters dialog box controls many aspects of animation.

By default, the animation is set to animate only the currently selected object. To animate all objects that have a path, click on Scene instead of Object in the Animation Parameters dialog box. Another item to note: The default endpoint of the animation will be the number of frames in the animation of the currently selected object. If the total animation has more frames, you can enter the number by hand.

To play the animation, click on the large upward-pointing arrowhead at the top right of the Animation Controller.

Right now, the animation is incomplete—some of the objects do not have paths. The outermost planet with the two moons is the culprit, and there's a reason. We want the two moons to orbit the planet while the planet orbits the sun. This involves hierarchical relationships.[(11)]

---

[11]Big words, but less intimidating than you might think. Like any hierarchy, there's one entity in charge, and one or more levels of responsibility lower down. A monarchy is a hierarchy taken to extremes, but it's a good model for most animation work: there's one central object in any hierarchy, and as many levels as it takes to get down to the peasants who do all the real work.

It's easy to create a hierarchy in trueSpace. Begin with the Big Cheese, the Parent, the King: the object that is at the top of the hierarchy. In this case, that's the outermost planet.[12]

Look closely at figure 11.43. A lot has happened to the animation, but it might not be immediately evident. First, notice that the outer planet has a path; that's no big deal—we've done this before. No, the really big news here is that the outer planet and the two little moons are all in white. White means selected. How did this happen?

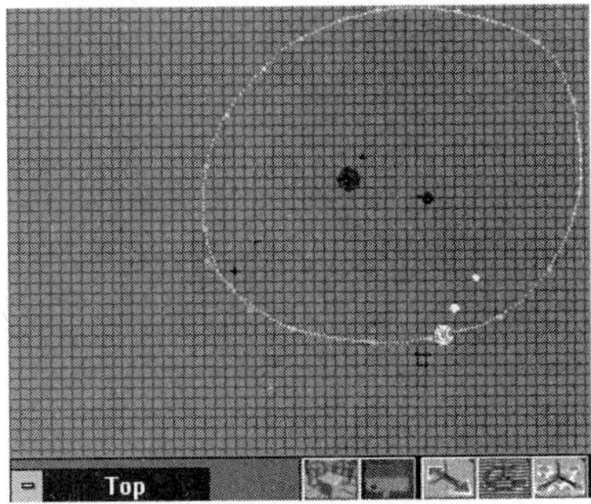

Figure 11.43. Creating a hierarchical animation.

The process is trivially easy. First, select the outermost planet by clicking on it. Now click the Glue Child button. Now click on the inner moon. Presto—you've just created a hierarchy; congratulations. Wasn't that easy? It was so easy, and so much fun, let's add another level to the hierarchy. If you haven't done any random clicking, the Glue Child button is still down. Now click on the second little moon. Wow—now we have a two-level hierarchy.

Now add the path, and the whole hierarchy will follow the path. That's what actually is going on in figure 11.43—those aren't the starting positions for any of the planets you can see. But the little moons need orbital paths of their very own. Again, it's easy. We just have to navigate up and down the hierarchy until we have selected only the member we want. Again, this is easy—just use the arrow keys. The left- and right-arrow keys move sideways in the hierarchy, and the up- and down-arrow keys move up and down. If the planet and its two little moons are all white (selected, in other words), press the down arrow. You will move down a level, and just the two little moons will be white; the planet will be beige. White means

[12]Strictly speaking, if we planned to move the sun around, it would be the Top Enchilada, so that the planets would follow it around like little Taquitos.

selected; beige means part of the current hierarchy, but not selected. In figure 11.44, only the inner little moon is selected. The process of moving around in the hierarchy couldn't be much easier. To select just the outer little moon, press the down arrow again.

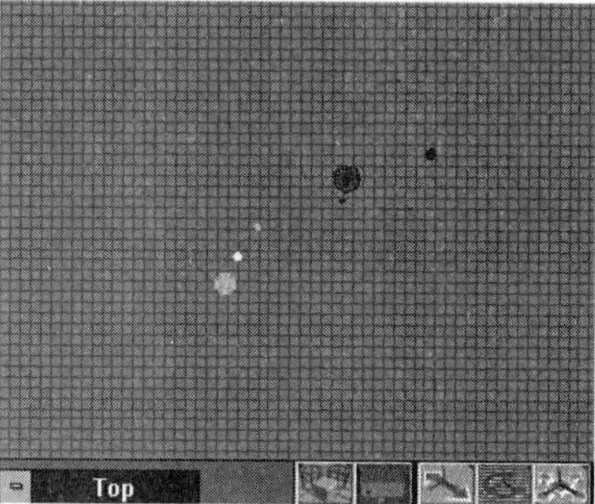

Figure 11.44. Selecting just one member of a hierarchy.

Figure 11.45 shows a nice elliptical path for the outer moon. Add a path for the inner moon, and, presto—a moving hierarchy.

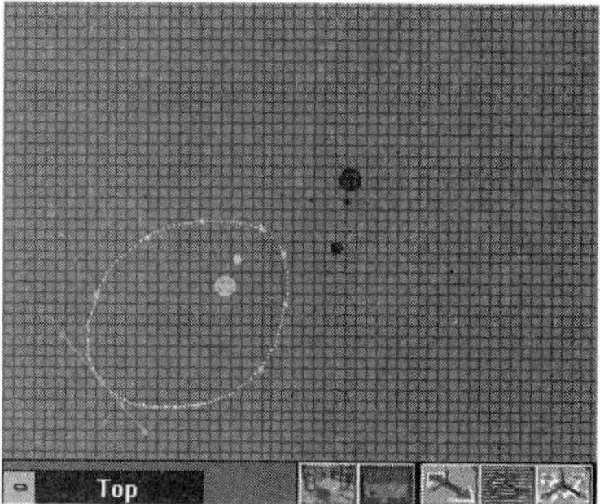

Figure 11.45. Adding a path for one of the little moons of the outermost planet.

All the animations we have been creating have different numbers of frames. The complete animation is as long as the longest individual animation. However, the object with the shortest animation will simply stop moving after one execution. The Animation Panel (see fig. 11.46) comes to the rescue. Each object (or hierarchy, such as our NoName hierarchy in fig. 11.46) has its own horizontal band in the panel. To create a repeating animation, just click the far right button on the bottom of the panel, and then click on the horizontal bar corresponding to the animation. We want everything to repeat, so repeat the process for all animations.

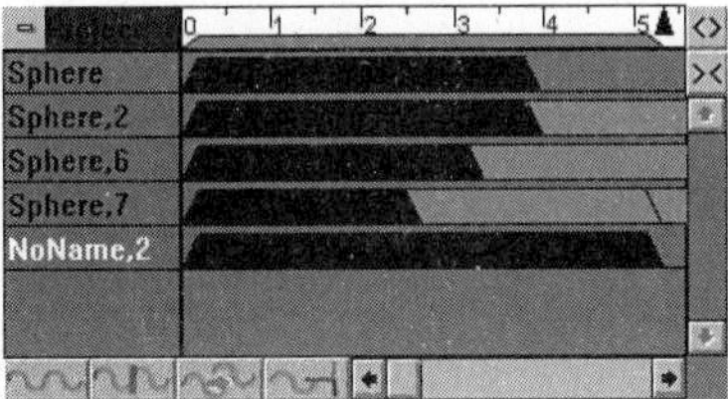

Figure 11.46. The Animation Panel.

We now have the basics of what we want: an animated solar system of our own design. Figures 11.47 and 11.48 show two frames from a wireframe animation. However, let's face it—it's a boring little solar system, full of pink planets and a pink sun,[13] with a dull gray background. All of our animation work deserves a much spicier color scheme. To do this, we must create materials or select from existing materials in the library.

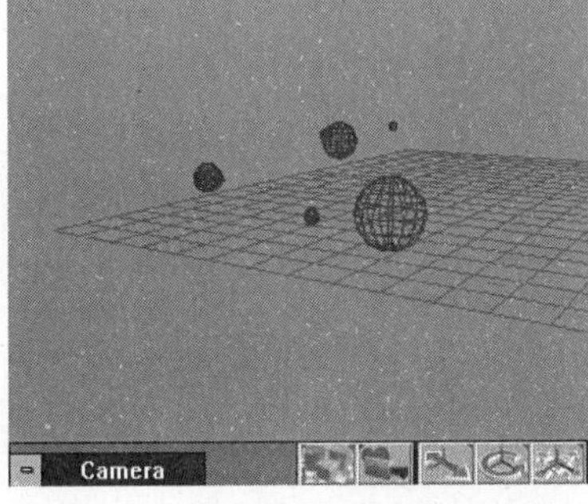

Figure 11.47. A frame from the animation, in Wireframe mode.

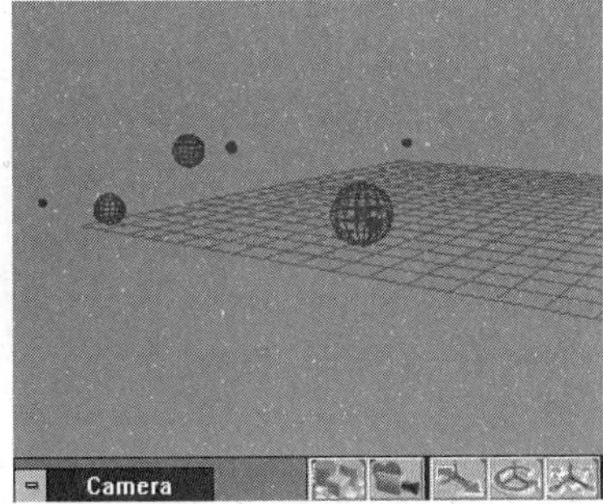

Figure 11.48. A frame from a different part of the animation.

---

[13]Refer back to the earlier rendering, which, while in black and white, is pretty darn boring.

To access the material controls, right-click the Paint tool. This displays several dialog boxes, shown in figures 11.49 through 11.52. This may look intimidating, but the dialog boxes work together in a simple way. When in doubt, pass the mouse cursor over a button or dialog box, and watch the status bar for helpful information. There are just too many buttons to remember here, and in trueSpace overall. This little trick makes it much easier to learn how to use trueSpace.

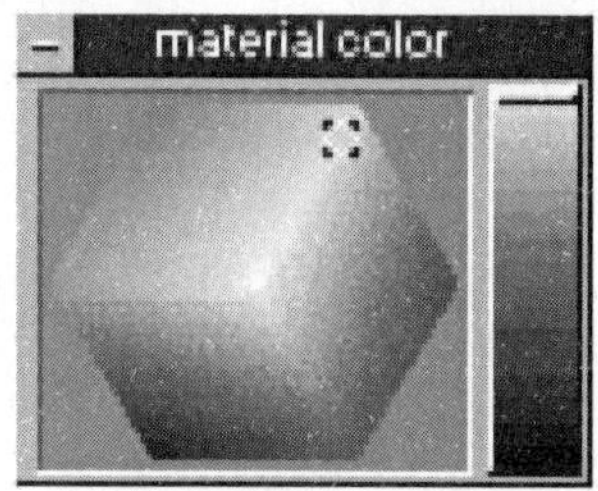

Figure 11.49. The color picker.

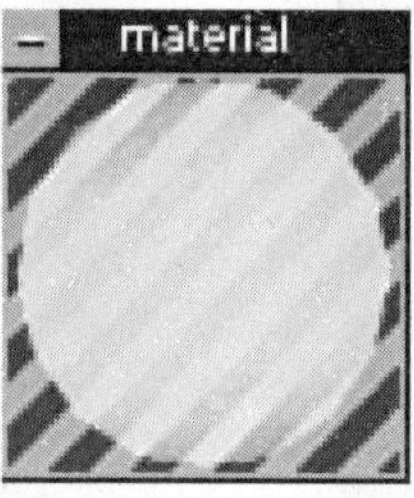

Figure 11.50. The current material.

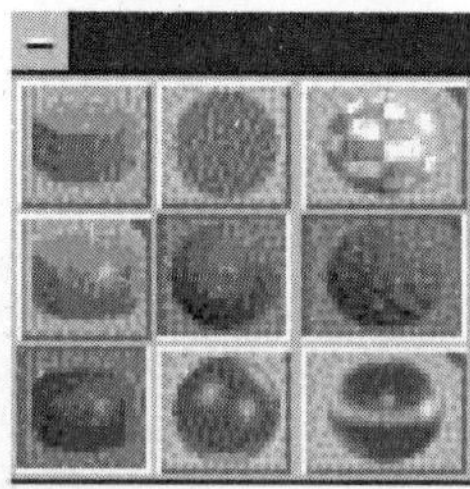

Figure 11.51. Setting material characteristics.

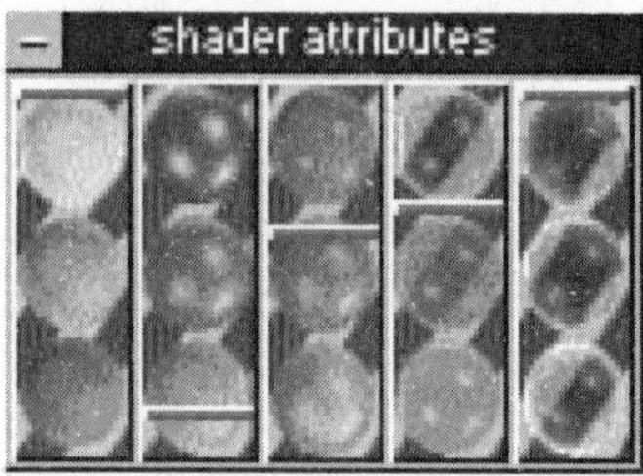

Figure 11.52. Adjusting the shader attributes.

The color picker is just like any other color picker. First, pick a color from the large hexagon. Then lighten or darken it by clicking in the vertical bar. This becomes the primary color for the material. If you change the color (or any other material parameter), you will see an immediate update in the Material dialog box.

The dialog box in figure 11.51 is unnamed, and perhaps that's wise, for it contains quite a variety of buttons and controls. They are arranged in three columns. The far-left column controls faceting. From top to bottom, you'll get facets, auto-smoothing, and all smooth surfaces.[14] The second column controls shading from simple to fancy metallic, and the third column controls surface texture/bumpiness.

The Shader Attributes dialog box provides visual cues for adjusting a variety of material properties. There are five columns, with a slider in each column. To vary a property, move the slider up or down as needed. The five properties are

Self-illumination

Shininess

Roughness

Transparency

Refraction

For the sun, we can take advantage of self-illumination—set it all the way to the top. You'll find that maximum self-illumination tends to override other settings, so you may not need to change anything else except color—yellow for my sun, and the color you want for yours. Figure 11.53 shows a rendering for the scene, with the sun glowing away nicely. But the background is still gray, and the planets are still smooth and, well, pink. However, they are nicely lit by the sun!

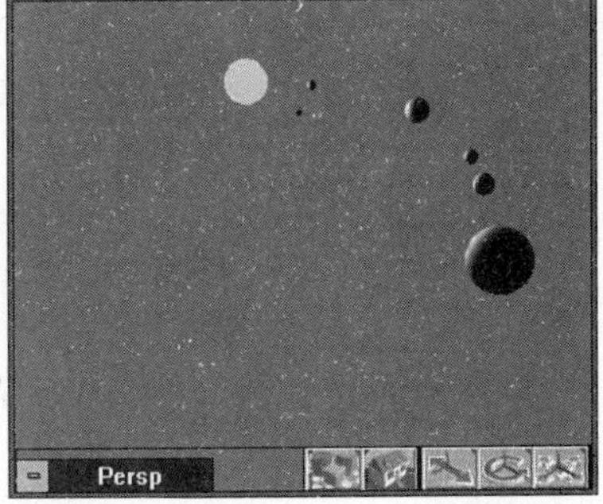

Figure 11.53. A rendering showing the sun as a self-illuminating object.

[14]Smooth means you won't see the edges between facets.

What we need now are some nice planetary textures and colors for the planets. You can, if you want, dig out planetary maps for your own solar system, but this is strictly a do-it-yourself solar system, so we'll have to improvise. Figure 11.54 shows a material that uses a bumpy texture. It has a nice planetary look, and I tuned it a bit by using the Shader Attributes dialog box. Figure 11.55 shows the dialog box that allows you to select various surface textures; I chose orange because it was the most planetary-looking.

Figure 11.54.
A material with a planet-like texture.

bump map			
ORANGE		Amp	0.26
U Repts	1	U Offset	0
V Repts	1	V Offset	0

Figure 11.55.
Selecting a surface texture for a material.

I used this texture, with some variations, for all the planets but the outermost one. I kind of liked the weird texture shown in figure 11.56, which I dug out of the sample textures supplied with trueSpace.

Figure 11.56.
A nice, exotic planetary texture.

Figure 11.57 shows a rendering of the scene with the planets and the sun all having textures. Nice, but, wow—that gray background has got to go!

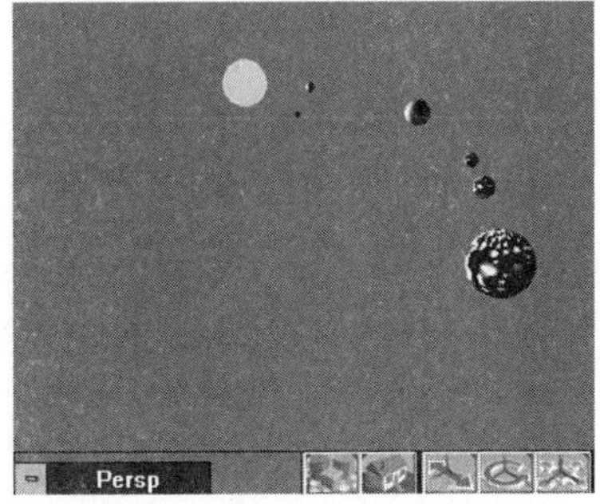

Figure 11.57. All the objects now have a material texture.

It's easy to do; just right-click the Render button in the Perspective window to display a few global settings (see fig. 11.58), one of which is the background. I created the background shown in figure 11.59 using an Image Editor—just some random white, blue, and red dots for stars, and then an airbrush to create a nebula or two. Instant space background.

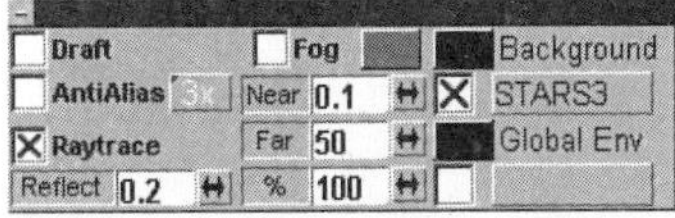

Figure 11.58. Adjusting the background.

Figure 11.59. A background that looks nice and spacey.

To save the animation as an AVI file, I simply clicked the Render to File button (a variant of the Render tool). Figure 11.60 shows the dialog box that allows you to set parameters for the AVI file. Make sure you click on All Frames in the Animation section of the dialog box, and enter a valid AVI file name. You'll also need to set a size for the animation (I used 320×240 because it's a standard size for video clips), as well as a frame rate (15 or 30), and verify that the Pixel Aspect Ration is 1.0. Click the Render button when all is ready.

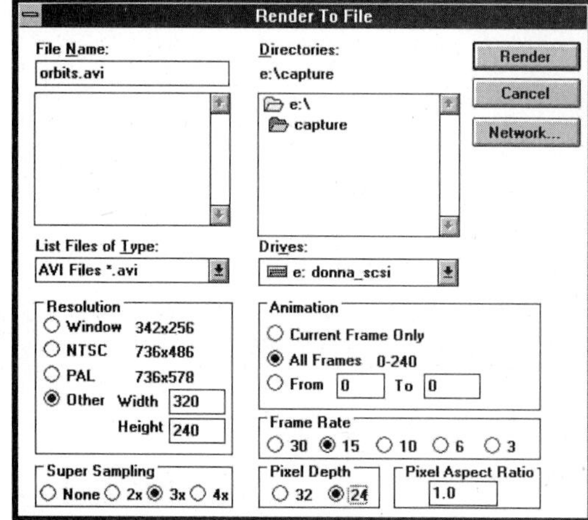

Figure 11.60. Setting values saving the animation to a file.

This will display YADB (Yet Another Dialog Box), shown in figure 11.61. You can accept the default, no compression, but you wind up with a huge file that no one can play. Compression makes it possible to hit frame rates of 30 per second with an animation that uses a steady background (that's this one). I have chosen Cinepak in the example, but any compression codec you favor will do (such as Indeo or MS Video 1). Set a quality level (the higher the number, the better the image, but the greater the demands it will put on your system during playback). Click OK when you have it all decided.

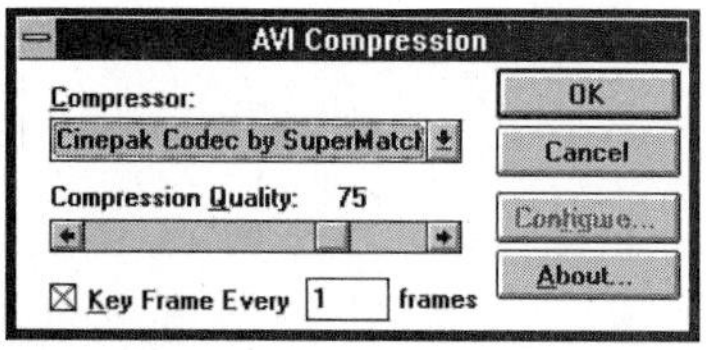

Figure 11.61. Setting the compression method.

AVI Compression
Compressor:
Cinepak Codec by SuperMatch
OK
Cancel
Compression Quality: 75
Configure...
About...
Key Frame Every 1 frames

Now, all you have to do is sit back and wait—compression may take anywhere from a few seconds to a minute per frame, depending on a variety of factors. But the end result is a lot of fun, as you can see from the sample rendered frame in figure 11.62. A full-size rendering is shown in figure 11.63.

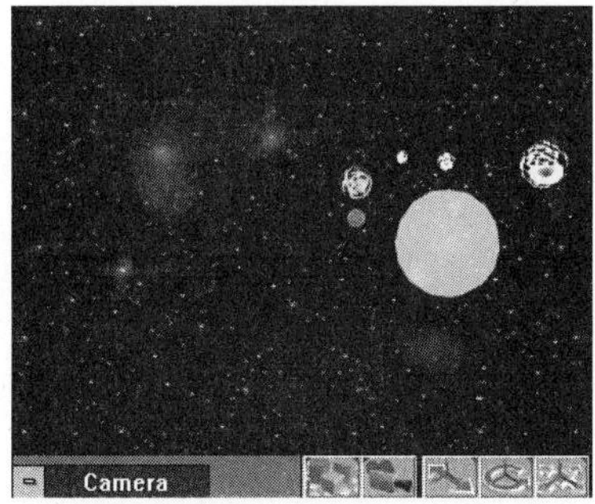

Figure 11.62. A sample frame from the animation.

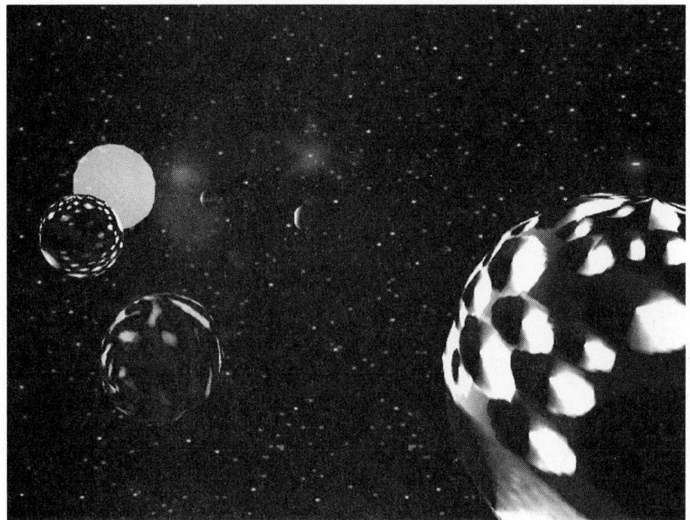

Figure 11.63. A larger rendering of a single frame, uncompressed for best image quality.

This is just the beginning of what you can do with trueSpace. The combination of a reasonably complete set of tools, a clever and easy-to-learn interface, and first-rate rendering make trueSpace an excellent startup tool for anyone interested in 3D animation, rendering, or artificial reality.

12

CYBERSPACE/CYBERPUNK

Reality may have already sprung a leak. To my knowledge, there is no little Dutch boy to put his finger in the dike and stem the flood—quite the contrary. There are hoards of cyberpunks scratching and clawing to widen the breach any way they can.

If that paragraph seems odd, or lacks meaning or a point of reference, read on. All will be made clear.

Let's begin with two words: *cyberspace* and *cyberpunk*. Both words owe their origin to the word *cybernetics*, a term coined decades ago by Norbert Wiener of MIT. This term originally referred to the study of control/feedback systems. It, in turn, is based on the Greek word *kybernetes*, meaning *helmsman*.

Over the years, the root portion of these words, *cyber*, gained a life of its own. Words such as *cyborg*—half man, half machine—began to crop up in the world of science fiction. In the last decade, William Gibson used the term *cyberspace* to describe what he calls "a consensual hallucination." It is "a graphic representation of data abstracted from the banks of every computer in the human system."

If you could connect all the computers in the world, and then find a way to put your own mind into that space, that would be cyberspace. In some ways, this is already happening, though not to the degree it has been depicted in science fiction. You can connect almost anywhere these days using Internet, a BBS, CompuServe, or just plain old electronic mail. But you can't insert yourself in a graphically vivid alternate reality composed of the very stuff of computers.

The Moral Dilemma

Even if the reality falls short of the virtual promise, there is a lot going on in the first bits[1] of cyberspace today. More and more people rely on some form of electronic communication and/or virtual presence to get work done, communicate about personal issues, or just raise a little hell. Cyberspace is uniquely suited to the latter—you are there, and you are not there. If you want to, you can walk away from an electronic conversation without anyone knowing who you are, or where you came from. This is just one way in which cyberspace reality is different from garden-variety, everyday *real* reality.

Given that the two are different, the question can be asked: What are the implications of virtual reality in general, and cyberspace in particular? The answer will

[1]Pun intended.

vary with your point of view. If you are JAC,[2] then the implications are nothing but joyous. If you are heavily invested in cable and phone stocks, well, the radical nature of cyberspace in general and cyberpunk in particular must give you pause.

VR versus TV

There is a vocal minority that would like us to believe that violence on television is ruining the youth of America. Whether you agree with that point of view or not, the same is likely to be said about virtual reality and cyberspace. The truth is that most of us alive now have grown up with television, and are either ruined or not, as the case may be. The generation coming along right now will be the first to grow up with virtual reality at their (literal) fingertips. What are the implications of that? Is VR just like TV? Or is the resemblance limited to the fact that both have two-letter acronyms?

The implications are more and less than you might think. I'll begin with less.

My son Justen is a good example of a typical Nintendo/Genesis child. He has access to both systems,[3] buys three or four games a year for each system,[4] and pesters his parents to death regarding every hot new game that is advertised. He will willingly spend hour after hour glued to the television playing the games. He will play them alone; he will play them with friends. He will play them when the weather outdoors is ideal; he will play them when it rains. In short, if someone doesn't come along and roust him from his reverie, he will play them until his thumbs fall off.

As a matter of fact, some of the most accessible VR technology can be found in games. Game vendors are competing with each other for the kids' parents' money, and the game that sounds, looks, or works more like reality— or, more often, some enhanced form of reality—is what catches the kids' attention. The picture I see is of kids hyper-excited about hyper-real games full of punching, kicking, and other forms of action. From what I've seen, the most popular games are the rockem-sockem ones, with dead bodies all over the place. The game player himself is often one of the dead until the game gets mastered.[5]

---

[2]Just Another Cyberpunk, and this pun is intended, too.

[3]And, just this week, the SuperNES arrived, so he's as cybernetically oriented as he can get.

[4]Lately, he has discovered that renting a game 10 times (total cost: $20-$30) is a better deal than buying the game (total cost: $50-$60). I guess his head isn't totally lost in cyberspace.

[5]The potential for religious significance is overwhelming, but even an analogy to Aesop's fables will make the point: Since time immemorial, kids have had far more stomach for mayhem than adults.

The Nature of Play

It's been said that we humans enjoy play because a small effort leads to a large reward, giving us pleasure. That's a dry description of play, but it makes a valid point. It also explains the allure of TV, video games, VR, and cyberspace. In the real world, a reward is married to effort. In any kind of artificial reality, the rules can be as artificial as the reality. The rules can be shaped to enhance the experience. A VR experience isn't like a vacation at all—it can rain on your vacation, or you can stub your toe on some coral while wading in a Caribbean lagoon. In VR, the experience is guaranteed. You fire the missile, you punch the bad guy, then you get the reward. In short, today's VR is predictable. Not entirely predictable, of course—there is always a need for some thrilling surprises.

Of course, I could go on endlessly about why kids, and some of us adults, enjoy video games. The bottom line is obvious: kids love them. The *why* may not be so important, but the results are.

The most serious potential problem with virtual reality is mistaking it for reality, and I think most of us are relatively immune to that mistake. In that sense, VR, cyberspace, cyberpunk, and so on are no more—and no less—dangerous than something like cigarettes or alcohol. Most people who use these things get enough pleasure out of them to offset both the risks and the potential for problems. Of course, there is a minority that does not find itself in this comfortable position.

There are going to be folks who get hooked on alternate realities, for whatever reason. There are going to be folks who indulge in it more than they know they should. And then there will be most folks, who will take it or leave it, as it suits them.

In other words, I don't think there's any more of a moral dilemma involved in virtual reality than in any other civilized pursuit. By *civilized*, I mean pursuits that are the fruit of civilization, not those that are tame. There are plenty of "civilized" activities that are fraught with danger, such as driving a car on a Friday afternoon on the way home from work. There are many "benefits" of civilization, both positive and negative:

- A teenage girl spending half her after-school day on the telephone giggling over stuff with her friends.
- An adult watching the evening news, and then turning the TV off in disgust when a vapid sitcom comes on.

- A teenage boy smoking when his parents aren't around.
- A book editor playing a game of Tetris to calm down after a lengthy editing session.

Here is what I see as the "real" bottom line:

> **Virtual reality will have the same joys and pitfalls as actual reality because the same user is running both operations: a human being.**

I must temper that opinion with another consideration, however. Without balance, without some actual reality to balance the virtual reality, sterility is a real concern. No one mistakes the urban jungle for the real jungle. Graffiti is nature's way of trying to put the equivalent of leaves on flat, sterile buildings. Unfortunately, it's a hopeless task. I would prefer that we do a better job with virtual reality than we have with actual reality, and I think I am not alone in that hope. I am also not alone in wondering how realistic such a hope is.

Ultimately, virtual reality appeals to, and satisfies, only a portion of the human psyche. If we as a society neglect to offer a balanced menu, or if individuals fail to choose a balanced menu, the end result can only be pain and trouble. We should do everything we can to avoid that.

More Questions than Answers

I relied on William Gibson for a definition of cyberspace, but I'll provide my own definition of cyberpunk. *Cyberpunk* is nothing more than young folks applying youthful energy and creativity to computers, art, and virtual reality. This isn't very different from what went into the beat generation, hippies, and yuppies. The beat generation applied its energy to finding the boundaries of imagination, hippies to finding the boundaries of personal freedom, yuppies to finding the boundaries of personal success. Each youthful generation is supplied with the enthusiasm and emotional tools for unremitting pursuit of the farther edge of some aspect of life. This generation is no different—it just wants to push what we take for granted to the edge, and then maybe a little bit farther.

This is the nature of adolescence. One effect of such single-minded pursuit is that it creates new territory. Whether that territory be jazz, beat poetry, acid rock, folk music, detailing of a BMW, surfing lingo, performance art, or virtual communities, it represents enormous vitality. It is the grass roots effort to build the future, and I believe it will have a profound effect on the nature and timing of our virtual future.

Where might that future lead? Consider the possibilities, both mundane and exotic, that follow.

Virtual Communities

A *virtual community* is a collection of individuals who communicate electronically. Such a community takes many, many forms. Within a company, several people may work together on a project without ever meeting face to face—they simply send electronic mail (e-mail) to one another during the course of the project to "talk" about goals, problems, and the like. Or a group of individuals interested in music of the later 18th century might communicate via their modems on a bulletin board. There are hundreds of such communities on the CompuServe Information Service, Genie, America Online, and other such services, as well as smaller, local bulletin boards.

The power of such virtual communities can be profound. Communication is a powerful tool. Not only does it transfer knowledge; it also acts as a catalyst for the generation of new ideas, and creates possibilities where none existed before.

The power of simple communication should not be missed or misunderstood. Science fiction defines cyberspace in grand and glorious terms. Books portray dramatic landscapes full of virtual objects, virtual travel, and virtual people doing all kinds of virtual things. Grand and glorious is, well, merely grand and glorious. Changing someone's mind, stimulating appreciation for art—these can happen in very mundane ways. Passionate e-mail, clearly written and widely read, may have far more impact than the grandest and most glorious artificial landscape.

Virtual Art

The range of art produced in the field of virtual reality is vast. Ranging from full-blown multimedia extravaganzas to intimate works, the field is hardly definable. Almost any aspect of computers, multimedia, or virtual reality is seen as a valid medium by many artists. And science fiction literature is rampant with cyber artists of every description, ranging from artists who sculpt with human emotion to creators of complete virtual systems.

I have worked in both the real and virtual worlds of art. I've always been handy with a pencil, and have lately taken to drawing several times a week just for recreation. I keep a few soft pencils around and a drawing notebook.

I also have a 12"×12" tablet with a pressure-sensitive pen, which I can use with software like Fractal Design Painter or Dabbler to draw. This, I suppose, qualifies me as a virtual artist. Having experienced both forms of creation, I can say that each has its merits.

Physically drawing with a pencil has an undeniable intimacy. The scratching of the pencil on paper, the ineradicable nature of a heavy line—these are things that virtual drawing cannot duplicate. I like being able to hold the final product in my hand, or tack it to the wall for further inspiration.

Virtual drawing requires greater technical skills, since I have to know how to use the hardware and software effectively. It takes a lot of time to learn the right touch for the pressure-sensitive pen, for example, and the software, while flexible, isn't as easy as picking up a brush or a pencil. For one thing, there are almost too many choices to make. But there is a good side, too—I never run out of a color, and my brush or pen can have an infinite supply of paint or ink. I can erase absolutely or minimally, as I choose. I have a greater degree of color because I can ignore the laws of physics if I want.

So the method I choose varies from day to day and mood to mood. That's a perfect example of the balance I spoke of earlier. Sometimes, it's good to really cut loose and ignore reality. Other times, the very limits of reality are reassuring and pleasant, and help me define what I want to draw.

Sensory Stimulation

So far, multimedia means only sight and sound.[6] The future holds the promise of adding stimulation of other senses, either directly or electronically. What would be the results of linking smell or touch to a computer simulation? How would it change our daily experience if such things became common—if the television migrated from "the box" to a suit you wear?

These possibilities are far down the road, but they could shake the foundations of what it means to be human. Even the writers of science fiction probably fall a good deal short of the potential for new ideas and ways of living from such technology.

Hypertext

Hypertext is the ability to link similar information by electronic means. Today, it is used by products like Encarta for more than text. You can, for example, look up

[6] At the cutting edge of VR, we find some opportunities for tactile feedback. At the consumer level, only extremely primitive methods are used, such as a vibrating stylus.

cat, and you will find not only references to specific breeds that you can access with a click of the mouse, but animations, sound recordings, and pictures as well. All are hyper-linked to the text.

The future possibilities for hyper-linking are endless. It could be applied to television, for example. You could be watching a program that reminds you of an old Jack Benny show, and you could jump to that show using a search tool, and then return to the show you were originally watching without missing a second of it.[7]

Medical Simulations

Today, the first simulations of the human body are appearing in medical schools. Sometimes referred to as a *virtual cadaver,* these simulations allow medical students to explore human anatomy without ever touching a real body, dead or otherwise. Surgeons can use such simulations to practice surgical techniques. Researchers can model activity in the human brain, and a diagnostician can compare images from a CAT scan to reference images from a "perfect" body.

At the far edge of such simulations is the conversion of data from CAT scans and other high-tech tools into 3D or virtual simulations. This allows a physician to examine the inside of a body as though the enclosing skin and muscle were not present.

Virtual Sex

Yes, there is virtual sex, too—whether you like it or not, this powerful human drive is very much a part of the virtual scene. You can already purchase 3D video tapes rated XXX, and there are interactive "games" that feature or emphasize sexual content. Simulated sex is as likely to find its way to market as any other kind of simulation.

The implications for virtual sex are legion. Sex is one of the most basic of human drives, and the idea that technology might create alternatives is pretty heady stuff. We might find ourselves right up against the edges of what humanity means.

Robotics

There are many uses for robots in places where it would be dangerous or difficult to put a human being. For example, robots are already being used to handle nuclear

[7]You could, in other words, get lost in virtual space without ever having to encounter a full-immersion, fully virtual system. Sort of the ultimate couch potato.

and chemical cleanup duties. The development of virtual reality and telepresence will enhance an operator's ability to maneuver such robots. Planetary exploration also offers a unique opportunity for development of virtual-reality techniques—it is much safer to send a robot probe controlled by a person to a planetary surface than that same person. In fact, planetary models are currently under development that would use miniature vehicles to allow researchers to explore a planet from a human perspective, and perhaps learn new ways of interpreting existing data.

The limitations of such a system are worth noting, however. For example, if such a miniature craft were on the surface of Mars, but its controller were seated in a lab in Houston, it would take minutes for the signals to go back and forth.[8] This time delay could prove disastrous. One solution is to put the Earthmen in orbit around the planet being probed, but that's expensive and dangerous. Besides, if you're that close, why not pop in for a visit?

You might be wondering why we don't simply program the robot to handle itself. To a certain degree, that can be done. For example, a robot can be pretty good about not running into objects that lie right in its path. However, robots are easy to fool and can get their signals mixed up, with disastrous results. False echoes and the like could destroy a robot probe more easily than we'd like.

In addition, it's exceedingly difficult for a robot to do many of the tasks that you and I handle quite easily. For example, a geologist can learn to make careful distinctions between various kinds of rocks in the field, and make intelligent choices about which ones to pick for later scientific study. A robot, on the other hand, would have a hard time distinguishing what was what—let alone making the kinds of fuzzy, intuitive connections that a geologist could make in his sleep.

Thus, remote-controlled robots make real sense. Such robots have enough intelligence to keep themselves from being smashed into little pieces, but they are basically there to enhance the perception of their distant operator. By acting as virtual eyes, ears, and hands, the robot, when integrated with a suitable virtual environment generator, becomes an extension of its operator.

Virtual Underground

And just as surely as there will be a virtual community, there will have to be a virtual underground—a place for the dissidents and rebels. This is evident even to-

[8]The speed of light, being finite, puts an upper limit on such technology. What good would it do for a human "teleoperator" to react to a falling rock when the rock will have already smashed the robot probe to pieces by the time he or she becomes aware of the object's fall? The delay in receiving images from even a nearby planet is measured in minutes.

day in the existence of the virtual equivalents of Greenwich Village, Berkeley, and Soho.

Hacker's Dream, Hacker's Nightmare

Whatever the future holds, I'll make one prediction: It's going to be more or less unpredictable. It will be a hacker's dream because there will be enormously interesting challenges to be met. It will be a hacker's nightmare because the proliferation of proprietary technologies likely to emerge will keep some technologies out of people's hands for decades.

Roots and Possibilities

If the roots of the future are already present, there is very little that is certain about where virtual reality is going. Talk about the info highway is now a common part of business discourse. Businesses are competing for these data highways the same as railroad barons competed for land to put railroads on. And just as the railroads changed forever how the American landscape was viewed and used, the data highways of the future will alter forever the nature of the human landscape, both inside and out.

Humankind must always keep one toe on the ground. That's where our roots are, and that's where our values are formed. It is our reference point, the measure of all things. If virtual reality is exciting or fun or useful or profound, it is in relation to what it adds to real experience, not the other way around.

CyberCity & the Info Highwaymen

Once upon a time, in a virtual city the size of the world, a bunch of virtual guys got together and dreamed The Really Big Dream: A world net of computers and cyberfolk. Everyone had a really good time, and then they went back to reality.

The truth: The realization of that dream isn't even close to happening. The result: Expectations are way ahead of reality.[9]

It can be hard to keep your head screwed on straight when talking and thinking about the future of virtual reality—or even of real reality, where the electronic

[9]Don't you just love the excessive mixed metaphors of those last two paragraphs? That's the trouble with virtual reality—it doesn't play by the same rules as the real reality. How about a more barbaric term, like *pseudo-space*, to refer to make-believe worlds?

landscape is undergoing tremendous change. On either side of the virtual curtain, it's hard to tell the stage from the players, the audience from the script. The reason: The human mind tends to get stuck in whatever rut it happens to be running in.

There's no reason to expect that VR won't be just as affected by the realities of human nature as real reality. Look at the majority of VR enthusiasts: They are young, and youth brings enthusiasm as well as a willingness to do and be new things.[10]

Of course, it goes well beyond just youth and age—what about crooks and cops? Here's a safe prediction: If there's an info highway, there will surely be infohighwaymen by its shoulders, armed and dangerous, and infocops to hold them at bay.

Why It's Called Cyberpunk

Let's face it: Virtual Reality isn't the domain of old fogies. If you've been driving your Oldsmobile on the concrete highways, it's going to be a major mind-bender to tool along the info highway by modem. I'm not talking about using the Internet or communicating over CompuServe:[11] I'm talking about pure pedal-to-the-metal, fast-lane action in communal virtual landscapes that defy most, if not all, of the logic of both physics and society. In other words, cyberpunk.

Cyberpunk is, and has always been, all about youth questioning authority. Hey—that's fun, and a normal part of adolescence. It's all about pushing the envelope to see what there is to see, to find new places to go and perhaps, for a lucky few, a new way of thinking about life. Now take that perfectly normal urge, expand the horizons a few thousand times, and remove the rulebook. That's the lure of cyberpunk.

Imagine painting your frustrations on a canvas bigger than life. Imagine ranting and raving free of the constraints of mere physical laws of nature. Imagine the boundaries of reality bursting at your whim, opening into dreams older generations couldn't have imagined.

If you have stayed with my train of thought, you now have a firm grip on the unreality of cyberpunk. It's fast, it's furious, it's got enough energy to fuel cyberspace forever. It's capable of replacing books and movies and TV and walks in the park. It's about dreaming and being free—the wanderlust of adolescence channeled into

---

[10]It also is noted for its lack of ruts, which are reserved for those of us who have been around for a while.

[11]Many of us old fogies do just fine at that.

the quantum states of electrons and amplified like a laser. It's power and coolness and radical rolled into one.

Now imagine doing this for a living. Imagine yourself as a citizen of the cyber metropolis, a card-carrying member of a virtual reality. Now we're talking about cyberformal, and the luster is gone. Wiped clean. We're talking about spending an hour in the morning reading e-mail. We're talking about your boss laying into you across the net about the mistakes in the contract you wrote up last week. We're talking boring. We're also talking about the universe in which things happen and have consequences. Cyberformal is not only a counterpoint to cyberpunk—it's a necessary one.

Cyberpunk is to e-mail as the '60s anti-war movement was to the ballot box. The first (cyberpunk, the movement) is exciting, the second (e-mail, voting) is about getting things done. The Wholly Virtual Person is going to have to live in both kinds of the virtual world.

So here's my prediction: 20 years from now, we'll all be reminiscing about the early days of cyberpunk, and we'll all still be sending boring old e-mail to get things done.

And maybe—just maybe—we'll still be able to cut loose in a virtual wonderland and do something utterly entertaining, completely incoherent, and unabashedly virtual. Just as there has always been a little kid inside every one of us looking for an excuse to play and have a good time, there's a little punk in there, too, angling for a joust with the outer boundaries of reality—aching to get a little virtual once in a while, to break the rules and soar with the imagination.

Look around, friend—the cyberpunks are making all the noise, but multimedia is where all the action is. Millions of us are listening to our computers, but how many can manage to jack into cyberspace whenever they want to? Let's get real here—you've got to walk before you can run. You've got to have a place to go before you can really *use* any kind of vehicle. There is no cyberspace yet, there is no alternate reality to plug into.

So what—VR and multimedia and all that stuff is still limited. The humanization of computers has begun, you're a party to it, and there's a lot of room to grow with all this cool stuff. So lose your hesitation, personalize your computer today, and get ready to boost your imagination into the stratosphere as this thing takes off.

If you ain't doin' VR, you're missin' out on the future.

13

THE VIRTUAL FUTURE

The virtual future holds a lot of promise, and there's no telling how much of the promise will actually come true. You can, however, get a real taste of that future today. You can even do it without spending a lot of money. Consider the recipe for this chapter.

RECIPE

1 PCVR parallel port interface
1 Pair LCD 3D goggles
1 Mattel Power Glove
1 3D software package

Instructions: This recipe looks much more intimidating than it really is. Over the last year, the ingredients have become much more economical. With only a little fine-tuning, you can attach a few cables and be virtual, interactive, and 3D all in one shot.

You might think it would cost a lot of money to acquire that list of ingredients, but that's not the case. For example, consider the costs of a basic 3D system from a company called 3DTV:

LCD[(1)] goggles	$150
3D software	Free or $$$[(2)]
Goggle interface	Included

[1]*LCD* stands for *Liquid Crystal Display*, and this is the same technology that is used in watches, laptop computer screens, and hand-held calculators. The idea is simple: When an electrical current is applied to and then removed from the liquid crystal, it toggles between transparent and opaque. In typical applications, the crystals are shaped into letters and numbers. Electrical currents are turned on and off to make portions of the LCD panel opaque, thus making readable text or numbers. Also, note that this price is a special one for readers of this book; standard prices are higher.

You can augment this basic setup with:

Mattel Power Glove[3] $50-$100

That means your total initial investment in 3D/VR can be from $150 to $250. At the time the first edition of this book was written (early 1993), the same equipment would have cost you about $500.

In the rest of this chapter, we'll be looking at a lot of products from the 3DTV company. You might think I'm favoring them, but the truth is there are very few companies offering this kind of hardware. 3DTV is something of a standard in the VR industry, and its long-standing support for 3D and VR technology makes it a relatively safe bet in this emerging market. 3DTV has made a serious effort to provide low-cost 3D and VR products, and I've been happy with the products it has offered. Some of them are downright fun, and I've always gotten the most bang for the buck out of its products.

Keep in mind that low cost means you won't be getting polished, full-color documentation with some products; keep your thinking cap on! If your idea of a good deal is to trade away the spit and polish, and get low prices and a photocopied manual, 3DTV is the place to shop for VR. Besides, the president (Michael Starks) is nuts about 3D and VR, and his enthusiasm comes across in the usefulness and design of his company's products.

Really Virtual

Of course, you don't have to stick with the basics. The next step up, at least until a few weeks before I wrote this, was about $2,000 for hardware, and $500 to $10,000 for software. A new product from 3DTV could create a stampede[4]—the Stereo Space

---

[2]That $$$ can be as much as you care to spend, or you can download shareware (Rend386, for example, from the CompuServe forum CYBERFORUM). Rend386 is explained later in this chapter, but only from the user-interface point of view. For complete information about Rend386, look for the book *Virtual Reality Creations* from the Waite Group Press. It is written by one of the authors of Rend386, David Stampe. If you want to spend a little money, you can create stereo images with Vistapro as well.

[3]This item is no longer manufactured, but it remains in heavy circulation among VR enthusiasts. You can find them locally by watching the classified section of your newspaper, or you can buy them on the very active VR market. Several companies are stocking large quantities of used Power Gloves. I ordered one, and when it arrived, it still had all the original equipment and manuals.

[4]At least on the hardware side! Software, of course, will still cost what it costs—although prices continue to drop in software, too.

Model 1. It's a little black box that allows you to use inexpensive LCD glasses with all kinds of really powerful VR and 3D software from VREAM to Superscape.

Why am I so excited about the Stereo Space? In basic terms, the biggest problem with LCD goggles in the past has been flicker. The Stereo Space allows the goggles to operate at twice the frequency of conventional design. The higher the frequency, the less the flicker, and the more effective the 3D effect. Let's look at the nature of LCD goggles, and then return to the Stereo Space.

LCD Goggles

LCD goggles work on a very simple principle. They are a pair of glasses with LCD panels in place of lenses. As explained in Chapter 8, most 3D systems must find a way to present different images to each eye. By switching electrical current to alternate LCD panels, the computer can control which eye sees the computer screen. Here's what's happening:

- The computer displays an image for the left eye on the monitor. At the same time, it sends a timing signal to the interface that controls the glasses, usually through the parallel port.
- When the glasses receive the timing signal, it opens one LCD panel and closes the other.[5]
- The computer displays the image for the right eye on the monitor and sends another timing signal.
- The glasses switch panels—the one that was open is now closed, and the one that was closed is now open.

This process continues at very high speed. If you were to view the monitor without the glasses, you would see both images at once—sort of like double vision. You need the glasses to make sure that each eye only sees what it is meant to see.

The glasses are often referred to by VR enthusiasts as *Sega goggles* because Sega was one of the first companies to come out with such a product. However, this is not an accurate name at all, because most such goggles are now used on computers, not game machines.

---

[5]This system does not guarantee that the correct panel will be open. Most such systems have a simple way for you to reverse the currently open panel—often nothing fancier than a simple toggle switch.

Figure 13.1[6] shows a pair of LCD goggles that I received from the 3DTV Corporation.

Figure 13.1. 3D LCD glasses from 3DTV Corporation.

I found it very easy to set up and use the glasses. In fact, it took just a few minutes to be up and running with the glasses. The glasses interface using several different available black boxes. I tested several, including the PCVR interface from 3DTV. It consists of a switch box (see fig. 13.2) and several cables. The PCVR is ideal if you will be using the Power Glove because you can connect both the glasses and the Power Glove to the PCVR. If you will not be using the Power Glove and just want 3D, you can try one of the less expensive products listed in one of the "Alternative" sections later in this chapter.

The front panel of the PCVR looks a bit intimidating, but most of what you see never needs any attention. To use the PCVR, you must make the following connections:

- Connect the PCVR to the parallel port of your computer, using the cable supplied.
- Connect the 3D goggles to the front of the PCVR (cable supplied).
- Connect the Power Glove cable (supplied) to the back of the PCVR.

---

[6]Many of the figures in this chapter were created using PC Video Capture technology. For those who are interested, the videos were recorded on Hi8 tape with a Canon A1 camcorder, and then captured with a Video Spigot card from Creative Labs. The images were captured at 640×480 as single frames and saved as 24-bit bitmaps.

- Connect the power cord (supplied) to the back of the PCVR, and plug it in.
- Optional: Connect your printer cable to the PCVR.
- Optional: Add a cable between your video display card and your normal video cable, and connect one end to the PCVR for better frame synchronization.

Figure 13.2. The PCVR interface unit for 3D glasses and Power Glove.

Figure 13.3 shows the rear panel of the PCVR, with the various connection ports just described.

The front panel of the PCVR has a large rotating switch. This works just like the rotating switch on a printer switch box—to use your parallel printer, rotate the switch to the Printer setting. To use the Power Glove, rotate the switch to the B 3D setting.

There are also two indicator lights. A red light indicates that the power is on, and a yellow light tells you when the proper synchronization signal is present for the glasses.[7] Just in case the timing signal is off, there's a switch you can use to make sure that the right and left eyes get into proper synchronization.

---

[7]The yellow light also lights up when data is being sent to your printer—just thought you should know.

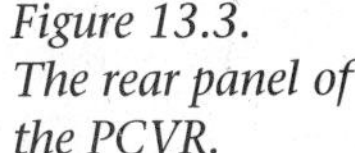

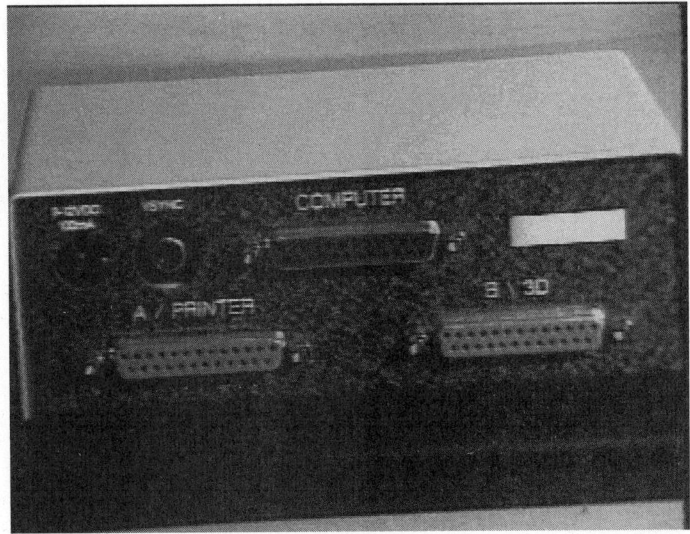

Figure 13.3. The rear panel of the PCVR.

The whole process is much simpler to do than it is to describe. Once you connect the cables, you should be up and running. One place where you can run into trouble is with a nonstandard port address for your parallel port, but that's easy to fix. If you connect everything correctly, and don't get a yellow light, check the "3D Software" section later in this chapter.

Figure 13.4 shows the goggles in use.[8] I expected the cable to get in the way, but it is light, thin, and very flexible, and wasn't much of a problem. However, a cable is a cable, and it is at best a minor annoyance.

There is a noticeable flicker when you use the goggles. This is not unexpected, considering that the goggles are basically flickering on and off to do their job. To reduce flicker, keep room lights low, and don't crank up the brightness setting on your monitor. Generally, I found that the 3D effect was quite good.

[8] That's Ron's wife and co-author of this book, Donna Brown, under those goggles.

Figure 13.4. The 3D LCD goggles in use. Note the connecting cable dangling from the left side of the goggles. This is the cable that connects to the PCVR.

Stereo Space Model 1

But if you really want to get the most out of a $150 pair of goggles, the Stereo Space and some serious VR software is really the way to go. I tested the Stereo Space with standard LCD goggles and two software packages: VREAM and Superscape.

You can use the Stereo Space with any software that supports the under-over method of 3D. As shown in figure 13.5, this technique outputs two completely separate images from your video card, with a black bar separating the two images. The top image is for the left eye, and the bottom image is for the right eye. The viewing hardware must pull apart the single video image and route the correct portion of the overall output to each eye. Most such hardware senses the black bar between the two images to tell when to switch from one eye to the other. In other words, the hardware reads each horizontal scan line in the video signal. If the scan line contains data, it continues sending lines to the current eye. When it encounters the black lines at the middle of the image, it stops sending to the current eye and gets ready to send to the other eye. When it encounters the first scan line of the second half of the image, it begins sending to the new eye.

There is an important advantage to using this technique, and it has to do with refresh rates. The average computer monitor is outputting data at about 60Hz-72Hz (cycles per second). If you were to take a complete image and route it to one eye, and then take another complete image and route it to the other eye, you cut that refresh rate in half. For example, if your computer outputs 60 screens per second

(60Hz vertical refresh), that means your eyes get a new image every 1/60th of a second. If you alternately route images to each eye, each eye sees a new image every 1/30th of a second—half as often. In short: flicker city.

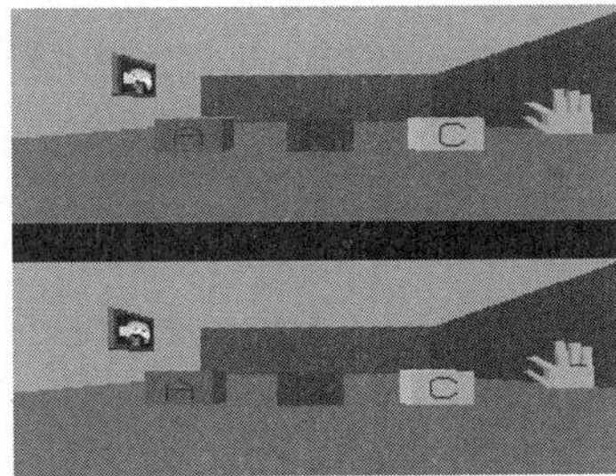

Figure 13.5. An over-under split-screen 3D image.

The over-under 3D format allows each eye to see a new image every 1/60th of a second. The obvious disadvantage: The resolution is cut in half.

Until recently, all LCD glasses have used the alternate technique; over-under was just for the Big Guys. The Stereo Space changes that. It takes as input the standard over-under video format. It then doubles the video rate to 120Hz, and then converts to alternate format. This means that each eye sees images updated at a full 60Hz—if you have a good multisync monitor that can handle the 120Hz refresh. I use a 17-inch Nanao F550i, and it works fine at this rate. The Stereo Space has a readout on the front panel that tells you what refresh rate it is working at.

If your monitor won't handle the full 120Hz, you can cut back your video card's output to a lower refresh rate (56Hz, 53Hz). However, you really do need a good, recent monitor to make use of the Stereo Space!

The front panel contains controls that allow you to tune the effect. You can adjust the vertical alignment of the two images, and you can easily toggle back and forth between standard mode (for viewing non-3D screens) and 3D mode.

Overall, I was extremely impressed with the results I got from using the combination of a true VR software, LCD goggles, and the Stereo Space. At $400 for readers of this book (goggles plus Stereo Space plus a few free, if simple, goodies), this is an excellent way to enjoy true 3D with your virtual reality software.[9]

---

[9] I spoke personally with the president of 3DTV and have arranged for readers of this book to receive two key discounts. First, if all you want is LCD goggles, you can get goggles, a PC interface (serial or parallel port), and some basic free software (what you get is up to 3DTV) for $150. Second, if you want to work with VR products, you can get goggles, Stereo Space Model 1, and basic free software for $400. Both these prices represent significant discounts (about 40 percent at the time of writing). You must mention this book to qualify for the discount; call 415-479-3516 to place orders or get more information.

Of course, you'll need to use software that supports the over-under format. To check if your software supports it, look for support for the Crystal Eyes HMD. That's one of the most common hardware units supporting the over-under format. If your software supports Crystal Eyes, it will support the Stereo Space. Then check the manual that comes with your monitor; if it supports 90Hz or better, there's a very good chance it will support the Stereo Space.[10] You'll also get better results using a recent vintage of video card; most high-quality video cards support a wide range of refresh rates.

The Mattel Power Glove

3D is fun, but getting right into the action is better. Using the Power Glove, you can interact with your computer in completely new ways.

However, before I get you all excited about the possibilities, a few words of caution are in order. The Power Glove, after all, started out as a toy. Real computer gloves use sophisticated tracking methods to allow fairly precise interpretation of your hand movements. For example, one model of a professional glove uses fiber-optic cables strung along your fingers. The surface of the cables is etched to allow a slight loss of light. The more the cable is bent by your finger, the greater the loss of light. Separate cables are used for each knuckle and joint on your hand. The result is a precision tool, and the cost is many thousands of dollars.

The Power Glove, on the other hand,[11] uses cruder techniques for detecting finger movements. The Power Glove offers much lower precision in tracking finger movement—it can detect when your fingers are straight and when they are bent, and that's about it. Instead of fiber optics, it uses resistive coated mylar—as your finger bends, the resistance of the coating changes. This is simply not as effective as fiber optics. But the price is much better: about $30-$50 for a typical used Power Glove. (They are no longer manufactured.) If you buy reconditioned Power Gloves from a reseller, you may pay as much as $100-$125, but you are guaranteed to get results. Power Gloves you purchase at garage sales will be as is—let the buyer beware. Try before you buy, or you could get a very fancy unmatched glove that won't even keep your fingers very warm in the winter.

Figure 13.6 shows the Mattel Power Glove. The unit consists of a glove for the hand, a sending unit attached to the back of the hand, and a data-entry section over the wrist. It is connected to the computer by a cable at the base of the wrist section.

---

[10]In most cases, you'll be able to achieve a better refresh rate than the rated maximum for your monitor. However, don't push your monitor too far past its rated capacity; such activity is seldom covered in your warranty!

[11]Pun, as usual, intended.

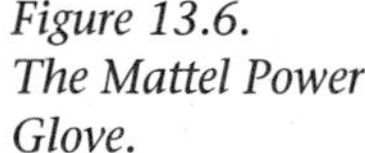

Figure 13.6.
The Mattel Power Glove.

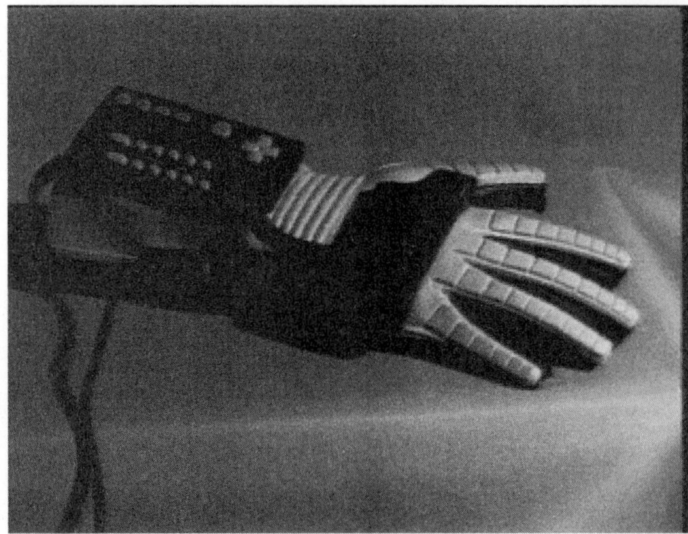

The underside of the glove is shown in figure 13.7, attached to a hand. The straps are easy to attach using the hook and eye (more commonly, but incorrectly known by the trademarked term Velcro) straps.

Figure 13.7.
The underside of the Power Glove.

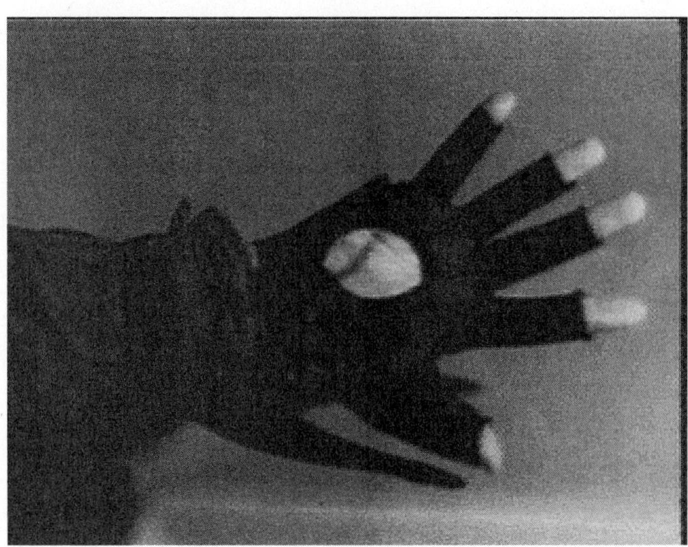

I have very long fingers, but I had no trouble using the glove—as you can see, the finger tips are open, allowing long fingers to simply stick out. This was not uncomfortable.

In normal use, you must do two things before using the glove with your software: flex and center. Flexing—making a fist a few times, as shown in figure 13.8—allows the glove to adjust to the size of your hand.

Figure 13.8. Flexing the glove to adjust to the size of your hand.

Centering is done by relaxing your hand and leveling it with the fingers spread in a relaxed manner (see fig. 13.9). When the glove is comfortable and level, press the Center button on the control panel of the glove with your other hand. A beep will confirm that you are centered.

Proper centering requires that you point the glove at the middle of the stationary receivers. The little black box attached at the back of the hand generates ultrasonic signals that the stationary receivers translate into positional information. Figure 13.10 shows the stationary receivers. There are three of them, and they must be oriented as shown. Normally, you drape them over your monitor. Because the average computer monitor is smaller than the average TV, you may need to add a book or something similar to balance the receiver properly on your monitor. Later illustrations show the use of a large dictionary for exactly this purpose.

To center properly, make sure that the glove points at the middle of a rectangle defined by the three black boxes of the receiver.(12)

---

12 Yes, you only need three points to define a rectangle.

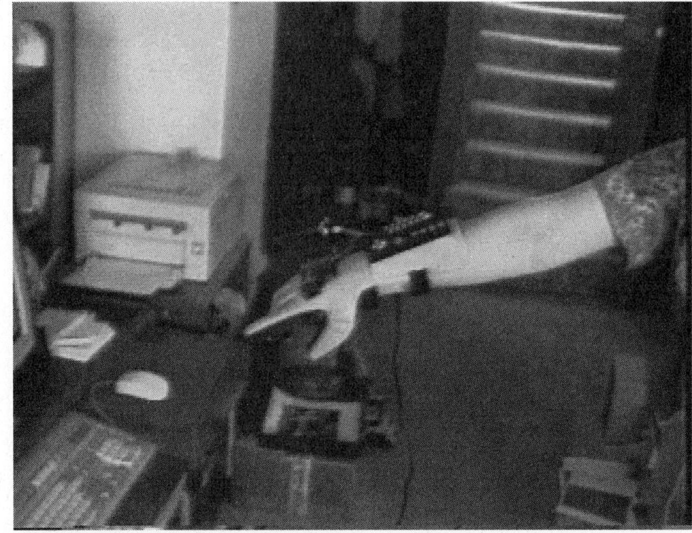

Figure 13.9. Centering the glove should be done with a relaxed hand.

Figure 13.10. The stationary receivers used with the Power Glove.

To verify that the glove is working properly, either plug it into a Nintendo Entertainment System (for which it was originally designed) or check to see that the LEDs[13] at the upper right of the receivers follow the movement of the glove.

---

[13]*LED* stands for *Light Emitting Diodes*, and are not to be confused with LCDs, which emit no light of their own.

You can also test the glove visually with your software, since Rend386 displays the current position and gesture of the glove on-screen. Pointing is a good test (see fig. 13.11). This is a gesture that is very useful in Rend386.

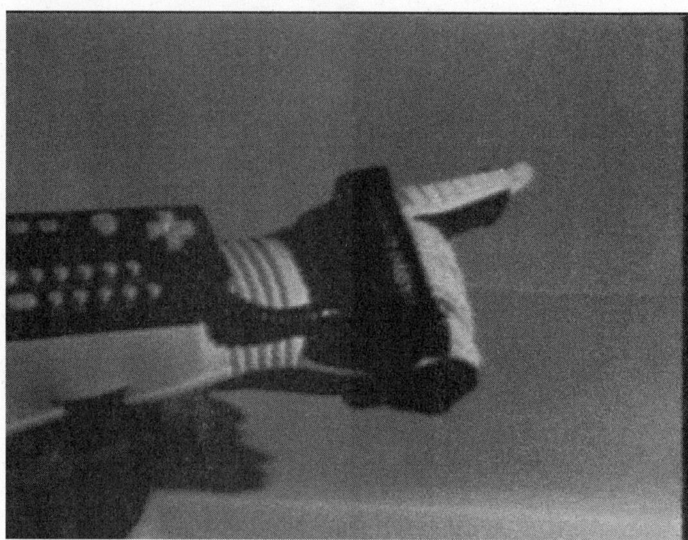

Figure 13.11. The pointing gesture.

Using the Power Glove

Once you have the Power Glove centered, you can begin using it with your software. Different software uses different glove gestures to manipulate objects. Figure 13.12 shows the glove in use.

In general, we found that the glove was easiest to use standing up. This makes typing awkward, and you can't type very well with the hand wearing the glove. This is part of the price you pay for using the glove.

Figure 13.13 shows the glove in use with the Rend386 program. The glove is in the centering position. If you look carefully, you can see that the glove on the screen matches the position and orientation of the real glove.

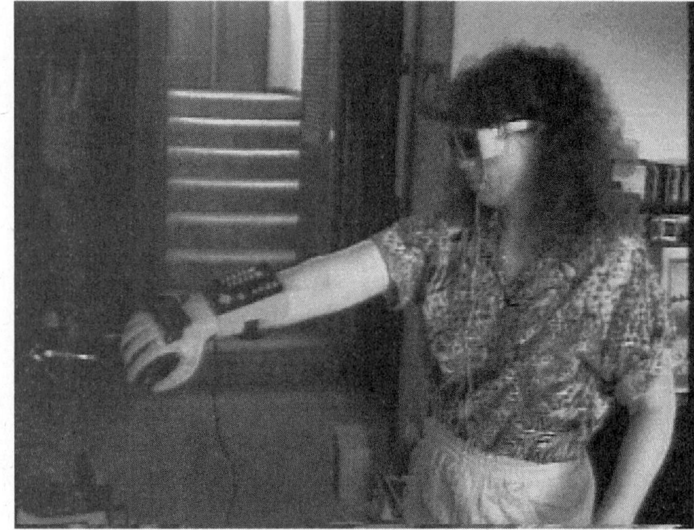

Figure 13.12. Using the Power Glove.

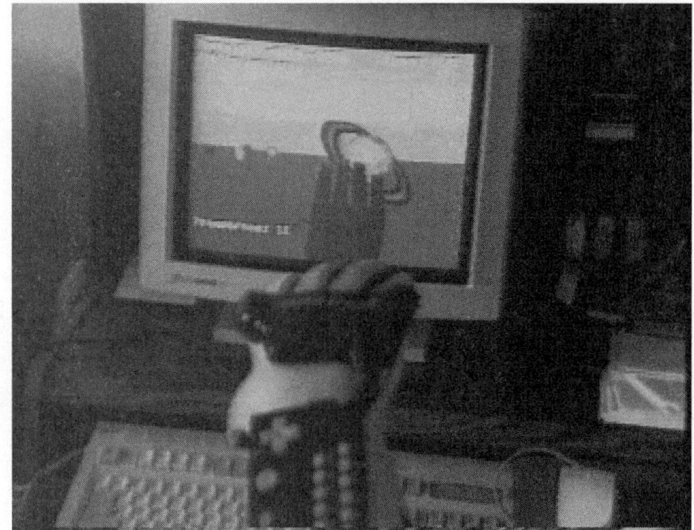

Figure 13.13. Using the Power Glove with software.

Figure 13.14 shows the glove made into a fist and the corresponding fist of the glove in the software.

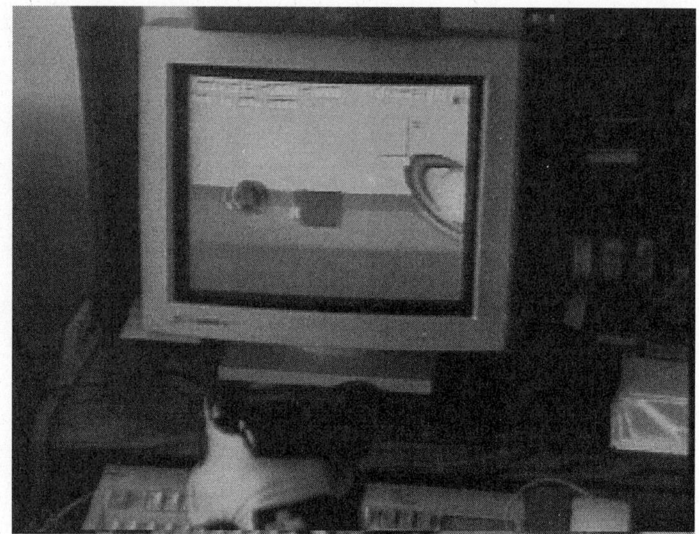

Figure 13.14. The physical glove and the on-screen glove match gestures.

If you move to the left of the screen (see fig. 13.15), the on-screen glove follows. If you make a pointing gesture (see fig. 13.16), the on-screen glove points, too.

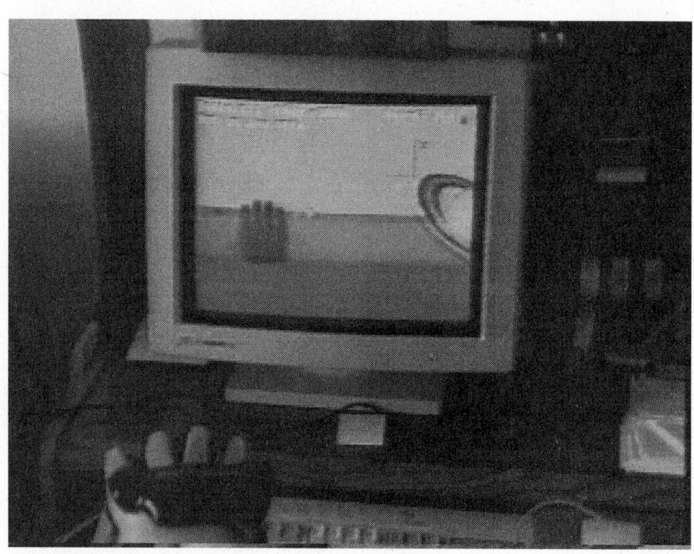

Figure 13.15. Moving the glove side to side.

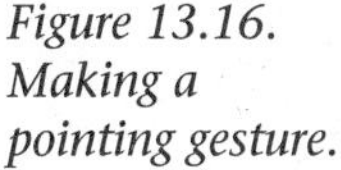

Figure 13.16. Making a pointing gesture.

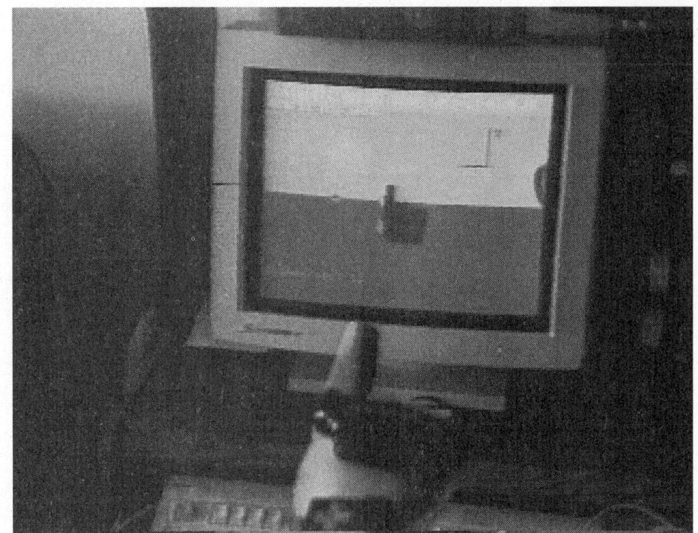

Moving the glove toward and away from the screen moves it into and out of the scene.

Connecting for 3D

The PCVR is just one way to connect your 3D goggles to your computer. The folks at 3DTV[14] make several other devices that work just as well—and if you won't be using a Power Glove, these are quite economical. In fact, they make a whole bunch of useful and interesting 3D/VR products; see the "Buyer's Guide" chapters for more information.

Alternative #1: The PC3D

The goggles kit that comes with the PC3D is normally $250, a full $100 less than the PCVR kit. As a reader of this book, you qualify for a purchase price of $150, but you must mention this book to get the deal.

The PC3D is a serial interface for the goggles and is extremely compact (see fig. 13.17). It is extremely easy to use. It takes its power from the serial port, so all you need to do to use it is to connect it to your serial port and plug in the 3D glasses.

---

[14]You may be wondering why I keep mentioning 3DTV—am I ignoring other companies? It's because this is an infant industry, and 3DTV is by far the most prominent supplier of inexpensive VR technology. If it weren't for 3DTV, VR would not be as accessible as it is.

As with the PCVR, if your computer doesn't use standard port addresses, or if you aren't using COM1 as your serial connection, you may have to edit a few lines in the configuration file of the software.

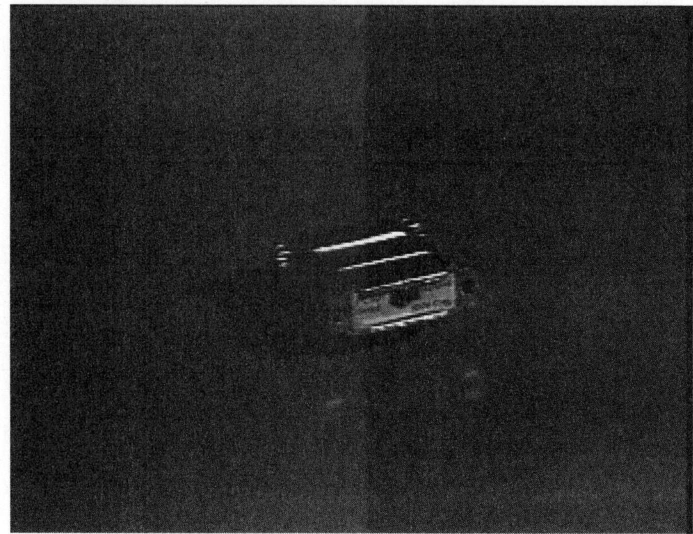

Figure 13.17. The PC3D serial interface for 3D goggles.

Alternative #2: The Model 3000

The Model 3000 is an interesting device. The unit I tested was a prototype (see fig. 13.18). This unit costs $175 (in addition to the cost of goggles).

The Model 3000 is an interesting hybrid. It interfaces your goggles with the video port only—there is no parallel port connection involved. It senses the sync signal by tapping into the video cable using an adapter supplied with the unit. It also comes with a power unit for its AC connection.

The Model 3000 also supports viewing of 3D video from your VCR. To use it in this manner, you need only run a cable from the video out of your VCR to the Model 3000. You can then plug the 3D goggles into the Model 3000. 3DTV markets a number of 3D videotapes, which are listed in the hardware buyer's guide, Chapter 14.(15)

How does 3D video look? When the source material is recorded using a 3D video camera, the effect is the best I have ever seen. Converting 3D movies to videotape is not as effective.

---

[15]The quality of the tapes is mixed, and the content is idiosyncratic. However, when the content and quality of the material is just right, the effects are some of the best 3D I have ever seen.

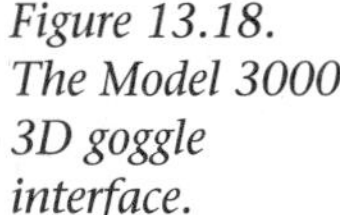

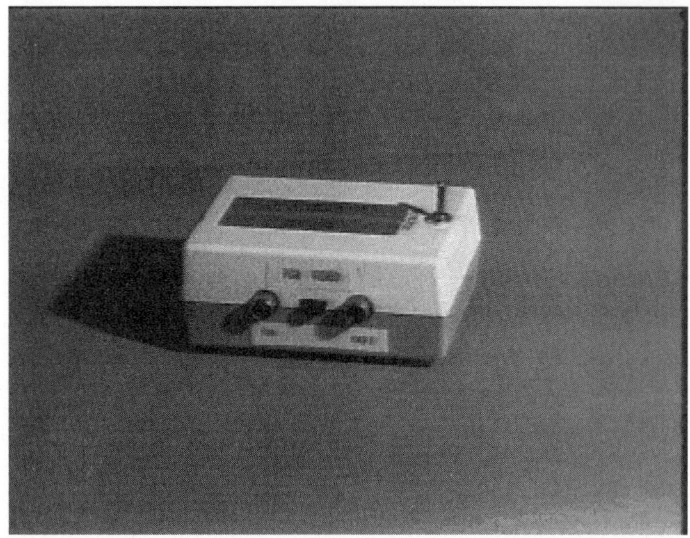

Figure 13.18. The Model 3000 3D goggle interface.

3D Software

The world of 3D software is in its infancy. It wasn't until 1993 that inexpensive hardware became commonly available, and, as in the past, software is busy trying to catch up to what the hardware can do.

Keep in mind that there is simply no way to provide adequate illustrations for 3D in the book. I have included some sample 3D software on the CD, but if you don't have at least LCD glasses and an interface, you won't be able to do much of anything with it.

Software Options

OK, so you spring for a set of LCD glasses and some kind of interface. What can you do with it? Software options are currently limited, but the range of products has increased significantly since the first edition of this book. Of course, if you had a lot to spend, the range was always better, but the list of products in the key under-$500 range has expanded enormously. Two of the more interesting ones are Vistapro, whose virtual-reality aspects were covered in Chapter 1, and Rend386 (shareware). Each program takes advantage of 3D goggles in a completely different way. Of the two, only Rend386 takes advantage of the Power Glove.

If you are willing to invest in a Stereo Space Model 1, your horizons open up. Many VR development and runtime tools support the over-under video format. I tested the Stereo Space with VREAM and Superscape, but many other VR products also support the format.

Stereo Pro

Stereo Pro is a simple product that does a simple job, but does it really well. Stereo Pro works with LCD glasses to display 3D still images.

A 3D still image is actually made up of two images, called a *stereo pair*. One image is for the left eye, and one image is for the right eye. The trick, as with all 3D products, is to make sure that each eye sees the image intended for it. Stereo Pro handles the process of alternating the presentation of the images and coordinates timing of the LCD glasses.

Figure 13.19 shows an image for the left eye, and figure 13.20 shows an image for the right eye. Figure 13.21 shows the two images superimposed; this is how they look on the computer monitor if you are not wearing the LCD glasses. If you are wearing the LCD glasses, of course, you see a single 3D image.[16]

Figure 13.19. The left-eye image.

[16]There is some slight ghosting of the image for the other eye, since LCD glasses are not perfectly opaque when the shutter is closed.

Figure 13.20. The right-eye image.

Figure 13.21. The combined images.

The Stereo Pro software ships with several 3D images, but to get good use out of this product, you will want to create your own 3D images. Vistapro, covered elsewhere in this chapter, is one of many different products you can use to create stereo pairs. Most 3D modeling and rendering software will create stereo pairs. For example, here is a stereo pair I created in 3D studio (see figs. 13.22 and 13.23). Figure 13.24 shows the overlapped version. trueSpace is also a good product for creating 3D stereo pairs.

Figure 13.22.
Left-eye image.

Figure 13.23.
Right-eye image.

The trick for stereo pairs is to set up two cameras that simulate the human eye. To get useful images, you can't simply position two cameras a few inches apart; the actual distance varies. In general, I find that an angle of about 2 to 5 degrees between the cameras is good; the focal points of the cameras should meet at about the middle of the depth of the field. Figure 13.25 shows a 3D Studio session with two cameras; this is the model that was used to create figures 13.22 and 13.23.

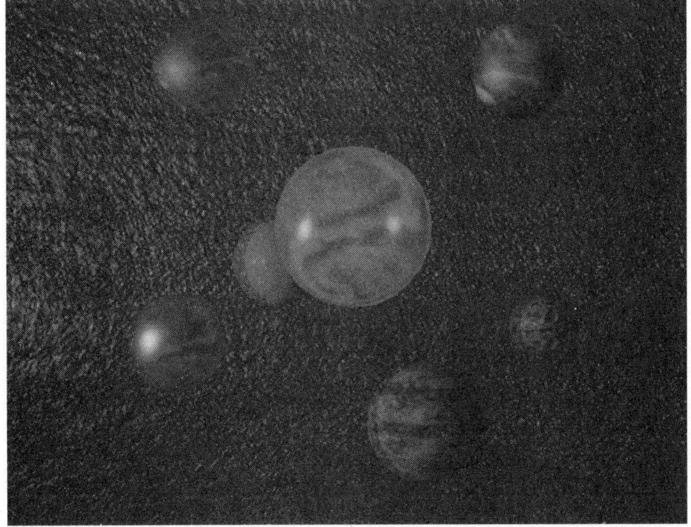

Figure 13.24. Overlapped images.

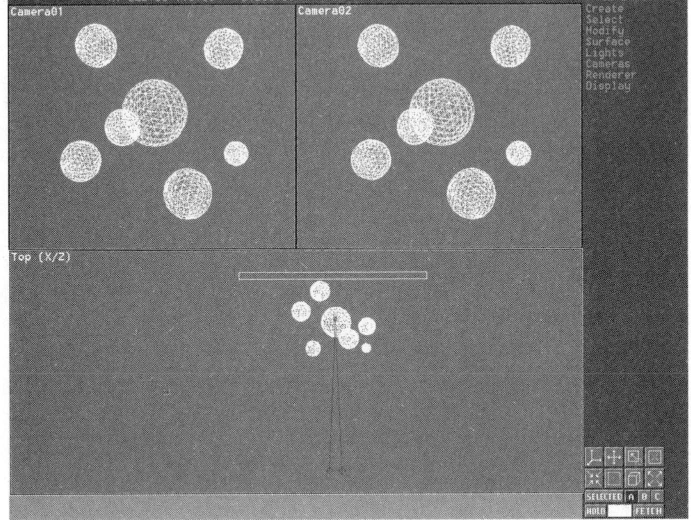

Figure 13.25. Setting up for a 3D stereo pair in 3D Studio; note camera angle at upper left.

3D Flic Player

Here's my basic position on 3D software: 3D is cool, but *moving* 3D is even cooler. The 3D Flic player is a perfect case in point. As much fun as stereo pair images are, creating an animation is a lot more fun for me.

If it's hard to convey the quality of a 3D still image in a book, it's even harder to do so with an animation. I created an animation in 3D studio of the comet Shoemaker-Levy 9 crashing into Jupiter. To make it a 3D animation, I added a second camera as I would for a still stereo pair, and then rendered the animation a second time.

That gave me two complete FLC files with perfect stereo alignment, but I needed a way to play them back. Good old 3DTV came to my rescue with a product called 3D Flic. This program will play back a right/left stereo pair of FLC files for viewing with LCD goggles.

Figure 13.26 shows a left frame from the animation, and figure 13.27 shows a right frame. The complete animation is provided on the CDs, as is the 3D Flic player. If you can create your own 3D FLC files (using Vistapro, trueSpace, 3D Studio, or any other software capable of creating camera positions), you can view them with 3D Flic.(17)

Figure 13.26. Left-eye frame from a 3D animation.

17 3DTV normally charges for 3D Flic, but they agreed to put a free copy on the CD for two reasons: one, so you can play with it; two, so you'll go out and buy LCD glasses from them. This is capitalism at its best, eh?

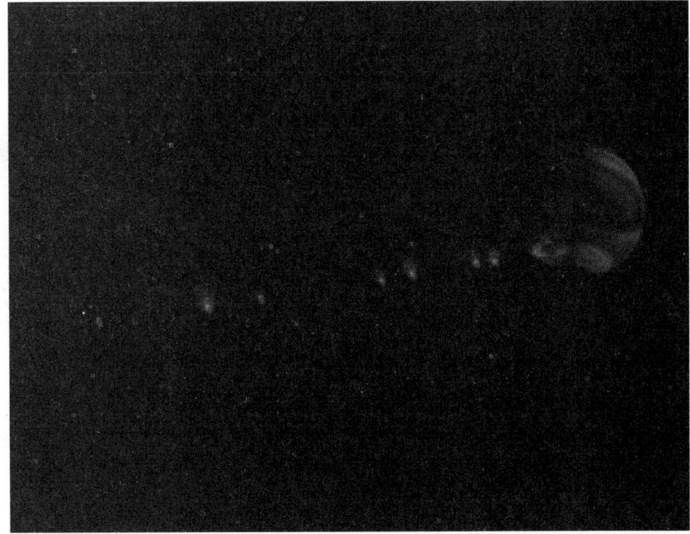

Figure 13.27. Right-eye frame from a 3D animation.

Games

There are several 3D games available, but I'm not entirely sold on any of them. Until the market grows—until there are at least a few hundred thousand of us wearing LCD goggles—game manufacturers won't take the time and trouble to put out 3D versions of their games.

There is a simple solution to this problem. If you own LCD goggles, call up the game manufacturers (or send e-mail, or snail mail, or whatever!) and tell them that you want 3D games. Unless they know the market exists, they won't create for it.

Personally, I would think that a 3D version of DOOM would be totally addicting; the lust for 3D would hit new heights.

Until then, you'll have to settle for things like 3D versions of the breakout game. One exception: 3DTV's 3D Go game (see fig. 13.28).

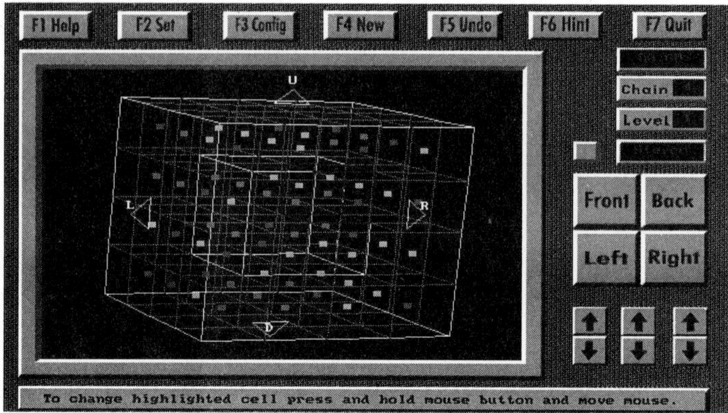

Figure 13.28. 3DTV's 3D Go game.

Vistapro

To use Vistapro with 3D glasses, you would create stereo pairs in the normal manner (see Chapter 1). However, instead of combining the pair into a single red/blue color image, you would convert each of the PCX files to the GIF format and then combine them using the PCGV program supplied by 3DTV for viewing with 3D goggles.

Rend386

Rend386 is a remarkable program. Created by David Stampe and Bernie Roehl, it is not available in any store. It isn't shareware either, and it isn't freeware. Rend386 is a collective project of many individuals and is available for downloading from Compuserve's Cyberforum.[18] The program is almost always evolving to support new stuff in virtual reality, so the features you see here may not reflect the state of the program when you download it.

Rend386 has two personalities. One is very friendly, and one is very technical.

The friendly side consists of a program you can use to move interactively through relatively simple 3D spaces. The technical side involves the creation of 3D spaces. Rend386 uses a fairly complicated mechanism to specify the objects in a 3D space and their properties. On the plus side, it is very powerful. On the minus side, it takes a lot of perseverance to create a 3D world for Rend386.[19]

---

[18]It is also available for downloading via anonymous FTP from SUNEE.UWATERLOO.CA in the PUB/REND386 directory—if you can handle such things using Internet.

[19]If you are interested in exploring world creation with Rend386, I strongly suggest you look into the book *Virtual Reality Creations* from The Waite Group Press. It is essential for a solid understanding of Rend386 at this level. Because of the unique nature of the development of Rend386, this book will actually serve, in effect, as the program's documentation.

Figure 13.29 shows a screen from the Rend386 program that you can use to tour a 3D world. The scene is one that comes with the Rend386 disk from 3DTV, called POOL.WLD. This is one of several worlds that are included. Another favorite is an animated version of the solar system, SOLARSYS.WLD, and is also highly recommended.

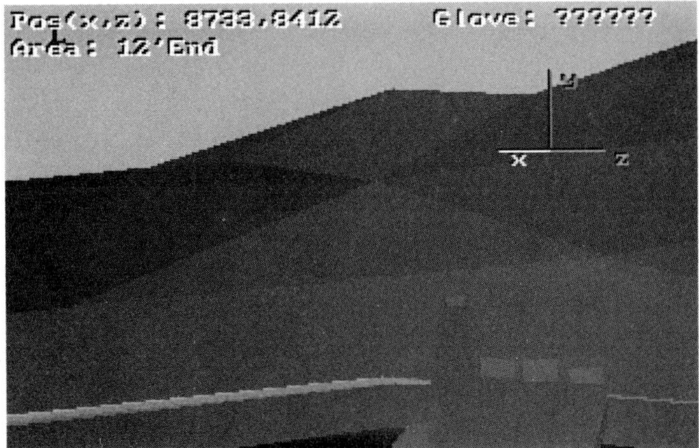

Figure 13.29. A Rend386 screen.

As you can see, the glove is shown on the screen. In this example, the glove is making the pointing gesture.

Setting Up Rend386 for the Goggles and the Power Glove

If you run Rend386, and the glove and/or goggles don't work properly, the most likely problem is that the default port settings aren't right for your setup. These can be edited with a text editor in the configuration file REND386.CFG.

The most common problems involve port addresses. For example, the default port address for LPT1, the parallel port, is 378 hex. In my case, my machine was using 3BC as the port address for LPT1. I simply edited the lines in REND386.CFG that reference this port address:

```
segaport 3BC 04 04 00 00 00
pgloveport 3BD 3BC 3 0 2 1 3 10 00
```

As you can see, the contents of REND386.CFG aren't exactly plain English, but there are lots of comments in the file to help you out. You probably won't need to change much to get yourself started. Don't try to change any lines that start with a pound sign (#)—it indicates a comment.

Exploring with Rend386

You can move around easily in Rend386. The arrow keys rotate your point of view left and right, and the up and down arrows move you into and out of the virtual space. There are also key combinations you can use for vertical and sideways movement.

You can also select objects in the virtual space and move them around. You can select with the mouse, or by pointing to objects with the glove. If an object is moving, selecting it with glove takes some dexterity—the first touch selects, and the second touch deselects. If the object is moving rapidly, a touch on the leading surface will select, but a touch on the trailing surface will deselect. Figure 13.30 shows the glove touching an object with the pointing gesture to select it.

Figure 13.30. Selecting an object by touching it with the glove.

Figure 13.31 shows a lounge chair near the pool that has been selected—the construction lines are now highlighted.

To move a selected object or objects, simply make a fist with the Power Glove and move it up or down, left or right, in or out of the virtual space. Figure 13.32 shows the lounge chair lifted up. Figure 13.33 shows the lounge chair pushed farther back into the scene using the glove.

In figure 13.34, a second lounge chair has been selected using the pointing gesture of the glove, and pulled toward the viewer.

Figure 13.31.
A selected item is highlighted. The glove can be seen at the right of the screen.

Figure 13.32.
An object moved upward with the Power Glove.

Figure 13.33.
An object moved farther back using the Power Glove.

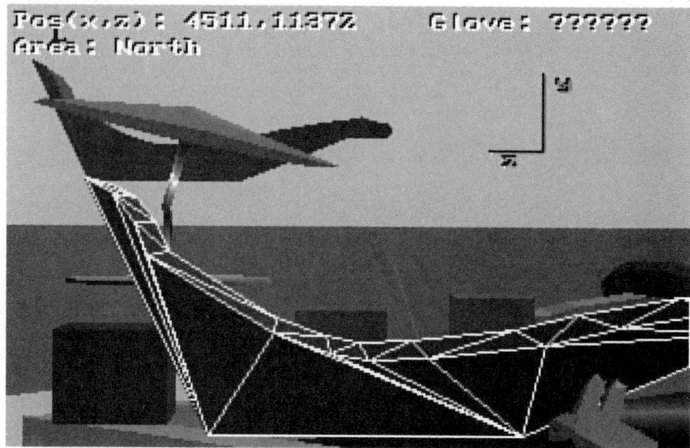

Figure 13.34.
An object moved forward using the glove.

Throughout these operations, the glove appears on the screen,[20] mimicking the current position and orientation of the real glove. For example, in figure 13.35, the glove can be clearly seen at the right of the screen.

Figure 13.35.
An object moved forward using the glove. The glove can be seen at the right of the screen.

Even if you move very far from the center of the scene, the glove still maintains the same relative proportion of the screen at various physical positions. For example, figure 13.36 shows the point of view moved thousands of units up and out from the pool, but the glove stays right with the point of view.

---

[20]If you move the glove too far in any direction, it will move off of the screen. To bring it back, simply move it back within the boundaries of the receivers.

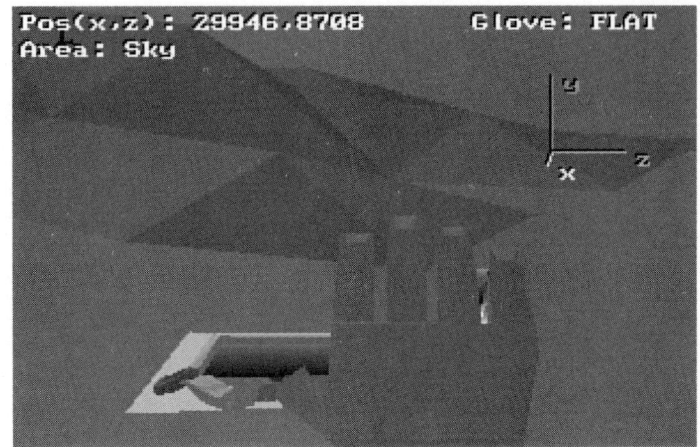

Figure 13.36. The glove maintains a constant relationship with the local point of view.

Summary

In this chapter, you learned about technology that is at the cutting edge of affordable VR hardware and software. Throughout this book, I have tried to present tools that are within the reach of the average computer user. The barriers—cost and complexity—that kept VR tools out of the mainstream of computing are falling all around us. You have the opportunity, right now, to get involved in the development and use of virtual worlds.

Whatever the implications of adding virtual-reality capabilities to personal computers may turn out to be, you are in a position to start finding out today.

IV

VR BUYER'S GUIDE

14

VR HARDWARE

Anyone with a budget of $10,000 or more can easily find some flashy VR hardware and have some fun. The rest of us have a bit less money to spend, but we still want to have fun with VR. This chapter covers a wide range of hardware—some costs a lot, and some is surprisingly affordable.

Wherever possible, we have tried to provide a complete description of the hardware. In some cases, only limited information was available. In the interest of being more complete, we have included product listings nonetheless.

Catalog Shopping

The following vendors offer a range of VR products. Several sample products and brief descriptions are listed under each company. For complete product offerings, call and ask for a catalog.

PCVR

PCVR
P.O. Box 475
Stoughton, WI 53589
608-877-0909

PCVR publishes "The Magazine Dedicated to PC-Based Virtual Reality." It features articles on subjects ranging from VR-rendering software like REND386 and VREAM, to how to build your own HMD (Head Mounted Display).

PCVR also offers a catalog of affordable virtual reality gear, software, interfaces, and connectors. You can order via phone, fax, or U.S. mail from the address and phone number shown here. Or e-mail to PCVR@fullfeed.com or VRmag@aol.com. A product listing from PCVR's Premier Catalog on PC-Based Virtual Reality follows. Read through this to learn about sample hardware offerings from the PCVR catalog.

Mattel Power Glove

The Mattel Power Glove is a low-cost way to interface to your PC. The Power Glove was originally marketed for the Nintendo Entertainment System, but Mattel discontinued production in 1991.

Cost: $30-$45 (call for latest price), plus shipping

Power Glove Interface

The Power Glove Interface Cable lets you attach a Power Glove to the parallel port of your PC without any cutting. All you need to do is plug the Nintendo connector of the Power Glove to the Nintendo connector on the Interface Cable, attach the DB25 to your parallel port, and supply +5-volt power to the 1/8" jack (Power Glove and power supply sold separately). The interface comes with a disk that provides Power Glove software that uses the Interface Cable.

Cost: $20 each, plus shipping

Interface Power Supply

The Power Glove Interface Cable requires a +5-volt power supply that will drive the electronics of the Power Glove.

Cost: $20 each, plus shipping

Power Glove Kit

The Power Glove Kit includes all the accessories needed to hook a Mattel Power Glove to your PC: a Power Glove, Power Glove Interface Cable, power supply, and a disk containing VR software.

Cost: $75 each (U.S./Canada); $95 each overseas. Shipping is included in the cost of both packages.

Shutter Glasses

Shutter Glasses let you see a true 3D stereoscopic image using an ordinary computer monitor. The Glasses work with VR computer software like REND386 to help you experience 3D in the comfort of your own home. These Shutter Glasses are manufactured by 3DTV Corporation, and can be fastened to your head using a built-in headband.

Cost: $125 each, plus shipping

Shutter Glasses Interface

The Shutter Glasses require an interface between the Glasses and your PC. PCVR provides an interface that can be used with Sega, Toshiba, and 3DTV Corporation's wired Shutter Glasses. The interface consists of a small box with two connectors: attach one connector to the serial port of a PC, and attach the other to the Shutter Glasses. The Interface comes with a disk containing software that will help get you started in stereo viewing.

Cost: $30 each, plus shipping

The Alternative HMD

The Alternative HMD (Head Mounted Display) is an affordable monoscopic HMD. The 4-inch color LCD has a resolution of 729×234. The optics, which are proprietary, provide an 80-degree horizontal and 60-degree vertical field of view. The HMD headphones create full stereo sound. The Alternative HMD includes a user manual and 30-day, money-back guarantee, and PCVR includes a 90-day warranty of the product. Inputs are NTSC (National Television Standards Committee) for video, 1/8-inch stereo plug for sound, and a DC power jack (which includes a power supply).

Cost: $750 each, plus shipping

VGA-to-NTSC Converter

PCVR's solution to an inexpensive conversion from VGA output to an NTSC signal is the Boffin Limited VIP-100. The VIP-100 lets you view your PC monitor and the NTSC signal simultaneously. And, it can be used with the Alternative HMD.

Cost: $199 each, plus shipping

StuntMaster Interface

StuntMaster is an HMD for Sega and Nintendo Entertainment Systems. This interface lets you connect the VictorMaxx Stuntmaster to your PC. The interface also lets you input an NTSC TV signal to the HMD, as well as sound.

Cost: $30 each, plus shipping

Simple Track

The Simple Track is an experimental head tracker that is designed for use with an HMD. The tracker is arm-based, and interfaces to a joystick port. It does not require a power connection. The tracker comes with software so you can interface with REND386 or other rendering systems.

Cost: $35 each for a kit; $75 each if already assembled. Shipping is extra.

3DTV Corporation

3DTV Corporation
Stereoscopic Video
P.O. Box Q
San Rafael, CA 94913-4316
415-479-3516
Fax: 415-479-3316

3DTV Corporation creates affordable stereoscopic virtual reality interfaces that can drive LCD stereo glasses and several models of low-cost StereoVisors (LCD viewing glasses). Several of these VR interfaces have ports for gloves and other devices. 3DTV Corporation also provides software drivers for the glasses and other devices. Additionally, 3DTV has complete systems for interactive stereo imaging or viewing, for about one-tenth the cost.

The following items are from the 3DTV catalog.

Home 3D Theater System

A stereoscopic television system that includes LCD glasses, 3D tapes and carrying cases, and interface for VCR and 3D videotape. Works with any TV, monitor, or projector (except those using LCDs).

Cost: $300-$400

PC3DTV

A 3D multimedia virtual reality system that includes the Model 3000 StereoDriver for PC or VCR with 3D cable, wired LCD glasses, stereoscopic videotape, and VR software for PC and video.

Cost: $350

SpaceMouse

A one-knob, three-axis mouse with tactile feedback.

Cost: $375

StereoPro

A kit for merging stereo pairs in several file formats, such as PCX or GIF, and a converter for other file formats. Includes LCD glasses, interface for PC (serial or parallel port), and software.

Cost: $250 ($150, software only)

Hot Product Alert!

3DTV also sells a wide variety of software and ancillary hardware. As we were going to press, 3DTV was ready to announce two new products that we had the good fortune to test. One is a small black box that allows you to use simple, inexpensive LCD glasses the same way that expensive products like CrystalEyes are used. This little box takes output from programs like VREAM (using CrystalEyes format), and converts it into field-sequential video at up to a 120Hz refresh rate. It then synchronizes the LCD glasses to this high rate, yielding the best results I've seen to date with LCD glasses.

Contact 3DTV directly for information about this new product—including its name. Highly recommended.

The other product worth note is an FLC player that displays 3D FLC files—left/right pairs of FLC files, actually. When combined with the 120Hz refresh rate mentioned earlier, the result is extremely effective 3D at a low cost. At press time, 3DTV was going to offer the combination of LCD glasses and little black box for under $500. Check with 3DTV for final prices. For the home VR or 3D enthusiast, this system offers a lot of bang for the buck. The ability to quickly interface with inexpensive VR software, such as VREAM, gives you a lot of power and fun for a relatively small investment. If you work with high-power packages such as Superscape, you can also do your design work in 3D—not just the runtime stuff!

As a general rule, if you are interested in low-cost VR, 3DTV is the best place to find new and interesting products. They are doing a lot to foster affordable VR. See the next chapter for interesting 3D and VR software.

3D Audio Cards

Beachtron

Crystal River Engineering
400 California Avenue, Suite 200
Palo Alto, CA 94306
415-323-8155
Fax: 415-232-8157

This is Crystal River's most affordable 3D audio system. Consists of a single-slot ISA-compatible signal-processing card, with an on-board sampled sound synthesizer, audio recording/playback capabilities, and a C software library. One Beachtron card allows two separate audio sources to be spatialized. Up to eight Beachtrons can be used in a single PC, allowing a maximum of 16 sources to be spatialized in real time. The processing creates the perception that the source is positioned at any specified location in three-dimensional space.

Sound can be fed to the Beachtron in three ways:

- External inputs, such as CD tracks, magnetic tapes, or live material.
- Sound files from hard disk or CD-ROM, played back by the on-card digital signal processor.
- MIDI sounds, selected from a repertoire of 16-bit samples, and played by an on-card synthesizer. The synthesizer can be controlled by software or by an external MIDI controller.

The Beachtron card is a customized version of the MultiSound Card from Turtle Beach Systems, Inc. It includes a Motorola DSP56001 chip (running at 40MHz) and a Proteus/1 XR synthesizer, providing audio recording, playback, and MIDI services. The PC-host software for controlling the card requires DOS 3.3 or later versions.

Beachtron's software simplifies the creation of virtual sound spaces, and ensures compatibility between all Crystal River Engineering products. It includes a test and demo program, and several small sample programs in source form. An example application from Sense8's WorldToolKit is distributed with the board, demonstrating how to use several of the board's important features. The Beachtron also comes with a high level ANSI C programming interface.

Imagine being inside a virtual room. You are facing an open window; the entrance to the room is behind you. A door opens and someone calls your name. Without 3D audio, you can't tell where the sound of the opening door came from, or if the voice is calling you from outside through the open window or from the door that just opened. The Beachtron spatializes sounds, which helps create a sense of immersion in a virtual environment.

Cost: $1,495 (includes card, software, and a manual)

Convolvotron

The Convolvotron is a 3D audio processor for any ISA-compatible, DOS-based PC. It brings 3D audio effects to VR applications, allowing up to four independent sound sources to be positioned in space, reflections from six surfaces with programmable acoustic characteristics, and Doppler shift effects.

The Convolvotron accepts sound inputs from conventional audio equipment, such as CDs, magnetic tapes, or microphones; and presents a three-dimensional sound space as output. A high level ANSI C programming interface simplifies both the development of acoustic models and the integration of 3D sound into existing applications.

Cost: $14,995

Focal Point 3D Audio

Focal Point 3D Audio
1402 Pine Ave., Suite 127
Niagara Falls, NY 14301
416-963-9188

The Focal Point is a CD-quality, convolved, binaural-sound system for VR audio displays, teleconferencing, and music. It is modular, so one host can position any number of sounds. Focal Point comes with a mouse, headtracking, and MIDI software; it is available for Mac and DOS-based PCs.

Cost: $1,260 (PCs); $1,795 (Macintosh II)

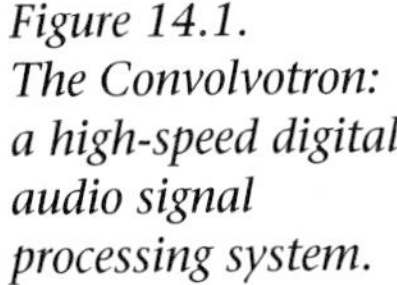

Figure 14.1.
The Convolvotron: a high-speed digital audio signal processing system.

Ultrasound Max

Advanced Gravis
#101-3750 North Fraser Way
Burnaby, BC Canada V5J 5E9
604-431-5020
Fax: 604-431-5155

Many people know Gravis for their joystick products, but Gravis is also one of the leading companies in 3D audio boards. The Ultrasound Max offers the VR enthusiast a good combination of quality sound and 3D effects. Nothing enhances the VR experience quite like adding 3D sound to a 3D image. The human brain reacts to sound cues in a visceral way, and this adds emotional depth to a VR experience.

The Ultrasound Max offers the following features:

- 32-voice wavetable synthesis
- 16-bit, 48kHz Stereo recording and playback
- 3D holographic sound
- 16 stereo digital channels
- Expandable 192 General MIDI instrument set
- DDSP dedicated digital/digital sound processor
- RAM-based sounds (512K to 1024K)
- CD-ROM interface built-in (Mitsumi, Sony, or Panasonic)
- Speed-compensating game port

- Stereo amplifier
- Line in, line out, amplified out, microphone in, MIDI/joystick adapter
- Sound Blaster, MT-32, and Windows Sound System compatible

Not all software products support the 3D features of the Ultrasound Max—games are the most likely to support it. One example: Hired Guns from DMA Designs and Psygnosis, Ltd.

Cost: $349, Ultrasound Max

Boards

Pixel Pump

RPI Advanced Technology Group
P.O. Box 14607
San Francisco, CA 94114
415-495-5671
Fax: 415-495-5124

This is a graphics board for stereoscopic immersive visualization. It is used in conjunction with a head-mounted device (HMD) to provide real-time 3D images. Contact RPI for information about currently supported hardware and software.

Cost: $954 to $1,500

Sapphire Interactive Multimedia Engine

Future Vision Technologies, Inc.
701 Devonshire Dr.
Champaign, IL 61820
217-355-3030
Fax: 217-355-3031

The Sapphire is a single-slot ISA board for IBM-compatible PCs. It is fully programmable for 3D graphics and stereo audio applications. The board offers built-in features like 48 bits per pixel; VGA, NTSC, PAL, and S-VHS output; and DAT-quality sound I/O with a quadruple frame buffer. The board has Gouraud shading processing with A-buffer processing, polygon-drawing processing with Z-buffer processing, 32M pixels/second Gouraud shaded fill, 16M pixels/second bitblt, and a floating point coprocessor.

The Sapphire is versatile, so you can start out with monoscopic graphic environments and upgrade to stereoscopic interactivity with StereoGraphics' CrystalEyes LCD shutter glasses. Sapphire supports CrystalEyes directly, so there's no need for a converter box.

The board is easy to use and currently supports Autodesk's Cyberspace Developer Kit, Sense8's WorldToolKit, and FVT's Sapphire Developer Library. Future versions will support other standard software packages such as VREAM, the Autodesk Device Interface, and Microsoft Windows.

Sapphire is targeted at the broadcast video, business multimedia, CAD, scientific visualization, and synthetic environment (VR) markets.

Cost: $3,495

Gloves

CyberGlove
Virtual Technologies
2175 Park Blvd.
Palo Alto, CA 94306
415-321-4900
Fax: 415-321-4912

The CyberGlove is a lightweight, flexible, instrumented glove with sensors in it that measure the positions and movements of the fingers. The glove contains up to 22 sensors: three bend sensors and an abduction sensor for each finger, a sensor to measure the extension of the thumb across the palm toward the pinkie finger, a sensor to measure the arch of the palm, and sensors to measure the flexion and abduction of the wrist joint. Sensor resolution is 0.5 degrees, and resolution remains constant over the entire range of joint motion.

VirtualHand software is included with the CyberGlove and utilizes CyberGlove's sensor data to calculate and display a 2600 polygon Gouraud-shaded graphical hand on a computer screen, which accurately reproduces the movements of the physical hand and fingers. The CyberGlove has a software-programmable switch and LED on the wristband to permit system software developers to provide the glove wearer with program input/output capability.

The CyberGlove comes with a lightweight instrumentation unit that is connected to the glove via a 10-foot flexible cable. The instrumentation unit connects to the host computer via an RS-232 serial link and operates at up to 115.2 kBaud. It has a selectable sampling rate to more than 100 Hz or polled I/O. The instrumentation unit provides a variety of other functions and features including Time-Stamp, CyberGlove Status, External Sampling Sync, and analog sensor outputs.

The fingertips and palm of the glove are removed to provide ventilation and allow you to type, write, or grasp. The glove material is 80/20 Nylon/Lycra blend, so the glove flows with finger movement. Virtual Technologies also markets custom-made CyberWear such as the full-body CyberSuit, which is instrumented clothing.

Also available is the GestureGlove, software that uses the latest Artificial Neural Network technology to recognize gestures. The software converts fingerspelling to synthesized speech. Also available soon is CyberForce, which provides computer-programmable grip force feedback to the CyberGlove user.

Real-world applications include Virtual environments, telerobotics, video games, CAD, sign-language recognition, graphical character animation, music generation, hand-function analysis, and more.

Cost: contact vendor

3D Visualization: CrystalEyes

StereoGraphics Corporation
2171 E. Francisco Blvd.
San Rafael, CA 94901
415-459-4500
Fax: 415-459-3020

The CrystalEyes PC system combines a pair of Golden LCS (liquid crystal shutters) with an infrared emitter that sits on top of the computer monitor. The system supports IBM PCs and compatibles, as well as some Apple Macintosh and Amiga computers.

The CrystalEyes eyewear allows you to see stereo or depth by using a fast switching technology that shutters 60 times per eye per second in synchronization with the alternating left- and right-eye views presented on the display. This lets each eye see the image with a unique perspective, which the brain then integrates into one high-resolution, full-color, flicker-free stereo image.

CrystalEyes PC delivers a minimum dynamic range of 250:1 for a ghost-free color image, and 120Hz screen refresh for flicker-free viewing. There are no wires, since the infrared emitter synchronizes CrystalEyes eyewear with the stereo image. This means that any number of users can simultaneously use the system with complete freedom of movement. The glasses are lightweight, weighing only 3 ounces (85 grams).

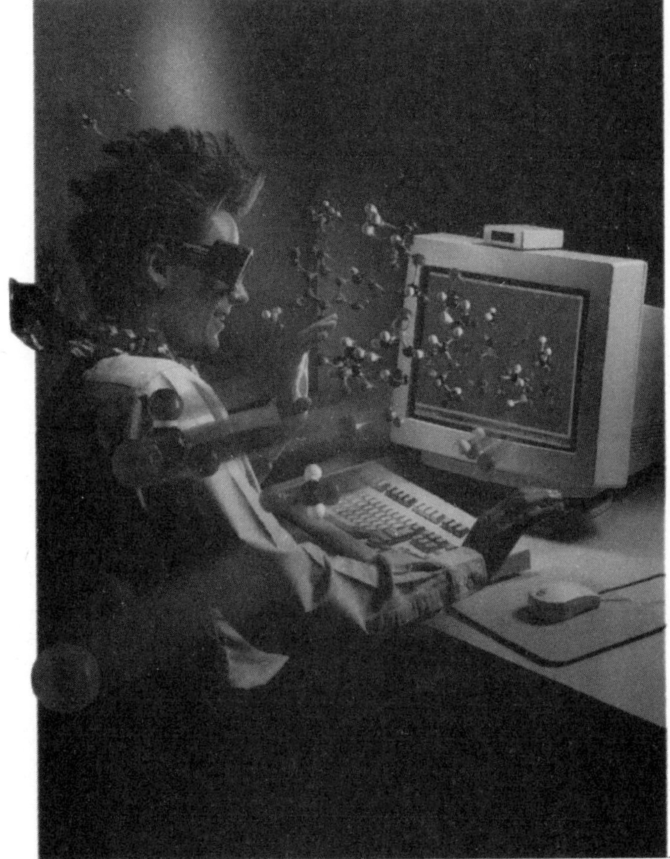

Figure 14.2. When you use StereoGraphics' CrystalEyes family of stereo depth-perception products, computer and video images leap from the screen in true 3D depth.

This stereo eyewear is well suited to real-world applications such as molecular modeling, scientific visualization, photogrammetric mapping, animation, mechanical CAD/CAE, flight simulation, architectural design and walk-throughs, prototype modeling, and all types of training.

Cost: $1,300 list price for model CE-PCE, *special introductory offer of $985*; or $2,695 for model CE-PCE/17M, which is bundled with a 17-inch stereo-ready monitor, *special introductory offer of $2,380.*

CrystalEyes VR

StereoGraphics also produces CrystalEyes VR systems, which enable viewers to see a stereo image through the CrystalEyes eyewear via a computer-directed, ultrasound, head-tracking device supporting all six degrees of head movement. So, if you move your head from side to side, up or down, or closer to or farther away from the monitor, the image on the display changes its perspective as well. The result is a convincing illusion that the image is a real object.

The user wearing the CrystalEyes VR—that is, the eyewear that is equipped with ultrasound microphones—interacts with the image. However, any number of viewers wearing CrystalEyes stereo eyewear can observe the first user's interactions.

Real-world applications for this eyewear are mission-planning, simulation, design and automation, tele-operations and robotic control, computational fluid dynamics, and entertainment.

Cost: $7,900 (includes CrystalEyes, ultrasound tracking device, and Sense8's WorldToolKit software).

CrystalEyes CAD

StereoGraphics and MicronGreen, a third-party VR software developer, jointly developed CrystalEyes CAD. By teaming up CrystalEyes CAD with Autodesk's AutoCAD, AveRender, AutoVision, and AnimatorPro, users now have the ability to rotate, texture, create volume surface, and animate AutoCAD stereo 3D models.

MicronGreen's CE CAD software creates a second, parallel image which, when viewed through CrystalEyes eyewear, lets you see three-dimensional models in stereo 3D. The lightweight (3 oz.) untethered glasses are synchronized with the stereo image by the infrared emitter. This allows you to view 3D screen images with complete freedom of movement.

Real-world applications include scientific visualization, mapping, architectural design and construction, global imaging, structural analysis, plant design, facilities management, and quality assurance.

Cost: $1,695, *special introductory offer $1,380.* Upgrades to CE CAD software for existing CrystalEyes users, $395.

CrystalEyes VideoSystem

The CrystalEyes VideoSystem is a self-contained 3D stereo video system that enables high resolution, full-color, video-true, stereoscopic 3D images to be simultaneously viewed and transmitted or recorded and played back with a single VCR. The Video System is NTSC- and PAL-compatible and works with virtually all video equipment worldwide. The system requires no external computer and uses standard video cameras, which are available as an option. The CrystalEyes VideoSystem is routinely used for minimally invasive surgery and for remote operation of vehicles.

Cost: $18,000

CrystalEyes Model 241

The self-contained Model 241 is a two-channel, full-color video multiplexing system. It allows two video images to be simultaneously transmitted or recorded and played back with a single VCR, so you can transmit two channels in the space usually occupied by a single NTSC channel.

The system works with all existing video-delivery systems such as VCRs and laser disc players. Real-world applications include video-broadcast transmission, cable systems, teleconferencing, education and training, entertainment, manufacturing, quality control, remote manipulation, and industrial and corporate video presentations.

Cost: $14,000

CrystalEyes Projection System

This product is a high-resolution, large-screen, 3D stereo projection system that projects images from any source, such as PCs and VCRs, to workstations. The system works with active or passive eyewear. The active system uses CrystalEyes stereo eyewear that is synched to the source's field rate via an infrared emitter. The passive system converts the CrystalEyes LCS technology to a high-performance Zscreen mounted over the projector lenses. This system uses inexpensive circular polarizing eyewear and is suitable for large audiences.

Real-world applications include presentations, virtual reality, simulation, video or computer graphics, virtual prototypes, entertainment, telecommunications, corporate video presentations, education, and training.

Cost: $25,150

Figure 14.3. The Virtual Vision Sport: A portable TV with a big-screen color image. In ultra-light 5-ounce eyeglasses.

Virtual Vision Sport

Virtual Vision Inc.
Professional Division
7659 178th Place, NE
Redmond, WA 98052
206-882-7878
800-755-4378
Fax: 206-882-7373

Virtual Vision Sport lets you watch big-screen television programming through portable five-ounce eyeglasses. The eyeware creates a large, NTSC color virtual image that appears to float in front of you in your lower field of vision. The image is mounted slightly below your normal field of vision on your dominant eye side, but the video image appears to be focused a comfortable distance (6 feet and beyond) in front of you. The Sport comes with indoor and outdoor eye shades, high-fidelity earphones, and a modular interface with VHF/UHF TV tuner.

Cost: $699 (one system); $1,999 (Developer Kit system, which includes right- and left-eye eyeware, modular interface, engineering interface breadboard, a TV tuner, a developer's manual, and spare parts)

Computer Display Development Kit

This includes hardware and software required to convert computer VGA output to NTSC video, and to modify screen layout for better legibility of text and graphics within the eyeware. The kit includes the following:

- Eyeware with light and dark eyeshades (right-eye or left-eye)
- A modular interface
- A developer's manual
- VGA-to-NTSC converter that has a small, extended box for laptop/notebook use; supports simultaneous display on eyeware and VGA monitor; and includes software drivers
- MAGic display magnification software that works with DOS and Windows applications; magnifies screen display by two times; and allows panning across the entire display via mouse or keyboard

Cost: $1,050 (specify right-eye or left-eye). Enhanced components are available at an additional cost for

- G-Lock VGA+ VGA to NTSC converter for flicker-free video output; mounts in PC card slot
- MAGic Deluxe Display Magnification Software that provides up to 8X magnifications and screen-locator features

View 100 (Monocular)

The View 100 delivers a color "floating" image in the lower part of vision of your dominant eye. You can look up and see normal surroundings (80 degrees + normal full field of vision), or glance down at the image (20 degrees peripheral placement). It comes with a rechargeable/modular interface that supplies audio, video, and power to the eyeware. Accessory products like a TV tuner, 900-MHz receiver, and interface development kit are available as modules.

Cost: $699; application developers kits $2,000

Binocular/Stereoscopic Development Kit

The binocular/stereoscopic system offers a wide field of view (30 degrees each eye) from two images in the center of your field of vision, which provides a more immersive experience. The kit provides a lab unit that enables you to produce a prototype of your concept or product, and Virtual Vision will work with you to develop this lab unit into a product.

This kit is appropriate for applications where little or no external environment input is required, such as remote stereoscopic vision, games, a portable theater, or virtual reality. The binocular/stereoscopic system includes high fidelity external earphones and a developer's manual.

Cost: $2,899

Interface Modules

The interface modules provide the power, audio/video signal, and controls for Virtual Vision's eyeware. The modules are interchangeable, working with any pair of eyeware. They have controls for on/off, volume, brightness, and mute. They also accept video and stereo inputs, and come with AC adapters. The IM 100 Modular Interface is for applications where portability and mobility are important. This module can be self-contained with a television tuner or radio frequency receiver and battery power. A belt carrying case is provided.

The rugged interface is for applications where mobility is less important or where rough handling is expected.

Cost: contact vendor

Wireless Interface

The Remote 900 is a 900-MHz FM system that provides a line-of-sight wireless link between any NTSC source and Virtual Vision's rechargeable/modular interface. The transmitter can easily be connected to any NTSC source via RCA jacks, and uses an external power source. It transmits full-color video and stereo audio. The mobile receiver snaps on the modular interface from which it draws its power.

This system is appropriate if you need mobility but can generally stay within the line of sight of the transmitter.

Cost: contact vendor

LCD Glasses

X-Specs 3D

Haitex Resources, Inc.
P.O. Box 20609
Charleston, SC 29413-0609
803-852-0750
Fax: 803-852-0650

Haitex offers a variety of stereoscopic vision tools for Amiga and other platforms. This is fancy talk for LCD glasses—one of the most economical means for realistic 3D viewing on your computer monitor.

Versions of X-Specs include the following:

X-Specs TV

This hardware device allows images to be recorded to videotape and then replaced with stereoscopic 3D depth. Ideal for animation or professional presentation. Compatible with NTSC, PAL, and SECAM composite or component video. Requires the use of X-Specs 3D glasses.

Cost: $169.95

X-Specs Composite Stereoscopic Multiplexer

Multiplexes the input of any two composite genlockable cameras providing a composite output in field-sequential 3D format. Use X-Specs TV for playback synch.

Cost: $995

X-Specs Component Stereoscopic Multiplexer

Multiplexes the input of any two composite or component (RGB, CAV, YC/SVHS/Hi8) genlockable cameras, providing a composite or component output in field-sequential 3D format. Switchable to external synch. Use X-Specs TV for playback synch.

Cost: $4,200

3D ImageTek Reality LCD Glasses

3D ImageTek Corporation
4525-B San Fernando Road
Glendale, CA 91204
714-455-1806
Fax: 714-455-1990

3D ImageTek sells LCD (Liquid Crystal Display) glasses for 3D viewing that are affordable and wireless. OEM pricing is available.

Cost: $265

3D ImageTek CyberScope

3D ImageTek also sells CyberScope, a patented, dual-cathode ray tube or LCD 3D display system. This system is autostereoscopic (no glasses), and displays bright, clear, 3D images. Licensing is available.

Cost: $11,450

Cyberscope 3D Hood

Cyberscope
Simsalabim Systems, Inc.
909D Madison Street
Albany, CA 94706
510-528-2021
Fax: 510-528-9499
Internet: scope@well.ss.ca.us

The Cyberscope is an inexpensive optical hood that attaches to a computer monitor. It creates stereo imagery on a computer by splitting the screen into two parts and displaying left and right images at the same time. Cyberscope orients the images so that the top of each points out the side of the monitor. A special hood containing mirrors is used to correctly orient the images.

Cost: $199

Tactile Feedback

Muscle Wires

Mondo-tronics, Inc.
524 San Anselmo Ave., #107
San Anselmo, CA 94960
415-455-9330
Fax: 415-455-9333

Mondo-tronics distributes a step-by-step guide called *The Muscle Wires Project Book* by Roger G. Gilbertson, president of Mondo-tronics, which explores applications for shape-memory wires, also known as *muscle wires*—robotic muscles that shorten when electrically powered.

Mondo-tronics markets TiNi Alloy Company's tactile feedback devices. Small tactors produce a direct fingertip signal using Muscle Wire technology, which provides electric action without motors or solenoids. The tactor, which measures 9mm × 20mm × 2.5mm, contains a small button that presses against the skin when powered. The tactor uses less than one volt, and can pulse at up to two cycles per second. The tactors mount easily inside gloves, on mouse buttons, joysticks, and other input devices. They provide direct physical signals to indicate contact with real or virtual objects, and even force feedback by variable pulse rates. This makes them well-suited for virtual reality and tele-operated systems.

The Tactor Demonstration Package and Software includes one tactor, a pocket-sized Driver Box (uses one 9-volt alkaline battery, not included), interface cable for PC-type serial ports (9-pin), and a 5 1/2-inch disk of PC demo programs.

Cost: $178

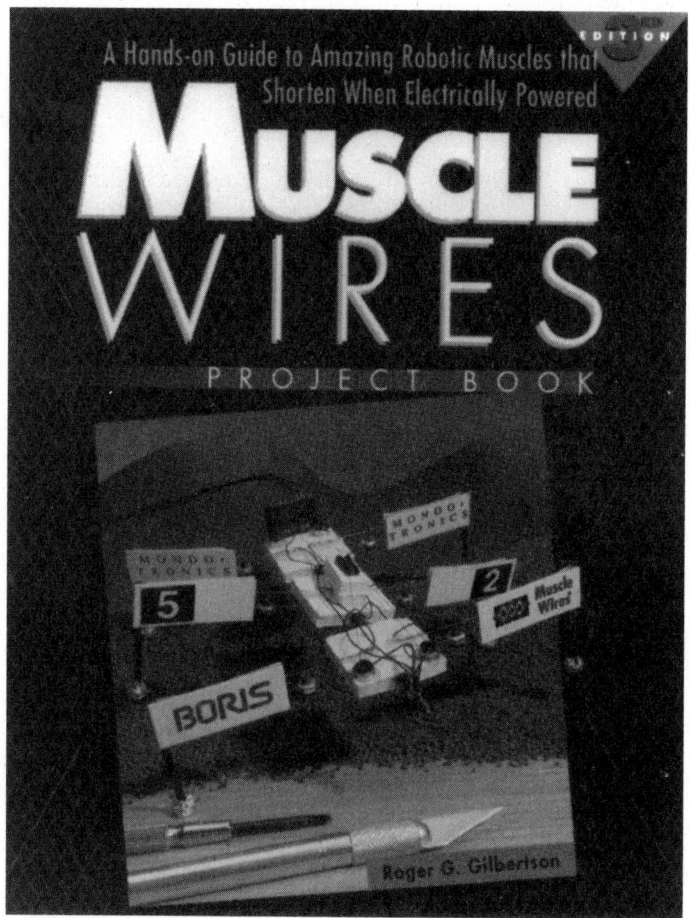

Figure 14.4. Mondo-tronics' Muscle Wires Project Book discusses shape memory wires, which are robotic muscles that shorten when electrically powered.

Tactools

Xtensory, Inc.
140 Sunridge Drive
Scotts Valley, CA 95066
408-439-0600
Fax: 408-439-8845

Figure 14.5. Tactools' Tactile Feedback System is comprised of two components: tactors and a controller.

Tactools is a tactile feedback system in which you receive tactile cues from tactors via computer control. Tactools is comprised of two components: tactors and a controller. SMA (shape memory alloy) actuators move the tactors, which permits forceful yet compact devices to be placed where they meet your fingertips. The tactors are small enough to permit unimpeded hand-grasp motions in gloves, and are compact enough to fit in pointing devices. Each tactor is individually controllable, and can be actuated in impulsive and vibratory modes.

The controller receives commands from the host and fires the appropriate tactors at the appropriate times. So the host is not burdened with actuator control overhead, and needs only to send out commands to fire the tactors. Tactools uses a simple protocol for communications, which makes it easy to connect them to workstations and PCs. Each Tactools controller can control up to 10 tactors, which can be distributed over single or multiple input devices.

Four inputs are provided: serial (EIA232), parallel, analog, and MIDI. The parallel input permits direct connection to VPL's Glove Box User Port or other devices with parallel ports, which saves host serial ports. The analog input permits reading sensors, which are useful for telepresence applications. The MIDI ports permit daisy-chaining of multiple Tactools systems, which also saves host serial ports. Xtensory provides custom engineering for special requirements.

Cost: $1,500

Xtensory VR Services (XVS)

Xtensory offers consulting to assist you in using VR technology to maximum advantage. Xtensory has a fully equipped VR lab where they perform hardware and software integration testing, and can help you integrate a new user interface or new approach to problems using VR technology. Some of the technologies they are evaluating follow:

- 3D visual displays (head-mounted displays and nonimmersive systems)
- 3D audio displays
- Xtensory tactile feedback displays
- 3D tracking systems (head, hands, and so on)
- Xtensory VR software toolkit

Integration projects are delivered in four phases, with specific deliverables for each:

Phase 1—Identifies business opportunities and organizes project team.

Phase 2—Targets specific information-management problems and determines meaningful business metrics for the project.

Phase 3—Helps assess effectiveness of current system interfaces and standards, and design new VR-based interface; helps you build a prototype system.

Phase 4—Develops a transition plan to enterprise-wide implementations.

Cost: contact vendor

3D Devices (Mice/Joystick)

Global 3D Controller

Global Devices
6630 Arabian Circle
Granite Bay, CA 95661
916-791-3533
Fax: 916-791-4358

The Global Controller is a 3D graphics controller that translates full 3D input from the user's hand to control 3D graphics or to move the user through any virtual environment. The Global 3D Controller has true six-degrees-of-freedom function, and can translate all possible combinations of linear and rotational vectors of the x, y, and z-coordinate system. The Global 3D Controller includes 32 levels of active tactile feedback within the handle.

Cost: $249

Immersion Probe

Immersion Corporation
P.O. Box 8669
Palo Alto, CA 94309
415-960-6882
Fax: 415-960-6977

The Probe is a pen-like stylus that manipulates a computer cursor in 3D "space" according to the movements of its mechanical linkage. The Probe replaces 3D mice, space balls, Polhemus sensors, and flying mice, which can be fatiguing to hold up in the air, difficult to hold steady, and awkward to grasp. The stylus is held between the fingers like a pencil, and reports position (x,y,z) and orientation (roll, pitch, and yaw) information to a host processor through a standard serial port. Because the stylus uses mechanical sensor elements, it eliminates the "shadow" interference of ultrasonically linked trackers that can occur when your hands come between those devices and their ultrasonic receivers.

Cost: Immersion Probe-IC, $999; Immersion Probe-IX, $1,495; Immersion Probe-MD, $2,495

Immersion Personal Digitizer

The Personal Digitizer is a high-performance 3D digitizer that allows you to trace the surface contours of three-dimensional objects with a stylus and store the profile in a standard data format. It interfaces with any standard computer system via a serial port, and reports the position and orientation of the stylus with position resolution as high as 3600 points per square inch. The Personal Digitizer reports the orientation of the stylus in 3D space, which allows it to be used as a six-degrees-of-freedom human-interface tool to manipulate 3D images. It is ideal for graphic artists, animators, and engineers. Real-world applications include CAD, virtual reality, graphic design, 3D animation, architecture, and medical imaging.

Cost: $1,595 (including software)

Immersion Interface Box

This product is a small electronics module that plugs peripherals such as foot pedals, hand controllers, and joysticks into the serial port of most computer systems. It lets you interface with up to eight human interface devices simultaneously: foot-pedals, knobs, sliders, and hand-grips.

The Interface Box is an ideal tool for rapid prototypes of unique user interface systems. Suppose that you are creating a unique system for moving through virtual environments using a gas pedal and brake pedal as the metaphor for controlling your speed. You could plug in the Immersion Interface Box to your serial port, and plug in two standard analog pedals, which are also distributed by Immersion Corp., and add this capability to your system. The Interface Box can connect up to four digital and four analog input signals simultaneously.

The Interface Box supports several platforms, such as PC, Macintosh, SGI, and UNIX. The basic unit includes a single foot pedal and software library.

Cost: $299

Digital Force Synthesizer

The Digital Force Synthesizer is an affordable force-reflecting interface for manual interaction with virtual environments and scientific visualization. It provides high bandwidth force information through a pen-like stylus. You can manipulate the pen-like interface to actually feel realistic sensations such as walls, springs, liquids, and even simulated body tissue for VR medical applications.

This tool is well-suited for software developers and VR research scientists to explore haptic display. Although it is designed for use outside the laboratory, the Digital Force Synthesizer allows for the generation of crisp-feeling walls and realistic spongy surfaces with minimal friction or inertia distortions.

Cost: $3,999

Cyberman

Logitech
6505 Kaiser Drive
Fremont, CA 94555
510-795-8500
Fax: 510-792-8901

Logitech produces 2D and 3D mice and a head tracker. These ultrasonic devices let you input 2D and 3D information into a computer. They are designed for CAD, robotics, computer simulation, high-end computer graphics and animation, scientific visualization, and VR applications. The Cyberman is a six-degrees-of-freedom input device.

Cost: $129

SpaceController

Spaceball Technologies, Inc.
600 Suffolk Street
Lowell, MA 01854
508-970-0330
800-490-3200 (Order)
Fax: 508-970-0199

The SpaceController is a 3D input device developed exclusively for DOS-based PCs. It is particularly useful for 3D CAD applications, and is awesome with PC action games. The ball is easy and intuitive to use, and can improve productivity moving models by 30 percent or more.

The SpaceController is comprised of a ball mounted on an ergonomic base. The ball lets you pan, scale (zoom), or rotate 3D design parts or models with full simultaneous six-degrees-of-freedom control. The SpaceController is easy and natural to use: Rest your wrist on the platform base, and grab the ball gently around its equator. Then, use fingertip pressure to push, pull, and twist the ball in any direction. The ball doesn't actually move, but senses the forces you apply to it. Twist the ball, and your image rotates. Pull on the SpaceController, and your image comes toward you. The harder the ball is pushed, the faster the object moves.

Two function buttons located on either side of the base provide additional functionality that is available using SpaceWare, which is interactive motion control (IMC) proprietary software. The software interfaces the SpaceController to your application for optimized performance. Initially, support was offered for the SpaceController in three PC-based CAD applications: CADKEY, MicroStation, and AutoCAD. Additional application support will be available in CAD, as well as applications in AEC, GIS, Science and Medicine, Multimedia, and Virtual Reality.

Cost: $795

Spaceball 2003

The Spaceball provides full, simultaneous six-axis control. It consists of a tennis ball-sized sphere mounted on a molded platform, occupying about 10" x 4" in desktop space. Unlike a trackball, the ball does not actually move but responds to the slightest fingertip pressures applied to it. Any combination of movements or pressures applied to the ball are resolved into X, Y, and Z translations and rotations of the image. The more pressure applied, the faster the object moves.

Figure 14.6. The Spaceball 2003 sports a high-tech design and ergonomic base.

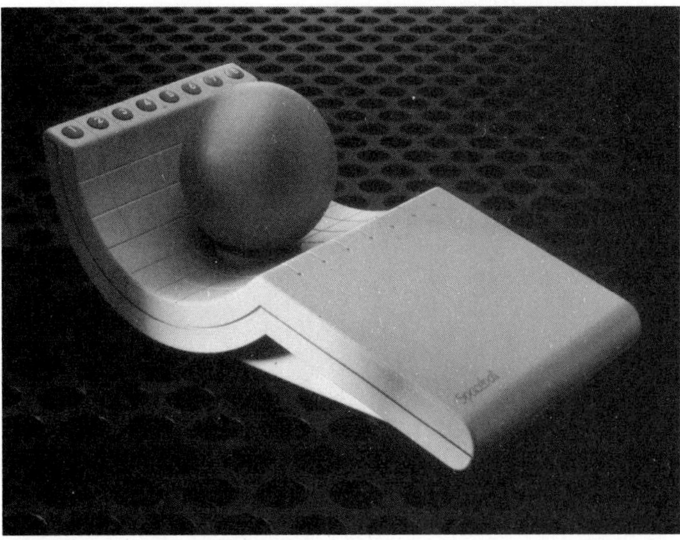

The base of the Spaceball has eight function buttons located at the top of the device that can be customized by defining key functions specific to your application. The Spaceball uses a proprietary software product called the SpaceWare Interactive Motion Control (IMC) interface. The software includes SpaceWare drivers for applications in areas such as AEC, Animation, CAD/CAM/CAE, Computational Fluid Dynamics, Geographic Information Systems, Molecular Modeling, Scientific Visualization, Virtual Reality, and Visual Simulation.

The Spaceball 2003 interfaces to your computer system via a standard RS-232C port. It is fully supported on all major UNIX 3D graphics platforms from PCs to high-end workstations like Apollo, DEC, Hewlett-Packard, IBM, Intergraph, Silicon Graphics, Stardent, and Sun.

Cost: contact vendor

Totally Immersed

Mandala Virtual World System

The Vivid Group
317 Adelaide Street W., Suite 302
Toronto, ON M5V 1P9 CANADA
416-340-9290
Fax: 416-348-9809

Figure 14.7. In Shark Bait, you find yourself among the creatures of the Great Barrier Reef. Using only body movement, you must move around the reef collecting treasure while avoiding sharks and eels.

The Mandala System uses a video camera to immerse your image into interactive video and computer graphics worlds. You see yourself on TV, and when you move, the virtual world responds to your presence. You don't have to wear, touch, or hold anything. Just reach out and, through "video gesture," trigger visible or invisible icons to score points, manipulate animations, bodypaint, or play a virtual drum kit.

The Vivid Group has produced several Mandala game environments, with themes ranging from science fiction adventures to skill-testing sports simulators. Recently, the Vivid Group released the VR Goalie game at the Hockey Hall of Fame in Toronto. The game is a goaltender simulator that allows players to step into a picture as a goalie and try to defend the goal against two opponents. One of the shooters in the game is Ron Ellis, who played for the Maple Leafs from 1963 through '81.

The Virtual Reality Basketball Simulator was created for the Basketball Hall of Fame in Springfield, Massachusetts. The game allows players to step onto a computer-generated court and go one-on-one against Hall of Famer Bill Walton, also a two-time NBA champ. Other games include a Tennis Experience created for CBS Sports, Soccer created in conjunction with Expo '93, golf, beach volleyball, and others.

Other Mandala systems include:

- SharkBait, which is an underwater adventure game that takes place in an animated Barrier Reef.
- Vincent John Vincent's Mandala dance and music performance, which combines interactive video and computer graphics to create surreal musical and visual performances.
- Nickelodeon Channel's "Arcade Show," which features the Mandala technology incorporated into an interactive game show environment.
- Virtual Cities, which is a teleconferencing project that brings students in different cities around the world into a networked common virtual environment. Virtual Cities allows a network of young people to study urban environments and the design of "green cities."
- Mandala's Virtual *Star Trek* simulation, which is an interactive exhibit created by the Vivid Group and Paramount Pictures. In the game, you enter a physical re-creation of *Star Trek*'s transporter room and are beamed from the transporter platform to a variety of interactive *Star Trek* experiences. Or, in the Ship's Holodeck, you are immersed in a jungle with an array of flora and fauna that react when touched.

The Vivid Group also produces custom worlds using story boards and video tests to produce worlds based on your specifications.

Cost: $15,000 to $42,000 (existing Mandala systems); $10,000 to $200,000+ (custom worlds)

Virtuality

Horizon Entertainment
501 N. Broadway
St. Louis, MO 63102
800-ILUSION
314-331-6000
Fax: 314-331-6002

Figure 14.8.
Mount the Cyber platform and slip your head into the Visette. Grab the spacestick, and you're whisked away to a 3D world.

Virtuality is a virtual reality entertainment system that allows you to replace your view of the real world with the fantasy dimension of cyberspace. Through a special combination of hardware and software, you can enter a computer-generated world and interact with other people and objects in that world.

Virtuality is distributed in the United States by a division of Edison Brothers Stores of St. Louis. The virtual-reality system is manufactured by W Industries of Leicester, England for use in video arcades and other entertainment spots, and the game software is provided by Spectrum Holobyte of Alameda, California.

Virtuality is available in two models: the 1000CS, which is a stand-up model, and the 1000SD, which is a sit-down model. Both models track the player's head movement, but the stand-up model tracks the player's hand movement also.

Model 1000CS

The stand-up model lets you navigate in cyberspace by turning your body. You can interact with other players and objects using your hand and arm. The system includes a Visette, which is exclusive headgear that immerses you in the experience. It includes two liquid-crystal screens, a quadrophonic (four-channel) sound system, a magnetic tracking system that monitors the position and angle of a player's head, and a microphone that lets players talk to each other. The system runs on the Expality, which is a multiprocessor computer system with three 25-33MHz processors, a 40-553M CD-ROM, and 100M hard disk that provides computer-generated images, multichannel sound, and motion outputs. An on-board LAN (Local Area Network) enables linking of multiple Virtuality systems for interactive play. Model 1000CS also has a Space Joystick, which becomes your hand, weapon, or wand in cyberspace. The system has an external monitor that shows the player's point of view.

Cost: Approximately $55,000 new ($29,000 used)

Model 1000SD

The sit-down model lets you fly, drive, or walk in cyberspace using a variety of mounted controls including joystick, foot pedals, steering wheel, and T-shift. It, too, includes a Visette, Expality, and external monitor.

Cost: Approximately $45,000 new ($25,000 used)

Virtuality Rentals

Horizon provides the addresses, telephone numbers, and quantity of Virtuality equipment at various locations. For updates, call 314-331-6051. The games can be rented for special events, such as trade shows, publicity tours, corporate events, and so on. Complete systems include the Virtuality pod (including software and hardware), themed cabinet, service, and support through the event or tour. Horizon also offers a turnkey package that includes transportation of two simulators to your event, a technician to set up units and install your choice of software, and two 25-inch monitors so that people nearby can view what the players are experiencing. Call the Event Marketing Department at 314-331-6005 for details.

Trackers

A Flock of Birds

Ascension Technology Corp.
P.O. Box 527
Burlington, VT 05402
802-860-6440
Fax: 802-860-6439

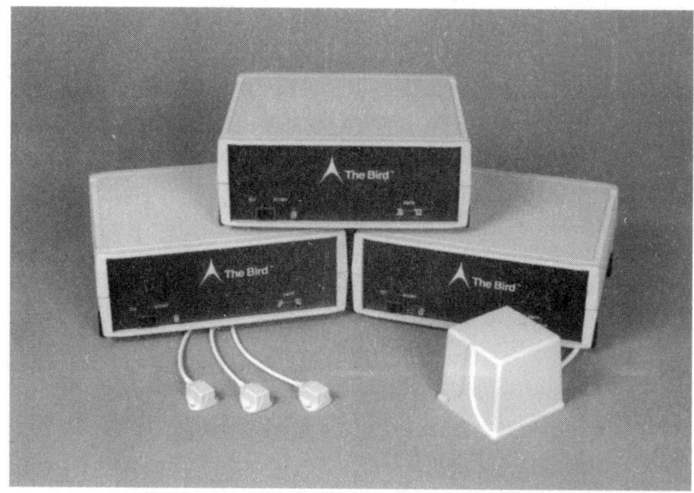

Figure 14.9. Ascension's Flock of Birds. Shown here is a three-receiver Flock tracker with a standard transmitter on the right.

A Flock of Birds provides six-degrees-of-freedom tracking without blocking or obstruction problems. The Flock is an easy-to-use modular tracker, which enables you to simultaneously track the position and orientation in space of up to 30 small receivers. These receivers may be attached to one's head, hands, arms, or legs. Each receiver makes up to 144 position and orientation measurements a second, and allows operation within about a three-foot radius. Range may be increased up to plus or minus eight feet with the Extended Range Transmitter, and is accurate to 0.1 inch and 0.5 degree. If linked together, the Flock's transmitters provide enough coverage for a virtual world to fill a 12-by-12-foot room.

Flock trackers use pulsed DC magnetic fields to reduce distortions by metallic objects like stainless steel, aluminum, tin, brass, and so on, and to overcome line-of-sight blocking problems. The trackers use multiprocessors to reduce computation time and a Fast Bird Bus (FBB) to speed data transmissions to a host computer. This minimizes the lag between spatial measurements and presentation of visual scenes. The result is real-time availability of sensed motions for graphics and measurement applications ranging from simulation and virtual reality to biomechanics and entertainment.

Long-range tracking has proved particularly useful to the entertainment and film industry. Long-range multireceiver tracking allows human actors to specify the motion paths of synthetic characters for animation purposes. Flock trackers were recently interfaced with Lamb's Wavefront software to produce the animation for the latest *Donnie Domino* pizza commercial. They were used at Mr. Film, a California-based production house that specializes in animation of computer-generated images, to provide natural motions for characters ranging from walking skeletons to break-dancing turtles.

Cost: $2,695 (one receiver)

DynaSight Sensor

Origin Instruments Corporation
854 Greenview Drive
Grand Prairie, TX 75050-2438
214-606-8740
Fax: 214-606-8741

The DynaSight sensor is a 3D optical position-tracking system for computer workstations. The sensor operates without wires or cumbersome head-mounted apparatus. It uses a tiny, paper-thin dot that is placed directly on your forehead or glasses, and can be worn for days at a time. The sensor package is about the size and shape of a trade paperback book and is mounted on top of the computer CRT monitor. A two-color LED on the front of the sensor indicates the tracking status.

The DynaSight sensor operates by measuring and reporting on the 3D movements of the tiny target on your forehead. The sensor uses small changes in head position and orientation to provide spatial context and reveal obscured details. With this information, the perspective of displayed graphics can be animated to be geometrically appropriate for the instantaneous positions of your eyes. When the tracking, rendering, and stereo display systems are working in concert, the result is a real-time, hologram-like display that provides a *virtual window* into a computer generated environment. An additional benefit of using the head to tune the visual perspective is that the hands are free to edit or control the object being displayed.

The DynaSight sensor is mounted above the viewable area of a real-time graphics display, such as the top of a computer monitor. The sensor's field of view is a nominal 75-degree cone, and the sensor is pointed so this field covers a comfortable range of head-eye positions. To cue the sensor, you place the adhesive-backed disposable target, weighing less than 10 milligrams, on your eyeglasses, stereoscopic goggles or, in some applications, on your forehead. This wireless, tiny target does not obscure vision or interfere with activities. Larger, high-performance targets are available that allow measurements at a sensor-to-target range of up to 20 feet.

The DynaSight sensor is compatible with a wide range of stereoscopic viewing accessories, including StereoGraphics CrystalEyes, the Tektronix line of wireless stereo viewing systems, Dimension Technologies' autostereoscopic displays, and 3DTV's low-cost tethered stereo glasses.

The DynaSight sensor can also be configured to emulate or filter the outputs from existing serial devices, including the Microsoft serial mouse and the Mouse Systems serial mouse.

Real-world applications include the following:

- Mechanical CAD
- Molecular modeling
- Telepresence
- 3D situation awareness
- Mission planning
- Training and simulation
- Medical imaging
- Desktop virtual reality
- Interactive projection displays
- Head-controlled pointing systems that augment the mouse and provide cursor positioning in three dimensions
- Computer access for persons with physical disabilities, including high-level quadriplegics
- Laboratory metrology and industrial automation systems

The DynaSight sensor is also available in the DynaSight Developer's Kit, which includes the sensor, an assortment of standard and high-gain infrared targets, cabling, accessories for most PCs and workstations, technical documentation, and an array of software-application examples. The kit provides implementation ideas and source code in ANSI C that can be used as a foundation for your own development.

Cost: $2,195 for DynaSight Sensor; $2,495 for DynaSight Developer's Kit

HeadMouse Sensor

Origin Instruments also distributes the HeadMouse Sensor, which is a head-controlled mouse for people with disabilities. The HeadMouse is a wireless optical sensor that tracks a tiny, disposable target that is placed on your forehead or glasses. This capability can be combined with an on-screen keyboard to replace the functions of a conventional keyboard. To emulate a key press, you position the mouse pointer over a key and dwell on that key for a set period of time. Or you can use a Remote Switch Interface to relay mouse-button inputs from a wheelchair to the computer. The HeadMouse resolution is sufficient to allow you to control the mouse pointer at the level of a pixel. This precision allows you to perform tasks such as drawing or computer-aided design.

Cost: $1,795

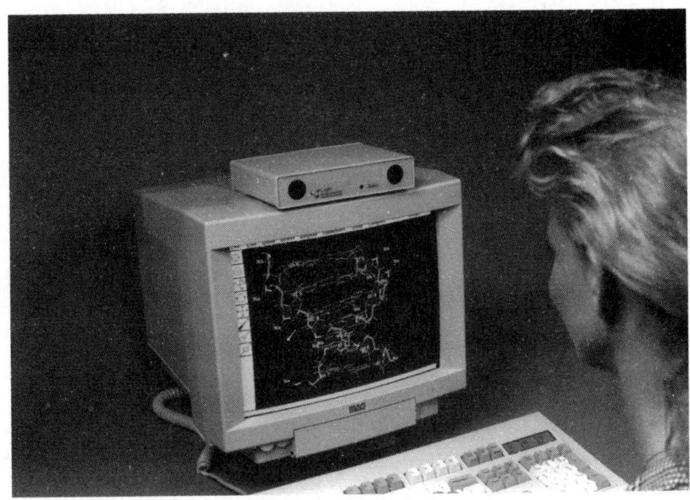

Figure 14.10. The HeadMouse sensor—a wireless optical sensor that tracks a tiny, disposable target on your forehead or glasses—is placed on top of the computer monitor.

GAMS

Acoustic Positioning Research
11514 77th Avenue
Edmonton, AB T6G 0M1 CANADA
403-438-5810
Fax: 403-438-5810

The Gesture and Media System (GAMS) is a wireless ultrasonic 3D tracking system that monitors position, velocity, and acceleration in 3D, plus the status of an optional user interface button over a wide tracking area. This information can be used by another computer platform or can be mapped to MIDI commands.

The wand can either be held in your hands or strapped to your body, and is responsive to 360 degrees—so there's no need to "point" the wand. Unlike laser or infrared controllers, the wand is designed to circumvent physical obstructions such as props, other people, or equipment.

GAMS comes with an IBM AT hardware card, ultrasonic speakers, a radio receiver, MIDI mapping/control software, and up to four wireless wands. It outputs data via a serial port to any computer platform similarly equipped. If you use the mapping software included with GAMS, you can generate MIDI commands to drive samplers, lighting controllers, laser disc players, slide projectors, or other MIDI controllable instruments and machines.

Real-world applications include the following:

- Location-based entertainment applications
- VR navigation tool
- Immersive data-visualization tasks
- Simulation and computer-modeling control
- Crowd-gathering sales tool at trade shows
- Large-scale baton for a MIDI orchestra
- Allows performing artists to control their staging, lighting, and media
- Telepresence applications
- 3D mouse

Host system requirements: Minimum configuration is 12MHz 286 AT compatible, 80287 numeric coprocessor, 640K RAM, EGA graphics, bus mouse, and an RS232 serial port. A Roland MPU 401 compatible MIDI card is required for MIDI applications. No serial port is needed if only MIDI output is desired. Operation with multiple wands requires a faster PC.

Cost: $6,500 (includes one wand, mapping software, ultrasonic speakers and their cabling, radio receiver, and AT interface hardware); $900 (single wand and radio receiver); $4,000 (upgrade to 4-wand system, does not include extra wands)

INSIDETRAK

Polhemus, Inc.
1 Hercules Drive
P.O. Box 560
Colchester, VT 05446
802-655-3159
Fax: 802-655-1439

Polhemus systems transmit very low-level magnetic fields, which are received by a small lightweight device attached to the object you want to measure. The position and orientation are rapidly computed and transmitted to your host computer. The object may be a head-mounted display (HMD) or a Polhemus-supplied stylus, which you can use to accurately digitize other objects. Polhemus technology is electromagnetic, so line of sight is not required between the transmitter and receiver.

Polhemus' 3SPACE INSIDETRAK is a 3D position/orientation measuring device that inserts into your PC (or any computer with an ISA slot). Since it plugs into the ISA slot on the motherboard, transport delays are minimized. The INSIDETRAK comes standard with a single receiver. An optional second receiver can be added by plugging it into the masterboard. Additional slave boards can be added, each one handling up to two receivers.

The INSIDETRAK accurately computes the position and orientation of a tiny receiver as it moves through three-dimensional space. The system provides real-time, six-degrees-of-freedom measurement of position (x,y,z Cartesian coordinates) and orientation (aximuth, elevation, and roll). It is accurate to 0.5 inch RMS for the X, Y, or Z position; and 2 degrees RMS for receiver orientation when the receivers are located within 30 inches of the transmitter; and has a range of up to five feet with slightly reduced performance.

INSIDETRAK uses Polhemus' patented, low-frequency magnetic transducing technology, so it is unnecessary to maintain a clear line of light between transmitter and receiver. The problems of signal blocking that are common with sonic or laser devices are eliminated. However, large metallic objects, such as desks or cabinets located near the transmitter or receiver, may adversely affect the performance of the system.

Real-world applications include

Virtual Reality—Polhemus' 3SPACE INSIDETRAK system is well-suited for head and body motion-tracking applications.

Simulators—INSIDETRAK can be used to track head-mounted displays utilized in simulator or trainer applications.

Biomechanical Analysis—Use INSIDETRAK to collect real-time relative movement data for gait and limb analysis. Perfect for leg, knee, joint, spinal, or shoulder rotational measurement.

The INSIDETRAK is Polhemus' low-end product.

Cost: $2,250

FASTRAK

The 3SPACE FASTRAK provides real-time, six-degrees-of-freedom tracking with virtually no latency. It's great for position/orientation measuring of 3D applications and environments. It is well-suited for measuring range of motion or limb rotation in biomedical research, as well as head tracking, biomechanical analysis, graphic and cursor control, and stereotaxic localization.

The 3SPACE FASTRAK includes a System Electronics Unit (SEU), power supply, one receiver, and one transmitter. The system's capabilities can be expanded by adding up to three additional receivers. Digital Signal Processing (DSP) technology provides 4ms latency, updated at 120Hz. It has a range of up to 10 feet with accuracy of 0.03 in RMS with a resolution of 0.0002 in/in. It permits measurement of up to 4 receivers on a single system, and up to 32 receivers at a time, utilizing 8 multiplexed systems.

Cost: $5,750

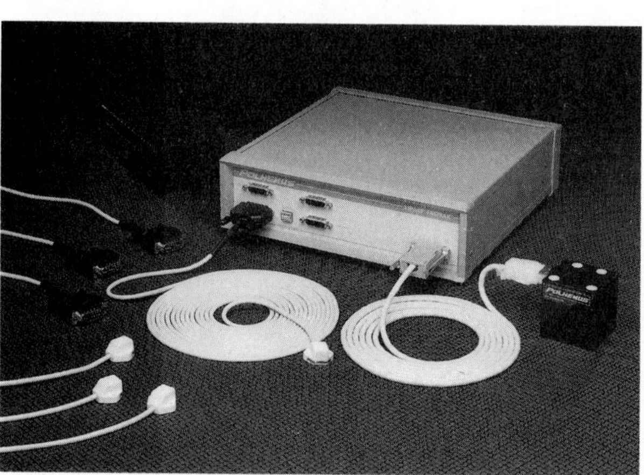

Figure 14.11. Polhemus' 3SPACE FASTRAK provides real-time six-degrees-of-freedom with minimal latency.

ISOTRAK II

This product is a six-degrees-of-freedom position sensor that supports up to two receivers. The system includes a System Electronics Unit (SEU), a power supply, one receiver, and one transmitter. The system can be expanded by adding an additional receiver.

The Isotrak II is two solutions in one: a 3D digitizer and a dual-receiver motion tracker. It provides dynamic, real-time 6DOF measurement of position and orientation. Because it measures position and orientation in real time, it can update data continuously, discretely (point by point), or incrementally. The ability to capture orientation of the receiver enables you to use the Isotrak II (with the optional 3BALL 3D mouse device) to rotate a captured database, act as a light for shading, or become the eye for perspective views.

Cost: $2,875

3DRAW

The 3DRAW captures and archives the dimensions of any nonmetallic object.

Cost: $6,500

Voice-Recognition Systems

SoundMaster II

Covox, Inc.
675 Conger Street
Eugene, OR 97042
503-342-1271
Fax: 503-342-1283

This sound card is compatible with AdLib, MIDI, and most other internal PC sound systems. It includes Voice Master speech-recognition software, which you can use to add voice commands to existing programs. It provides high-speed digital sampling and direct-to-RAM or direct-to-disc digital recording and playback software, and it includes MIDI cables and twin mini-speakers.

Cost: $149

Head-Mounted Devices

CyberEye

General Reality Company
P.O. Box 8873
San Jose, CA 95159-8873
408-289-8340
Fax: 408-289-8258

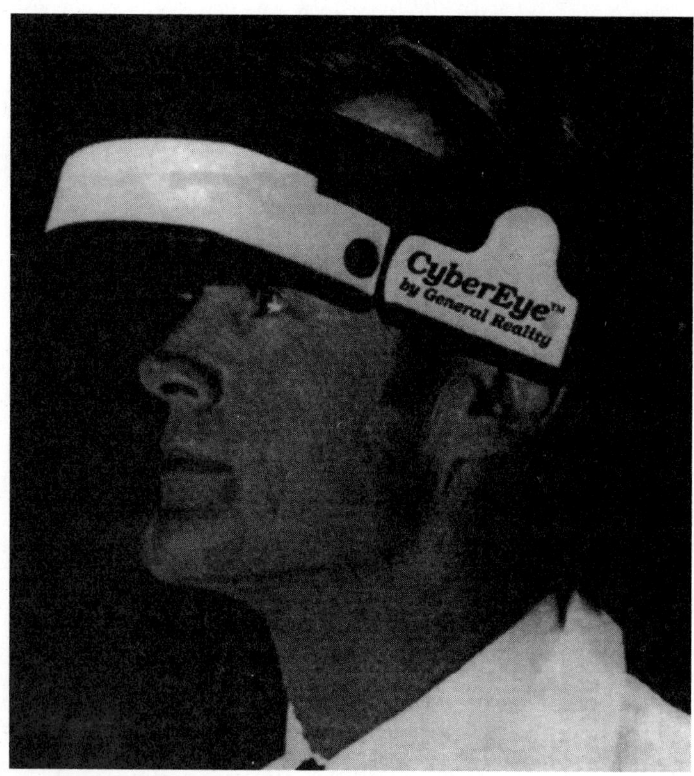

Figure 14.12. Model 100 & Stereo 100S head-mounted-display for Professional Applications. The CyberEye has eight adjustment points to accommodate eyeglasses, full immersion, and simultaneous immersive/desktop work.

The CyberEye HMD is a lightweight (14 ounces) HMD that mounts on your head using a headband and overhead strap. It includes CyberEye's 3D-ready dual in-ear stereo privacy buds that plug in right behind your ear, and comes with a beltpack that provides power, brightness, volume, and mute controls. CyberEye is designed for comfortable extended wear in professional applications ranging from minimally invasive surgery to VR content development.

CyberEye's field of vision is just below 30 degrees, which provides crisp, undistorted images equivalent to a 7-foot-wide TV screen just 12 feet away. The HMD's optics focus at "near-infinity," which is the most relaxed point for your eyes.

The CyberEye HMD has eight individual adjustment points that support a wide range of user requirements, including eyeglasses, full immersion, and simultaneous immersive/desktop work.

Cost: $1,995 (mono) and $2,495 (stereo)

CyberMaxx

VictorMaxx Technologies, Inc.
510 Lake Cook Road, Suite 100
Deerfield, IL 60015
708-267-0007
Fax: 708-267-0037

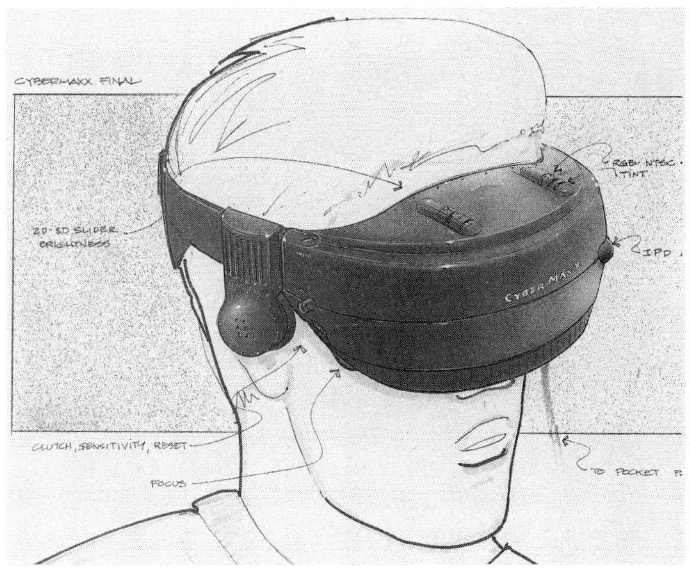

Figure 14.13. The CyberMaxx provides a completely immersive stereoscopic environment in which to play computer games.

The CyberMaxx is an HMD specifically designed for IBM and Macintosh PCs, though it functions monoscopically with Sega, Nintendo, Jaguar, and Amiga game systems. CyberMaxx is intended to provide an immersive stereoscopic environment in which to play computer games.

The HMD includes twin 120,000-pixel, active-matrix color liquid crystal displays (LCDs), and weighs only 14 ounces. It offers proprietary optics with a 70-degree horizontal field of view, and lets you adjust the eye focus individually (for those with corrective lenses). The CyberMaxx includes real-time sourceless head tracking with a lag time of less than 75 milliseconds for pitch, yaw, and roll head tracking, so when you move your head, the game environment moves with you in full color with 3D stereo sound and visuals. The CyberMaxx comes with high fidelity, adjustable headphones that provide immersive sound.

VictorMaxx Technologies is currently working with independent software developers to produce virtual-reality games for the CyberMaxx.

Cost: Around $700

Forte VFX1

FORTE Technologies, Inc.
1057 E. Henrietta Road
Rochester, NY 14623
716-427-8595
Fax: 716-292-6353

The VFX1 combines all three sought-after features in a standard unit—3D color imaging, 3D stereo sound, and 3-axis head tracking. It does all of this at a price that sets a new standard for HMDs—under $1,000. We would have liked to test a unit, but they were not shipping as of press time. At this price point, and with these features, the VFX1 could well be a significant step forward in VR technology for the masses. Like most HMDs, it takes a standard NTSC signal for input.

Here are some details on the VFX1:

3D stereo imaging—Two color LCDs featuring high-resolution images (428x244). According to material from Forte, "each eye sees different images, but both eyes work as a team. It is the equivalent of sitting in a movie theater near the front row." This suggests that there are some compromises at the low price point, but only a test drive will reveal how well the concept works.

3D VOS head tracker—VOS stands for Virtual Orientation System, and it is a proprietary Forte technique for tracking head movements. All hardware is self-contained in the HMD; there are no external tracking modules.

3D sound—The VFX1 uses the Gravis Ultrasound to provide 3D holographic sound.

Smart visor—The visor flips up so you can access your PC monitor when not immersed in a VR space.

VFX1 interface card—This allows the VFX1 to interface with VGA cards, such as Diamonds Stealth and Speedstar cards. The interface card uses a standard VGA feature connector.

Virtual Research HMDs

Virtual Research
3193 Belick Street, Suite 2
Santa Clara, CA 95054
408-748-8712
Fax: 408-748-8714

The EyeGen3 is an HMD that uses monochrome CRTs with color wheels instead of LCDs. The NTSC video signal is divided into its three color components (red, blue, and green). These are displayed at three times the normal rate (180 fields per second instead of 60). A spinning color wheel between the CRT and the optics is synchronized so that it places a red filter in front of the LCD when the red image is displayed, a blue filter when the blue image is displayed, and so on. The eye perceives a full-color image.

This gives an effective resolution of 493 NTSC lines by 250 resolvable lines. The field of view is 40 degrees diagonal, and interpupillary distance can be varied from 50mm to 74mm. Overlap between the images is user adjustable from 100 percent to 55 percent.

The EyeGen3 also supports audio inputs. The weight of the unit is counterbalanced by the cable that extends down the user's back.

Cost: $7,900

VR4

The VR4 is a more advanced HMD than the EyeGen3. It is the unit we tested ourselves; see Chapter 7 for our experiences with the unit. The VR4 uses the same physical chassis as the EyeGen3, but it uses two standard color LCDs and covers the eyes with a full shield to increase ruggedness. The field of view is larger than the EyeGen—60 degrees versus 40 degrees.

The VR4 is intended for high-performance multiuser applications and quick-fit applications (arcades and trade shows). The EyeGen3 is the preferred selection where higher resolution is the paramount consideration.

The outer shell of the VR4 is easily adjustable for a wide range of users. We had no trouble quickly fitting the unit to our needs. There are adjustments for how low the unit sits on the head, interpupillary distance, distance of optics from the user's eyes, and so on. The VR4, like the EyeGen3, includes headphones for audio.

Cost: Approximately $7,000

MRG2 HMD

Liquid Image Corporation
659 Century Street
Winnipeg, MB R3H 0L9 CANADA
204-772-0137
Fax: 204-772-0239

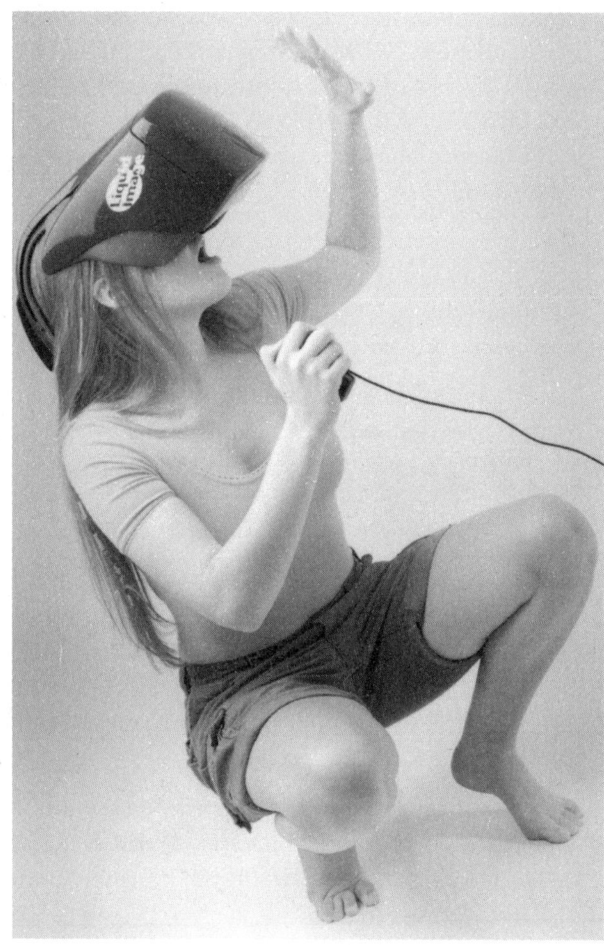

Figure 14.14. Immerse yourself in Cyberspace with the MRG2, a biocular head-mounted display.

The MRG2 is an effective way for you to be immersed in a computer-generated world, or Cyberspace, through the use of a head-mounted display (HMD). The MRG2 has attempted to solve many of the problems that currently plague HMDs such as resolution, picture quality, comfort, field of view, and weight.

The MRG2 is a biocular HMD that uses a 5.7-inch thin film transistor (TFT), active matrix LCD display. It has a resolution of 240×240 pixels, and uses over 16 million colors. The new active matrix system eliminates "ghosting" effects, flicker, and striping. Using new cold cathode backlight, which lasts twice as long as hot cathode backlights, the MRG2 is less subject to breakdown or maintenance.

The MRG2 has a custom-built controller box that accepts video and audio inputs from several different sources and requires no additional add-ons. The controller box will allow for RGB or composite signals, conforming to the NTSC standard, to be input. The signal to the HMD can then be output to an external monitor or projection system for public viewing. The system comes with Sony stereo headphones, Model #MDRV400 digital, to ensure high-quality audio.

The shell provides a horizontal field of view of approximately 85 degrees, slips on and off easily, and is lightweight. The MRG2 comes with a one-year warranty on parts and labor, door-to-door delivery, and a competitive price that includes taxes, delivery, duty, and broker's fees.

Cost: $6,500 (educational and/or volume discounts available)

Tier 1 Visor

Frontier Worlds of Stoughton, Inc.
809 E. South Street
Stoughton, WI 53589
608-873-8523
Fax: 608-877-0575

An HMD with two four-inch LCD screens. The unit was undergoing redesign as we went to press, and details were unavailable.

Cost: $2,400

VIM Personal Viewer

Kaiser Electro-Optics, Inc.
2752 Loker Avenue West
Carlsbad, CA 92008
619-438-9255
Fax: 619-438-6875

The Model 500pv Personal Viewer is a lightweight headset (less than 15 ounces) that looks like a visor. It has a removable, hygienic head mount that can be sterilized and is eyeglasses compatible. The center of gravity is placed just behind the eyes, avoiding the off-balance feeling of some VR helmets and headsets. The Model 500pv was developed using the patented Vision Immersion Module (VIM) technology, which is the same technology that was used in developing the Model 1000pv that runs on high-end workstations.

The Personal Viewer has a 50-degree field of view that uses multiple, tiled, active-matrix LCDs with 232,300 color elements (77,433 color groups). Because the Vision Immersion Module is tiled, the headset provides better angular resolution than conventional optical approaches.

VIM provides an exceptionally large viewing eye box ("VIM Sweet Spot") and long eye relief. It includes built-in Sennheiser 3D stereo headphones, which provide high fidelity sound. It also comes with a built-in intercom.

The Personal Viewer includes a Polhemus sensor to enable head-position tracking, and other sensors are available by special order. The Personal Viewer has a standard 4:3 aspect ratio and uses NTSC 2-channel video input.

Cost: $2,985

Figure 14.15. The VIM personal viewer is great looking, comfortably balanced, and easy to clean—with a removable head mount.

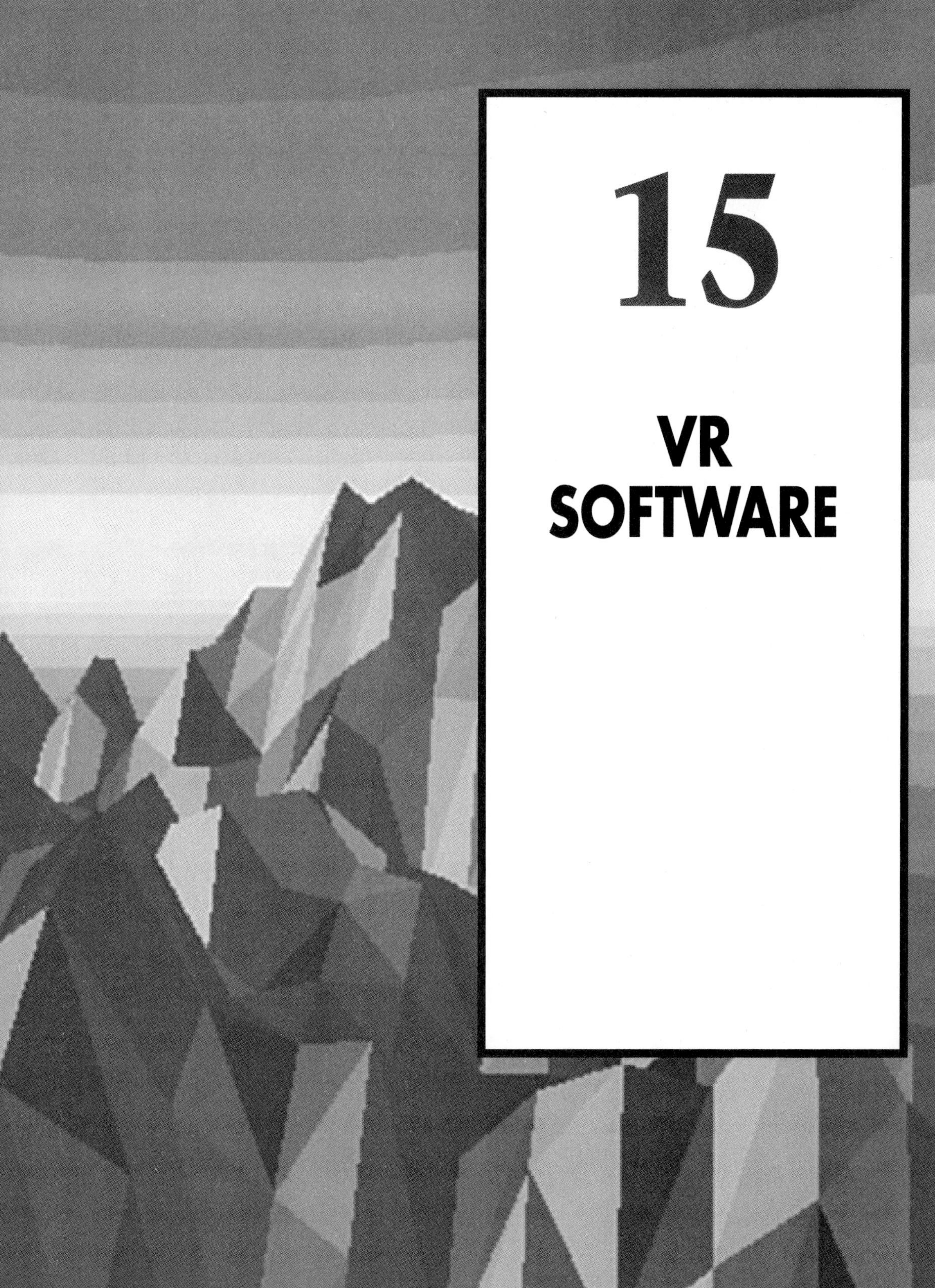

15

VR SOFTWARE

VR-related hardware gets a lot of attention, but software is just as important in developing interesting virtual worlds. Granted, hardware like HMDs and data gloves is impressive, but so are the things you can do on your very own PC with many of the VR software packages included in this chapter.

'Zines, Shareware, and More

One of the best places to begin your search for software that combines the power and price is in the various magazines that feature articles on VR. Some, like *PCVR*, are ideal because they are practically a VR catalog.

We have listed a number of intriguing software products we saw in issues of *PCVR Magazine* in the next section—and many of them are affordable. Other magazines and catalogs to keep an eye out for:

- AI Expert publishes occasional special reports on Virtual Reality. For subscription inquiries, call 800-274-2534 (303-447-9330 in Colorado or outside the United States).
- *CyberEdge Journal* is a VR newsletter that covers news on technological developments, business deals, new products, conferences, book reviews, and other VR-related topics. For information, call 415-331-3343.
- *The Virtual Reality Sourcebook* is a collection of all kinds of VR-related materials, including 3D sound, computer animation, displays, interactive gaming, real-time image generation, etc. It's not cheap at $129 per year, but it is comprehensive. For information, call 800-487-7687.
- CereBel Information Arts publishes the *Complete Guide to VR,* a catalog of VR products. Phone: 617-576-6700.
- Meckler Publishing has two magazines related to VR. *Virtual Reality World* is a monthly magazine dedicated to VR issues, and *Virtual Reality Report* is a newsletter published 10 times a year. Phone: 203-226-6967.
- 3DTV offers an excellent catalog selection of VR software, ranging from high-tech systems to some at amazingly low prices (if budget is your primary concern). A sample of the offerings from 3DTV are listed later in this section. For a catalog, call 415-479-3516. We have been fans of 3DTV for several years because founder Michael Starks is a real VR enthusiast and comes up with some fascinating hardware and software at affordable prices.

The following vendors—PCVR and 3DTV—offer a range of VR products. Several sample products and brief descriptions are listed under each company. For complete product offerings, call and ask for a catalog.

PCVR

PCVR publishes "The Magazine Dedicated to PC-Based Virtual Reality." It features articles on subjects ranging from VR-rendering software like REND386 and VREAM to how to build your own HMD (Head Mounted Display).

PCVR also offers a catalog of affordable virtual reality gear, software, interfaces, and connectors. You can order via phone, fax, or U.S. mail from the address and phone number listed below. Or, e-mail to PCVR@fullfeed.com or VRmag@aol.com. A product listing follows from their Premier Catalog on PC-Based Virtual Reality.

PCVR
P.O. Box 475
Stoughton, WI 53589
608-877-0909

PCVR Magazine

PCVR Magazine is published bimonthly and presents informative articles, projects, tutorials, columns, and up-to-date information about VR hardware and software for PC users.

Cost: \$26 per year in the U.S. and Canada, and \$38 per year for overseas subscribers. You can order back issues for \$4.50 per issue (U.S. and Canada), or \$6.50 per issue (overseas).

REND386

A freeware Virtual Reality rendering system for the PC. REND386 lets you create worlds and interact with them using any number of input devices. The set includes three disks and the complete source code for Versions 4.01 and 5.00.

Cost: \$10 (U.S. and Canada) or \$15 (overseas). Shipping is included.

VREAM

An affordable, complete, off-the-shelf VR system that allows you to create virtual worlds using a mouse. The package includes a 3D world editor that lets you apply textures. VREAM supports a full range of VR equipment, including a standard mouse, joystick, and monitor for desktop Virtual Reality.

Cost: $755, plus shipping, for the basic VREAM development package. (Runtime systems available for world distribution.)

VR Sampler

A five-disk set that includes Virtual Reality demonstration programs, text files, and source code. The majority of files in the set were taken from Internet archive sites and are considered public domain. These files are being offered to help facilitate the flow of information. They include information on Power Gloves, Shutter Glasses, REND386, Virtual Reality Studio, VREAM demo, and so on.

Cost: $20 each, plus shipping (U.S. and Canada)

The Virtual Reality Construction Kit

This is a project book that provides detailed instructions on how to build 18 inexpensive pieces of virtual reality gear. It covers subjects like adapting existing hardware to work on a PC, building your own 3D goggles, motion trackers, 3D sound systems, and more from scratch. The kit includes software to test, calibrate, and run the gear you build.

Cost: $26, plus shipping

3DTV Corporation

3DTV Corporation
Stereoscopic Video
P.O. Box Q
San Rafael, CA 94913-4316
415-479-3516
Fax: 415-479-3316

If you have a burning desire to play with stuff out on the cutting edge of VR but have a limited budget, 3DTV is often your best bet for products. 3DTV does a great job of offering low-cost products that borrow from the leading edge of technology. You won't find a $100 HMD, of course, but you will find stuff that is fun and interesting.

Depth

A software development system that creates stereoscopic (3D) VR software that drives LCD glasses. The software runs on DOS-based PCs with VGA graphics and CRT monitor.

Cost: $125.

Stereo Pro

This is a fun product that is similar to Depth but is intended for viewing stereo pairs of images.

3D Magic

A 3D game for IBM PCs or compatibles with color VGA graphics, CRT monitor, and 2M of free hard disk space. A mouse is essential for playing the game. Includes LCD glasses and parallel or serial interface. The kit includes a variety of stereo images, several interactive stereo demos controllable with cursor keys or mouse, and the game Ricochet.

Cost: $300, $200 without glasses, $90 for software only

3DFLIC

Merges right and left stereo animation in FLI format and drives LCD glasses for stereo viewing. This is a great program if you have the ability to generate FLC files in stereo pairs. Any 3D program that allows you to position a camera and outputs FLC files will work just fine. I used 3D Studio and trueSpace, for example, to generate pairs of FLC files for various kinds of animations. The process is simple:

- Position the camera where you want it to be to observe the animation. Now shift it to the left a small amount (2-5 degrees), and record the animation to an FLC file.
- Reposition the camera to the right a small, matching amount (2-5 degrees from the base position). Record to an FLC file.
- Play the flic files with 3DFlic, using a pair of LCD glasses to view the result in 3D.

For each animation, you will need to experiment to determine the best camera angle for 3D viewing. Rather than waste time generating a complete FLC file, generate a single stereo pair of images, and view it with 3DTV's Stereo Pro, a stereo pair viewer. Adjust the distance between the two camera positions until you get the best 3D effect. Look ahead to figure 15.4 to see how this was done in 3D Studio.

You can also use the Depth program (above) for generating stereo pairs, but 3D modeling and animation packages are your best bet for 3D flics.

Animation

Animator Pro

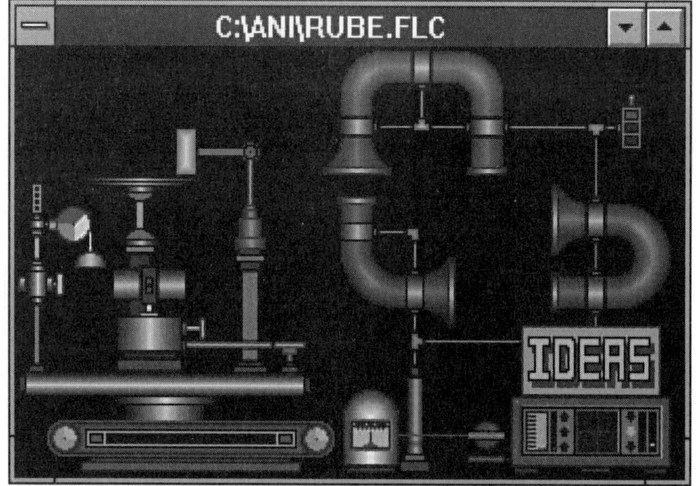

Figure 15.1. An imported sample file from Animator Pro.

Autodesk, Inc.
2320 Marinship Way
Sausalito, CA 94965
800-525-2763
415-332-2344
Fax: 415-491-8303

Autodesk Animator Pro includes extensive paint capabilities for creating the elements you want to animate. All standard 2D animation tools are represented in eight modules, and special effects are available. Overall, Animator Pro is a comprehensive animation tool. Animator Pro has an awkward interface, but the painting tools and animation functions make up for the steep learning curve. Animator Pro runs in protected mode and includes the POCO utility, a C-language-based interpreter that you can use to extend Animator Pro's functions.

System requirements: 386SX-based PC or better, 4M RAM, 11M hard disk space, VGA display or better, DOS 3.3 or higher, and a mouse. If you are working with Windows, make sure that you get version 1.3 of Animator Pro. It adds support for BMP files and Postscript fonts.

Cost: $795 ($659 through IBM Ultimedia Tools Series, 800-887-7771)

trueSpace

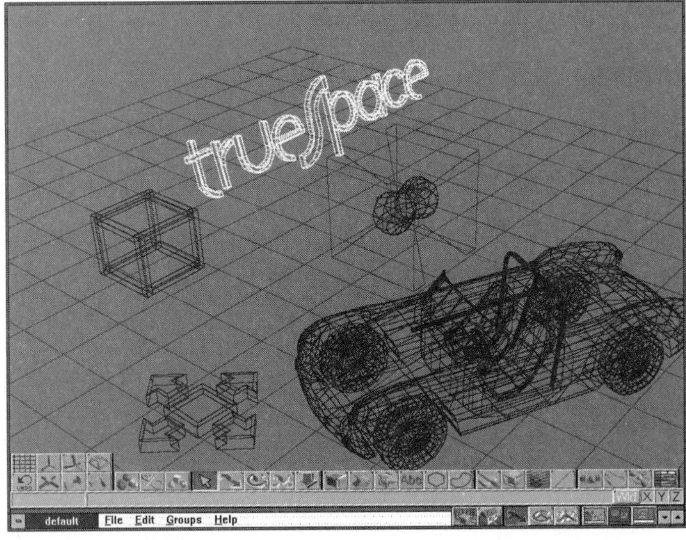

Figure 15.2. Opening screen shot of trueSpace. Notice the menus are at the bottom of the screen. That's intentional, but you can change it.

Caligari Corporation
1955 Landings Drive
Mountain View, CA 94043
415-390-9600
Fax: 415-390-9755

Caligari trueSpace is a 3D modeling, rendering, and animation program for graphic artists, designers, multimedia authors, or video professionals who use Windows. Draw in 3D, paint on surfaces, shape objects like clay, and use real-time preview to direct your characters like actors on a film set. Render final slides or produce video animation at workstation speeds with the touch of a button.

trueSpace allows you to do the following things:

- Work in a perspective-based interface, not in the three-view interface of products like 3D Workshop
- Move objects in real time
- Glue primitives to create more complex objects
- Draw freehand and then sweep shapes into objects

- Create hierarchical objects in two modes: structured (plane, bicycle) and jointed (robot, animal)
- Stretch and squeeze objects during animation
- Assign materials interactively
- Manipulate local and direction lights
- Use textures and bump maps for realistic effects
- Support 3D formats such as DXF, 3D Studio, WaveFront, LightWave, and Imagine
- Import standard image formats like BMP and TGA for texture and bump mapping
- Output BMP, TGA with alpha channel or AVI/Video for Windows

Caligari trueSpace supports output of animations to video tape. You will need a video output card (an encoder) to perform the actual output, and an appropriate VCR for recording. Both real-time and timecode output are supported. The package includes a videotape tutorial.

System requirements: Windows 3.1 or greater, 386 or higher CPU with FPU, 4M or more RAM, 6M free hard disk space.

Imagine 3.0

Impulse, Inc.
6870 Shingle Creek Parkway
Minneapolis, MN 55430
617-566-0221

Imagine, originally an Amiga program, is a bit of an odd duck. It is an extremely powerful 3D animation program, but the interface is difficult to learn and even harder to master. However, if you take the necessary time to learn this program, you can produce some amazing 3D animations. I have used it myself and am impressed with both the difficulty of learning how to use it and the power of its unique interface. If you tend toward the artistic rather than the scientific, you'll do better with this package. However, I think you should also look at Playmation, which offers even better tools for designing 3D animations.

PhotoMorph 2

Figure 15.3.
A warp of the author created in Photomorph 2, in progress.

North Coast Software
P.O. Box 459
265 Scruton Pond Road
Barrington, NH 03825
603-664-6999
Fax: 603-664-7872

PhotoMorph 2 is an extremely well-designed and well-thought-out product. It has a great, easy-to-use interface that will have you morphing and warping quickly, and it also delivers smooth, realistic morph files. You can generate AVI, FLC, or bitmap sequences.

In addition to morphing, PhotoMorph gives you warps, transitions, and storyboards; and it also chains multiple clips. It includes sample 24-bit movies and still images. A runtime version of Video for Windows is supplied so you can distribute your files. PhotoMorph supports the following formats: AVI, GIF, TIFF, Targa, PCX, BMP, JPEG, PICT, and IFF.

Cost: $149.95

Playmation

Hash Enterprises
2800 E. Evergreen Blvd.
Vancouver, WA 98661
206-750-0042
Fax: 206-576-7186

Playmation bears some similarity to products like 3D Studio and Imagine, but only because all these programs enable you to model 3D objects in wire-frame and then render them. Playmation adds some clever and useful twists to the process—sometimes quite literally! For example, Playmation enables you to create spines and muscles for your objects, and you can control them much more easily than with other products. Playmation is thus more of a character animation program—it gives life to whatever you create, from pitchers and airplanes to cartoon characters. Unlike many other 3D rendering/animation products, Playmation uses *patches* and *splines* in place of *polygons*.

Patch—A Surface (curved or flat) defined by three or four splines. A patch can have an infinite number of shapes and curves.

Spline—A curved line defined mathematically and infinitely editable to any degree of curvature.

Polygon—A three-sided flat object. When polygons are combined, they form complex 3D shapes. Rendering capabilities are limited because each polygon is flat, and curved surfaces require tricks to render correctly.

Using patches and splines enables Playmation to generate more realistic shapes more quickly. They also enable you to define complex animated behaviors with minimal effort. The addition of spines and skeletal hierarchies gives you even more modeling power.

As with any 3D modeling program, you should expect to spend some time learning how to apply Playmation's techniques—3D modeling is a complex art. The hardest part of 3D animation, in fact, is creating good-looking characters/objects. However, once you have applied your artistic talents to creating them, you will find that animating them is remarkably easy.

3D Studio, Release 3

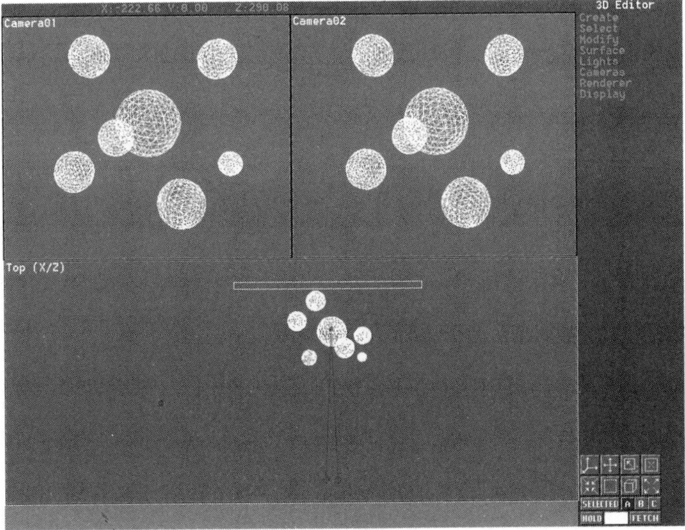

Figure 15.4. Four views of a sample object.

Autodesk, Inc.
2320 Marinship Way
Sausalito, CA 94965
800-525-2763
415-332-2344
Fax: 415-491-8303

3D Studio is the top of the line when it comes to 3D imaging—its latest version offers stunning realism. It also enables you to animate the objects in a 3D scene in complex ways using a wide variety of tools. 3D Studio is a professional product in every respect (including price). However, if you are serious about animation, there aren't too many programs that compete. In many ways, 3D Studio is about as much fun as you can have with a computer. The interface is complex and therefore complete, but count on taking some serious time to learn your way around.

3D Studio's strength is in what I'll call architectural realism—if you can do it as an engineering drawing, 3D Studio is ideal. If you are interested more in organic objects and animation, you can probably force 3D Studio to do what you want, but a product like Playmation might be better for your needs.

Cost: $2,995

vrTrader for Windows

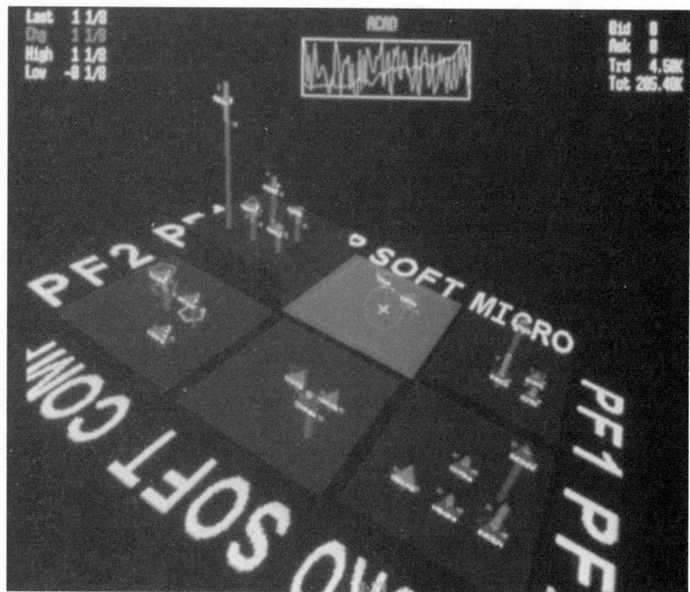

Figure 15.5. View of virtual reality Trader, a stock market visualization product built with AmberC++.

Avatar Partners
13090 Central Avenue, Suite 3
Boulder Creek, CA 95006
408-338-6460
Fax: 408-338-6462

Virtual Reality 3D software for Windows that tracks financial markets for subscribers to Data Broadcasting Corporation's (DBC) PC-based Signal quote service. Avatar's vrTrader software uses DBC's Signal receiver box to receive real-time data from one of three DBC networks: FM radio, direct satellite, or the vertical blanking interval of several cable TV networks. Using vrTrader under Windows, a subscriber can view up to 300 stocks from a choice of over 9,500 from the NYSE, AMEX, and NASDAQ exchanges.

The software presents stock-market data as 3D objects with graphics and text around them. Stocks are projected onto a matrix that resembles a three-dimensional football field, with each security represented by a color-coded pole coming out of the ground. The color and behavior of each stock object dynamically indicates a buying or selling opportunity. Each pole can grow, spin, blink, or emit a sound that indicates the movement of that security. The software further updates related factors, such as when stock reaches a certain price, or when news about the stock is released. The software supports both real-time and delayed (15 minute) quotes. You can assign visual thresholds and auditory alerts to monitor each stock's volume and price.

System requirements: 386, 486, or Pentium-based system with Microsoft Windows. Audio alerts require an optional sound card. 8M of RAM. DBC's Signal receiver and quotation subscription service are also required.

Cost: $495 for Windows software; data receiver and subscription services sold separately.

Virtual Environment Navigator

Figure 15.6. Pick wand in Navigator is attached to red box, which lets you move objects. In this example, you could move the water tower in Boynton Beach, Florida model city, and put it anywhere.

MicronGreen, Inc.
1240 N.W. 21st Ave.
Gainesville, FL 32069
904-376-1529
Fax: 904-376-0466

The Navigator is a software tool that brings real-time interactive simulations of 3D worlds to the DOS platform. It is designed for PC AutoCAD 3D modelers but accepts DXF or 3DS files. The Navigator supports a wide range of peripherals and you can begin experiencing Virtual Environments with just a monitor, keyboard, and a mouse. Later, you can upgrade to high-end HMDs and 6D motion sensors.

Virtual hand tools—which can be used from a mouse, joystick, or 6D sensors—are included with the system for interactively manipulating worlds. You can use these tools to change colors, objects, and lights as you move your hand; or fly around using both head and hand movements.

Object animations allow you to define ongoing or selective activities. The Navigator includes several utilities, such as an external ray-tracing renderer for high quality images of finished environments. And you can use worlds created in the Navigator by other CAD and animation packages as final output to stills or videos.

Real-world applications in the past have been military and aviation. However, the Navigator will open new opportunities for architects, interior designers, engineers, manufacturers, and educators. The Navigator can be used by architects and engineers for design and presentations, as well as for simulated experiences for non-technical users.

This package requires no programming experience and can run as a standalone or as an ADS application inside AutoCAD.

System requirements: 386/486 PCs (486 recommended), and 8M RAM (10M recommended). 10M available disk space, DOS 3.3 or higher, mouse or tablet and joystick, VESA VGA (local bus preferred).

Optional support is available for SPEA Fire Boards, Division Boards, or any graphics board with an ADI 4.2 3D compliant driver. Also supports CrystalEyes Stereo Eyewear and HMDs, Polhemus and Logitech 6D sensors (Sapphire, Matrox, Artist, and Pellucid boards are under development).

Cost: $1,495

Vistapro 3.0

Virtual Reality Laboratories, Inc.
2341 Ganador Ct.
San Luis Obispo, CA 93401
805-545-8515
Fax: 805-781-2259

Vistapro is one of those programs that is simultaneously extremely different from anything else you've seen, and perfectly done. Vistapro enables you to create lush, detailed landscapes that literally take your breath away. I made a special effort to put some sample landscapes on the CD-ROM. You also can purchase some add-on products, such as Flight Director, to create animations that simulate flying or driving through a landscape.

This is absolutely addictive, must-have software. You can get a simplified version of the software with this book.

CD-ROM Libraries

ImageCEL CD-ROM

Figure 15.7. Left: A 3D model of a home rendered without fancy textures (or good lighting!). Right: the same 3D model rendered with textures from the ImageCEL CD-ROM.

Imagetects
P.O. Box 4
Saratoga, CA 95071
408-252-5487
Fax: 408-252-7409

A royalty-free library of 1,150 seamless photorealistic, high-resolution texture maps, full-screen backgrounds, and images used to create realistic virtual worlds. Consists of building materials, environmental objects, designer patterns, landscaping, and industrial finishes. Has 14 multiplatform file formats in 8-, 16-, and 24-bit for PCs, Macintosh, UNIX, and Amiga on one ISO-9660 formatted CD-ROM. Color photo index is included.

Cost: $495

ImageCELs' Designer Package

Contains more than 900 photo-realistic images and seamless texture maps. The Designer Package, which is a subset of ImageCELs' CD-ROM, is available in 16-bit TGA file format for PCs, includes a color photo flipchart index, and is used in conjunction with graphics software. The Designer Package is royalty-free.

Cost: $395

ImageCELs' VGA CD-ROM

Contains 240 seamless, photo-realistic texture maps, full-screen backgrounds, and landscape images in 10 multiplatform 9-bit file formats for PCs, Macintosh, UNIX, and Amiga. The VGA CD-ROM is designed for all VR applications, is royalty free, and dual formatted with ISO-9660 and System 7 HFS.

Cost: $99

ImageCELs' VGA Library PC/Mac

A royalty-free library of 180 seamless, photo-realistic, high-resolution texture maps to enhance virtual world design. Installs texture maps to enhance virtual world design. Installs as PCX or TGA files for PCs, and TIFF for Macintosh users. The VGA library offers on-screen icons for the Macintosh version and comes with a color photo flipchart index. This package is a subset of ImageCELs' VGA CD-ROM and ImageCELs' CD-ROM. Upgrades are available.

Cost: $99

ImageCELs' Botanicals

Real trees and shrubs for virtual worlds. ImageCELs' Botanicals are high-resolution, photo-realistic plant materials from all regions. 32-bit TGA files with Alpha channel. ImageCELs Botanicals are available individually through DesigNetwork, an online service: 202-686-2373.

Cost: $10 each, quantity discounts available

Educational

Control System/Control Lab

Figure 15.8. LEGO Dacta's Control System, which turns your computer into a hands-on science and math lab.

LEGO Dacta
555 Taylor Road
P.O. Box 1600
Enfield, CT 06083-1600
800-527-8339
203-749-2291
Fax: 302-763-2466

LEGO Dacta, the educational division of the LEGO Group, distributes computerized LEGO sets. In 1993, they introduced Control Lab, which teaches hands-on technology with computers. LEGO Dacta developed Control Lab in response to a growing movement away from traditional shop classes to technology education in the schools. The Control Lab combines LEGO bricks with a Macintosh or MS-DOS computer, a special version of the Logo programming language, and technology curriculum materials for grades 7 through 12.

With Control Lab, students can build things like a temperature-controlled greenhouse, a pick-and-place robot arm, a motorized vertical lift bridge, a motorized car and dynamometer, and a color code reader. Once the model is built, students write a program to control it. For instance, they can program the greenhouse door to open and close, depending on the temperature inside the greenhouse.

Control Lab models and programming address the important technology concepts of manufacturing, bio-related technology, communication, construction, and transportation. The computer controls the models through an interface box connected to a serial port. Teacher and student guides, reference guides, and setup guides are all included with the Control Lab starter pack.

In 1994 LEGO Dacta released the Control System, which is a product that integrates science and math for the upper elementary grades (7 through 12). The Control System combines LEGO elements with a Macintosh or MS-DOS computer, and a special version of the Logo programming language.

Students can use the Control System to build their own data-collecting models and control them with a computer. For example, they can use the computer to control the motion of a motorized vehicle. Then they use data collected by an angle sensor on the vehicle to determine the average speed.

The Control System concentrates on exploration, investigation, and invention activities in the science concept area of linear motion (distance time and average speed). Also included are activities for work, power, energy, and for generation of electricity. Mathematics-related concepts include computation, estimation, measurement, graphing, and pattern recognition.

Cost: $450, Control System Starter Pack (includes building elements, step-by-step building instructions, computer interface box, sensors, software, and curriculum materials); $599, Control Lab Starter Pack.

Entertainment

Beyond the Mind's Eye

Miramar
200 Second Avenue West
Seattle, WA 98119-4204
206-284-4700
Fax: 206-286-4433

Miramar produces a series of computer animation videos that combine musical scores with visual settings and animation. Miramar uses a unique approach to creating their videos. They start with a storyboard of a particular visual topic, like the sun, and then write music to fit. Miramar then finds more visuals to fit the music. This approach is time-consuming, and production can take anywhere from three months to a year.

The first video album, *Natural States*, was a nature video that featured scenic views of the Northwest, as well as forest scenes from Big Sur in Northern California. The music for this video was provided by Paul Speer and David Lanz. The next two nature videos were *Desert Vision*, filmed in the Southwest desert and in 10 U.S. parks; and *Canyon Dreams*, which explored the Grand Canyon. Tangerine Dream provided the musical score for the *Canyon Dreams* video; they also contributed to the score of *True North*, which was filmed entirely in Alaska and was nominated for a Grammy award.

Miramar also produces *The Mind's Eye* and *Beyond the Mind's Eye*, which are outstanding computer animated videos. *Beyond the Mind's Eye* offers state-of-the-art computer graphics to the music of Jan Hammer. Their newest video, *Imaginaria*, is a computer animation music video for children, with original music produced by Gary Powell. It offers an imaginative journey to 15 worlds with ships, trains, and cartoon characters.

Cost: Contact vendor (ranges from $14.95 to $19.98 each)

Virtual Adventures

Figure 15.9. Capsule in the Loch Ness Expedition.

Iwerks Entertainment
4540 W. Valerio St.
Burbank, CA 91505
818-840-6133
Fax: 818-841-7847

Virtual Adventures is an advanced VR ride that offers an immersive experience using real-time computer graphics to create a 3D world without the use of a helmet. Each of the vehicles in the ride contain a 3D, digital-audio system that delivers sound effects in real-time in sync with each vehicle's movements. The imagery is rear projected onto the ship's large 3D video display screen. Passengers wear polarized glasses, which permit stereoscopic three-dimensional viewing of high resolution graphics. A spatial, four-channel sound system surrounds the players, which enhances their sense of being immersed in this virtual reality. Players use all these audio-visual cues to navigate through the real world and manipulate it.

The first attraction features *The Loch Ness Expedition*. Six players enter an enclosed "submersible" capsule, and each of the players riding in the vehicle are assigned a specific task during the underwater expedition. The goal of the crew is to work as a team to save the eggs of the endangered Loch Ness monster from evil bounty hunters and hungry prehistoric prey. The outcome of the journey depends on the actions of each member and the crews in the other vehicles.

The commander is stationed at a computer map of the entire Loch, equipped with an intercom to communicate with other vessels. He also has touch screen controls that execute a variety of functions. Two periscope operators can view the Loch through 360-degree periscopes, so they can scout for bounty hunters or creatures lying in wait ahead or behind. Two robotic arm operators control the "hands" of the ship, which are used to retrieve the Loch Ness monster's eggs. The arm and periscope operators also are responsible for defending the ship by shooting an immobilizing gel at any hazards. The pilot steers the ship using aircraft-like controls to maneuver the ship through a continuously changing environment. The ship can navigate around, over, under, and through myriad objects in the virtual world.

The goal of Iwerks Entertainment and Evans & Sutherland, the ride's creators, was to offer an alternative to combat-based attractions. The players work in collaboration with passengers in another vehicle as they compete with two other groups, which makes the experience both competitive and cooperative. While Virtual Adventures will rouse a player's competitive spirit, it does not depend on violence as a prime motivator.

The Virtual Adventures vehicle was designed as a multipurpose control platform, and the attraction can be re-themed with new software. It can be transformed into a submarine, a spaceship, aircraft, or subterranean vehicle that goes beneath the earth's surface. The possibility for new adventures is limitless, exploring different periods of time, as well as different places.

Fun and Games

Blake Stone

Figure 15.10. British military agent Blake Stone in a life-and-death struggle with the forces of evil.

Apogee Software
P.O. Box 496389
Garland, TX 75049
800-GAME-123

From the company that gave you Wolfenstein 3D, this is another shareware game in which you are the British military agent, Blake Stone, in deadly combat against a malevolent scientist, Dr. Goldfire, and the insidious mutant army under his command. Dr. Goldfire, driven by insanity and bent on annihilating mankind, won't rest until he rules the known universe. The game is rated PC-13 and is not recommended for younger viewers due to realistic depictions of violence.

Blake Stone uses 3D texture mapping in 256 colors. It makes use of diminished lighting effects and movie-like animations and effects, such as liquid aliens that slither along the floor and rise to strike, or electro-aliens that emerge from wall-mounted sockets. It includes a built-in auto-mapping feature so you can see where you've been. The game includes over 20 different guards, aliens, mutants, and bosses, and you can choose from five futuristic weapons—from silent-shot to grenade launcher. It includes AdLib and Sound Blaster digital stereo sound effects and intense, action-oriented theme music. There are 60 main levels, plus many secret levels. The game comes with a manual and 11-page Blake Stone comic book.

System requirements: Minimum system configuration requires an IBM or 100-percent compatible computer 25 MHz 386, 640K RAM, 8M of free hard disk space, and a VGA graphics card.

Cost: $59.95, plus $5 shipping and handling

Blake Stone and the following Apogee Games are but a few that are available. Call Apogee for a copy of their catalog.

Halloween Harry

Figure 15.11. Halloween Harry: the only thing between you and an evil army of slobbering zombies.

Alien invaders are blasting New York City, shattering city blocks, and turning its inhabitants into an evil army of slobbering zombies. As Halloween Harry, you must penetrate the alien warrens, free the hostages, and find the invaders' buried mothership.

The game includes parallax scrolling graphics in 256 colors, digital music, and Sound Blaster effects. Duke Nukem fans will love this game.

Cost: $29 95 plus shipping and handling

Duke Nukem II

Figure 15.12. Duke Nukem is back in action!

Duke Nukem, the world's most ruthless warrior, has been abducted by aliens. He must escape the SuperMega EncephaloSucker and battle to end the hideous plans of the evil Rigelatins. Confused? Good—the game is more interesting that way.

The game uses parallaxing VGA graphics, AdLib music, and digitized sound effects for Sound Blaster or compatible cards. There are 32 levels and four episodes.

Cost: $34.95, plus shipping and handling

Raptor

Figure 15.13. You are a mercenary in the Mega-Corps. You know what you have to do, and have the arsenal and guts to do it.

You are a mercenary in the Mega Corps, with turbine-powered engines and wing cannons to defeat the enemy.

Raptor supports 256-color graphics and cinematic sequences for 27 levels of intense combat. It supports AdLib, Sound Blaster, Roland, Gravis Ultra Sound, and Pro Audio Spectrum 16 sound cards. You can use a mouse, joystick, Thrustmaster, or a Gravis game pad.

Cost: $34.95, plus shipping and handling.

Bio Menace

Figure 15.14. Super agent Lake Logan fights to save the world from Dr. Mangle's mutants.

Doctor Mangle is intent on ruling the world with an army of mutants released from his laboratory. You are Snake Logan, super agent and weapons expert, fighting to save the world from a fate worse than death.

The game offers colorful, smooth scrolling graphics, multiple high-powered weapons, and AdLib music and sound effects. The game has three levels of skill, ranging from novice to pro.

Cost: $29.95, plus shipping and handling

Word Rescue

Figure 15.15. Helping Benny Bookworm retrieve words stolen by the Gruzzles.

Benny Bookworm needs your help to stop the mean ol' Gruzzles. They can't read, and they don't want anyone else to, either. So they've stolen the words out of all our books! Benny needs you to help rescue the stolen words with their meanings, and he will put them back into the books.

Word Rescue has multilevel adventures with 330 words to rescue. Skill levels are based on age. Play the game as a boy or girl! Learn reading, word spelling, word meanings, and logic solving. The game comes with AdLib and Sound Blaster music, save/restore functions, joystick support, built-in help, a high score list, and more.

System requirements: 80286+ PC and EGA/VGA adapter; joystick and Adlib/Sound Blaster card optional.

Cost: $29.95, plus shipping and handling. ($55 for both Math Rescue and Word Rescue.)

Math Rescue

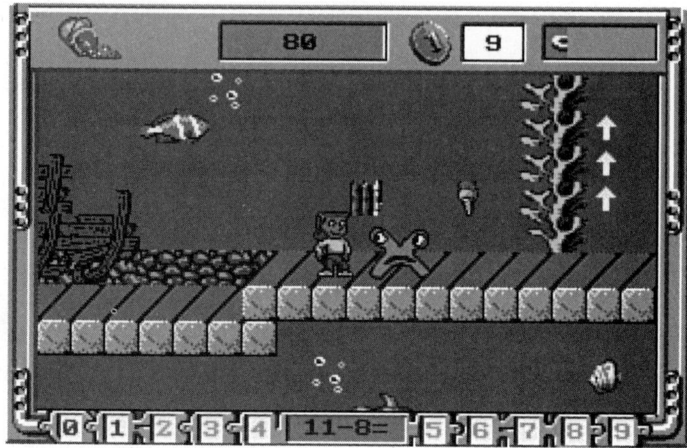

Figure 15.16. More fun with the mean ol' Gruzzles.

A bone-chilling crisis has struck the world. Reports are pouring in from all corners of the globe: Missing numbers! Drivers are in peril because the speed limit signs have gone blank. You try to call your best friend, but the buttons on your phone are blank!

This madness can only be the work of...the Gruzzles. You tangled with them in Word Rescue. Now the Gruzzles are taking all the numbers, and it's up to you to get them back.

This educational software is fun to play, as a boy or girl character! Learn the four arithmetic functions: add, subtract, multiply, and divide. Includes AdLib and Sound Blaster music, save/restore, joystick support, built-in help, high score list, etc.

System requirements: 80286+ PC and EGA/VGA adapter; joystick and Adlib/Sound Blaster card optional.

Cost: $29.95, plus shipping and handling (or order both for $55)

DOOM Version 1.2

Figure 15.17. It's DOOMSday: let the game begin.

id Software
c/o Star Pak
P.O. Box 1230
Greeley, CO 80632
800-IDGAMES (800-434-2637)
Fax: 303-330-7553

Shareware virtual reality action game, consisting of DOOM Trilogy: *Knee-Deep in the Dead, The Shores of Hell*, and the *Inferno*. The object of the game is to shoot your way through a monster-infested holocaust, living to tell the tale, if possible. The game is action-oriented, and requires brains and a killer instinct in order to escape.

You use the keyboard, mouse, or joystick to navigate through the corridors or to fire your weapons. At first, you may run into walls or objects, but it doesn't take long to learn to move smoothly. You open doors and operate switches by pressing the space bar. The game includes locked doors that require a color-coded security card or skull key to open hidden doors, elevators, and teleporters.

You can load or save games at any time during gameplay, or use the quicksave feature without interrupting your game. Messages are displayed at the top of the screen during the game and can be toggled on and off. You can adjust the screen detail from high to low if the action is too jerky, and you can adjust the screen size as well. There is also an Automap device to help you find your way around DOOM.

There are seven different weapons for you to use, and you pick up ammunition and weapons as you play. You pick up items by walking over them. You can also replenish your health and armor.

System requirements: IBM-compatible 386 or better with 4M of RAM, a VGA graphics card, and a hard disk drive. Recommended configuration is a 486 or better, and a Sound Blaster Pro or 100-percent compatible sound card. Network game players require a network that uses IPX protocol.

Cost: $40, plus shipping and handling.

Myst

Figure 15.18. A scene from Myst.

Broderbund
500 Redwood Blvd.
Novato, CA 94948-6121
415-382-4600

Myst is a surrealistic adventure game that takes you on a journey to an island world that is full of mystery. The game includes a Journal in which you are encouraged to record every scrap of evidence you find, no matter how insignificant it may appear. The clues may be a rock, a scrap of paper, or a sound. You are encouraged to combine keen observation and logic to unlock the secrets of Myst.

An earlier inhabitant of the island discovered many fantastic worlds, which are being destroyed by someone's greed. You are encouraged to use your wits and imagination to uncover the betrayer.

The game lets you walk through 3D photorealistic graphics, and includes an original soundtrack with sound effects and music that enhance the sense of realism. You are able to experience a first-person point of view with no windows or controls to distract you. If you want to zip from one place to another, simply place your cursor at the top of the screen to access a hidden menu. You can easily save or load a game, or use any of the other features of the menu—and you determine when to display the menu.

System requirements: IBM/Tandy PC or 100-percent compatible, 386DX 33MHz processor or higher (486 recommended), 4M of RAM, Windows 3.1, MS/PC-DOS 5.0 or higher, Super VGA graphics card (640×480, 256 colors), MPC-compliant sound card, mouse, hard disk with 4M free space, CD-ROM drive.

Return to Zork

Figure 15.19. A scene from Zork.

ActiVision
P.O. Box 67713
Los Angeles, CA 90067
312-207-4500

An epic adventure game in the Great Underground Empire. The game combines several elements found in an adventure game: exploration, meeting interesting characters, scavenger hunting, puzzle solving, and the gradual revelation of a compelling story in which you play the central character.

The object is to navigate through this unknown world, gathering clues along the way. You must look at, listen to, and read everything presented to you. Pick up objects along the way, examine them closer, show them to characters you meet, and try combining them in new and unusual ways. You will be able to solve problems by experimenting and trying new things.

But be careful; you may die or be killed at any time. For this reason, it is wise to save your adventure often. You can start up where you left off at any time. If you try something that doesn't work, you can always go back and try something else.

Get your friends or family to help puzzle out a problem if you reach a dead end. Everyone has a different approach to problem solving, and our family has a lot of fun sharing our solutions to a tricky situation. Enjoy!

SimCity 2000

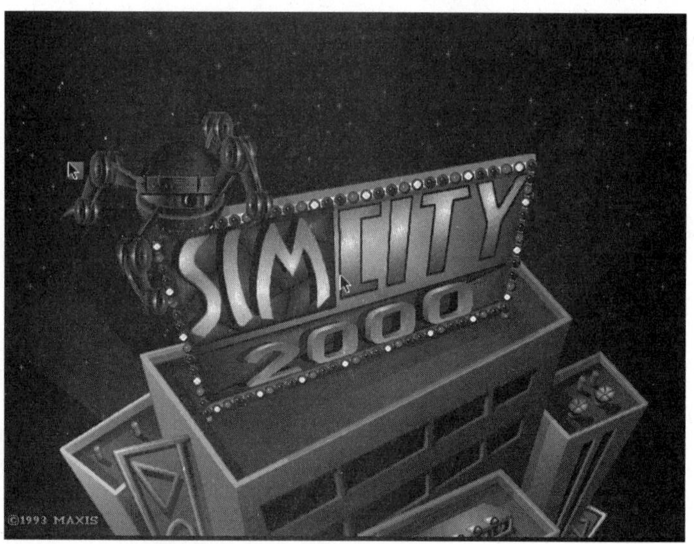

Figure 15.20. A city created with SimCity 2000.

Maxis
Two Theater Square, Ste. 230
Orinda, CA 94563-3041
510-254-9700

With SimCity, you can govern your own city, determine zoning and road construction, and build houses and parks. You become the planner, designer, and mayor. Take over and run any of the included scenario cities, or build your own from the ground up.

One of your biggest challenges is to maintain a huge city without sacrificing the Sims' quality of life, without going broke maintaining the infrastructure, and without raising taxes so high that businesses relocate. Think you can do a better job than the politicians? Prove it!

Or you can destroy your cities, using bulldozers or natural disasters, such as tornadoes, earthquakes, fire, flood, or even monsters.

On-Line Services

CyberForum

CompuServe Inc.
5000 Arlington Centre Blvd.
Columbus, OH 43220
800-848-8199
614-457-8650

The CompuServe Information Service provides online information services for personal computer users worldwide. To access CompuServe, you need a PC, a terminal or communicating word processor, a modem (connects the computer to the telephone), communications software, and a telephone. CompuServe Mail lets members send and receive messages 24 hours a day. An upload feature lets you compose messages offline and send files from a personal computer. CompuServe Mail provides links to AT&TMail, AT&T Easylink, MCI Mail, and Internet, which is an electronic mail system linking government institutions, military branches, educational institutions, and commercial companies. The cost for sending or reading an Internet message is 15 cents for the first 7,500 characters and 5 cents for each additional 2,500 characters.

CompuServe's special interest forums, such as CyberForum, provide members with three means of communication:

- Via a message board on which you can post messages, ask questions, carry on discussions, and list items you'd like to learn more about
- Through libraries, which contain software and information files that can be downloaded
- By means of the online conference capability that allows you to communicate with other members in real-time by typing messages on your computer keyboard

When you initially sign on, leave a message for the *sysop* (system operator). The sysop can direct you to special Help files that can be downloaded to help new members get the most out of the forum. For example, if you are new to the CyberForum, be sure you get the file WHATVR.ZIP in Lib 3, which includes a text file called "What is VR?" by Jerry Isdale.

Other forums relating to virtual reality are the Autodesk Software Forum (ASOFT), Gamers Forum (GAMERS), Graphics Developers Forum (GRAPHDEV), Graphics Vendor Forum (GRAPHVEN), The Absolut Museum (ABS)—which is free, and the Computer Art Forum (COMART). COMART and GRAPHDEV have some great computer-generated images.

One of the biggest benefits from using a forum is the ability to access the collection of public domain software and shareware available to CompuServe members. Members are encouraged to share programs with other forum members and are not charged when uploading a program to the forum.

Cost: $8.95/month, Standard Pricing Plan (waived first month of membership); $2.50/month plus connect-time and network-access charges, Alternative Pricing Plan. Note: If you use CompuServe more than half an hour a month, it is more cost effective to use the basic services with the Standard Pricing Plan.

Diaspar Virtual Reality Network

Diaspar Virtual Reality Network
424 Glenneyre
Laguna Beach, CA 92651
714-831-1776
Fax: 714-499-3449

Diaspar offers on-line electronic mail, conferencing, and talk/chat facilities that include a no-charge multimedia communications program called Dmodem. Virtual Networks, or on-line offices, can be rented by geographically distributed groups.

Cost: $10 per month subscription fee; $5 a month minimum for Virtual Network

Resource Guides

Explore the Realm of Virtual Reality

CAD Institute
4100 E. Broadway
Phoenix, AZ 85040
800-658-5744
602-437-0405

A complete video/seminar program that includes two video cassette tapes, a curriculum workbook, and a Virtual Reality Resource Guide. Contact the CAD Institute for further details—we were unable to review these materials personally.

Cost: Introductory price of $149

VR Authoring Systems

PhotoVR

Figure 15.21. Furnished office in a virtual reality building.

StrayLight Corp.
150 Mt. Bethel Rd.
Warren, NJ 07059
908-580-0086
Fax: 908-580-0092

PhotoVR is a PC-based, interactive, 3D, walk-through software package. It is a menu-driven application that imports files directly from Autodesk's 3D Studio or AutoCAD/AutoShade design products. It is capable of displaying real-time views of complex scenes in excess of 100,000 polygons that show textures, colors, reflections, shadows, multiple lights, procedural textures, bump maps, and numerous other rendering attributes. Straylight also offers PhotoVR in a run-time system that has all the capabilities of the full system, except that you can't create new environments.

PhotoVR provides support for HMDs, video tape recorders, NTSC, and VGA monitors. Input devices include Logitech 6D, SpaceBall, Polhemus Isotrak, Ascension Bird, Trackball, Joystick, and Mouse. PhotoVR supports a wide variety of output devices such as VGA and 15.75 khz, a flat screen monitor or projection system, or one of several popular head-mounted displays. You can add an NTSC encoder to make PhotoVR video ready.

System requirements: PC equipped with 386/25 or above with a 387 numeric processor, or 486SX with an Intel numeric processor. The PhotoVR run-time system will run with 1M of RAM, but the precalculation process may require more RAM. DOS 4.01 or greater and a Microsoft compatible mouse.

Cost: starts at $995

Cybertron

A new VR arcade game created with Straylight's PhotoVR software. Participants are strapped into a gyro wheel 7.5 feet in diameter that resembles the one shown in the movie *The Lawnmower Man*. The game uses a head-mounted display that immerses people in various VR scenarios that were created with the PhotoVR software. The arcade game is bundled with one game, which is a single-user version, although networked versions are expected at a later time.

Cost: $54,000

Superscape VRT3

Dimension International
Zephyr One, Calleva Park
Aldermaston, Berkshire RG7 4QZ ENGLAND
44-734-810077
Fax: 44-734-816940

Provides both a graphical environment for object and world creation, and a lower level C library. Superscape is super in every sense of the word—it has great tools, it can mimic most aspects of reality (from gravity to friction), and it allows you to program motion and interactivity for objects in your world. It's also very expensive, so it's not for everyone. If you have the budget, however, you can create some very sophisticated models. See Chapter 5 for detailed information about Superscape.

Cost: £3,450, plus run-time distribution fees

Superscape Networks

An upgrade/extension to Superscape VRT3 that facilitates creation of networked virtual worlds.

Cost: £2,950

Superscape Developer's Kit

Optional extension to Superscape VRT3 for interfacing virtual worlds with third-party devices, applications, or data.

Cost: £5,950

Superscape Visualizer

An integrated software system that supports networked virtual worlds and applications written with Superscape Developer's Kit.

Cost: £650

Virtual Reality Studio Version 2.0

Domark Software Inc.
1900 S. Norfolk St., #202
San Mateo, CA 94403
415-513-8929
Fax: 415-571-0437

A low-cost VR authoring system that lets you design and manipulate your own virtual worlds. Uses a graphic interface and simple scripting language, which simplifies the process of creating or editing objects. VRS 2.0 includes a paint program, sound effects, animation program, and clip-art library. Use the VCR playback function to create a movie, and play it back in slow motion or fast forward—or do a fly-through. Spheres and flexicubes are available; you just point and click. VRS 2.0 includes 2D bitmaps, including sprites and animation cells.

Cost: $99.95

Virtus WalkThrough for Windows

Virtus Corp.
117 Edinburgh St., Suite 204
Cary, NC 27511
919-467-9700
Fax: 919-460-4530

Virtus WalkThrough is a drawing and design package that provides an object-oriented, real-time, 3D graphics environment. WalkThrough for Windows allows PC users to "walk through" their ideas on projects like interior remodeling, factory floor layout, trade show booth planning, theater set design, product displays, and animated client presentations. Virtus WalkThrough has also been used for film storyboarding and was employed in the development of major motion pictures such as *The Abyss* and *The Firm*. Assisted by computer technology consultant Frank Dutro, director Sydney Pollack used Virtus WalkThrough to plan each day's shots, develop sets, and pre-visualize individual scenes for *The Firm* in order to make decisions about lighting, camera angles, movement, space design, and other production and creative issues.

Virtus WalkThrough uses a tool palette from which you can select specific drawing and editing tools, and a drawing window where the tools are used to create and edit two-dimensional object outlines. The Walk View window automatically displays a 3D version of the 2D object outlines from the drawing window. You can use the mouse to view these 3D objects from any angle, inside or outside, or you can walk through the 3D design in real-time. You can record your movements in the 3D environment, which can be saved with the model and played back at a later time.

WalkThrough for Windows offers the capability to export the recorded walk path to the Animator Pro presentation format, so it can be integrated into multimedia productions. WalkThrough supports import options 2D DXF, 3D DXF, and BMP (trace layer option) so you can combine 3D models with other graphics packages, or view objects created in other packages. It provides export/SnapShot options like 2D DXF, 3D DXF, BMP, EPS, Illustrator 1.1, BMP, and TIFF so you can combine your 3D models with other graphics and CAD packages.

System requirements: IBM/PC or compatible with 386/486/Pentium with 4M RAM, VGA monitor, and Microsoft Windows version 3.1 or later. Recommended system is 486/33+ with 8M+ RAM.

Cost: Virtus WalkThrough for Windows, $195; for Macintosh, $495

Virtus VR

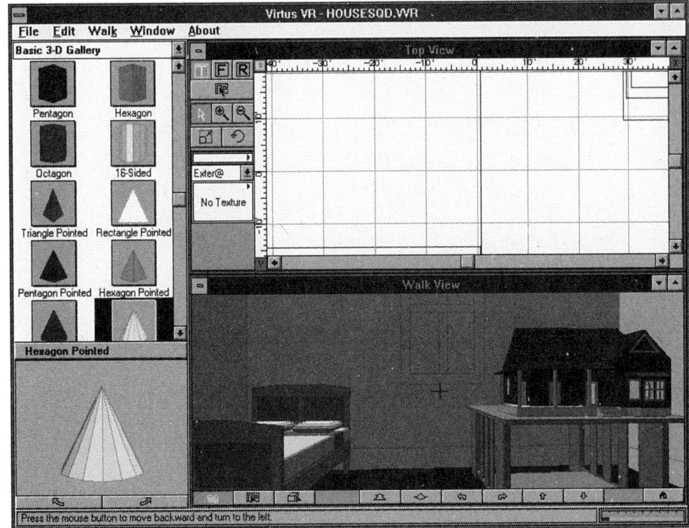

Figure 15.22. A scene from Virtus VR of a house within a house.

A consumer, entertainment-oriented software package that includes six VR scenes; a gallery of sample three-dimensional objects; and tools that let you explore, alter, model, and invent 3D environments. Virtus VR comes with five prefab worlds: the White House, a futuristic ocean floor apartment and research complex, the Hindenberg blimp, a mystery house (within a house, within another house...), and Dealey Plaza—site of John F. Kennedy's assassination.

You can select real-world objects from Virtus VR's galleries and add them to these scenes. The galleries are displayed as 3D icons, which can be dragged into the 3D scene. Virtus VR automatically sizes the object, making it the right proportion for the current environment. Or create your own worlds from scratch using Virtus VR's basic building blocks like cubes, squares, and pyramids. For complex models, however, use Virtus's high-level product, Virtus WalkThrough.

System requirements: 80368-based (or later) personal computer, 4M RAM, VGA or SuperVGA display adapter, Microsoft Windows 3.1. Recommended configuration: 80486-based (or later) PC, 8M+ RAM, VGA or SVGA display adapter, Microsoft Windows 3.1.

Cost: Virtus VR, $99; Virtus VR upgrade to WalkThrough for Windows, $69

Virtus also distributes add-ons, which contain additional sites and object galleries. Each add-on package includes five worlds and over 100 objects. The first two add-ons include a gallery of homes and a science fiction gallery. Sample homes include a mountain retreat, a beach house, a country club estate, and a model of Frank Lloyd Wright's Pope-Leighy House. The add-on also includes a gallery of rooms: a bathroom, kitchen, living room, bedroom, and basement. Scenes from the science fiction gallery include a lunar penitentiary, a space colony, and a Mount Rushmore from the future that lets you look inside the heads of Presidents Nixon, Carter, Reagan, and Clinton.

Cost: $39 each

VREAM Virtual Reality Development System

Figure 15.23. Inside the living room of a virtual house.

VREAM Inc.
2568 N. Clark Street, Suite 250
Chicago, IL 60614
312-477-0425
Fax: 312-477-9702

An off-the-shelf VR system for DOS-based PCs. Provides a GUI environment for creation of objects and worlds, as well as a fairly powerful scripting language. Supports a very wide variety of input and output devices, including low-end interface devices like joystick and mouse, or high-end interface devices like HMDs and gloves.

Cost: $795

VREAM Runtime System

Lets you enter and interact with virtual worlds created with the VREAM Virtual Reality Development System. Works with standard VGA display using a joystick, mouse, and keyboard.

Cost: $59

VREAM Advanced Runtime System

An advanced version of the Runtime System that lets you use any of the devices supported by the VREAM System, including HMDs, 3D tracking systems, and gloves.

Cost: $295

Programming Tool Kits

AmberC++

Avatar Partners
13090 Central Avenue, Suite 3
Boulder Creek, CA 95006
408-338-6460
Fax: 408-338-6462

A set of C++ classes that extend Sense8 Corporation's WorldToolKit (WTK) software with an object-oriented library of reusable C++ tools. Amber provides WTK users with access to Sense8's Application Programmer's Interface (API). Amber is intended for use by experienced world builders and C++ programmers.

AmberC++ provides a library of reusable C++ components that will be available as a complete package, or sold separately in "Class Bundles." Licensed AmberC++ developers will be able to sell class bundles that they developed without any runtime fees. Third-party class bundles will be sold through the Amber product catalog.

Cost: $495

Genesys Virtual Lightning

Genesys Research & Technologies, Inc.
15600 San Pedro, Suite 302
San Antonio, TX 78232-3738
210-490-8210
Fax: 210-490-1566

Virtual Lightning is a C-callable library of procedures designed for a wide variety of virtual reality (VR)-based tasks. The library presents C programmers with a variable level of abstraction, which differentiates it from other virtual reality C libraries. This provides programmers with the freedom to develop alternate solutions to things like collision detection, perspective transformations, shading algorithms, and networking. Or, use procedures included with the library if you don't want to be concerned with them.

Virtual Lightning currently provides library support for the following DOS compilers: Borland C/C++ version 3.1, Microsoft C/C++ version 7.0, and WATCOM C/C++ version 9.5.

The library is packaged with a set of display drivers, but since the drawing procedures are generic, additional display support is simple. Virtual Lightning includes display drivers for the following hardware:

- VGA mode 13h (320 × 200 × 8-bit color depth)
- Diamond Viper using the Weitek P9000 (selectable resolutions)
- Matrox MGA Impression series (selectable resolutions)

Ready-to-use procedures are included for the Input/Output devices. Similar to the display drivers, there is little difficulty importing other devices. The following I/O devices are currently supported:

- Mattel PowerGlove
- StereoGraphics CrystalEyes
- Gravis Ultrasound
- Origin Instruments Dynasight
- Null modem communications
- Netware IPX communications

Virtual Lightning is a powerful simulation tool for applications in areas like education, training, entertainment, communication, medicine, architecture, data visualization, and the abstract sciences. It runs on low-end, VGA-based PCs, as well as high-powered PCs with graphics coprocessors.

Cost: Contact vendor

Lepton VR Toolkit

Lepton Graphics Systems
2118 Central S.E., Suite 45
Albuquerque, NM 87106
505-843-6719
Fax: 505-843-9394

A collection of C programming libraries for real-time 3D data modeling on DOS systems. It provides a library of over 100 C-callable functions that speed and simplify the process of writing virtual reality and interactive 3D graphics programs. It contains functions for rendering and drivers for many affordable input and output devices.

Cost: $150

WorldToolKit Version 2.0

Sense8 Corporation
4000 Bridgeway, Suite 101
Sausalito, CA 94965
415-331-6318
Fax: 415-331-9148

A platform-independent library of over 400 C-language functions for building interactive, real-time 3D graphics and virtual reality applications. WorldToolKit developers can rapidly prototype applications; a fully functional "walkthrough" application can be built from 20 lines of code. Though WorldToolKit is intended for C programmers, it is shipped with several compiled applications.

3D objects are created with WorldToolKit using tools such as AutoCAD, 3D Studio, Swivel 3D, Wavefront, or any other 3D modeler that generates DXF or 3DS files. WorldToolKit imports these files so you can interact with and explore 3D models in real-time using your PC hardware. Although WorldToolKit is not a 3D-modeling program, it contains functions for interactively creating spheres, cubes, cylinders, polygons, and so on. You can use these functions to dynamically create shapes within your virtual environment.

WorldToolKit's features include 24-bit color; anti-aliasing filter for improved image quality; wireframe, flat, Gouraud-shaded and texture-mapped polygons; transparent, shaded and perspective-corrected textures; and improved terrain generation, and rendering. It now interfaces to more modelers, such as 3D Studio, MultiGen, and Wavefront. Dual boards can be used in a single PC to generate stereo images. WorldToolKit supports new input/output devices like StereoGraphics CrystalEyes LCD shutter glasses.

WorldToolKit integrates a real-time rendering pipeline, 3D modelers, sensors, input and output devices, and graphics display devices for the creation of virtual world and other 3D graphics applications. At the core of a WorldToolKit application is a real-time activity loop, where a 3D graphical world responds continuously to the user's input. WorldToolKit also supports real-time texture mapping when used with the SPEA Fire Board (a single i860 graphics accelerator) on an 80486 PC or above.

WorldToolKit encapsulates the operation of 3D real-time rendering in a simple-to-use library so models or data can be easily imported, rendered, and manipulated. The input from head-mounted position sensors can be used to update the stereoscopic WorldToolKit display for head position and orientation. A wide range of other supported input devices can be incorporated for gesture tracking and manipulation of objects in a virtual world.

Cost: $2,400 for DOS

WorldToolKit for Windows

A VR development tool that helps Microsoft Windows developers build real-time VR and graphics-simulation applications for business and professional use. Helps you create interactive 3D applications under Windows that present information more effectively. Rather than using a spreadsheet or two-dimensional tool, you can provide real-time, multidimensional data. You can create graphical objects with attributes such as position (x,y,z), size, orientation (roll, pitch, yaw), color, shape, and behaviors (spin, vibration, sound) that extend the dimensions of data space from three to 12 dimensions or more.

WorldToolKit for Windows easily links to mainstream applications such as Microsoft Excel. You can abstract information from a simple spreadsheet and present it in a 3D virtual "room" where elements move or change colors to reflect changes in the data. Users can navigate around the room to see views of the data that are not apparent on a 2D spreadsheet.

WorldToolKit for Windows includes several precompiled demonstration programs (including source code)—any of which can be used to accelerate your own development efforts:

- How to create a WorldToolKit application that communicates with an Excel spreadsheet using DDE techniques.

- A simple game with wandering fish you can spear, and special portals that lead to other worlds.
- A multifunction demonstration program that loads DXF and 3DS files, allows you to interactively apply textures or change colors, and works with many interface devices (such as the Cyberscope, joysticks, mouse).

Sense8's WorldToolKit for Windows offers support for inexpensive interface devices that attach to your PC, such as joysticks, mice, 6DOF, and 3DOF trackers. The following products are currently supported, or under consideration:

Stereoscopic Viewers—Cyberscope 3D viewer (mounts on monitor), and StereoGraphics LCD shutter glasses

3D Sound—Gravis UltraSound 3D sound board

2D Sound—Access to Windows multimedia devices (MIDI, etc.)

Head-Trackers—Logitech ultrasonic head-tracking device

Navigation—2D mice, joysticks, Spaceball, Logitech Space Controller and Cyberman, and more

Wired-Gloves—Mattel PowerGlove device

Real-world applications include the following:

Architectural Walkthroughs—Load a 3D Studio model of your new house or remodeled kitchen, and interactively move around and view it from different directions. Use a mouse to select a cabinet surface and apply different wood textures or paint colors. Link the 3D model to a Microsoft Excel spreadsheet so you can change the height or width of a wall from Excel.

Educational Simulations—Build a world where the laws of physics apply, or make up your own rules and see what happens. Create a simulation of the moon or take a trip through the solar system.

Entertainment—Create a 3D race-car game or air-combat simulation. Use existing Windows for Workgroups networking or WorldToolKit's serial port capabilities to play against a friend or group of friends.

Data Visualization—Extract stock market data from a remote database using SQL queries and create a virtual world where stocks are represented as virtual rooms containing additional price and trend information on the walls.

System requirements: 486DX PC running Windows 3.1 or NT with either a 16K, 256K, 32K, 64K, or 16.7M color graphics driver. 4M RAM (8M suggested) and a numeric coprocessor. PCs with VESA or PCI local bus graphics will improve performance by about 30 percent or better over equivalent ISA-bus systems. Runs on any PC equipped with standard VGA driver, but uses hardware-accelerated graphics for maximum performance.

To develop applications with WorldToolKit for Windows, you need an appropriate Windows 3.1, Win32s or NT development environment. Applications created with WorldToolKit are Win32s compliant—that is, they will run under Windows NT or Windows 3.1. Most Windows-based compilers (including 16-bit compilers) should be able to access the 32-bit Win32s DLLs that comprise WorldToolKit for Windows. Integrated development environments provided by tools like Microsoft's Visual C++ NT, Borland 4.0, or Symantec's C++ Professional are fully supported by WorldToolKit's Win32s DLL.

Cost: $795

Voice-Recognition Software

Listen for Windows

Verbex Voice Systems, Inc.
119 Russell Street
Littleton, MA 01460
800-ASK-VRBX
508-486-8886
Fax: 508-486-9654

Listen for Windows is a continuous speech-recognition system for business, professional, or home use. Listen for Windows recognizes any language, accent, or dialect with a high degree of accuracy. It lets you speak to your computer naturally, in sentences, without pausing between words. For example, it understands phrases such as "switch to card file" or "copy entry and paste."

Listen can recognize any language, accent, jargon, or dialect accurately because you train Listen by speaking sample command words and phrases into a microphone. Listen's unique sound-sampling process enables it to perform well in quiet, noisy, or variable noise environments.

Verbex Listen is available with different levels of speech-recognition coprocessing assistance, and you choose the level you want depending on the speed of your PC.

Listen comes with Ready-to-Listen speech interfaces for major Windows applications including Microsoft Office, Lotus SmartSuite, WordPerfect, Microsoft Word, Intuit Quicken, CorelDRAW!, Asymetrix Compel, Maxis SimCity Classic, and more.

Sold separately is a manual that explains how to set up your own speech interface, a desk/monitor-mount microphone for quiet environments, or a headset microphone that performs well in noisy environments. Or a professional headset microphone for improved noise canceling, quick disconnect, or multiple-wearing options. Also available is a runtime upgrade kit for digitized speech playback, or coprocessing boards to offload all speech-recognition tasks from your host PC.

VOICE BLASTER

Covox, Inc.
675 Conger St.
Eugene, OR 97042
503-342-1271
Fax: 503-342-1283

The developers of the U.S. Air Force's "Bionic Ear" created VOICE BLASTER—voice-recognition software for popular sound cards. With VOICE BLASTER, you can add voice commands to educational, business, and entertainment programs such as WordPerfect, F117A, Lotus 1-2-3, Secret Weapons of the Luftwaffe, DAC Easy, and more.

VOICE BLASTER comes with a high-fidelity headset/microphone that connects to your PC via the parallel port. The software includes recording, editing, and playback programs.

Cost: $120

A
THE
VIRTUAL
REALITY
MADNESS
AND MORE!
CD-ROMs

The two CD-ROMs that accompany this book contain a wealth of VR-related software, including three complete award-winning virtual-reality programs:

- *Virtus WalkThrough, Special Edition*
- *Vistapro version 1*
- *Virtual Reality Studio version 1*

These programs have a combined value of more than $200. They are included on the CD-ROM through special arrangements with Virtus Corporation, Virtual Reality Laboratories, and Domark Software. For more information on installing and using these products, read Appendixes B, C, and D.

In addition to these amazing programs, these two discs contain:

- Test-drive versions of VR games
- Virtual worlds to explore
- Demos of commercial programs
- Animations and videos
- Color pictures from the book
- And a whole lot more...

The DOS and Windows menu programs on the discs allow you to easily navigate through the included software—you can run or install programs, explore worlds, play animations and videos, and view pictures. The DOS and Windows menu programs only allow you to explore the software that runs under either DOS or Windows, respectively.

The Windows Menu Program

Before you can run the Windows software on the CD-ROMs, you need to run the setup program on each disc. This program will create a Program Manager group with icons for running the software. It will also copy software drivers for animation to your hard drive.

Start Windows, if you haven't already done so, and follow these steps:

1. Insert Disc One in your CD-ROM drive.
2. Switch to Program Manager or File Manager. Select File from the menu, and then select Run.
3. In the Run dialog box, type ***D*:\VRSETUP.EXE** in the Command Line box and click on OK. If your CD-ROM drive is not drive D, then substitute the correct letter. For instance, if your CD-ROM drive is G, type **G:\VRSETUP.EXE**.

4. The opening screen of the setup program will appear. Click on the Continue button.
5. The program will install animation drivers to your hard drive and create a Program Manager group named *VR Madness Disc One.*

When the setup for Disc One is complete, the setup program for Microsoft Video for Windows will automatically start. Follow the prompts within this program, and video playback drivers will be installed on your system. When the Video for Windows setup is complete, it will restart Windows to allow the new drivers to load.

If the first setup has completed successfully, you're ready to explore the first CD-ROM! To explore Disc Two, insert it into your CD-ROM drive, follow the preceding steps, and a group named *VR Madness Disc Two* will be created.

Running the Windows Menu Program

When you start the Windows menu program, you'll see an opening screen—click on the button to begin exploring the disc. Each different screen of the menu program will be referred to as a page. Just think of the program as being like a multimedia book. You can jump directly to sections that interest you, or you can move through the program one page at a time.

Your Windows video setup must be capable of displaying at least 256 colors, or the menu program and animation clips will not display properly. Graphics with lots of colors look pretty ugly on a 16 color display; if you can only display 16 colors, consult your system's manual for information on how to switch to a different video driver with more colors. If you can switch to a driver that displays 16-bit or 24-bit color, graphics and animations will look like they were intended to look.

You can navigate through the disc in several different ways. In the bottom right area of each page, you'll find yellow navigation buttons. To move to the next or preceding page, click on one of the left or right arrow buttons.

If you click on the question mark symbol in the lower right area, a Help screen will appear. Pressing the F1 key will also display this Help screen. Click anywhere on the Help screen to make it disappear.

On some pages, you won't see the arrows that let you move to the next or preceding page; you'll see an upward-pointing arrow instead. Each upward-pointing arrow moves back to the preceding level of the menu.

If you choose Index from the menu, you can choose any of the major sections and jump immediately to that page.

To exit from the menu, choose File and then Exit from the menu.

If you experience any problems with running the menu program, double-click on the Troubleshooting icon in either of the Program Manager groups. This will open a file with hints and tips for solving your Windows problems.

The DOS Menu Program

The DOS software on the disc can be explored using the DOS menu program. Follow these steps to start the menu:

1. Insert either CD-ROM into your drive.
2. If you're running Windows, exit to DOS.
3. At a DOS prompt, switch to the drive containing the CD-ROM. For example, if your CD-ROM is in drive D, type ***D*:** and press Enter.
4. Type **MENU** and press Enter. This will start the menu program.

The opening screen of the menu contains buttons that represent the major categories of DOS software on the disc. Click on any button to see more options. At the bottom of the screens are several buttons:

Quit—Exits the menu program. You can also exit by pressing the Escape key.

Help—Opens a file with information on how to use the menu program.

Up and down arrows—Moves up and down through the screens of the menu.

Windows Demos

The software demos in this section are special versions of commercial products that let you take the full product for a test drive.

Elastic Reality

Elastic Reality
925 Stewart Street
Madison, WI 53713
608-273-6585

Elastic Reality has been used to create astonishing special-effects sequences in films like *Wolf* and *Forrest Gump*, TV shows like *Star Trek: Deep Space Nine* and *Babylon 5*, and numerous commercials. It offers professional quality morphing and warping effects, along with a nearly unlimited variety of other effects.

trueSpace

Caligari Corporation
1955 Landings Dr.
Mountain View, CA 94043
415-390-9600

Caligari trueSpace for Windows is an advanced 3D package that offers organic modeling, fast rendering, and broadcast-quality animation. This program is remarkably easy to use for software with this kind of power.

World Toolkit

Sense8
4000 Bridgeway, Suite 101
Sausalito, CA 94965
415-331-6318

This demo is designed to show some of the more general capabilities of World ToolKit for Windows. You can "drag and drop" models and textures into the universe or simply use the dialog boxes to load models and apply textures to polygons. You can interactively fly around your models and change the color or texture of various surfaces or polygons.

You can also load AutoCAD DXF, 3D Studio 3DS, or Wavefront OBJ files. If you load any of these files, there will be an automatic timeout after 90 seconds of viewing the files.

Typestry

Pixar
1001 W. Cutting Blvd.
Point Richmond, CA 94804
510-236-4000

Typestry turns TrueType and Type 1 fonts into 3D images and animations. The software uses RenderMan® technology to apply textures and 3D lighting effects.

PhotoMorph 2

North Coast Software
P.O. Box 459
265 Scruton Pond Rd.
Barrington, NH 03825
603-664-7871
800-274-9674

PhotoMorph is the easy-to-use Windows-based morphing software from North Coast Software. PhotoMorph can easily create morphs of various types and in different formats, including Video for Windows AVI format. The quality of morphs created with this software can rival what you see in movies and on television.

MacroModel

Macromedia
600 Townsend St., Suite 310 W
San Francisco, CA 94103
415-252-2000

MacroModel is a 3D modeling program that combines CAD accuracy with 2D drawing tools. It provides real-time visualization from any angle for feedback. You can import and export polygon-based objects for compatibility with other 3D modelers.

Visual Reality

Visual Software
21731 Ventura Blvd.
Woodland Hills, CA 91364
818-593-3500

This interactive presentation shows you detailed information about the suite of programs within Visual Reality, including Visual Model, Visual Font, Renderize Live, and Visual Image. You can also view a gallery of professionally rendered images.

Distant Suns

Virtual Reality Laboratories, Inc.
2341 Ganador Court
San Luis Obispo, CA 93401
805-545-8515
800-829-VRLI

Distant Suns is the Windows-based desktop planetarium that displays the night sky from anywhere on the planet from 4173 BC to 10000 AD. One of the new features in Distant Suns 2.0 is the Off Earth mode that can display the heavens from anywhere in the solar system.

DOS Demos

The software demos in this section are special versions of commercial products that let you take the full product for a test drive.

Mars Explorer

Virtual Reality Laboratories, Inc.
2341 Ganador Court
San Luis Obispo, CA 93401
805-545-8515
800-829-VRLI

This software is a sample version of the full Mars Explorer package from Virtual Reality Laboratories, the makers of Vistapro. The full package contains low to high resolution images of the surface of Mars pieced together from NASA's Viking missions.

Vistapro 3

Virtual Reality Laboratories, Inc.
2341 Ganador Court
San Luis Obispo, CA 93401
805-545-8515
800-829-VRLI

This demo is an interactive tutorial and trial version Vistapro 3. After working with the full version of Vistapro 1, included on these CD-ROMs, this demo will give you a feel for how version 3 works (there was no version 2 of Vistapro).

NeoBook

NeoSoft Corporation
354 NE Greenwood Avenue, Suite 108
Bend, OR 97701-4631
503-389-5489

NeoSoft publishes the NeoBook Pro software that was used to create the DOS menu system for these CD-ROMs. You can install a trial version from the DOS menu program itself.

Virtual Worlds

In this section, you'll find dozens of interesting virtual worlds to explore, nearly all of them interactive. Most of these worlds were created with commercial virtual-reality products. Some were even created with Virtual Reality Studio, which is included on Disc One.

Virtual Reality Studio Creations

You'll find a number of interactive virtual worlds on the discs that were created with versions 1 and 2 of Virtual Reality Studio. Some of them are complex games, while others are worlds meant for exploration.

These creations will give you a taste of the types of virtual-reality worlds that can be put together with Virtual Reality Studio.

fLAtDiSk Dreams (various)
Rich LaBonte

EYELAND worlds (various)
Teran Skye

City Project
Douglas Faxon

3D House
Charles Carr

Noah '92
Domark Software

Superscape VR

Dimension International
Zephyr One, Calleva Park
Aldermaston
Berkshire
ENGLAND RG7 4QZ
+44-734-810077

This software is a demo of the commercial Superscape virtual-reality software. The demo allows you to control one of several objects in an industrial complex. You have your choice of driving around in one of two cars (either from the driver's seat or from above), flying a helicopter, or controlling a walking man.

This demo was created specifically for VGA cards, but the actual product is a high-resolution interactive environment that runs on high-end graphical workstations. In the back of the book you'll find an advertisement for this software.

RenderWare Creations

Criterion Software, Ltd.
20, Alan Turing Road
Guildford, GU2 5YF
United Kingdom
+44-483-448833 (sales)
+44-483-448800 (voice)

These Windows and DOS creations demostrate the power of RenderWare software for creating animated game and VR environments. Be sure to read the documentation for each demo before running it; some of them have special requirements.

VREAM

VREAM, Inc.
2568 N. Clark St. #250
Chicago, IL 60614
312-477-0425

The VREAM Virtual Reality Development System allows users to create fully interactive, textured, virtual-reality worlds, without doing any programming. This very simple virtual world illustrates some of the fundamental capabilities of worlds developed with the VREAM System.

Stunt Island Movies

Disney Computer Software
500 S. Buena Vista St.
Burbank, CA 91521
818-973-4015

These movies are examples of the types of interaction that can be created with Stunt Island, from Disney Software. Stunt Island allows you to become your own movie director by creating complex action scenes and stunts. After setting up the action, you film it from different angles and locations, edit the film, and view the final result.

Fly the Grand Canyon

Hyacinth
5508 Chimney Hollow
Norcross, GA 30093

This program is a demo version of Fly the Grand Canyon. This is a flight simulator type program that lets you take a flying tour of the Grand Canyon. You can let the program fly you around, or take your chances at flying yourself.

The Grand Canyon appears as wireframe contours, and you can use 3D glasses to view the scene in three dimensions. This demo shows just a part of the complete program. The full program allows you to fly through the entire Grand Canyon, not just a small portion of it. The complete Fly the Grand Canyon also has other added features, such as a Record mode and more detailed graphics.

FlightSim Toolkit Creations

Domark Software

These samples were created with FlightSim Toolkit, the software that lets you design your own interactive flight simulator.

VR Games

Arcade-type virtual-reality games are beginning to appear in places like shopping malls and video arcades. Sophisticated virtual-reality games are also beginning to be available for home computers. In this section, you'll find a variety of virtual-reality games, from action games to interactive games that can be played over phone lines.

Some of these games are marketed as shareware. This is nearly the same as the limited demos from commercial retail companies, but you must order the full registered product directly from the shareware company. You generally can't buy shareware products in stores.

When you register or purchase a shareware game, you'll get the complete version along with a number of other bonuses. See the documentation for each shareware product for more information.

Myst

Brøderbund Software
P.O. Box 6125
Novato, CA 94948
415-382-4400

Myst has taken the gaming world by storm, and this demo will give you a feel for why this has happened. The game is not like most games you've played—it features amazing 3D computer-generated scenery in a virtual environment that you must explore to solve a great mystery.

Under a Killing Moon

Access Software
4910 W. Amelia Earhart Dr.
Salt Lake City, UT 84118
800-800-4880

Under a Killing Moon is a hot new CD-ROM game that combines 3D computer-generated scenes with smooth-scrolling action, video actors, and liberal doses of humor. The demo version lets you explore one small area and get a feel for the action in the complete game.

Return to Zork

Activision/Infocom
11440 San Vincente Blvd., Suite 300
Los Angeles, CA 90049
310-207-4500

Return to Zork was one of the first CD-ROM games to incorporate live video actors into the scenes. It's based on the classic text adventure games from Infocom. Liberal doses of humor help make this a fun game to experience.

Rebel Assault

LucasArts Entertainment Company
P.O. Box 10307
San Rafael, CA 94912
415-721-3300

Rebel Assault is the best-seller computer game based on the George Lucas' *Star Wars* movies. It puts you in the seat of rebel aircraft, where you can recreate battle scenes from the movie.

VR Slingshot

Virtual Entertainment, Inc.
1335 N. Northlake Way, Suite 102
Seattle, WA 98103
800-707-1VRS (orders only)

VR Slingshot is a unique game that allows two people to compete in two sports through the telephone. It incorporates aspects of dogfighting planes, boxing, bumper cars, lacrosse, and handball. If you purchase the complete version, you'll be able to use VR stereoscopic headsets to view the action. You must have a joystick to sample the games in this demo; if you don't, you'll be able to observe several games.

DOOM

id Software
c/o StarPak
P.O. Box 1230
Greeley, CO 80632
800-IDGAMES (434-2637)

DOOM was a breakthrough in 3D gaming graphics, and it's become quite a phenomenon. The game is a fast-moving virtual-reality adventure in which you're plunged into a brutal 3D world. Note: DOOM portrays graphic violence.

Ravenloft: Strahd's Possession

Strategic Simulations, Inc.
675 Almanor Ave., Suite 201
Sunnyvale, CA 94086
408-737-6800

Ravenloft was one of the earliest games to incorporate the 3D first-person approach. It's a classic group-adventure game that pits you against all sorts of perils.

Shadowcaster

Origin Systems
12940 Research Blvd.
Austin, TX 78750
512-335-5200

Shadowcaster is another game that shows the action from a first-person perspective, but it also features sophisticated 3D graphics with an illusion of real depth. Your character has the ability to morph into several other creatures, each with unique powers.

Ultima Underworld

Origin Systems
12940 Research Blvd.
Austin, TX 78750
512-335-5200

Ultima Underworld is a part of the popular Ultima series of adventure games. This installment features a first-person perspective as you explore the dark recesses of an underground world.

Blake Stone—Aliens of Gold

Apogee Software Productions
P.O. Box 496389
Garland, TX 75049
214-278-5655

First came Wolfenstein 3D, then Blake Stone—Aliens of Gold. It features a 3D environment like Wolfenstein, but one that's more sophisicated. You'll battle in the future against a madman who has hatched an army of mutants, biodroids, and demons.

Mate

VRontier Worlds
809 E. South Street
Stoughton, WI 53589

Mate is a true virtual-reality chess game that allows two players to interact in a single virtual environment. In addition, you don't have to live close to your opponents. You can call them with your modem and play over the telephone lines. All the telephone functions are built into the program.

Megatron

John Dee Stanley
6959 California Ave. SW
Seattle, WA 98136

Megatron is a two-player combat game. The object of the game is to simply hunt down your adversary and destroy his assault robot. You can play against the computer, or you can use your modem to play against another computer over the phone lines.

Ken's Labyrinth

Epic Megagames
10406 Holbrook Dr.
Potomac, MD 20854
301-983-9771

Ken's Labyrinth is a 3D arcade maze game featuring high-resolution 256-color graphics, music, and digital sound effects. Before playing, you need to run SETUP to tell the game what hardware you have. Simply type **SETUP** and press Enter, then go through the menu and select your hardware from the lists of choices.

Wolfenstein 3D

Apogee Software Productions
P.O. Box 496389
Garland, TX 75049
214-278-5655

Wolfenstein 3D was a technology breakthrough in PC games—one of the first games where you play your character in first-person perspective in a 3D world.

Alone in the Dark, 1 and 2

Interplay Productions
17922 Fitch Avenue
Irvine, CA
800-969-4263

Alone in the Dark, versions 1 and 2, are sophisticated virtual reality–based commercial games, which feature 3D ray-traced characters that interact with each other in a gothic-horror novel setting. These demo versions allow you to play out one scene from the many rooms and scenarios in the full game.

Spectre VR

Velocity Development
5 Embarcadero Center, Suite 3100
San Francisco, CA 94111
415-776-8000

SpectreVR comes in both DOS and Windows versions. It's a game that combines elements of tank battles and racing, taking place in a futuristic 3D wireframe environment. The complete version of the game allows you to play head-to-head with another player via modem.

DragonSphere

MicroProse Entertainment Software
P.O. Box 509
Hunt Valley, MD 21030
410-771-0440

This is an interactive demonstration of the fantasy adventure game, DragonSphere. This game uses rotoscoped animations and painted backgrounds for a nice feel of realism and beauty. After watching a short opening animation, you can play a little of the game.

MechWarrior 2: The Clans

Activision/Infocom
11440 San Vincente Blvd., Suite 300
Los Angeles, CA 90049
310-207-4500

MechWarrior 2: The Clans puts you in the seat of a futuristic battle robot, where you'll do battle with other similar robots.

Animations and Videos

There are hundreds of animations, video clips, and images on the two *VR Madness* CD-ROMs. You'll also find many of the illustrations from the book. Most of these clips and images must be viewed from the Windows menu program.

To view the video clips on the discs, you must have the latest version of Microsoft Video for Windows installed on your system. These video playback drivers are normally installed during the setup for each CD-ROM. If you didn't allow these drivers to be installed, you can install them by double-clicking on the Install Video for Windows

CompuServe Information Service

Virtual Reality is a quickly evolving field. That makes it important to have access to the latest information. One of the best ways I have found to provide that access is on the CompuServe Information Network. If you are not already a member of CompuServe, you are missing out on a great source of information.

You can access CompuServe with your modem. As a reader of this book, you'll receive a free membership to CompuServe and a $15 usage credit upon joining. CompuServe's Windows access software (WinCIM) is also included on Disc One. If you don't own a modem, you can get even a very fast (9600 or 14.4k baud) modem very cheaply.

More than 1 million computer users are a part of CompuServe Information Service, and for good reason. CompuServe has special-interest areas for nearly any subject you're interested in, including Virtual Reality. And you'll find users from across the United States and around the World.

WinCIM

Windows CompuServe Information Manager (WinCIM) is the communications software that makes being on-line easy. Instead of typing commands, you can click on icons or choose from menu items to explore forums, download files, read and create messages, send and receive electronic mail, and much more.

WinCIM contain extensive on-line help, which is always available by pressing the F1 key. You can even browse through a list of the forums on CompuServe without being on-line. You can install your free copy of WinCIM by double-clicking from within the VR Madness menu program.

Contacting the Author

You can find me in the Multimedia forum of CompuServe (GO MULTIMEDIA). You can send me e-mail at my CompuServe ID: 75530,3711, or you can send me a message in the Hands-on Multimedia section of the Multimedia forum (or use section 1 if you are new and don't know your way around yet). I prefer receiving messages in the Multimedia forum because when I answer your questions there, other people also get to learn things. Please only use e-mail for private messages.

You may also want to visit the CYBERFORUM, where you will find ongoing discussions about virtual reality. There are a number of interesting shareware applications in both the Multimedia and Cyber forums.

B

VISTAPRO

In this appendix, you'll find information on installing and getting started with Vistapro, which is included on the *Virtual Reality Madness and More!* CD-ROMs.

Vistapro is a three-dimensional landscape-simulation program. Using data from the U.S. Geological Survey (USGS) Digital Elevation Model (DEM), Vistapro can accurately recreate real-world landscapes in vivid detail. As a fractal landscape generator, Vistapro can create landscapes from a random seed number.

Vistapro supports more than four billion fractal landscapes. Simply by changing a number, you can simulate whole new worlds. These virtual worlds can then be customized. For instance, by clicking on several buttons, rivers and lakes can be created in a landscape where none existed previously.

The Vistapro software included with this book is the complete version of Vistapro 1.0. You can upgrade to the newest version for a special price—see the Vistapro registration card in the back of the book.

You might want to refer back to Chapter 1, "Virtual Realiy has Arrived" which goes into more detail about how virtual landscapes can be created with Vistapro. That chapter talks about the latest version of Vistapro, but most of what's shown in the chapter can be duplicated with Vistapro 1.0.

License Agreement

Vistapro is being provided to you through a special arrangement with Virtual Reality Laboratories, Inc. This software is not public domain and you must abide by the terms of the company's license agreement:

> *The program Vistapro and the related user manual are copyrighted. You may not copy, modify, distribute, transfer, or transmit this program or the related manual except as is expressly provided in this agreement.*
>
> *You have the non-exclusive right to use this program on a single computer. You may make one backup copy of this program to protect against media damage. Call Virtual Reality Laboratories for use on local area networks—usually there is no charge.*
>
> *This program is sold as entertainment, without warranty as to its suitability to be used as any other purpose.*
>
> *This license agreement shall be governed by the laws of the United States of America and the State of California.*

How Vistapro Works

Vistapro uses a combination of artificial intelligence, chaotic math, and a user-definable set of values to simulate landscapes in their natural state. At present, the USGS has converted about 40 percent of the United States to DEM files that potentially may be used with Vistapro. Vistapro is a single frame generator, meaning that it acts like a camera; point and click the camera, and Vistapro will render a new view of the landscape.

Landscapes can be viewed from a practically infinite combination of heights, angles, and distances. Using the combination of user-controllable values and Vistapro's built-in routines, landscapes can be made as realistic or as surreal as desired. It is easy to alter tree and snow lines, haze, exposure, rivers, lakes, and light sources to customize the appearance of the landscape.

For generating its images, Vistapro uses data derived from United States Geologic Survey Digital Elevation Mapping files. These files contain coordinate and elevation data at 30-meter (roughly 100 feet) increments. Each file used in Vistapro contains about 65,000 elevation points and 130,000 polygons.

Vistapro doesn't know anything about what covers the terrain. It doesn't know where the trees, roads, or buildings are. It does its best to color each polygon (based on a few numbers that you input) in a realistic way, but it still can't draw each rock and tree where they are in reality.

Installing Vistapro

At a minimum, you must have the following hardware and software to run Vistapro:

- IBM PC-compatible computer with 640K memory
- MS-DOS or PC DOS operating system
- Microsoft compatible mouse and driver
- VGA, Extended VGA, or Super VGA graphics capability
- DOS hard-disk partition with at least 3M free space

Vistapro must be installed on a hard disk before it can be run. You can install Vistapro by running the DOS menu program on Disc one. The installation files for Vistapro are located in the \VISTAPRO directory.

If you want to install the program manually, place the *Virtual Reality Madness and More!* Disc one in your CD drive and follow these steps:

1. From the DOS prompt, type ***drive:*\VISTAPRO\INSTALL** and press Enter. For example, if your CD drive is D, type **D:\VISTAPRO\INSTALL** and press Enter.
2. You'll be given the option to change the drive where the programs will be installed. Use the arrow keys to select drive C or D and then press Enter.
3. The install program will display an introductory message; press any key to begin installing files.
4. A message will appear when the program is finished.

The following section provides more details on the memory requirements of Vistapro.

Memory Usage by Vistapro

Vistapro requires a lot of memory (RAM) to run. It must have about 540K of free memory. You can determine how much memory is free at the DOS prompt by using the DOS CHKDSK command. DOS 5 and DOS 6 users can also use the MEM program to obtain the total and free amounts of memory.

The amount of free memory should be greater than 540,000 bytes for Vistapro to run properly. Most users should have enough memory available, but if you don't, you will have to do something to free up some memory.

The simplest option is to remove some memory-resident programs from memory. You might also try removing unused device drivers. ANSI.SYS is often installed but not used. A RAM disk may be eating up some conventional memory, and even though it is desirable to have Vistapro put its temporary files on the RAM disk, you may want to remove it if the existence of the RAM disk eats up too much memory.

All these solutions require editing your CONFIG.SYS or AUTOEXEC.BAT files and rebooting your computer. **Caution:** If you are not familiar with these files, we don't recommend fiddling with them.

Another good way to free up some memory on 80286, 80386, and 80486 systems is to upgrade to DOS 5, DOS 6, or DR DOS 6.0. All these solutions require that you buy these packages and then spend the time installing them—and probably backing up your hard disk, too.

Advanced Setup Options

Vistapro uses several temporary files while it is running. These files contain data that is used internally and a copy of the graphics screen after a picture is rendered. We recommend placing these files on the fastest available drive or partition.

If the environmental variable VTEMPDIR is not defined, Vistapro will create these files in its default directory, usually C:\VISTAPRO. If VTEMPDIR is set to a valid drive and path name, Vistapro will place these working files at that location. These files may consume as much as 1.2M of memory.

If you can spare the memory, we suggest setting VTEMPDIR to point to a RAM disk that is big enough to hold all the temporary files. For example, if your RAM disk is drive D and is 1.2M or greater, type

```
SET VTEMPDIR=D:\
```

Vistapro will run a little faster and more smoothly with its temp file on RAM disk. If VTEMPDIR is set to a drive or directory that doesn't exist, Vistapro will complain and abort. You can erase the environmental variable with the following command:

```
SET VTEMPDIR=
```

This will force Vistapro to return to using the default directory for its temporary files.

The screen modes you plan to use (see table B.1) will determine how big a RAM disk you need for the temp files.

Table B.1. RAM Disk Sizes for Each Graphics Mode.

Graphics Mode	*Bytes Needed*
320×200	520K
640×400	700K
640×480	750K
800×600	930K
1024×768	1.17M

For example, if you will only be using the lowest resolution graphics mode (320×200), your RAM disk need only be 520,000 bytes.

Note that the RAM disk must be in EMS or XMS, and that Vistapro will still need about 540K bytes of DOS program memory.

You may also use VTEMPDIR to select another hard disk for the temp files. Many people keep their permanent files on one disk or partition and their transitory files on another disk or partition. We suggest putting the temp files (via VTEMPDIR) on your fastest available device.

Graphics Modes

The 320×200 VGA graphics mode can be used with a standard VGA system. For resolutions that are higher than this, you must have either a VESA-compatible VGA system or a system that has VESA capability.

With systems that have VESA capability, a special VESA software driver must be run before starting Vistapro. Your video card manufacturer may have supplied you with such a driver with the video card. If not, there are a number of VESA drivers supplied with Vistapro.

The VESA drivers are located in the VESA subdirectory of your Vistapro directory. The drivers are arranged by manufacturer; for example, the drivers for ATI cards are located in the \VISTAPRO\VESA\ATI subdirectory. Read the text file in the subdirectory for your card manufacturer. This file will explain how to set up the driver for your card.

Getting Started

To start Vistapro, you need to be at the DOS prompt. Type the following commands, pressing Enter after each line:

```
C:
CD \VISTAPRO
VISTAPRO
```

If you installed Vistapro to a hard drive other than C, substitute that drive letter for C in the preceding commands.

You will be ready to start when you see a screen with the gray Control Panels on the right side and the empty green topographical map on the left.

Vistapro Menus

Vistapro's menus are accessed via the buttons at the top left of the main screen (see fig. B.1). To see the menus, place the mouse cursor over one of the buttons and press the left mouse button. A menu with several selections appears immediately below the button. This menu will remain on-screen as long as the left mouse button is held down.

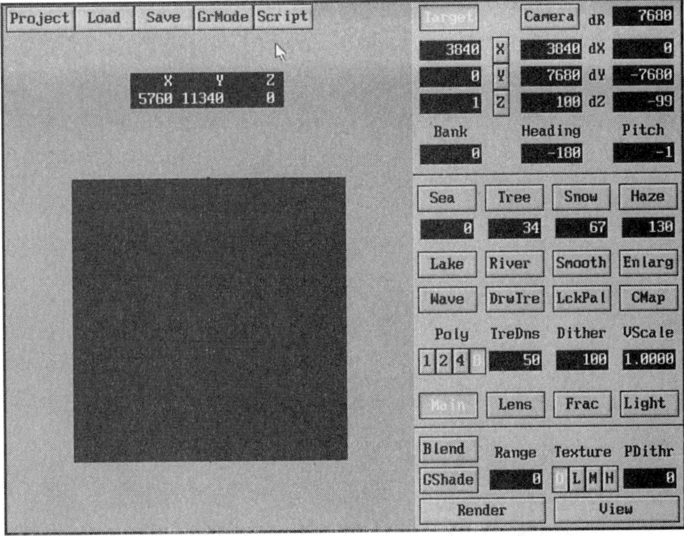

Figure B.1. The opening screen of Vistapro.

To select a menu item, move the mouse pointer down over the menu and release it when the cursor is over the desired item. (For more general information on using the menus, see the Graphical User Interface section that is located in Chapter 2 of the online manual. This manual is installed to your hard drive when you install Vistapro from the CD-ROM.)

There are five menus in Vistapro:

Project menu—Accesses DOS, information about Vistapro, information about the currently loaded landscape, and the Quit Vistapro function.

Load menu—Loads landscapes, colormaps, and pictures.

Save menu—Saves landscapes, colormaps, and pictures.

GrMode menu—Selects graphics and animation modes.

Script menu—Creates and executes Scripts.

Loading a Landscape

When Vistapro is first loaded, it starts out with a flat landscape. To quickly view an actual landscape, you can load one of the DEM (Digital Elevation Model) files included with Vistapro. These files are in a format used to represent landscape data.

To load a landscape, position the mouse pointer over the Load button at the top of the screen. Press and hold the left mouse button. The Load menu will drop down to reveal several options. Move the mouse pointer (while still holding the left button) to the first option, Load DEM, and release the button.

Now you will see the Load Vista DEM *File Requestor* (see fig. B.2). The File Requestor is used anytime a file is to be loaded or saved.

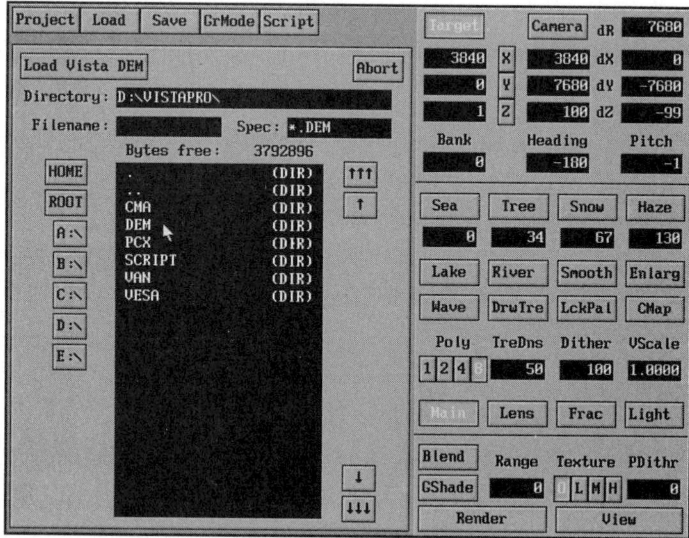

Figure B.2. The Load Vista DEM File Requestor screen.

The Load Vista DEM button is this File Requestor's confirm button. Clicking on it means to go ahead and load the file. The label on the confirm button varies, depending on the File Requestor. The Abort button is used to exit the File Requestor without taking an action.

The single up-arrow button scrolls up one line, and the single down-arrow button scrolls down one line. The three up arrows scroll up one page, and the three down arrows scroll down one page.

Find the DEM directory in the list, position the mouse pointer over it, and click the left mouse button. You will now be presented with a list from the DEM directory.

Find the file HALFDOME.DEM, and click it. Click the confirm button, which is the button labeled Load Vista DEM at the top left of the File Requestor.

The screen will switch back to the topographical map, and Control Panel and Vistapro will begin loading the landscape. It could take several seconds to complete.

Once Vistapro is finished loading the landscape, you will see a topographical view of the landscape in the box near the left side of the screen. The topographic map is colored by elevation. Dark greens represent the lowest altitudes, browns represent the middle altitudes, and gray-whites are the highest altitudes.

Locate the Render button at the lower left corner of the lower control panel. Press and release this button with the mouse, and Vistapro will begin to render the scene you loaded.

After a few seconds, you'll see the screen switch to the View screen. At first it will be blank, and then you will see Vistapro draw the sky and ground. Then it will draw a landscape.

At the current settings (assuming that you haven't changed anything), this landscape of Halfdome in Yosemite will look very blocky. As you learn more about Vistapro, you'll learn how to make scenes like this more photo-realistic. You'll also learn how to create fly-throughs and animated sequences.

To switch back to the Control Panels and topographical map, just click the left mouse button.

You now need to read the Vistapro online manual, which is discussed in the following section. It contains full details on how to use the many features of Vistapro.

The Online Vistapro Manual

When you install the Vistapro software from the CD-ROM, the online user's manual will also be installed. It will be located in the \VISTAPRO\MANUAL subdirectory of your hard drive.

The manual comprises the following series of text files, arranged by chapters and appendixes:

CH1.TXT
CH2.TXT
CH3.TXT
CH4.TXT
CH5.TXT
CH6.TXT

CH7.TXT
APPA.TXT
APPB.TXT
APPC.TXT
TUTOR1.TXT
TUTOR2.TXT
TUTOR3.TXT
TUTOR4.TXT

The file TUTORIAL.TXT steps you through the creation of Vistapro landscapes, explaining about most of the controls and features of the program.

To view the manual, change to the \VISTAPRO subdirectory, type **MANUAL**, and press Enter. You will see a menu of choices, which represents a table of contents for the manual. When you select a choice, the text for that chapter will be displayed.

You can also read these files into your favorite text editor or word processor and then print them.

C

VIRTUAL REALITY STUDIO

In this appendix, you'll find information on installing and getting started with Virtual Reality Studio, which is included on the *Virtual Reality Madness and More!* CD-ROM Disc One.

Virtual Reality Studio allows you to create interactive virtual-reality worlds on your home computer. You can even add animation, sound, and teleportation effects to your worlds.

You can use the Editor to create, test, and edit your custom worlds. Then, you can create stand-alone versions of the worlds that can be run on any compatible computer.

The version included with this book is version 1 of Virtual Reality Studio; you can upgrade to the newest version for a special price—see the advertisement in the back of the book.

You'll find more details of how Virtual Reality Studio can be used in Chapter 2, "Virtual Possibilities." That chapter deals with the latest version of the software, but much of what's shown there can be duplicated with version 1.

License Agreement

Virtual Reality Studio is being provided to you through a special arrangement with Domark Software. This software is not public domain and you must abide by the terms of the company's license agreement:

> *This computer software product (the "Software") is provided to the customer under license from Domark. The Software and the on-line manual are subject to the following terms and conditions, to which the customer agrees by opening the package of the software.*
>
> *The software is copyrighted 1991 by Incentive Software. The user manual is copyrighted 1991 by Domark. All rights are reserved. Neither the software or the manual may be duplicated or copied for any reason. The Customer may not transfer or resell the software or the user manual. Except as provided above, Incentive Software makes no warranties, either express or implied, with respect to the Software. Domark makes no warrantees either express or implied, with respect to the user manual. Incentive and Domark expressly disclaim all implied warranties, including without limitation, the warranty of merchandisability and/or fitness for a particular purpose.*

Installing Virtual Reality Studio

At a minimum, you must have the following hardware and software to run Virtual Reality Studio:

- IBM PC-compatible computer
- MS-DOS or PC DOS operating system, version 2.0 or higher
- Microsoft-compatible mouse and driver
- VGA, EGA, CGA, or Tandy graphics

The software also supports a mouse, joystick, and Ad Lib-compatible sound boards.

Virtual Reality Studio must be installed on a hard disk before it can be run. You can install the software by running the DOS menu program on Disc One. If you want to install the program manually, place the *Virtual Reality Madness and More!* Disc One in your CD drive and follow these steps:

1. From the DOS prompt, change to the drive that holds the CD-ROM. For example, if this drive is D, type **D:** and press Enter.
2. Type **\VRSTUDIO\INSTALL** and press Enter.
3. You will see a menu that asks you to choose the VGA, EGA, CGA, or Tandy version of the install program. Use the arrow keys to highlight the choice that corresponds to the type of video display you have, and then press Enter.
4. You'll be given the option to change the drive where the programs will be installed. Use the arrow keys to select drive C or D, and press Enter.
5. The install program will display an introductory message; press any key to begin installing the files to your hard drive.
6. A message will appear when the program is finished. Press any key to continue.

Running Virtual Reality Studio

After you've installed the software from the CD-ROM, you can start Virtual Reality Studio by typing the following commands at the DOS prompt (remember to press Enter after each line):

```
C:
CD\STUDIO
STUDIO
```

If you installed the software to a drive other than C, substitute that drive letter for C in the preceding commands.

This will bring up the Virtual Reality Studio Editor, which is where you will create and test your virtual creations. The following section of this appendix gives you an overview of how the Editor operates. (You'll find more details on how to create and program worlds in the special online documentation, which is discussed later in this appendix.)

You can get a good feel for the kinds of worlds this software can create by looking at the Virtual Reality Studio creations that are included on the CD-ROM. Refer to Appendix A for more information on these virtual worlds.

The Virtual Reality Studio Editor

Virtual Reality Studio is designed to be user-friendly, with icons and pull-down menus enabling the user to quickly understand the working environment. When you load the program, you will see the main screen (see fig. C.1), which is divided into several areas.

The menu selector is the top text line, which contains the headings for various menus. To access one of the menus, simply move the mouse pointer over the desired heading and the relevant menu will open below the heading. Moving the mouse pointer over the options within the menu will highlight them, and then pressing the mouse button will select the option currently highlighted. Moving the pointer out of the boundary of the menu will cause it to retract.

You can use Virtual Reality Studio without a mouse, although it will be more cumbersome. The cursor keys on the numeric keypad will move the mouse cursor around the screen. To move faster, press either Shift key at the same time. The Insert and Delete keys on the numeric keypad act exactly like the left and right mouse buttons.

The joystick options act in a similar manner—the stick moves the cursor and the buttons correspond to the mouse buttons.

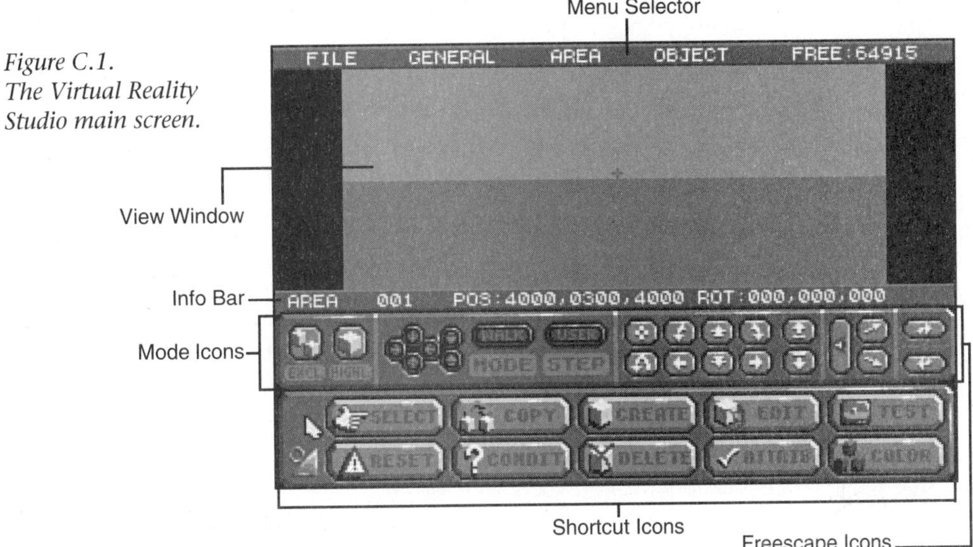

Figure C.1.
The Virtual Reality Studio main screen.

View Window

Below the menu selector you will see the main View window. This area is always used to display the current Freescape view, as seen from whichever camera is currently selected. Here is where you will see the objects in the world you are creating and editing.

Information Bar

Below the View window is the Information bar. This shows the current area, your present viewpoint coordinates (x,y,z), and the angle of view (yaw, pitch, and roll). When in Edit mode, this line will change to read the object name you are editing, its position in the environment, and its size. This information will be especially useful when animation or other more advanced uses of the system are used.

Icons

Immediately below the Information bar, you will see a series of icons, comprising the Mode and Freescape group of icons. The Mode group is on the left half of the screen.

EXCL is useful when editing objects. Clicking on this icon will exclude all background information and leave the currently selected object to be edited.

Just to the right of this you see HIGHL, which highlights the selected object for ease of identification during work.

To the right of these icons, you see a set of small icons in the form of arrows. These icons are very useful. When an object is selected, if these arrows are activated, they lock onto the current object from the front, rear, sides, top, or bottom.

To the right of the arrows, you see the MODE and STEP icons. MODE toggles between the following modes, which affect your movement:

> WALK allows you to move along the ground, with the restriction of gravity. You can climb onto objects and fall off them. Your height above the floor is restricted to between 64 and 280 units, corresponding to a crouched and standing position.
>
> FLY1 removes restrictions on gravity. You can now fly as if you were in a helicopter, with complete freedom in three dimensions. Forward motion is restricted to a horizontal plane, so that you can fly forward and look down at the same time.
>
> FLY2 is very similar to FLY1, except that you can now fly in exactly the direction you are looking, as though you were in an airplane.
>
> CAM1 through CAM5 control five "cameras" that can be placed anywhere. Control is similar to FLY1, except that the cameras are allowed inside objects and outside the area. When you change to another view, the camera's position is saved, so that on returning to that camera, the view position is retained.
>
> WALK, FLY1, and FLY2 have built-in collision detection. They will not travel through solid objects. These modes are the only three possible modes within a runnable program or the test screen.

STEP toggles between USER and FINE, which affect the size of movements as follows:

> USER affects the standard speed of operation and movement, which is initially set by the PREFERENCES menu on the GENERAL menu bar item.
>
> FINE is used for fine work when only a small movement is required in editing or movement.

To the right of the Mode icons, you will find the Freescape icons. The first of these is a set of directional arrows that are used for your movement in an environment. Using these arrows, you can move left, right, forward, or backward, rotate left, rotate right, make a complete U-turn, move up or down, and toggle the cross-hair cursor on and off.

To the right of these icons, you see the rest of the Freescape icons, which control your view movement. These allow you to look up, look down, and roll. Clicking on the center "eye" icon returns your view to the center view.

The Edit and Freescape icons remain on-screen and can be used at most times during editing.

Below the Mode and Freescape icons, you will see the shortcut icons (see table C.1). These icons duplicate the more commonly used functions, which are also available from the menus.

Table C.1. The Editor's Shortcut Icons.

Shortcut Icon	*Menu*
SELECT	OBJECT
COPY	OBJECT
CREATE	OBJECT
EDIT	OBJECT
TEST	GENERAL
RESET	GENERAL
CONDITION	OBJECT
DELETE	OBJECT
ATTR	OBJECT
COLOR	OBJECT

The Studio Game

The Studio Game is a Virtual Reality Studio world that has been included as an illustration of some of the possible environments that can be constructed. The object of the game is to escape from the mysterious world in which you find yourself and return to Earth. Some sort of space vehicle will probably come in handy. See if you can complete the game without cheating.

This game features advanced use of animations and conditions, and these can be examined and edited using the relevant functions of the editor. In addition, the tutorial section at the end of the online manual takes you through the beginning of the game and explains how the program was written.

To load the game, follow these steps at the main screen of the Editor:

1. Go to the File menu and select Load Data. When the file selector box appears, click on the DATA directory.
2. Select the Studio game file name. The file is named VGAGAME.STU for VGA installations, EGAGAME.STU for EGA or Tandy, and CGAGAME.STU for CGA.
3. Go to the File menu and select Load Border. When the file selector box appears, click the box-shaped icon next to the file list. This moves you up one directory level, back to \STUDIO.
4. Select the BORDERS directory.
5. Select the appropriate file for your system. The border file is named SGVGAPIC.LBM for VGA installations, SGEGAPIC.LBM for EGA or Tandy, and SGCGAPIC.LBM for CGA.
6. Press F1 or select the TEST icon. This starts the game.

To exit the game, press F1, go to the File menu, and select Clear All.

The Online Virtual Reality Studio Manual

When you install the Virtual Reality Studio software from the CD-ROM, the online user's manual will also be installed. It will be located in the same \STUDIO\MANUAL subdirectory of your hard drive.

The manual is a series of text files, arranged by chapter, as shown in table C.2.

Table C.2. Online Manual Files.

File Name	*Contents*
CH1.TXT	Introduction
CH2.TXT	Introduction to Freescape
CH3.TXT	Introduction to the Editor
CH4.TXT	Creating and editing your first object
CH5.TXT	The user interface
CH6.TXT	File menu options

File Name	*Contents*
CH7.TXT	General menu options
CH8.TXT	Area menu options
CH9.TXT	Object menu options
CH10.TXT	The Freescape Command Language (FCL)
CH11.TXT	The Animation Controller
CH12.TXT	Examples and variables
CH13.TXT	Sound effects
CH14.TXT	Studio game tutorial
CH15.TXT	Additional information

To view the manual, change to the \STUDIO\MANUAL subdirectory, type **MANUAL**, and press Enter. You will see a menu of choices, which represents a table of contents for the manual. When you select one of the choices, the text for that chapter is displayed.

You can also read these files into your favorite text editor or word processor and then print them.

D

VIRTUS WALKTHROUGH, SPECIAL EDITION

Virtus WalkThrough, Special Edition, is a Windows program that allows you to create and navigate through 3D worlds. You can also cruise the completed worlds that are included with the software.

To install the software, click the Install WalkThrough SE button in the Windows menu program. You can also install it by double-clicking the Install WalkThrough SE icon in the VR Madness Disc One group. After the program is installed, you can view the online version of the WalkThrough manual by clicking the manual icons in the Virtus group.

In addition to the Virtus WalkThrough, Special Edition application and its related files, you will find MANUAL, MODELS, and LIBRARY subdirectories within the VIRTUS directory. The MODELS subdirectory contains Virtus WalkThrough, Special Edition models that depict a variety of subjects. These include archaeological ruins, entire homes, and various rooms (bathrooms, kitchens, and living rooms). The LIBRARY subdirectory contains sample libraries of objects that can be placed and used in the worlds you create.

What makes this version of WalkThrough a "Special Edition?" It's the same WalkThrough program that has won dozens of computer-industry awards, with a few expert-level functions changed. See the manual for more details.

Don't miss the animations created with the new WalkThrough Pro product. This revolutionary software has dozens of completely new features, including texture mapping, shading, video insertion, and much more. If you decide to upgrade to WalkThrough Pro, don't miss the Virtus special offer in the back of the book.

License Agreement

Virtus WalkThrough, Special Edition for Windows 1.0, was developed for Sams Publishing by Virtus Corporation. The software is for use by a single user only. You may not copy or distribute any or all of the included files (listed later in this appendix) without written permission from Virtus Corporation. In short, please do not give, sell, share, trade, or reproduce this software without written permission from Virtus Corporation.

To receive technical assistance for Virtus WalkThrough, Special Edition for Windows 1.0, you must complete and return the Product Registration Card included with your book.

The WalkThrough SE Interface

There are two main components to the WalkThrough interface: windows and menus. Within Windows are elements such as Views, Tools, and Editors. Menus contain command functions and options.

There are two kinds of views in WalkThrough: the Walk View and the Design Views. The Walk View displays a three-dimensional rendering of the objects that you draw in a Design View, and it allows you to walk through and around the objects.

A Design View is a two-dimensional area in which you draw objects. There are six possible Design Views: Top, Bottom, Front, Back, Left, and Right. You can draw, view, or edit your drawings in any of the Design Views.

Within the Design Views are two editors that perform specific operations on the objects you draw: the Surface Editor and the Tumble Editor. You can read more about these editors in the online manual included with this software. This manual also contains tutorials that help you learn how to use WalkThrough to create and manipulate worlds.

Windows

Each view, or *editor*, is displayed in a window that can be resized or repositioned. See your Windows documentation for more about window manipulation and standard Windows interface operations.

Tools Window—Each of the two kinds of views and each editor has its own set of tools that appear in the Tools window. The view or editor that you are working in determines which tools are displayed.

Active Window—Only one window may be active at any time. To make a window active, click anywhere inside its boundaries, or select a view name from the View menu, or select a window name from the Window menu. You can tell whether a window is active by looking at its title bar; if the title bar is dark, the window is active.

Title Bar—The title bar of a view window displays the name of the view or editor with which the window is associated. If a window is active, its title bar is dark and the text is light. If a window is not active, its title bar is light and the text is dark.

Walk View

The Walk View displays a three-dimensional rendering of the objects that you draw in a Design View. In the Walk View, you can walk around and through objects by moving the mouse. The Walk View has a set of tools specific to the Walk View. These tools are displayed when the Walk View is active. In addition to the regular menus, the Walk menu is visible when the Walk View window is active. The Walk menu contains commands and options that affect the appearance of the Walk View and the objects within it.

Navigation Methods

Movement through the Walk View is in response to your movement of the mouse pointer relative to the crosshair in the center of the Walk View screen. Press the mouse button to begin movement and release the mouse button to stop. Speed increases as the cursor is pointed farther from the crosshair. Direction is determined by the position of the pointer relative to the crosshair. By using a combination of the Ctrl key or Shift key and the mouse, movements like tilting your head, sliding from side to side, or increasing and decreasing your altitude are also possible.

The crosshair in the middle of the Walk View is used as a reference point for navigation. The crosshair can be hidden with the Cross Hair option under the Walk menu.

Velocity Grid

Velocity Grid marks are the horizontal and vertical marks in the Walk View that display the points at which walk speed changes. The default for the Velocity Grid marks is Off (not visible), but they can be turned on and off by selecting Velocity Grid from the Walk Menu or by selecting Velocity Grid in the Preferences, Navigation dialog box from the Edit menu. Novice users may find the Velocity Grid helpful while learning to navigate.

Walk View Tools

When the Walk View is active, the Walk View Tools appear in the Tools window. The Walk View Tools allow you to change the Walk View background color, adjust the lens of the Observer, and record and play back a walk path. You can hide the Tools window by choosing Tools Window from the Window menu.

Recording and Playing Back a Walk Path

As you navigate through a model in the Walk View, you can use the Record tool and Playback tool to record and later play back the walk path. The length of a recording is limited only by memory; however, it is unlikely that you will run out of memory.

When you save a file, the recorded walk path is also saved. When you open the file again, you can click the Play button and view the recording. Only one recorded path can be saved with each model. If you record another, the previous path will be erased.

Recording does not take a picture of the screen each time the Observer takes a step; it records movement through the Virtus world. This means that if you record a walk path and then change your model, the playback follows the same recorded path and you see the changes you made to the model.

To record the walk path, click inside the Walk View to make it active; then click the Record Tool. Navigate the Observer through the Walk View. You may also record a path by selecting Record from the Walk menu. This menu option is helpful when running in full-screen mode or when the Tools window is hidden.

To stop recording, click the Stop tool. The Stop tool also stops a playback in progress. You may also stop recording by selecting Stop from the Walk menu. This menu option is helpful when running in full-screen mode or when the Tools window is hidden.

To play back a recording, click the Playback Tool. If the playback reaches the end of the recording, it loops automatically and starts from the beginning until you either click the mouse button anywhere on the computer screen or click the Stop tool. You may also play back a recorded path by selecting Play from the Walk menu. This menu option is helpful when running in full-screen mode or when the Tools window is hidden.

The Design Views

There are three sets of skills to learn in WalkThrough: creating objects, editing/modifying objects, and navigating in and around objects. The Design Views are used for creating and editing/modifying objects.

A Design View is a drawing area where you draw or view object outlines in two dimensions. There are six different Design Views: Top, Bottom, Front, Back, Left, and Right. You may draw in any Design View. More than one Design View can be open at any time; however, only one view can be active at any time.

The Design Views have a specific set of tools. When a Design View is active, the Design View tools are displayed in the Tools window.

The Virtus World is a cube (six sides). Each of the Design Views corresponds to a side of the cube. The three dimensions of the cube—X, Y, and Z—are based on the Top View, since the Top View opens as the default when you start the program. X is the left/right dimension, Y is the front/back dimension, and Z is the top/bottom dimension.

The Observer

The Observer is a small circle that represents your eyes in the WalkThrough environment. In a Design View, the Observer is shown as a circle with a line that indicates the viewing direction. In different Design Views, the appearance of the Observer is different. As you navigate in the Walk View, the Observer position changes in the Design View.

You can use the Select Object tool to drag the Observer to a desired location. You can also rotate the Observer, thus changing the viewing direction, by holding down the Ctrl key and dragging from the center of the Observer outward to the direction of the desired view. As you drag outward, a dotted line appears, representing the apparent viewing direction of the Observer. The farther you drag, the more control you have over the angle of view.

Design View Tools

The tools on the upper half of the Tools window allow you to create, edit, and orient objects and surfaces. Some tools have other tools nested beneath them. Nested tools are indicated by a small arrowhead to the lower right of a tool.

To select a tool, point to the desired tool and click. To make a nested tool available, click on the tool to reveal the nested tools, drag to the desired tool, and release the mouse button. You can also cycle through the nested tools by selecting a tool, holding down the Ctrl key and pressing the space bar.

I
INDEX

SYMBOLS

A

B

C

D

E

F

G

H

I

K

L

M

N

O

P

R

T

U

V

W

X-Z

Book ISBN 0-672-30604-2

Virtual Reality Madness and More! Disk Offer

If you don't have access to a CD-ROM drive, you can order the Virtual Reality Studio and Vistapro software on floppy disks. The disks contain the complete software for these programs, including the special on-line manuals.

The cost is only $12 (add $4 for international orders).

You can order these disks only by mail, and you **must** return this page with your order—photocopies of this page will not be accepted.

To order the disks, complete this form and mail it to

Sales Department—Disk Offer
Sams Publishing
Virtual Reality Madness!
201 West 103rd Street
Indianapolis, IN 46032

Enclose a money order or check for $12 (add $4 for international orders).

Name____

Company (for company address)_______________________

Street____

City____

State____________________ ZIP or Postal Code____________

Country (outside USA)_________________________________

ISBN # 0-672-30604-2

The Virtual Reality Madness and More! CD-ROMs

The CD-ROMs contain **two** award-winning commercial virtual reality programs, which retail for more than **$150**. You'll find a complete version of these award-winning VR programs—*not* demos!

> ***Virtual Reality Studio***
> *by Domark Software and New Dimension International*
>
> The leading virtual reality creation software for home computers. You can design your own interactive virtual reality worlds. Version 1.
>
> ***Vistapro***
> *by Virtual Reality Laboratories*
>
> The three-dimensional landscape simulation program. Create and explore real-world landscapes with vivid details. Version 1.

Both programs include special on-line versions of their complete manuals.

If you don't have access to a CD-ROM drive, you can order floppy disk versions of Virtual Reality Studio and Vistapro. Use the order form at the back of this book.

Plus—The CD-ROMs are a treasure chest of additional virtual reality demos, programs, and samples—more than 400 megabytes of software. Here's just a sample of what you'll find:

- Demo versions of popular commercial VR programs
- VR worlds you can explore and interact with
- VR games, including programs that feature two-player interaction over phone lines
- Animated fly-bys of virtual worlds
- Videos of virtual worlds
- A complete multimedia presentation of VR creations with animations, video, graphics, and sound

For information regarding the CD-ROMs and how to use the programs on them, read Appendix A in the book.

On the CD in this book,
you'll find a full working copy of

Vistapro 1.0

the incredible virtual reality landscape generator

Turn in this registration card for version 1.0 to become eligible to upgrade to Vistapro 3.0

Please see coupon opposite.

cut along this line.

VISTAPRO 1.0 IBM REGISTRATION CARD

Please take a few moments to register your FREE software.

Date ______________________

Contact Name ______________________

Business Name ______________________

Street Address/P.O. Box ______________________

City ______________________ State/Province __________ Zip/PC __________

Country ______________________ Phone ______________ FAX __________

Where did you hear about VISTAPRO? ☐ Store ☐ Review ☐ BBS ☐ Friend ☐ VRLI

☐ User Group (which?) __________ ☐ Trade Show ☐ Magazine (which?) __________

Where did you buy VISTAPRO?

☐ Store ☐ Mail Order ☐ VRLI ☐ Trade Show ☐ User Group ☐ Other __________

What processor do you have? ☐ 386 ☐ 486 ☐ 586

How much memory does your PC have? __________ What size is your hard drive? __________

Do you own a CD ROM drive? ☐ Yes ☐ No

Comments ______________________

____

What is your primary use for Vistapro? ______________________

____

NO POSTAGE
NECESSARY
IF MAILED
IN THE
UNITED STATES

BUSINESS REPLY MAIL
FIRST CLASS MAIL PERMIT NO. 496 SAN LUIS OBISPO CA

VIRTUAL REALITY LABORATORIES, INC.
2341 GANADOR COURT
SAN LUIS OBISPO, CA 93401-9826